# Fodor's

# ROME
## 6TH EDITION

---

**Where to Stay and Eat
for All Budgets**

---

**Must-See Sights
and Local Secrets**

---

**Ratings You Can Trust**

---

Fodor's Travel Publications   New York, Toronto, London, Sydney, Auckland
**www.fodors.com**

**FODOR'S ROME**
**Editor:** Robert I. C. Fisher

**Editorial Production:** Bethany Cassin Beckerlegge
**Editorial Contributors:** Valerie Hamilton, Dana Klitzberg, Margaret Stenhouse
**Maps:** David Lindroth, *cartographer;* Bob Blake and Rebecca Baer, *map editors*
**Design:** Fabrizio La Rocca, *creative director;* Moon Sun Kim, *cover design;* Guido Caroti, *art director;* Melanie Marin, *senior picture editor*
**Production/Manufacturing:** Angela L. McLean
**Cover Photo:** Andreas Achmann/Fototeca 9 × 12

**COPYRIGHT**
Copyright © 2006 by Fodors LLC

Fodor's is a registered trademark of Random House, Inc.

All rights reserved under International and Pan-American Copyright Conventions. Published in the United States by Fodor's Travel Publications, a unit of Fodors LLC, a subsidiary of Random House, Inc., and simultaneously in Canada by Random House of Canada Limited, Toronto. Distributed by Random House, Inc., New York.

*No maps, illustrations, or other portions of this book may be reproduced in any form without written permission from the publisher.*

Sixth Edition

ISBN: 1–4000–1586–3

ISBN-13: 978–1–4000–1586–3

ISSN: 0276–2560

**SPECIAL SALES**
Fodor's Travel Publications are available at special discounts for bulk purchases for sales promotions or premiums. Special editions, including personalized covers, excerpts of existing guides, and corporate imprints, can be created in large quantities for special needs. For more information, contact your local bookseller or write to Special Markets, Fodor's Travel Publications, 1745 Broadway, New York, New York 10019. Inquiries from Canada should be directed to your local Canadian bookseller or sent to Random House of Canada, Ltd., Marketing Department, 2775 Matheson Boulevard East, Mississauga, Ontario L4W 4P7. Inquiries from the United Kingdom should be sent to Fodor's Travel Publications, 20 Vauxhall Bridge Road, London SW1V 2SA, England.

**AN IMPORTANT TIP & AN INVITATION**
Although all prices, opening times, and other details in this book are based on information supplied to us at press time, changes occur all the time in the travel world, and Fodor's cannot accept responsibility for facts that become outdated or for inadvertent errors or omissions. So **always confirm information when it matters,** especially if you're making a detour to visit a specific place. Your experiences—positive and negative—matter to us. If we have missed or misstated something, **please write to us.** We follow up on all suggestions. Contact the Rome editor at editors@fodors.com or c/o Fodor's at 1745 Broadway, New York, New York 10019.

PRINTED IN THE UNITED STATES OF AMERICA

10 9 8 7 6 5 4 3 2 1

# Be a Fodor's Correspondent

Your opinion matters. It matters to us. It matters to your fellow Fodor's travelers, too. And we'd like to hear it. In fact, we *need* to hear it.

When you share your experiences and opinions, you become an active member of the Fodor's community. That means we'll not only use your feedback to make our books better, but we'll publish your names and comments whenever possible. Throughout our guides, look for "Word of Mouth," excerpts of your unvarnished feedback.

Here's how you can help improve Fodor's for all of us.

Tell us when we're right. We rely on local writers to give you an insider's perspective. But our writers and staff editors—who are the best in the business—depend on you. Your positive feedback is a vote to renew our recommendations for the next edition.

Tell us when we're wrong. We're proud that we update most of our guides every year. But we're not perfect. Things change. Hotels cut services. Museums change hours. Charming cafés lose charm. If our writer didn't quite capture the essence of a place, tell us how you'd do it differently. If any of our descriptions are inaccurate or inadequate, we'll incorporate your changes in the next edition and will correct factual errors at fodors.com *immediately.*

Tell us what to include. You probably have had fantastic travel experiences that aren't yet in Fodor's. Why not share them with a community of like-minded travelers? Maybe you chanced upon a cozy *trattoria* or irresistible bookshop that you don't want to keep to yourself. Tell us why we should include it. And share your discoveries and experiences with everyone directly at fodors.com. Your input may lead us to add a new listing or highlight a place we cover with a "Highly Recommended" star or with our highest rating, "Fodor's Choice."

Give us your opinion instantly at our feedback center at www.fodors.com/feedback. You may also e-mail editors@fodors.com with the subject line "Rome Editor." Or send your nominations, comments, and complaints by mail to Rome Editor, Fodor's, 1745 Broadway, New York, NY 10019.

You and travelers like you are the heart of the Fodor's community. Make our community richer by sharing your experiences. Be a Fodor's correspondent.

*Buon viaggio!*

**Tim Jarrell, Publisher**

# CONTENTS

# ABOUT THIS BOOK

## Our Ratings

Sometimes you find terrific travel experiences and sometimes they just find you. But usually the burden is on you to select the right combination of experiences. That's where our ratings come in.

As travelers we've all discovered a place so wonderful that its worthiness is obvious. And sometimes that place is so experiential that superlatives don't do it justice: you just have to be there to know. These sights, properties, and experiences get our highest rating, Fodor's Choice, indicated by orange stars throughout this book.

Black stars highlight sights and properties we deem Highly Recommended, places that our writers, editors, and readers praise again and again for consistency and excellence.

By default, there's another category: any place we include in this book is by definition worth your time, unless we say otherwise. And we will.

Disagree with any of our choices? Care to nominate a place or suggest that we rate one more highly? Visit our feedback center at www.fodors.com/feedback.

## Budget Well

Hotel and restaurant price categories from ¢ to $$$$ are defined in the opening pages of each chapter. For attractions, we always give standard adult admission fees; reductions are usually available for children, students, and senior citizens. Want to pay with plastic? AE, D, DC, MC, V following restaurant and hotel listings indicate if American Express, Discover, Diner's Club, MasterCard, and Visa are accepted.

## Restaurants

Unless we state otherwise, restaurants are open for lunch and dinner daily. We mention dress only when there's a specific requirement and reservations only when they're essential or not accepted—it's always best to book ahead.

## Hotels

Hotels have private bath, phone, TV, and air-conditioning and operate on the European Plan (a.k.a. EP, meaning without meals), unless we specify that they use the Continental Plan (CP, with a Continental breakfast), Breakfast Plan (BP, with a full breakfast), or Modified American Plan (MAP, with breakfast and dinner) or are all-inclusive (AI, including all meals and most activities). We always list facilities but not whether you'll be charged an extra fee to use them, so when pricing accommodations, find out what's included.

### Many Listings

| | |
|---|---|
| ★ | Fodor's Choice |
| ★ | Highly recommended |
| ✉ | Physical address |
| ↔ | Directions |
| 🕮 | Mailing address |
| ☎ | Telephone |
| 🖷 | Fax |
| ⊕ | On the Web |
| ✆ | E-mail |
| 🎟 | Admission fee |
| ⊙ | Open/closed times |
| ► | Start of walk/itinerary |
| Ⓣ | Metro stations |
| 💳 | Credit cards |

### Hotels & Restaurants

| | |
|---|---|
| 🏨 | Hotel |
| 🛏 | Number of rooms |
| ⚲ | Facilities |
| ❍ | Meal plans |
| ✕ | Restaurant |
| ⌖ | Reservations |
| ⌂ | Dress code |
| ⦨ | Smoking |
| ⦿ | BYOB |
| ✕🏨 | Hotel with restaurant that warrants a visit |

### Outdoors

| | |
|---|---|
| 🏌 | Golf |
| ⛺ | Camping |

### Other

| | |
|---|---|
| ♺ | Family-friendly |
| ✆ | Contact information |
| ⇨ | See also |
| ✉ | Branch address |
| ☞ | Take note |

# ABOUT OUR WRITERS

Valerie Hamilton has been turning Rome inside out for Fodor's since 1996, comparing churches, sampling spaghetti, and wrangling with more nuns than she cares to admit. When she's done bouncing quarters off of hotel beds, she steps out of the phone booth as a clipboard-brandishing, mike-wielding TV news producer, dedicated to the pursuit of truth, justice, and La Dolce Vita. After more than a decade in the Eternal City, Valerie has finally turned over all of her insider tips to Fodor's—you'll find her favorite restaurant, park and museum in this book, as well as the hotel where she puts her friends and family. For this edition, Valerie completely revamped our lodging chapter and updated our exploring chapter.

When Dana Klitzberg wound up spending more time in restaurants and kitchens than checking out Botticellis and Michelangelos during her college semester break in Florence, she knew which way her life was headed. After attending Peter Kump's New York Cooking School and a stint at the famous San Domenico restaurant in Manhattan, Dana returned to Rome to work as executive chef and line cook in several restaurants there, even starting an American-style brunch with her friends (helping spread the trend for this in Italy in the process). Rome is paradise for Dana, offering her a chance to be "a culinary professional in a country obsessed with extraordinary food," as she puts it. As she holds a degree in English Literature from the University of Virginia, authoring articles for many publications on food and travel marries her two loves perfectly. Today, she runs her culinary venture in Rome, Blu Aubergine, through which she gives private cooking classes and culinary tours, provides catering and personal chef services, and writes on food and style. For this edition, Dana completely revamped our dining chapter and also updated our nightlife/arts chapter.

After developing a passion for Renaissance art in high school, Margaret Stenhouse knew she was bound to call Italy her home one day. While she set off to explore the Boot, La Dolce Vita proved so irresistible that her intended six-month sojourn in Rome stretched on to become forty years. Her lifelong stay—from early years in an attic at Piazza Navona (which she shared with the odd rat) to her family home next to the Roman Forum—has allowed her to acquire an intimate knowledge of practically every corner of the city. An award-winning travel writer, she has also worked as a tour guide. In the past, she has been Rome correspondent for *The Herald,* Scotland's leading daily, and a contributor to the *International Herald Tribune*'s "Italy Daily" supplement and the monthly magazine, *Italy Italy.* Recently, she moved permanently to her weekend house in the Castelli Romani hills south of Rome, where she lives with her husband, three sons, two grandchildren, a cat, and a very large and woolly Maremmano sheepdog. For this edition, she completely revamped our shopping chapter and updated our Smart Travel Tips and side trips chapters.

New York–based editor Robert I. C. Fisher considers Rome his spiritual home. Since studying its Renaissance art under the tutelage of the "pope"—Sir John Pope-Hennessy, that is—at the Institute of Fine Arts in the 1980s, he has visited Mamma Roma many times, including a trip to write up the Capitoline Hill palazzo of Count and Countess Ferdinando Pecci-Blunt for *Town & Country.*

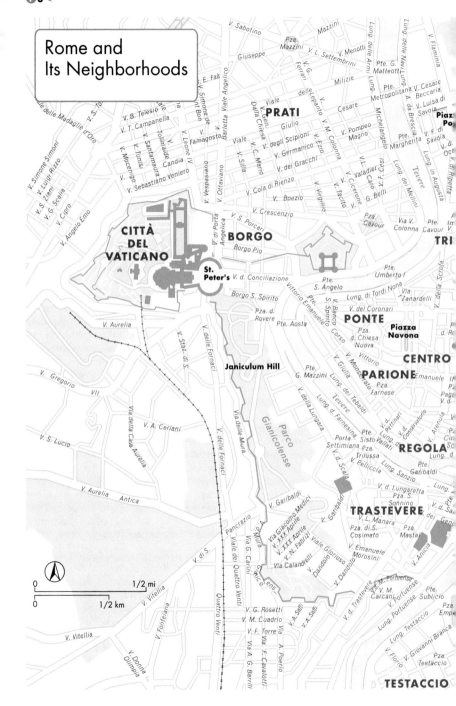

# Rome and Its Neighborhoods

Viale delle Belle Arti

Vle. G. Washington

V. Pietro Raimondi

Botanical Gardens

Villa Borghese

Museo e Galleria Borghese

**PARIOLI**

V. Salaria

Viale Regina Margherita

Via Arno

V. di Villa Albanini

Via Savoia

Via Nizza

V. Nomentana

V. dei Villini

Pza. V. Alessandria

Viale d. Policlinico

Pincio

V. d. Magnolie

V. P. Canonica

Viale Canonica

Galoppatoia

Viale del Muro

Villa Medici

Viale d. Museo Borghese

Porta Pinciana

Corso d' Italia

Pza. Fiume

Alessandria

Pte. di Porta Pia

Piazza del Popolo

V. di Ripetta

V. del Corso

V. del Babuino

V. dei Greci

V. di Pta. Pinciana

V. G. Annunzio

V. Medici

Torto

Campania

**LUDOVISI**

Vitt. Veneto

V. Ludovisi

V. Liguria

V. Pinciana

V. Boncompagni

V. Romagna

V. Piave

V. Quintino Sella

Settembre

V. Castelfidardo

V. Goito

V. Montebello

Viale d.

**CASTRO PRETORIO**

**SAN LORENZO**

Pza. Augusto Imperatore

V. Tomacelli

Pza. di Spagna

**Spanish Steps**

V. della Croce

V. delle Carozzi

V. Condotti

V. Borgognona

V. Frattina

V. di Due Macelli

**TRIDENTE**

V. della Vite

V. d. Mercede

V. del Tritone

V. d. Umiltà

Vitt. Veneto

Nicola

V. Sistina

Purificazione

Pza. Barberini

San Nicola

Tolentino

V. Barberini

V. Sallustiana

V. Bissolati

V. Firenze

V. Orlando

V. XX

V. Cernaia

V. Gaeta

V. S. Martino

Pza. di Cinquecento

V. Volturno

V. Vicenza

Palestro

V. Marghera

V. Milazzo

V. Castro Pretorio

Viale Pretoriano

**COLLE QUIRINALE**

Giardini del Quirinale

**Trevi Fountain**

V. d. Muratte

V. d. Scuderie

Pza. Colonna

V. d. del Corso

V. di Campo Marzio

V. d. Quattro Fontane

V. Napoli

V. A. Depretis

V. Torino

V. Viminale

Via d'Aveglio

V. Cavour

V. Manin

**Piazza della Reppublica**

**Stazione Termini**

V. Marsala

**Palazzo del Quirinale**

V. del Quirinale

Pza. Rotonda

**Pantheon**

V. Nazionale

V. Pilotta

V. Novembre

SS. Apostoli

Milano

V. d. Serpenti

Panisperna

V. d. S. Maria Maggiore

V. Cavour

V. G. Amendola

V. Giolitti

V. Gioberti

V. Carlo Cattáneo

G. Giovanni Giolitti

V. Napoleone III

V. Pr. Umberto

**ISTORICO**

V. d. Plebiscito

V. d. Battisti

Pza. Aracanica d. B. Oscure

**Piazza Venezia**

Pza. d'Aracoeli

**Vittoriano**

V. d. Fori Imperiali

**COLLE VIMINALE**

V. d. Zingari

V. Leonina

V. d. Cantoni

V. Quattro

V. Sforza

V. Giovanni Lanza

Pza. Vittoria Emanuele II

V. Carlo Alberto

V. d. Statuto

**ESQUILINO**

V. Pr. Eugenio

V. Conte Verde

V. Cairoli

V. Emanuele Filiberto

Pza. Manzoni

**GHETTO**

V. d. Funari

Pza. Cinque Scole

d. Cenci

Pte. Fabricio

**Campidoglio**

V. d. Marcello

**COLLE CAPITOLINO**

Teodoro

V. Madonna d. Monti

V. Cavour

**COLLE ESQUILINO**

Viale del Monte Oppio

**Domus Aurea**

V. d. Domus Aurea

V. Terme di Traiano

V. Mecenate

V. Botta

V. Merulana

V. Giusti

V. Ferruccio

Pza. Dante

V. Ruggero Bonghi

V. Murator

V. Petrarca

V. Galilea

V. Ariosto

V. Tasso

V. M. Bolardo

V. Labicana

V. S. Giovanni in Laterano

V. S. S. Quattro

Via Annia

**CAMPITELLI**

**Roman Forum**

**Colosseum**

V. Claudia

V. d. S. Gregorio

Pza. SS. Giovanni e Paolo

**COLLE CELIO**

**CELIO**

V. di S. Stefano

Rotondo

V. d. Erasmo

Villa Fonseca

Pza. Giovanni XXIII

**S. Giovanni in Laterano**

V. Amba Aradam

V. Funari

Lung. Ripa

Tevere

Lung. Aventino

V. dei Cerchi

V. del Circo Massimo

Pza. Ugo Saffi la Maifa

**Circo Massimo**

V. di Valle d. Camene

Via d. Terme d. Caracalla

Pza. di Porta Metronia

V. Ipponio

V. Druso

V. Sibari

Merruvio

V. Gallia

**COLLE AVENTINO**

Pza. d. Tempio

V. d. S. Sabina

V. di S. Anselmo

V. d. Decii

V. d. Diane

**RIPA/ ARENTINO**

Parco di Porta Capena

**Terme di Caracalla**

Pza. Numa Pompilio

Antoniniana

Pza. Albania

L. Fioritto

G. Baccelli

V. d. Porta Latina

V. Marmorata

V. M. Gelsomini

V. Ponzio Femuria

Guido Baccelli

Aventina

Rome is a veritable Grand Canyon of culture, built up with stratified layers of pagan, medieval, Baroque, and modern influences. Most everyone begins by discovering the grandeur that was Rome: the Colosseum, the Forum, and the Pantheon. Then many move on to the Vatican, the closest thing to heaven on earth for some. The historical pageant continues with the 1,001 splendors of the Baroque era: glittering palaces, jewel-studded churches, and Caravaggio masterpieces. Arrive refreshed—thanks to an espresso at Antico Caffè Greco—at the foot of the Spanish Steps, where the picturesque world of the classic Grand Tour (peopled by such spirits as John Keats and Tosca) awaits you. To help you catch your historic breath along the way, Rome provides delightful ways to relax: a walk through the cobblestone valleys of Trastevere; a campari-break in a café facing a timeless piazza; an hour stolen alongside a splashing Bernini fountain, under the balm of Roman sunshine. A visit to the Eternal City will live up to its name in memory.

Although 3 million Romans live in the city and its wide-ranging suburbs, the good news is that practically all of the capital's myriad sights are in the *centro storico,* or historic center, a relatively small part of that area. Historic Rome is defined by the impressive Aurelian Wall that encompasses the city's core. In AD 7, the emperor Augustus organized ancient Rome into 14 *regiones,* administrative divisions that were the origin of the historic *rioni* (districts), many of which still have Latin-sounding names, such as Suburra, Esquilino, and Monti. The outline of most of the city's seven original hills has been dulled by landfill and development, but the Palatino and Aventino are still prominent heights. Modern Rome's neighborhoods may be known by ancient names, or by the names of key streets or piazzas. It's possible to walk from the leafy Villa Borghese park above Piazza del Popolo to the Gianicolo Hill on the other side of town, two of the most stunning vantage points of the historic center of Rome, in less than an hour and a half.

### Ancient Rome

Like a remnant of some forgotten Cecil B. DeMille movie-set, the massive late-19th-century Vittorio Emanuele monument—-the "eighth hill of Rome"—looms over the geographic center of the city, the **Piazza Venezia.** Just to its south rises the **Campidoglio** hill, crowned by Michelangelo's magnificent piazza and the **Capitoline museums.** Below them extends the most evocative ruins of the ancient city: the **Roman Forum,** bookended by two great triumphal arches, the **Arch of Constantine** and the **Arch of Titus.** Beyond Titus's monument lies the fabled **Colosseum** and the **Baths of Caracalla.** The cliff face that shadows the Forum is the **Palatine Hill**—the "Beverly Hills of ancient Rome"—this is where the emperors used to live and gaze down on the **Circus Massimo.** As an archaeological park of enormous dimensions, all this comprises one of the world's most striking and significant concentrations of historic remains. Except on the fringes, this area has no residents besides lazy lizards and complacent cats (be sure to take some packets of cat food to feed them). Stand at the back of the Campidoglio overlooking the Roman Forum and take in 2,500 years of history at a glance. Scattered throughout the city are many more ruins, reminders of just how vast ancient Rome really was.

## The Vatican

Seat of Roman Catholicism and residence of the popes, Vatican City has religious resonance and artistic splendors. Mostly enclosed within high walls that recall the papacy's stormy history, the Vatican opens the spectacular arms of **Bernini's Colonnade** to embrace the world at **Piazza San Pietro**, an immense meeting place for the faithful and scene of the pope's public appearances. The Basilica di San Pietro, or **St. Peter's Basilica**, is astounding for its size and glorious (mainly 18th-century) interior, studded with artistic masterpieces from Michelangeo's *Pietà* to Bernini's great bronze *baldacchino* canopy over the main altar. A good walk away from the main nave you can find the entrance to the **Vatican Museums**; the blisters will be worth it as the endless collections here contain many fabled artworks, ranging from the Apollo Belvedere to Leonardo's *St. Jerome* and Raphael's *Transfiguration*. The **Sistine Chapel** is Michelangelo's magnificent artistic legacy. Given that the Vatican is home to many of Rome's (and the world's) greatest art treasures, as well as being the spiritual home of a billion Catholics, this area of the city is full of tourists and pilgrims almost year-round. Between the Vatican and the once-moated bulk of **Castel Sant'Angelo**—erstwhile mausoleum of Emperor Hadrian and now a gorgeous relic of medieval Rome—the pope's covered passageway flanks an enclave of workers and craftspeople, the old Borgo neighborhood, whose workaday charm is beginning to succumb to gentrification.

## Old Rome

This is the Rome of your dreams: terra-cotta-hued palazzi, relentlessly picturesque squares and fountains, with one brauara Baroque architectural blockbuster after another. Here you can time-travel back to the 17th century and watch the world pass by on **Piazza Navona**—the "living room of Rome"—where you'll find Bernini's most lighthearted tribute to the Baroque style, the Fountain of the Four Rivers and Borromini's showiest showpiece, the church of **Sant'Agnese**. To either side of the piazza are more 17th-century wonders: one block to the west is the adorable piazza and church of **Santa Maria della Pace** designed by Pietro da Cortona; one block to the east lies the church of **San Luigi dei Francesi**, which has three of Caravaggio's greatest paintings. Continuing over to the Tiber you'll find **Via Giulia**, which, lined with palazzi, is still a 16th-century diorama. First laid out by Pope Julius II, Michelangelo's fiery patron, it remains the address of choice of some of Rome's princeliest families. Via Giulia leads south to the Piazza Farnese, where the **Palazzo Farnese** (the French embassy) still shelters the legendary landmark of the Baroque style, the Galleria painted by Annibale Caracci. One block to the east lies **Campo de' Fiori**, whose piazza is home to the city's lively food market. Continuing five blocks eastward you'll wind up at the magnificent **Pantheon**, one of the world's greatest buildings, which, along with the 3rd-century BC temples at **Largo Argentina** and the great antique sculptures on view at **Palazzo Altemps**, evokes ancient Rome. Other prelates' palaces, especially **Palazzo della Cancelleria,** make strong statements about the riches and power of the papal court. Churches such as **Il Gesù** tell even more about an era of religious triumph and turmoil. In between are narrow streets and intriguing little shops, interspersed with eating places and cafés that are a focus of Rome's easygoing, itinerant nightlife.

## The Spanish Steps & Trevi Fountain

The Rome of the Grand Tour era, this region was colonized by English lords and ladies in the 19th century and it still remains one of the most picturesque areas of the city. Back when, artists used to troll the area around the **Spanish Steps** for models; today, it remains a magnet all day and well into the night for teenage Romans and camera-toting tourists. At the foot of the steps are two relics of that period: the **Keats-Shelley Memorial House** and **Babington's Tea Rooms.** Fanning out from its **Piazza di Spagna** are streets that remain a shopper's paradise. In the triangle that extends north of Via del Tritone to Piazza del Popolo, the density of high-fashion boutiques and trendy little shops leaves little room for residents (although the neighborhoods on either side of honky-tonk Via del Tritone are sparsely populated). **Via Condotti** is perhaps the best-known shopping street in Italy, with many of the designer names that have made the Italian fashion industry a world leader; **Antico Caffè Greco**—one-time haunt of Franz Lizst, Mark Twain, and Hans Christian Andersen—is here. Especially on weekends, the Via Condotti–Via del Corso zone is sometimes jammed with swarms of Rome's young and very young, in from the city's outlying districts for a ritual stroll that resembles a chaotic migration of lemmings in blue jeans. But hordes of tourists make the scene around the Fontana di Trevi equally crowded, forcing the wishful to toss their coins into the fountain from center field. Art lovers will make a beeline for two of the most aristocratic palaces in Rome: the **Palazzo Doria Pamphilj** and the **Palazzo Colonna.** Each contains splendorous 17th-century rooms hung with great Old Master paintings, although, for pomp and ceremony, even they are trumped by the glitter of **Sant'Ignazio,** Rome's most opulent Baroque church.

## The Quirinale to Piazza della Repubblica

Pompous ministry buildings, government palaces, and a plethora of offices and banks mark this area as central Rome's principal business district, but you can also find some glorious monuments of Rome's artistic legacy here. The massive **Palazzo Quirinale** marks the more sober limit of this district laid out in the late 19th century, after the unification of Italy under the Savoy kings and the pope's retreat to the Vatican, which left the city free to become the capital of the new kingdom. Home to Italy's president, it has a panoply of over-the-top spectacular salons you can see on a tour. For more venerable treasures, head over a few blocks to the north; on ugly, frantic **Piazza Barberini,** you can catch Bernini's Fontana del Tritone, while just up the road is one of Rome's biggest 17th-century extravaganzas, the **Palazzo Barberini.** Continue a few blocks to the north and you'll find the quintessence of Roman Baroque in the Cappella Cornaro of **Santa Maria della Vittoria:** Bernini's *Ecstasy of St. Theresa.* A few blocks to the west, **Piazza della Repubblica** is another example of how Rome's history is revealed in layers: the vast ruins of the Baths of Diocletian, the **Terme di Diocleziano,** were transformed into a Renaissance monastery and the church of Santa Maria degli Angeli, designed by Michelangelo, while the piazza itself, a paragon of late-19th-century urban planning, echoes the outline of the ancient baths. Today one of Rome's hippest hotels, the Exedra, occupies part of the mammoth palazzo, which overlooks the piazza's gigantic fountain. Meanwhile, an oasis of ease appears on **Via Veneto,** where a former Savoy palace is now the American Embassy and where grand hotels and elegant cafés bask in the afterglow of La Dolce Vita.

## Villa Borghese to the Ara Pacis

Much of this district accommodates Rome's most central park, dotted with pines and fountains and neoclassical faux ruins. The lush park of **Villa Borghese** is a happy conjunction of the pleasure gardens and palaces of Renaissance prelates on the site of ancient Roman villas. It's expanse of greenery is studded with world-class museums. The most celebrated is the **Galleria Borghese,** set in a regal palazzo built by Cardinal Scipione Borghese to house his fabulous art collection. Great paintings by Titian and Raphael, a slew of Bernini statues, and some of the most sumptuous 17th-century salons ravish the eye here. Near the northwest end of the park, the Villa Giulia also has a history of its own, as it was built for Pope Julius II around 1550 and today houses the **Museo Etrusco,** a fairly dry collection of Etruscan artifacts. Nearby is the Neoclassical gallery that somewhat incongruously houses collections of modern art, the **Galleria Nazionale d'Arte Moderna.** Moving to the south of the park, the **Pincio** hill is a belvedere over the city. Here you'll find the elegantly picturesque **Villa Medici,** whose gardens were once painted by Velásquez, Fragonard, and Ingres. Once a favored place for the 19th-century rich and famous to take their promenades, the Pincian remains a lovely vantage point over elegantly planned **Piazza del Popolo.** The piazza's cafés are, in turn, vantage points from which to enjoy the variegated passersby. Crossing the piazza are dedicated shoppers heading for Via del Corso's emporia, art students on mopeds veering toward Via Ripetta and the local school for the arts, and more subdued types on their way to the art and antiques galleries on Via del Babuino or Via Margutta. In the opposite direction, art lovers hurry to **Santa Maria del Popolo,** a church with famous chapels decorated by Raphael and Caravaggio. Five blocks to the south is the great **Ara Pacis Augustae,** an ancient Roman altar decorated with sculpted reliefs of the ruling imperial families.

## Trastevere & the Ghetto

The charming little island of the Tiber, the **Isola Tiberina,** with bridges on either side, links two of the city's most distinctive neighborhoods: the Jewish Ghetto on the Tiber's left bank and Trastevere across the river. Both were bustling neighborhoods even in the earliest Roman times. What was to become the **Ghetto** in the 1500s was at the edge of ancient Rome's river port and wholesale marketplace. Trastevere was the place where immigrants from the empire's eastern colonies lived, among them ancient Rome's large Jewish community, which moved across the Tiber during the Middle Ages. Despite creeping gentrification, the Ghetto still preserves the flavor of Old Rome and a sense of community revolving around Via Portico d'Ottavia and the nearby Synagogue. There may be few public signs of Jewish life left in this quarter, but it's still the symbolic center of the city's Jewish community, and architecturally one of Rome's most charming rioni. The most venerable landmark is the ancient Roman **Portico d'Ottavia,** built into the church of Sant'Angelo in Pescheria. Nearby is another of ancient Rome's most evocative relics, the **Teatro di Marcello,** an ancient theater that now contains some posh apartments. Somewhat schizophrenic, **Trastevere** is trying to find its equilibrium on a fine line between its historic, authentic Roman character and a pseudo-folksy sensibility. It's afflicted with too many cute little restaurants and pizzerias, clubby tearooms and trendy shops, and noisy late-night activity. But it still hides some lovely medieval alleyways and no one can dismiss its beautiful piazza, **Santa Maria in Trastevere,** or its namesake church, whose sublimely gilded nave conjures up the splendor of ancient Rome better than any other in the city. At night, both the piazza's fountain and the church's mosaic facade are spotlit: Rome at its postcard best. Several blocks to the north lie two famous palaces, the **Palazzo Corsini,** with a fine art collection, and the **Villa Farnesina,** with some great Raphael frescoes. To top things off, bus up (and hike down) the tallest of Rome's hills, the **Gianicolo** (Janiculum) for a view that puts all Rome at your feet.

## The Aventine Hill to St. Paul's

Gateway to the Aventino area is the evocative **Piazza Bocca della Verità,** where three enormously appealing monuments sit shoulder to shoulder: two ancient dollhouse-size Roman temples, the **Temple of Fortuna Virilis** and the circular **Temple of Vesta,** both shadowed by the soaring campanile of **Santa Maria in Cosmedin,** a Romanesque masterpiece and candidate for the city's most poetic church (its portico shelters the famous Roman "Mouth of Truth" that once so scared Audrey Hepburn in *Roman Holiday*). Moving south, you begin to climb the Aventino, one of Rome's seven hills, now an upscale residential neighborhood lush with private gardens, several early churches—notably, the medieval **San Saba** and the stirringly handsome early Christian **Santa Sabina**—the famous keyhole with a view of St. Peter's found on the **Piazza Cavalieri di Malta,** and Parco Savelli, known for orange trees and a great view up the Tiber toward Old Rome. The view of the Palatino from the northern approaches to the Aventino gives an insight into the scale of Imperial Rome's palaces. Beyond, **Testaccio** is a working-class neighborhood that has been transformed into a trendy place to eat and club-hop into the wee hours of the morning. It's at the foot of Mount Testaccio, a man-made hill that served once as a dump for shards of the amphorae that the ancient Romans used to transport foodstuffs. Other than the **Piramide,** a monumental Roman tomb, and the **Cimitero Acattolico**—the exquisitely picturesque resting spot of poet John Keats and other English expatriates—there's not much to see between here and the Basilica of **San Paolo fuori le Mura,** which is about 2 km (1 mi) down the drab Via Ostiense.

## The Celian Hill & the Baths of Caracalla

Almost entirely given over to parks, churches, and ruins, the area encompassing the Celio (Celian Hill) and the ancient Terme di Caracalla includes islands of quiet that seem far removed from the streams of traffic swirling around it. Several early Christian churches and the towering brick structures of the baths provide historical interest. South of the Colosseum area stretches the verdant **Villa Celimontana** park; hidden here is a place where time seems to be holding its breath, the **Piazza Santi Giovanni e Paolo**, accessed by the ancient Clivo di Scauro arched pathway. To the south, bowered by the park trees, lies the church of **San Gregorio Magno**, fronted with one of Rome's most nobly Baroque facades. On the eastern edge of the park lie two fine historic churches, **Santa Maria in Domnica** and the circular **Santo Stefano Rotondo**, which is filled with the goriest frescoes ever painted. Five blocks to the north are **Santi Quattro Coronati**—The Four Crowned Saints, a magisterial relic of Rome's medieval period—and the early Christian splendors of **San Clemente**.

## Monti & San Giovanni in Laterano

Monti was the Roman neighborhood of Suburra, where the plebs of ancient Rome lived in dark tenements, with a high wall between their mean streets and the glories of the Imperial Fora. The neighborhood has a workaday, pleasant part along Via Panisperna and Via dei Serpenti, streets that follow the declivity of the Esquilino (Esquiline Hill) and are lined with offbeat shops and little restaurants. Artistic treasures appear in out-of-the-way corners, such as Michelangelo's *Moses* in the church of **San Pietro in Vincoli** and the extraordinary early Christian mosaic of Christ with the Apostles found in the church of **Santa Pudenziana** and the later Byzantine mosaic chapel at **Santa Prassede** (both saints were martyred daughters of a Roman senator who was friendly to Peter and Paul—yes, these are proven historic links to the earliest Christian days). The great basilicas of **Santa Maria Maggiore** and **San Giovanni in Laterano** loom at the end of the broad avenues laid out centuries ago by the popes to make the pilgrims' way through Rome a little easier. Via Nazionale, instead, is a 19th-century thoroughfare that cuts a straight line from Piazza della Repubblica down to Via IV Novembre and Piazza Venezia. It's home to dozens of Rome's more affordable clothing shops. The **Termini Station** neighborhood is a patchwork of dignified and seamy blocks; the patterns shift from time to time, but the area in general seems to be putting its better face forward in the wake of urban renewal projects. The Piazza Vittorio area is an ethnic kaleidoscope, full of African, Asian, and Middle Eastern shops and restaurants.

## Via Appia Antica

The ancient Via Appia starts at Porta San Sebastiano and extends across the Italian Peninsula to the Adriatic. The first portion of the road, rich with ruins, will someday be the core of a proposed archaeological park encompassing many of ancient Rome's most majestic sites. To the east lies the Via Appia Nuova, which starts in front of the basilica of San Giovanni in Laterano and cuts through miles of highly developed residential neighborhood to reach the Capannelle racetrack, Ciampino Airport, and points southeast. The Via Appia Antica, so called to distinguish it from the modern thoroughfare, leads past the landmark church of Domine Quo Vadis and walled gardens to the Catacombs—notably the two most famous, the **Catacombe di San Callisto** and the **Catacombe di San Sebastiano.** Past the Jewish Catacombs lies the **Circus of Maxentius,** while a bit farther looms the **Tomba di Cecilia Metella,** where the lush countryside is dotted with evocative ruins and the arches of ancient aqueducts. It's long been a favored spot among Romans for a Sunday stroll, when a stretch of it is sealed off from traffic. This exclusive area is home to such personalities as Gina Lollobrigida and Franco Zeffirelli.

## Side Trips from Rome
Romans are undeniably lucky. For just beyond their city gates lie the wonders and splendors of the region called Lazio, filled with superb destinations that make great day trips. You can visit **Ostia Antica,** the "Pompeii of Rome"—an entire ancient Roman port city preserved without the help of a volcano. Thirty miles to the north lies Tuscia, which is fabled for its Renaissance-era villas and gardens, including the **Villa Lante, Bomarzo,** and **Caprarola,** along with **Viterbo,** with its famous medieval town center. Head east of Rome to find **Tivoli,** home to two showstoppers: the **Villa Adriana** (Hadrian's Villa) and the **Villa d'Este,** whose spectacular fountains make this possibly the most beautiful garden in the world. Nearby **Palestrina** has some extensive ancient Roman ruins, while **Subiaco** has a sublime medieval monastery. Directly south of Rome lies the **Castelli Romani.** Here the **Villa Aldobrandini** is just one of the palatial estates that dot **Frascati,** the "Beverly Hills" of the 17th century. Nearby is **Castelgandolfo,** famed for its **Villa Pontifica**—the country retreat of the pope—and the town's lakeside lido. **Arricia** is an overlooked Baroque jewel of a town, studded with palaces and Bernini designs. **Nemi** is the smallest and prettiest town of the area.

Contact the Italian Government Tourist Board (⇨ Visitor Information, *in* Smart Travel Tips) for exact dates and further information on all the festivals held in Rome.

| | |
|---|---|
| **ONGOING**<br>Mid-June–Oct. | The French Academy at Villa Medici holds a festival of performing arts called RomaEuropa (⊕ www.romaeuropa.net). It's Rome's biggest international arts festival. The curtain rises in June, but most of the main events are in September and October. |
| **WINTER**<br>Dec. 8 | This is the day of the Festa dell'Immacolata Concezione, (Feast of the Immaculate Conception), when Rome's fire department replaces the garland atop the statue of the Virgin Mary in Piazza di Spagna and the pope comes to pay his respects. |
| Mid-Dec. | Rome's opera season begins. |
| Late Dec. | Presepi (Christmas crèches) go on display in many churches; some of them are antique and quite elaborate. They often remain into the new year. |
| Dec. 24 & 25 | Natale (Christmas) is very much a family holiday in Rome. There are no public celebrations other than solemn religious rites, beginning on Christmas Eve; these are especially beautiful in the city's older churches and in St. Peter's Basilica, where the pope officiates both at midnight mass and at the late-morning mass on Christmas Day before imparting his blessing to the faithful in the square (for tickets for the basilica mass, fax the Pretfettura della Casa Pontificia at 06/6988–5863). Rome has more churches per square foot than any other city in the world. A Christmas service in one of the city's ancient places of worship is not to be missed. |
| Dec. 31 | To celebrate New Year's Eve, San Silvestro, the city mounts a free concert and fireworks in the Piazza del Popolo. A concert is also held on the Quirinale Hill. |
| Jan. 5 & 6 | On the eve of Epifania (Epiphany Celebrations), Piazza Navona's toy fair finishes with much noise and rowdiness to encourage Befana, an old woman who brings toys to good children and pieces of coal (represented by similar-looking candy) to the naughty. |
| Feb. | Carnivale celebrations reach a peak of masquerading fun on the Sunday and Tuesday before Lent begins. On the evening of Martedí Grasso (Mardi Gras) many restaurants hold special carnival parties—you'll need to make reservations well in advance. |
| Late Feb.–<br>early Mar. | Watch for the Settimana Beni Culturali (Museum Week), a week of cultural heritage when museums and archaeological sites are free. |
| **SPRING**<br>Mar. & Apr. | Pasqua (Easter) is the big event of the season, preceded by the solemn rites of Holy Week, or Settimana Santa, in which the pope takes an active part (⊕ www.vatican.va). Concerts of sacred music abound |

in churches all around town. The Good Friday procession of the Stations of the Cross, led by the pope near the Colosseum, is both moving and spectacular. The Monday after Easter, known as Pasquetta, is a holiday and traditionally a day for an outing into the country. This is one of the busiest weeks of the year in Rome; make reservations well in advance.

| | |
|---|---|
| Late Apr. | The Piazza di Spagna bursts into bloom, with the Spanish Steps covered by azaleas. Nearby, Via Margutta holds an outdoor art show. |
| May | The Primo Maggio outdoor concert extravaganza is a blast organized by Italy's biggest labor unions. Held on Piazza di San Giovanni in Laterano on May 1, this free concert attracts hundreds of thousands. The Festival Internazionale delle Letterature hosts some of the world's great writers in outdoor readings in the fabled setting of the Basilica of Maxentius. Last year, Salman Rushie, Jonathan Safran Foer, and Amos Oz participated. An antiques fair is held in the beautiful old Via dei Coronari in Old Rome. Shops stay open late and the street is lighted by torches. Don't expect to find many bargains among the seductive antiques shops. The fair is repeated in October. In late May, the Federazione Italiana Tennis (Italian International Tennis Tournament; ✉ Viale Tiziano 74 ☎ 06/36858510) is held at the Foro Italico. |
| **SUMMER** June & July | In June and July there are concerts of classical, jazz, and ethnic music every Wednesday evening in the gardens of Villa Mazzanti on the hill of Monte Mario northwest of the Vatican. |
| June–Aug. | Movie buffs can choose from half a dozen film festivals in the summer—the most interesting being the Massenzio in the Parco dell'Appia Antica, the L'Isola del Cinema on the Gianicolo Hill near Trastevere, and the outdoor screenings on the Tiber Island. Consult local magazine listings for details. |
| June–Sept. | The Estate Romana program, sponsored by several of the national academies in the city, consists of outdoor concerts, plays, and movies throughout the city at such venues as the Baths of Caracalla and church cloisters (⊕ www.estateromana.it). Check with the local tourist office for schedules. The Jazz & Image series brings together hot-cool players for 9 PM concerts in the beautifully illuminated gardens of the Villa Celimontana, near the Colosseum, during the summer months. |
| June 23 | On the eve of the Festa di San Giovanni (Feast of St. John the Baptist, June 24) the neighborhood of San Giovanni bursts with festive activities, mainly gastronomic. |
| June 29 | The Festa di San Pietro (Feast of St. Peter), patron saint of Rome, is marked by solemn celebrations in St. Peter's Basilica, when the interior of the church is ablaze with light, and by showy fireworks over the Aventine Hill. |

| | |
|---|---|
| July–August | Ballet, opera, and concert lovers can take in the Festival EuroMediterraneo performances at the ancient Roman Villa Adriana in Tivoli, outside Rome. To get here, use the special bus that leaves from Via Marsala at 7 PM on event days. The famous opera performances in the Baths of Caracalla are presented by Rome's Teatro dell'Opera (⊕ www.opera.roma.it). |
| Mid-July | The Cosmophonies music festival hosts grand concerts in the amphitheater in Ostia Antica during July (⊕ www.cosmophonies.com). The Festa di Noantri in Trastevere combines religious processions with concerts of traditional Roman music and a sidewalk fair. |
| Aug. 5 | The Festa della Madonna della Neve (Feast of the Madonna of the Snow) is marked in the Basilica of Santa Maria Maggiore by a high mass, during which white rose petals are thrown to represent the miraculous August snowfall that indicated where the church should be built. |
| Aug. 15 | Ferragosto marks the height of the summer vacation period. Most shops, restaurants, and museums are closed; public transport is at a minimum; and the city is the quietest it will ever be. There are special celebrations in the church of Santa Maria in Trastevere. |
| **FALL** <br> Sept. | The Enzimi festival hosts the newest talents in the arts—for Italians, tomorrow's stars are often born here. |
| Late Sept.– early Oct. | A Mercatino di Via dell'Orso (Handicrafts Fair) in Rome brings torchlight, street stalls, and animation to Via dell'Orso. |
| Early Oct. | In the Alban Hills southeast of Rome, Marino's La Sagra dell'Uva (Grape Harvest Festival) features parades and fountains spouting wine. |
| Oct. | Look for the fall version of the semiannual antiques fair on Via dei Coronari in Old Rome. |

Romans are fond of reminding visitors that Rome wasn't built in a day. Neither can it be seen in a day, or even two or three. In a city with as many richly stocked museums and marvels as Mamma Roma, tourists risk seeing half of everything and all of nothing. So use the itineraries below as suggestions to keep you on track as you explore both the famous sights and those off the beaten path. Remember to be Nero-esque in your rambles—and fiddle while you roam: people who stop for a caffè occasionally get more out of these breaks than those who breathlessly try to make every second count. After all, there's no way to see everything. The Italian author Silvio Negro said it best: *"Roma, non basta una vita"* (Rome, a lifetime is not enough).

## If You Have 2 Days

So you want to taste Rome, gaze at its beauty, and inhale its special flair, all in one breathtaking (literally) day? Think Rome 101, and get ready for a spectacular sunrise-to-sunset span. Begin with the Grandeur that Was (and is) Rome: the **Colosseum**. No need to arrive by chariot, as there is a handy Colosseo metro stop. Get there by 9 AM when the gates open. After an hour, head past the gigantic **Arch of Constantine** across Via di San Gregorio and find the "back exit" to the **Roman Forum**. Actually, this is the best way to enter, since you'll be parading down the ancient Via Sacra past the small but gorgeous **Arch of Titus**. On your right, notice the vast **Basilica of Maxentius** and the impressive colonnaded front of the Temple of Antoninus and Faustina; to your left looms the graceful circular Temple of Vesta, shrine of the Vestal Virgins. Continue along the ancient Roman paving stones toward the Capitoline Hill on the horizon. Here, under its cliff, you can see some of the Forum's greatest remnants, including the redbrick **Curia** and, to its right, the **Rostra** platform where Mark Antony once eulogized Julius Caesar. Straight ahead is the magnificent **Arch of Septimius Severus.** To its left up the hill are the eight remaining Ionic columns of the mighty **Temple of Saturn**— a favorite icon of Grand Tour visitors. Around this temple winds the Clivus Capitolinus, the ancient stone path that leads up to the top of the **Capitoline Hill.** Today, this leads into the Via di Monte Tarpeo, which will take you to the top and the complex of museums and palazzi that comprise Michelangelo's glorious Campidoglio; if that street is closed, exit by the Via del Foro Romano entrance to the Forum and wind your way over. Tour the **Musei Capitolini**'s legendary ancient sculptures (and some opulent Baroque salons), including the *Dying Gaul,* the *Capitoline Wolf,* the gigantic stone face of Constantine, and the Sala degli Imperatori, where ancient marble busts of no less than 48 Roman emperors gaze at you. Head off the Campidoglio down the Cordonata stairway back down to busy Via di Teatro di Marcello.

By now, your feet may be calling for a sit-down strike, so break for lunch. If you're up for it, one of the city's most quintessential feasting spots, Vecchia Roma, is a few blocks to the northwest, on lovely Piazza Campitelli (you'll need to reserve, dress accordingly, and spend money— but remember that many Romans make luncheon the main meal of the day). After your time out at Vecchia Roma—or a corner café—continue on Via di Teatro di Marcello, passing **Santa Maria in Aracoeli,** which sits atop its 137 steps ("the grandest loafing place of mankind," as Henry James described it); this is the perch that inspired Gibbon to write his history of the fall and decline of the Roman empire. Looming up over all is now the gigantic **Vittorio Emanuele Monument,** the "Altar of the Nation." Although it looks like some leftover from a Hollywood spectacular, it does offer great views from its top.

In front of the monument roars the central traffic hub of Rome, **Piazza Venezia.** Work your way around to its opposite end to find the Corso, the main drag of the center city. One block up the left side you can find the **Palazzo Doria Pamphilj,** the palace of one of Rome's most aristocratic families—tour its gigantic salons, which are virtually wallpapered with fine Old Master paintings (including a great Velázquez portrait of the "family" pope). Take the first left down Via Lata past the Piazza del Collegio Romano and turn right on Via Sant' Ignazio to **Sant' Ignazio,** a church that exults in hyperopulent Roman Baroque. Note the cute stage-set piazza out front, then return to Via Sant' Ignazio to Via Pie' Di Marmo, which leads into Via di S. Caterina di Siena to wind up at Piazza della Minerva, graced by Bernini's unique elephant obelisk monument. The church of **Santa Maria sopra Minerva** has Michelangelo's *Risen Christ* and the gorgeous Renaissance-era Carafa Chapel. Head north one block up Via di Minerva to the massive bulk of the **Pantheon.** After exploring this most complete temple extant from the days of the emperors, head west from the Piazza della Rotonda along Via Giustiniani to **San Luigi dei Francesi,** whose Cerasi Chapel has three unforgettable Caravaggio paintings, probably the greatest works of the Italian Baroque period. From here it's two blocks over to **Piazza Navona,** the most beautiful urban set piece of Rome and the perfect place for a cappuccino soak. This is a prime area to watch Romans enjoy their sunset passeggiata promenade. Join them as you walk in search of an evening meal but head back in the direction in which you came. Some 14 blocks eastward lies the spotlit-at-night **Trevi Fountain,** which you should enjoy with a gelato cone in one hand and a euro coin in the other.

To start your second day, use the convenient metro stop of Via Cipro/ Musei Vaticano to deposit you a few blocks from the entrance to the great art collections of the **Vatican Museums.** Michelangelo's Sistine Ceiling, Raphael's Stanze rooms, and Leonardo da Vinci's *St. Jerome* are just three of the hundreds of treasures you'll savor here. If you're lucky the entrance to **St. Peter's Basilica** from the Sistine Chapel will be open; if not, you'll have to take a hike of some 10 blocks around to the main entrance of St. Peter's proper, Bernini's spectacular **Piazza di San Pietro.** If you keep moving, you should be able to do the museums and the basilica by lunch time; a tour of the Vatican gardens or a climb up to the church's dome will require more stamina. After touring the Vaticano, hike eight blocks north of the piazza to the Ottaviano metro stop and take it three stops to the Spagna stop. Here you'll surface right at the feet of that living postcard: the **Spanish Steps.** Tackle all those steps for the view at the top and Via Gregoriana, a very posh street where you can find (and photograph!) Rome's most amusing house, the **Palazzetto Zuccari,** a Mannerist-style masterwork (the door is a mouth, etc.). Back down at the foot of the steps is the **Keats–Shelley House**—to keep that 19th-century vibe going, repair to Babington's Tea Rooms for a Victorian-era cup of tea or head down **Via Condotti** to Antico Caffè Greco, Rome's oldest coffeehouse. This street is lined with Rome's most famous luxury stores, as are the surrounding sidestreets, especially Via Bocca di Leone and Via Bogognona. Have dinner, then opt perhaps for an orchestra concert at the gilded Baroque church or frug down memory lane at that landmark disco, Jackie O's.

## If You Have 5 Days

Rome at its most charming awaits you on Day 3. Begin at **Piazza Bocca della Verità** and three sights that sit shoulder to shoulder: the beautiful medieval church of **Santa Maria in Cosmedin** (where you'll find the famous ancient Roman "Mouth of Truth" manhole cover) plus two pagan temples, the **Tempio della Fortuna Virilis** and the **Tempio di Vesta.** Head up north along the embankment of the Tiber River past the **Theater of Marcellus** to Via di Portico d'Ottavia, the heart of the old **Jewish Ghetto,** where the streets are particularly time-burnished (catch pretty Renaissance-era Piazza Mattei one block north). Head back to the river and cross the Ponte Fabricio, which delightfully anchors the **Tiber Island** to the mainland. You'll now enter **Trastevere,** once known as Rome's Greenwich Village, and threaded with little alleys and tiny piazze. Travel north to Piazza **Santa Maria in Trastevere,** where the gilded mosaics on its church facade pale in comparison to the splendor of those within. Yes, this is probably Rome's most spectacular church nave. Return to the fountain-adorned piazza, then continue north to two grand palaces: the **Palazzo Corsini** and the **Villa Farnesina,** with great frescoes by Raphael, then break for lunch at Raphael's old watering hole, Romolo's. Head back south a few blocks to the end and cross Ponte Sisto to pick up the beginning of **Via Giulia;** laid out during the Renaissance by Pope Julius II and lined with palazzi, it's still one of Rome's most noble addresses. Follow the razor-straight road to the end (a good 12 blocks) to emerge at the river embankment, where you can turn right to find **Ponte Sant'Angelo,** adorned with Bernini's angel statues, and the great **Castel Sant'Angelo** fort. If you wish more ancient splendors, head to the **Palazzo Altemps** on nearby Piazza Sant'Apollinare; for red-velvet, 19th-century luxury, go to the **Museo Napoleonico** (in the same building you'll find that connoisseur's delight, the Mario Praz apartment museum). Enjoy dinner and a sunset back at Piazza Navona.

For Day 4, opt for a holiday from your Roman holiday: take a day trip out to **Tivoli** to be regaled by the **Villa d'Este** and its hundreds of breathtaking fountains. Lovers of all things antique will make a side trip to the **Villa Adriana**—Emperor Hadrian's pleasure palace—just outside town. For a stunning sunset repast, take in a dinner at Ristorante Sibilla, where two ancient Roman temples frame the terrace set over a gorge and a famous waterfall.

Day 5 may give you a bout of museum feet but the blisters will be well worth it, for beautiful masterpieces are as common as bricks on this tour, which offers more visual excitement than most cities possess in their entire environs. Along the way, Villa Borghese, Rome's largest park, can prevent gallery gout by offering an oasis of trees and lakes. Begin by taking the metro to the Repubblica stop to take in the fabulous ancient Greek and Roman art treasures in the gigantic **Palazzo Massimo alle Terme**; for the real thing, walk two blocks north to the **Baths of Diocletian**. If big barnlike spaces don't turn you on, skip it and forge instead past the Piazza della Repubblica's circular fountain along Via V. Emanuele Orlando past the Acqua Felice fountain to Via XX Settembre: here you'll find **Santa Maria della Vittoria**, home to Bernini's amazing *St. Theresa in Ecstasy.* Take Via Bissolati over to Via Veneto, lined with grand Belle Epoque hotels, and hike past seven blocks to the Porta Pinciana and the entrance to the **Villa Borghese** park. Hang a right and go north about four blocks to the **Galleria Borghese**, perhaps Rome's most spectacular palace, crammed to the gills with priceless Old Master paintings and a bevy of Bernini statues. Picnic under the park's ilex trees or find a neighborhood café or *tavola calda.* Then wander south through the park down to the Pincian Hill, where you can book a tour of the enchanting gardens of the **Villa Medici**, before ending up at **Piazza del Popolo.** Hopefully, the masterpiece-jammed church of **Santa Maria del Popolo** will still be open for evening services. For dinner why not book a luxe blowout at Dal Bolognese, right across the square? After all, congratulations are in order: you've just completed a grand tour across two millennia and viewed some of the greatest works of western civilization in only five days.

# PLEASURES & PASTIMES

**The Art of Enjoying Art** Travel veterans will tell you that the endless series of masterpieces in Rome's churches, palaces, and museums can cause first-time visitors—eyes glazed over from a heavy downpour of images, dates, and names—to lean, Pisa-like, on their companions for support. After a surfeit of Bernini and Canova and the 14th Raphael, even the greatest of the Italian masters may begin to pall. The secret, of course, is to act like a turtle—not a hare—and take your sweet time. Instead of trotting after briskly efficient tour guides, allow the splendors of Rome to unfold—slowly. Museums are only the most obvious places to view art; there are always the trompe l'oeil renderings of Assumptions that float across Baroque church ceilings and piazza scenes that might be Renaissance paintings brought to life. Of course, there may be many art treasures that will not quicken your pulse, but one morning you may see a Caravaggio so perfect, so beautiful, that your knees will buckle.

**Il Caffè** The Roman day begins and ends with coffee, and more cups of coffee punctuate the time in between. To live like the Romans do, drink as they drink, standing at the counter or sitting at outdoor tables of the corner bar. (In Italy, the term *bar* always means coffee bar—establishments serving primarily alcoholic beverages are called *pubs* or *American bars*.) A primer: *caffè* means coffee, and Italian standard issue is what Americans call espresso—short, strong, and usually taken very sweet. *Cappuccino* is a foamy half-and-half of espresso and steamed milk; cocoa powder (*cacao*) on top is acceptable, cinnamon not. If you're thinking of having a cappuccino for dessert, think again—Italians drink only caffè or *caffè macchiato* (with a spot of steamed milk) after lunchtime. Confused? Homesick? Order *caffè americano* for a reasonable facsimile of good old filtered joe.

**La Passeggiata** A favorite pastime in Rome (and throughout Italy) is the *passeggiata,* literally, the promenade. In the late afternoon and early evening, especially on weekends, couples, families, and packs of teenagers stroll the city's main streets and piazzas. It's a ritual of exchanged news and gossip, window-shopping, flirting, and gelato eating that adds up to a uniquely Italian experience. To join in, simply hit the streets for a bit of wandering. You may feel more like an observer than a participant, until you realize that observing is what la passeggiata is all about.

**Parks & Gardens of Lazio** Dating back to antiquity, the Lazio region has been dotted with the country retreats of wealthy Romans, places where they could escape the city to relax in expansive surroundings and indulge their grand and sometimes eccentric gardening tastes. Today one of the primary pleasures of the region is visiting these estates: Hadrian's Villa and Villa d'Este are must-see destinations, but you can also be richly rewarded by visits to lesser-known spots, such as Bomarzo, where a 16th-century prince created a bizarre theme park.

# The Roman Table

By the standards of Italian cuisine, which is first and foremost dedicated to perpetuating regional cooking traditions, the Roman restaurant scene is distinctly cosmopolitan. Although Rome maintains its own unique culinary heritage, it's also a place where you can sample the cooking styles of Tuscany, Puglia, Sardinia, and virtually every other region of Italy, the cultural baggage of countless immigrants who have been drawn to the city but still long for the flavors of home. In recent years this phenomenon has gone international: Italian restaurants still predominate, but you can now find more than passable renditions of everything from sushi to Ethiopian. Although good food is of course essential to a fine Roman meal, the experience is as much about what happens at the table as in the kitchen. Romans are masters at lingering over a long lunch or dinner, savoring both the food they eat and the company they keep. Capturing that experience as an outsider can be a tricky proposition in a city that draws millions of tourists every year. We've taken care in selecting the restaurants that appear in the Where to Eat chapter of this book to guide you to places where Romans themselves dine with gusto.

# Shopping

The city's most famous shopping district is conveniently compact, fanning out at the foot of the Spanish Steps in a galaxy of boutiques offering gorgeous wares with glamorous labels. Here you can ricochet from Gucci to Prada to Valentino to Versace with less effort than it takes to pull out your credit card. Even if your budget is designed for lower altitudes, you can find great clothes and accessories at prices you can afford. But buying is not necessarily the point. The greatest pleasure is in browsing, admiring window displays that are works of art, imagining you or yours in a little red dress by Valentino or a lean Armani suit, and dreaming that all this could be yours—on only *half* the budget of Bill Gates.

# Il Gelato

During warmer months, *gelato*—the Italian equivalent of ice cream—is a Roman obsession. It's considered a snack rather than a dessert, bought at stands and shops in piazzas and on street corners, and consumed on foot, usually at a leisurely stroll. Gelato is softer, less creamy, and more intensely flavored than its American counterpart. It comes in simple flavors that capture the essence of the main ingredient. (You won't find Chunky Monkey or Cookies 'n' Cream.) At most gelaterias standard choices inlude pistachio, nocciola (hazelnut), caffè, and numerous fresh-fruit varieties; the surest sign that you've hit on a good spot is a line at the counter.

# FODOR'S CHOICE

The sights, restaurants, hotels, and other travel experiences on these pages are our editors' top picks—our Fodor's Choices. They're the best of their type in the area covered by the book—not to be missed and always worth your time. In the chapters that follow, you will find all the details.

## QUINTESSENTIAL ROME

**Via Giulia.** A "virtual painting" of the Renaissance, this magnificent street was created at the bequest of Pope Julius II (he also had Michelangelo whip up the Sistine Ceiling). Home to some of Rome's grandest palaces, it remains "the salon of Rome."

**Gianicolo.** The climb to the top of this hill rewards you with a marvelous vista of the entire city and the Castelli Romani. Add a sunset and you have a perfect Roman moment.

**Via Gregoriana.** Climbing up to the top of the Spanish Steps, this elegant street has always been an address of note—Hans Christian Andersen and Ingres were among the great who have lived here—and is still crowned with the Palazzetto Zuccari, the city's bizarrest residence.

**Piazza Navona.** The exuberant spirit of the Baroque age is embodied in Bernini's fantastic Fontana dei Quattro Fiumi (Fountain of the Four Rivers), set off by the curves and steeples of Borromini's church of Sant'Agnese, and admired by colorful crowds devouring gelati.

## AMAZING ANTIQUITIES

**Colle Palatino.** Wander through the ages of Rome, from imperial palaces to a peaceful Renaissance garden, and take in the city from ahigh.

**Colosseo.** The shouts of gladiators, the cries of the crowd, and wails of pitiless persecutions (though Christians were probably martyred elsewhere) echo across these ancient stones.

**Ostia Antica**, Lazio. Perhaps even more than Pompeii, the excavated port city of ancient Rome conveys a picture of everyday life in a busy commercial center.

**The Pantheon.** Take time to absorb the harmonious proportions of this pagan temple that was later consecrated as a church, and stand under the oculus (opening in the roof) to look up at the eye of heaven.

## GLORIOUS CHURCHES

**Basilica di San Pietro.** The largest church in the world, built over the tomb of St. Peter, is also the most imposing and breathtaking architectural achievement of the Renaissance.

**San Clemente.** Delve deep into the excavations below this church to get a sense of how Rome, and its religions, grew.

**San Ignazio.** Gold and jewels create an overwhelming statement of splendor here—Roman Baroque in its apotheosis.

**San Luigi dei Francesi.** Adorning the Chapel of Saint Matthew are the three greatest Caravaggio paintings in the world.

**Santa Maria della Vittoria.** Bernini's *St. Theresa in Ecstasy* reposes here—the most eye-knocking sculpture of the Baroque, period.

**Santa Maria in Trastevere.** Gilded mosaics from the 12th and 13th centuries give a unique glow to what is purportedly Rome's oldest church dedicated to the Virgin Mary.

**Santi Quattro Coronati.** An enclave of peace where nuns chant their prayers, this is one of the most unusual and unexpected corners of Rome, a quiet oasis that has resisted the tide of time and traffic outside its doors.

**MAGNIFICENT MUSEUMS**

**Museo e Galleria Borghese.** Resplendent with frescoes and stuccoes, this museum harbors Canova's *Pauline Borghese* and several Bernini works that define the essence of Baroque sculpture.

**Musei Vaticani.** The sheer size of the Vatican Museums is daunting, but with the Sistine Chapel, the Raphael Rooms, and scores of masterpieces on view, this is one of the world's great repositories of art.

**Palazzo Altemps.** The restored interior hints at the splendid Roman lifestyle of the 16th through 18th centuries and serves as a stunning showcase for the most illustrious pieces from the Museo Nazionale Romano's collection of ancient Roman sculpture.

**Palazzo Doria Pamphilj.** Get a taste of the lifestyles of the rich and famous—17th-century version—at this fabulous palace, still lived in by the Pamphilj heirs. Stare down the famous Velàzquez portrait of Pope Innocent X—the finest portrait ever painted.

**TOP HOTELS**

$$$$ **Ponte Sisto.** With one of the prettiest patio-courtyards in Rome, this hotel offers its own blissful definition of *Pax Romana*. Inside, the palazzo has been given a modern makeover inside but you're just a second away from gorgeously time-burnished Via Giulia.

$$$$ **D'Inghilterra.** Lizst, Mendelssohn, Hans Christian Andersen, Mark Twain, Hemingway—and now you? Set on a potted-palm cobblestone stretch of posh Via Bocca di Leone, this "albergo" has a staff that is as warm as the surroundings are velvety.

$$$$ **Hassler.** Set atop the Spanish Steps, this famous landmark was built to take advantage of the spectacular views, so come here to have all Rome at your feet. The hotel exterior may be ugly but the interiors have enough tufted velvets, satin drapes, and passementerie to please even Valentino.

| | |
|---|---|
| $$$–$$$$ | Aleph. The most unfalteringly fashionable of Rome's new class of design hotels, this has a just-this-side-of-kitsch theme that plays on Dante's Divine Comedy: enjoy walking the line between heaven and hell through the Angelo bar, the red-red-red Sin restaurant, and Paradise spa. |
| $$–$$$$ | Locarno. While this has been a longtime choice for art aficionados and people in the cinema, everyone will appreciate this hotel's fin de siècle charm, intimate feel, and central location off Piazza del Popolo. |
| $$–$$$ | Britannia. Set in a very regal white villa, smartly fitted out with black shutters (and a not so smart neon sign), this spot exults in attention to detail. |
| $$ | Hotel Santa Maria di Trastevere. This Trastevere treasure has a pedigree going back four centuries: an ivy-covered, mansard-roofed, and rosy-brick-red Renaissance-era convent now transformed into a charmer, set around a monastic porticoed courtyard. |
| $–$$ | Margutta. For location in the Spanish Steps area, good value, and friendly owner-managers, the Margutta is outstanding. |
| $ | Casa di Santa Francesca Romana. Not far from some of the sweetest nooks and crannies of medieval Trastevere, this former monastery—centered around an impressive ochre-colored courtyard—has a fabulous location and is a great buy. |
| $ | Panda. A night at this comfortable spot will cost you less than most of the baubles for sale in the surrounding Piazza di Spagna shopping district. |
| $ | Smeraldo. Superb location (in the Campo de' Fiori area) at a reasonable price makes the "Emerald" hotel a gem. |
| **TEMPTING RESTAURANTS**<br><br>$$$$ | Il Convivio Troiani. Quietly redefining the experience of Italian *alta cucina* for many years, this spot is run by the three Troiani brothers with spectacular results in the kitchen: "roast beef" of tuna fillet laquered with chestnut honey or the squid ink risotto with baby cuttlefish will sate the appetites of those with dreams of *fantasia*. |
| $$$$ | La Pergola. The most celebrated restaurant in Rome, with the fantastic creations of chef Heinz Beck, is one of the best places in the ancient city (well, it's in the Hilton on the modern outskirts) that to indulge in haute and nouvelle cuisine. |
| $$$–$$$$ | Agata e Romeo. For the perfect marriage (pun intended) of fine dining, creative cuisine, and rustic Roman tradition, the husband-and-wife team of Agata Parisella and Romeo Caraccio is the top. The signature style is both simple and elegant, perhaps best seen in the *sformato di formaggio di fossa* (a soufflé-tart of sheep's cheese aged in special caves) with a pear sauce and Acacia honey—a perfect balance between sweet and sharp. |

|          |                                                                                                                                                                                                                                                                                                                                            |
| -------- | -------------------------------------------------------------------------------------------------------------------------------------------------------------------------------------------------------------------------------------------------------------------------------------------------------------------------------------------- |
| $$-$$$$  | **Dal Bolognese.** The darling of the media, film, and fashion communities (yes, that was Scorsese . . . and Valentino, you're looking tan!), this classic restaurant on Piazza del Popolo is not only an "in-crowd" dinner destination but also happens to be the place for rich, wonderful Bolognese-style cuisine. |
| $$-$$$$  | **Il Simposio di Costantini.** At perhaps the most upscale wine bar in town, you can sit at the bar and sip and chat with the owners about why you prefer pinot nero to merlot (*alla* "Sideways"), or order a full meal at this enoteca-turned-restaurant. |
| $$—$$$   | **Antico Arco.** Attracting foodies with its culinary inventiveness and high style, this spot—high up on the Janiculum Hill—is set in a precious little villa, making for a homey ambience that's difficult to come by elsewhere in the city. The molten chocolate soufflé is justly famous among chocoholics all over the city. |
| $$-$$$   | **Romolo.** Raphael use to court his love, La Fornarina, here while he painted up a storm at the Villa Farnesina across the way. A summer evening at one of the garden candlelit tables is magic. |
| $$-$$$   | **Nino.** Just down the block from the Spanish Stepts, this has been a favorite among international journalists and fashionistas for decaees. With its yellow walls, dark-wood paneling, and a plethora of framed prints, the ambience is both cultured and cozy. |
| $$       | **Ditirambo.** Feel the pulse of Campo de' Fiori street life as you sample surprising variations on traditional Mediterranean cuisine. |
| $-$$     | **Ōbikā.** If you've ever wanted to take in a "mozzarella bar," here's your chance. Mozzarella is featured here much like sushi bars showcase fresh fish—even the decor is modern Japanese minimalism-meets-ancient Roman grandeur. |
| ¢–$      | **Dar Poeta.** Who makes the best pizza in Rome is a dispute that will never be settled, but Dar Poeta is a perennial contender. |
| ¢        | **Tazza d'Oro.** Italy's national coffee habit is a key to its character, and there's no better place to take a cup of caffè than here. Do as the Romans do: order a glass of water as a chaser. |

# WHEN TO GO

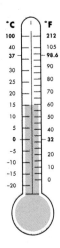

| °C | | °F |
|---|---|---|
| 100 | | 212 |
| 40 | | 105 |
| 37 | | 98.6 |
| 30 | | 90 |
| 25 | | 80 |
| 20 | | 70 |
| 15 | | 60 |
| 10 | | 50 |
| 5 | | 40 |
| 0 | | 32 |
| –5 | | 20 |
| –10 | | 10 |
| –15 | | 0 |
| –20 | | |

The main tourist season in Rome starts shortly before Easter (when the greatest number of visitors flock to the city) and runs through October. In July and August, come if you like, but learn to do as the Romans do—get up and out early, seek shady refuge from early afternoon heat, take a nap if you can, resume activities in the late afternoon, and stay up late to enjoy the nighttime breeze. During August many shops and restaurants close, and on the August 15 holiday Rome is a ghost town. During the winter months, especially January–March, you have a better chance of getting into the major tourist attractions without having to wait in line.

## Climate

Spring and fall are the best seasons in Rome, as far as the weather goes, though tourist attractions are crowded. It's neither too hot nor too cold, there's usually plenty of sun, and the famous Roman sunsets are at their best. Summers can be sweltering—recent ones have been among the hottest and driest on record. Roman winters are relatively mild, with some persistent rainy spells.

Below are average daily maximum and minimum temperatures by month for Rome.

𝌆 Forecasts **Weather Channel Connection** ⊕ www.weather.com.

## ROME

| | | | | | | | | |
|---|---|---|---|---|---|---|---|---|
| Jan. | 52F | 11C | May | 74F | 23C | Sept. | 79F | 26C |
| | 40 | 5 | | 56 | 13 | | 62 | 17 |
| Feb. | 55F | 13C | June | 82F | 28C | Oct. | 71F | 22C |
| | 42 | 6 | | 63 | 17 | | 55 | 13 |
| Mar. | 59F | 15C | July | 87F | 30C | Nov. | 61F | 16C |
| | 45 | 7 | | 67 | 20 | | 49 | 10 |
| Apr. | 66F | 19C | Aug. | 86F | 30C | Dec. | 55F | 13C |
| | 50 | 10 | | 67 | 20 | | 44 | 6 |

# SMART TRAVEL TIPS

*Half the fun of traveling is looking forward to your trip—but when you look forward, don't just daydream. There are plans to be made, things to learn about, serious work to be done. This chapter will give you helpful pointers on many of the questions that arise when planning your trip and also when you're on the road. Finding out about your destination before you leave home means you won't squander time organizing everyday minutiae once you've arrived. You'll be more streetwise when you hit the ground as well, better prepared to explore the aspects of Rome that drew you here in the first place. The organizations in this chapter can provide information to supplement this guide; contact them for up-to-the-minute details. Many trips begin by contacting the Italian Government Tourist Board (ENIT): consult their listings under Visitor Information below. Happy landings!*

## ADDRESSES

Addresses in Italy are fairly straightforward: the street is followed by the street number. However, you might see an address with a number plus "bis" or "A"; for instance, "Via Verdi 3/bis" or "Via Mazzini 8/A." This indicates that 3/bis and 8/A are the next doors down from Via Verdi 3 and Via Mazzini 8. It's worth noting that the streets of Rome, even in the newer outskirts, are numbered erratically. Numbers can be even on one side of the street and odd on the other; sometimes numbers are in ascending consecutive order on one side of the street and descending order on the other.

## AIR TRAVEL TO & FROM ROME

Price is just one factor to consider when booking a flight: frequency of service and even a carrier's safety record are often just as important. Major airlines offer the greatest number of departures. Smaller airlines—including regional and no-frills airlines—usually have a limited number of flights daily. On the other hand, so-called low-cost airlines usually are cheaper, and their fares impose fewer restrictions, such as advance-purchase requirements. In terms of safety, low-cost carriers as a group have a good history—about equal to that of major carriers.

## BOOKING

When you book, look for nonstop flights and remember that "direct" flights stop at least once. Try to avoid connecting flights, which require a change of plane. Two airlines may operate a connecting flight jointly, so ask whether your airline operates every segment of the trip; you may find that the carrier you prefer flies you only part of the way. To find more booking tips and to check prices and make online flight reservations, log on to ⊕ www.fodors.com.

## CARRIERS

When flying internationally, you must usually choose between a domestic carrier, the national flag carrier of the country you're visiting, and a foreign carrier from a third country. You may, for example, choose to fly Alitalia to Rome. National flag carriers have the greatest number of nonstops. Domestic carriers may have better connections to your hometown and serve a greater number of gateway cities. Third-party carriers may have a price advantage.

Charters usually have the lowest fares but are the least dependable. Departures are infrequent and seldom on time, and flights can be delayed for up to 48 hours or can be canceled for any reason up to 10 days before you're scheduled to leave. Itineraries and prices can change after you've booked your flight.

In the United States, the Department of Transportation's Aviation Consumer Protection Division has jurisdiction over charters and provides a certain degree of protection. The DOT requires that money paid to charter operators be held in escrow, so if you can't pay with a credit card, **always make your check payable to a charter carrier's escrow account.** The name of the bank should be in the charter contract. If you have any problems with a charter operator, contact the DOT (⇨ Airline Complaints). If you buy a charter package that includes both air and land arrangements, remember that the es-

crow requirement applies only to the air component.

🛪 **To & from Rome** **Alitalia** ☎ 800/223-5730, 0870/544-8259 in U.K. ⊕ www.alitalia.it. **British Airways** ☎ 0845/773-3377 in U.K. ⊕ www.britishairways.com. **Continental** ☎ 800/231-0856 ⊕ www.flycontinental.com. **Delta** ☎ 800/241-4141 ⊕ www.deltaairlines.com. **Northwest** ☎ 800/225-2525 ⊕ www.nwa.com. **Ryanair** ☎ 0871/246-000 ⊕ ryanair.com. **US Airways** ☎ 800/622-1015 ⊕ www.usairways.com.
🛪 **Charter Carriers Tower Air** ☎ 800/348-6937.
🛪 **Within Rome** **Air One** ☎ 199/207080 ⊕ www.flyairone.it. **Meridiana** ☎ 199/111333 in Italy ⊕ www.meridiana.it.

## CHECK-IN & BOARDING

Always **find out your carrier's check-in policy.** Plan to arrive at the airport about two hours before your scheduled departure time for domestic flights and 2½ to 3 hours before international flights. You may need to arrive earlier if you're flying from one of the busier airports or during peak air-traffic times. To avoid delays at airport-security checkpoints, try not to wear any metal. Jewelry, belt and other buckles, steel-toe shoes, barrettes, and underwire bras are among the items that can set off detectors.

Assuming that not everyone with a ticket will show up, airlines routinely overbook planes. When everyone does, airlines ask for volunteers to give up their seats. In return, these volunteers usually get a several-hundred-dollar flight voucher, which can be used toward the purchase of another ticket, and are rebooked on the next flight out. If there are not enough volunteers, the airline must choose who will be denied boarding. The first to get bumped are passengers who checked in late and those flying on discounted tickets, so get to the gate and check in as early as possible, especially during peak periods.

Always **bring a government-issued photo ID** to the airport; even when it's not required, a passport is best.

## CUTTING COSTS

The least expensive airfares to Rome are priced for round-trip travel and must usually be purchased in advance. Airlines generally allow you to change your return date for a fee; most low-fare tickets, however, are nonrefundable. It's smart to call a number of airlines and check the Internet; when you are quoted a good price, book it on the spot—the same fare may not be available the next day, or even the next hour. Always check different routings and look into using alternate airports. Also, price off-peak flights, which may be significantly less expensive than others. Travel agents, especially low-fare specialists ( ⇨ Discounts & Deals), are helpful.

Consolidators are another good source. They buy tickets for scheduled flights at reduced rates from the airlines, then sell them at prices that beat the best fare available directly from the airlines. Sometimes you can even get your money back if you need to return the ticket. Carefully read the fine print detailing penalties for changes and cancellations, purchase the ticket with a credit card, and confirm your consolidator reservation with the airline.

**▮ Consolidators AirlineConsolidator.com** ☎ 888/468-5385 ⊕ www.airlineconsolidator.com, for international tickets. **Best Fares** ☎ 800/576-8255 or 800/576-1600 ⊕ www.bestfares.com; $59.90 annual membership. **Cheap Tickets** ☎ 800/377-1000 or 888/922-8849 ⊕ www.cheaptickets.com. **Expedia** ☎ 800/397-3342 or 404/728-8787 ⊕ www.expedia. com. **Hotwire** ☎ 866/468-9473 or 920/330-9418 ⊕ www.hotwire.com. **Now Voyager Travel** ⊠ 45 W. 21st St., 5th fl., New York, NY 10010 ☎ 212/459-1616 ⊟ 212/243-2711 ⊕ www.nowvoyagertravel. com. **Onetravel.com** ⊕ www.onetravel.com. **Orbitz** ☎ 888/656-4546 ⊕ www.orbitz.com. **Priceline. com** ⊕ www.priceline.com. **Travelocity** ☎ 888/709-5983, 877/282-2925 in Canada, 0870/111-7060 in U.K. ⊕ www.travelocity.com.

**▮ Courier Resources Air Courier Association/ Cheaptrips.com** ☎ 800/282-1202 ⊕ www. aircourier.org or www.cheaptrips.com; $29 annual membership. **International Association of Air Travel Couriers** ☎ 308/632-3273 ⊕ www.courier. org; $45 annual membership.

### ENJOYING THE FLIGHT

State your seat preference when purchasing your ticket, and then repeat it when you confirm and when you check in. For more legroom, you can request one of the few emergency-aisle seats at check-in, if you are capable of lifting at least 50 pounds—a Federal Aviation Administration requirement of passengers in these seats. Seats behind a bulkhead also offer more legroom, but they don't have underseat storage. Don't sit in the row in front of the emergency aisle or in front of a bulkhead, where seats may not recline.

Ask the airline whether a snack or meal is served on the flight. If you have dietary concerns, request special meals when booking. These can be vegetarian, low-cholesterol, or kosher, for example. It's a good idea to pack some healthful snacks and a small (plastic) bottle of water in your carry-on bag. On long flights, try to maintain a normal routine, to help fight jet lag. At night, get some sleep. By day, eat light meals, drink water (not alcohol), and **move around the cabin** to stretch your legs. For additional jet-lag tips consult *Fodor's FYI: Travel Fit & Healthy* (available at bookstores everywhere).

Smoking policies vary from carrier to carrier. Many airlines prohibit smoking on all of their flights; others allow smoking only on certain routes or certain departures. Ask your carrier about its policy.

### FLYING TIMES

Flying time to Rome is 7½–8½ hours from New York, 10–11 hours from Chicago, 12–13 hours from Los Angeles, and 2½ hours from London.

### HOW TO COMPLAIN

If your baggage goes astray or your flight goes awry, complain right away. Most carriers require that you **file a claim immediately.** The Aviation Consumer Protection Division of the Department of Transportation publishes *Fly-Rights,* which discusses airlines and consumer issues and is available online. You can also find articles and information on mytravelrights.com, the Web site of the nonprofit Consumer Travel Rights Center.

**▮ Airline Complaints Aviation Consumer Protection Division** ⊠ U.S. Department of Transportation, C-75, Room 4107, 400 7th St. SW, Washington, DC 20590 ☎ 202/366-2220 ⊕ airconsumer.ost.dot.gov. **Federal Aviation Administration Consumer Hotline** ⊠ For inquiries: FAA, 800 Independence Ave.

SW, Washington, DC 20591 ☎ 800/322-7873
⊕ www.faa.gov.

## RECONFIRMING

Check the status of your flight before you leave for the airport. You can do this on your carrier's Web site, by linking to a flight-status checker (many Web booking services offer these), or by calling your carrier or travel agent.

Always confirm international flights at least 72 hours ahead of the scheduled departure time. Although the trend on international flights is to drop reconfirmation requirements, many airlines still ask you to reconfirm each leg of your international itinerary. Failure to do so may result in your reservation's being canceled. When flying out of Italian airports, always check with the airport or tourist agency about upcoming strikes, which are frequent in Italy and often affect air travel.

## AIRPORTS & TRANSFERS

The principal airport for flights to Rome is **Leonardo da Vinci Airport,** commonly known by the name of its location, **Fiumicino** (FCO). It's 30 km (19 mi) southwest of the city, on the coast. It has been enlarged and equipped with computerized baggage handling and has a direct train link with downtown Rome. Rome's other airport is **Ciampino (CIA),** on Via Appia Nuova, 15 km (9 mi) south of downtown. Ciampino is a civil and military airport used by some international flights and most charter companies.

🔁 Airport Information Ciampino ☎ 06/794941 ⊕ www.adr.it. **Leonardo da Vinci Airport/ Fiumicino** ☎ 06/65951 ⊕ www.adr.it.

## TRANSFERS BETWEEN FIUMICINO & DOWNTOWN

When approaching by car, **follow the signs for Rome and the GRA** (the ring road that circles Rome). The direction you take on the GRA depends on where your hotel is located. If it's in the Via Veneto area, for instance, you would take the GRA in the direction of the Via Aurelia, turn off the GRA onto the Via Aurelia, and follow it into Rome. **Get a map and directions** from the car-rental desk at the airport.

A taxi ride to the center of Rome costs about €50, including *supplementi* (extra charges) for airport service and luggage, and takes about 30–45 minutes. Private limousines can be booked at booths in the Arrivals hall; they charge a little more than taxis but can carry more passengers. There's a taxi stand in front of the International Arrivals hall and a booth inside for taxi information. Use only licensed white or older yellow taxis. **Avoid drivers who may approach you in the Arrivals hall;** they charge exorbitant, unmetered rates.

Two trains link downtown Rome with Fiumicino. Inquire at the APT tourist information counter in the International Arrivals hall or train information counter near the tracks to determine which takes you closest to your destination in Rome. The 30-minute nonstop Airport-Termini express (called the Leonardo Express) goes directly to Track 25 at Termini Station, Rome's main train station, which is well served by taxis and is a hub of Metro and bus lines. The ride to Termini takes 30 minutes; departures are every half hour beginning at 6:37 AM from the airport, with a final departure at 11:37 PM. Trains depart Termini to the airport starting at 5:52 AM and run until 11:52 PM. Tickets cost €9.50.

FM1, the other airport train, leaves from the same tracks and runs to Rome and beyond, serving commuters as well as air travelers. The main stops in Rome are at Trastevere (35 minutes), Ostiense (40 minutes), and Tiburtina (50 minutes); at each you can find taxis and bus and/or Metro connections to other parts of Rome. FM1 trains run from Fiumicino between 5:57 AM and 11:27 PM, with departures every 15–30 minutes; the schedule is similar going to the airport. Tickets cost €4.70. For either train, **buy your ticket at a vending machine or at ticket counters** at the airport and at some stations (Termini Track 22, Trastevere, Tiburtina). At the airport, stamp the ticket at the gate. Remember when using the train at other stations to **stamp the ticket** in the little yellow or red machine near the track before you board. During the night, **take COTRAL buses** from the airport to Tiburtina Station in Rome (45 minutes); they depart from in front of the International Arrivals hall at 1:15, 2:15, 3:30, and 5 AM. Buses leave Tiburtina Station for the airport at 12:30, 1:15, 2:30, 3:45, and 5 AM. Tickets either way cost €3.60 or €5 if bought on board. The two stations are connected by bus 40N.

### TRANSFERS BETWEEN CIAMPINO & DOWNTOWN

By car, **go north on the Via Appia Nuova** into downtown Rome.

A taxi from Ciampino to the center of Rome can cost between €35 and €40, and the ride takes about 20 minutes. Take only official cabs with the TAXI sign on top; unofficial cabs often overcharge disoriented travelers.

A COTRAL bus connects the airport with the Anagnina Station of Metro line A or Ciampino railway station, which takes you into the center of the city. Buses depart from in front of the airport terminal around 25 times a day between 6 AM and 11:40 PM. The fare is €1 and tickets can be bought on the bus.

🚍 Transfer Contacts **COTRAL** ☎ 800/150008. **Trenitalia** ☎ 166/105050.

### DUTY-FREE SHOPPING

Among European Union (EU) countries there's no duty-free shopping. Visitors traveling from Italy to a non-EU country, however, can avail themselves of duty-free privileges.

### BIKE TRAVEL

Rome is not the easiest place to get around on a bike, especially in heavy traffic. However, you can have pleasant trips around the many large public parks, like the Villa Borghese or the Appia Antica Park. You can pick up a free guide to recommended cycle routes at any of the tourist information kiosks. Rental rates for standard bikes are about €3 for four hours to a maximum €12 for a full day. Remember to take your passport or ID card with you as you may be asked to leave an identity document as a guarantee until you return the bike.

🚲 Bike Rentals **Collalti** ✉ Via del Pellegrino 82 ☎ 06/68801084. **I Bike Rome** ✉ Underground parking lot at Villa Borghese, Via del Galoppatoio 33

☎ 06/322524 ✉ Piazza del Cinquecento parking lot ☎ 06/48905823. **Parco Appia Antica (Sunday only)** ✉ Via Appia Antica 42 ☎ 06/5126314.

### BIKES IN FLIGHT

Most airlines accommodate bikes as luggage, provided they are dismantled and boxed; check with individual airlines about packing requirements. Some airlines sell bike boxes, which are often free at bike shops, for about $15 (bike bags can be considerably more expensive). International travelers often can substitute a bike for a piece of checked luggage at no charge; otherwise, the cost is about $100. U.S. and Canadian airlines charge $40–$80 each way.

## BUSINESS HOURS

### BANKS & OFFICES

Banks are open weekdays 8:30–1:30 and 2:45–3:45 or 3–4. Exchange offices are open all day, usually 8:30–8.

Post offices are open Monday–Saturday 8–2; central and main district post offices stay open until 8 or 9 PM on weekdays for some operations. You can buy stamps at tobacconists.

### GAS STATIONS

Only a few gas stations are open on Sunday, and most close during weekday lunch hours and at 7 PM for the night. Many, however, have self-service pumps that are operational 24 hours a day, and gas stations on autostrade are open 24 hours.

### MUSEUMS & SIGHTS

Museum hours vary and may change with the seasons. Many important national museums are closed one day a week, often on Monday. The Roman Forum, other sites, and some museums may be open until late in the evening during the summer. **Always check locally.**

Most churches are open from early morning until noon or 12:30, when they close for two hours or more; they open again in the afternoon, generally around 4 PM, closing about 7 PM or later. Major cathedrals and basilicas, such as the Basilica di San Pietro, are open all day. Note that sightseeing in churches during religious rites is usually discouraged. Be sure to **have some**

**coins handy** for the *luce* (light) machines that illuminate the works of art in the perpetual dusk of ecclesiastical interiors. A pair of binoculars will help you get a good look at painted ceilings and domes.

A tip for pilgrims and tourists keen to get a glimpse of the pope: avoid the weekly general audience on Wednesday morning in Piazza di San Pietro, and **go to his Sunday angelus instead.** This midday prayer service tends to be far less crowded (unless beatifications or canonizations are taking place) and is also mercifully shorter, which makes a difference when you're standing.

### PHARMACIES

Most pharmacies are open Monday–Saturday 8:30–1 and 4–8; some are open all night. A schedule posted outside each pharmacy indicates the nearest pharmacy open during off-hours (afternoons, through the night, and Sunday).

### SHOPS

Shop hours vary. Many shops in downtown Rome are open all day during the week and also on Sunday, as are some department stores and supermarkets. Alternating city neighborhoods also have general once-a-month Sunday opening days. Otherwise, most shops throughout the city are closed on Sunday. Shops that take a lengthy lunch break are open 9:30–1 and 3:30 or 4–7 or 7:30. Many shops close for one half day during the week: Monday morning in winter and Saturday afternoon in summer.

Food shops are open 8–2 and 5–7:30, some until 8, and most are closed on Sunday. They also close for one half day during the week, usually Thursday afternoon from September to June and Saturday afternoon in July and August.

**Termini Station has a large, modern shopping mall** with over a hundred stores, many of which are open late in the evening. Pharmacies, bookstores and boutiques, as well as cafés, toilets, ATMs, and money-changing services, a first aid station, and an art gallery and exhibition center can all be found here. The Drug Store here is open every day between 6 AM and midnight. It sells sandwiches, fresh fruit, gourmet snacks, toiletries, gifts, and things like cameras, electric razors, and bouquets of fresh flowers (useful if you get an unexpected invitation to someone's home).

Traditionally the worst days to arrive in Rome, or do anything that hasn't been preplanned, are Easter Sunday, May 1 (Labor Day), Christmas Day, and New Year's Day. Expect to find many shops and businesses closed, and only a skeleton transport system working. Ferragosto (the middle weekend of August) will also be challenging.

### BUS TRAVEL TO & FROM ROME

An extensive network of bus lines that cover all of the Lazio region is operated by COTRAL (Consorzio Trasporti Lazio). There are several main bus stations. Long-distance and suburban COTRAL bus routes terminate either near Tiburtina Station or at outlying Metro stops, such as Rebibbia and Ponte Mammolo (Line B) and Anagnina (Line A).

Fares are reasonable, especially with the BIRG (Bigiletto Integrale Regionale Giornali), which allows you to travel on all of the lines (and some railroad lines) up to midnight on the day of the ticket's first validation. The cost of a BIRG depends upon the distance to your destination and how many "zones" you travel through. Because of the extent and complexity of the system, it's a good idea to consult with your hotel concierge or to telephone COTRAL's central office when planning a trip.

🚍 Bus Information **COTRAL** ☎ 800/150008 ⊕ www.cotral.it.

### CAMERAS & PHOTOGRAPHY

Be on the lookout for signs indicating that photographs are not allowed; some museums and other institutions retain the sole right to photograph their works. Do not use flash when in museums or when photographing paintings or sculptures. The *Kodak Guide to Shooting Great Travel Pictures* (available at bookstores everywhere) is loaded with tips.

🚍 Photo Help **Kodak Information Center** ☎ 800/ 242-2424 ⊕ www.kodak.com.

## EQUIPMENT PRECAUTIONS

**Don't pack film or equipment in checked luggage,** where it is much more susceptible to damage. X-ray machines used to view checked luggage are extremely powerful and therefore are likely to ruin your film. Try to ask for hand inspection of film, which becomes clouded after repeated exposure to airport X-ray machines, and keep videotapes and computer disks away from metal detectors. Always keep film, tape, and computer disks out of the sun. Carry an extra supply of batteries, and be prepared to turn on your camera, camcorder, or laptop to prove to airport security personnel that the device is real.

## FILM & DEVELOPING

All types of film for common use is readily available throughout the city. A roll of 35 mm film costs about €6, depending on the speed. One-hour photo developers are common in the city center and around the Vatican; they charge around €12 for a 24-exposure roll of 35 mm print film.

## VIDEOS

The European norm for videotape is PAL, and unless you have a special machine you will not be able to play videos bought in Italy back in the States. So **bring your own videotapes from home.**

## CAR RENTAL

Rates in Rome begin at around $100 a day for an economy car with air-conditioning, a manual transmission, and unlimited mileage. This includes the 20% tax on car rentals. Note that Italian legislation now permits certain rental wholesalers, such as Auto Europe, to drop the value-added tax (V.A.T.). Rental rates vary according to the period. Look out for special deals and offers. All international car rental agencies in Rome have a number of locations. Call and inquire about the one closest to you.
🚗 Major Agencies **Alamo** ☎ 800/522-9696 ⊕ www.alamo.com. **Avis** ☎ 800/331-1084, 800/879-2847 in Canada, 0870/606-0100 in U.K., 02/9353-9000 in Australia, 09/526-2847 in New Zealand ⊕ www.avis.com. **Budget** ☎ 800/527-0700, 0870/156-5656 in U.K. ⊕ www.budget.com. **Dollar** ☎ 800/800-6000, 0124/622-0111 in U.K., where it's affiliated with Sixt, 02/9223-1444 in Australia ⊕ www.dollar.com. **Hertz** ☎ 800/654-3001, 800/263-0600 in Canada, 0870/844-8844 in U.K., 02/9669-2444 in Australia, 09/256-8690 in New Zealand ⊕ www.hertz.com. **National Car Rental** ☎ 800/227-7368, 0870/600-6666 in U.K. ⊕ www.nationalcar.com.

## CUTTING COSTS

It's usually cheaper to rent a car in advance through your local agency than to rent on location in Italy. Within Italy, local rental agencies and international ones offer similar rates.

For a good deal, book through a travel agent who will shop around.

Do look into wholesalers, companies that do not own fleets but rent in bulk from those that do and often offer better rates than traditional car-rental operations. Prices are best during off-peak periods. Rentals booked through wholesalers often must be paid for before you leave home.
🚗 Wholesalers **Auto Europe** ☎ 207/842-2000 or 800/223-5555, 800/876272 in Italy 📠 207/842-2222 ⊕ www.autoeurope.com. **Europe by Car** ☎ 212/581-3040 or 800/223-1516 📠 212/246-1458 ⊕ www.europebycar.com. **Destination Europe Resources** (DER) ✉ 9501 W. Devon Ave., Rosemont, IL 60018 ☎ 800/782-2424 ⊕ www.der.com. **Kemwel** ☎ 800/678-0678 📠 207/842-2124 ⊕ www.kemwel.com.

## INSURANCE

When driving a rented car you are generally responsible for any damage to or loss of the vehicle. Collision policies that car-rental companies sell for European rentals typically don't cover stolen vehicles. Indeed, all car-rental agencies operating in Italy require that you buy a theft-protection policy. Before you rent—and purchase collision coverage—see what coverage you already have under the terms of your personal auto-insurance policy and credit cards.

## REQUIREMENTS & RESTRICTIONS

In Italy your own driver's license is acceptable. An International Driver's Permit is a good idea; it's available from the American or Canadian Automobile Association and, in the United Kingdom, from the Automobile Association or Royal Automobile Club. These international permits are universally recognized, and having one in your wallet may save you a problem with the local authorities.

In Italy you must be 21 years of age to rent an economy or subcompact car, and most companies require customers under the age of 23 to pay by credit card. Upon rental, all companies require credit cards as a warranty; to rent bigger cars (2,000 cc or more), you must often show two credit cards. Call local agents for details. There are no special restrictions on senior-citizen drivers.

Car seats are required for children under three and must be booked in advance. The rental cost is €5 upward, depending on the type of car.

### SURCHARGES

Before you pick up a car in one city and leave it in another, ask about drop-off charges or one-way service fees, which can be substantial. Note, too, that some rental agencies charge extra if you return the car before the time specified in your contract. To avoid a hefty refueling fee, fill the tank just before you turn in the car, but be aware that gas stations near the rental outlet may overcharge. It's almost never a deal to buy the tank of gas that's in the car when you rent it; the understanding is that you'll return it empty, but some fuel usually remains. The cost for an additional driver is about €5 per day.

### CAR TRAVEL

The main access routes from the north are A1 (Autostrada del Sole) from Milan and Florence and the A12–E80 highway from Genoa. The principal route to or from points south, including Naples, is the A2. All highways connect with the Grande Raccordo Anulare Ring Road (GRA), which channels traffic into the city center. Markings on the GRA are confusing: take time to study the route you need. Be extremely careful of pedestrians when driving: Romans are casual jaywalkers and pop out frequently from between parked cars.

### EMERGENCY SERVICES

There are phone boxes on highways to report breakdowns. Major rental agencies often provide roadside assistance, so **check**

**your rental agreement** if a problem arises. Also, ACI (Auto Club of Italy) Service offers 24-hour road service. **Dial 803–116 from any phone,** 24 hours a day, to reach the nearest ACI service station. When speaking to ACI, ask and you will be transferred to an English-speaking operator. Be prepared to tell the operator which road you're on, the direction you're going, for example, "*verso* (in the direction of) Pizzo," and the *targa* (license plate number) of your car.

🚘 Auto Club of Italy (ACI) ☎ 803–116.

### GASOLINE

Only a few gas stations are open on Sunday, and most close for a couple of hours at lunchtime and at 7 PM for the night. Many, however, have self-service pumps that accept both currency and credit cards and are operational 24 hours a day. Gas stations on autostrade are open 24 hours. Gas costs about €1.20 per liter.

### PARKING

Be warned: parking in Rome can be a nightmare. The situation is greatly compounded by the fact that private cars are not allowed access to the entire historic center during the day, except for residents with resident permits. Space is at a premium and your car may be towed away if it's illegally parked. When you book your hotel, inquire about parking facilities. There's limited free parking space in the city. Meter parking costs €1 per hour with limited stopping time allowed in many areas. Parking facilities near the historic sights exist at the Villa Borghese underground car park (entrance at Viale del Muro Torto) and the Vatican (entrance from Piazza della Rovere).

### ROAD CONDITIONS

Italians drive fast and are impatient with those who don't, a tendency that can make driving on the congested streets of Rome a hair-raising experience. Traffic is heaviest during morning and late-afternoon commuter hours, and on weekends. Watch out for mopeds.

### ROAD MAPS

Most bookstores such as Feltrinelli sell maps, as do most highway gas stations.

The Touring Club Italiano's shops sell maps (road, bicycle, hiking, among others). Probably the best road maps are those produced by Michelin.

## RULES OF THE ROAD

Driving is on the right, as in North America. Regulations are largely as in Britain and America, except that the police have the power to levy on-the-spot fines. Although honking abounds, the use of horns is forbidden in many areas; a large sign, ZONA DI SILENZIO, indicates where. Speed limits are 50 kph (31 mph) in Rome, 130 kph (80 mph) on autostrade, and 110 kph (70 mph) on state and provincial roads, unless otherwise marked. The blood-alcohol content limit for driving is 0.5 gr/, with fines up to €5,000 and the possibility of six months' imprisonment for surpassing the limit. Fines for speeding are uniformly stiff: 10 kph (6 mph) over the speed limit can warrant a fine of up to €500; over 10 kph, and your license could be taken away from you.

## CHILDREN IN ROME

Although Italians love children and are generally very tolerant and patient with them, they provide few amenities for them. Discounts do exist. **Always ask about a sconto bambino** (child's discount) before purchasing tickets. Children under a certain height ride free on municipal buses and trams. Children under 18 who are EU citizens are admitted free to state-run museums and galleries, and there are similar privileges in many municipal or private museums. Discounts on concert tickets may be available for young people with student ID.

*Fodor's Around Rome with Kids* (available in many English language bookstores) can help you plan your days together. If you're renting a car, don't forget to arrange for a car seat when you reserve. For general advice about traveling with children, consult *Fodor's FYI: Travel with Your Baby* (available in bookstores everywhere).

🖪 Vacation Packages with Children **Grandtravel** ✉ 6900 Wisconsin Ave., Suite 706, Chevy Chase, MD 20815 ☎ 301/986-0790 or 800/247-7651. For people traveling with grandchildren ages 7–17,

contact **Rascals in Paradise** ✉ 650 5th St., Suite 505, San Francisco, CA 94107 ☎ 800/872-7225 or 415/978-9800 🖷 415/442-0289. **Young Family Travelers** ✉ 235 Wanaque Ave., Suite 201, Pompton Lakes, NJ 07442 ☎ 888/968-6432 🖷 973/616-4654.

## BABYSITTING

Your hotel may have recommendations for babysitters. Crescere Insieme is an agency that offers qualified, experienced babysitters who speak English.

🖪 Agencies **Crescere Insieme** ☎ 06/65742319.

## WHERE TO STAY

Most hotels in Rome allow children under a certain age to stay in their parents' room at no extra charge, but others charge for them as extra adults; be sure to **find out the cutoff age for children's discounts.**

## PRECAUTIONS

Mosquitoes are not common in the city but in recent years Italy has been invaded by the troublesome Tiger Mosquito, which can give a nasty bite. Travel with your usual brand of children's insect repellent. There are several Italian brands—Autun, for instance—that also do the trick. They're available in pharmacies and supermarkets.

## SIGHTS & ATTRACTIONS

Historic sites that give kids space to run around in and explore include the Colosseum and the Roman forum and adjacent Palatine Hill. The Musei Capitolini provides a children's audio guide and special room where kids can draw and play interactive computer games. Children also tend to find the catacombs, which are dark and mysterious, exciting sites to visit. The Museo dei Bambini (Children's Museum) at Via Flaminia 82, the Biopark (animal research center) in the Villa Borghese Park, and the Luneur Amusement Park at EUR are all havens where little ones can let off steam and give exhausted parents some breathing space. Boat trips on the Tiber are fun and, in summer, don't forget that the beach at Ostia Lido is only a short train journey away. The APT information kiosks supply information about special children's activities, many of them free.

Places that are especially appealing to children are indicated by a rubber-duckie icon (🦆) in the margin.

## SUPPLIES & EQUIPMENT

The cost of diapers in Italy is similar to that in other places, though American brands such as Pampers and Huggies are slightly higher than in the United States. COOP is a reliable brand; you'll pay about €10 for 50 diapers.

Italian formula (both in premixed and powder forms) generally contains more vitamins than its American counterparts; Plasmon is a good brand. Italian bottles are identical to American ones, but it's difficult to find no-spill glasses for toddlers; it's best to bring a couple along with you.

## COMPUTERS ON THE ROAD

Getting online in Rome isn't difficult: public Internet stations and Internet cafés, some open 24 hours a day, are common. Prices differ from place to place, so **spend some time to find the best deal.** This isn't always readily apparent: a place might have higher rates, but because it belongs to a chain you won't be charged an initial flat fee again when you go to a different location of the same chain. Some hotels have in-room modem lines, but, as with phones, using the hotel's line is relatively expensive. Always check modem rates before plugging in. You may need an adapter for your computer for the European-style plugs. As always, if you're traveling with a laptop, carry a spare battery and an adapter. Never plug your computer into any socket before asking about surge protection. IBM sells a pea-size modem tester that plugs into a telephone jack to check whether the line is safe to use.

🖳 Internet Cafés **Call Net** ✉ Galleria Stazione Termini ☎ 06/87406008. **Easy Everything** ✉ Via Barberini 2 ☎ 06/42020118. **Internet Café** ✉ Via Cavour 208 ☎ 06/474-0068. **Pantheon Internet Point** ✉ Via di Santa Caterina da Siena ☎ 06/6920-0501. **Tourist Friend** ✉ Via Crescenzio 41 ☎ 06/6821-0410. **TreviNet Place** ✉ Via in Arcione 103 ☎ 06/6992-2320.

## CONCIERGES

Concierges, found in many hotels, can help you with theater tickets and dinner reservations: a good one with connections may be able to get you seats for a hot show or prime-time dinner reservations at the restaurant of the moment. You can also turn to your hotel's concierge for help with travel arrangements, sightseeing plans, services ranging from aromatherapy to zipper repair, and emergencies. **Always tip** a concierge who has been of assistance.

## CONSUMER PROTECTION

Whether you're shopping for gifts or purchasing travel services, **pay with a major credit card** whenever possible, so you can cancel payment or get reimbursed if there's a problem (and you can provide documentation). If you're doing business with a particular company for the first time, contact your local Better Business Bureau and the attorney general's offices in your state and (for U.S. businesses) the company's home state as well. Have any complaints been filed? Finally, if you're buying a package or tour, always consider travel insurance that includes default coverage (⇨ Insurance).

🖳 BBBs **Council of Better Business Bureaus** ✉ 4200 Wilson Blvd., Suite 800, Arlington, VA 22203 ☎ 703/276-0100 🖷 703/525-8277 ⊕ www. bbb.org.

## CUSTOMS & DUTIES

When shopping abroad, keep receipts for all purchases. Upon reentering the country, **be ready to show customs officials what you've bought.** Pack purchases together in an easily accessible place. If you think a duty is incorrect, appeal the assessment. If you object to the way your clearance was handled, note the inspector's badge number. In either case, first ask to see a supervisor. If the problem isn't resolved, write to the appropriate authorities, beginning with the port director at your point of entry.

### IN AUSTRALIA

Australian residents who are 18 or older may bring home A$400 worth of souvenirs and gifts (including jewelry), 250 cigarettes or 250 grams of cigars or other tobacco products, and 1,125 ml of alcohol (including wine, beer, and spirits). Residents under 18 may bring back A$200 worth of goods. Members of the same family traveling together may pool their allowances. Prohibited items include meat products. Seeds, plants, and fruits need to be declared upon arrival.

**🛈 Australian Customs Service** ⌂ Regional Director, Box 8, Sydney, NSW 2001 ☎ 02/9213-2000 or 1300/363263, 02/9364-7222 or 1800/803-006 quarantine-inquiry line 🖷 02/9213-4043 ⊕ www.customs.gov.au.

## IN CANADA

Canadian residents who have been out of Canada for at least seven days may bring in C$750 worth of goods duty-free. If you've been away fewer than seven days but more than 48 hours, the duty-free allowance drops to C$200. If your trip lasts 24 to 48 hours, the allowance is C$50. You may not pool allowances with family members. Goods claimed under the C$750 exemption may follow you by mail; those claimed under the lesser exemptions must accompany you. Alcohol and tobacco products may be included in the seven-day and 48-hour exemptions but not in the 24-hour exemption. If you meet the age requirements of the province or territory through which you reenter Canada, you may bring in, duty-free, 1.5 liters of wine *or* 1.14 liters (40 imperial ounces) of liquor *or* 24 12-ounce cans or bottles of beer or ale. Also, if you meet the local age requirement for tobacco products, you may bring in, duty-free, 200 cigarettes and 50 cigars. Check ahead of time with the Canada Customs and Revenue Agency or the Department of Agriculture for policies regarding meat products, seeds, plants, and fruits.

You may send an unlimited number of gifts (only one gift per recipient, however) worth up to C$60 each duty-free to Canada. Label the package UNSOLICITED GIFT—VALUE UNDER $60. Alcohol and tobacco are excluded.

**🛈 Canada Customs and Revenue Agency** ✉ 2265 St. Laurent Blvd., Ottawa, Ontario K1G 4K3 ☎ 800/461-9999, 204/983-3500, or 506/636-5064 ⊕ www.ccra.gc.ca.

## IN ITALY

Of goods obtained anywhere outside the EU or goods purchased in a duty-free shop within an EU country, the allowances are as follows: (1) 200 cigarettes or 100 cigarillos or 50 cigars or 250 grams of tobacco; (2) 2 liters of still table wine or 1 liter of spirits over 22% volume or 2 liters of spirits under 22% volume or 2 liters of fortified and sparkling wines; and (3) 50 ml of perfume and 250 ml of toilet water.

Of goods obtained (duty and tax paid) within another EU country, the allowances are (1) 800 cigarettes or 400 cigarillos (under 3 grams) or 200 cigars or 1 kilogram of tobacco; (2) 90 liters of still table wine or 10 liters of spirits over 22% volume or 20 liters of spirits under 22% volume or 110 liters of beer.

**🛈 Italian Customs, Fumicino Airport** ✉ Circoscrizione Doganale Roma 2 ☎ 06/65951.

## IN NEW ZEALAND

All homeward-bound residents may bring back NZ$700 worth of souvenirs and gifts; passengers may not pool their allowances, and children can claim only the concession on goods intended for their own use. For those 17 or older, the duty-free allowance also includes 4.5 liters of wine or beer; one 1,125-ml bottle of spirits; and either 200 cigarettes, 250 grams of tobacco, 50 cigars, *or* a combination of the three up to 250 grams. Meat products, seeds, plants, and fruits must be declared upon arrival to the Agricultural Services Department.

**🛈 New Zealand Customs** ✉ Head office: The Customhouse, 17–21 Whitmore St., Box 2218, Wellington ☎ 09/300-5399 or 0800/428-786 ⊕ www.customs.govt.nz.

## IN THE U.K.

If you are a U.K. resident and your journey was wholly within the EU, you probably won't have to pass through customs when you return to the United Kingdom. If you plan to bring back large quantities of alcohol or tobacco, check EU limits beforehand. In most cases, if you bring back more than 200 cigars, 3,200 cigarettes, 10 liters of spirits, 110 liters of beer, and/or 90 liters of wine, you have to declare the goods upon return.

**🛈 HM Customs and Excise** ✉ Portcullis House, 21 Cowbridge Rd. E, Cardiff CF11 9SS ☎ 0845/010-

9000 or 0208/929-0152, 0208/929-6731 or 0208/910-3602 complaints ⊕ www.hmce.gov.uk.

### IN THE U.S.

U.S. residents who have been out of the country for at least 48 hours may bring home, for personal use, $800 worth of foreign goods duty-free, as long as they haven't used the $800 allowance or any part of it in the past 30 days. This exemption may include 1 liter of alcohol (for travelers 21 and older), 200 cigarettes, and 100 non-Cuban cigars. Family members from the same household who are traveling together may pool their $800 personal exemptions. For fewer than 48 hours, the duty-free allowance drops to $200, which may include 50 cigarettes, 10 non-Cuban cigars, and 150 ml of alcohol (or 150 ml of perfume containing alcohol). The $200 allowance cannot be combined with other individuals' exemptions, and if you exceed it, the full value of all the goods will be taxed. Antiques, which the U.S. Bureau of Customs and Border Protection defines as objects more than 100 years old, enter duty-free, as do original works of art done entirely by hand, including paintings, drawings, and sculptures. This doesn't apply to folk art or handicrafts, which are in general dutiable.

You may also send packages home duty-free, with a limit of one parcel per addressee per day (except alcohol or tobacco products or perfume worth more than $5). You can mail up to $200 worth of goods for personal use; label the package PERSONAL USE and attach a list of its contents and their retail value. If the package contains your used personal belongings, mark it AMERICAN GOODS RETURNED to avoid paying duties. You may send up to $100 worth of goods as a gift; mark the package UNSOLICITED GIFT. Mailed items do not affect your duty-free allowance on your return.

To avoid paying duty on foreign-made high-ticket items you already own and will take on your trip, register them with Customs before you leave the country. Consider filing a Certificate of Registration for laptops, cameras, watches, and other digital devices identified with serial numbers or other permanent markings; you can keep the certificate for other trips. Otherwise, bring a sales receipt or insurance form to show that you owned the item before you left the United States.

🛂 **U.S. Bureau of Customs and Border Protection** ⊠ For inquiries and equipment registration, 1300 Pennsylvania Ave. NW, Washington, DC 20229 ⊕ www.customs.gov ☎ 877/287-8667 or 202/354-1000 ⊠ For complaints, Customer Satisfaction Unit, 1300 Pennsylvania Ave. NW, Room 5.5D, Washington, DC 20229.

## DISABILITIES & ACCESSIBILITY

### ACCESS IN ROME

Facilities such as ramps, telephones, and restrooms for people with disabilities are the exception, not the rule. Travelers' wheelchairs must be transported free of charge, according to Italian law, but the logistics of getting a wheelchair on and off trains and buses can make this requirement irrelevant. High, narrow steps for boarding trains create problems. Seats are reserved for people with disabilities on public transportation, but few buses have lifts for wheelchairs. Rome's newer gray-and-red city buses are equipped for easy boarding and securing of wheelchairs. A handful of subway stops in the Rome subway system are accessible to wheelchair users. The terminals of the Fiumicino Airport–Rome Ostiense rail connection have elevators for wheelchairs.

Throughout Rome parking spaces near major monuments and public buildings are reserved for cars transporting people with disabilities. The narrow streets of the city's center, parked cars hugging the buildings, the lack of sidewalks, and uneven cobblestone pavement add up to hard going.

Bringing a guide dog into Italy requires an import license, a current certificate detailing the dog's inoculations, and a letter from your veterinarian certifying the dog's health. Contact the nearest Italian consulate for particulars.

The Italian Government Tourist Board (ENIT) can provide a list of accessible hotels and the addresses of Italian associations for travelers with disabilities.

🛂 Local Resources **Italian Government Tourist Board** (ENIT) ⊠ 630 5th Ave., New York, NY 10111

☎ 212/245-4822 ⊟ 212/586-9249; *see* Visitor Information for a list of other ENIT locations.

## WHERE TO STAY
There are a large number of Rome hotels that can accommodate guests with disabilities. Contact Rome APT tourist office or ENIT for a full list, or call the Information Line for the Disabled (☎ 800/271027).

## SIGHTS & ATTRACTIONS
In many monuments and museums, even in some hotels and restaurants, architectural barriers make it difficult, if not impossible, for people with disabilities to gain access. St. Peter's, the Sistine Chapel, the Castel Sant'Angelo, and the Musei Vaticani (Vatican Museums) are all accessible by wheelchair (but the Colosseum and Forum are not).

🖪 Complaints **Aviation Consumer Protection Division** (⇨ Air Travel) for airline-related problems. **Departmental Office of Civil Rights** ⊠ For general inquiries, U.S. Department of Transportation, S-30, 400 7th St. SW, Room 10215, Washington, DC 20590 ☎ 202/366-4648 ⊟ 202/366-9371 ⊕ www.dot.gov/ost/docr/index.htm. **Disability Rights Section** ⊠ NYAV, U.S. Department of Justice, Civil Rights Division, 950 Pennsylvania Ave. NW, Washington, DC 20530 ☎ ADA information line 202/514-0301 or 800/514-0301, 202/514-0383 TTY or 800/514-0383 TTY ⊕ www.ada.gov. **U.S. Department of Transportation Hotline** ☎ For disability-related air-travel problems, 800/778-4838 or 800/455-9880 TTY.

## DISCOUNTS & DEALS
If you're visiting more than several archaeological sites and museums, it's worthwhile purchasing special multisite tickets that offer entrance to several sites. The Museo Nazionale Romano ticket costs €7. It lasts three days and is valid for four museums. The Roma Archaeologia Card costs €20. It covers nine museums and archaeological sites and is valid for seven days. EU citizens between 18 and 25 can purchase these cards at half price. The tickets are on sale at the sites where they can be used.

## DISCOUNT RESERVATIONS
To save money, look into discount reservations services with Web sites and toll-free numbers, which use their buying power to get a better price on hotels, airline tickets

(⇨ Air Travel), even car rentals. When booking a room, always **call the hotel's local toll-free number** (if one is available) rather than the central reservations number—you'll often get a better price. Always ask about special packages or corporate rates.

When shopping for the best deal on hotels and car rentals, look for guaranteed exchange rates, which protect you against a falling dollar. With your rate locked in, you won't pay more, even if the price goes up in the local currency.

🖪 Airline Tickets **Air 4 Less** ☎ 800/AIR4LESS; low-fare specialist.

🖪 Hotel Rooms **Accommodations Express** ☎ 800/444-7666 or 800/277-1064 ⊕ www.accommodationsexpress.com. **Hotels.com** ☎ 800/246-8357 ⊕ www.hotels.com. **Steigenberger Reservation Service** ☎ 800/223-5652 ⊕ www.srs-worldhotels.com. **Turbotrip.com** ☎ 800/473-7829 ⊕ www.turbotrip.com.

## PACKAGE DEALS
Don't confuse packages and guided tours. When you buy a package, you travel on your own, just as though you had planned the trip yourself. Fly/drive packages, which combine airfare and car rental, are often a good deal. In cities, ask the local visitor's bureau about hotel packages that include tickets to major museum exhibits or other special events. If you **buy a rail/drive pass,** you may save on train tickets and car rentals. All Eurailpass holders get a discount on Eurostar fares through the Channel Tunnel and often receive reduced rates for buses, hotels, ferries, and car rentals.

## ELECTRICITY
To use electric-powered equipment purchased in the United States or Canada, **bring a converter and adapter.** The electrical current in Italy is 220 volts, 50 cycles alternating current (AC); wall outlets take Continental-type plugs, with two or three round prongs.

If your appliances are dual-voltage, you'll need only an adapter. Don't use 110-volt outlets marked FOR SHAVERS ONLY for high-wattage appliances such as blow-dryers. Most laptops operate equally well on 110 and 220 volts and so require only an adapter.

## EMBASSIES

🚩 Australia **Australian Embassy** ✉ Via Alessandria 215, 00198 Rome ☎ 06/852721 ⊕ www. australian-embassy.it.

🚩 Canada **Canadian Embassy** ✉ Via G.B. de Rossi 27, 00161 Rome ☎ 06/445981 ⊕ www.dfait-maeci.gc.ca/canadaeuropa/italy.

🚩 New Zealand **New Zealand Embassy** ✉ Via Zara 28, 00198 Rome ☎ 06/4417171.

🚩 United Kingdom **British Embassy** ✉ Via XX Settembre 80A, 00187 Rome ☎ 06/42200001 ⊕ www.britain.it.

🚩 United States **U.S. Embassy** ✉ Via Veneto 121 00187 Rome ☎ 06/46741 ⊕ www.usembassy.it.

## EMERGENCIES

No matter where you are in Italy, **dial 113 for all emergencies,** or find somebody (your concierge, a passer-by) who will call for you, as not all 113 operators speak English; the Italian word to use to draw people's attention in an emergency is *Aiuto!* (Help!, pronounced ah-*you*-toh). *Pronto soccorso* means "first aid". When confronted with a health emergency, head straight for the Pronto Soccorso department of the nearest hospital or dial 118. To call a Red Cross ambulance *(ambulanza)* dial 06/5510. At night, or on Sunday and holidays, you can call on the services of the *Guardia Medica,* or First Aid Station, at the following number: 06/58201030. If you just need a doctor, you should ask for *un medico*; most hotels will be able to refer you to a local doctor *(medico).* Don't forget to ask the doctor for *una ricevuta* (an invoice) to show to your insurance company to get a reimbursement. Other useful Italian words to use are *Al fuoco!* (Fire!, pronounced ahl fuh-*woe*-co) and *Al ladro!* (Follow the thief!, pronounced ahl *lah*-droh).

Italy has a national police force *(carabinieri)* as well as local police *(polizia).* Both are armed and have the power to arrest and investigate crimes. **Always report any theft or the loss of your passport to either the carabinieri or the police,** as well as to your embassy. Local traffic officers are known as *vigili* (though their official name is *polizia municipale*)—they are re-

sponsible for, among other things, giving out parking tickets and clamping cars, so before you even consider parking the Italian way, make sure you are at least able to spot their white (in summer) or black uniforms (many are women). Should you find yourself involved in a minor car accident, you should contact the vigili. Call the countrywide toll-free number 113 if you need the police.

Most pharmacies are open Monday–Saturday 8:30–1 and 4–8; some are open all night. A schedule posted outside each pharmacy indicates the nearest pharmacy open during off-hours (afternoons, through the night, and Sunday). Farmacia Internazionale Capranica, Farmacia Internazionale Barberini (open 24 hours), and Farmacia Cola di Rienzo are pharmacies that have some English-speaking staff. The hospitals listed below have English-speaking doctors. Rome American Hospital is about 30 minutes by cab from the center of town.

For a full listing of doctors and dentists in Rome who speak English, consult the English Yellow Pages at ⊕ www. englishyellowpages.it or pick up a copy at any English-language bookstore. Your embassy will also have a recommended list of medical professionals.

🚩 Emergencies ☎ 113. Police ☎ 113.

🚩 Hospitals **Rome American Hospital** ✉ Via Emilio Longoni 69, Via Prenestina ☎ 06/22551 ⊕ www.rah.it. **Salvator Mundi International Hospital** ✉ Viale delle Mura Gianicolensi 66, Trastevere ☎ 06/588961 ⊕ www.ministerosalute.it.

🚩 Hotlines **Crime Victims Services** ☎ 840/002244. **Highway Police** ☎ 06/22101. **Road Breakdown** ☎ 116. **Women's Rights and Abuse Prevention** ☎ 06/37511362.

🚩 Pharmacies **Farmacia Cola di Rienzo** ✉ Via Cola di Rienzo 213, San Pietro ☎ 06/3243130. **Farmacia Internazionale Barberini** ✉ Piazza Barberini 49, Via Veneto ☎ 06/4825456. **Farmacia Internazionale Capranica** ✉ Piazza Capranica 96, Pantheon ☎ 06/6794680.

## ENGLISH-LANGUAGE MEDIA
### BOOKS

English-language books in Rome are expensive; most are imported from England, and reflect the strong pound and shipping costs. The Anglo-American Bookstore has the widest selection of genres. Trastevere's The Almost Corner Bookstore carries off-beat new fiction and has a vast history section. For used books, try the Open Door. The nationwide chain Feltrinelli International has a large selection of English-language books.

**⚑ Bookstores Almost Corner Bookstore** ⊠ Via del Moro 45, Trastevere ☏ 06/5836942. **Anglo-American Bookstore** ⊠ Via della Vite 102, Piazza di Spagna ☏ 06/6795222 ⊕ www.aab.it. **Feltrinelli International** ⊠ Via Vittorio Emanuale Orlando 78/81, Termini ☏ 06/4870171. **Lion Bookshop** ⊠ Via dei Greci 33/36, Piazza di Spagna ☏ 06/32654007. **Open Door** ⊠ Via della Lungaretta 23, Trastevere ☏ 06/5896478.

## NEWSPAPERS & MAGAZINES

A monthly booklet called *L'Evento,* available free at tourist information kiosks, lists all concerts, exhibitions, shows, and other cultural events in both Italian and English. Rome's English-language biweekly, *Wanted in Rome,* on sale at newsstands, also carries information about current events. Major English and American news-magazines and a few daily papers are available at most newsstands in the city center. You can find the Sunday *New York Times* in some places, but be prepared to pay a lot for it.

## RADIO & TELEVISION

Radio broadcasts are almost completely in Italian. Unless you have satellite TV (with access to CNN or SkyNews), or unless you speak Italian, Italian television is completely inaccessible, as everything is either spoken in Italian or dubbed into Italian. MTV is sometimes broadcast in English with Italian subtitles—but that's the exception, not the rule. Vatican Radio broadcasts world news in English three times a day throughout Italy, with Vatican news included.

## ETIQUETTE & BEHAVIOR

Italy is teeming with churches, many with significant works of art in them. Because they are places of worship, care should be taken with appropriate dress. Shorts, cropped tops, miniskirts, and bare midriffs are taboo at St. Peter's in Rome, and in many other churches throughout Italy. So, too, are short shorts anywhere. When touring churches—especially in summer when it's hot and no sleeves are desirable—it's wise to carry a sweater, or scarf, to wrap around your shoulders before entering the church. **Do not enter a church with food,** and do not drink from your water bottle while inside. **Do not go in if a service is in progress.** And if you have a cellular phone, **turn it off before entering.**

Italians who are friends greet each other with a kiss, usually first on the right cheek, and then on the left. When you meet a new person, shake hands.

## GAY & LESBIAN TRAVEL

Local gays and lesbians generally maintain low visibility in Rome; favorite clubs and bars are usually mixed rather than exclusively homosexual. Some mainstream bars and nightclubs have a gay night during the week; inquire at the local tourist office.

**⚑ Gay Awareness Organizations Arcilesbica** ⊠ Via Monti Pietralata 16, Piazza Fiume ☏ 06/418021. **Circolo di Cultura Omosessuale Mario Mieli** ⊠ Via Corinto 5, Testaccio ☏ 06/59604622 ⊕ www.mariomieli.org. **Circolo di Cultura Omosessuale** ⊠ Via Efeso 2, San Paolo ☏ 06/5413985.

**⚑ Gay- & Lesbian-Friendly Travel Agencies Different Roads Travel** ⊠ 8383 Wilshire Blvd., Suite 520, Beverly Hills, CA 90211 ☏ 323/651-5557 or 800/429-8747 (Ext. 14 for both) 🖷 323/651-3678 ✉ lgernert@tzell.com. **Kennedy Travel** ⊠ 130 W. 42nd St., Suite 401, New York, NY 10036 ☏ 212/840-8659 or 800/237-7433 🖷 212/730-2269 ⊕ www. kennedytravel.com. **Now, Voyager** ⊠ 4406 18th St., San Francisco, CA 94114 ☏ 415/626-1169 or 800/255-6951 🖷 415/626-8626 ⊕ www.nowvoyager. com. **Skylink Travel and Tour** ⊠ 1455 N. Dutton Ave., Suite A, Santa Rosa, CA 95401 ☏ 707/546-9888 or 800/225-5759 🖷 707/636-0951, serving lesbian travelers.

## GUIDEBOOKS

Plan well and you won't be sorry. Guidebooks are excellent tools—and you can take them with you. You may want to check out color-photo-illustrated *Fodor's See It Rome,* thorough on culture and history; pocket-size *Rome's 25 Best,* which includes a supersize foldout map; or

*Fodor's Holy Rome,* a photo-filled guide to the city's Christian sights. All are available at online retailers and bookstores everywhere.

## HEALTH

### FOOD & DRINK

Tap water is drinkable across Rome itself, and the city is renowned for the high quality of its water that comes from plentiful underground springs. Throughout the city, in almost every square and side street, you'll find drinking fountains, which the Romans call *nasoni* because of the shape of their little bronze or brass drinking spout. The only water you should not drink is the water that gushes into ornamental fountains, which often has cleansing chemicals in it, and any fountain that has the words *non potabile,* meaning undrinkable, written over it.

Cows' meat is now considered safe to eat throughout the EU and Italians are once more enjoying traditional beef dishes, like the prized *bistecca alla fiorentina,* the thick T-bone steak cut from Tuscan beef, or the succulent *osso buco* (braised veal shank), oxtail, and offal specialties that are prepared throughout the country. Alternative meats, such as *struzzo* (ostrich) and *canguro* (kangaroo), which became available during the mad cow scare, have not proved lastingly popular and have largely disappeared from restaurant menus.

### OVER-THE-COUNTER REMEDIES

It's always best to **travel with your own tried and true medicines.** The regulations regarding what medicines require a prescription are not likely to be exactly the same in Italy and in your home country—all the more reason to bring what you need with you. Aspirin (*l'aspirina*) can be purchased at any pharmacy, but Tylenol and Advil are unavailable. Note that over-the-counter remedies, including cough syrup, antiseptic creams, and headache pills are only sold in pharmacies.

### HOLIDAYS

If you can avoid it, don't travel at all in Italy in August, when much of the population is on the move, especially around *Fer-*

*ragosto,* the August 15 national holiday, when cities such as Rome are deserted and many restaurants and shops are closed.

National holidays are New Year's Day; January 6 (Epiphany); Easter Sunday and Monday; April 25 (Liberation Day); May 1 (Labor Day or May Day); June 29 (Sts. Peter and Paul, Rome's patron saints); August 15 (Assumption of Mary, also known as Ferragosto); November 1 (All Saints' Day); December 8 (Immaculate Conception); Christmas Day and the feast of Saint Stephen (December 25 and 26).

## INSURANCE

The most useful travel-insurance plan is a comprehensive policy that includes coverage for trip cancellation and interruption, default, trip delay, and medical expenses (with a waiver for preexisting conditions).

Without insurance you'll lose all or most of your money if you cancel your trip, regardless of the reason. Default insurance covers you if your tour operator, airline, or cruise line goes out of business. Trip-delay covers expenses that arise because of bad weather or mechanical delays. Study the fine print when comparing policies.

If you're traveling internationally, a key component of travel insurance is coverage for medical bills incurred if you get sick on the road. Such expenses aren't generally covered by Medicare or private policies. U.K. residents can buy a travel-insurance policy valid for most vacations taken during the year in which it's purchased (but check preexisting-condition coverage). British and Australian citizens need extra medical coverage when traveling overseas.

Always **buy travel policies directly from the insurance company**; if you buy them from a cruise line, airline, or tour operator that goes out of business, you probably won't be covered for the agency or operator's default, a major risk. Before making any purchase, review your existing health and home-owner's policies to find what they cover away from home.

🎫 Travel Insurers In the U.S.: **Access America** ✉ 6600 W. Broad St., Richmond, VA 23230 ☎ 800/284-8300 🖷 804/673-1491 or 800/346-9265 🌐 www.accessamerica.com. **Travel Guard Interna-**

**tional** ✉ 1145 Clark St., Stevens Point, WI 54481 ☎ 715/345-0505 or 800/826-1300 🖷 800/955-8785 ⊕ www.travelguard.com. 🔝 In the U.K.: **Association of British Insurers** ✉ 51 Gresham St., London EC2V 7HQ ☎ 020/7600-3333 🖷 020/7696-8999 ⊕ www.abi.org.uk. In Canada: **RBC Insurance** ✉ 6880 Financial Dr., Mississauga, Ontario L5N 7Y5 ☎ 800/565-3129 🖷 905/813-4704 ⊕ www.rbcinsurance.com. In Australia: **Insurance Council of Australia** ✉ Insurance Enquiries and Complaints, Level 3, 56 Pitt St., Sydney, NSW 2000 ☎ 1300/363683 or 02/9251-4456 🖷 02/9251-4453 ⊕ www.iecltd.com.au. In New Zealand: **Insurance Council of New Zealand** ✉ Level 7, 111-115 Customhouse Quay, Box 474, Wellington ☎ 04/472-5230 🖷 04/473-3011 ⊕ www.icnz.org.nz.

## LANGUAGE

You can always find someone who speaks at least a little English in Rome, albeit with a heavy accent. Remember that the Italian language is pronounced exactly as it's written—many Italians try to speak English as it's written, with bewildering results. You may run into a language barrier in the countryside, but a phrase book and close attention to the Italians' astonishing use of pantomime and expressive gestures will go a long way.

Try to **master a few phrases for daily use,** and familiarize yourself with the terms you'll need to decipher signs and museum labels. Some museums have exhibits labeled in both English and Italian, but this is the exception rather than the rule. Most exhibitions have multilanguage headphones you can rent and English-language guidebooks are generally available at museum shops. Many newsstands and bookstores stock a useful guide called *Rome, Past & Present.* It has photos of the most famous ancient monuments, together with drawings of what they originally looked like, and is particularly useful to get children interested in what seems (to them) just heaps of old stones.

### LANGUAGES FOR TRAVELERS

A phrase book and language-tape set can help get you started. *Fodor's Italian for Travelers* (available at bookstores everywhere) is excellent.

### LANGUAGE-STUDY PROGRAMS

Private language schools and U.S.- and U.K.-affiliated educational institutions offer a host of Italian language study programs in Rome. 🔝 Language Schools **American University of Rome** ✉ Via Pietro Rosselli 4 ☎ 06/58330919 ⊕ www.aur.edu. **Arco di Druso** ✉ Via Tunisi 4 ☎ 06/39750984 ⊕ www.arcodidruso.com. **Berlitz** ✉ Via Torre Argentina 21 ☎ 06/6834000 ⊕ www.berlitz.com. **Centro Linguistico Italiano Dante Alighieri** ✉ Piazza Bologna 1 ☎ 06/44231490. **Ciao Italia** ✉ Via delle Frasche 5 ☎ 06/4814084 ⊕ www.ciao-italia.it. **Dilit International House** ✉ Via Marghera 22 ☎ 06/4462592 ⊕ www.dilit.it.

## MAIL & SHIPPING

The Italian mail system has improved tremendously with the introduction of a two-tier postal system. A **posta prioritaria stamp** (first class stamp) costs €0.62 and usually guarantees delivery to EEC destinations within three days. A posta prioritaria stamp within Italy costs € 0.60. Most mailboxes have a separate posta prioritaria compartment.

The Vatican postal service has a reputation for efficiency and many foreigners prefer to send their mail from there, with Vatican stamps. You can buy these in the post offices on either side of Piazza di San Pietro, one next to the information office and the other under the colonnade opposite. During peak tourist seasons a Vatican Post Office mobile unit is set up in Piazza di San Pietro. 🔝 Post Offices **Main Rome post office** ✉ Piazza San Silvestro 19 ☎ 06/6798495.

### OVERNIGHT SERVICES

Although DHL and UPS offices are far out of the city center, FedEx has walk-in service on Via Barberini; all three companies will pick up packages from anywhere in Rome. 🔝 Major Services **DHL** ☎ 199199345. **Federal Express** ✉ Via Barberini 115, Via Veneto ☎ 800/123800. **UPS** ☎ 800/877877.

### POSTAL RATES

Letters and postcards to the United States and Canada cost €0.80 for up to 20 grams and automatically go airmail. Letters and postcards to the United Kingdom cost €0.62. You can buy stamps at tobacconists.

### RECEIVING MAIL

Correspondence can be addressed to you in care of the Italian post office. Letters should be addressed to your name, "c/o Ufficio Postale Centrale," followed by "Fermo Posta" on the next line, and "00187 Rome" on the next. You can **collect it at the central post office** at Piazza San Silvestro by showing your passport or photo-bearing ID and paying a small fee. American Express also has a general-delivery service. There's no charge for cardholders, holders of American Express traveler's checks, or anyone who booked a vacation with American Express.

### SHIPPING PARCELS

Air shipping takes about two weeks, and surface anywhere up to three months. If you have purchased antiques, ceramics, or other objects, **most vendors will arrange to do the shipping.** Buy antiques or art works only from a reputable dealer who can organize export permits and customs clearance for you, if necessary. (See our note on Consumer Protection).

## MONEY MATTERS

Rome's prices are comparable to those in other major capitals, such as Paris and London. Unless you dine in the swankiest places, you'll still find Rome one of the cheapest European capitals in which to eat. Clothes and leather goods are also generally less expensive than in northern Europe. Public transport is relatively cheap.

A Rome 2 km (1 mi) taxi ride costs €5.25. An inexpensive hotel room for two, including breakfast, is about €100; an inexpensive dinner for two is €30. A simple pasta item on the menu is about €8, and a ½-liter carafe of house wine €3.50. A McDonald's Big Mac is €2.80, with prices doubled if you sit down. A pint of beer in a pub is around €4.

Admission to the Musei Vaticani is €10. The cheapest seat at Rome's Opera House runs €17; a movie ticket is €6. A daily English-language newspaper is about €2.

Prices throughout this guide are given for adults. Substantially reduced fees are almost always available for children, students, and senior citizens. For information on taxes, *see* Taxes.

### ATMS

ATMs are common in Rome and are the easiest way to get euros. The word for ATM in Italian is *bancomat,* for PIN, *codice segreto.* Four-digit PINs are the standard, though in some machines longer numbers will work.

### CREDIT CARDS

Although increasingly common, credit cards aren't accepted at all establishments, and some require a minimum expenditure. If you want to pay with a card in a small hotel, store, or restaurant, it's a good idea to ask before conducting your business. Visa and MasterCard are preferred to American Express, but in tourist areas American Express is usually accepted. Acceptance of Diners Club is rare.

Throughout this guide, the following abbreviations are used: **AE,** American Express; **DC,** Diners Club; **MC,** MasterCard; and **V,** Visa.

Reporting Lost Cards **American Express** ☎ 336/668–5110 international collect. **Diners Club** ☎ 702/797–5532 collect. **MasterCard** ☎ 800/870866 toll-free in Italy. **Visa** ☎ 800/877232 toll-free in Italy.

### CURRENCY

The euro is the main unit of currency in Italy, as well as in 11 other European countries. Under the euro system, there are eight coins: 1, 2, 5, 10, 20, and 50 *centesimi* (at 100 centesimi to the euro), and 1 and 2 euros. There are seven notes: 5, 10, 20, 50, 100, 200, and 500 euros.

### CURRENCY EXCHANGE

At press time, the exchange rate was about 0.86 euros to the U.S. dollar; 0.65 euros to the Canadian dollar; 1.46 euros to the pound sterling; 0.61 euros to the Australian dollar; and 0.53 euros to the New Zealand dollar.

For the most favorable rates, **change money through banks.** Although ATM transaction fees may be higher abroad than at home, ATM rates are excellent because they're based on wholesale rates offered only by major banks. You won't do as well at exchange booths in airports or rail and bus stations, in hotels, in restaurants, or in stores. To avoid lines at airport exchange booths, get a bit of local currency before you leave home.

**Exchange Services** **International Currency Express** ✉ 427 N. Camden Dr., Suite F, Beverly Hills, CA 90210 ☎ 888/278-6628 orders 🖷 310/278-6410 ⊕ www.foreignmoney.com. **Thomas Cook International Money Services** ☎ 800/287-7362 orders and retail locations ⊕ www.us.thomascook.com.

## TRAVELER'S CHECKS

Lost or stolen checks can usually be replaced within 24 hours. To ensure a speedy refund, buy your own traveler's checks—don't let someone else pay for them: irregularities like this can cause delays. The person who bought the checks should make the call to request a refund.

## MOPEDS

As bikes are to Beijing, so mopeds are to Rome; that means they are everywhere. Riders are required to wear helmets, and traffic police are tough in enforcing this law. Producing your country's driver's license should be enough to convince most rental firms that they're not dealing with a complete beginner; but if you're unsure of exactly how to ride a moped, think twice, and at least ask the assistant for a detailed demonstration.

If you don't feel up to braving the Roman traffic on a moped, you can hire an electric car to scoot around the city. The MELEX is a four-seater, golf-cart-style car, with battery power lasting up to eight hours. To rent the MELEX, you need a valid driver's licence. Cost: €18 per hour.

**Rental Agencies** **Auto City** ✉ Via Collina 22, Termini ☎ 06/42020207. **Free Rome(MELEX cars)** ✉ Via Ludovisi 60, Via Veneto ☎ 06/42013110. **Happy Rent** ✉ Via Farini 3, Termini ☎ 06/4818185. **Scoot-a-Long** ✉ Via Cavour 302, Termini ☎ 06/6780206. **St. Peter Moto** ✉ Via di Porta Castello 43, San Pietro ☎ 06/6875714.

## PACKING

Plan your wardrobe in layers, no matter what the season. Rome generally has mild winters and hot, sticky summers. Heavy rain showers are common in spring and late fall. Take a medium-weight coat for winter; a lightweight all-weather coat for spring and fall; and a lightweight jacket or sweater for summer evenings, which may be cool. Brief summer thunderstorms are common, so take a folding umbrella, and keep in mind that anything more than light cotton clothes is unbearable in the humid heat. Few public buildings in Rome, including museums, restaurants, and shops, are air-conditioned. Interiors can be cold and sometimes damp in the cooler months, so take woolens or flannels.

Dress codes are strict for visits to the Basilica di San Pietro, the Musei Vaticani, and some churches: for both men and women, shorts, scanty tops, and bare midriffs are taboo. Shoulders must be covered. Women should carry a scarf or shawl to cover bare arms if the custodians insist. Those who do not comply with the dress code are refused admittance. Although there are no specific dress rules for the huge outdoor papal audiences, you'll be turned away if you're in shorts or a revealing outfit. The Vatican Information Office in Piazza di San Pietro will tell you the dress requirements for smaller audiences.

Don't keep your passport and large sums of money in your handbag or hip pocket. Any kind of bag, shoulder bag, or camera case is a target. If you must carry one, choose one with long straps that you can sling across your body, bandolier style. Avoid carrying a bag if you can, or carry one that is obviously just a tote for your guidebook and sundries.

In your carry-on luggage, pack an extra pair of eyeglasses or contact lenses and enough of any medication you take to last a few days longer than the entire trip. You may also ask your doctor to write a spare prescription using the drug's generic name, as brand names may vary from country to country. In luggage to be checked, **never pack prescription drugs, valuables, or undeveloped film.** And don't forget to carry with you the addresses of offices that handle refunds of lost traveler's checks. Check *Fodor's How to Pack* (available at online retailers and bookstores everywhere) for more tips.

To avoid customs and security delays, carry medications in their original packaging. Don't pack any sharp objects in your carry-on luggage, including knives of any size or material, scissors, and corkscrews, or anything else that might arouse suspicion.

To avoid having your checked luggage chosen for hand inspection, don't cram bags full. The U.S. Transportation Security Administration suggests packing shoes on top and placing personal items you don't want touched in clear plastic bags.

### CHECKING LUGGAGE

You're allowed to carry aboard one bag and one personal article, such as a purse or a laptop computer. Make sure what you carry on fits under your seat or in the overhead bin. Get to the gate early, so you can board as soon as possible, before the overhead bins fill up.

Baggage allowances vary by carrier, destination, and ticket class. On international flights, you're usually allowed to check two bags weighing up to 70 pounds (32 kilograms) each, although a few airlines allow checked bags of up to 88 pounds (40 kilograms) in first class. Some international carriers don't allow more than 66 pounds (30 kilograms) per bag in business class and 44 pounds (20 kilograms) in economy. On domestic flights, the limit is usually 50 to 70 pounds (23 to 32 kilograms) per bag. In general, carry-on bags shouldn't exceed 40 pounds (18 kilograms). Most airlines won't accept bags that weigh more than 100 pounds (45 kilograms) on domestic or international flights. Check baggage restrictions with your carrier before you pack.

### PASSPORTS & VISAS

When traveling internationally, carry your passport even if you don't need one (it's always the best form of ID) and **make two photocopies of the data page** (one for someone at home and another for you, carried separately from your passport). If you lose your passport, promptly call the nearest embassy or consulate and the local police.

U.S. passport applications for children under age 14 require consent from both parents or legal guardians; both parents must appear together to sign the application. If only one parent appears, he or she must submit a written statement from the other parent authorizing passport issuance for the child. A parent with sole authority must present evidence of it when applying; acceptable documentation includes the child's certified birth certificate listing only the applying parent, a court order specifically permitting this parent's travel with the child, or a death certificate for the non-applying parent. Application forms and instructions are available on the Web site of the U.S. State Department's Bureau of Consular Affairs (⊕ www.travel.state.gov).

### ENTERING ITALY

All U.S., Canadian, U.K., Australian, and New Zealand citizens, even infants, need only a valid passport to enter Italy for stays of up to 90 days.

### PASSPORT OFFICES

The best time to apply for a passport or to renew is in fall and winter. Before any trip, check your passport's expiration date, and, if necessary, renew it as soon as possible.

**Australian Citizens Passports Australia** ☎ 131-232 ⊕ www.passports.gov.au.
**Canadian Citizens Passport Office** ✉ To mail in applications: 200 Promenade du Portage, Hull, Québec J8X 4B7 ☎ 819/994-3500 or 800/567-6868 ⊕ www.ppt.gc.ca.
**New Zealand Citizens New Zealand Passports Office** ☎ 0800/22-5050 or 04/474-8100 ⊕ www.passports.govt.nz.
**U.K. Citizens U.K. Passport Service** ☎ 0870/521-0410 ⊕ www.passport.gov.uk.
**U.S. Citizens National Passport Information Center** ☎ 900/225-5674 or 900/225-7778 TTY (calls are 55¢ per minute for automated service or $1.50 per minute for operator service), 888/362-8668 or 888/498-3648 TTY (calls are $5.50 each) ⊕ www.travel.state.gov.

### PUBLIC TRANSPORTATION: BUS, TRAM & METROPOLITANA

Although most of Rome's sights are in a relatively circumscribed area, the city is too large to be seen solely on foot. Try to avoid rush hours when taking the Metro (subway) or a bus, as public transport can be extremely crowded. Mid-morning or the middle of the day up until early afternoon tend to be less busy. Otherwise, it's best to take a taxi to the area you plan to visit if it is across town. But you should always expect to do a lot of walking in Rome (especially considering how limited the subway stops are) and so plan on wearing a pair of comfortable, sturdy shoes to cushion the impact of the *sampietrini* (cobblestones). Get away from the noise and polluted air of heavily trafficked streets by taking parallel streets whenever possible. You can get free city and transportation-route maps at municipal information booths.

Rome's integrated transportation system includes buses and trams (ATAC), Metropolitana (subway, often nicknamed the Metro) and suburban trains and buses (COTRAL), and some other suburban trains (Trenitalia) run by the state railways. A ticket (BIT) valid for 75 minutes on any combination of buses and trams and one entrance to the Metro costs €1.

Tickets are sold at tobacconists, newsstands, some coffee bars, automatic ticket machines in Metro stations, some bus stops, and ATAC and COTRAL ticket booths (in some Metro stations and at a few main bus stops). You can buy them singly or in quantity; it's always a good idea to **have a few tickets handy** so you don't have to hunt for a vendor when you need one. **Time-stamp your ticket when boarding the first vehicle,** stamping it again when boarding for the last time within 75 minutes. You stamp the ticket at Metro turnstiles and in the little machines near the stops for buses and trams.

A BIG ticket—or *Biglietto integrato giornaliero* (integrated daily ticket)—is valid for one day (only for the day it is stamped, not 24 hours) on all public transport and costs €4. A three-day pass (BTI)—or *Biglietto turistico integrato*—costs €11. A weekly ticket (*settimanale,* also known as CIS) costs €16 and gives unlimited travel on ATAC buses, COTRAL urban bus services, COTRAL trains for the Lido and

Viterbo, the subway, and one trip on FS trains. There's an ATAC kiosk at the bus terminus in front of Termini station.

If you're going farther afield, or planning to spend more than a week in Rome, think about getting a BIRG regional ticket or a CIRS (regional weekly ticket) from the railway station. These give you unlimited travel on all state transport throughout the region of Lazio. This can take you as far as the Etruscan city of Tarquinia or medieval Viterbo.

## BUS & TRAM TRAVEL

Not as fast as the Metropolitana, bus travel is more scenic. With reserved bus lanes and numerous tram lines, surface transportation is surprisingly efficient, given the volume of Roman traffic. At peak times, however, buses can be very crowded. If the distance you have to travel is not too great, walking can be a more comfortable alternative. ATAC city buses and trams are orange, gray-and-red, or blue-and-orange. Remember to board at the rear and to exit at the middle; you must **buy your ticket before boarding, and stamp it in a machine as soon as you enter.** If you find the bus too crowded to get to the ticket machine, manually cancel the ticket by writing on it the date and time you got on. The ticket is good for a transfer within the next 75 minutes. Buses and trams run from 5:30 AM to midnight, plus there's an extensive network of night buses throughout the city.

**ATAC urban buses** ☎ 06/48915, Freephone 800/431784, 8 AM–8 PM except Sunday ⊕ www.atac.roma.it. **COTRAL** ☎ 800/150008 ⊕ www.cotral.it. **Trenitalia suburban trains** ⊕ www.trenitalia.it.

## METROPOLITANA

The Metropolitana (or Metro) is the easiest and fastest way to get around Rome. There are stops near most of the main tourist attractions (street entrances are marked with red "M" signs). The Metro has two lines—A and B—which intersect at Termini Station. Line A runs from the eastern part of the city, with stops, among others, at San Giovanni in Laterano, Piazza Barberini, Piazza di Spagna, Piazzale Flaminio (Piazza del Popolo), and Ottaviano/San Pietro,

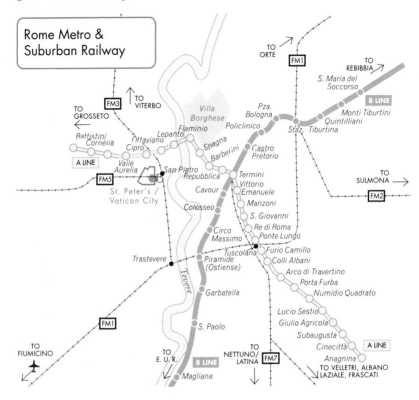

Rome Metro & Suburban Railway

near the Basilica di San Pietro and the Musei Vaticani. At press time, due to reconstruction, the Metro A line underground services end at 9 PM, at which time they are substituted by buses at the terminals that run until 11:30 PM. Work is estimated to take at least a year. Line B has stops near the Colosseum, the Circus Maximus, the Pyramid (Ostiense Station and trains for Ostia Antica), and the Basilica di San Paolo Fuori le Mura. The Metro opens at 5:30 AM, and the last trains leave the last station at either end at 11:30 PM (on Saturday night the last train leaves at 12:30 AM).

### SMOKING

Smoking is not permitted on Rome buses, trams, or subway trains.

### RESTROOMS

Public restrooms are rather rare in Rome. Although there are public toilets in Piazza di San Pietro, Piazza di Spagna, at the

Roman Forum, and in a few other strategic locations (all with a charge of €0.50–€0.70), the locals seem to make do primarily with well-timed pit stops and rely on the local bar. Most bars will allow you to use the restroom if you ask politely. Alternatively, it's not uncommon to pay for a little something—a mineral water or espresso—to get access to the facilities. Standards of cleanliness and comfort vary greatly. Restaurants, hotels, department stores like La Rinascente and Coin, and McDonald's restaurants tend to have the cleanest restrooms. Pubs and bars rank among the worst. In general, it's in your interest to carry tissues with you. There are bathrooms in all airports and train stations (in major train stations you'll also find well-kept pay toilets for €0.70) and in most museums. Carry a selection of coins as some turnstiles do not give change. There are also free facilities at highway rest stops and gas stations: a small tip to the cleaning person is always appreciated. There are no bathrooms in churches, post offices, public beaches, or subway stations.

## SAFETY

Don't wear a money belt or a waist pack, both of which peg you as a tourist. Distribute your cash and any valuables (including your credit cards and passport) between a deep front pocket, an inside jacket or vest pocket, and a hidden money pouch. Do not reach for the money pouch once you're in public.

Wear a bag or camera slung across your body bandolier style, and don't rest your bag or camera on a table or chair at a sidewalk café or restaurant. In Rome, **beware of pickpockets** on buses, especially Line 64 (Termini–St. Peter's train station); the Line 40 Express, which takes a faster route and takes you closer to the basilica; and subways—and when making your way through the corridors of crowded trains. Pickpockets may be active wherever tourists gather, including the Roman Forum, Piazza Navona, and Piazza di San Pietro. Purse snatchers work in teams on a single motor scooter or motorcycle: one drives and the other grabs.

## LOCAL SCAMS

Groups of gypsy children and young women (often with babes in arms) are present around sights popular with tourists and on buses and are adept pickpockets. One well-tried method is to approach a tourist and proffer a piece of cardboard with writing on it. While the unsuspecting victim attempts to read the message *on* it, the children's hands are busy *under* it, trying to make off with wallets and valuables. If you see such a group, do not even allow them near you—they are quick and know more tricks than you do. The phrases *Vai via!* (Go away!) and *Chiamo la polizia* (I'll call the police) usually keep them at bay. The colorful characters dressed as Roman legionaries, who hover round the Colosseum and other monuments, expect a tip if you photograph them. The amount of €5 is quite sufficient.

## SENIOR-CITIZEN TRAVEL

Senior-citizen discounts are not widely offered in Italy unless they're part of a tour package. EU citizens over 65 are entitled to free admission to state museums as well as to many other museums, as are Canadians and New Zealanders with their passports—always ask at the ticket office. Older travelers may be eligible for special fares on Alitalia and other airlines. When renting a car, **ask about promotional car-rental discounts,** which can be cheaper than senior-citizen rates.

Wheelchairs are available for free for use at the Vatican Museums.

**f** Educational Programs **Elderhostel** ⊠ 11 Ave. de Lafayette, Boston, MA 02111-1746 ☎ 877/426-8056, 978/323-4141 international callers, 877/426-2167 TTY 🖷 877/426-2166 ⊕ www.elderhostel.org. **Interhostel** ⊠ University of New Hampshire, 6 Garrison Ave., Durham, NH 03824 ☎ 603/862-1147 or 800/733-9753 🖷 603/862-1113 ⊕ www.learn.unh.edu.

## SHOPPING

The notice PREZZI FISSI (fixed prices) means just that: in shops displaying this sign it's a waste of time to bargain unless you're buying a sizable quantity of goods or a particularly costly object. *Saldi* (sales) happen just after the New Year and run as late as March, and then again in July through early September. Always bargain at outdoor markets (except food markets) and when buying from street vendors. For information on V.A.T. refunds, *see* Taxes.

## FUN SOUVENIRS

From the holy to the kitsch, Rome has no shortage of keepsakes. For rose-scented rosary beads or reproductions of Raphael's angels, head for the shops that line Borgo Pio, near St. Peter's. These shops will also arrange to have a papal blessing sent anywhere in the world for a wedding, christening, or special anniversary. Smart bottle openers and other household articles in cutting-edge Italian design make useful mementos. Miniature alabaster or plaster copies of famous sculptures abound, as well as calendars of Roman cats. Aprons emblazoned with naked Davids make an inexpensive gift for a friend with a sense of humor. Vatican stamp sets and coins are prized souvenirs for collectors. It's also possible to buy old Roman coins quite cheaply in specialized numismatic shops. One of the most fun places to shop for little Roman gifts is the hip stationery store near the Spanish Steps, the Cartotecnica Romana.

## SIGHTSEEING TOURS

### ORIENTATION TOURS

Some might consider them campy and kitschy, but guided bus tours can prove a blissfully easy way to enjoy a quick introduction to the city's top sights. Sitting in a bus, with friendly tour guide commentary (and even friendlier fellow sightseers, many of whom will be from every country under the sun), can make for a delightful and fun experience—so give one a whirl *even* if you're an old Rome hand. Of course, you'll want to savor these incredible sights at your own leisure later on.

Appian Line, Carrani, Vastours (in collaboration with American Express), and other operators offer half-day and full-day tours in air-conditioned buses with English-speaking guides. The four main itineraries are: "Ancient Rome," "Classic Rome," "Christian Rome," and "The Vatican Museums and Sistine Chapel." Half-day tours cost around €32.50 and full-day tours (including lunch and entrance fees) are between €88 and €100. The Musei Vaticani tour costs €45.50, but offers the advantage of not having to queue (sometimes for an hour or more) at the museum doors, awaiting your turn for admission. All the companies pick you up at centrally located hotels.

All operators can provide a luxury car for up to three people, a limousine for up to seven, or a minibus for up to nine, all with an English-speaking driver, but guide service is extra. Almost all operators offer "Rome by Night" tours, with or without dinner and entertainment. You can book tours through travel agents.

Various sightseeing buses following a continuous circle route through the center of town operate daily. Stop-'n'-Go has eight daily departures and makes 14 scheduled stops at important sites, where you can get on and off at will. Check with the Rome tourist information kiosks

or inquire at your hotel for prices and further information.

The least expensive organized sightseeing tour of Rome is that run by ATAC, the municipal bus company. Double-decker bus 110 leaves from Piazza dei Cinquecento, in front of Termini Station, but you can pick it up at any of its 10 stopover points. A day ticket costs €13 and allows you to stop off and get on as often as you like. The price includes an audio guide system in six languages. The total tour takes about two hours and covers the Colosseum, Piazza Navona, St. Peter's, the Trevi Fountain, and Via Veneto. Tickets can be bought on board. Two-day and three-day tickets are also available. Tours leave from Termini Station every 20 minutes between 9 AM and 8:30 PM.

The Archeobus, which takes you to the Old Appian Way, the Catacombs, and the new Park of the Aqueducts in the open countryside also operates with the stop n' go formula. Little 15-seater buses leave from Piazza della Cinquecento every hour between 10 AM and 4 PM. Tickets cost €8 and are valid all day. A combined 110 + Archeobus ticket costs € 20 and is valid for one day.

Of course, you get a real bargain if you do your sightseeing "tours" of Rome by public transport. Many buses and trams pass major sights. With a single €1 ticket you can get in 75 minutes of sightseeing (or an entire day, with a €3.10 *giornaliero* ticket). Time your ride to avoid rush hours. The little electric bus 116 scoots through the heart of Old Rome, with stops near the Pantheon, the Spanish Steps, and Piazza del Popolo, among others. The route of bus 117 takes in San Giovanni in Laterano, the Colosseum, and the Spanish Steps.

Since certain parts of the historic center are open to pedestrians only, some walking is involved in most escorted bus tours of the city. Don't forget to dress appropriately for visits to churches (see the Etiquette & Behavior section). Tour operators can also organize minibus tours for small parties.

🚌 Bus Line **ATAC** ☎ 800/431784 toll-free ⊕ www.atac.roma.it.

⚐ Tour Operators **American Express** ☎ 06/67641. **Appian Line** ☎ 06/48786601 ⊕ www.appianline.it. **Carrani** ☎ 06/4742501 ⊕ www.carrani.com. **Ciao Roma Trolley Tour** ☎ 06/48976161. **Vastours** ☎ 06/4814309 ⊕ www.vastours.it/roma. **Stop-'n'-go City Tours** ☎ 06/48905729.

## SPECIAL-INTEREST TOURS

You can make your own arrangements (at no cost) to attend a public papal audience at the Vatican or at the pope's summer residence at Castel Gandolfo. You can also book through a travel agency for a package that includes coach transportation to the Vatican for the audience and some sightseeing along the way, returning you to your hotel, for about €32.50. The excursion outside Rome to Castel Gandolfo on summer Sundays for the pope's blessing costs about €39. Agencies that arrange these tours include Appian Line and Carrani.

Tourvisa Italia organizes boat trips on the Tiber, departing and returning to Ponte Sant'Angelo. Boats leave four times daily for a cruise lasting an hour and a half. Tickets cost €10. The company also does combined bus and boat tours lasting two and one half hours and an evening cruise with dinner on board.

A ride in a horse-drawn carriage is the Rome equivalent of a gondola ride in Venice. Coachmen can be contacted directly at popular sights like St. Peter's Square and the Colosseum. An hour's ride for four passengers to view the fountains of Rome will cost around €150, depending on your bargaining skills.

If heights thrill you, you can enjoy a unique trip up in the Aerophile 5500. This air balloon carries 30 passengers to 500 feet above the ground for a 15-minute eagle's view of Rome. The balloon is tethered in the Villa Borghese Park at the Galoppatoio (near Via Veneto) and flies daily between 9:30 AM and sunset. Tickets cost €15, except Tuesday when you can go for €11. Weekends cost €18. Children and teenagers get discounts.

Centro Studi Cassia organizes courses in Italian cooking, art, music, and current events in simple Italian. This is an enjoyable way to learn to speak some of the language and, at the same time, find out more about the culture and traditions of the country.

⚐ Tour Operators **Aerophile Italia** ☎ 06/3211-1511 ⊕ www.aerophile.it/. **Appian Line** ☎ 06/487861 ✉ appian@appianline.it ⊕ www.appianline.it. **Carrani** ☎ 06/474-2501 ✉ carrani.viaggi@tiscalinet.it ⊕ www.carrani.com. **Centro Studi Cassia** ☎ 06/3325-3852 ⊕ www.centrostudicassia.it. **Tourvisa Italia** ☎ 06/678-9361.

## WALKING TOURS

All About Rome, Enjoy Rome, Scala Reale, Through Eternity, and Argiletum Tour offer walking tours of the city and its sights. Argiletum and the cultural association Genti e Paesi offer regular walking tours and museum visits in English, including private tours of the Sistine Chapel before all the hordes arrive. Book at least one day in advance. If you have a reasonable knowledge of Italian, you can take advantage of the free guided visits and walking tours organized by Rome's cultural associations and the city council for museums and monuments. These usually take place on weekends. Programs are announced in the daily papers and in weekly magazine *roma c'è*.

⚐ Tour Operators **All About Rome** ☎ 06/7100823 ✉ allaboutromewalks@yahoo.com. **Argiletum Tour** ✉ Via Madonna dei Monti 49 ☎ 06/47825706 ⊕ www.argiletumtour.com. **Enjoy Rome** ✉ Via Marghera 8A, Termini ☎ 06/4451843. **Genti e Paesi** ✉ Via Adda 111 ☎ 06/85301758 ⊕ www.romeguide.it. **Scala Reale** ✉ Via dell'Olmata 30, Termini, 00184 ☎ 06/4745673 or 800/732-2863 Ext. 4052 ⊕ www.scalareale.org. **Through Eternity** ☎ 06/7009336 ⊕ www.thro..heternity.com.

## EXCURSIONS

Most operators offer half-day excursions to Tivoli to see the fountains and gardens of Villa D'Este. Appian Line's afternoon tour to Tivoli includes a visit to Hadrian's Villa, with its impressive ancient ruins, as well as the many fountained Villa D'Este. Most operators also have full-day excursions to Assisi, to Pompeii and/or Capri, and to Florence.

⚐ Tour Operator **Appian Line** ☎ 06/48786601 ⊕ www.appianline.it.

## PERSONAL GUIDES

You can arrange for a personal guide through the main APT (Azienda Per Turismo) Tourist Information Office.

**ℹ Tour Operator APT** ✉ Via Parigi 11 ☎ 06/488991 ⊕ www.romaturismo.it.

## SMOKING

From March 2005, smoking has been banned in Italy in all public places. This includes trains, buses, offices, and waiting rooms, as well as restaurants, pubs, and discotheques (unless the latter have separate smoking rooms). If you're an unrepentant smoker, you would be advised to check with restaurants before making a booking, as very few can offer smokers' facilities. Fines for breaking the law are so stiff that they have succeeded (for the moment) in curbing the Italians' propensity to light up everywhere. Outside dining is exempt from the rule, so if smoking annoys you, you may even find it better to eat indoors in warm weather. Many restaurants are now equipped with air-conditioning. There are no smoking cars on any FS (Italian state railway) trains.

## STUDENTS IN ROME

Students from member nations in the EU possessing valid ID cards are entitled to discounts at state or municipal museums, galleries, exhibitions, and entertainment venues, and on some transportation. Students who aren't EU citizens pay the usual entrance fees.

## LOCAL RESOURCES

The Centro Turistico Studentesco (CTS) is a student and youth travel agency with offices in major Italian cities; CTS helps its clients find low-cost accommodations and bargain fares for travel in Italy and elsewhere and also serves as a meeting place for young people of all nations. CTS is also the Rome representative for Euro-Train International.

**ℹ Agency Centro Turistico Studentesco** ✉ Via Andrea di Vesalio 6, northeast of Termini Station, Termini ☎ 06/441111 ✉ Via Genova 16, Termini ☎ 06/4620431.

**ℹ IDs & Services STA Travel** ✉ 10 Downing St., New York, NY 10014 ☎ 212/627-3111, 800/777-0112 24-hr service center ⊠ 212/627-3387 ⊕ www.sta.

com. **Travel Cuts** ✉ 187 College St., Toronto, Ontario M5T 1P7, Canada ☎ 800/592-2887 in U.S., 416/979-2406 or 866/246-9762 in Canada ⊠ 416/979-8167 ⊕ www.travelcuts.com.

## TAXES

### HOTELS

The service charge and IVA, or value-added tax (V.A.T.), are included in the rate except in five-star deluxe hotels, where the IVA (15% on luxury hotels) may be a separate item added to the bill at departure.

### RESTAURANTS

Many, but not all, Rome restaurants have eliminated extra charges for service and for *pane e coperto* (a cover charge that includes bread, whether you eat it or not). If it is an extra, the service charge may be 12%–15%. Only part, if any, of this amount goes to the waiter, so an additional tip is customary ( ⇨ Tipping).

**Always ask for an itemized bill** and a *scontrino,* or receipt. Officially you have to keep this receipt with you for 600 feet from the restaurant or store and be able to produce it if asked by the tax police. Sound absurd? It's something of a desperate measure for the country with the highest taxes in Europe and the highest levels of tax evasion/avoidance, and there have been cases of unwitting customers falling foul of the law, even though this practice is meant to catch noncompliant restaurants.

### VALUE-ADDED TAX

Value-added tax (IVA in Italy, V.A.T. to English-speakers) is 20% on luxury goods, clothing, and wine. On most consumer goods, it's already included in the amount shown on the price tag; on services, such as car rentals, it's an extra item. If a store you shop in has a "Euro Tax Free" sign outside and you make a purchase above €155 (before tax), present your passport and request a "Tax Free Shopping Check" when paying, or at least an invoice itemizing the article(s), price(s), and the amount of tax.

To get an IVA refund when you're leaving Italy, take the goods and the invoice to the customs office at the airport or other point of departure and have the invoice stamped. (If you return to the United States or Canada directly from Italy, go through the procedure at Italian customs; if your return is, say, via Britain, take the Italian goods and invoice to British customs.) Once back home—and within 90 days of the date of purchase—mail the stamped invoice to the store, which will forward the IVA rebate to you.

A refund service can save you some hassle, for a fee. Global Refund is a Europe-wide service with 190,000 affiliated stores and more than 700 refund counters—located at every major airport and border crossing. Its refund form is called a Tax Free Check. The service issues refunds in the form of cash, check, or credit-card adjustment, minus a processing fee. If you don't have time to wait at the refund counter, you can mail in the form instead.

**7** V.A.T. Refunds **Global Refund** ✉ 99 Main St., Suite 307, Nyack, NY 10960 ☎ 800/566-9828 📠 845/348-1549 ⊕ www.globalrefund.com.

## TAXIS

Taxis in Rome do not cruise, but if free they will stop if you flag them down. They wait at stands but can also be called by phone, in which case you're charged a supplement. The various taxi services are considered interchangeable and are referred to by their phone numbers rather than names. Only some taxis are equipped to take credit cards. Inquire when you phone to make the booking.

The meter starts at €2.33 during the day, €4.91 after 10 PM, and €3.36 on Sunday and holidays. There's a supplement of €1.04 for each piece of baggage. Unfortunately, these charges do not appear on the meter, causing countless misunderstandings. If you take a taxi at night and/or on a Sunday, or if you have baggage or have had the cab called by phone, the fare will legitimately be more than the figure shown on the meter. Use only licensed, metered white or yellow cabs, identified by a numbered shield on the side, an illuminated taxi sign on the roof, and a plaque next to the license plate reading SERVIZIO PUBBLICO. Avoid unmarked, unauthorized, unmetered gypsy cabs (numerous at Rome airports and train stations), whose drivers actively solicit your trade and may demand astronomical fares.

**7** Taxi Companies **Cab** ☎ 06/6645, 06/3570, 06/4994, 06/5551, or 06/4157.

## TELEPHONES

### AREA & COUNTRY CODES

The country code for Italy is 39. The area code for Rome is 06. When dialing an Italian number from abroad, **do not drop the initial 0 from the local area code.**

The country code is 1 for the United States, 61 for Australia, 1 for Canada, 64 for New Zealand, and 44 for the United Kingdom.

### DIRECTORY & OPERATOR ASSISTANCE

For general information in English, dial 176. To place international telephone calls via operator-assisted service (or for information), dial 170 or long-distance access numbers ( ⇨ *Long Distance Services*).

### INTERNATIONAL CALLS

Hotels tend to overcharge, sometimes exorbitantly, for long-distance and international calls. Use your AT&T, MCI, or Sprint card or buy an international phone card, which supplies a local number to call and gives a low rate. Or make your calls from Telefoni offices, designated TELECOM, where operators will assign you a booth, sell you an international telephone card, and help you place your call. You can make collect calls from any phone by dialing ☎ 800/172444, which will get you an English-speaking AT&T operator. Rates to the United States are lowest round the clock on Sunday and 10 PM–8 AM, Italian time, on weekdays.

### LOCAL CALLS

Phone numbers in Rome, and throughout Italy, don't have a set number of digits. All calls in Rome are preceded by the city code 06, with the exception of three-digit numbers (113 is for general emergencies). Emergency numbers can be called for free from pay phones.

### LONG-DISTANCE CALLS

Throughout Italy, long-distance calls are dialed in the same manner as local calls: the city code plus the number. Rates vary, depending on the time of day, with the lowest late at night and early in the morning.

## LONG-DISTANCE SERVICES

AT&T, MCI, and Sprint access codes make calling long-distance relatively convenient, but you may find the local access number blocked in many hotel rooms. First ask the hotel operator to connect you. If the hotel operator balks, ask for an international operator, or dial the international operator yourself. One way to improve your odds of getting connected to your long-distance carrier is to travel with more than one company's calling card (a hotel may block Sprint, for example, but not MCI). If all else fails, call from a pay phone.

📞 **Access Codes AT&T Direct** ☎ 800/172-444. **MCI WorldPhone** ☎ 800/172-401/404. **Sprint International Access** ☎ 800/172-405. From cell phones call 892-176.

## PUBLIC PHONES & PHONE CARDS

Few pay phones now accept coins only. Most require *carte telefoniche* (phone cards). You buy the card (values vary—€2.50, €5, and so on) at Telefoni offices, post offices, newsstands (called *edicole*), and tobacconists. Tear off the corner of the card and insert it in the slot. When you dial, its value appears in the window. After you hang up, the card is returned so you can use it until its value runs out. The best card for calling North America or Europe is the €5 or €10 Europa card, which gives you a local number to dial and a pin number, and roughly 180 minutes and 360 minutes, respectively, of calling time.

## TIME

Rome is one hour ahead of London, six ahead of New York, seven ahead of Chicago, and nine ahead of Los Angeles. Rome is nine hours behind Sydney and 11 behind Auckland. Like the rest of Europe, Italy uses the 24-hour (or "military") clock, which means that after 12 noon you continue counting forward: 13:00 is 1 PM, 23:30 is 11:30 PM.

## TIPPING

Many Rome restaurants have done away with the service charge of about 12%–15% that used to appear as a separate item on your check—now service is almost always included in the menu prices. It's customary to leave an additional 5%–10% tip for the waiter, depending on the quality of service. Tip checkroom attendants €1 per person, restroom attendants €0.50. In both cases tip more in expensive hotels and restaurants. Tip €0.05–€0.10 for whatever you drink standing up at a coffee bar, €0.25 or more for table service in a café. At a hotel bar tip €1 and up for a round or two of cocktails, more in the grander hotels.

Tip taxi drivers 5%–10% of the meter amount. Railway and airport porters charge a fixed rate per bag. Tip an additional €0.50, more if the porter is very helpful. Not all theater ushers expect a tip; if they do, tip €0.25 per person, more for very expensive seats. Give a barber €1–€1.50 and a hairdresser's assistant €1.50–€4 for a shampoo or cut, depending on the type of establishment and the final bill; 5%–10% is a fair guideline.

On sightseeing tours, tip guides about €1.50 per person for a half-day group tour, more if they're very good. In museums and other places of interest where admission is free, a contribution is expected; give anything from €0.50 to €1 for one or two people, more if the guardian has been especially helpful. Service station attendants are tipped only for special services.

In hotels, give the *portiere* (concierge) about 15% of his bill for services, or €2.50–€5 if he has been generally helpful. For two people in a double room, leave the chambermaid about €1 per day, or about €4–€6 a week, in a moderately priced hotel; tip a minimum of €1 for valet or room service. Increase these amounts by one half in an expensive hotel, and double them in a very expensive hotel. In very expensive hotels, tip doormen €0.50 for calling a cab and €1 for carrying bags to the check-in desk, bellhops €1.50–€2.50 for carrying your bags to the room, and €2–€2.50 for room service.

## TRAIN TRAVEL TO & FROM ROME

State-owned Trenitalia trains are part of the Metrebus system ( ⇨ Public Transportation) and also serve some destinations on side trips outside Rome. The main Trenitalia stations in Rome are Termini, Tiburtina, Ostiense, and Trastevere. Suburban trains use all of these stations. The Ferrovie COTRAL line departs from a terminal in Piazzale Flaminio, connecting Rome with Viterbo.

## CLASSES
Trenitalia trains do not have first and second class. Local trains can be crowded early morning and evening as many people commute to and from the city, so try to avoid these times. On long-distance routes (to Florence and Venice, for instance), you can either travel by the cheap, but slow, *diretto* trains, or the fast, but more expensive *Intercity,* or the first-class only *Eurostar.* Seat reservations are obligatory on both Intercity and Eurostar trains. This can be done directly at the station when you buy your ticket, or through a travel agent.

## CUTTING COSTS
To save money, **look into rail passes.** But be aware that if you don't plan to cover many miles, you may come out ahead by buying individual tickets.

## FARES & SCHEDULES
For destinations within 200 km (124 mi) of Rome, you can buy a *kilometrico* ticket. Like bus tickets, they can be purchased at some newsstands and in ticketing machines, as well as at Trenitalia ticket windows. Buy them in advance so you won't waste time in line at station ticket booths. Like all train tickets, they must be date-stamped in the little yellow or red machines near the track before you board. Within a range of 200 km (124 mi) they're valid for six hours from the time they're stamped, and you can get on and off at will at stops in between for the duration of the ticket's validity.
🚆 Train Information **Trenitalia** ☎ 166/105050 ⊕ www.trenitalia.it.

## TRAVEL AGENCIES
A good travel agent puts your needs first. Look for an agency that has been in business at least five years, emphasizes customer service, and has someone on staff who specializes in your destination. In addition, **make sure the agency belongs to a professional trade organization.** The American Society of Travel Agents (ASTA)—the largest and most influential in the field with more than 20,000 members in some 140 countries—maintains and enforces a strict code of ethics and will step in to help mediate any agent-client disputes involving ASTA members if necessary. ASTA (whose motto is "Without a travel agent, you're on your own") also maintains a Web site that includes a directory of agents. (If a travel agency is also acting as your tour operator, *see* Buyer Beware *in* Tours & Packages.)
🚆 Local Agent Referrals **American Society of Travel Agents (ASTA)** ✉ 1101 King St., Suite 200, Alexandria, VA 22314 ☎ 703/739-2782 or 800/965-2782 24-hr hotline 🖶 703/739-3268 ⊕ www.astanet.com. **Association of British Travel Agents** ✉ 68-71 Newman St., London W1T 3AH ☎ 020/7637-2444 🖶 020/7637-0713 ⊕ www.abta.com. **Association of Canadian Travel Agencies** ✉ 130 Albert St., Suite 1705, Ottawa, Ontario K1P 5G4 ☎ 613/237-3657 🖶 613/237-7052 ⊕ www.acta.ca. **Australian Federation of Travel Agents** ✉ Level 3, 309 Pitt St., Sydney, NSW 2000 ☎ 02/9264-3299 🖶 02/9264-1085 ⊕ www.afta.com.au. **Travel Agents' Association of New Zealand** ✉ Level 5, Tourism and Travel House, 79 Boulcott St., Box 1888, Wellington 6001 ☎ 04/499-0104 🖶 04/499-0786 ⊕ www.taanz.org.nz.

## VISITOR INFORMATION
Learn more about foreign destinations by checking government-issued travel advisories and country information. For a broader picture, consider information from more than one country.

## TOURIST INFORMATION
Rome has an APT (Azienda Per Turismo) Tourist Information Office in the city center. Green APT information kiosks with multilingual personnel are situated near the most important sights and squares, as well as at Termini Station and Leonardo da Vinci Airport. They're open between 9:30 AM and 7:30 PM and provide information about cultural events, museums, opening hours, city transportation, and so

on. You can also pick up free tourist maps and brochures.

🚩 Government Advisories **U.S. Department of State** ⊠ Overseas Citizens Services Office, Room 4811, 2201 C St. NW, Washington, DC 20520 ☎ 202/647-5225 interactive hotline or 888/407-4747 ⊕ www.travel.state.gov; enclose a cover letter with your request and a business-size SASE. **Consular Affairs Bureau of Canada** ☎ 800/267-6788 or 613/944-6788 ⊕ www.voyage.gc.ca. **U.K. Foreign and Commonwealth Office** ⊠ Travel Advice Unit, Consular Division, Old Admiralty Bldg., London SW1A 2PA ☎ 020/7008-0232 or 020/7008-0233 ⊕ www.fco.gov.uk/travel. **Australian Department of Foreign Affairs and Trade** ☎ 02/6261-1299 Consular Travel Advice Faxback Service ⊕ www.dfat.gov.au. **New Zealand Ministry of Foreign Affairs and Trade** ☎ 04/439-8000 ⊕ www.mft.govt.nz.

🚩 At Home **Italian Government Tourist Board (ENIT)** ⊠ 630 5th Ave., New York, NY 10111 ☎ 212/245-4822 🖷 212/586-9249 ⊠ 401 N. Michigan Ave., Chicago, IL 60611 ☎ 312/644-0990 🖷 312/644-3019 ⊠ 12400 Wilshire Blvd., Suite 550, Los Angeles, CA 90025 ☎ 310/820-0098 🖷 310/820-6357 ⊠ 1 Pl. Ville Marie, Suite 1914, Montréal, Québec H3B 3M9 ☎ 514/866-7667 🖷 514/392-1429 ⊠ 1 Princes St., London W1R 8AY ☎ 020/7408-1254 🖷 020/7493-6695.

🚩 In Rome **APT Tourist Information Office** ⊠ Via Parigi 5-11, Termini ☎ 06/46952027 ⊕ www.romaturismo.it, open Monday-Saturday 9 AM-7 PM. **Call Center Ufficio Tourismo** ☎ 06/36004399. **ENIT (Italian Government Tourist Board)** ⊠ Via Marghera 2-6, Termini ☎ 06/48899253 or 06/36004399 ⊕ www.italiantourism.com/.

## WEB SITES

Do check out the World Wide Web when planning your trip. You'll find everything from weather forecasts to virtual tours of famous cities. Be sure to visit Fodors.com (⊕ www.fodors.com), a complete travel-planning site. You can research prices and book plane tickets, hotel rooms, rental cars, vacation packages, and more. In addition, you can post your pressing questions in the Travel Talk section. Other planning tools include a currency converter and weather reports, and there are loads of links to travel resources.

The APT (Rome tourist board) Web site is ⊕ www.romaturismo.it and is packed with information about events and places to visit. Particularly provocative, fascinating, and up-to-date are the monthly web issues of *The American*, a popular English-magazine based in Rome; their web site is ⊕ www.theamericanmag.com. A fine web site on all things Roman is ⊕ www.romecity.it. Magnificent is the only word to describe this passionate writer's ode to the city's treasures of art and archecture, replete with hundreds of photos and little known facts: ⊕ www.romeartlover.it/new.htm. An official web site for many of Rome's most famous sights is: ⊕ www.pierreci.it/ Rome is located in the province of Lazio and that web site is ⊕ www.turislazio.it/index.php/turismo_eng. A dynamic organization offering unusual tours and news about what's happening in Rome is ⊕ www.nerone.cc; ⊕ www.museionline.it has invaluable links to almost all the city's many museums and galleries together with news of the latest exhibitions, opening hours, and prices. For more information specifically on Italy, visit ⊕ www.italiantourism.com/, ⊕ www.initaly.com, and ⊕ www.wel.it. Other particularly useful sites are ⊕ www.romeguide.it and ⊕ www.unospitearoma.it, both of which have English versions. You may also like to consult ⊕ www.italyhotel.com. The state railways' excellent and user-friendly site at ⊕ www.trenitalia.com will help you plan any rail trips in the country.

# Exploring
# Rome

## WORD OF MOUTH

Once we got our "Rome legs," we loved the place. My philosophy is "don't try to do Rome, let Rome do you."

—SallyJo

I love Rome's extremes. I love the fact that it is a modern city yet does not ignore its past by compartmentalizing all its treasures in museums. It is a city that lives in its past and its future at the same time.

—DawnRainbows

"Rome is the cradle of civilization"? Ah . . . so THAT explains all the Roman babies!

—capo

Updated by
Valerie
Hamilton

**COMING OFF THE AUTOSTRADA AT ROMA NORD OR ROMA SUD,** you know by the convergence of heavily trafficked routes that you are entering a grand nexus: All roads lead to Rome. And then the interminable suburbs, the railroad crossings, the intersections—no wonder they call it the Eternal City. As you enter the city proper, features that match your expectations begin to take shape: a bridge with heroic statues along its parapets; a towering cake of frothy marble decorated with allegorical figures in extravagant poses; a piazza and an obelisk under an umbrella of pine trees. Then you spot what looks like a multistory parking lot; with a gasp, you realize it's the Colosseum. With traffic encircling the great stone arena of the Roman emperors, the broad girdle of tarmac seems to still be a racetrack, as it must have been in charioteering days. Not surprisingly, the motorists behind the wheels of their Fiats seem to display the panache of so many Ben-Hurs.

You have arrived. You're in the city's heart. You step down from your excursion bus onto a manhole cover stamped SPQR, "The Senate and Populace of Rome." This is an expression that links the citizen with his ancestor of 23 centuries ago and gives the arriving visitor the eerie feeling that the dust he stirs has been stirred by the togas of Cato, Cicero, and Seneca. In Rome, 23 centuries are just a few generations back.

When 18th-century aristocrats traveled to Rome on their Grand Tours, it was because Rome *was* history: an unparalleled repository of Western culture's greatest hits. To see Rome was to see our past, and revel in its greatness. Since then, a kingdom has fallen, a republic risen, and Rome has lived through three wars to a new era of Europe and a globalized world. What's most thrilling for visitors, and sometimes frustrating for residents, is how little has changed.

This is a city built—literally—on its own history, whose reputation has preceded it for the better part of three millennia. And its legacy is magnificent: ancient Rome rubs shoulders with the medieval, the modern runs into the Renaissance, and the result is like nothing so much as an open-air museum, a city that glories in its glories and is a monument to itself. Senators, emperors, Vandals, popes and the Borgias, Napoléon, and Mussolini all left their physical, cultural, and spiritual stamps on the city. More than Florence, more than Venice, Rome is Italy's treasure trove, packed with masterpieces from more than two millennia of artistic achievement. It's here that the ancient Romans made us heirs-in-law to what we call Western Civilization; where centuries later Michelangelo painted the Sistine Chapel; where Gian Lorenzo Bernini's Baroque nymphs and naiads still dance in their marble fountains; and where, at Cinecittà Studios, Fellini filmed *La Dolce Vita* and *8½*.

But it's also a real city, where the present is in many ways slave to the past. Winding medieval alleys are snarled with parked cars. Efforts to expand Rome's limited Metro are stymied by the cultural impossibility of digging tunnels through the ancient city, and the result is some of Europe's worst traffic. The famously proud descendants of the ancient Romans are famously disrespectful of their beautiful city, littering and writing graffiti as they have for millennia. And Rome's enduring popularity on tourists' itineraries feeds a gluttonous tourism industry that can feel more like *National Lampoon's European Vacation* than *Roman Holiday*. As tour buses belch black smoke and the line at the Vatican Museums stretches on into eternity, even the steeliest of sightseers have been known to wonder, why am I here?

The answer, with apologies to Dorothy, is: There's no place like Rome. Yesterday's Grand Tourists thronged the city for the same reason today's Expedians do. Majestic, complicated, enthralling, romantic, chaotic, monumental Rome is one of the world's great cities—past, present, and, probably, future. To visit is to bathe in its memory, to travel in time. Students walk dogs in the park that used to be the mausoleum of the family of the Emperor Augustus; Raphaelesque madonnas queue up for buses on busy corners; a priest in flowing robes walks through a medieval piazza talking on a cell phone. "When you first come here you assume that you must burrow about in ruins and prowl in museums to get back to the days of Numa Pompilius or Mark Antony," Maud Howe observes in her book *Roma Beata*. "It is not necessary; you only have to live, and the common happenings of daily life—yes, even the trolley car and your bicycle—carry you back in turn to the Dark Ages, to the early Christians, even to prehistoric Rome." Modern Rome has one foot in the past, one in the present—a delightful stance that allows you to have an espresso in a square designed by Bernini, then take the Metro back to your hotel room in a renovated Renaissance palace.

Rome can never be regarded as merely an Introduction or a Farewell: Some tourists arrive at Rome's airport, stay a night or two, then depart for a tour of Italy. But there are too many Romes—Early Christian, Ancient, Baroque, Neoclassical, Papal—to treat the city as just a jumping-off point. Whether your Roman visit turns out to be a short or long one, keep your sightseeing schedule flexible. Plan your days to take into account the wide diversity of opening times—which usually means mixing classical and Baroque, museums and parks, the center and the environs. No one will fault you for choosing a lazy ramble through a picturesque quarter of Old Rome over a deadly earnest trek through marbled miles of museum corridors.

Remember, *Bisogna vivere a Roma coi costumi di Roma* ("When you are in Rome, do as Rome does"). Don't feel intimidated by the press of art and culture. Instead, contemplate the grandeur from a table at a sun-drenched caffè on Piazza Navona; let Rome's colorful life flow around you without feeling guilty because you haven't seen everything. It can't be done, anyway. There's just so much here that you will have to come back again, so be sure to throw a coin in the Trevi Fountain. It works.

## Touring Rome

With more masterpieces per square foot than any other city in the world, Rome presents a particular challenge for visitors: just as they are beginning to feel hopelessly smitten by the spell of the city, they realize they don't have the time—let alone the stamina—to see more than a frac-

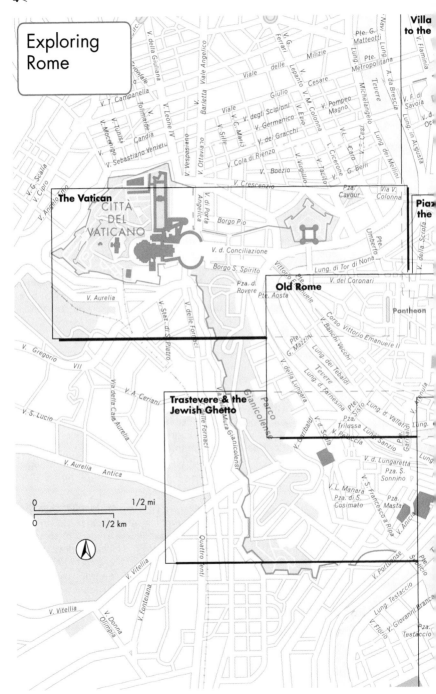

Exploring
Rome

The Vatican

CITTÀ
DEL
VATICANO

Old Rome

Pantheon

Trastevere & the
Jewish Ghetto

Villa
to the

Piaz
the

0        1/2 mi
0        1/2 km

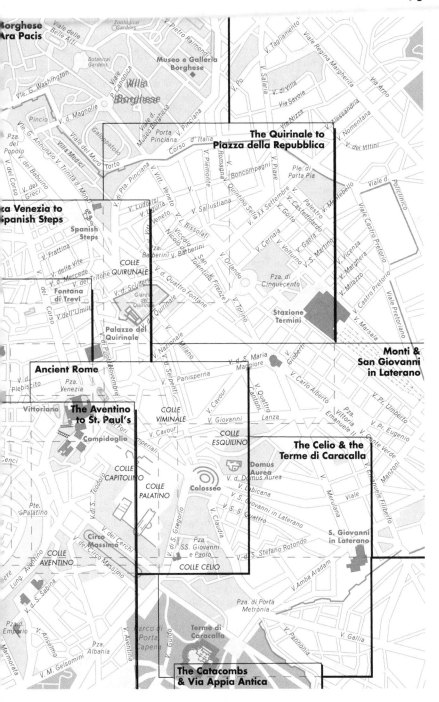

tion of its treasures. It's wise to start out knowing this, and to have a focused itinerary. These 10 tours of clustered sightseeing encapsulate quintessential Rome while allowing roamers to make minidiscoveries of their own.

We begin where Rome itself began—amid the Campigdoglio and the ancient ruins of the Roman Forum—and then follow up with a look at St. Peter's and the Vatican. Combined with strolls around central Rome— the *centro istorico* (historic center) and its indescribably sumptuous Baroque artworks—these tours introduce you to the sights highest on practically everybody's list of priorities. The **first** section is an introduction to "The grandeur that was Rome": the Capitoline Hill, Roman Forum, Colosseum, and Palatine Hill. The **second** section takes you to the incomparable sights of St. Peter's Basilica, the Sistine Chapel, and the Vatican Museums. The **third** section covers the heart of Baroque Rome—jewel-encrusted churches, Caravaggio paintings, and urban showstoppers such as Piazza Navona (plus the ancient Pantheon).

The **fourth** section goes deep into Rome's postcard-country of the Spanish Steps and the Trevi Fountain and includes visits to two of Rome's grandest palaces, the Palazzo Doria-Pamphili and the Palazzo Colonna. The **fifth** section ranges from the Quirinal Hill to the Piazza della Republica—site of the Baths of Diocletian and the ancient art treasures of the Museo Nazionale Romano—and includes some of the city's finest Baroque-era monuments, such as Bernini's Sant'Andrea al Quirinale, Borromini's San Carlo alle Quattro Fontane, as well as a pageant of palaces: the Palazzo del Quirinale, the Palazzo Barberini (home to the Galleria Nazionale and Raphael's *Fornarina*), and the Palazzo Pallavinci-Rospigliosi. In the northern sector of the city, the **sixth** section begins with Rome's great park, the Villa Borghese, home to three museums: the dazzlingly opulent Galleria Borghese, the late-Renaissance Villa Medici, and the Villa Giulia, and then moves south down the Pincio hill to Piazza del Popolo and the ancient Roman Ara Pacis monument. The **seventh** section explores the Jewish Ghetto and then crosses the Tiber to explore Trastevere, Rome's "Greenwich Village"—don't miss Santa Maria in Trastevere, to some observers the one church that best distills the grandeur of Rome's past.

The **eighth** section tours the Aventine Hill, beginning with the famous Piazza Bocca della Verità, home to two tiny Roman temples and the magnficiently medieval Santa Maria in Cosmedin, then passes Santa Sabina and San Saba on the way to Rome's newly gentrifying "Left Bank," the Testaccio neighborhood. The **ninth** section takes in the magical and oft overlooked Celian Hill, studded with extraordinary churches like Santi Giovanni e Paolo, Santo Stefano Rotondo, San Clemente, and Santi Quattro Coronati, before ending at the Baths of Caracalla. The **10th** section brings you to the Monti neighborhood and a tour through some landmark churches, including Santa Maria Maggiore, Santa Pudenziana, Santa Prassede, San Giovanni in Laterano, Santa Croce in Gerusalemme, some of which are studded with Early Christian and Byzantine mosaics (showing how much older this section of the city is from the 17th-century Baroque quarter), plus San Pietro in Vincoli, home to Michelangelo's

*Moses.* The 11th, and final, section takes you from the atmosphere-rich Catacombs to the Appian Way.

# ANCIENT ROME: GLORIES OF THE EMPERORS

Rome was famously built on seven hills—Capitolino (commonly known as Campidoglio), Palatino, Esquilino, Viminale, Celio, Quirinale, and Aventino. Two of these historic hills—the Campidoglio and the Palatine—formed the hub of ancient Rome, the center of the civilized world. The Campidoglio has always been the seat of Rome's government; its Latin name is echoed in the designation of national and state capitol buildings. On the Palatine the earliest recorded inhabitants of Rome lived in modest mud huts; later, its position made it Rome's most exclusive residential zone, site of the emperors' vast and luxurious palaces. Between the hills, in the Forum, the Romans worshipped, discussed politics, and carried on commerce. Between the Palatine and the Tiber were the markets where livestock and produce arrived by boat. Though it remained the heart of monumental and religious Rome, the Forum was later dwarfed by the Imperial Fora, built by a succession of emperors to augment the original, overcrowded Forum and to make sure that the people would have tangible evidence of their generosity.

More than any other, this part of Rome exemplifies that layering of historic eras, the overlapping of ages, of religions, of a past that is very much a part of the present. Christian churches rise on the foundations of ancient pagan temples. An immense marble monument to a 19th-century king shares a square with a medieval palace built by a future pope. Still, the history and memory of ancient Rome dominate the area. The ruins and monuments, the Colosseo, and the triumphal arches have stood through the centuries as emphatic reminders of the genius and power that made Rome the fountainhead of the Western world.

You can save some money by purchasing an all-in-one ticket for €20. It's good for five days and provides you access to many of the major sights, including the Colosseum, the Palatine Hill, the Baths of Caracalla, Palazzo Massimo, and Palazzo Altemps—the two leading museums of Roman antiquities—and the Crypta Balbi. You can buy one at any of the sights to which it provides access.

*Numbers in the text and margin correspond to points of interest on the Ancient Rome map.*

## The Campidoglio

a good walk

Begin your walk on the **Campidoglio ❶** ☞—the Capitoline Hill—famed as the site of Michelangelo's spectacular Piazza del Campidoglio and Rome's ceremonial city hall, **Palazzo Senatorio ❷**. First head around the Palazzo to the belvederes situated along the sides of the building to gaze down on what was once the center of the known world: the Roman Forum. The Palatine Hill and the Colosseum loom in the background. The rubblescape of marble fragments scattered over the area of the Forum makes all but students of archaeology ask: Is this the grandeur that was Rome? Just consider that much of the history fed to the world over happened right here. This square—once an enormous banquet hall where the entire population of a city could be simultaneously entertained (as our times have often observed, thanks to such Hollywood epics as *Quo Vadis, Ben-Hur,* and *Cleopatra*)—was the birthplace of much of Western civilization. Roman law and powerful armies were created here, banishing the Barbarian world for a millenium. Here, all Rome shouted as one, "Caesar has been murdered," and crowded to hear Mark Antony's eulogy for the fallen leader. Legend has it that St. Paul traversed the Forum en route to his audience with Nero. After a more than 27-century-long parade of pageantry, it's not surprising that Shelley and Gibbon reflected on the sense of *sic transit gloria mundi* (thus pass the glories of the world) on these same grounds.

Back in center of the piazza, head to the right of the replica of the ancient bronze statue of Marcus Aurelius and the **Musei Capitolini** ❸, home to one of the city's finest and most famous collections of ancient sculpture and Baroque painting. Off the southeast flank of Palazzo Nuovo, head to the formidable flight of steps that leads up to the ancient redbrick church of **Santa Maria di Aracoeli** ❹, the national church of Italy.

From the southwest flank of Palazzo Senatorio, take Via del Campidoglio and then Via del Tempio di Giove for a look at the Roman Forum from the **Belvedere Tarpeo** ❺, the Tarpean Rock, from which prisoners were dispatched in ancient times; try to imagine what the area looked like when most of these magnificent ruins were covered over by marshy pastureland, and cows grazed beside half-buried columns and trod on 2,000-year-old marble paving slabs. From the belvedere on the northeast side of Palazzo Senatorio, descend Via San Pietro in Carcere, which is actually a flight of stairs, to the gloomy **Carcere Mamertino** ❻, once prison to St. Peter and the Gaul warrior, Vercingetorix.

TIMING This walk can be done in about two hours, but allow an extra hour and a half to two hours if you plan to visit the Musei Capitolini. Take the walk, as well as those exploring the Foro Romano and Palatino, on one of your first days in Rome to get a sense of how the city began, and how it evolved. Fair weather helps, but is not essential. Late evening is an option for this walk; though the church is closed, the museums are open until 9 PM, and the lighted-up city and the illuminated Victor Emmanuel II Monument and Foro Romano are striking sights at night.

## What to See

❺ **Belvedere Tarpeo.** This was the infamous Tarpeian Rock from which traitors were hurled to the ground in Roman times. In the 18th and 19th centuries, it became a popular stop for people doing the Grand Tour, because of the view it gave of the Palatine Hill. Here, in the 7th century BC, Tarpeia betrayed the Roman citadel to the early Romans' sworn enemies, the Sabines, only asking in return for the heavy gold bracelets they wore on their left arms. The scornful Sabines did indeed shower her with their gold, but also added the crushing weight of their heavy shields, also carried on their left arms. ✉ *Via del Tempio di Giove, Piazza Venezia.*

**➤ ❶ Campidoglio.** Spectacularly transformed by Michelangelo's late-Renaissance designs, the Campidoglio was once the epicenter of the Roman
★ empire, the place where the city's first and holiest temples stood, including
its most sacred, the Temple of Jupiter. Originally, the Capitoline Hill consisted of two peaks: the Capitolium and the Arx. The hollow between
them was known as the Asylum, and it was here, in the days before the
Roman Republic was founded in 509 BC, that prospective settlers came
to seek the protection of Romulus, legendary first king of Rome—hence
the term "asylum." Later, during the Republic, temples occupied both
peaks, and, later still, in 78 BC, the Tabularium, or Hall of Records, was
erected to house the city archives. Throughout the Middle Ages an earlier incarnation of Palazzo Senatorio that stood over the Tabularium was
just about the only building remaining on the Campidoglio, then an un-
kempt hill strewn with the classical rubble of temples and used mainly
as a goat pasture. Nonetheless, the fame of the spot lingered on. Petrarch,
the 14th-century Italian poet, was just one of many to extol its original
splendor, though its sumptuous marble palaces and temples had long
since crumbled.

In 1536 Michelangelo was charged with restoring the piazza on the summit of the Campidoglio to its former glory, in preparation for the im-
pending visit of Holy Roman Emperor Charles V, triumphant after the
empire's victory over the Moors. In emulation of ancient Roman triumphal processions, it was decided that Charles V should follow what
was believed to have been the route of the Roman emperors, through
the city to the fully restored Campidoglio. Much of Michelangelo's
plans for refurbishment were not completed for several centuries, but
almost everything visible today follows his original designs, including
the distinctive stellate pattern set into the pavement, added in 1940.

You approach the piazza on the *cordonata* (a gently graded ramp), designed by Michelangelo to allow a carriage to be drawn up the hill with
minimal difficulty. As you climb, the buildings and visual effects of the
site gradually reveal themselves. The equestrian statue of Marcus Aurelius at the center is a copy of the original, from the 2nd century AD,
which stood on this spot from the 16th century until 1981. It was
placed here as a visual reference to the corresponding glory of Charles
V and the ancient emperor; it's said that Michelangelo was so impressed
by the statue's vivid naturalism that, after it was in place, he commanded it to walk. Although bronze statues of emperors were usually
melted down after the decline of Rome, this one is thought to have survived because it was mistaken for a likeness of the Christian emperor
Constantine, rather than of the pagan Marcus Aurelius. A legend fore-
tells that some day the statue's original gold patina will return, herald-
ing the end of the world. The city's authorities had it restored and
placed in the courtyard of the Museo Capitolino, saving not only what
was left of the gold but also the statue's bronze, which had been seriously damaged by air pollution. The copy was placed on the original
pedestal in 1997.

**❻ Carcere Mamertino** (Mamertine Prison). Hidden amid the glories of ancient Rome, the Mamertino consists of two gloomy subterranean cells

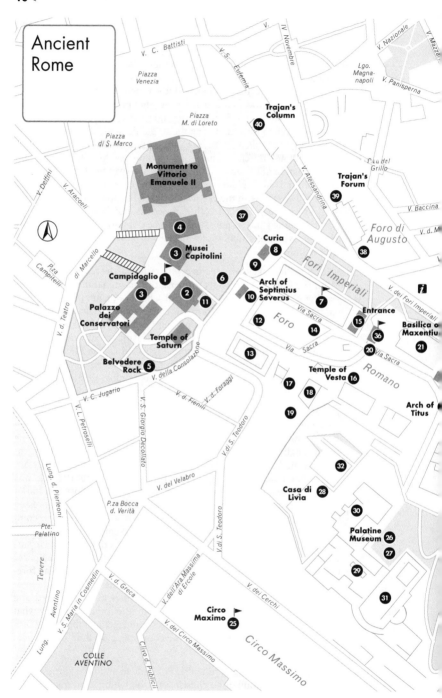

Ancient Rome

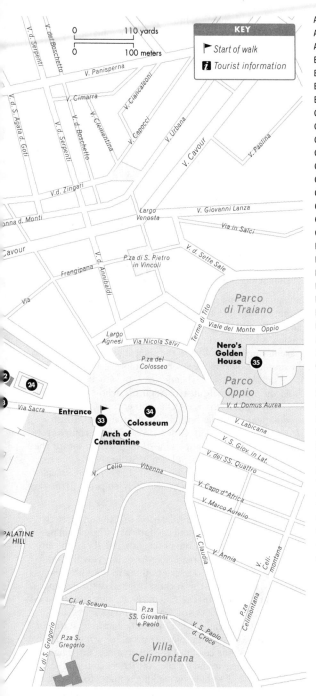

where Rome's vanquished enemies, most famously the Goth Jugurtha and the indomitable Gaul Vercingetorix, were imprisoned and died, of either starvation or strangulation. In the lower cell, St. Peter himself is believed to have been held prisoner and to have miraculously brought forth a spring of water, from which to baptize his jailers. That explains why a church, San Giuseppe dei Falegnami, now stands over the prison. ⊠ *Via del Tulliano, Piazza Venezia* 🗺 *Donations requested* ⊙ *Daily 9–12:30 and 2–5.*

**❸** **Musei Capitolini** (Capitoline Museums). Surpassed in sheer size and rich-

Fodor'sChoice ness only by the Musei Vaticani, this immense collection is a greatest

★   hits collection of Roman art through the ages, from the ancients to the Baroque. Housed in the twin Museo Capitolino and Palazzo dei Conservatori that bookend Michelangelo's piazza, you'll find some of antiquity's most famous sculptures here, such as the poignant *Dying Gaul,* the regal *Capitoline Venus,* and the *Exquiline Venus* (identified as another Mediterranean beauty, Cleopatra herself). Although some pieces in the collection—first assembled by Sixtus IV (1414–84)—may excite only archaeologists and art historians, others are unforgettable, including the original bronze statue of Marcus Aurelius whose copy sits in the piazza.

Although many ancient Roman treasures were merely copies of Greek originals, portraiture was one area in which the Romans took precedence. In the **Museo Capitolino,** the hundreds of Roman busts of emperors in the Sala degli Imperatori and of philosophers in the Sala dei Filosofi are a fascinating Who's Who of the ancient world, and a major highlight of the museum. Within these serried ranks are 48 Roman emperors, ranging from Augustus to Theodosius (AD 346–395). On one console, you'll see the handsomely austere Augustus, who "found Rome a city of brick and left it one of marble." On another rests Claudius "the stutterer," an indefatigable builder brought vividly to life in the history-based novel *I, Claudius* by Robert Graves. Also in this company is Nero, one of the most notorious emperors—though by no means the worst—who built for himself the fabled Domus Aurea. And, of course, there are the standout baddies: cruel Caligula (AD 12–41) and Caracalla (AD 186–217), and the dissolute, eerily modern boy-emperor, Heliogabalus (AD 203–222).

Unlike the Greeks, whose portraits were idealized, the Romans preferred the "warts and all" school of representation. Many of the busts that have come down to us, notably that of Commodus (AD 161–192), the emperor-gladiator, are almost brutally realistic. Movie-lovers will want to search out this bust of the man who added nothing to the Roman way of life except new ways of dying—this was the original of the man portrayed by Christopher Plummer in *The Fall of the Roman Empire* and by Joquin Phoenix in *Gladiator.* As you leave the museum, be sure to stop in the courtyard. To the right is the original equestrian statue of Marcus Aurelius that once stood in the piazza outside, now restored and safely kept behind glass. At the center of the courtyard is the gigantic, reclining figure of Oceanus, found in the Roman Forum and later dubbed *Marforio,* one of Rome's famous "talking statues" to which citizens from the 1500s to the 1900s affixed anonymous satirical verses and notes of political protest. (Another talking statue still in use today sits at Piazza Pasquino, near Piazza Navona.)

The **Palazzo dei Conservatori** is a trove of ancient and Baroque treasures. Lining the courtyard are the colossal fragments of a head, leg, foot, and hand—remains of the famous statue of the emperor Constantine the Great, who believed that Rome's future lay with Christianity. These immense effigies were much in vogue in the latter days of the Roman Empire. The resplendent Salone dei Orazi e Curiazi (Salon of Horatii and Curatii) on the first floor is a ceremonial hall with a magnificent gilt ceiling, carved wooden doors, and 16th-century frescoes. At both ends of the hall are statues of the Baroque era's most charismatic popes: a marble Urban VIII (1568–1644) by Gian Lorenzo Bernini (1598–1680) and a bronze Innocent X (1574–1655) by Bernini's rival, Algardi (1595–1654). The renowned symbol of Rome, the *Capitoline Wolf*, a 6th-century BC Etruscan bronze, holds a place of honor in the museum; the suckling twins were added during the Renaissance to adapt the statue to the legend of Romulus and Remus. The museum's *pinacoteca*, or painting gallery, holds some noted Baroque masterpieces, including Caravaggio's *La Buona Ventura* (1595) and *San Giovanni Battista* (1602), Peter Paul Rubens's (1577–1640) *Romulus and Remus* (1614), and Pietro da Cortona's (1627) sumptuous portrait of Pope Urban VIII. The Capitoline Museum includes the adjacent **Palazzo Caffarelli,** where temporary exhibitions are mounted and where you can enjoy both the view and refreshments on a large open terrace. ⊠ *Piazza del Campidoglio, Piazza Venezia* ☏ *06/39967800* ⊕ *www.museicapitolini.org* ▭ €6.20, free last Sun. of month ☉ Tues.–Sun. 9–8.

❷ **Palazzo Senatorio.** Rome's city hall thrusts its foundations deep into the Tabularium, the ancient city's hall of records. During the Middle Ages it looked like the medieval town halls you can see in Tuscan hill towns, part fortress and part assembly hall. The building was entirely rebuilt in the 1500s as part of Michelangelo's revamping of the Campidoglio for Pope Paul III; the master's design was adapted by later architects, who wisely left the front staircase as the focus of the facade. The ancient statue of Minerva in the niche at the center was opportunely renamed the Goddess Rome, and the river gods (the River Tigris remodeled to symbolize the Tiber, to the right, and the Nile, to the left) were hauled over from the Terme di Costantino on the Quirinal Hill. ⊠ *Piazza del Campidoglio, Piazza Venezia.*

❹ **Santa Maria di Aracoeli.** Sitting atop its 137 steps—"the grandest loafing place of mankind," as Henry James put it, and the spot on which Gibbon was inspired to write his great history of the decline and fall of the Roman empire—Santa Maria di Aracoeli perches on the north slope of the Capitoline Hill (where you can also access the church using a less challenging staircase from the left of Michelangelo's piazza). Basically a venerated monument of the Middle Ages period, it rests on the site of the ancient Roman temple of Juno Moneta (Admonishing Juno), which also housed the Roman mint (hence the origin of the word "money"). According to legend, it was here that the Sibyl (a prophetess) predicted to Augustus the coming of a Redeemer. The emperor supposedly responded by erecting an altar, the Ara Coeli (Altar of Heaven). This was eventually replaced by one of Rome's medieval convent churches. The church passed to the Benedictines in the 10th century, and in 1250 to the Franciscans, who restored and enlarged it in Romanesque-Gothic style. In the Middle Ages, citizens used to meet here to discuss current affairs, just as the ancient Romans had met in the Forum.

Today, the Aracoeli is best known for the **Santa Bambino,** a much-revered wooden figure of the Christ Child (today a copy of the 15th-century original). During the Christmas season, everyone pays homage to the Bambi Gesù as children recite poems from a miniature pulpit. In true Roman style, the church interior is a historical hodgepodge, with materials and decorations dating from ancient times all the way to the 19th century. There are classical columns and large marble fragments from pagan buildings, as well as a 13th-century Cosmatesque pavement—so called because, like many brilliantly colored mosaics of the period, it's the work of the prolific Cosmati family, who used bits of the precious marbles of ancient Rome in their compositions. The richly gilded Renaissance ceiling commemorates the naval victory at Lepanto in 1571 over the Turks. Among these artistic treasures, the first chapel on the right is noteworthy for Pinturicchio's frescoes of San Bernardino of Siena (1486). There's a Byzantine Madonna over the main altar of the church: the emperor Augustus and the Sibyl are depicted in the apse amid saints and angels (a most unusual position for a pagan emperor). In the third chapel on the left you can admire Benozzo Gozzoli's (1420–97) 15th-century fresco *St. Anthony of Padua*; on the right of the main portal there's a handsome polychrome monument to Cardinal D'Albret by Bregno. ✉ *Via del Teatro di Marcello, on top of steep stairway, Piazza Venezia* ☎ *06/6798155.*

## The Roman Forum

From the main entrance on Via dei Fori Imperiali, descend into the extraordinary archaeologial complex that is the **Foro Romano** (Roman Forum). This was once the heart of Republican Rome, the austere enclave that preceded the hedonistic society that grew up under the emperors in the 1st to the 4th century AD, but was soon transformed by the pleasure-crazed citizens of imperial Rome. It began life as a marshy valley between the Capitoline and Palatine hills—a valley crossed by a mud track and used as a cemetery by Iron Age settlers. Over the years a market center and some huts were established here, and after the land was drained in the 6th century BC, the site eventually became a political, religious, and commercial center—namely, the Forum. The original Roman Forum is only one part of the labyrinthine archaeological complex that goes by that name. It can also be confused with the later Imperial Forums (or, more properly, Fora), built by Julius Caesar and other emperors as the city's needs grew.

Hundreds of years of plunder and the tendency of later Romans to scavenge what was left of the better building materials reduced the Forum to its current desolate state. It's difficult to imagine that this enormous area was once Rome's pulsating heart, filled with stately and extravagant temples, palaces, and shops, and crowded with people from all corners of the empire. Adding to the confusion is the fact that the Forum developed over many centuries; what you see today are not the ruins from just one period but from a span of almost 900 years, from about 500 BC to AD 400. Archaeological digs continue to discover more about the site, but for the uninitiated, making sense of these gaunt and craggy ruins isn't easy. It's worth investing in the famous book, *Rome Then and Now,* which superimposes plans of many of the Forum buildings onto photos of the present sites (it can be purchased at the Colosseo bookshop, among other places, for €10). Nonetheless, the enduring romance of the place, with its lonely columns and great, broken fragments of sculpted marble and stone, makes for a quintessential Roman walk. ⊠ *Entrances at Via dei Fori Imperiali and Piazza del Colosseo* ☎ *06/ 39967700* ⊕ *www.pierreci.it* ☑ *Free, guided tour €3.50, audio guide €4* ☉ *Daily 9–1 hr before sunset.*

**a good walk**

Head for Via dei Fori Imperiali and the entrance to the Foro Romano. Here you can find what remains of the various buildings in the Forum: the **Basilica Emilia** ❼ ▶, which was not a church but a grand civic hall; the **Curia** ❽, where the Senate met and one of the most complete buildings of ancient Rome still standing; and the **Comitium** ❾ rostrum, where Mark Antony eulogized Caesar. Although the **Arco di Settimio Severo** ❿— the most spectacular arch of triumph extant from antiquity—the remaining columns of the **Tempio di Vespasiano** ⓫ (Temple of Vespasian), and the **Colonna di Foca** ⓬ rise above the ruins, the **Basilica Giulia** ⓭ is little more than a large raised platform. The **Tempio di Cesare** ⓮ (Temple of Caesar), on the spot where Caesar was cremated, is hardly distinguishable. The **Tempio di Antonino e Faustina** ⓯ met with better luck; incorporated into a church, its column front has been well preserved. Nearby are the three famous columns of the partially reconstructed, round **Tempio di Vesta** ⓰. The **Tempio di Castore e Polluce** ⓱ and the **Fonte di Giuturna** ⓲ have to be imagined, as little is left of them. Off to one side, you can see, but not visit, the church of **Santa Maria Antiqua** ⓳, built into what was originally a vestibule of the imperial palace on the Palatino.

Stroll east along the **Via Sacra** ⓴, and turn left into the **Basilica di Massenzio** ㉑, built by Emperor Maxentius to be one of the grandest meeting halls of ancient times. The 10th-century church of **Santa Francesca Romana** ㉒ stands atop a rise next to the basilica. The Via Sacra ends at the **Arco di Tito** ㉓, the triumphal arch built by Emperor Titus and famed for its carved menorah (recalling Rome's recapture of Jerusalem after the great Jewish revolt). The **Tempio di Venere e Roma** ㉔, one of the projects of the architecturally savvy emperor Hadrian, was begun on the site of the vast vestibule of Nero's grandiose Domus Aurea in AD 121.

TIMING   It takes about one hour to explore the Forum and identify the principal ruins. With the exception of mobile refreshment stands along Via dei Fori Imperiali and cafés on Largo Corrado Ricci, there are few places within easy reach where you can take a break for lunch or a snack. It might be easier to bring along your own food for sustenance during this outing. As this walk is almost entirely outdoors, good weather is a must; the beaten-earth paths of the Foro Romano become muddy and slippery in the rain. The route is a magical one for a late-evening stroll, when the site and surrounding monuments are illuminated. In summer, the Forum is sometimes open for midnight (guided) tours—look for signs at the entrances in July and August, or ask at the tourist office or your hotel.

## What to See

★ ❿ **Arco di Settimio Severo** (Arch of Septimius Severus). One of the grandest arch of triumphs erected by a Roman emperor, this richly decorated monument was built in AD 203 to celebrate Severus's victory over the Parthians. It was once topped by a bronze statuary group of a chariot drawn by four or perhaps as many as six life-size horses. Masterpieces of Roman statuary, the stone reliefs on the arch were probably based on huge painted panels depicting the event, a kind of visual report on his foreign campaigns that would have been displayed during the emperor's triumphal parade in Rome to impress his subjects (and, like all statuary back then, were painted in florid, lifelike colors). ⊠ *West end of Foro Romano.*

㉓ **Arco di Tito** (Arch of Titus). Standing at a slightly elevated position at
FodorśChoice  the northern approach to the Palatine Hill on the Via Sacra, this triumphal
★  arch was erected in AD 81 to celebrate the sack of Jerusalem 10 years earlier, after the great Jewish revolt. The view of the Colosseum from the arch is superb, and reminds us that it was the emperor Titus who helped finish the vast amphitheater, begun earlier by his father, Vespasian. Under the arch are the two great sculpted reliefs, both showing scenes from Titus's triumphal parade along this very Via Sacra, including the spoils of war plundered from Herod's Temple—a gigantic seven-branched candelabrum (menorah) and silver trumpets. In his sack, Titus killed or deported most of the Jewish population, thus initiating the Jewish diaspora, an event that would have historical consequences for millenia. Only the central section dates back to Roman times; the side pylons were heavily restored in the 18th century. ⊠ *East end of Via Sacra.*

★ ㉑ **Basilica di Massenzio** (Basilica of Maxentius). What remains of this gigantic basilica—or meeting-hall—is only about one-third of the original, so you can imagine what a wonder this building was when erected. Today, the great arched vaults of this structure still dominate the north side of the Via Sacra. Begun under the emperor Maxentius about AD 306, the edifice was a center of judicial and commercial activity, the last of its kind to be built in Rome. Over the centuries, like so many Roman monuments, it was exploited as a quarry for building materials and was stripped of its sumptuous marble and stucco decorations. Its coffered vaults, like the coffering inside the Pantheon's dome, were later copied by many Renaissance artists and architects. ⊠ *Via Sacra.*

▶ ❼ **Basilica Emilia.** Once a great colonnaded hall, this served as a meeting place for merchants and a kind of community center of the 2nd century BC; it was later rebuilt in the 1st century AD by Augustus. The term "basilica" refers not strictly to the purpose of a church, but to a particular architectural form developed by the Romans. A rectangular hall flanked by colonnades, it could serve as a court of law or a center for business

# CAPITAL HILLS

**A**LTHOUGH IT'S BEEN THE CAPITAL of the Republic of Italy only since 1946, Rome has been the capital of something for more than 2,500 years, and it shows. The magnificent ruins of the Palatino, the ancient complexity of the Forum, the Renaissance harmony of the Campidoglio, not to mention St. Peter's Basilica, capital of Catholic Christianity, are all part of Rome's longest-lasting identity as a seat of government—one of the world's most enduring. The Roman Republic, founded in the 6th century BC, was the philosophical base of modern republics; the Roman Senate the inspiration for modern senates (complete with dynastic rule and seat-buying). Even the language of modern government comes from Rome: the English words "capitol" and "palace" come from the names of the Capitoline (Campidoglio) and Palatine (Palatino) Hills, the ancient sites of, respectively, the government halls and imperial residences.

This is not to say that it's been an easy 2½ millennia. Whereas senators of the Roman Republic contented themselves with buying influence, would-be emperors of later centuries found much more permanent ways of getting their opponents out of office. The end of the Roman Republic was marked by the ambush and murder of Julius Caesar, and Nero ascended to the throne with the help of his mother, who cleared the way by poisoning Claudius with death's-head mushrooms. Popes elected to rule in medieval times were frequently challenged by anti-popes, rival pontiffs chosen in opposition elections. Hundreds of years later, with the advent of the democratic Italian Republic, political methods have become tamer, and, perhaps for this reason, the turnover rate has increased: there's been a new government, on average, every 11½ months since 1946. What that means is that there's a chance for everyone— everyone—to participate. In 1987, porn star Ilona Staller, aka Cicciolina ("Cuddles"), was elected to a term in Italy's lower house of Parliament, after a campaign spent, Godiva-like, in undraped public appearances. For 2006, she's announced her candidacy for mayor of Milan. At the other end of the spectrum, the far-right Northern League hopes to establish a new country, "Padania," in Italy's wealthy north while fascist dictator Benito Mussolini's granddaughter Alessandra represented Naples in the lower house until recently. Looming over all is troubled media billionaire Silvio Berlusconi who, as prime minister, seems to be undeterred by his string of legal troubles, including charges of tax evasion, bribery, and fraud.

Rome's major sights constitute a tour through the governments of the ages. The Imperial Fora, monuments to the power and wealth of the emperors, nestle up against the monument to Vittorio Emanuele II, the first king of a united Italy; next door is the Campidoglio, home of the municipal records building in Republican times, now the site of modern Rome's City Hall. Across the street on Piazza Venezia is the Palazzo Venezia, from whose balcony Mussolini gave his most famous addresses, and up the Quirinal Hill is the Palazzo Quirinale, once home to popes, then kings, and now to the Italian president. Modern Italian politics are played right in the center of it all: at Palazzo Madama (the Italian Senate), next to Piazza Navona; Palazzo Chigi (the prime minister's office), on Piazza Colonna; and the Chamber of Deputies, next door at Piazza Montecitorio.

and commerce. Some Roman basilicas were later converted into churches, and the early models proved remarkably durable in the design of later Roman churches; there are 13th-century churches in the city that are fundamentally no different from many built during the 5th and 6th centuries AD. ⊠ *On right as you descend into Roman Forum from Via dei Fori Imperiali entrance.*

⓭ **Basilica Giulia.** The Basilica Giulia owes its name to Julius Caesar, who ordered its construction. One of several such basilicas in the center of Rome, it was where the Centumviri, the hundred-or-so judges forming the civil court, met to hear cases. The open space between the Basilica Emilia and this basilica was the heart of the Forum proper, prototype of Italy's famous piazzas, and center of civic and social activity in ancient Rome. ⊠ *Via Sacra.*

⓬ **Colonna di Foca** (Pillar of Phocas). The last monument to be added to the Forum was erected in AD 608 in honor of a Byzantine emperor who had donated the Pantheon to Pope Boniface IV. It stands 44 feet high and remains in good condition. ⊠ *West end of Foro Romano.*

❾ **Comitium.** The open space in front of the Curia was the political hub of ancient Rome. Julius Caesar had rearranged the Comitium, moving the Curia to its current site and transferring the imperial **Rostra,** the podium from which orators spoke to the people (decorated originally with the prows of captured ships, or *rostra,* the source for the term "rostrum"), to a spot just south of the Arch of Septimius Severus. It was from this location that Mark Antony delivered his funeral address in Caesar's honor. Also here, under protective roofing (visitors are not allowed to enter), is the legendary burial place of Romulus, first king of Rome. The patch of black pavement actually marks a sacred area of undetermined origin, identified by fragments of inscription found on an underlying stone—the earliest known Latin inscription written in an archaic Greek alphabet. On the left of the Rostra stands what remains of the **Tempio di Saturno,** which served as ancient Rome's state treasury. ⊠ *West end of Foro Romano.*

★❽ **Curia.** The best preserved building of the Forum, this large brick building next to the Arch of Septimius Severus was built during the era of Diocletian in the late 3rd century AD. By that time the Senate, which met here, had lost practically all of the power and prestige that it had possessed during the Republican era, becoming a mere echo chamber for the decisions reached in other centers of power. Still, this gives one a haunting image of Roman life back when. ⊠ *Via Sacra, northwest corner of Foro Romano.*

⓮ **Fonte di Giuturna.** Legend says that as Castor and Pollux carried the news of a great victory to Rome, they paused to water their horses at the rectangular, marble-lined pool near what became their temple. The remains of the pool are still visible, as are remains of the temple, outlined by a concrete base of the podium and three columns. ⊠ *Via Sacra.*

㉒ **Santa Francesca Romana.** This church, a 10th-century edifice with a Renaissance facade, is dedicated to the patron saint of motorists; on her feast day, March 9, cars and taxis used to crowd the roadway below for a special blessing—a practice that died out with the advent of increased traffic restrictions. The incomparable setting continues to be a favorite for weddings. ⊠ *Piazza di Santa Francesca Romana, next to Colosseum.*

**⑲ Santa Maria Antiqua.** The earliest Christian site in the Forum was originally part of an imperial temple, before it was converted into a church some time in the 5th or 6th century. Within are some exceptional but faded 7th- and 8th-century frescoes of the early church fathers, saints, and popes; the styles vary from typically classical to Oriental, reflecting the empire's expansion eastward. ⊠ *South of Tempio di Castore and Polluce, at foot of Palatine Hill.*

**⑮ Tempio di Antonino e Faustina.** Erected by the Senate in honor of Faustina, deified wife of emperor Antoninus Pius (AD 138–161), Hadrian's successor, this temple was rededicated to the emperor himself upon his death. Because it was transformed into a church, it's one of the best-preserved ancient structures in the Forum. ⊠ *North of Via Sacra.*

★ **⑰ Tempio di Castore e Polluce.** One of the most evocative icons of ancient Roman architecture, the sole three remaining Corinthian columns of this temple beautifully conjure up the former elegant grandeur of the Forum. This temple was dedicated in 484 BC to Castor and Pollux, the twin brothers of Helen of Troy who carried to Rome the news of victory at Lake Regillus, southeast of Rome, the definitive defeat of the deposed Tarquin dynasty. The twins flew on their fabulous white steeds over the 20 km (12 mi) distance between the lake and the city to bring the news to the people before mortal messengers could arrive. Rebuilt over the centuries before Christ, the temple suffered a major fire and was reconstructed by Emperor Tiberius in 12 BC, the date of the three standing columns. ⊠ *West of House of the Vestals.*

**⑭ Tempio di Cesare.** Built by Augustus, Caesar's successor, the temple stands over the spot where Julius Caesar's body was cremated. A pyre was improvised by grief-crazed citizens who kept the flames going with their own possessions. ⊠ *Between 2 forks of Via Sacra.*

**㉔ Tempio di Venere e Roma.** The now-truncated columns of this temple, dedicated to Venus and Rome, begun by Hadrian in AD 121, frame a view of the Colosseum. ⊠ *East of Arco di Tito.*

**⑪ Tempio di Vespasiano.** All that remains of Vespasian's temple are three graceful Corinthian columns. They marked the site of the Forum through the centuries while the rest was hidden beneath overgrown rubble. Nearby is the ruined platform that was the **Tempio di Concordia.** ⊠ *West end of Foro Romano.*

★ **⑯ Tempio di Vesta.** The "iconic" image of the Forum, the three magnificent extant columns of this circular temple loom over the center of the Forum. This is where the highly privileged vestal virgins kept the sacred vestal flame alive. Next to the temple, the ruins of the **Casa delle Vestali** give no hint of the splendor in which the women lived out their 30-year vows of chastity. Inside was the garden courtyard of their palace, surrounded by lofty colonnades, behind which extended at least 50 rooms. Chosen when they were between 6 and 10 years old, the six vestal virgins dedicated the next 30 years of their lives to keeping the sacred fire, a tradition that dated back to the very earliest days of Rome, when guarding the community's precious fire was essential to its well-being. Their standing in Rome was considerable; indeed, among women, they were second in rank only to the empress. Their intercession could save a condemned man, and they did, in fact, rescue Julius Caesar from the lethal vengeance of his enemy Sulla. The virgins were handsomely maintained by the state, but if they allowed the sacred fire to go out, they were scourged by the high priest, and if they broke their vows of celibacy, they were buried alive. The vestal virgins were one of the last of ancient Rome's institutions to die out, enduring as late as the end of the 4th century AD, even after Rome's emperors had become Christian. They were finally suppressed by Theodosius. ⊠ *South side of Via Sacra.*

**㉕ Via Sacra.** The celebrated basalt-paved road that loops through the Roman Forum, lined with temples and shrines, was also the traditional route of religious and triumphal processions. It's now little more than a dirt track, but there are occasional patches of the paving stones—stones once trod by Caesars and plebs—rutted with the ironclad wheels of Roman wagons. If you ever wanted to walk where Mark Antony did.

## The Palatine Hill

Just beyond the Arch of Titus lies the Clivus Palatinus, which rises up a slight incline to the heights of the **Colle Palatino** (Palatine Hill), the oldest inhabited site in Rome. Despite its location overlooking the Forum's traffic and attendant noise, the Palatine was the most coveted address for ancient Rome's rich and famous. More than a few of the Twelve Caesars called the Palatine home, including Caligula, who was murdered in the still-standing and unnerving (even today) tunnel, the Cryptoporticus. The palace of Tiberius was the first to be built here; others followed, notably the gigantic extravaganza constructed for Emperor Domitian. But perhaps the most famous lodging goes back to Rome's very beginning. Once upon a time, early skeptics termed Romulus a solar myth. About a century ago, however, Rome's greatest archaeologist, Rodolfo Lanciani, excavated a site on the hill and uncovered the remains of an Iron Age settlement dating back to the 9th century BC, supporting the belief that Romulus, founder of Rome, lived here. The story goes that the twins Romulus and Remus were abandoned as infants but were suckled by a she wolf on the banks of the Tiber and adopted by a shepherd. Encouraged by the gods to build a city, the twins chose a site in 735 BC, fortifying it with a wall that Lanciani identified by digging on the Palatine. During the building of the city, the brothers quarreled, and, in a fit of anger, Romulus killed Remus.

During the Republican era the hill was an important religious center, housing the Temple of Cybele and the Temple of Victory, as well as an exclusive residential area for wealthy families. Hortensius, Cicero, Catiline, Crassus, and Agrippa all had homes here. Augustus was born on the hill, and as he rose in power he bought up surrounding estates and transformed them into private libraries, halls, and a temple to the god Apollo; the House of Livia, reserved for Augustus's wife, is the best preserved structure. Her son by a previous marriage, Emperor Tiberius, was one of the first to build a palace here, and other emperors followed suit. The structures most visible today date back to the late 1st century AD, when the Palatine experienced an extensive remodeling under Emperor Domitian. His architects put up two separate palaces, called Domus Augustana and Domus Flavia, as well as a stadium. The palaces were enlarged again under Septimius Severus in the early 2nd century AD. The lack of undeveloped space forced his workers to reshape the hill, razing old structures, filling in hollows, and building terraces. During the Renaissance, the powerful Farnese family built gardens atop the ruins overlooking the Forum. Known as the Orti Farnesiani, they were Europe's first botanical gardens, and were partly destroyed during 19th-century excavations. The hill has undergone extensive restorations, with a layout that allows visitors to appreciate the hill in its entirety—from the Iron Age to the Renaissance pleasure gardens.

**a good walk**

There are few more atmospheric places in Rome to wander about in than the Palatine Hill, with its hidden corners and shady lanes. Though picnicking is frowned on, some diehard visitors to the Domus Flavia area insist on enjoying a circumspect snack while sitting on the very stone banquettes in the sunken Triclinium where emperors once feasted on truffled peacock (the room is by the cliff overlooking the Circus Maximus—in all events, don't forget to bring some fixings for the famous stray cats of the Forum). Ticket offices and entrances to Colle Palatino are inside the Forum at the base of the hill near the Arco di Tito and on Via di San Gregorio. To visit the Palatine's ruins in a roughly chronological order, start from the southeast area facing the Aventine. The Belvedere offers panoramic views of the famous Roman arena, the **Circo Massimo** ㉕ ▶ (Circus Maximus), the green slopes of the Aventine and Celian hills, and the picturesque bell tower of Santa Maria in Cosmedin. You can then proceed to the **Museo Palatino** ㉖ or the adjacent Iron Age **Capanne Arcaiche** ㉗ settlement, moving on to the temples there and to the legendary **Casa di Livia** ㉘, no less the house of the wife of Emperor Augustus. Then visit the ruins of two more grand palaces, the **Domus Augustana** ㉙ and the **Domus Flavia** ㉚, taking in the **Stadio Palatino** ㉛, before winding up at the lovely **Orti Farnesiani** ㉜ gardens, overlooking the Forum and the Capitoline Hill.

TIMING   A leisurely stroll on the Palatino, with stops for the views and a visit to the Museo Palatino, takes about two hours. Fair weather is a must, as are good walking shoes for dusty slopes that are slippery when damp.

## What to See

㉗ **Capanne Arcaiche.** On a bank of volcanic tufa stone, archaeologists discovered the remains of an Iron Age settlement. Oval-shape wattle huts had thatched roofs resting on wooden poles, which were lodged into holes dug in the tufa. These holes and the canals dug out to channel off rainwater are visible at the site, together with the remains of two archaic circular water cisterns. A reconstruction of the village is displayed in the Antiquarium nearby. ⊠ *Northwest crest of Palatino.*

★ ㉘ **Casa di Livia** (House of Livia). Yes, this is the notorious Livia that made a career of dispatching half of the Roman imperial family—if Robert Graves' *I, Claudius* can be believed. She was the wife of perhaps the greatest emperor of them all, Augustus. Once he defeated Anthony and Cleopatra, he inaugurated the Imperial age, when Roman civilization exploded across the world. Back at home, Livia was busy dispatching successors to the royal line to ensure her son Tiberius, product of an earlier marriage, would take the throne. Here, atop the Palatine, she hatched her plots in this Casa—this was her private retreat and living quarters, not part of her state apartments. The delicate, delightful frescoes reflect the sophisticated taste of wealthy Romans, whose love of beauty and theatrical conception of nature were revived by their descendants in the Renaissance age. You'll need to call or fax several days ahead for special permission to visit. ☒ *Northwest crest of Palatino* ☎ 06/6990110 🖷 06/6787689.

➤ ㉕ **Circo Massimo** (Circus Maximus). From the palace belvedere of the Domus Flavia, you can see the Circus Maximus, the giant arena where more than 300,000 spectators watched chariot races while the emperor looked on from this very spot. Ancient Rome's oldest and largest racetrack lies in a natural hollow between two hills. The oval course stretches about 650 yards from end to end; on certain occasions, there were as many as 24 chariot races a day and competitions could last for 15 days. The noise, the color, and the excitement of the crowd must have reached astonishing levels. The central ridge was the site of two Egyptian obelisks (now in Piazza del Popolo and Piazza San Giovanni in Laterano). Picture the great chariot race scene from MGM's *Ben-Hur* and you have an inkling of what this all looked like. ☒ *Valley between Palatine and Aventine hills.*

㉙ **Domus Augustana.** In the Palazzi Imperiali complex, this palace consisted of private apartments for Emperor Domitian and his family. ☒ *Southern crest of Palatino.*

㉚ **Domus Flavia.** This palace in the Palazzi Imperiali complex was used by Domitian for official functions and ceremonies. Also called Palazzo dei Flavi, it included a basilica where the emperor could hold judiciary hearings. There were also a large audience hall, a peristyle (a columned courtyard), and the imperial triclinium (dining room), the latter set in a sunken declivity overlooking the Circus Maximus—some of its mosaic floors and stone banquettes are still in place. ☒ *Southern crest of Palatino.*

㉖ **Museo Palatino.** The Palatine Museum charts the history of the hill from Archaic times (ground floor) through its history (ground and upper floors). On display are painted terra-cotta moldings and decorations from various temples, as well as splendid sculptures, frescoes, and mosaic intarsia. Upon request, museum staff will accompany visitors to see the 16th-century frescoes of the Loggia Mattei. Portions of the paintings have been returned here from the Metropolitan Museum of Art of New York City. In the same building are frescoes detached from the Aula Isaica, one of the chambers belonging to the House of Augustus. ☒ *Northwest crest of Palatino.*

**32** **Orti Farnesiani.** Alessandro Farnese, a nephew of Pope Paul III, commissioned the 16th-century architect Vignola to lay out this archetypal Italian garden over the ruins of the Palace of Tiberius, up just a few steps from the House of Livia. The views over the main part of the Roman Forum are most impressive here. ⊠ *Monte Palatino.*

**31** **Stadio Palatino.** Domitian created this vast open space immediately adjoining his palace. It may have been his private hippodrome, or it may simply have been an immense sunken garden; alternatively, perhaps it was used to stage games and other amusements for the benefit of the emperor. ⊠ *Southeast crest of Palatino.*

## Around the Colosseum

The Eternal City's yardstick of eternity, the Colosseum, looms over a group of the Roman Empire's most magnificent monuments to imperial wealth and power, set side by side in a cobblestone piazza and adjacent park just south of the Forum complex. The most famous monument of ancient Rome, the Colosseum, was the gigantic sports arena built by Vespasian and Titus. Next to its western flank is the Arch of Constantine, a majestic, ornate triumphal arch, built solely as a tribute to the emperor Constantine; victorious armies purportedly marched under it on their return from war. On the eastern side of the Colosseum, hidden under the Colle Oppio, is Nero's opulent Domus Aurea, a palace that stands as testimony to the lavish lifestyle for which the emperors were known.

**a good walk**

The exit of the Palatino leads to the Arch of Titus, where you turn east toward the Colosseum. To the right is the **Arco di Costantino** **33** ☞ (Arch of Constantine). Next, you can explore the **Colosseo** **34** (Colosseum), one of antiquity's most celebrated monuments. Cross Piazza del Colosseo and stroll through the park on the Colle Oppio (Oppian Hill), where most of Nero's fabulous palace, the **Domus Aurea** **35** (Golden House), is hidden under the remains of the monumental baths that were built over it. The park has some good views over the Colosseum; one of the best vantage points is from Via Nicola Salvi, which climbs uphill from the Colosseum.

TIMING A look at the Arco di Costantino won't take up more than 15 minutes of your time, but the Colosseum deserves more. You can give it a cursory look in 30 minutes, but if you want to climb to the upper tiers, allow another 20 minutes or so. To avoid long lines, arrive early.

### What to See

☞ **33** **Arco di Costantino** (Arch of Constantine). This majestic arch was erected in AD 315 to commemorate Constantine's victory over Maxentius at the Milvian Bridge. It was just before this battle, in AD 312, that Constantine—the emperor who converted Rome to Christianity—had a vision of a cross in the heavens and heard the words "In this sign thou shalt conquer." The economy-minded Senate ordered that many of the rich marble decorations for the arch be scavenged from earlier monuments. It's easy to picture ranks of Roman legionnaires marching under the great barrel vault. ⊠ *Piazza del Colosseo.*

**❸❹ Colosseo** (Colosseum). The most spectacular extant edifice of ancient
★
Rome, this sports arena was designed to hold more than 50,000 spectators for gory entertainments such as combats between wild beasts and
gladiators. Here, before the imperial box, gladiators would salute the
emperor and cry *Ave, imperator, morituri te salutant* ("Hail, emperor,
men soon to die salute thee"); it's said that when one day they heard
the emperor Claudius respond, "or maybe not," they became so offended
that they called a strike. Scene of countless Hollywood spectacles—Deb-
orah Kerr besieged by lions in *Quo Vadis,* Victor Mature laying down
his arms in *Demetrius and the Gladiators,* Anthony Quinn doing battle in *Barrabas,* and Russell Crowe fighting an emperor in a computer-
generated stadium in *Gladiator,* to name just four—the Colosseum still
awes onlookers today with its power and might.

The proportions of the Colosseum, like those of many a classical building, are so perfect you do not appreciate its grandeur until you look up
from close under the walls, or its outside arches. These external arches—
called *fornices*—put a word into the English language, as they were the
haunts of young ladies of the night. Just now they are mostly abandoned
to cats, mostly tawny (having taken on some of the protective coloring
of the soft Roman brick they love to sprawl on). One can almost believe them to be miniature offspring of the gladiatorial beasts which performed here—but let's not let our imagination run away with us.

The arena has a circumference of 573 yards and was faced with stone
from nearby Tivoli. Its construction was a remarkable feat of engineering, for it stands on marshy terrain reclaimed by draining an artificial lake on the grounds of Nero's Domus Aurea, done to make amends
to the Roman people for Nero's earlier confiscation of the land. Originally known as the Flavian amphitheater, it came to be called the Colosseum by later Romans who identified it with the site of the Colossus of
Nero, a 115-foot-tall gilded bronze statue of the emperor in the guise
of the sun god that stood at the entrance to what is now Via dei Fori
Imperiali. Twelve pairs of elephants were needed to transport the statue
to the spot; it was toppled and destroyed by order of Pope Gregory the
Great at the end of the 6th century.

Designed by order of the Flavian emperor Vespasian in AD 72, the
Colosseum was inaugurated by Titus eight years later with a program
of games and shows lasting 100 days. On the opening day alone, 5,000
wild beasts perished. Among the stadium's many wonders was a *velar-
ium,* an ingenious system of sail-like awnings rigged on ropes and ma-
neuvered by sailors from the imperial fleet, who would unfurl them to
protect the arena's occupants from sun or rain.

In one of the arches on the Metro station side, look for the traces of ancient Roman stucco decoration that once adorned most of the arena.
Once inside, you can take the wooden walkway across the arena floor
for a gladiator's-eye view, then explore the upper levels, where behind
glass you can see a scale model of the Colosseum as it was, sheathed
with marble and decorated with statues. From the upper tiers there's a
good view of the labyrinthine passageways on the subterranean level of

the arena. The walkway over the floor of the arena and the stage at one end were constructed for special concerts given (only) during the Jubilee year of 2000; Paul McCartney, Simon & Garfunkel, and Elton John have recently performed just outside the Colosseo, not within it.

Legend has it that as long as the Colosseum stands, Rome will stand; and when Rome falls, so will the world. This prophecy didn't deter Renaissance princes from using the Colosseum as a quarry for building materials for such noble dwellings as Palazzo Barberini and Palazzo Farnese. Earlier, the Colosseum had been seriously damaged by earthquakes and, during the Middle Ages, had been transformed into a fortress. Some experts maintain that it was in Rome's circuses, and not here, that thousands of early Christians were martyred. Still, tradition has reserved a special place for the Colosseum in the story of Christianity, and it was Pope Benedict XIV who stopped the use of the building as a quarry when, in 1749, he declared it sanctified by the blood of the martyrs. A tiny chapel built in the 6th century under one of the Colosseum's arches was restored and reconsecrated for the 1983 Holy Year. A guided tour in English is available; there is now a small exhibition space and bookshop on site. During the 19th century, romantic poets lauded the glories of the amphitheater when viewed by moonlight. Now its arches glow at night with mellow golden spotlights, less romantic, perhaps, but still unforgettable. ✉ *Piazza del Colosseo* ☎ *06/39967700* ⊕ *www.pierreci. it* ✆ *€8* ☉ *Daily 9–1 hr before sunset.*

> **need a break?**
>
> About half a block east of the Colosseum is **Pasqualino** (✉ Via dei Santi Quattro 66 ☎ 06/67004576), a neighborhood trattoria with sidewalk tables providing a view of the arena's marble arches. For delicious gelato try **Ristoro della Salute** (✉ Piazza del Colosseo 2/a ☎ 06/77590465), on the east side of the Piazza del Colosseo, one of Rome's best gelaterias (ice-cream parlors).

★ ③⑤ **Domus Aurea** (Golden House of Nero). Legend has it that Nero famously fiddled while Rome burned. Fancying himself a great actor and poet, he played, as it turns out, his harp to accompany his recital of "The Destruction of Troy" while gazing at the flames of Rome's catastrophic fire of AD 64. Anti-Neronian historians propagandized that Nero, in fact, had set the Great Fire to clear out a vast tract of the city center to build his new palace. Today's historians discount this as historical folderol (going so far as to point to the fact that there was a full moon on the evening of July 19th, hardly the propitious occasion to commit arson). But legend or not, Nero did get to build his new palace, the extravagant Domus Aurea (Golden House). The fire was so devastating an entire ridge of the Esquiline Hill was cleared, which the capricious emperor quickly confiscated, drawing the animosity of most of his subjects. The new palace was huge and sumptuous, with a facade of pure gold, seawater piped into the baths, decorations of mother-of-pearl, fretted ivory and other precious materials, and vast gardens. It was said that after completing this gigantic house Nero exclaimed "Now I can live like a human being!" Lovers of all things Greek, happiest when he could devote himself to the arts, Nero has come down to us as a monster, but

# CloseUp

## AN EMPEROR CHEAT SHEET

OCTAVIAN, *later known as* CAESAR AUGUSTUS, *was Rome's first emperor (27 BC– AD 14), and his rule began a 200-year peace known as the Pax Romana.*

*The name of* **NERO** *(AD 54–68) lives in infamy as a violent persecutor of Christians, and as the murderer of his wife, his mother, and countless others. Although it's not certain whether he actually fiddled as Rome burned in AD 64, he was well known as an actor.*

**DOMITIAN** *(AD 81–96) declared himself "Dominus et Deus," Lord and God. He stripped away power from the Senate, and as a result after his death he suffered "Damnatio Memoriae"—the Senate had his name and image erased from all public records.*

**TRAJAN** *(AD 98–117), the first Roman emperor to be born outside Italy (in southern Spain), enlarged the empire's boundaries to include modern-day Romania, Armenia, and Upper Mesopotamia.*

**HADRIAN** *(AD 117–138) is best known for designing and rebuilding the Pantheon, constructing a majestic villa at Tivoli, and initiating myriad other constructions, including the famed wall across Britain.*

**MARCUS AURELIUS** *(AD 161–180) is remembered as a humanitarian emperor, a Stoic philosopher whose Meditations are still read today. Nonetheless, he was devoted to expansion and an aggressive leader of the empire.*

**CONSTANTINE I** *(AD 306–337) made his mark by legalizing Christianity, an act that changed the course of history, legitimizing the once-banned religion and paving the way for the papacy in Rome.*

that image was created by hostile historians of his age, like Suetonius and Tacitus. Today, scholars draw a more balanced picture.

Not much has survived of Nero's palace; a good portion of the buildings and grounds was buried under the public works with which subsequent emperors sought to make reparation to the Roman people for Nero's phenomenal greed. The largest of the buildings put up by later emperors over the Domus Aurea was the great complex of baths built by Trajan. As a result, the site of the Domus Aurea itself remained unknown for many centuries until they were rediscovered during the Renaissance era. In 1998 the city of Rome mounted a massive restoration of the archaeological site. Unfortunately, all of the fabulous decors designed by Fabullus have vanished but you can still be awed by the famous Octagon Room, topped by an oculus, where Nero once displayed the famous Greek statues of the *Dying Gaul* and the *Dying Gaul Killing Himself and His Wife* (now on view at Rome's Palazzo Altemps museum). Elsewhere are soaring vaults covered with faded remnants of Pompeiian-style frescoes, some of which came to inspire Raphael, who later used these models—known as *grotesques* because they were found in the so-called ruined grottoes of the palace—in his decorative motifs for the Vatican Loggia. Keep in mind that the temperature underground is about 50°F all year round. Reservations are strongly recommended. ✉ *Via della Domus Aurea* ☎ *06/39967700 reservations* ⊕ *www. pierreci.it* ⌨ *€5, €10 with tour, €2 for audio guide* ⊘ *Wed.–Mon. 9–7:45.*

## The Imperial Forums

A complex of five grandly conceived squares flanked with colonnades and temples, the **Fori Imperiali** (Imperial Fora) formed the magnificent monumental core of ancient Rome, together with the original Roman Forum. Excavations at the start of the 21st century have revealed more of the Imperial Fora than has been seen in nearly a thousand years.

**a good walk**

From Piazza del Colosseo, head northwest on Via dei Fori Imperiali toward Piazza Venezia. On the walls to your left, maps in marble and bronze put up by Benito Mussolini show the extent of the Roman Republic and Empire. The dictator's own dreams of empire led him to construct this avenue, cutting brutally through the Imperial Fora area, so that he would have a suitable venue for parades celebrating his expected military triumphs. Beginning in the 1990s, part of the historical neighborhood ravaged by Mussolini has been revealed by new digs. Beyond the ancient brick walls behind the Imperial Fora lay the Suburra, the mean streets of ancient Rome, where the plebs lived in crowded tenements. Opposite the brick wall, look through an archway into the huge Basilica di Massenzio. Next door is the church of **Santi Cosma e Damiano** 36, a little gem that started life as a library in the Forum of Vespasian and holds a marvelous early Christian mosaic. Among the Fori Imperiali along the avenue you can see the **Foro di Cesare** 37 (Forum of Caesar) and the **Foro di Augusto** 38 (Forum of Augustus). The grandest of all the Imperial Fora was the **Foro di Traiano** 39 (Forum of Trajan), with its huge semicircular Mercati Traianei and the **Colonna di Traiano** 40 (Trajan's Column).

TIMING   The walk along Via dei Fori Imperiali, with a stop at the church of Santi Cosma e Damiano and a look at the Imperial Fora from sidewalk level, takes only about 30 minutes. To explore the fora more closely, allow another 30 minutes or so. The fora are illuminated at night and on rare occasions are open for evening visits, when guided tours in English may also be offered (check with the tourist office).

### What to See

★ 40 **Colonna di Traiano** (Trajan's Column). The remarkable series of reliefs spiraling up this column celebrate the emperor's victories over the Dacians in what is today Romania. It has stood in this spot since AD 113. The scenes on the column are an important primary source for information on the Roman army and its tactics. An inscription on the base declares that the column was erected in Trajan's honor and that its height corresponds to the height of the hill that was razed to create a level area for the grandiose Foro di Traiano. The emperor's ashes, no longer here, were kept in a golden urn in a chamber at the column's base, and his statue stood atop the column until 1587, when the pope had it replaced with a statue of St. Peter. ✉ *Via del Foro di Traiano.*

38 **Foro di Augusto** (Forum of Augustus). These ruins, along with those of the **Foro di Nerva,** on the northeast side of Via dei Fori Imperiali, give

only a hint of what must have been impressive edifices. ☒ *Via dei Fori Imperiali.*

**㊲ Foro di Cesare** (Forum of Caesar). Julius Caesar was the first to attempt to rival the original Roman Forum, when he had this forum built in the middle of the 1st century BC. Each year without fail, on the Ides of March, an unknown hand lays a bouquet at the foot of Caesar's statue. Call several days in advance to arrange a visit. ☒ *Via dei Fori Imperiali* 🕾 06/69780532.

★ **㊴ Foro di Traiano** (Forum of Trajan). Of all the Imperial Fora complexes, Trajan's was the grandest and most imposing, a veritable city unto itself. Designed by architect Apollodorus of Damascus, it comprised a vast basilica, two libraries, and a colonnade laid out around the square, all once covered with rich marble ornamentation. Adjoining the forum were the **Mercati Traianei** (Trajan's markets), a huge, multilevel brick complex of shops, walkways, and terraces that was one of the marvels of the ancient world.

To build a complex of this magnitude, Apollodorus and his patron clearly had to have great confidence, not to mention almost unlimited means, centuries of experience, and cheap labor at their disposal. Very little is known about the markets' original function: they may have been the Roman equivalent of a multipurpose commercial center, with shops, taverns, and depots, as well as offices for regulating Rome's enormous food supplies. They also contained two semicircular lecture halls, one at either end, which were likely associated with the libraries in Trajan's Forum. The markets' architectural centerpiece is the enormous curved wall, or hexedra, that shores up the side of the Quirinal Hill exposed by Apollodorus's gangs of laborers. Covered galleries and streets were constructed at various levels, following the hexedra's curves and giving the complex a strikingly modern appearance.

As you enter the markets, a large, vaulted hall stands in front of you. Two stories of shops or offices rise up on either side. It's thought that they were either a bazaar or an administrative center for food handouts to the city's poor. Head for the flight of steps at the far end that leads down to Via Biberatica. (*Bibere* is Latin for "to drink," and the shops that open onto the street are believed to have been taverns.) Then head back to the three tiers of shops that line the upper levels of the great hexedra and look out over the remains of the forum. Though empty and bare today, the cubicles were once ancient Rome's busiest market stalls. Wine, oils, flowers, perfumes, shoes, clothing, and household goods were all sold in this thriving market—everything a burgeoning and sophisticated population desired. There's evidence that the market was equipped with fresh- and saltwater tanks so the Romans could buy their fish live. Though it seems to be part of the market, the **Torre delle Milizie** (Tower of the Militia), the tall brick tower, which is a prominent feature of Rome's skyline, was built in the early 1200s. In those times wealthy families vied with one another to build the strongest, highest defensive towers. Pope Boniface VIII bought this one from the Conti family so that he could use it as a stronghold to defend his Roman territory against his arch-enemies, the Colonnas. ⊠ *Entrance: Via dei Fori Imperiali and Via IV Novembre 6* ☎ *06/820771* ⊕ *www.romabeniculturali.it/mercatitraianei* ⊠ *€3.10* ⊗ *Tues.–Sun. 9–6.*

★ ❸ **Santi Cosma e Damiano.** Home to one of the most striking early Christian mosaics in the world, this church was adapted in the 6th century from two ancient buildings: the library in Vespasian's Forum of Peace and a hall of the Temple of Romulus (dedicated to the son of Maxentius). It was restored in the 17th century by the Barberini Pope Urban VIII, who added a few bees from his family's coat of arms to the lower left-hand side of the mosaic in the apse. In the apse is the famous 6th-century mosaic (circa 530) of Christ in Glory. It reveals how popes at the time strove to re-create the splendor of imperial audience halls in Christian churches, for Christ wears a gold, Roman-style toga, and his pose recalls that of an emperor addressing his subjects. He floats on a blue sky streaked with a flaming sunset—a miracle of tesserae mosaic-work. To his side are the figures of Sts. Peter and Paul, who present Cosmas and Damian, two Syrian benefactors whose charity was such they were branded Christians and condemned to death. Beneath this awe-inspiring work is an enchanting mosaic frieze of holy lambs. There's also a Neapolitan *presepio*, or Christmas crèche, on permanent display. ⊠ *Off Via Sacra, opposite Tempio di Antonino e Faustina* ☎ *06/6920441* ⊗ *Daily 9–1 and 3–7.*

# THE VATICAN: ROME OF THE POPES

The Vatican is a place where some people go to find a fabled work of art—Michelangelo's frescoes, rare archaeological marbles, or Bernini's statues. Others go to find their soul. In between these two extremes lies an awe-inspiring landscape that offers a famous sight for every taste and inclination. Rooms decorated by Raphael, antique sculptures like the Apollo Belvedere and the Laocoon, walls daubed by Fra Angelico, famous paintings by Giotto and Leonardo, and chief among revered non plus ultras, the ceiling of the Sistine Chapel: For the lover of beauty, few places are as historically important as this epitome of faith and grandeur. What gave all this impetus was a new force that emerged as the emperors of ancient Rome presided over their declining empire: Christianity came to Rome, and the seat of the popes was established over the tomb of St. Peter, thereby making the Vatican the spiritual core of the Roman Catholic Church. Today, there are two principal reasons for sightseeing at the Vatican. One is to visit the Basilica di San Pietro, the largest church in the world and the most overwhelming architectural achievement of the Renaissance; the other is to visit the Vatican Museums, which contain collections of staggering richness and diversity.

The massive walls surrounding Vatican City strongly underscore the fact that this is an independent, sovereign state, established by the Lateran Treaty of 1929 between the Holy See—the pope—and the Italian government. Vatican City covers 108 acres on a hill west of the Tiber and is separated from the city on all sides, except at Piazza di San Pietro, by high walls. Within the walls, about 1,000 people are permanent residents. The Vatican has its own daily newspaper (*L'Osservatore Romano*), issues its own stamps, mints its own coins, and has its own postal system. Within its territory are administrative and foreign offices, a pharmacy, banks, an astronomical observatory, a print shop, a mosaic school and art restoration institute, a tiny train station, a supermarket, a small department store, and several gas stations. Radio Vaticana broadcasts in 35 languages to six different continents.

The sovereign of this little state is the pope, Benedict XVI (elected April 2005). He has full legislative, judicial, and executive powers, with complete freedom under the Lateran Treaty to organize armed forces within the state (the Swiss Guards and the Vatican police) and to live in or move through Italian territory whenever he so desires.

Your first view of the Vatican will be your most memorable—Piazza di San Pietro (St. Peter's Square) is not only the grand entrance to Vatican territory but is one of the world's most spectacular urban showpieces, created in 1667 by Italy's greatest Baroque artist, Gian Lorenzo Bernini. Framed by a magnificent curving pair of quadruple colonnades, which are topped by a balustrade and statues of 140 saints, these gigantic enfolding "arms" welcome you to enter the great church, whose facade and dome—another Michelangelo masterstroke—remain one of Rome's most impressive sights.

*Numbers in the text and margin correspond to numbers on the Vatican map.*

**a good walk**

To enter the Musei Vaticani, the Sistine Chapel, and the Basilica di San Pietro you must comply with the Vatican's dress code, or you will be turned away by the implacable custodians stationed at the doors. For both men and women, shorts and tank tops are taboo, as are miniskirts and other revealing clothing. Wear a jacket or shawl over sleeveless tops, and avoid T-shirts with writing or pictures that could risk giving offense. Start at the **Musei Vaticani** ❶ ☛ (Vatican Museums). The entrance on Viale Vaticano (there's a separate exit on the same street) can be reached by Bus 49 from Piazza Cavour, which stops right in front; or on foot from Piazza del Risorgimento (Bus 81 or Tram 19) or a brief walk from the Via Cipro–Musei Vaticani stop on Metro line A. The collections of the museums are immense, covering about 7 km (4½ mi) of displays. You can rent a taped commentary in English explaining the Sistine Chapel and the Raphael Rooms. You're free to photograph what you like, barring use of flash, tripod, or other special equipment, for which permission must be obtained. To economize on time and effort, once you've seen the frescoes in the Raphael rooms, you can skip the collections of modern religious art in good conscience and get on with your tour. Lines at the entrance to the **Cappella Sistina** ❷ (Sistine Chapel) can move slowly, as custodians block further entrance when the room becomes crowded. Keep in mind that sometimes it's possible to exit the museums from the Sistine Chapel into St. Peter's, saving time and legwork. A sign at the entrance to the museums indicates whether the exit is open.

# CHURCH & STATE

ALONG WITH THE COLOSSEUM, the Forum, and its countless other unique sights, Rome has another characteristic that sets it apart: it's the only Catholic diocese in the world with an elected bishop. And he's not just any bishop—the bishop of Rome is none other than the pope, chosen for life by the members of the College of Cardinals in an election that arguably affects more of the world's people than any other. Although the pope's primary role is as the leader of the Catholic Church, this job title brings with it sovereignty over Vatican City and ecclesiastical responsibility for the city of Rome from Rome's cathedral, San Giovanni in Laterano.

The complicated accord between Rome and the Vatican was laid down in 1929 in the terms of the Lateran Concordat and Treaty, signed by Fascist strongman Benito Mussolini and Cardinal Gasparri, on behalf of Pope Pius XI. Under Italian unification in 1870, the land controlled by the Church, the Papal States, had been annexed by the Kingdom of Italy, giving rise to complaints that dependence on a political body compromised the pope's ability to direct the Church. The treaty remains in effect today, and it's responsible for the unquestionably unique relationship between Italy and the world's smallest country, tucked away in the center of Rome.

Vatican City is completely surrounded by the city of Rome, and although it's possible to pass through without ever knowing you've left the sovereignty of the Italian state, closer inspection reveals a number of differences more striking than the brick walls that mark the city limits. The Vatican is an autonomous political body, with independent leadership and diplomatic relationships like any other nation. The country is ruled by the pope and the various papally appointed Pontifical Councils that advise him; although technically the pope is an elected official, the electorate is not the population of Vatican City but the College of Cardinals.

Drop a soda can inside the Vatican walls, and it's the Vatican police who will give you a ticket for littering; anything more serious and you might make headlines in L'Osservatore Romano, the Vatican's own newspaper. Although its population is just over 1,000 (including the pope, who lives in the Apostolic Palace), the Vatican has its own postal system, reputedly more reliable than the Posta Italiana (look for blue or yellow boxes marked POSTA VATICANA). To use the Vatican Post, you'll have to buy special stamps at the Posta Vaticana, with offices at both sides of St. Peter's Square and in the Vatican Museums near the exit. Within the Vatican's territory are administrative and foreign offices, a pharmacy, banks, an astronomical observatory, a print shop, a mosaic school and art restoration institute, a tiny train station, a supermarket, a small department store, and several gas stations.

With two autonomous nations so closely linked, it can get messy when they disagree. In recent years, Italy has clashed with the Vatican over such diverse issues as artificial insemination, gay pride, the war in Iraq, electronic pollution from Radio Vaticana transmission towers, and the eternally thorny issue of the Vatican's tax-exempt status. It remains an uneasy balance between the two states.

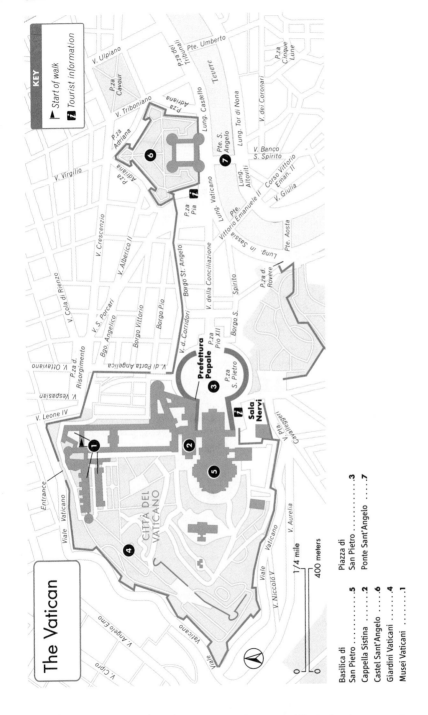

# The Vatican

**KEY**

▶ Start of walk

🛈 Tourist information

CITTÀ DEL VATICANO

Prefettura Papale

Sala Nervi

1/4 mile

400 meters

**Piazza di San Pietro** ❸ is at the west end of Via della Conciliazione. If you have the stamina, take the tour of the **Giardini Vaticani** ❹ (Vatican Gardens); then enter the **Basilica di San Pietro** ❺ (St. Peter's Basilica), visiting the Museo Storico-Artistico e Tesoro and the Grotte Vaticane. Take the elevator to the roof of the basilica, a strange fairy-tale landscape of little cupolas and towers. Climb the short staircase to the gallery inside the base of the huge dome for a dove's-eye view of the papal altar below. If you can't handle a steep, claustrophobic, one-way-only climb, don't attempt the ascent to the lantern, the small, topmost cupola of the dome.

You can continue your walk to **Castel Sant'Angelo** ❻, on Borgo Pio, where there are a number of trattorias and cafés. The huge medieval fortress, built over the tomb of emperor Hadrian, saved at least one pope's life, when Clement VII took refuge here during the Sack of Rome in 1527. From Castel Sant'Angelo's terraces you can get a bird's-eye view of **Ponte Sant'Angelo** ❼, the graceful bridge adorned with glorious statues designed by Bernini, and the rooftops of central Rome.

TIMING  If possible, break up this itinerary into two half days. Keep in mind that tours of the Giardini Vaticani start at 10 AM; it's possible to visit St. Peter's beforehand, but you won't have time for the Vatican Museums. You could do St. Peter's Basilica and Castel Sant'Angelo one day and devote another day to the museums. To do all three on the same day takes stamina and dedication; even if you rush through to the Sistine Chapel, you run the risk of cultural burn-out. Because the Vatican is close to the Via Cola di Rienzo and Via Ottaviano shopping areas, you might want to combine sightseeing with shopping. Another option would be to add Castel Sant'Angelo to the end of an Old Rome tour.

The crowds at the museums, and especially the Sistine Chapel, can be overwhelming; a good strategy is to get there either very early, before the pressure builds up, or late, as the crowds thin out. Plan on about 90 minutes for even the most cursory visit to the Vatican Museums and the Sistine Chapel. Allow an hour for St. Peter's Basilica and an hour for Castel Sant'Angelo. To do all three sights, including a lot of walking from one to another, would take five to six hours, not counting breaks.

## What to See

★ ❺ **Basilica di San Pietro** (St. Peter's Basilica). The largest church in the world, built over the tomb of St. Peter, is also the most imposing and breathtaking architectural achievement of the Renaissance (although much of the lavish interior dates to the Baroque). The physical statistics are impressive: it covers 18,000 square yards, runs 212 yards in length, and carries a dome that rises 435 feet and measures 138 feet across its base. Its history is equally impressive: No less than five of Italy's greatest artists—Bramante, Raphael, Peruzzi, Antonio Sangallo the Younger, and Michelangelo—died while striving to erect this new St. Peter's.

The history of the original St. Peter's goes back to AD 349, when the emperor Constantine completed a basilica over the site of the tomb of St. Peter, the Church's first pope. The original church stood for more than 1,000 years, undergoing a number of restorations and alterations,

# Basilica di San Pietro

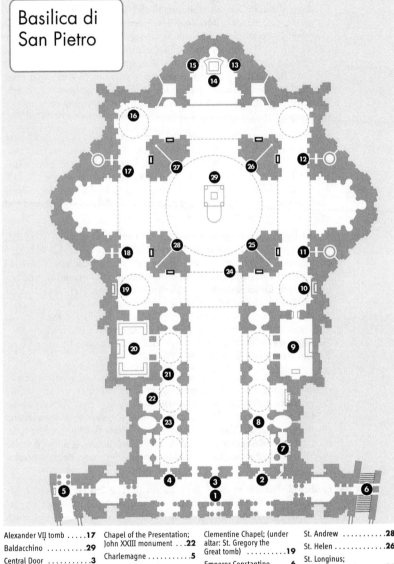

until it was in danger of collapse toward the middle of the 15th century. In 1452 a reconstruction job began but was quickly abandoned for lack of money. In 1503 Pope Julius II instructed the architect Bramante to raze all the existing buildings and to build a new basilica, one that would surpass even Constantine's for grandeur. It wasn't until 1626 that the basilica was completed and consecrated.

Though Bramante made little progress in rebuilding St. Peter's, he succeeded nonetheless in outlining a basic plan for the church, and, a crucial step, he built the piers of the crossings—the massive pillars supporting the dome. After Bramante's death in 1514, Raphael, the Sangallos, and Peruzzi all proposed variations on the original plan at one time or another. Again, however, lack of finances, rivalries between the architects, and, above all, the turmoil caused by the Sack of Rome in 1527 and the mounting crisis of the Reformation conspired to prevent much progress from being made. In 1546, however, Pope Paul III turned to Michelangelo and more or less forced the aging artist to complete the building. Michelangelo, in turn, insisted on having carte blanche to do as he thought best. He returned to Bramante's first idea of having a centralized Greek-cross plan—that is, with the "arms" of the church all the same length—and completed most of the exterior architecture except for the dome and the facade. His design for the dome, however, was modified after his death by Giacomo della Porta (his dome was much taller in proportion). The nave, too, was altered after Michelangelo's death. Pope Paul V wanted a Latin-cross church (a church with one "arm" longer than the rest), so Carlo Maderno lengthened one of the arms to create a longer central nave. He was also responsible for the facade. This was much criticized at the time because it hides the dome from observers below. It's also wider than it is high.

As you climb the shallow steps up to the great church, flanked by the statues of Sts. Peter and Paul, you'll see the **Loggia delle Benedizioni** (Benediction Loggia) over the central portal. This is the balcony where newly elected popes are proclaimed and where they stand to give their apostolic blessing on solemn feast days. The vault of the vestibule is encrusted with rich stuccowork, and the mosaic above the central entrance to the portico is a much-restored work by the 14th-century painter Giotto that was in the original basilica. The bronze doors of the main entrance also were salvaged from the old basilica. The sculptor Filarete worked on them for 12 years; they show scenes from the martyrdom of St. Peter and St. Paul, and the life of Pope Eugene IV (1431–47), Filarete's patron. In the basilica, look at the inside of these doors for the amusing "signature" at the bottom in which Filarete shows himself and his assistant dancing with joy, tools in hand, upon having completed their task. To the left are two modern bronze doors, the so-called Doors of Death, in both of which you'll see Pope John XXIII. On the right of the main entrance are the Door of the Sacraments and the Holy Door, opened only during Holy Years.

Pause a moment to appraise the size of the great building. The people near the main altar seem dwarfed by the incredible dimensions of this immense temple. The statues, the pillars, and the holy-water stoups borne by colossal cherubs are all imposing—walk over to where the cherub clings to a pier and place your arm across the sole of the cherub's foot; you will discover that it's as long as the distance from your fingers to your elbow. It's because the proportions of this giant building are in such perfect harmony that its vastness may escape you at first. Brass inscriptions in the marble pavement down the center of the nave indicate the approximate lengths of the world's other principal Christian churches, all of which fall far short of the 186-meter span of St. Peter's Basilica. In its megascale—inspired by the spatial volumes of ancient Roman ruins—the church reflects Roman grandiosità in all its majesty.

As you enter the great nave from the entrance, you'll find immediately to your right Michelangelo's *Pietà,* one of the world's most famous statues. Could you question whether this moving work, sculpted when he was only 22, owes more to man's art than to an artist's faith? As we contemplate this masterpiece we are able to understand a little better that art and faith sometimes partake of the same impulse.

In the entrance to the second chapel on the right aisle, the **body of Pope John XXIII** is laid out in a glass case, his skin waxed to prevent decay. It was brought up from his tomb in the burial area below the basilica in 2000 (*see* Grotte Vaticane, *below*), to celebrate the pope's beatification, and John Paul II now lies in his place. Exquisite bronze grilles and doors by Borromini open into the third chapel in the right aisle, the **Cappella del Santissimo Sacramento** (Chapel of the Most Holy Sacrament), with a Baroque fresco of the Trinity by Pietro da Cortona and carved angels by Bernini. At the last pillar on the right (the pier of St. Longinus) is a bronze statue of St. Peter, whose big toe is ritually kissed by the faithful. In the right transept, over the door to the **Cappella di San Michele** (Chapel of St. Michael), usually closed, Canova created a brooding Neoclassical monument to Pope Clement XIII.

In the central crossing, Bernini's great bronze *baldacchino*—a huge, spiral-columned canopy—rises high over the *altare papale* (papal altar). Bernini's Barberini patron, Pope Urban VIII, had no qualms about stripping the bronze from the Pantheon to provide Bernini with the material to create this curious structure. The Romans reacted with the famous quip *"Quod non fecerunt barbari, fecerunt Barberini"* ("What the barbarians didn't do, the Barberini did"). A curious legend connected with the baldacchino, which swarms with Barberini bees (the bee was the Barberini family symbol), relates that the pope commissioned it in thanks for the recovery of a favorite niece who had almost died in childbirth. The story is borne out by the marble reliefs on the bases of the columns: the Barberini coat of arms is surmounted by a series of heads, all but two of which seem to represent a woman in what might be the pain of labor, while a smiling baby's face appears on the base at the right front.

The splendid gilt-bronze **Cattedra di San Pietro** (throne of St. Peter) in the apse above the main altar was designed by Bernini to contain a wooden and ivory chair that St. Peter himself is said to have used, though in fact it doesn't date from further back than medieval times. (You can see a copy of the chair in the treasury.) Above it, Bernini placed a window of thin alabaster sheets that diffuses a golden light around the dove, symbol of the Holy Spirit, in the center.

Two of the major papal funeral monuments in St. Peter's Basilica are on either side of the apse and unfortunately are usually only dimly lighted. To the right is the **tomb of Pope Urban VIII;** to the left is the **tomb of Pope Paul III.** Paul's tomb is of an earlier date, designed between 1551 and 1575 by Giacomo della Porta, the architect who completed the dome of St. Peter's Basilica after Michelangelo's death. The nude figure of Justice was widely believed to be a portrait of the pope's beautiful sister, Giulia. The charms of this alluring figure were such that in the 19th century, it was thought that she should no longer be allowed to distract worshippers from their prayers, and she was swathed in marble drapery. It was in emulation of this splendid late-Renaissance work that Urban VIII ordered Bernini to design his tomb. The **tomb of Pope Alexander VII,** also designed by Bernini, stands to the left of the altar as you look up the nave, behind the farthest pier of the crossing. This may be the most haunting memorial in the basilica, thanks to the frightening skeletonized figure of Death Bernini has added, which holds an hourglass up in its hand.

With advance notice you can take a 1¼–hour guided tour in English of the **Vatican Necropolis** (☎ 06/69885318 🖷 06/69873017 ⊕ www.vatican.va ✉ €10 ☾ Ufficio Scavi Mon.–Sat. 8–5), under the basilica, which gives a rare glimpse of early Christian Roman burial customs. Apply by fax or e-mail (scavi@fsp.va) at least 10 days in advance, specifying the number of people in the group (all must be age 15 or older), preferred language, preferred time, available dates, and your contact information in Rome.

Under the Pope Pius V monument, the entrance to the sacristy also leads to the **Museo Storico-Artistico e Tesoro** (Historical-Artistic Museum and Treasury; ✉ €9 ☾ Apr.–Sept., daily 9–6; Oct.–Mar., daily 9–5), a small collection of Vatican treasures. They range from the massive and beautifully sculptured 15th-century tomb of Pope Sixtus IV by Pollaiuolo, which you can view from above, to a jeweled cross dating from the 6th century and a marble tabernacle by the Florentine mid-15th-century sculptor Donatello. Among the other priceless objects are a platinum chalice presented to Pope Pius VI by Charles III of Spain in the middle of the 18th century and an array of sacred vessels in gold, silver, and precious stones.

Continue on down the left nave past Algardi's **tomb of St. Leo.** The handsome bronze grilles in the **Capella del Coro** (Chapel of the Choir) were designed by Borromini to complement those opposite in the Cappella del Santissimo Sacramento. The next pillar holds a rearrangement of the Pollaiuolo brothers' austere monument to Pope Innocent VIII, the only major tomb to have been transferred from the old basilica. The next chapel contains the handsome bronze monument to Pope John XXIII by contemporary sculptor Emilio Greco. On the last pier in this nave stands a monument by the late-18th-century Venetian sculptor Canova marking the burial in the crypt below of the ill-fated Stuarts—the 18th-century

Roman Catholic claimants to the British throne, who were long exiled in Rome.

Above, the vast sweep of the basilica's dome is the cynosure of all eyes. To reach the dome of St. Peter's, proceed from the vestibule and follow the signs; you can either take the elevator or climb the long flight of shallow stairs to the **roof of the church** (☎ 06/69883462 ⛟ Elevator €5, stairs €4 ⊘ Daily 8–5; closed during ceremonies in piazza). From here you'll see a surreal landscape of vast sloping terraces punctuated by cupolas that serve as skylights over the various chapels. The roof affords unusual perspectives on the dome above and the piazza below. The terrace is equipped with the inevitable souvenir shop and restrooms. A short flight of stairs leads to the entrance of the *tamburo* (drum)—the base of the dome—where, appropriately enough, there's a bust of Michelangelo, the dome's principal designer. Within the drum, another short ramp and staircase give access to the **gallery** encircling the base of the dome. From here you have a dove's-eye view of the interior of the church. It's well worth the slight effort to make your way up here—unless you suffer from vertigo.

Only if you're of stout heart and strong lungs should you then make the taxing climb from the drum of the dome up to the *lanterna* (lantern) at the very apex of the dome. A narrow, seemingly interminable staircase follows the curve of the dome between inner and outer shells, finally releasing you into the cramped space of the lantern balcony for an absolutely gorgeous panorama of Rome and the countryside on a clear day. There's also a nearly complete view of the palaces, courtyards, and gardens of the Vatican. Be aware, however, that it's a tiring, slightly claustrophobic climb. There's one stairway for going up and a different one for coming down, so you can't change your mind halfway and turn back.

The entrance to the **Grotte Vaticane** (Tombs of the Popes; ⛟ Free ⊘ Apr.–Sept., daily 7–6; Oct.–Mar., daily 7–5) is at the base of the pier dedicated to St. Longinus. Because the only exit from the crypt leads outside St. Peter's Basilica, it's best to leave this visit for last. The crypt is lined with marble-face chapels and simple tombs occupying the area of Constantine's basilica and standing over what is believed to be the tomb of St. Peter himself. Other tombs and graves include those of Queen Christina of Sweden, the only woman buried in the church, and Pope John Paul II, buried in a simple grave nearby. ⊠ *Piazza di San Pietro, Vatican* ⛟ *Free* ⊘ *Basilica: Apr.–Sept., daily 7–7; Oct.–Mar., daily 7–6. Free 1-hr guided tours in English available; inquire at Centro Servizi (information office), as times vary.*

> **need a break?**
>
> **Insalata Ricca** (⊠ Piazza Risorgimento 6, Vatican ☎ 06/39730387), about halfway between the Vatican Museums and St. Peter's Basilica, offers light meals, chiefly pasta, salads, and pizza. As a dining experience, it's unremarkable, but keep this one in mind on a hot day—its air-conditioning is the best in the neighborhood.

**❷ Cappella Sistina** (Sistine Chapel). In 1508, the redoubtable Pope Julius
FodorśChoice   II commissioned Michelangelo to fresco the more than 10,000 square
★   feet of the Sistine Chapel's ceiling. (*Sistine,* by the way, is simply the ad-
jective from *Sixtus,* in reference to Pope Sixtus IV, who commissioned
the chapel itself.) The task took four years, and it's said that for many
years afterward Michelangelo couldn't read anything without holding
it up over his head. The result, however, was a masterpiece. A pair of
binoculars helps greatly, as does a small mirror—hold the mirror facing the ceiling and look down to study the reflection.

Before the chapel was consecrated in 1483, its lower walls had been decorated by a group of artists including Botticelli, Ghirlandaio, Perugino,
Signorelli, and Pinturicchio. They had painted scenes from the life of
Moses on one wall and episodes from the life of Christ on the other.
Later, Julius II, dissatisfied with the simple vault decoration—it consisted
of no more than stars painted on the ceiling—decided to call in Michelangelo. At the time, Michelangelo was carving Julius II's resplendent
tomb—a project that never came near completion. He had no desire to
give the project up to paint a ceiling, considering the task unworthy of
him. Julius was not, however, a man to be trifled with, and Michelangelo reluctantly began work. The project proceeded in fits and starts until
Michelangelo decided to dedicate himself wholeheartedly to it.

His subject was the story of humanity before the coming of Christ. It's
told principally by means of the scenes depicted in nine central panels.
These show, starting from the altar: the *Separation of Light from Darkness,* the *Creation of the Heavenly Bodies,* the *Separation of Land and
Sea,* the *Creation of Adam,* the *Creation of Eve,* the *Fall of Man and
the Expulsion from Paradise,* the *Sacrifice of Noah,* the *Flood,* and the
*Drunkenness of Noah.* The scenes appear in an architectural framework,
further embellished with Old Testament figures, prophets, Sibyls, and
20 *ignudi,* or nude youths (one may well wonder what these muscle-
bound men are doing up there, but the art historians tell us they refer
to the "athletes of virtue" and were meant as iconographical symbols
of asceticism). In the lunettes below, the spaces between the windows,
Michelangelo painted the ancestors of Christ.

The ceiling was cleaned and restored in the early 1990s, revealing vibrant colors that proved a startling contrast to the previously dark and
veiled tones. The cleaning, which was not without controversy, has led
art historians to reevaluate Michelangelo's influence on the later Man-
nerists, who favored similarly vivid colors. What remains unchanged,
however, is the remarkable power and imagination of the ceiling. Notice the way that the later scenes—the *Creation of Adam* is a good example—are larger and more simply painted than the earlier ones. As the
work advanced, Michelangelo became progressively bolder in his treatment, using larger forms and simpler colors. The Adam also reveals how
much Michelangelo brought to the field of painting from the discipline
of sculpture.

More than 20 years later, Michelangelo was called on again, this time
by the Farnese Pope Paul III, to add to the chapel's decoration by paint-

ing the *Last Judgment* on the wall over the altar. The subject was well suited to the aging and embittered artist, who had been deeply moved by the horrendous Sack of Rome in 1527 and the confusions and disturbances of the Reformation. The painting stirred up controversy even before it was unveiled in 1541, shocking many Vatican officials, especially one Biagio di Cesena, who criticized its "indecent" nudes. Michelangelo retaliated by painting Biagio's face on the figure with donkey's ears in Hades, in the lower right-hand corner of the work. Biagio pleaded with Pope Paul to have Michelangelo erase his portrait, but the pontiff replied that he could intercede for those in purgatory but had no power over hell. As if to sign this, his late great fresco, Michelangelo painted his own face on the wrinkled human skin in the hand of St. Bartholomew. ⊠ *Vatican Palace; entry only through Musei Vaticani.*

☺ ➏ **Castel Sant'Angelo.** Standing between the Tiber and the Vatican, this circular and medieval "castle" has long been one of Rome's most distinctive landmarks. Opera-lovers know it well as the setting for the final scene of Puccini's *Tosca*; on the upper terrace is the rampart from which the tempestuous diva throws herself to end the opera. In fact, the structure was built as a mausoleum for the emperor Hadrian. Work began in AD 135 and was completed by the emperor's successor, Antoninus Pius, about five years later. When first finished, it consisted of a great square base topped by a marble-clad cylinder on which was planted a ring of cypress trees. Above them towered a gigantic statue of Hadrian. From about the middle of the 6th century AD the building became a fortress, the military key to Rome for almost 1,000 years and the place of refuge for numerous popes during wars and sieges. Its name dates from 590, when Pope Gregory the Great, during a procession to plead for the end of a plague, saw an angel standing on the summit of the castle in the act of sheathing its sword. Taking this as a heavenly sign that the plague was at an end, the pope built a small chapel atop the castle on the spot where he had seen the angel, and next to it had placed a statue of the angel. Henceforth, it became known as Castel Sant'Angelo. Notwithstanding poor Tosca's demise, Castel Sant'Angelo's loggias and terraces have wonderful views.

Enter the building from the former moat, and through the original Roman door of Hadrian's tomb. From here you pass through a courtyard that was enclosed in the base of the classical monument. You enter a vaulted brick corridor that hints at grim punishments in dank cells. On the right, a spiral ramp leads up to the chamber in which Hadrian's ashes were kept. Where the ramp ends, the Borgia Pope Alexander VI's staircase begins. Part of it consisted of a wooden drawbridge, which could isolate the upper part of the castle completely. The staircase ends at the Cortile dell'Angelo, a courtyard that has become the resting place of the marble angel that stood above the castle. (It was replaced by a bronze sculpture in 1753.) The stone cannonballs piled in the courtyard look like oversize marble snowballs. In the rooms off the Cortile dell'Angelo, there's a small collection of arms and armor; on the left are some frescoed halls, which are used for temporary exhibitions, and the **Cappella di Papa Leone X** (Chapel of Pope Leo X), with a facade by Michelangelo.

In the courtyard named for Pope Alexander VI, a wellhead bears the Borgia coat of arms. The courtyard is surrounded by gloomy cells and huge storerooms that could hold great quantities of oil and grain in case of siege. Benvenuto Cellini, the rowdy 16th-century Florentine goldsmith, sculptor, and boastful autobiographer, spent some time in Castel Sant'Angelo's foul prisons; so did Giordano Bruno, a heretical monk who was later burned at the stake in Campo de' Fiori, and Beatrice Cenci, accused of patricide and incest and executed just across Ponte Sant'Angelo. (Beatrice's story forms the lurid plot of Shelley's verse drama *The Cenci*.)

Take the stairs at the far end of the courtyard to the open terrace. From here, you have some wonderful views of the city's rooftops and of the lower portions of the castle. You can also see the Passetto, the fortified corridor connecting Castel Sant'Angelo with the Vatican. Pope Clement VII used it to make his way safely to the castle during the Sack of Rome in 1527. Opening off the terrace are more rooms containing arms and military uniforms. There's also a café here where you can pause for refreshments.

Continue your walk along the perimeter of the tower and climb the few stairs to the ***appartamento papale*** (papal apartment). Though used by the popes mainly in times of crisis, these splendid rooms are far from spartan. The sumptuous Sala Paolina (Pauline Room), the first you enter, was decorated in the 16th century by Pierino del Vaga and his assistants with lavish frescoes of scenes from the Old Testament and the lives of St. Paul and Alexander the Great. Look for the trompe l'oeil door with a figure climbing the stairs. From another false door, a black-clad figure peers into the room. This is believed to be a portrait of an illegitimate son of the powerful Orsini family. The Camera del Perseo (Perseus Room), next door, is named for a frieze in which del Vaga represents Perseus with damsels and unicorns. The classical theme is continued in the next room, the Camera d'Amore e Psiche (Cupid and Psyche Room), used by the popes as a bedroom. You can continue on to the upper terrace at the feet of the bronze angel to take in a magnificent view. ✉ *Lungotevere Castello 50, Vatican* ☎ *06/39967700* ⊕ *www. pierreci.it* ✎ *€5* ☉ *Tues.–Sun. 9–8.*

**need a break?**

A tiny take-out pastry shop, **Dolceborgo** (✉ Borgo Pio 162, Vatican ☎ No phone) offers traditional cakes, pies, and confections of fresh fruit, custard, and cream that will give you a boost after a day of pounding the pavement. Walk three blocks down Borgo Pio from Via Porta Angelica; you will find it on the left.

**❹ Giardini Vaticani** (Vatican Gardens). Extending over the hill behind St. Peter's Basilica is Vatican City's enclave of neatly trimmed lawns and flower beds, which are dotted with some interesting constructions and other, duller ones that serve as office buildings. The Vatican Gardens occupy almost 40 acres of land on the Vatican hill, behind St. Peter's Basilica. The mandatory tour begins in front of the Centro Servizi on Piazza San Pietro. It takes about two hours and includes a visit to the little-used Vatican railroad station, which now houses a museum of coins and stamps made in the Vatican, and the Torre di San Giovanni (Tower of St. John), restored by Pope John XXIII as a place where he could retreat to work in peace, and now used as a residence for distinguished guests. The tower is at the top of the hill, which you explore on foot. The plantings include a formal Italian garden, a flowering French garden, a romantic English landscape, and a small forest. Photography is not allowed, but souvenir photos and postcards are available. The visit includes considerable walking and climbing of stairs and slopes. Wear good walking shoes and observe the Vatican dress code. Call for a reservation (which is required) two or three days in advance. ⊠ *Centro Servizi, south side of Piazza San Pietro, Vatican* ☎ *06/69884466* 🖷 *06/ 69885100* ⊕ *www.vatican.va* 🖃 *€9 for Gardens tour, €19 for Gardens and Sistine Chapel* 🕙 *Mon.–Sat.*

▶ ❶ **Musei Vaticani** (Vatican Museums). Other than the pope and his papal
Fodor'sChoice court, the occupants of the Vatican are some of the most famous art works
★ in the world. The museums that contain them are part of the **Vatican Palace,** residence of the popes since 1377. The palace consists of a number of individual buildings containing an estimated 1,400 rooms, chapels, and galleries. The pope and his household occupy only a small part of the palace, most of the rest of which is given over to the Vatican Library and Museums. Beyond the glories of the Sistine Chapel, the collection is so extraordinarily rich you may just wish to skim the surface, but few will want to miss out on the great antique sculptures, the Raphael Stanze, and Old Master paintings, such as Leonardo da Vinci's *St. Jerome.*

Among the collections on the way to the chapel, the **Egyptian Museum** (in which Room II reproduces an underground chamber tomb of the Valley of Kings) is well worth a stop. The **Chiaramonti Museum** was organized by the Neoclassical sculptor Canova and contains almost 1,000 copies of classical sculpture. The gems of the Vatican's sculpture collection are in the **Pio-Clementino Museum,** however. Just off the hall in Room X, you can find the *Apoxyomenos* (Scraper), a beautiful 1st-century AD copy of a bronze statue of an athlete. There are other even more famous pieces in the **Octagonal Courtyard,** where Pope Julius II installed the greatest pieces from his private collection: on the left stands the celebrated *Apollo Belvedere.* In the far corner, on the same side of the courtyard, is the *Laocoön* group, found on Rome's Esquiline Hill in 1506, held to be possibly the single most important antique sculpture group in terms of its influence on Renaissance artists.

An adjacent hall dedicated to animals is filled with sculpture and mosaics done in colored marble, some of them very charming. There's a gallery of classical statues and a **Gallery of Busts;** the smallish **Mask Room** displays a lively mosaic pavement from the emperor Hadrian's Villa at Tivoli just outside Rome, and a copy of the 4th-century BC Greek sculptor Praxiteles' *Cnidian Venus.* In the **Hall of the Muses,** the *Belvedere Torso* occupies center stage: this is a fragment of a 1st-century BC statue, probably of Hercules, all rippling muscles and classical dignity, much admired by Michelangelo. The lovely neoclassical room of the **Rotonda** has an ancient mosaic pavement and a huge porphyry basin from Nero's palace, as well as several colossal statues. The room on the Greek-cross plan contains two fine porphyry sarcophagi (great marble burial caskets), one of Costantia and one of St. Helena, mother of the emperor Constantine.

Upstairs, the **Etruscan Museum** holds many objects from the Regolini-Galassi find near Cerveteri, and a wealth of other material as well. Adjacent are three sections of limited interest: the **Antiquarium,** with Roman originals; three small rooms of Greek originals (followed by a broad staircase lined with Assyrian reliefs); and a vase collection. The domed **Sala della Biga** comes next. The *biga* (chariot) group at the center was extensively reconstructed in 1780. The chariot itself is original and was used in the church of San Marco as an episcopal throne.

In the **Candelabra Gallery,** the tall candelabra—immense candlesticks—under the arches are, like the sarcophagi and vases, of ancient origin. The walls facing the windows of the **Tapestry Gallery** are hung with magnificent tapestries executed in Brussels in the 16th century from designs by Raphael. On the window walls are tapestries illustrating the life of Pope Urban VIII. They were done in a workshop that the Barberini family set up in Rome in the 17th century expressly for this purpose.

The long **Gallery of Maps** is frescoed with 40 maps of Italy and the papal territories, commissioned by Pope Gregory XIII in 1580. On each map is a detailed plan of the region's principal city. The ceiling is decorated with episodes from the history of the regions.

In the **Apartment of Pius V** is a small hall hung with tapestries. Facing the windows are the precious 15th-century *Passion* and *Baptism of Christ* from Tournai, in Belgium. The **Sobieski Room** gets its name from a huge painting by the Polish artist Matejko. It shows the *Victory of Vienna,* a decisive defeat of the invading Ottoman forces in the late 17th century. A massive display case in the **Hall of the Immaculate Conception** shows some preciously bound volumes containing the text of the papal bull promulgating that particular dogma.

Rivaling the Sistine Chapel for artistic interest are the **Stanze di Raffaello** (Raphael Rooms), which are directly over the Borgia apartments and can be very crowded. Pope Julius II moved into this suite of rooms in 1507, four years after his election. Reluctant to continue living in the Borgia apartments with their memories of his ill-famed predecessor, Alexander VI, he called in Raphael to decorate his new quarters. When people talk about the Italian High Renaissance—thought to be the very pinnacle of Western art—it's Raphael's frescoes they're probably thinking about. The theme of the **Segnatura Room,** the first to be frescoed, was painted almost entirely by Raphael himself (as opposed to the other rooms, which were painted in large part by his assistants). The theme of the room—which may broadly be said to be "enlightenment"—reflects the fact that this was Julius's private library.

Theology triumphs in the fresco known as the *Disputa,* or *Debate on the Holy Sacrament,* on the wall behind you as you enter. Opposite, the *School of Athens* glorifies philosophy in its greatest exponents. Plato

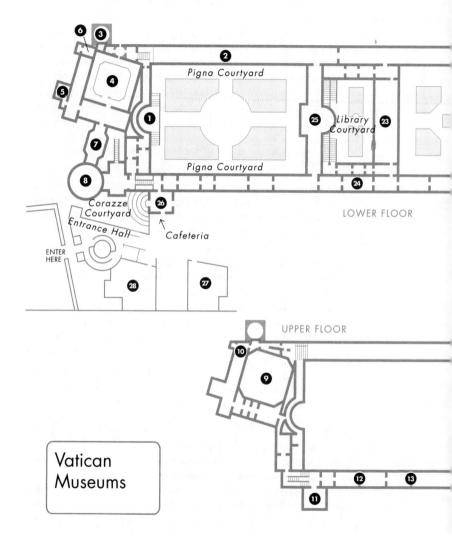

Pigna Courtyard

Pigna Courtyard

Library Courtyard

LOWER FLOOR

Corazze Courtyard

Entrance Hall

ENTER HERE

Cafeteria

UPPER FLOOR

Vatican Museums

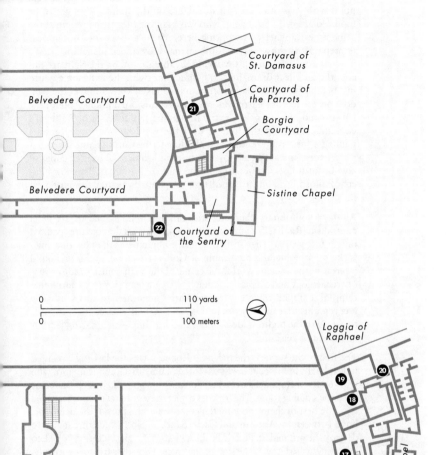

Courtyard of
St. Damasus

Courtyard of
the Parrots

Borgia
Courtyard

Belvedere Courtyard

㉑

Sistine Chapel

Belvedere Courtyard

㉒ Courtyard of
the Sentry

0                    110 yards
0                    100 meters

Loggia of
Raphael

⑲  ⑳

⑱

⑰

⑯

Sistine Chapel

⑭        ⑮

(perhaps a portrait of Leonardo da Vinci), in the center, is debating a point with Aristotle. The pensive figure on the stairs is thought to be modeled after Michelangelo, who was painting the Sistine ceiling at the same time Raphael was working here. Michelangelo does not appear in preparatory drawings, so Raphael may have added his fellow artist's portrait after admiring his work. In the foreground on the right are Euclid, the architect Bramante, and, on the far right, the handsome youth just behind the white-clad older man is Raphael himself. Over the window on the left are Parnassus, who represents poetry, and Apollo, the Muses, and famous poets, many of whom are likenesses of Raphael's contemporaries. In the lunette over the window opposite, Raphael painted figures representing and alluding to the Cardinal and Theological Virtues, and subjects showing the establishment of written codes of law. Beautiful personifications of the four subject areas, Theology, Poetry, Philosophy, and Jurisprudence, are painted in circular pictures on the ceiling above.

All the revolutionary characteristics of High Renaissance art are here: naturalism (Raphael's figures lack the awkwardness that pictures painted only a few years earlier still contained); humanism (the idea that man is the most noble and admirable of God's creatures); and a profound interest in the ancient world, the result of the 15th-century rediscovery of archaeology and classical antiquity. There's a tendency to go into something of a stupor when confronted with "great art" of this kind. The fact remains that the frescoes in this room virtually dared its occupants to aspire to the highest ideas of law and learning—an amazing feat for an artist not yet 30.

The first in the series is the **Incendio Room**; it was the last to be painted in Raphael's lifetime, and was executed mainly by Giulio Romano, who worked from Raphael's drawings for the new pope, Leo X. It served as the pope's dining room. The frescoes depict stories of previous popes called Leo, the best of them showing the great fire in the Borgo (the neighborhood between the Vatican and Castel Sant'Angelo), which threatened to destroy the original St. Peter's Basilica in AD 847; miraculously, Pope Leo IV extinguished it with the sign of the cross. The other frescoes show the coronation of Charlemagne by Leo III in St. Peter's Basilica, the *Oath of Leo III,* and a naval battle with the Saracens at Ostia in AD 849, after which Pope Leo IV showed clemency to the defeated.

The **Eliodoro Room** is a private antechamber. Working on the theme of Divine Providence's miraculous intervention in defense of endangered faith, Raphael depicted Leo the Great's encounter with Attila; it's on the wall to your left as you enter. The *Expulsion of Heliodorus from the Temple of Jerusalem,* opposite the entrance, refers to Pope Julius II's insistence on the Church's right to temporal possessions. He appears on the left, watching the scene. On the left window wall, the *Liberation of St. Peter* is one of Raphael's best-known and most effective works.

Adjacent to the Raphael Rooms, the **Hall of Constantine** was decorated by Giulio Romano and other assistants of Raphael after the master's untimely death in 1520. The frescoes represent various scenes from the life of the emperor Constantine. Don't miss the tiny **Chapel of Nicholas V,** aglow with Fra Angelico (1395–1455) frescoes of episodes from the life of St. Stephen (above) and St. Lawrence (below), one of the greatest gems of Renaissance art. If it weren't under the same roof as Raphael's and Michelangelo's works, it would undoubtedly draw greater attention.

Returning downstairs, you enter the **Borgia apartments,** where some intriguing historic figures are depicted in the elaborately painted ceilings, designed but only partially executed by Pinturicchio at the end of the 15th century, and greatly retouched in later centuries. It's generally believed that Cesare Borgia murdered his sister Lucrezia's husband, Alphonse of Aragon, in the Room of the Sibyl. In the Room of the Saints, Pinturicchio painted his self-portrait in the figure to the left of the possible portrait of the architect Antonio da Sangallo. (His profession is made clear by the fact that he holds a T-square.) The lovely picture of St. Catherine of Alexandria is said to be a representation of Lucrezia Borgia herself. The resurrection scene in the next room, the Room of the Mysteries, offers excellent portraits of the kneeling Borgia pope, of Cesare Borgia (the soldier with a lance at the center), and of the young Francesco Borgia (the Roman at the soldier's side), who also was probably assassinated by Cesare. These and the other rooms of the Borgia apartments have been given over to exhibits of the Vatican's collection of modern religious art, which continues interminably on lower levels of the building.

In the frescoed exhibition halls that are part of the Vatican Museums, the **Vatican Library** displays precious illuminated manuscripts and documents from its vast collections. The **Aldobrandini Marriage Room** contains beautiful ancient frescoes of a Roman nuptial rite, named for their subsequent owner, Cardinal Aldobrandini.

The **Braccio Nuovo** (New Wing) holds an additional collection of ancient Greek and Roman statues, the most famous of which is the *Augustus of Prima Porta,* in the fourth niche from the end on the left. It's considered a faithful likeness of the emperor Augustus, who was 40 years old at the time. Note the workmanship in the reliefs on his armor. The two gilt bronze peacocks in the gallery were in the courtyard of the original basilica of St. Peter's. Before that it's likely that they stood in the emperor Hadrian's mausoleum, today Castel Sant'Angelo. To the ancient Romans the peacock was a symbol of immortality.

The paintings in the **Pinacoteca** (Picture Gallery) are almost exclusively of religious subjects and are arranged in chronological order, beginning with works of the 11th and 12th centuries. Room II has a marvelous Giotto triptych, painted on both sides, which formerly stood on the high altar in the old St. Peter's. In Room III you'll see Madonnas by the Florentine 15th-century painters Fra Angelico and Filippo Lippi. The Raphael Room contains some of the master's greatest creations, including the exceptional *Transfiguration,* the *Coronation of the Virgin,* and the *Foligno Madonna* as well as the tapestries that Raphael designed to hang in the Sistine Chapel. The next room contains Leonardo's beautiful (though unfinished) *St. Jerome* and a Bellini *Pietà.* In the courtyard outside the

Pinacoteca you can admire the reliefs from the base of the Colonna di Marco Aurelio, the column in Piazza Colonna.

In the **Museo Pio Cristiano** (Museum of Christian Antiquities), the most famous piece is the 3rd-century AD statue called the *Good Shepherd,* much reproduced as a devotional image. The **Museo Missionario-Etnologico** (Ethnological-Missionary Museum), usually open only Wednesday and Saturday, has artifacts from exotic places all over the world. There are some precious Asian statuettes and vases, scale models of temples, and full-scale Melanesian spirit huts. The **Museo Storico** (Historical Museum) displays a collection of state carriages (including an early version of the Popemobile, an ordinary car adapted to hold an armchair in the back), uniforms, arms, and banners. *Vatican Museums ⊠ Viale Vaticano ☎ 06/69883332 ⊕ www.vatican.va ☜ €12, free last Sun. of month; audio guide €5.50 ☉ Mid-Mar.–Oct., weekdays 8:45–4:45, no admission after 3:45; Sat. and last Sun. of month 8:45–1:45, no admission after 12:20; Nov.–mid-Mar., Mon.–Sat. and last Sun. of month 8:45–1:45, no admission after 12:20 ☉ Closed Catholic holidays ☞ Note: ushers at entrance of St. Peter's and Vatican Museums will bar entry to people with bare knees or bare shoulders.*

**need a break?** About five minutes from the Vatican Museums exit are two good neighborhood trattorias that are far less touristy than those directly opposite the museums. At **Dino e Toni** (⊠ Via Leone IV 60, Vatican ☎ 06/39733284) you can dine on typical Roman fare, fresh from the nearby outdoor market on Via Andrea Doria, and pizza. **La Caravella** (⊠ Via degli Scipioni 42, at Via Vespasiano, off Piazza Risorgimento, Vatican ☎ 06/39726161) serves classic Roman food and pizza.

❸ **Piazza di San Pietro** (St. Peter's Square). Actually an oval, this magnifi-
FodorśChoice cent square is the vast main entrance into the Vatican. It's one of
★ Bernini's most spectacular masterpieces, completed in 1667 after 11 years' work—a relatively short time in those days, considering the vastness of the task—and capable of holding 400,000 people. It's surrounded by a pair of quadruple colonnades, gloriously studded with more than 140 statues of saints and martyrs. Look for the two disks set into the piazza's pavement on either side of the central obelisk. If you stand on either disk, a trick of perspective makes the colonnades seem to consist of a single row of columns. Bernini had an even grander visual effect in mind when he designed the square. By opening up this immense, airy, and luminous space in a neighborhood of narrow, shadowy streets, he created a contrast that would surprise and impress anyone who emerged from the darkness into the light, in a characteristically Baroque metaphor. But in the 1930s, Mussolini ruined the effect. To celebrate the "conciliation" between the Vatican and the Italian government under the Lateran Treaty of 1929, he conceived of the Via della Conciliazione, the broad, rather soulless avenue that now forms the main approach to St. Peter's and gives the eye time to adjust to the enormous dimensions of the square and church, nullifying Bernini's grand conception.

The 85-foot-high Egyptian **obelisk** was brought to Rome by Caligula in AD 38 and was probably placed in his circus, believed to have been near here. It was moved to its current site in 1586 by Pope Sixtus V. According to legend, the monumental task of raising it almost ended in disaster when the ropes started to give way. In the absolute silence—the spectators had been threatened with death if they made a sound—a voice called out "Water on the ropes!" Strengthened by having water poured on them, the ropes held, and thus a Genoese sailor who dared to speak up had saved the day. He was rewarded with the papal promise that thereafter the palms used in St. Peter's Basilica on Palm Sunday should come from Bordighera, the sailor's hometown.

The emblem at the top of the obelisk is the Chigi star, placed here in honor of Alexander VII, a member of the powerful Chigi family who was pope when the piazza was built. Alexander had been categorical in dictating to Bernini his requirements for the design of the piazza. It had to make the pope visible to as many people as possible from the Benediction Loggia and from his Vatican apartments; it had to provide a covered passageway for papal processions; and it had to skirt the various existing buildings of the Vatican, while incorporating the obelisk and the fountain already there. (The fountain was moved to its current position, and a twin fountain was installed to balance it.)

Piazza San Pietro is the scene of large papal audiences as well as special commemorations, masses, and beatification ceremonies. When he's in Rome, the pope makes an appearance every Sunday around 11 AM (call the Vatican Information office to find out if the pope is in town and the exact time) at the window of the Vatican Palace. He addresses the crowd and blesses all present. The pope holds mass audiences on Wednesday morning about 10 (at 9 in the hotter months). Whether or not they are held in the square depends on the weather. There's an indoor audience hall adjacent to the basilica. While the pope is vacationing at Castel Gandolfo in the Castelli Romani hills outside Rome, he gives a talk and blessing from a balcony of the papal palace there. For admission to an **audience** (⌓ Prefettura della Casa Pontefice, 00120 Vatican City ☎ 06/69883273 🖷 06/69885863), apply for free tickets by mail or fax in advance, indicating the date you prefer, the language you speak, and the hotel in which you will stay. Or apply for tickets on the Monday or Tuesday before the Wednesday audience at the Prefettura della Casa Pontifice, open Monday and Tuesday 9–1, which you reach through the Portone di Bronzo (Bronze Door) at the end of the right-hand colonnade. You can also arrange to pick up free tickets on Tuesday from 5 to 6:45 at the **Santa Susanna American Church** (✉ Via XX Settembre 15, Near Termini ☎ 06/42014554); call first. For a fee, travel agencies make arrangements that include transportation. Arrive early, as security is tight and the best places fill up fast.

On the south side of the square are the **Centro Servizi Vaticani** (Vatican Information Office; ☎ 06/69881662 ⊙ Mon.–Sat. 8:30–7) and the **Vatican Bookshop** (⊙ Weekdays 8:30–7, Sat. 8:30–2). There are Vatican post offices (known for fast handling of outgoing mail) on both sides of St. Peter's Square and inside the Vatican Museums complex. You can also buy Vatican stamps and coins at the shop annexed to the information office. Although postage rates are the same at the Vatican as elsewhere in Italy, the stamps are not interchangeable, so any material stamped with Vatican stamps must be placed into a blue or yellow Posta Vaticana box. Public toilets are near the Information Office, under the colonnade opposite, and outside the exit of the crypt. Religious objects and souvenirs are sold at shops in the surrounding neighborhood. ⊠ *West end of Via della Conciliazione, Vatican.*

❼ **Ponte Sant'Angelo.** One of the most beautiful of central Rome's 20 or so bridges is lined with angels designed by Bernini, Baroque Rome's most prolific architect and sculptor. Bernini himself carved only two of the angels, both of which were moved to the church of Sant'Andrea delle Fratte shortly afterward for safekeeping. Though copies, the angels on the bridge today convey forcefully the grace and characteristic sense of movement—a key element of Baroque sculpture—of Bernini's best work. ⊠ *Between Lungotevere Castello and Lungotevere Altoviti, San Pietro.*

# OLD ROME: GOLD AND GRANDEUR

The most important clue to the Romans is their Baroque art—not its artistic technicalities, but its spirit. When you understand that, you'll no longer be a stranger in Rome. Flagrantly emotional, heavily expressive, and sensuously visual, the 17th-century artistic movement known as the Baroque was born in Rome, the creation of three geniuses, the sculptor and architect Gian Lorenzo Bernini and the painters Annibale Caracci and Caravaggio. Ranging from the austere drama found in Caravaggio's painted altarpieces to the jewel-encrusted, gold-on-gold decoration of 17th-century Roman palace decoration, the Baroque sought to both shock and delight by upsetting the placid, "correct" rules of the Renaissance masters. By appealing to the emotions, it became a powerful weapon in the hands of the Counter-Reformation. Although this tour includes such sights as the Pantheon—ancient Rome's most perfectly preserved building—it's mainly an excursion into the 16th and 17th centuries, when Baroque art triumphed in Rome.

We wend our way through one of Rome's most beautiful districts—**Vecchia Roma** (Old Rome), thick with narrow streets with curious names, airy Baroque piazzas, and picturesque courtyards. Occupying the horn of land that pushes the Tiber westward toward the Vatican, it has been an integral part of the city since ancient times, and its position between the Vatican and Lateran palaces, both seats of papal rule, puts it in the mainstream of Rome's development from the Middle Ages onward. For centuries, artisans and shopkeepers toiled in the shadow of the huge palaces built to consolidate the power and prestige of the leading figures in the papal court. Writers and artists, such as the satirist Aretino and the goldsmith-sculptor Cellini, made sarcastic comments on the alternate fortunes of the courtiers and courtesans who populated the area. Artisans and artists still live in Old Rome, but their numbers are diminishing as the district becomes gentrified and posh. Two of the liveliest piazzas in Rome, Piazza Navona and Piazza del Pantheon, are the local lodestars in a constellation of cafés, trendy stores, eating places, clubs, and wineshops.

The walk here is a long one and could well be divided into two or even three sections, to include other sights on the fringes, such as Castel Sant'Angelo, the Palazzo Doria Pamphilj, or the Ghetto. You can give free rein to your curiosity, poking into corners, peeking into courtyards, stepping into esoteric shops, and finding eye-catching vistas at every turn.

*Numbers in the text and margin correspond to points of interest on the Old Rome map.*

**a good walk**

The grandmother of all Rome's churches, **Il Gesù ❶** ▶, kicks off this tour. Take in the Baroque splendor—notably, the spiraling ceiling frescoes—then head out into the piazza. Cross Corso Vittorio and take Via del Gesù, turning left onto Via Piè di Marmo (literally, Street of the Marble Foot, named for the broken-off foot of what must have been a very large classical statue that was found here; the foot is at the corner of Via Santo Stefano del Cacco). Via Piè di Marmo leads into Piazza Santa Caterina di Siena and into Piazza della Minerva. On the right is the church of **Santa Maria sopra Minerva ❷**, the only major church in Rome built in Gothic style—it glitters and shines, so it was chosen for one of Andrea Bocelli's televised concerts—and is famous as the home of Michelangelo's *Risen Christ* and frescoes by Filippino Lippi, some of the most beautiful Renaissance works in Rome. Right outside the church is the astounding 17th-century elephant memorial sculpted by Bernini.

Straight ahead is the curving, brick-bound mass of the **Pantheon ❸**, one of the wonders of the ancient world and the most complete surviving building from antiquity. What you see is the side and rear of the building, where you can observe how the Romans built a series of weight-carrying arches into the walls of the building to support the huge dome, a technique later taken up by Renaissance architects. Follow Via della Minerva to Piazza della Rotonda and go to the north end of the square to get an overall view of the temple's columned portico. Inside, the oculus opens the ancient temple to the skies—a great photo-op. Back out on the piazza you'll find a busy café scene that starts in the late morning and continues until late at night. Streets throughout this area are lined with gelaterias, pubs, pizzerias, restaurants, clubs, and discos.

Take Via degli Orfani north to Piazza Capranica and follow Via della Guglia into Piazza Montecitorio. Off the west side of the piazza, head into Via Uffizi del Vicario. Continue west on Via della Stelletta. Ahead of you, across Via della Scrofa, is Via dei Portoghesi and the picturesque **Torre della Scimmia ❹**, the "Monkey Tower." More a piazza than a street, Via dei Portoghesi leads almost immediately into Via dell'Orso, lined with the shops of artisans, cabinetmakers, and antiques restorers. It ends at Via dei Soldati; climb the short flight of street stairs in front of the Hostaria dell'Orso, which has been serving guests since the 15th century, to see a museum devoted to the Italian-based branch of the French emperor, the **Museo Napoleonico ❺**; inside, a group of salons conjure up all the red-velvet-crystal-chandelier charm of the 19th century. Highly conspicuous across the Tiber is the huge Palazzo di Giustizia (Court Building), a bombastic late-19th-century travertine marble monster.

Instead of heading south on heavily trafficked Via Zanardelli, go back down the street stairs and follow Via dei Soldati to **Palazzo Altemps** ❻, renovated a decade ago to house a famous collection of classical antiquities. Piazza Navona is just across Piazza Sant'Apollonia, but you can save it for later. Instead, head east, under the arch, to the church of **Sant'Agostino** ❼, which harbors a Caravaggio masterpiece. To see the most legendary Caravaggios, turn right on Via della Scrofa to reach Via della Dogana Vecchia and the church of **San Luigi dei Francesi** ❽—his three gigantic paintings devoted to the story of St. Matthew had the same effect on 17th-century art that Picasso's *Demoiselles d'Avignon* had on 20th-century painters. Continue south on Via della Dogana Vecchia to Piazza Sant'Eustachio, pausing to admire the bizarre pinnacle crowning the dome of Sant'Ivo alla Sapienza, which you can see from the piazza (the church's rear entrance is on the west side of Piazza Sant'Eustachio). Via del Salvatore skirts the flank of **Palazzo Madama** ❾, Italy's Senate building, and leads to Corso Rinascimento. Go left on Corso Rinascimento to number 40, where you can get a frontal view of the church of **Sant'Ivo alla Sapienza** ❿, considered the finest structure devised by Borromini, the second most famous Baroque architect after Bernini. The huge church looming at the end of Corso Rinascimento is **Sant'Andrea della Valle** ⓫, setting of the first act of *Tosca*. The slightly curved, columned facade on the north side of Corso Vittorio Emanuele is that of **Palazzo Massimo alle Colonne** ⓬, one of Rome's oldest patrician homes and still the residence of members of the Massimo family. On the south side of this major traffic artery is the **Museo Barracco** ⓭, a small collection of antiquities housed in a fine Renaissance building.

From Piazza San Pantaleo, Via della Cuccagna (Street of the Greased Pole, site of a favorite game) gives access to **Piazza Navona** ⓮, a celebrated 17th-century example of Baroque exuberance, with Bernini's **Fontana dei Quattro Fiumi** ⓯, or Fountain of the Four Rivers, as its centerpiece. This is easily Rome's most glorious piazza so be sure to grab a café table, order a gelato or lunch, and take in the spectacle. Flanking the piazza are **Palazzo Pamphilj** ⓰ and the church of **Sant'Agnese in Agone** ⓱, whose Borromini facade is considered the quintessence of Roman Baroque.

From the west side of Piazza Navona, enter Via di Tor Millina and turn right at pretty Piazza della Pace. Narrow alleys curve around either side of the church of **Santa Maria della Pace** ⓲, set on a tiny piazzina and one of the city's cutest streetscapes. They lead to Via dei Coronari (Street of the Rosary Makers, where craftsmen fashion rosaries and wreaths for sacred images, a flourishing business in papal Rome). In addition, this attractive street is lined with art galleries and antiques shops. About halfway along Via dei Coronari is large Piazza San Salvatore in Lauro and on it the church of **San Salvatore in Lauro** ⓳. Continue west along Via dei Coronari to Via di Panico. Turn right and follow Via di Panico to Ponte Sant'Angelo and a good frontal view of Castel Sant'Angelo.

Next, turn left, away from the river, onto Via del Banco di Santo Spirito. On the right-hand side of this byway is an arched passageway, the Arco dei Banchi, entrance to Renaissance financier Agostino Chigi's counting rooms. A marble inscription on the left pillar of the arch says that the street was often flooded by the Tiber, a problem finally solved in the late 1800s when embankments were put up along the course of the river. In the pretty little edifice on the corner of Via dei Banchi Nuovi, Rome's oldest bank, the Banco di Santo Spirito (Bank of the Holy Spirit, now Banca di Roma), has operated since the early 1600s.

Cross Largo Tassoni to the west side of Corso Vittorio, where both Via del Consolato and Via dei Cimatori lead to the graceful church of **San Giovanni dei Fiorentini** ⑳, on Piazza dell'Oro (Gold Square), once the heart of Renaissance Rome's gold district. The interior of the church seems lifted from one of Raphael's paintings—he once lived in this quarter—and is imbued with 16th-century grace. One of Old Rome's most stately and historic streets, **Via Giulia** ㉑—a Renaissance painting come to life—begins at the south end of Piazza dell'Oro. It's lined with regal palaces and opulent antiques shops.

Stroll down Via Giulia, almost to the end, and take a left onto Via dei Farnese, which flanks the magisterial **Palazzo Farnese** ㉒—once home to the hyperwealthy Farnese family, great Baroque art patrons—and leads to the piazza of the same name. On the south side of Piazza Farnese, Via Capo di Ferro leads to **Palazzo Spada** ㉓, which houses a superb collection of paintings in gilded 17th-century salons. From Piazza della Quercia take Via dei Balestrari or Vicolo delle Grotte east to **Campo de' Fiori** ㉔ (Field of Flowers), one of Rome's most colorful piazzas and home to the historic center's open-air market. North of Campo de' Fiori is the immense **Palazzo della Cancelleria** ㉕, headquarters of the Vatican's high court. Head northwest on Via del Pellegrino (the route pilgrims took to reach St. Peter's Basilica). Turn right onto Via Larga to reach busy Corso Vittorio Emanuele, dominated here by the huge **Santa Maria in Vallicella** ㉖ and the **Oratorio dei Filippini** ㉗. To return to Piazza Navona, go east on Via del Governo Vecchio. The street takes its name from the 15th-century Palazzo Nardini, at No. 39, once seat of Rome's papal governors and later a law court.

TIMING    Not a walk for a rainy day, this tour can, however, be interrupted and resumed again to suit your program and energy. To do the entire walk, spending about 40 minutes in Palazzo Altemps, would take about five hours, not counting breaks. But taking breaks is what this walk is all about: the route takes you past a plethora of piazzas to linger in and cafés where you can sit and take in the sights over coffee or a gelato. Campo de' Fiori is best seen on mornings Monday–Saturday, when it hosts a lively outdoor market.

## What to See

㉔ **Campo de' Fiori** (Field of Flowers). A bustling marketplace in the morning (Mon.–Sat. 8 AM–1 PM) and bohemian haunt the rest of the day (and night), this piazza has plenty of earthy charm. Except for the pizzerias and gelaterias, it looks much as it did in the early 1800s. Brooding over the piazza is a hooded statue of the philosopher Giordano Bruno, who was burned at the stake here in 1600 for heresy. His was the first of the executions that drew Roman crowds to Campo de' Fiori in the 17th century. Now the area is crowded with shops selling crafts and secondhand furniture. ⊠ *Junction of Via dei Baullari, Via Giubbonari, Via del Pellegrino, and Piazza della Cancelleria.*

▶ ★ ❶ **Il Gesù.** The mother church of the Jesuits in Rome is the prototype of all Counter-Reformation churches. Its architecture (the overall design was by Vignola, the facade by della Porta) influenced ecclesiastical building in Rome for more than a century and was exported by the Jesuits throughout Europe. Though consecrated in 1584, the church wasn't decorated inside for 100 years or more. It had been intended originally that the interior be left plain to the point of austerity—but, when it was finally embellished, no expense was spared. Its interior drips with gold and lapis lazuli, gold and precious marbles, gold and more gold, all covered by a fantastically painted ceiling by Baciccia. Unfortunately, the church is also one of Rome's most crespuscular, so its tone of visual magnificence is considerably dulled by lack of light.

The architectural significance of Il Gesù extends far beyond the splendid interior. The first of the great Counter-Reformation churches, it was put up after the Council of Trent (1545–63) had signaled the determination of the Roman Catholic Church to fight back against the Reformed Protestant heretics of northern Europe. The church decided to do so by using overwhelming pomp and majesty to woo believers. As a harbinger of ecclesiastical spectacle, Il Gesù spawned imitations throughout Italy and the other Catholic countries of Europe as well as the Americas.

The most striking element is the ceiling, covered with frescoes swirling down from on high to merge with the painted stucco figures at their base, the illusion of space in the two-dimensional painting becoming the reality of three dimensions in the sculpted figures. Baciccia, their painter, achieved extraordinary effects in these frescoes, especially in the *Triumph of the Holy Name of Jesus,* over the nave. Here, the figures representing evil cast out of heaven seem to be hurtling down onto the observer. Further grandeur is represented in the altar in the Chapel of St. Ignatius in the left-hand transept. This is surely the most sumptuous Baroque altar in Rome; as is typical, the enormous globe of lapis lazuli that crowns it is really only a shell of lapis over a stucco base—after all, Baroque decoration prides itself on achieving stunning effects and illusions. The heavy bronze altar rail by architect Carlo Fontana is in keeping with the surrounding opulence. ⊠ *Piazza del Gesù, off Via del Plebiscito, Piazza Venezia* ☎ *06/697001* ☉ *Daily 7–noon and 4–7.*

❸ **Museo Barracco.** This small but select museum offers a compact overview of sculpture from the ancient civilizations of the Mediterranean area, including Egyptian, Assyrian, and Greek works. The chronologically ordered collection is housed in a Renaissance building commissioned by a French prelate, a member of the papal court. Lilies—symbols of France—are prominent in the frieze circling the exterior. ⊠ *Corso Vittorio Emanuele II 166, Campo de' Fiori* ☎ *06/68806848* ⊕ *http://www2.*

*comune.roma.it/museobarracco* 🖾 *€2.50* ⓧ *Closed at least through 2005 for restoration.*

**❺ Museo Mario Praz.** On the top floor of the Palazzo Primoli—the same building (separate entrance) that houses the Museo Napoleonico—is one of Rome's most unusual museums. As if in amber, the apartment in which the famous Italian essayist Mario Praz lived is preserved intact, decorated with a lifetime's accumulation of delightful Baroque and Neoclassical art and antiques. As author of *The Romantic Sensibility* and *A History of Interior Decoration,* Praz was fabled for his taste for the arcane and the bizarre, although the apartment, prettily done up in Empire style, is a bit on the staid side. That noted, it's a rare chance to view a private Roman collection and no connoisseur will want to miss it. 🖾 *Via Zanardelli 1, Piazza Navona* ☎ *06/68806286* 🖾 *€2.60* ⓧ *Tues.–Sun. 9–7.*

**★ ❺ Museo Napoleonico.** Housed in an opulent collection of velvet-and-crystal salons that hauntingly capture the fragile charm of early-19th-century Rome, this small museum in the Palazzo Primoli contains a specialized and rich collection of Napoléon memorabilia, including a bust by Canova of the general's sister, Pauline Borghese (as well as a plaster cast of her left bust). You may well ask why this outpost of Napoléon in Rome but in 1809, the French emperor had made a grab for Rome, kidnapping Pope Pius VII in 1809 and proclaiming his young son the King of Rome. All came to naught a few years later, when the emperor was routed off his French throne. Upstairs is the Museo Mario Praz. 🖾 *Museo Napoleonico: Palazzo Primoli, Piazza di Ponte Umberto I, Piazza Navona* ☎ *06/ 68806286* ⓦ *www2.comune.roma.it/museonapoleonico* 🖾 *€2.58* ⓧ *Tues.–Sat. 9–7, Sun. 9–1:30.*

**㉗ Oratorio dei Filippini.** Housed in a Baroque masterwork by Borromini, this religious residence is named for Rome's favorite saint, Philip Neri, founder in 1551 of the Congregation of the Oratorians. Like the Jesuits, the Oratorians—or Filippini, as they were commonly known—were one of the new religious orders established in the mid-16th century as part of the Counter-Reformation. Under Neri's benign leadership, the Oratorians lived by a code of humility and good works. Neri, a man of rare charm and wit, insisted that the members of the order—most of them young noblemen whom he had recruited personally—not only renounce their worldly goods, but also work as common laborers in the building of Neri's great church of Santa Maria in Vallicella. The Oratory itself, headquarters of the order, was built by Borromini between 1637 and 1662. Its gently curving facade is typical of Borromini's insistence on introducing movement into everything he designed. 🖾 *Piazza della Chiesa Nuova (Corso Vittorio Emanuele), Piazza Navona* ☎ *06/6892537* ⓧ *Daily 8–noon.*

**❻ Palazzo Altemps.** Containing some of the finest ancient Roman statues
FodorśChoice in the world, this collection formerly formed the core of the Museo
★ Nazionale Romano. As of 1995, it was moved to these new, suitably grander digs. The palace's sober exterior belies a magnificence that appears as soon as you walk into the majestic courtyard, studded with statues and covered in part by a retractable awning. It's a reconstruction of a nicety used in many a patrician abode, a throwback to the type of

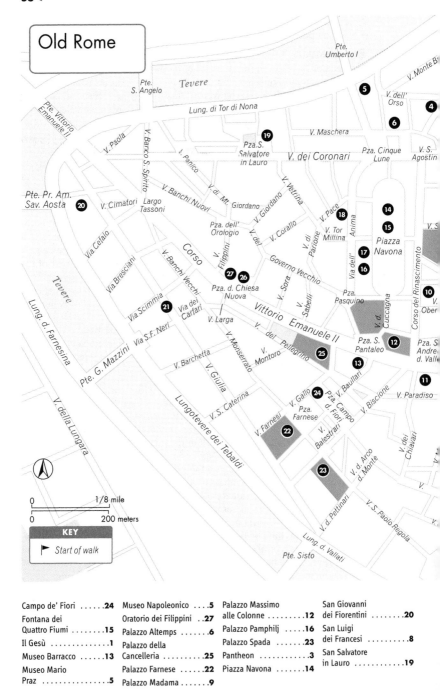

# Old Rome

Pte. Umberto I

Tevere

Pte. S. Angelo

V. Monte B

Lung. di Tor di Nona

V. dell' Orso

**5**

**4**

**6**

Pte. Vittorio Emanuele II

V. Paola

V. Barco S. Spirito

I. Panico

V. Maschera

Pza.S. Salvatore in Lauro

**19**

V. dei Coronari

Pza. Cinque Lune

V. S. Agostin

Pte. Pr. Am. Sav. Aosta

**20**

V. Cimatori

Largo Tassoni

V. Banchi Nuovi

V. di Mt. Giordano

V. Giordano

V. Vettina

V. Pace

V. Corallo

V. di Parione

V. Tor Millina

**18**

Anima

Via dell'

**14**

**15**

V. S

Via Cefalo

Pza. dell' Orologio

V. del

Corso

V. Filippini

V. Banchi Vecchi

Governo Vecchio

**17**

**16**

Piazza Navona

**10**

V. Ober

Via Bresciani

Tevere

Lung. d. Farnesina

Via Scimmia

**21**

Via dei Carfari

Pza. d. Chiesa Nuova

**27** **26**

V. Sora

V. Sabelli

Vittorio Emanuele II

Pza. Pasquino

Corso del Rinascimento

V. Cuccagna

Via S.F. Neri

V. Larga

V. del Pellegrino

Pza. S. Pantaleo

**12**

Pza. S Andre d. Vall

Pte. G. Mazzini

V. Barchetta

V. Monserrato

V. Montoro

**25**

**13**

**11**

V. della Lungara

Lungotevere dei Tebaldi

V. Giulia

V. S. Caterina

V. Gallo

**24**

Pza. v. Baullari

V. Biscione

V. Paradiso

V. dei Chiavari

Pza. Campo d. Fiori

V. Farnesi

**22**

Pza. Farnese

V. Balestrari

**23**

V. d. Arco d. Monte

V. d. Pettinari

V. S. Paolo Regola

V.

Lung. d. Vallati

Pte. Sisto

0 — 1/8 mile

0 — 200 meters

**KEY**

► Start of walk

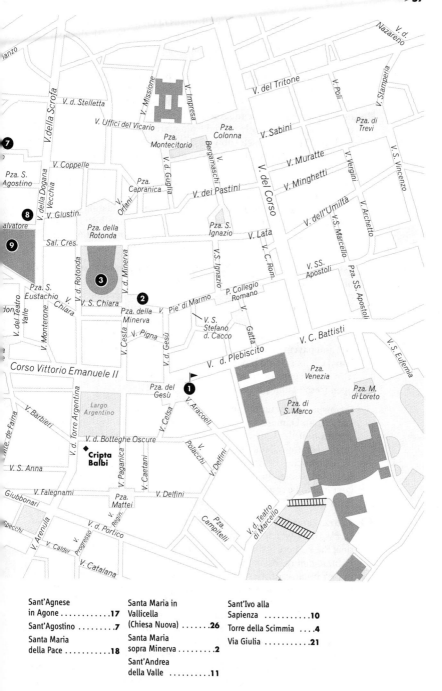

awning that shaded the ancient Romans in the Colosseum. The restored interior hints at the splendid Roman lifestyle of the 16th through 18th centuries and serves as a stunning showcase for the most illustrious pieces from the Museo Nazionale's collection of ancient Roman sculpture, which includes famous pieces from the Ludovisi family collection. In the frescoed salons you can see the *Galata,* a poignant work portraying a barbarian warrior who chooses death for himself and his wife rather than humiliation by the enemy. Another highlight is the large Ludovisi sarcophagus, magnificently carved from marble. In a place of honor is the Ludovisi Throne, which shows a goddess emerging from the sea being helped by her acolytes. For centuries this was heralded as one of the most sublime statues of Greek sculpture but, today, at least one authoritative art historian considers it a colossally overrated fake. Look for the framed explanations of the exhibits that detail (in English) how and exactly where Renaissance sculptors, Bernini among them, added missing pieces to the classical works. In the lavishly frescoed Loggia stand busts of the Caesars. ⊠ *Piazza Sant'Apollinare 46, Piazza Navona* ☎ *06/39967700* ⊕ *www.pierreci.it* ✍ *€5* ⊙ *Tues.–Sun. 9–7:45.*

**㉕ Palazzo della Cancelleria.** Occupying a massive site in a neighborhood of splendid palazzos, this is the largest and one of the most beautiful of the city's Renaissance palaces. It was built for a nephew of the Riario Pope Sixtus IV toward the end of the 15th century and reputedly paid for by the winnings of a single night's gambling. The Riario family symbol of the rose appears on the windows of the main floor and in the pillars and pavement of the courtyard. The palace houses the offices of the Papal Chancery and is part of the Vatican's extraterritorial possessions. You can step inside to see the courtyard; some salons are occasionally open to the public as concert venues.

Inconspicuously tucked into a corner of the palace, the church of **San Lorenzo in Damaso** was probably added by Bramante during the construction of the Cancelleria at the beginning of the 16th century. The original church of that name, on another part of the site, was one of the oldest churches of Rome, founded in the 4th century. When Napoléon occupied Rome, the 16th-century church was used as a law court and later had to be reconsecrated. ⊠ *Piazza della Cancelleria, off Corso Vittorio Emanuele II, Campo de' Fiori.*

**㉒ Palazzo Farnese.** Famous for the grandeur of its rooms, notably the Carracci gallery, which has the second greatest ceiling in Rome after the Sistine, the Farnese is the most beautiful Renaissance palace in Rome. The Farnese family rose to great power and wealth during the Renaissance, in part because of the favor Pope Alexander VI showed to the beautiful Giullia Farnese. The large palace was begun when, with Alexander's aid, Giullia's brother became cardinal; it was further enlarged on his election as Pope Paul III in 1534. The uppermost frieze decorations and main window overlooking the piazza are the work of Michelangelo, who also designed part of the courtyard, as well as the graceful arch over Via Giulia at the back. The facade on Piazza Farnese has recently been cleaned, further revealing geometrical brick configurations that have long been thought to hold some occult meaning. When looking up at the palace,

FodorśChoice
★

try to catch a glimpse of the splendid frescoed ceilings, including the **Galleria Carracci** vault painted by Annibale Carracci between 1597 and 1604. The Carracci gallery depicts the loves of the gods, a supremely pagan theme that the artist painted in a swirling style that announced the birth of the Baroque style. It's said that Carracci was so dismayed at the miserly fee he received—the Farnese family was extravagantly rich even by the standards of 15th- and 16th-century Rome's extravagantly rich—that he took to drink and died shortly thereafter. Those who sympathize with the poor man's fate will be further dismayed to learn that the French government pays one euro every 99 years as rent for their sumptuous embassy (actually, the Italian embassy has the same arrangement). Due to demand, the embassy now offers free tours (in French and Italian only) of their palace's historic rooms four times a week. You'll need to send a letter or e-mail to reserve tickets, specifying the number in your party, when you wish to visit, and a local phone number, for confirmation a few days before the visit. ⊠ *Servizio Culturale, French Embassy, Piazza Farnese 67* ☎ *06/6889–2818* ⊕ *ambafrance-it.org* ⊠ *Free* ☉ *Tours only, Mon. and Thurs., 4 and 5 PM.*

**❾ Palazzo Madama.** The handsome 17th-century palace is a onetime Medici residence, now seat of the Italian Senate. It is most admired for its Baroque facade, with exotic cornice and roof detail. ⊠ *Corso Rinascimento, Piazza Navona.*

**⓬ Palazzo Massimo alle Colonne.** A curving, columned portico identifies this otherwise inconspicuous palace on a traffic-swept bend of busy Corso Vittorio Emanuele. In the 1530s the noted Renaissance architect Baldassare Peruzzi adapted the structure of an earlier palace belonging to the Massimo family, transforming it to suit the clan's high rank in the papal aristocracy and its status as the oldest of Rome's noble families, older than even the Colonna and Orsini clans. If you're here on March 16, you'll be able to go upstairs in the palace, seeing the antique livery on the servants and the courtyard and loggias on your way to the family chapel. On this day the public is invited inside to take part in commemorations of a prodigious miracle performed here in 1583 by Philip Neri, who is said to have recalled a young member of the family, one Paolo Massimo, from the dead. ⊠ *Corso Vittorio Emanuele II 141, Piazza Navona.*

**⓰ Palazzo Pamphilj.** Not to be confused with the art-filled Doria Pamphilj palace on the Corso, this palazzo is adjacent to the family's church of Sant'Agnese on the Piazza Navona and now houses the Brazilian Embassy. Sometimes in the evening you can get a tantalizing glimpse of Pietro da Cortona's magnificent ceiling frescoes through the great illuminated windows of this palace. ⊠ *Piazza Navona 14.*

**★ ㉓ Palazzo Spada.** In this neighborhood of huge, austere palaces, Palazzo Spada strikes an almost frivolous note, with its upper stories covered with stuccos and statues and its pretty ornament-encrusted courtyard. The little garden gallery is a delightful example of the sort of architectural games rich Romans of the 17th century found irresistible. Even if you don't go into the gallery, step into the courtyard and look through the glass window of the library to the colonnaded corridor in the adjacent courtyard, which appears to stretch for a great distance with a large statue at the end. In fact the distance is an illusion: the corridor grows progressively narrower and the columns progressively smaller as they near the statue, which is just 2 feet tall. The illusion of depth multiplies the space by a factor of four. It was long thought that Borromini was responsible for this ruse; in fact it's now known that it was designed by an Augustinian priest, Giovanni Maria da Bitonto. Upstairs is a seignorial picture gallery, housed in period rooms. Outstanding works include Brueghel's *Landscape with Windmills,* Titian's *Musician,* and Andrea del Sarto's *Visitation.* ✉ *Piazza Capo di Ferro 13, Campo de' Fiori* ☎ *06/6832409* ⊕ *www.galleriaborghese.it* ✆ €5 ☉ *Tues.–Sun. 8:30–7:30.*

**❸ Pantheon.** This onetime pagan temple, a marvel of architectural harmony and proportion, is the best-preserved monument of imperial Rome. It was entirely rebuilt by the emperor Hadrian around AD 120 on the site of an earlier pantheon (from the Greek *pan,* all, and *theon,* gods) erected in 27 BC by Augustus's general Agrippa. The majestic circular building was actually designed *by* Hadrian, as were many of the temples, palaces, and lakes of his enormous villa outside the city at Tivoli. Hadrian nonetheless retained the inscription over the entrance from the original building that named Agrippa as the builder, in the process causing enormous confusion among historians until, in 1892, a French architect discovered that all the bricks used in the Pantheon dated from Hadrian's time.

*Fodor'sChoice* ★

The most striking thing about the Pantheon is not its size, immense though it is (until 1960 the dome was the largest ever built), nor even the phenomenal technical difficulties posed by so vast a construction; rather, it's the remarkable unity of the building. You don't have to look far to find the reason for this harmony: the diameter described by the dome is exactly equal to its height. It's the use of such simple mathematical balance that gives classical architecture its characteristic sense of proportion and its nobility and timeless appeal. The great opening at the apex of the dome, the oculus, is nearly 30 feet in diameter and was the temple's only source of light. It was intended to symbolize the "all-seeing eye of heaven."

The Pantheon is by far the best preserved of the major monuments of imperial Rome, a condition that is the result of it being consecrated as a church in AD 608. No building, church or not, escaped some degree of plundering through the turbulent centuries of Rome's history after the fall of the empire. In 655, for example, the gilded bronze covering the dome was stripped. Similarly, in the early 17th century, Pope Urban VIII removed the bronze beams of the portico, using the metal to produce the baldacchino (canopy) that covers the high altar at St. Peter's Basilica. Most of its interior marble facing has also been stripped and replaced over the centuries. Nonetheless, the Pantheon suffered less than many other structures from ancient Rome.

The Pantheon serves as one of the city's important burial places. Its most famous tomb is that of Raphael (between the second and third chapels on the left as you enter). The inscription reads "Here lies Raphael; while he lived, mother Nature feared to be outdone; and when he died, she feared to die with him." Two of Italy's 19th-century kings are buried here, too: Vittorio Emanuele II and Umberto I. The tomb of the former was partly made from bronze that had been taken from the Pantheon by Urban VIII to cast as cannon. Thankfully, the temple's original bronze doors have remained intact for more than 1,800 years. Be sure to ponder them as you leave. ⊠ *Piazza della Rotonda* ☎ *06/68300230* 🖃 *Free* ☽ *Mon.–Sat. 8:30–7:30, Sun. 9–6.*

**need a break?**

On Via degli Orfani, on the east side of Piazza del Pantheon, the **Tazza d'Oro** coffee bar (no tables, no frills) is the place for serious coffee drinkers, who also indulge in *granita di caffè con panna* (coffee ice with whipped cream). The Pantheon area is ice-cream heaven, with some of Rome's best gelaterias within a few steps of each other. Romans consider **Giolitti** (⊠ Via Uffizi del Vicario 40 ☎ 06/6991243) superlative; the scene at the counter often looks like the storming of the Bastille. Remember to pay the cashier first, and hand the stub to the counterperson when you order your cone. Giolitti has a good snack counter, also.

**⑭ Piazza Navona.** Here everything that makes Rome unique is compressed

**Fodor'sChoice** into one beautiful Baroque piazza. It has antiquity, Bernini sculptures,

★ three gorgeous fountains, a magnificently Baroque church (Sant'Agnese in Agone) and, above all, the excitement of people out to enjoy themselves—strolling, café-loafing, seeing, and being seen. Piazza Navona has been an entertainment venue for Romans down through the centuries. It stands over the ruins of Domitian's circus; you can see a section of the ancient arena's walls by walking out of the long end of the piazza (toward Piazza Sant'Apollinare) and taking a quick left. The square still has the carefree air of the days when it was the scene of Roman circus games, medieval jousts, and 17th-century carnivals. Even now it's the site of a lively Christmas fair and the place where revelers gather for many other entertainment events throughout the year.

**⑮** Piazza Navona still looks much as it did during the 17th and 18th centuries, after the Pamphili pope Innocent X decided to make it over into a monument to the Pamphili family that would rival the Barberini's palace at the Quattro Fontane. The piazza's most famous work of art, planted right in the center, is the **Fontana dei Quattro Fiumi**, created for Innocent X by Bernini in 1651. The obelisk rising out of the fountain, a Roman copy, had stood in the Circo di Massenzio on Via Appia Antica. Bernini's powerful figures of the four rivers represent the four corners of the world: the Nile; the Ganges; the Danube; and the Plata, with its hand raised. One story has it that the figure of the Nile—the figure closest to Santa' Agnese in Agone—is hiding its head because it can't bear to look upon the church's "inferior" Borromini facade; in fact, the facade was built after the fountain, and the statue hides its head because it represents a river whose source was unknown until relatively recently.

One of Rome's most spectacular settings, the piazza is often the venue for glamorous televised fashion events but most of the time the square is simply Rome's most popular place to meet, have ice cream and coffee, take the children and dogs for a walk, and watch the passing parade. The piazza still looks much as it did during the 17th and 18th centuries. The piazza dozes in the morning, when small groups of pensioners sun themselves on stone benches and children pedal tricycles around the big fountain. In the late afternoon, the sidewalk cafés fill up for the aperitif hour. In the evening, especially in good weather, Piazza Navona comes to life with a colorful throng of vendors, street artists, tourists, and Romans out for their evening *passeggiata* (promenade). Life is a piazza, no? ⊠ *Junction of Via della Cuccagna, Corsia Agonale, Via di Sant'Agnese, and Via Agonale.*

**need a break?**  The sidewalk tables of the **Tre Scalini** (⊠ Piazza Navona 30 ☎ 06/6879148) café offer a grandstand view of the piazza and the action. This is the place that invented the *tartufo,* a luscious chocolate ice-cream specialty. The restaurant-pizzeria annex (the menu features Pizza Navona) has the same view.

★ ⑳ **San Giovanni dei Fiorentini.** Imbued with the supreme grace of the Florentine Renaissance, this totally overlooked church dedicated to Florence's patron saint, John the Baptist, stands in what was the heart of the Florentine colony in Old Rome. Many of these Florentines were goldsmiths, bankers, and money-changers who contributed to the building of the church. Talented goldsmith and sculptor Benvenuto Cellini of Florence, known for his vindictive nature as much as for his genius, lived nearby. While the church was designed by Sansovino, Raphael (yes, he was also an architect) was among those who competed for this commission. Today, the church interior makes you feel you have wandered inside a perfect Renaissance space, one so harmonious it seems to be a Raphael pop-up 3-D painting. Borromini executed a splendid altar for the Falconieri family chapel in the choir. He's buried under the dome, despite the fact that those who committed suicide normally were refused a Christian burial. The animal-loving pastor allows well-behaved pets to keep their owners company at services. ⊠ *Via Accaioli 2 (Piazza dell'Oro), Vatican* ☎ *06/68892059* ⊙ *Daily 9–1 and 4–7.*

⑧ **San Luigi dei Francesi.** A pilgrimage spot for art lovers everywhere, San Luigi is home to the Cerasi Chapel, adorned with three stunningly dramatic works by Caravaggio (1571–1610), the Baroque master of the heightened approach to light and dark. Set in the Chapel of St. Matthew (at the altar end of the left nave), they were commissioned for San Luigi, the official church of Rome's French colony (San Luigi is St. Louis, patron of France). The inevitable coin machine will light up his *Calling of St. Matthew, Matthew and the Angel,* and *Matthew's Martyrdom,* seen from left to right, and Caravaggio's mastery of light takes it from there. When painted, they caused considerable consternation to the clergy of San Luigi, who thought the artist's dramatically realistic approach was scandalously disrespectful. A first version of the altarpiece was rejected; the priests were not particularly happy with the other two,

**Fodor's**Choice
★

either. Time has fully vindicated Caravaggio's patron, Cardinal Francesco del Monte, who secured the commission for these works and stoutly defended them. They're now recognized to be among the world's greatest paintings. ⊠ *Piazza San Luigi dei Francesi, Piazza Navona* ☎ *06/ 688271* ⊘ *Daily 8:30–12:30, Fri.–Wed. also 3:30–5.*

**⑲ San Salvatore in Lauro.** Outside and in, this church looks more Venetian than Roman. It was designed along the lines of models by the Venetian architect Palladio. If the church is not open, ring the bell at number 15 for admission to the interior and to the charming little 15th-century cloister that is now used by a civic association. ⊠ *Piazza San Salvatore in Lauro 15, Piazza Navona* ☎ *06/6875187* ⊘ *Daily 8–12:30 and 3:30–7:30.*

**★ ⑰ Sant'Agnese in Agone.** The absolute quintessence of Baroque architecture, this church has a facade that remains a wonderfully rich melange of bell towers, concave spaces, and dovetailed stone and marble, the creation of Francesco Borromini (1599–1667), a contemporary and rival of Bernini. Built by the regal Doria-Pamphili family and the family pope, Innocent X, the church bears a name that comes from *agona,* the source of the word *navona* and a corruption of the Latin *agonalis,* describing the type of games held there in Roman times. The saint associated with the church is Agnes, who was martyred here in the piazza's forerunner, the Stadium of Domitian. As she was stripped nude before the crowd, hair miraculously grew to maintain her modesty before she was killed. The interior is a marvel of modular Barqoue space and is ornamented by giant marble reliefs sculpted by Raggi and Ferrata. ⊠ *Piazza Navona* ☎ *06/68192134* ⊘ *Tues.–Sun. 8–noon and 4–7.*

**❼ Sant'Agostino.** Caravaggio's celebrated *Madonna of the Pilgrims*—which scandalized all of Rome because a kneeling pilgrim is pictured, all too realistically for the taste of the time, with dirt on the soles of his feet, and the Madonna stands in a less than majestic pose in a dilapidated doorway—is in the first chapel on the left. In a niche just inside the door of the church is Sansovino's sculpted *Madonna and Child,* known to the Romans as the Madonna del Parto (of Childbirth) and piled high with ex-votos. Above it looms a prophet painted by Raphael. ⊠ *Piazza Sant'Agostino, Piazza Navona* ☎ *06/68801962* ⊘ *Daily 8–noon and 4–7:30.*

**⑱ Santa Maria della Pace.** In 1656, Pietro da Cortona (1596–1669) was
FodorsChoice commissioned by Pope Alexander VII to enlarge the tiny Piazza della
★ Pace in front of the 15th-century church of Santa Maria (to accommodate the carriages of its wealthy parishioners). His architectural solution was to design a new church facade complete with semicircular portico, demolish a few buildings here and there to create a more spacious approach to the church, add arches to give architectural unity to the piazza, and then complete it with a series of bijou-size palaces. The result was one of Rome's most delightful little architectural stage sets. Within the church are two great Renaissance treasures: Raphael's fresco of the Sibyls above the first altar on your right, and the fine decorations of the Cesi Chapel, second on the right, designed in the mid-16th century by Sangallo. Behind the church proper is its cloister, designed by Bramante (architect of St. Peter's) as the very first expression of High Renaissance

style in Rome. The church is usually closed but if you take the alleylike Vicolo along the left-hand side of the church and ring the bell at the first entryway on the right, the nuns will usually permit you to enter. At times, the cloister is the venue for modern art shows and, thanks to the Caffè alla Pace, the little piazza has become the core of a trendy café scene. ⊠ *Via Arco della Pace 5, Piazza Navona* ☎ *06/6861156.*

**㉖ Santa Maria in Vallicella.** This church, also known as Chiesa Nuova (New Church), was built toward the end of the 16th century at the urging of Philip Neri, and like Il Gesù is a product of the fervor of the Counter-Reformation. It has a sturdy baroque interior, all white and gold, with ceiling frescoes by Pietro da Cortona and three magnificent altarpieces by Rubens. An enormous statue of Mary is in the sacristy. ⊠ *Piazza della Chiesa Nuova, Corso Vittorio Emanuele II, Piazza Navona* ☎ *06/ 6875289* ⊙ *Daily 8–noon and 4:30–7.*

**❷ Santa Maria sopra Minerva.** The name of the church reveals that it was built *sopra* (over) the ruins of a temple of Minerva, ancient goddess of wisdom. Erected in 1280 by the Dominicans on severe Italian Gothic lines, it has undergone a number of more or less happy restorations to the interior. Certainly, as the city's major Gothic church, it provides a refreshing contrast to Baroque flamboyance. Have some coins handy to illuminate the **Cappella Carafa** in the right transept, where Filippino Lippi's (1457–1504) glowing 15th-century frescoes are well worth the small investment. Under the main altar is the tomb of St. Catherine of Siena, one of Italy's patron saints. Left of the altar you'll find Michelangelo's *Risen Christ* and the tomb of the gentle artist Fra Angelico, behind a modern sculptured bronze screen. Bernini's unusual and little-known monument to the Blessed Maria Raggi is on the fifth pier from the door on the left as you leave the church. In front of the church, the little obelisk-bearing elephant carved by Bernini is perhaps the city's most charming sculpture. An inscription on the base makes reference to the church's ancient patroness, reading something to the effect that it takes a strong mind to sustain solid wisdom. ⊠ *Piazza della Minerva, Piazza Navona* ☎ *06/6793926* ⊙ *Daily 7:30–7.*

**⓫ Sant'Andrea della Valle.** Topped by the highest dome in Rome (designed by Maderno) after St. Peter's, this huge and imposing 17th-century church is remarkably balanced in design. Note the early-17th-century frescoes in the choir vault by Domenichino and those by Lanfranco in the dome, one of the earliest ceilings in full Baroque style. Richly marbled and decorated chapels flank the nave, and in such a space, Puccini set the first act of *Tosca.* Puccini lovers have been known to hire a horse-drawn carriage at night for an evocative journey that traces the course of the opera: from Sant'Andrea up Via Giulia to Palazzo Farnese— Scarpia's headquarters—to the locale of the opera's climax, Castel Sant'Angelo. ⊠ *Piazza Vidoni 6, Corso Vittorio Emanuele II, Piazza Navona* ☎ *06/6861339* ⊙ *Daily 7:30–12:30 and 4:30–8.*

**❿ Sant'Ivo alla Sapienza.** The main facade of this eccentric Baroque church, probably Borromini's best, is on the stately courtyard of an austere building that once housed Rome's university. Sant'Ivo has what must surely be one of the most delightful domes in all of Rome—a golden spiral said to have been inspired by a bee's stinger. The bee symbol is a reminder that Borromini built the church on commission from the Barberini Pope Urban VIII (a swarm of bees figure on the Barberini family crest). The interior, open only for two hours on Sunday, is worth a look, especially if you share Borromini's taste for complex mathematical architectural idiosyncrasies. ⊠ *Corso Rinascimento 40, another entrance is off Piazza Sant'Eustachio, Piazza Navona* ☎ *06/6864987* ☉ *Sun. 10–noon.*

❹ **Torre della Scimmia** (Monkey Tower). The medieval tower atop the building that stands at the junction of Via dei Portoghesi with Via dei Pianellari figures in a chapter in the lore of Old Rome. In the building, so the story goes, a pet monkey ran amok one day, seizing a baby and carrying it to the top of the tower. Here the crazed animal seemed about to dash the child to the street below. A crowd of neighbors and bystanders invoked the Madonna's intercession, and the monkey carefully descended, carrying the baby to safety. In gratitude, the father placed a statue of the Madonna on the tower, along with a vigil light, both of them still neighborhood landmarks. The building is not open to the public. ⊠ *Via dei Portoghesi, Piazza Navona.*

㉑ **Via Giulia.** Still a Renaissance-era diorama and one of Rome's most exclusive addresses, Via Giulia was the first street since ancient times to be laid out in a straight line. Named for Pope Julius II (of Sistine Chapel fame) who commissioned it in the early 1500s as part of a scheme to open up a grandiose approach to St. Peter's Basilica (using funds from the taxation of prostitutes), it became flanked with elegant churches and palaces. Though the pope's plans to change the face of the city were only partially completed, Via Giulia became an important thoroughfare in Renaissance Rome. Today, after more than four centuries, it remains the "salon of Rome," address of choice for Roman aristocrats. A stroll will reveal elegant palaces and old churches (one, **San Eligio,** at No. 18, reputedly designed by Raphael himself). The area around Via Giulia is a wonderful section to wander through and get the feel of daily life as carried on in a centuries-old setting. Among the buildings that merit your attention are **Palazzo Sacchetti** (⊠ Via Giulia 66), with an imposing stone portal (inside are some of Rome's grandest state rooms, still, after 300 years, the private quarters of the Marchesi Sacchetti), and the forbidding brick building that housed the **Carceri Nuove** (New Prison; ⊠ Via Giulia 52), Rome's prison for more than two centuries. Near the bridge that arches over the southern end of Via Giulia is the church of **Santa Maria dell'Orazione e Morte** (Holy Mary of Prayer and Death), with stone skulls on its door. These are a symbol of a confraternity that was charged with burying the bodies of the unidentified dead found in the city streets. Best viewed from around the block along the Tiber embankment, the **Palazzo Falconieri** (⊠ Via Giulia 1) was designed by Borromini—note the architect's roof-top belvedere adorned with statues of the family "falcons." Remnant of a masterplan by Michelangelo, the arch over the street was meant to link massive Palazzo Farnese, on the east side of Via Giulia, with the building across the street and a bridge to the Villa Farnesina, directly across the river. ⊠ *Between Piazza dell'Oro and Piazza San Vincenzo Pallotti, Campo de' Fiori.*

**Fodor's Choice**
★

# VISTAS AND VIEWS: FROM PIAZZA VENEZIA TO THE SPANISH STEPS

The scenic-hungry traveler will delight in this area, which covers one of the city's most varied and historic districts. It begins at Piazza Venezia, the square in front of the elaborate marble confection that is the monument to Vittorio Emanuele II, and heads up the Corso, one of the busiest shopping streets in the city. Along the way you'll see stately palaces, Baroque ballrooms, and the greatest example of portraiture in Rome, Velázquez's incomparable Innocent X. Those with a taste for the sumptuous theatricality of Roman ecclesiastical architecture, and in particular, for heroic illusionistic ceiling painting, will find this a rewarding area. But for most, the highlights will be the Trevi Fountains and the Scalinata di Trinità dei Monti (a.k.a. the Spanish Steps), 18th-century Rome's most famous example of city planning.

*Numbers in the text and margin correspond to points of interest on the Piazza Venezia to the Spanish Steps map.*

a good walk

Begin at **Piazza Venezia** ❶ ⌐, the square in front of the elaborate marble mountain that is the **Monumento a Vittorio Emanuele II** ❷, sometimes jokingly referred to as "the eighth hill of Rome." On the west side of the piazza is **Palazzo Venezia** ❸, a grand palace Mussolini once requisitioned and whose balcony he liked to strut about on. It was built for Pope Paul II, who totally renovated the facade of the adjacent church of **San Marco** ❹, on Piazza San Marco on the south side of the palace. From Piazza Venezia, head north on Via del Corso, making sure to walk on the right-hand side of the street so that you can get a good view of the attractive facade of **Palazzo Doria Pamphilj** ❺, one of Rome's grandest palaces. The entrance to its sumptuous art gallery and state apartments is on Piazza del Collegio Romano. After a look at its priceless Old Master paintings and a peek at how an aristocratic family once lived (or lives—one occupant is the current prince), take Via di Sant'Ignazio to the enchanting 18th-century Rococo Piazza di Sant'Ignazio, designed by architect Raguzzini as if it were a stage set. But then, of course, theatricality was a key element of almost all the best Baroque and Rococo art. Nowhere is this more evident than in the hyperopulent church of **Sant'Ignazio** ❻, where the ceiling frescoes hold a surprise or two.

Behind the "stage set," Via del Burrò leads to Piazza di Pietra, where the onetime Rome Stock Exchange is set inside the columns of an ancient temple. From here it's just a few steps along Via dei Bergamaschi to Piazza Colonna, named for the celebrated **Colonna di Marco Aurelio** ❼ (Column of Marcus Aurelius) at its center. North of the column, Palazzo Chigi, a 16th- and 17th-century building, serves as the seat of the prime minister. Next door is **Palazzo Montecitorio** ❽, where the Chamber of Deputies (lower house) of the Italian Parliament meets.

Just off Via del Tritone is little **Santa Maria in Via** ❾, where the well water in the church is said to have miraculous powers. Across Via del Tritone,

# THREE COINS & A TRITON

A NYONE WHO'S THROWN A COIN backward over his or her shoulder into the Fontana di Trevi to ensure a return to Rome appreciates the magic of the city's fountains. From the magnificence of the Fontana dei Quattro Fiumi in Piazza Navona to the graceful caprice of the Fontana delle Tartarughe in the Ghetto, the water-spouting sculptures seem as essential to the piazzas they inhabit as the cobblestones and ocher buildings that surround them.

Rome's original fountains date back to ancient times, when they were part of the city's remarkable aqueduct system, but from AD 537 to 1562 the waterworks were in disrepair and the city's fountains lay dry and crumbling—Romans were left to draw their water from the Tiber and from wells. During the Renaissance, the popes brought running water back to the city as a means of currying political favor.

To mark the restoration of the Virgin Aqueduct, architect Giacomo della Porta designed 18 unassuming, functional fountains, each consisting of a large basin with two or three levels of smaller basins in the center, which were built and placed throughout the city at points along the water line. Although nearly all of della Porta's fountains remain, their spare Renaissance design is virtually unrecognizable, because most were elaborately redecorated with dolphins, obelisks, and sea monsters, in the flamboyant style of the Baroque.

Of this next generation of Baroque fountaineers, the most famous is Gian Lorenzo Bernini. Bernini's writhing, muscular creatures of myth adorn most of Rome's most visible fountains, including the Fontana di Trevi (so named for the three streets—tre vie—that converge at its

piazza); the Fontana del Nettuno, with its tritons, in Piazza Barberini; and, in Piazza Navona, the Fontana dei Quattro Fiumi, whose hulking figures represent the four great rivers of the known world: the Nile, the Ganges, the Danube, and the Rio de la Plata.

The most common type of fountain in Rome is a kind rarely noted by visitors: the small, inconspicuous drinking fountains that burble away from side-street walls, old stone niches, and fire hydrant–like installations on street corners. You can drink this water—many of these fontanelle even have pipes fitted with a little hole from which water shoots up when you hold your hand under the main spout. To combine the glorious Roman fountain with a drink of water, head to Piazza di Spagna, where the Barcaccia fountain (designed by Pietro Bernini, Gian Lorenzo's father) is outfitted with spouts from which you can wet your whistle.

Anita Ekberg and Marcello Mastroianni made cinematic history with their midnight dip in the Fontana di Trevi in the Fellini classic La Dolce Vita. On hot summer nights—and days—the temptation to follow in their soggy footsteps can be almost unbearable. Be forewarned: police guard the fountain 24 hours a day to keep out movie buffs and lovebirds alike, and transgressors risk a fine of up to €500. Far safer, and cheaper, is to emulate Dorothy McGuire, Jean Peters, and Maggie McNamara in Three Coins in the Fountain—your Roman fountain fantasy will cost no more than the change in your pocket, and who knows? Your wish might come true.

a busy thoroughfare that climbs to Piazza Barberini and Via Veneto, Piazza San Silvestro is a hub of public transportation and location of the main post office. It's also on the edge of a shopping district that has few equals elsewhere in the world. From Via del Tritone on the south to Piazza del Popolo on the north, from the Tiber on the west to Villa Borghese on the east, this is a fabulous trove of specialty shops and boutiques offering all types of fashions, jewelry, household goods, and anything else you might want—including the well-maintained restroom facilities in the Rinascente department store, which occupies the block at the corner of Via del Corso and Largo Chigi. You can detour in and out of the area's narrow byways as your fancy takes you, attracted by handsome window displays.

At some point, head north on Via del Corso again to Piazza San Lorenzo in Lucina to see the Bernini works in **San Lorenzo in Lucina** ❿ and perhaps linger in one of the fashionable cafés on this pretty square. At the west end of the piazza, take Via del Leone to Largo Fontanella Borghese to see the portal of the grandiose **Palazzo Borghese** ⓫ and browse at the stalls selling old books and prints around the corner in airy Piazza della Fontanella Borghese, where you can get an even better idea of the palace's size. Follow Via della Fontanella Borghese, lined with smart shops, to Largo Goldoni, site of an information kiosk.

From Largo Goldoni you enter Via Condotti and get a head-on view of that post-card icon, the **Piazza di Spagna** ⓬ and the church of **Trinità dei Monti** ⓭, which are connected by the Spanish Steps. Enjoy the great views atop the steps but don't forget to debouch slightly to the right from Piazza Trinità dei Monti onto posh Via Gregoriana to discover that amazing Mannerist-era mastework, the **Palazzetto Zuccari** ⓮, configured to look like a face. Back down the steps on Via Condotti you can get from Bulgari to Gucci to Valentino to Ferragamo with no effort at all, except perhaps that of navigating the crowds. On weekend and holiday afternoons the square, along with Via del Corso and neighboring streets, is packed with teenagers out for a mass stroll. They perch on the steps and around Bernini's low-lying **Fontana della Barcaccia** ⓯ in the middle of the piazza. To the right of the Spanish Steps, the **Keats–Shelley House** ⓰ gives you an idea of how England's Romantic poets lived in what was then Rome's bohemian quarter. Two doors down is **Casa Museo G. De Chirico** ⓱, the house and studio of the Metaphysical painter Giorgio De Chirico (1888–1978), now a museum. The column at the far end of the piazza, adjacent to the American Express office, supports a statue dedicated to the Immaculate Conception. Each December 8, a crack unit of the Rome Fire Department sends one of its best men up a ladder to replace the garland crowning the Madonna, and the pope usually stops by in the afternoon to pay his respects. Just in front of the column stands **Palazzo di Propaganda Fide** ⓲, brain center of the far-flung missionary activities of the Jesuits.

Follow Via di Propaganda to the church of **Sant'Andrea delle Fratte** ⓳, a sumptuous Baroque concoction, where you can pause under the orange trees in the cloister. From Via Sant'Andrea delle Fratte, turn left onto Via del Nazareno and cross busy Via del Tritone to Via della Stamperia. On the right-hand side of Via della Stamperia is **Palazzo Poli** ⑳, which houses the Calcografia dello Stato. A few paces beyond is the old building in which the **Accademia di San Luca** ㉑, with a gallery of Old Masters, is located. As you near the end of Via della Stamperia, you can probably hear the sound of **Fontana di Trevi** ㉒ (Trevi Fountain), a Baroque extravaganza of sculpture and cascading waters. From the fountain, Via Lucchesi leads you to Piazza della Pilotta and Via della Pilotta, where ornate bridges overhead connect **Palazzo Colonna** ㉓—site of Rome's most spectacular ballroom—with the Colonna family's gardens on the slope of the Quirinal Hill. The west side of the palace is flanked by the church of **Santi Apostoli** ㉔. On the ceiling, the early-18th-century artist Baciccia painted one of his swooping, swirling illusionist frescoes. Opposite the church is another of Rome's splendid patrician palaces, 17th-century Palazzo Odescalchi, used as a model for aristocratic palaces throughout Europe.

TIMING    Not counting shopping, this walk could take from 3½ to 5 hours, allowing for visits to the galleries and for a few coffee or ice-cream breaks. It certainly should be done on days when the shops are open, even if you're only window-shopping. Though the Palazzo Doria Pamphilj is open most days of the week, the Galleria in Palazzo Colonna is open only on Saturday morning.

## What to See

㉑ **Accademia di San Luca.** Founded by a group of painters in the 1400s, this private academy of the arts is housed in 16th-century Palazzo Carpegna. Its gallery is open to the public (though currently closed for restoration) and contains some fine Renaissance paintings, including a charming putto by Raphael as well as his *Madonna of St. Luke.* ⊠ *Piazza dell'Accademia di San Luca 77, Piazza di Trevi* ☎ *06/6798850* 🎟 *Free* ⊙ *Closed indefinitely for restoration.*

⑰ **Casa Museo G. De Chirico.** This small museum was the home of Italian surrealist artist Giorgio De Chirico (1888–1978) while he lived with his second wife, Isa. It's been kept as it was when De Chirico lived and worked here, and displays about 70 oil paintings in a range of styles, plus various sculptures by the artist. The second-floor studio gives a frozen-in-time glimpse of one of Italy's great modern artists at work. Call ahead to book a tour in English, available at no extra charge. ⊠ *Piazza di Spagna 31* ☎ *06/6796546* 🎟 *€5* ⊙ *Weekdays 10–1.*

❼ **Colonna di Marco Aurelio** (Column of Marcus Aurelius). Inspired by Trajan's Column, this 2nd-century AD column is composed of 27 blocks of marble covered with a series of reliefs recording Marcus Aurelius's victory over the Germans. At the top is a bronze statue of St. Paul, which replaced the effigy of Marcus Aurelius in the 16th century. The column is the centerpiece of Piazza Colonna. ⊠ *Piazza Colonna, Piazza di Trevi.*

❶❺ **Fontana della Barcaccia** (Leaky Boat Fountain). At the center of Piazza di Spagna and at the bottom of the Spanish Steps, this curious, half-sunken boat gently spills out water rather than cascading it dramatically into the air; it may have been designed that way to make the most of the area's low water pressure. It was thanks to the Barberini pope Urban

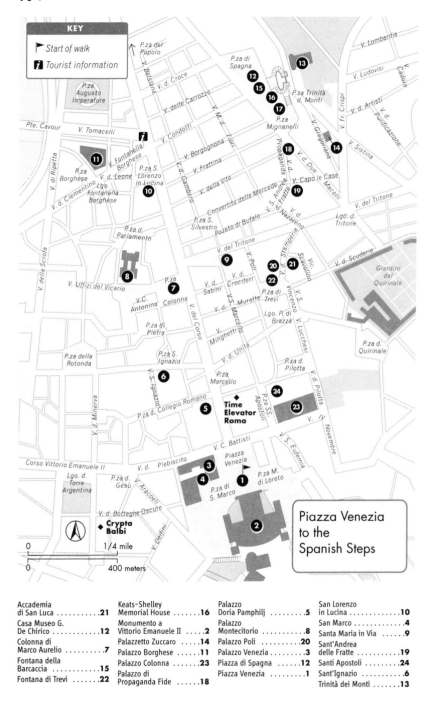

Piazza Venezia
to the
Spanish Steps

VIII, who commissioned the fountain, that there was any water at all in this area, which was becoming increasingly built up during the 17th century. He restored one of the ancient Roman aqueducts that once channeled water here. The bees and suns on the boat constitute the Barberini motif. Some insist that the Berninis (Pietro and his more famous son Gian Lorenzo) intended the fountain to be a reminder that this part of town was often flooded by the Tiber; others that it represents the Ship of the Church; and still others that it marks the presumed site of the emperor Domitian's water stadium in which sea battles were reenacted in the glory days of the Roman Empire. ⊠ *Piazza di Spagna.*

**need a break?** You may prefer to limit your shopping on Via Condotti to the window variety, but there's one thing here that everybody can afford—a stand-up coffee at the bar at the **Antico Caffè Greco** (⊠ Via Condotti 86, Piazza di Spagna ☎ 06/6791700), set just off the Piazza di Spagna and the Fontana della Barcaccia. With its tiny marble-top tables and velour settees, this 200-year-old institution has long been the haunt of artists and literati; it's closed Sunday. Johann Wolfgang van Goethe, Byron, and Franz Liszt were habitués; Buffalo Bill stopped in when his road show hit Rome. It's still a haven for writers and artists, and for ladies carrying Gucci shopping bags. The tab picks up considerably if you decide to sit down to enjoy table service.

**㉒** **Fontana di Trevi** (Trevi Fountain). Alive with rushing waters and marble
Fodor'sChoice sea creatures commanded by an imperious Oceanus, this aquatic mar-
★ vel is one of the city's most exciting sights. The work of Nicola Salvi— though it's thought that Bernini may have been responsible for parts of the design—was completed in 1762 and is a perfect example of the Rococo taste for dramatic theatrical effects. The water comes from the Acqua Vergine aqueduct, and is so called because of the legend that it was a young girl, a *vergine,* who showed its source to thirsty Roman soldiers. The story is pictured in the relief on the right of the figure of Oceanus. Usually thickly fringed with tourists tossing coins into the basin to ensure their return to Rome (the fountain grosses about €120,000 a year, most of it donated to charity), the fountain took center stage for Anita Ekberg's famous dip in *La Dolce Vita.* Unfortunately, the fountain is turned off during the wee hours and occasionally at other times for cleaning. If that's the case when you arrive, make a point of returning another day to see it in full gush. Some connoisseurs rue the day when the urban authorities cleaned the fountain off for the 2000 Holy Year celebrations and managed to wash off two centuries of golden, glorious patina almost overnight. ⊠ *Piazza di Trevi.*

**need a break?** **Gelateria San Crispino** (⊠ Via della Panetteria 42, Piazza di Trevi ☎ 06/6793924), closed Tuesday, has won the hearts of Rome's gelato fans. Flavors are true to life, thanks to the use of only natural ingredients.

**⓰** **Keats–Shelley House.** To help fight off the effect of consumption, the English Romantic poet John Keats lived here in what was the colorful bohemian quarter of 18th- and 19th-century Rome, especially favored by the English. Keats had become celebrated through such poems as "Ode to a Nightingale" and "She Walks in Beauty" but his trip to Rome was for naught, for he died here on February 23, 1821, aged only 25, forevermore the epitome of the doomed poet. In this "Casina di Keats," you can visit his rooms, which have been preserved as they were when he died here in 1821. Little is left of his furnishings (not that he had many) but they contain a rather quaint collection of memorabilia of English literary figures of the period—Lord Byron, Percy Bysshe Shelley, Joseph Severn, and Leigh Hunt as well as Keats—and an exhaustive library of works on the Romantics. For total immersion, inquire about the house's apartment for rent (three days to six months). ⊠ *Piazza di Spagna 26, next to Spanish Steps* ☎ *06/6784235* ⊕ *www.keats-shelley-house.org* ⌑ *€3* ⊗ *Weekdays 9–1 and 3–6, Sat. 11–2 and 3–6.*

**②** **Monumento a Vittorio Emanuele II, or Altare della Patria** (Victor Emmanuel Monument, or Altar of the Nation). The huge white mass of the "Vittoriano" is an inescapable landmark—Romans say you can avoid seeing it only if you're standing on it. Some have likened it to a huge wedding cake; others, to an immense typewriter. Though not held in the highest esteem by present-day citizens, it was the source of great civic pride at the time of its construction at the turn of the 20th century. To create this elaborate marble monster and the vast piazza on which it stands, architects blithely destroyed many ancient and medieval buildings and altered the slope of the Capitoline Hill, which abuts it. Built to honor the unification of Italy and the nation's first king, Victor Emmanuel II, it also shelters the eternal flame at the tomb of Italy's Unknown Soldier, guarded day and night by sentinels, and the (rather dry) Institute of the History of the Risorgimento—relics of the struggle for the unification of Italy in the 19th century.

The views from the top are unforgettable—some of Rome's best. Before you climb up, stop at the museum entrance to get a pamphlet identifying the sculpture groups on the monument and the landmarks you see from the top. Opposite the monument, note the enclosed wooden veranda fronting the palace on the corner of Via del Plebiscito and Via Corso. For the many years that she lived in Rome, Napoléon's mother had a fine view from here of the local goings-on. ⊠ *Entrance at Piazza Ara Coeli, next to Piazza Venezia* ☎ *06/6991718* ⊕ *www.ambienterm. arti.beniculturali.it/vittoriano/index.html* ⌑ *Monument free, museum €5* ⊗ *Daily 9:30–5:30.*

**⑭** **Palazzetto Zuccaro.** Shaped to form a monster's face and the most amus-
FodorśChoice ing house in all of Italy, this Mannerist-era folly was designed in 1591
★ by noted painter Federico Zuccaro (1540–1609), whose home this was. Typical of the outré style of the period, the eyes are the house's windows; the entrance portal is through the monster's mouth (this is one of the best photo-ops in Rome—have someone photograph you standing in front of the door with your own mouth gaping wide). Zuccaro—whose frescoes adorn many Roman churches, including Trinità del Monti just up the block—sank all of his money into this bizarre creation, dying in debt before his curious memorial, as it turned out to be,

was completed. Today, it is the property of the Biblioteca Hertziana, Rome's prestigous fine arts library. Leading up to the quaint Piazza Trinità del Monti, Via Gregoriana is a real charmer and has long been one of Rome's most elegant addresses, with residents ranging from French 19th-century painters Ingres and David to famed couturier Valentino. ✉ *Via Gregoriana 30.*

**⓫ Palazzo Borghese.** One of the princely palaces of Rome's aristocratic families, this is a huge, rambling Renaissance building that goes on for blocks and has several portals. Nicknamed *il cembalo*—"the harpsichord"—for its shape, the palace was begun in 1590 for a Spanish cardinal by architect Martino Longhi, who designed the sturdy facade facing Largo Fontanella Borghese. In 1605 Cardinal Borghese celebrated his election as Pope Paul V by purchasing the palace; it later passed to his nephew, Cardinal Scipione Borghese, who assembled his magnificent art collection here. Still used by the Borghese family, though part of it is rented out to the Circolo Romano della Caccia, a private club for Rome's nobles, the palace is closed to the public. You can get as far as the gate inside the main portal on Largo Fontanella Borghese to take a peek at the splendid double courtyard. ✉ *Largo Fontanella Borghese, Piazza di Spagna.*

**㉓ Palazzo Colonna.** Rome's grandest family built itself Rome's grandest FodorśChoice palazzo in the 18th century—it's so immense, it faces Piazza Santi Apos-★ toli on one side and the Quirinal Hill on the other (a little bridge over Via della Pilotta links the palace with the gardens on the hill). While still home to some Colonna patricians, the palace also holds the family picture gallery, open to the public one day a week. The galleria is itself a setting of aristocratic grandeur; you'll recognize the **Sala Grande** as the site where Audrey Hepburn meets the press in *Roman Holiday.* At one end looms the ancient red marble column (*colonna* in Italian), which is the family's emblem; above the vast room is the spectacular ceiling fresco of the Battle of Lepanto painted by Giovanni Coli and Filippo Gherardi in 1675—the center scene almost puts the computer-generated special effects of Hollywood to shame. Adding redundant luster to the opulently stuccoed and frescoed salons are works by Poussin, Tintoretto, and Veronese, and a number of portraits of illustrious members of the family such as Vittoria Colonna—Michelangelo's muse and longtime friend— and Marcantonio Colonna, who led the papal forces in the great naval victory at Lepanto in 1577. ✉ *Via della Pilotta 17, Piazza di Trevi* ☎ *06/6784350* ⊕ *www.galleriacolonna.it* ✉ *€7* ☉ *Sept.–July, Sat. 9–1; free guided tour in English with reservation.*

**⓲ Palazzo di Propaganda Fide** (Palace of the Propagation of the Faith). Jesuit missionary activity is headquartered here. Bernini created the simpler facade on the piazza in 1644; his archrival Borromini designed the more elaborate one on Via di Propaganda not long before his death in 1667. ✉ *Piazza di Spagna 48.*

**❺ Palazzo Doria Pamphilj.** Along with the Palazzo Colonna and the Galle- FodorśChoice ria Borghese, this family palace provides the best glimpse of aristocratic ★ Rome. Here, the main attractions are the legendary Old Master paintings, including treasures by Velázquez and Caravaggio, the splendor of the main galleries, and a unique suite of private family apartments. The beauty of the graceful 18th-century facade of this patrician palace may escape you unless you take time to step to the opposite side of the street for a good view; it was designed by Gabriele Valvassori in 1730. The foundations of the immense complex of buildings probably date from classical times. The current building dates from the 15th century, with the exception of the facade. It passed through several hands before it became the property of the famous seafaring Doria family of Genoa, who had married into the Roman Pamphilj (also spelled Pamphili) clan. As in most of Rome's older patrician residences, the family still lives in part of the palace but rents out some of its 1,000 rooms, five courtyards, and four monumental staircases to various public and private enterprises.

The picture gallery is housed in four *braccia* (wings) that line the palace's courtyard. The first large salon is nearly wallpapered with paintings, and not just any paintings: on one wall, you'll find no less than three pictures by Caravaggio, including his *Magdalen* and his breathtaking early *Rest on the Flight to Egypt*. Off the glittering centerpiece of the palazzo, the **Galleria degli Specchi** (Gallery of Mirrors), set like the family jewels that they are in an alcove, are the famous Velázquez portrait and the Bernini bust of the Pamphiji pope Innocent X. You'll also find a Titian and some noted 17th-century landscapes by Claude Lorrain and Gaspar Dughet. The guided tour of the **private apartments** includes a Baroque chapel, a ballroom, and three authentically furnished 18th-century salons, as well as other art treasures, including an *Annunciation* by Filippo Lippi, a family portrait by Lotto, and a stately portrait of Andrea Doria by Sebastiano del Piombo. While these private rooms are special in themselves, they can't compete—little could—with the great painting galleries of the family collection. ⊠ *Piazza del Collegio Romano 2, Near Piazza Venezia* ☎ *06/6797323* ⊕ *www.doriapamphilj.it* ⊠ *Galleria Doria Pamphilj* €7.30, *includes audio guide* ⊘ *Fri.–Wed. 10–5.*

**⑧ Palazzo Montecitorio** (Italian Parliament). The Chamber of Deputies, the lower house of the Italian Parliament, meets in this huge palace. The main facade on Piazza Montecitorio was designed by Bernini and is adorned with a 6th-century BC Egyptian obelisk. ⊠ *Piazza Montecitorio, Piazza Navona* ☎ *06/67601* ⊠ *Free* ⊘ *1st Sun. of month 10–5:30.*

**⑳ Palazzo Poli.** The palazzo is home to the Calcografia dello Stato (National Graphics Institute). Together with similar institutes in Paris and Madrid, the Calcografia preserves the world's most important collections of copper engraving plates by artists from the 1500s to the present. There's an exhibition space on the ground floor, where samples of its historic treasures and contemporary work may be on display. The collection includes invaluable antique presses and more than 1,400 engraving plates by 18th-century Roman artist Piranesi. ⊠ *Via della Stamperia 6, Piazza di Trevi* ☎ *06/699801* ⊠ *Free* ⊘ *Daily 9–1.*

**❸ Palazzo Venezia.** Centerpiece of Palazzo Venezia, this palace was originally built for Venetian cardinal Pietro Barbo, who became Pope Paul II. It was also the backdrop used by Mussolini to harangue crowds with dreams of empire from the balcony over the main portal. The palace shows a mixture of Renaissance grace and heavy medieval lines, and today houses an eclectic collection of decorative objects, paintings, sculptures, and ceramics in handsome salons, some of which Mussolini used as his offices. Lights were left on all night during Mussolini's reign, to suggest that the Fascist regime worked without pause. Important temporary exhibitions are often held here. The café on the loggia has a pleasant view over the garden courtyard. ⊠ *Piazza San Marco 49, Piazza Venezia* ☎ *06/69994319* ☞ *€4* ⊗ *Tues.–Sun. 9–7.*

☾ ⓬  **Piazza di Spagna** (Spanish Steps). Those icons of postcard Rome, the Span-
**Fodor's**Choice   ish Steps, and the piazza from which they ascend both get their names
★   from the Spanish Embassy to the Vatican on the piazza, opposite the American Express office—in spite of the fact that the staircase was built with French funds in 1723. In an allusion to the church of Trinità dei Monti at the top of the hill, the staircase is divided by three landings (beautifully banked with azaleas from mid-April to mid-May). For centuries, the Scalinata ("staircase," as natives refer to the Spanish Steps) has always welcomed tourists: 18th-century dukes and duchesses on their Grand Tour, 19th-century artists and writers in search of inspiration— among them Stendhal, Honoré de Balzac, William Makepeace Thackeray, and Byron—and today's enthusiastic hordes. Bookending the bottom of the steps are two monuments to the 18th-century days when the English colonized the area: to the right, the Keats-Shelley House, to the left, Babington's Tea Rooms, both beautifully redolent of the Grand Tour era. ⊠ *Junction of Via Condotti, Via del Babuino, and Via Due Macelli.*

---

**need a break?**

On the left at the foot of the Spanish Steps is **Babington's Tea Rooms,** (⊠ Piazza di Spagna 23 ☎ 06/6786027), which has catered to the refined cravings of Anglo-Saxon travelers since its establishment by two genteel English ladies in 1896. The "Inglesi" had long been a mainstay of Grand Tour visitors to Rome so Anna Maria Babington found her "corner of England" a great sucess from the start. Inside, it is as charming as all get-out and you half expect to see Miss Lavish buttering a scone for Lucy Honeychurch, but it's not a budgeteer's cup of tea. At weekday lunches, you're likely to find yourself next to a Bulgari, Fendi, or Agnelli. During the winter months, the fireplace makes this place (closed Monday) *molto* cozy.

---

▶ ❶  **Piazza Venezia.** The geographic heart of Rome, this is the spot from which all distances from Rome are calculated, and the principal crossroads of city traffic. Piazza Venezia stands at what was the beginning of Via Flaminia, the ancient Roman road that leads east across Italy to Fano on the Adriatic Sea. Via Flaminia was, and still is, a vital artery. The initial tract of Via Flaminia, from Piazza Venezia to Piazza del Popolo, is now known as the Corso (Via del Corso, one of the busiest shopping streets in the city), after the horse races (*corse*) that were run here during the wild Roman carnival celebrations of the 17th and 18th centuries. The podium near the beginning of the Corso is the sometime domain of Rome's most practiced traffic policemen, whose imperious gestures and imperative whistles are a spectacle not to be missed. The massive female bust, a fragment of antiquity near the church of San Marco in the corner of the piazza, is known to the Romans as Madama Lucrezia. It was one of the "talking statues" on which anonymous poets hung verses pungent with political satire, a practice that has not entirely disappeared. ⊠ *Junction of Via del Corso, Via Plebiscito, and Via Cesare Battisti.*

**⑩ San Lorenzo in Lucina.** This church was probably founded on the site of an early Christian meeting place under the aegis of a Roman matron named Lucina, whose name was added to that of St. Lorenzo (Lawrence) to distinguish it from other churches dedicated to him. Behind its 12th-century portico and campanile (bell tower), the interior is not especially interesting. There's one exception, however: the **Cappella Fonseca** (Fonseca Chapel), the fourth on the right, was designed by Bernini. ⊠ *Piazza San Lorenzo in Lucina, Piazza di Spagna* ☎ *06/6871494* ⊘ *Daily 8–noon and 4–8.*

**④ San Marco.** Venetian pope Paul II used this ancient church, next door to the palace where he resided, for official ceremonies. Tradition relates that St. Mark wrote his gospel in Rome, and the church is dedicated to the evangelist, as well as to the 4th-century Pope Mark, whose relics are under the main altar. One of many Roman churches built as a basilica, the original edifice was destroyed by fire and replaced in the 6th century. The third church, the one you see today, was built in the 9th century by Pope Gregory IV, as the dedication in the Byzantine apse mosaics testifies.

The church is a perfect example of Rome's layering of history, of periods and styles built up one upon another. From the early Christian architectural motifs to the Romanesque bell tower, from the Byzantine mosaics to the windows in the nave, nearly 1,500 years of architectural styles are represented here. There's the full flowering of Renaissance and Baroque styles in the magnificent gilt ceiling and the ample portico that Pope Paul II built to provide shelter for himself and his retinue during outdoor rites in bad weather. On the right wall of the portico is the tombstone of Vannozza Cattanei. The mistress of the Borgia pope Alexander VI, she bore him three children, including the infamous Lucrezia and Cesare. ⊠ *Piazza San Marco, off Piazza Venezia* ☎ *06/6795205* ⊘ *Daily 7:30–1 and 4–7.*

**⑨ Santa Maria in Via.** This small 16th-century church is like many others, except for one well-kept secret—under the foundations hides a bona fide natural spring, out of which bubbles purportedly curative water you can drink in the chapel on the right. In addition to mineral water, it's claimed the spring once brought forth the icon of the Madonna that's now over the altar. ⊠ *Via del Mortaro 24 (Via del Tritone), Piazza di Trevi* ☎ *06/6976741* ⊘ *Daily 8–1 and 4–8.*

**⑲ Sant'Andrea delle Fratte.** On either side of the choir in this floridly Baroque church are the two original angels that Bernini himself carved for the Ponte Sant'Angelo, where copies now stand. The door in the right aisle leads into one of Rome's hidden gardens, where orange trees bloom in the cloister. Borromini's fantastic contributions—the dome and a curious bell tower—are best seen from Via Capo le Case, across Via Due Macelli. ⊠ *Via Sant'Andrea delle Fratte 1 (Via della Mercede), Piazza di Spagna* ☎ *06/6793191* ⊘ *Daily 6:15–12:30 and 4–7.*

**㉔ Santi Apostoli.** The Basilica of the Holy Apostles is a mixture of architectural styles, the result of successive restorations of an ancient church. The grandiose ceiling fresco by Baciccia, who did an even grander one for the Jesuits at Il Gesù, celebrates the founding of the Franciscan Order. One of the church's best features is the lovely double portico on the facade, dating from the 15th century. The church is often the scene of the weddings and funerals of Rome's aristocracy, and the piazza frequently serves as a gathering place for heated political rallies and demonstrations. ⊠ *Piazza SS. Apostoli, Piazza Venezia* ☎ *06/59602716* ⊙ *Open only for mass: Mon.–Sat. 8 AM, 9 AM, and 6 PM, Sun. 8:30 AM, 11 AM, and 6 PM.*

**➏ Sant'Ignazio.** This 17th-century church harbors some of the most magnificent illusions typical of the Baroque style. To get the full effect of the marvelous illusionistic ceiling by priest-artist Andrea Pozzo, stand on the small disk set into the floor of the nave. The heavenly vision above you, seemingly extending upward almost indefinitely, represents the *Glory of St. Ignatius Loyola* and is part of Pozzo's cycle of works in this church exalting the early history of the Jesuit Order, whose founder was the reformer Ignatius of Loyola. The artist repeated this illusionist technique, so popular in the late 17th century, in the false dome, which is actually a flat canvas. The overall effect of the frescoes is dazzling (be sure to have coins handy for the machine that switches on the lights) and was fully intended to rival that produced by Baciccia in the nearby church of Il Gesù. Scattered around the nave note the awe-inspiring altars—soaring columns, gold-on-gold decoration, and gigantic statues make these the last word in splendor. The church is often host to concerts of sacred music performed by choirs from all over the world; look for posters at the church doors for more information. ⊠ *Piazza Sant'Ignazio, Piazza Venezia* ☎ *06/6794406* ⊙ *Daily 7:30–12:30 and 4–7:15.*

FodorsChoice
★

**⓭ Trinità dei Monti.** Standing high above the Spanish Steps, this church is beautiful not so much in itself but for its dramatic location and magnificent views. It's occasionally used as a concert venue. ⊠ *Piazza Trinità dei Monti, Piazza di Spagna* ☎ *06/6794179* ⊙ *Daily 8–8.*

# GO FOR BAROQUE: FROM THE QUIRINALE TO THE PIAZZA DELLA REPUBBLICA

Although this section takes you from ancient Roman sculptures to early Christian churches, it's mainly an excursion into the most Roman of styles—the Baroque, which triumphed in the 16th and 17th centuries. Spiritual excitement and intensity, theatrically presented, were to become the dominant themes in these centuries' art—most obviously in Bernini's chapel in Santa Maria della Vittoria, where members of the Cornaro family look out from their boxes at an ethereal vision of the ecstasy of St. Theresa. Along the way, other highlights include some of Rome's key Baroque buildings, notably the churches of Sant'Andrea del Quirinale, San Carlo alle Quattro Fontane, and the imposing Palazzo Barberini.

Around many of these older monuments, however, a newer Rome had sprung up—the area owes its broad avenues and dignified palazzi to the city's transformation after 1870, when it became the capital of a newly unified Italy. The influx of ministries set off a frenzied building boom and distinguished turn-of-the-20th-century architecture became the neighborhood's hallmark. Piazza della Repubblica was laid out to serve as a monumental foyer between the rail station and the rest of the city. After World War II the old Termini Station was replaced with a then-daring modern structure, and the huge Piazza dei Cinquecento was laid out in front of it.

*Numbers in the text and margin correspond to points of interest on the Quirinale to Piazza della Repubblica map.*

**a good walk**

Begin your walk at **Piazza del Quirinale ❶** ▶, studded with major Baroque sights. The square marks the summit of the Quirinal Hill, highest of the seven hills of Rome. The front of the largest palace on the plaza, **Palazzo del Quirinale ❷** (easily identified by the sentinels at the portal), is quite plain, though it houses the president of Italy. Make a brief detour onto Via XXIV Maggio, which links Piazza del Quirinale with Via Nazionale. On the right, a double ramp of stairs and an ornate stone portal mark the entrance to the gardens of Villa Colonna (closed to the public), domain of the Colonna family, whose palazzo is at the foot of the hill, on Piazza Santi Apostoli. Opposite, on the east side of Via XXIV Maggio, **Palazzo Pallavicini-Rospigliosi ❸** belongs to another of Rome's aristocratic clans.

Take Via del Quirinale, on the right of the presidential palace. The featureless, 1,188-foot-long wing of the palace on the left side of the street hides the Quirinale gardens (open to the public on June 2 only). On the right is Bernini's favorite architectural creation, the church of **Sant'Andrea al Quirinale ❹**. Borromini's perfectly proportioned church of **San Carlo alle Quattro Fontane ❺** stands at the end of Via del Quirinale, at the **Quattro Fontane ❻** intersection.

Turn northwest, or left, onto Via Quattro Fontane, where the **Galleria Nazionale d'Arte Antica/Palazzo Barberini ❼** (National Gallery of Historic Art) stands about halfway down the hill. This grandest of 17th-century Rome's stately palaces was decorated with illusionist frescoes by Pietro da Cortona. Downhill from the palace (turn right when you leave) you'll come upon frantic **Piazza Barberini ❽**, a handy starting point for exploring the 19th-century Ludovisi district and Via Veneto. On the east corner of Via Veneto, the tree-lined, uphill avenue at the north end of the piazza, is the **Fontana delle Api ❾** (Fountain of the Bees), attributed in part to Bernini. Walk uphill into the sedate lower reaches of Via Veneto. At the church of **Santa Maria della Concezione ❿**, thousands of bones are on morbidly artistic display, a reminder of the impermanence of earthly life. The broad avenue curves up the hill past travel agencies and hotels, with a sidewalk café or two where the only clients seem to be tired tourists and bank employees. At the intersection with Via Bissolati, the pace picks up. The big white palace on the right is **Palazzo Margherita ⓫**, built in 1890 as the residence of Italy's Queen Margherita. It's now the U.S. Embassy.

Turn right and follow Via Bissolati to the end and cross Largo Santa Susanna to the intersection with Via XX Settembre. On Piazza San Bernardo, the Baroque church of **Santa Susanna** ⑫ is Rome's American Catholic church. On the northeast corner of Via XX Settembre, the **Fontanone dell'Acqua Felice** ⑬ (Fountain of Happy Water) smugly spouting lions. On the northwest corner, the church of **Santa Maria della Vittoria** ⑭ harbors Bernini's surprisingly earthy interpretation of a mystical vision. At this point you can elect to make a detour to the early Christian churches of Sant'Agnese and Santa Costanza, 3 km (2 mi) northeast of here, beyond the old city walls. You can walk to **Porta Pia** ⑮ and then take a taxi or the bus, or take one directly from Via Vittorio Emanuele Orlando. As you walk or ride northeast along Via Nomentana, you'll hit Via Reggio Emilia, where Rome's new **MACRO** ⑯ contemporary art museum is. Continue on Nomentana to pass through some of Rome's pleasant residential suburbs and **Villa Torlonia** ⑰, a public park, on the right; inside the park is the Casina delle Civette, decorated with Art Nouveau stained glass.

Return to Piazza della Repubblica (Bus 60 stops near the church of Santa Maria della Vittoria) by way of Via Vittorio Emanuele Orlando, passing the historic Grand Hotel and the **Aula Ottagonale** ⑱ (Octagonal Hall), on the corner of Via Parigi. In **Piazza della Repubblica** ⑲, two Neoclassical exedrae (semicircular recesses) stand over similar, ancient exedrae that were part of the Baths of Diocletian. A simple cross high on stark brick walls identifies the church of **Santa Maria degli Angeli** ⑳, once the great hall of the Roman baths. You can see how parts of the ancient bath complex were adapted to serve as a monastery as you visit the halls and cloister of the **Terme di Diocleziano** ㉑, a section of the Museo Nazionale Romano. Off the southeast end of Piazza della Repubblica, Via delle Terme di Diocleziano leads to **Palazzo Massimo alle Terme** ㉒, where you'll see more of the fabulous antiquities that make up the Museo Nazionale Romano's collections.

TIMING    This is a long walk, involving some major museums and a lengthy detour to the church of Sant'Agnese. If the length of your stay in Rome permits, break it up into two shorter walks. The walk from Piazza del Quirinale to Piazza della Repubblica, not counting the detour to Sant'Agnese, takes about two hours, plus 10–15 minutes for every church visited, and at least 90 minutes each for visits to the Galleria Nazionale d'Arte Antica in Palazzo Barberini and the section of the Museo Nazionale Romano in Palazzo Massimo alle Terme.

## What to See

⑱ **Aula Ottagonale** (Octagonal Hall). Once part of the Terme di Diocleziano, this eight-sided hall had a twin on what is now the middle of Viale Einaudi, the street leading toward Termini Station. The hall was once used as a planetarium and now serves as a display space for several well-preserved Roman-era bronze sculptures. ⌧ *Via Romita, Piazza della Repubblica, Termini* ☎ *06/39967700* ⌦ *Free* ☉ *Daily 10–7.*

⑨ **Fontana delle Api** (Fountain of the Bees). Decorated with the famous heraldic bees of the Barberini family, the upper shell and the inscription

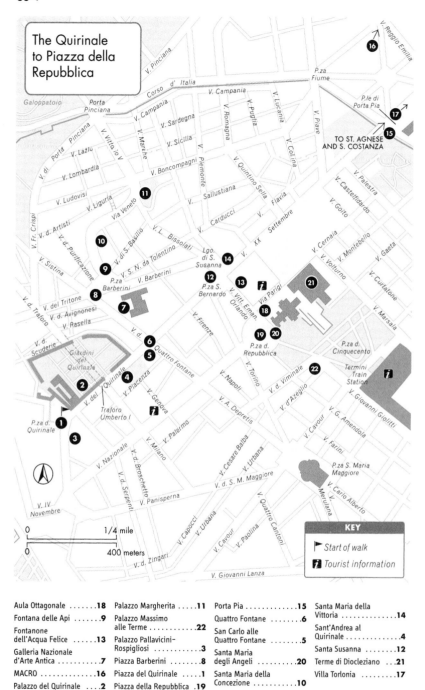

# The Quirinale to Piazza della Repubblica

**KEY**

▶ Start of walk

🛈 Tourist information

are from a fountain that Bernini designed for Pope Urban VIII; the rest was lost when the fountain had to be moved to make way for a new street. This inscription was the cause of a considerable scandal when the fountain was first put up in 1644. It said that the fountain had been erected in the 22nd year of the pontiff's reign, although in fact the 21st anniversary of Urban's election to the papacy was still some weeks away. The last numeral was hurriedly erased, but to no avail—Urban died eight days before the beginning of his 22nd year as pope. The superstitious Romans, who had immediately recognized the inscription as a foolhardy tempting of fate, were vindicated. ⊠ *Via Veneto at Piazza Barberini.*

**need a break?** Along Via degli Avignonesi and Via Rasella (both narrow streets off Via delle Quattro Fontane, opposite Palazzo Barberini) there are some good, moderately priced trattorias. One of the most popular with Romans is **Gioia Mia** (⊠ Via degli Avignonesi 34, Via Veneto ☎ 06/4882784); it's closed Wednesday.

**⑬ Fontanone dell'Acqua Felice** (Fountain of Happy Water). When Pope Sixtus V completed the restoration of the Acqua Felice aqueduct toward the end of the 16th century, Domenico Fontana was commissioned to design this commemorative fountain. As the story goes, a sculptor named Prospero da Brescia had the unhappy task of executing the central figure, which was to represent Moses (Sixtus liked to think of himself as, like Moses, having provided water for his thirsting population). The comparison with Michelangelo's magnificent *Moses* in the church of San Pietro in Vincoli was inevitable, and the largely disparaging criticism of Prospero's work is said to have driven him to his grave. Perhaps the most charming aspects of the fountain are the smug little lions spewing water in the foreground. ⊠ *Piazza San Bernardo, Quirinale.*

**★ ❼ Galleria Nazionale d'Arte Antica/Palazzo Barberini.** The city's noted collection of paintings from the 13th to the 18th century is installed in one of Rome's grandest palaces, the Palazzo Barberini. Both Bernini and Borromini worked on this massive building, but its overall plan was produced by Carlo Maderno. Pope Urban VIII had acquired the property and given it to a nephew, who was determined to build an edifice worthy of his generous uncle and the ever-more-powerful Barberini clan. You'll get an idea of the grandeur of the place as you visit the museum.

Entering the palace, you climb a broad marble staircase designed by Bernini. On the main floor (keep your ticket handy, because you'll have to show it again upstairs) you'll find several magnificent paintings, including Raphael's *Fornarina*, a luminous portrait of the artist's lover, cleaned and restored to reveal a jeweled ring and a bracelet on her upper arm bearing Raphael's name. A dramatic Caravaggio depicts a lovely young Judith wearing an expression of defiance and horror as she severs the head of Holofernes. There's a Holbein portrait of Henry VIII in the finery he donned for his wedding to Anne of Cleves in 1540, and two small but striking El Grecos. The showstopper here is the palace's **Gran Salone**, a vast ballroom whose ceiling was decorated in the 1630s by Pietro da Cortona. His *Glorification of Urban VIII's Reign* is a spectacular and sur-prisingly early example of the Baroque practice of glorifying patrons by depicting them on ceilings as part of the heavenly host. In this case, Pope Urban VIII appears as the agent of Divine Providence, who is being crowned by Immortality and escorted by a "bomber squadron"—to quote art historian Sir Michael Levey—of some huge Barberini bees, the heraldic symbol of the family. Upstairs you'll find an array of 17th- and 18th-century paintings, including some pretty little views of Rome by Van-vitelli, and four handsome Canalettos. Don't miss the stunning suite of rooms redecorated in 1728 for the marriage of a Barberini heiress to a scion of the Colonna family. ✉ *Via Barberini 18, Via Veneto* ☎ *06/32810* ⊕ *www.galleriaborghese.it* ✑ *€6* ✆ *Tues.–Sun. 9–7.*

**⑯ MACRO.** Formerly known as Rome's Modern and Contemporary Art Gallery, and before that formerly known as the Peroni beer factory, this redesigned industrial space has brought new life to the gallery and mu-seum scene of a city formerly known for its then, not its now. The col-lection here covers Italian contemporary artists from the 1960s through today. Its sister museum, **MACRO al Mattatoio** (✉ Piazza O. Giustiniani) is housed in a renovated slaughterhouse in the up-and-coming Testac-cio district, and features temporary exhibits and installations by cur-rent artists, open until midnight, with free admission. The goal of both spaces is to bring current art to the public in nontraditional museum spaces, and, not incidentally, to give support and recognition to Rome's contemporary art scene, which labors in the shadow of the city's artis-tic heritage. After a few days—or millennia—of dusty marble, it's a breath of fresh air. ✉ *Via Reggio Emilia 54, Termini* ☎ *06/671070400* ⊕ *www.macro.roma.museum* ✑ *€1* ✆ *Tues.–Sun. 9–7.*

**★ ❷ Palazzo del Quirinale.** For centuries home of the popes, now official res-idence of the president of Italy, this spectacular palace was begun in 1574 by Pope Gregory XIII, who planned to use it as a summer residence, choosing the hilltop site mainly for the superb view. However, as early as 1592 Pope Clement VIII decided to make the palace the permanent home of the papacy, at a safe elevation above the malarial miasmas shroud-ing the low-lying Vatican. It remained the official papal residence until 1870, in the process undergoing a series of enlargements and alter-ations by a succession of architects. When Italian troops under Garibaldi stormed the city in 1870, making it the capital of the newly united Italy, the popes moved back to the Vatican and the Quirinale became the of-ficial residence of the kings of Italy. When the Italian people voted out the monarchy in 1946, the Quirinal Palace passed to the presidency of the Italian Republic.

You get a fair idea of the palace's splendor from the size of the building, especially the interminable flank of the palace on Via del Quirinale. Seen on tour, the state reception rooms are some of Italy's most majestic. Be-hind this wall are the palace gardens, which, like the gardens of Villa d'Este in Tivoli, were laid out by Cardinal Ippolito d'Este when he summered here. At 4 PM daily you can see the changing of the military guard, and occasionally you can glimpse the *corazzieri* (presidential guard). All extra-tall, they are a stirring sight in their magnificent crimson-and-blue uniforms, their knee-high boots glistening, and their embossed steel helmets adorned with flowing manes. ⊠ *Piazza del Quirinale* ☎ *06/46991* ⊕ *www.quirinale.it* 🎟 *€5* ⊙ *Sept.–July, Sun. 8:30–noon.*

⓫ **Palazzo Margherita.** Built in 1890 as the residence of Italy's Queen Margherita, the white building is now the U.S. Embassy. American citizens on routine business (including replacing lost passports) are directed to the consulate building next door. The embassy and consulate are part of a heavily guarded complex that includes U.S. Information Service offices and the American Library. ⊠ *Via Veneto 119* ☎ *06/46741.*

★ ㉒ **Palazzo Massimo alle Terme** (Museo Nazionale Romano). The enormous collections of the Roman National Museum—which range from striking classical Roman sculptures and paintings to marble bric-a-brac and fragments picked up in excavations over the centuries—have been organized in four locations: Palazzo Massimo alle Terme, Palazzo Altemps, Aula Ottagona, and the Terme di Diocleziano. The vast structure of the Palazzo Massimo alle Terme holds the archaeological collection and the coin collection. Highlights include the *Niobid*, a masterpiece from the 5th century BC as well as the Roman marble of the *Discobolus Lancelloti*. Pride of place goes, however, to the great ancient frescoes on view. These include decorative stuccos and wall paintings found in the area of the Villa della Farnesina (in Trastevere) and the legendary frescoes from Empress Livia's villa at Prima Porta, delightful depictions of a garden in bloom and an orchard alive with birds. Their colors are remarkably well preserved. These delicate decorations covered the walls of cool, sunken rooms in Livia's summer house outside the city. ⊠ *Largo Villa Peretti1, Termini* ☎ *06/480201* ⊕ *www.archeorm.arti.beniculturali. it/sar2000/default.asp* 🎟 *€6, includes Museo delle Terme di Diocleziano* ⊙ *Tues.–Sun. 9–7:15.*

❸ **Palazzo Pallavicini-Rospigliosi.** A patrician palace built for Cardinal Scipione Borghese, this is now the residence of another of Rome's aristocratic families and is, unfortunately, closed to the public. However, in the large garden enclosed by the wings of the palace, a summer pavilion has a famous ceiling fresco of Aurora painted by 17th-century artist Guido Reni and once a month, when the family admits visitors to see the fresco, you can get a peek at the garden. ⊠ *Via XXIV Maggio 43, Quirinale* ☎ *06/4744019* 🎟 *Free* ⊙ *1st day of month, 10–noon and 3–5.*

❽ **Piazza Barberini.** One of Rome's more modern quarters, this district was built during the late-19th-century construction boom on the site of the lush gardens of Villa Ludovisi, a patrician family's estate that had in turn been built over the celebrated ancient Roman gardens of Sallust. The piazza, a picturesque marketplace during the 17th and 18th centuries, has lost its original charm in the rush of progress. Undistinguished modern buildings overshadow the older ones, and traffic circles the Bernini **Fontana del Tritone** (Triton Fountain). Bernini's Baroque centerpiece in Piazza Barberini was created in 1637 for Pope Urban VIII, whose Barberini coat of arms is at the base of the large shell. The fountain's triton blows into his conch shell with gusto, sending an arc of water into the air. In a city of beautiful fountains, this is one of the most vivacious.

Too bad about the setting. ⊠ *Junction of Via del Tritone, Via Veneto, Via Quattro Fontane, and Via Sistina.*

▶ **①** **Piazza del Quirinale.** This strategic location atop the Quirinal Hill has long been of great importance. It served as home of the Sabines in the 7th century BC, then deadly enemies of the Romans, who lived on the Capitoline and Palatine Hills (all of 1 km [½ mi] away). Today it's the foreground for the presidential residence, Palazzo del Quirinale, and home to **Palazzo della Consulta,** where Italy's Constitutional Court sits. The open side of the piazza has an impressive vista of the rooftops and domes of central Rome and St. Peter's in the distance. The **Fontana di Montecavallo** or Fontana dei Dioscuri, is composed of a huge Roman statuary group and an obelisk from the tomb of the emperor Augustus. The group of the Dioscuri trying to tame two massive marble steeds was found in the Baths of Constantine, which occupied part of the summit of the Quirinal Hill. Unlike just about every other ancient statue in Rome, this group survived the Dark Ages intact and accordingly became one of the city's great sights, especially during the Middle Ages. Next to the figures, the ancient obelisk from the Mausoleo di Augusto (Tomb of Augustus) was put here by Pope Pius VI at the end of the 18th century. ⊠ *Junction of Via del Quirinale and Via XXIV Aprile.*

**⑲** **Piazza della Repubblica.** Often the first view that spells "Rome" to weary travelers walking from the Stazione Termini, this broad square was laid out in the late 1800s and includes the exuberant **Fontana delle Naiadi** (Fountain of the Naiads). This pièce de résistance is draped with voluptuous bronze ladies wrestling happily with marine monsters. The nudes weren't there when the pope unveiled the fountain in 1870, sparing him any embarrassment. But when the figures were added in 1901, they caused a scandal, for it's said that the sculptor, Rutelli, modeled them on the ample figures of two musical comedy stars of the day. The piazza owes its curved lines to the structures of the Terme di Diocleziano; the curving, colonnaded neoclassic buildings on the southwest side trace the underlying form of the ancient baths. Today, one of them is occupied by the superdeluxe Hotel Exedra—which shows you how much the fortunes of the formely tatterdemalion part of the city have changed. ⊠ *Junction of Via Nazionale, Via Vittorio Emanuele Orlando, and Via delle Terme di Diocleziano, Termini.*

**⑮** **Porta Pia.** Though it owes its current name to Pope Pius IV, this is one of the principal city gates in the Aurelian walls, built on order of the emperor Aurelianus in the 3rd century. They owe their survival for 16 centuries to the fact that the popes had to maintain them in good order to defend the city from invaders. Porta Pia is also Michelangelo's last piece of architecture—he completed a facade for it in 1564. Nearby, a monument marks the breach in the walls created by Italian troops when they stormed into Rome in 1870 to claim the city from the pope for the new Italian state. ⊠ *Northeast end of Via XX Settembre.*

**⑥** **Quattro Fontane** (Four Fountains). The intersection takes its name from its four Baroque fountains, representing the Tiber (on the San Carlo corner), the Arno, Juno, and Diana. Sadly, the fumes from constant heavy traffic have managed to deface them to the point where they're unrecognizable. Despite the traffic, it's worthwhile to take in the views from this point in all four directions: to the southwest as far as the obelisk in Piazza del Quirinale; to the northeast along Via XX Settembre to the Porta Pia; to the northwest across Piazza Barberini to the obelisk of Trinità dei Monti; and to the southeast as far as the obelisk and apse of Santa Maria Maggiore. This extraordinary prospect is a highlight of Pope Sixtus V's campaign of urban beautification and a typical example of the Baroque influence on city planning. ⊠ *Junction of Via delle Quattro Fontane, Via Quirinale, and Via XX Settembre, Quirinale.*

★ ❺ **San Carlo alle Quattro Fontane.** San Carlo (sometimes identified by the diminutive San Carlino because of its tiny size) is one of Borromini's masterpieces. In a space no larger than the base of one of the piers of St. Peter's Basilica, he created a church that is an intricate exercise in geometric perfection, with a coffered dome that seems to float above the curves of the walls. Borromini's work is often bizarre, definitely intellectual, and intensely concerned with pure form. In San Carlo, he invented an original treatment of space that creates an effect of rippling movement, especially evident in the double-S curves of the facade. Characteristically, the interior decoration is subdued, in white stucco with no more than a few touches of gilding, so as not to distract from the form. Don't miss the **cloister,** a tiny, understated Baroque jewel, with a graceful portico and loggia above, echoing the lines of the church. ⊠ *Via del Quirinale 23, Quirinale* ☎ *06/4883261* ☉ *Daily 9–1 and 4–6.*

⑳ **Santa Maria degli Angeli.** The curving brick facade on the northeast side of Piazza della Repubblica is one small remaining part of the colossal Terme di Diocleziano, erected about AD 300 and the largest and most impressive of the baths of ancient Rome. The baths extended over what is now Piazza della Repubblica and covered much of the area. In 1561 Michelangelo was commissioned to convert the vast *tepidarium,* the central hall of the baths, into a church. His work was altered by Vanvitelli in the 18th century, but the huge transept, which formed the nave in Michelangelo's plan, has remained as he adapted it. The eight enormous monolithic columns of red granite that support the great beams are the original columns of the tepidarium, 45 feet high and more than 5 feet in diameter. The great hall is 92 feet high. Though the interior of the church is small in comparison with the vast baths Diocletian built here, it gives a better impression of the remarkable grandeur of ancient Rome's most imposing public buildings than any other edifice in the city. ⊠ *Via Cernaia 9, Termini* ☎ *06/4880812* ☉ *Daily 7–7.*

★ ❿ **Santa Maria della Concezione.** Although not for the easily spooked, the crypt under the main Capuchin church holds the bones of some 4,000 dead Capuchin monks. Arranged in odd decorative designs around the shriveled and decayed skeletons of their kinsmen, a macabre reminder of the impermanence of earthly life, the crypt is actually touching and oddly beautiful. Signs declare, "What you are, we once were. What we are, you someday will be." Upstairs in the church, the first chapel on the right contains Guido Reni's mid-17th-century *St. Michael Trampling the Devil.* The painting caused great scandal after an astute contemporary observer remarked that the face of the devil bore a surprising resemblance to the Pamphili Pope Innocent X, archenemy of Reni's Barberini patrons. Compare the devil with the bust of the pope that you saw in the Palazzo Doria Pamphilj and judge for yourself. ⊠ *Via Veneto 27* ☎ *06/4871185* 💲 *Donation expected* ⊙ *Church daily 6:30–noon and 3–7, crypt daily 9–noon and 3–6.*

**⑭ Santa Maria della Vittoria.** Like the church of Santa Susanna across Piazza San Bernardo, this church was designed by Carlo Maderno, but this one is best known for Bernini's sumptuous Baroque decoration of the **Cappella Cornaro** (Cornaro Chapel), on the left as you face the altar, where you'll find his interpretation of heavenly ecstasy in the statue of St. Theresa. In this chapel, Bernini produced an extraordinary fusion of architecture, painting, and sculpture, with the *Ecstasy of St. Theresa* as the focal point. Your eye is drawn effortlessly from the frescoes on the ceiling down to the marble figures of the angel and the swooning saint, to the earthly figures of the Cornaro family (which commissioned the chapel), to the two inlays of marble skeletons in the pavement, representing the hope and despair of souls in purgatory.

**Fodor'sChoice ★**

As evidenced in other works of the period, the theatricality of the chapel is the result of Bernini's masterly fusion of elements. This is one of the key examples of the mature Roman High Baroque. Bernini's audacious conceit was to model the chapel as a theater: Members of the Cornaro family—sculpted in colored marbles—witness watch from theater boxes as, center stage, the great moment of divine love is played out before them. The swooning saint's robes appear to be on fire, quivering with life, and the white marble group seems suspended in the heavens as golden rays illuminate the scene. An angel assists at the mystical moment of Theresa's vision as the saint abandons herself to the joys of heavenly love. Bernini represented this mystical experience in what, to modern eyes, may seem very earthly terms. Or, as the visiting dignitary President de Brosses put it in the 19th century, "If this is divine love, I know what it is." No matter what your reaction, you'll have to admit it's great theater. ⊠ *Via XX Settembre 17, Largo Santa Susanna, Quirinale* ☎ *06/42740571* ⊙ *Mon.–Sat. 8:30–11 and 3:30–6, Sun. 3:30–6.*

**★ ④ Sant'Andrea al Quirinale.** Designed by Bernini, this is an architectural gem of the Baroque. His son wrote that Bernini considered it one of his best works and that he used to come here occasionally just to sit and enjoy it. Bernini's simple oval plan, a classic of Baroque architecture, is given drama and movement by the church's decoration, which carries the story of St. Andrew's martyrdom and ascension into heaven, starting with the painting over the high altar, up past the figure of the saint over the chancel door, to the angels at the base of the lantern and the dove of the Holy Spirit that awaits on high. ⊠ *Via del Quirinale 29* ☎ *06/48903187* ⊙ *Wed.–Sun. 10–noon and 4–7.*

**⑫ Santa Susanna.** This is Rome's American Catholic church. The building's foundations incorporate parts of a Roman house where Susanna was martyred, but the frescoes, carved ceiling, and stucco decorations all date from the late 16th century. Maderno's 1603 facade masterfully heralded the beginning of the Baroque era in Roman architecture. To the left of the main door is the entrance to Santa Susanna's English-language lending library. ⊠ *Via XX Settembre 14, Quirinale* ☎ *06/42013734* ⊘ *Daily 7–noon and 4–6.*

㉑ **Terme di Diocleziano** (Baths of Diocletian). Though part of the ancient structure is now the church of Santa Maria degli Angeli, and other parts were transformed into a Carthusian monastery or razed to make room for later urban development, a visit gives you an idea of the scale and grandeur of this ancient bathing establishment. Upon entering the church you see the major structures of the baths, partly covered by 16th and 17th century overlay, some of which is by Michelangelo. The monastery cloister is filled with the lapidary collection of the Museo Nazionale Romano. ⊠ *Viale E. De Nicola 79, Termini* ☎ *06/39967700* ⊠ *€5* ⊘ *Tues.–Sun. 9–7:45.*

★ ☾ ⑰ **Villa Torlonia.** Built for one of the newest (and certainly wealthiest) of the Roman aristocratic families, the Torlonias, this villa became Mussolini's residence as prime minister under Italy's king and is now a public park. Long neglected, the park's vegetation and buildings are gradually being refurbished. The first of the buildings to be fully restored is now open to the public as a charming example of the Stil Liberty (Art Nouveau) style of the early 1900s: the gabled, fairy-tale-like cottage-palace, the **Museo della Casina delle Civette** (Museum of the Little House of Owls) displays majolica and stained-glass decorations, including windows with owl motifs, and is a stunning, overlooked find for lovers of 19th-century decorative arts. ⊠ *Villa Torlonia, Via Nomentana 70* ☎ *06/44250072* ⊕ *www.romabeniculturali.it/casinadellecivette/* ⊠ *Museum €2.60, free last Sun. of month* ⊘ *Tues.–Sun. 9–7.*

off the beaten path

**MAUSOLEO DI COSTANZA AND SANT'AGNESE** – From Largo Santa Susanna, take a 40-minute bus ride—or 20-minute taxi ride—back to the early Christian era. The journey is definitely worth it, as your reward is two of Rome's most beautiful mausoleo, one with stunning mosaics and a circular design that mirrors ancient Roman tombs. The histories of these sites are intertwined. Sant'Agnese (St. Agnes) was martyred around AD 304, and her catacomb became an important site for Rome's early Christians. After the conversion of Rome to Christianity under Constantine, the emperor's family built a church over the catacomb, and later an adjoining tomb (now used as a church) was erected for Constantine's daughter Constantia (Costanza) close to the burial site of St. Agnes herself. St. Agnes's church is of interest for its antique columns, 7th-century mosaics, and murky catacombs underneath (entrance to the left of church, €4.15). On January 21 each year, two flower-bedecked lambs are blessed before Agnes's altar. (*Agnus* means lamb in Latin.) They are then carried to the pope, who blesses them again before they're sent to the nuns of St. Cecilia in Trastevere. The nuns use the lambs' wool to make the episcopal *pallia*, bands of white wool that are conferred by the pope on archbishops.

Uphill from the catacomb, Santa Costanza has an unusual—and magical—circular format, echoing the format of the ancient Roman tombs of Augustus and Cecelia Metella. Twelve pairs of columns support the drum of the dome and the vaults are covered with 4th-century mosaics, among Rome's oldest and most beautiful. Their grapevine motif seems more bacchic than Christian. The figures on either side of the entrance probably represent Constantia and her husband. Opposite the entrance is a copy of the original heavy porphyry sarcophagus that is in the Vatican Museums. Its carved decorations are an adaptation of pagan symbols to Christian use, such as the sheep and the peacock, whose flesh was held to be incorruptible. ⊠ *Via Nomentana 349, from Piazza Repubblica, take Bus 84 8 stops up Via Nomentana; get off immediately after Via Carlo Fea and follow signs* ☏ *06/8610840* ☉ *Mon. 9–noon, Tues.–Sat. 9–noon and 4–6, Sun. 4–6.*

# A TALE OF TWO ROMES: FROM THE VILLA BORGHESE TO PIAZZA DEL POPOLO

From the umbrella pines of Rome's largest park—the Villa Borghese—to the cosmopolitan cafés lining Via Veneto, the northern sector of Rome offers up dazzling views of both the city's sylvan and urban sides. Some of the city's finest sights are tucked away in or next to green lawns and pedestrian piazzas, offering a breath of fresh air for weary sight-seers. As you make your way north toward the park, you'll pass the Pin-cian Hill. In ancient times, the city's most lavish host, Lucullus, staged fabulous alfresco banquets in his terraced villa on the heights here. On the plain below, called the Campus Martius, not far from today's bustling Piazza del Popolo by the banks of the Tiber, Augustus laid out a vast public garden, celebrating his own glory in his mausoleum and the Ara Pacis, and setting up an Egyptian obelisk that served as pointer in a huge sundial. Villa Borghese itself, the 17th-century pleasure gardens created by Cardinal Scipione Borghese, holds several treasures, the most precious at the Galleria Borghese, one of the finest and most beautiful museums in the city.

On the other side of the park are Villa Giulia, a late-Renaissance papal summerhouse now containing an enormous collection of Etruscan art, and the Galleria Nazionale d'Arte Moderna, with intriguingly varied collections of modern art in a vast neoclassical palace that has a fashionable terrace café. These are the three major museums in the area, but the past is also palpably preserved in the triangle that has its apex at Piazza del Popolo and extends to the Mausoleum of Augustus and the Spanish Steps. Here 17th-century buildings and churches are interspersed with art and antiques galleries and a plethora of boutiques. Together with the Via Condotti area, this constitutes Rome's most vibrant shopping district.

We start on the Via Veneto, which, after its 1950s and early '60s hey-day as the focus of dolce vita excitement, fell out of fashion as the "in" crowd headed elsewhere. Basically unchanging, the Via Veneto neigh-borhood has preserved its solid, bourgeois palaces and enormous ministries. And it keeps trying to woo back the mainstream of Roman sidewalk café society from the lively scenes at Piazza del Pantheon and Piazza Navona—as yet to no avail.

*Numbers in the text and margin correspond to points of interest on the Villa Borghese to the Ara Pacis map.*

**a good walk**

If you're staying on Via Veneto, this walk begins at your front door. Start if you want with a cappuccino in one of this famous street's famous cafés. The southern end of Via Veneto snakes upward from Piazza Barberini to the Porta Pinciana through the Ludovisi neighborhood, known for palatial hotels and stately residences that transformed patrician estates into commercial real estate in the 1880s. In the upper reaches of Via Veneto, near the flower vendors and big newsstands at the corner of Via Ludovisi, is the Café de Paris, erstwhile hub of la dolce vita. Past the big cafés, Via Veneto continues in a succession of more newsstands, boutiques, expensive shops, and a snack bar or two, and then debouches into the Villa Borghese park, the official start of our walk. If you intend to picnic under the ilex trees, this is your chance to pick up some supplies, whether ready-to-go from the snack bars or do-it-yourself from the *alimentari* (grocery stores) on the side streets. (There are some expensive mobile snack carts in the park and a café in the Galleria Borghese.)

**Porta Pinciana ❶** ☞ is one of the historic city gates in the Aurelian walls, built by Emperor Aurelianus late in the 3rd century AD to protect Rome. Take care crossing the thoroughfares on either side of the gate: the traffic here comes hurtling in from all directions. Now that you're inside the **Villa Borghese ❷** park, first look to the left, across the Galoppatoio (riding ring). The handsome 16th-century palace that you can see across the lawns is **Villa Medici ❸**, since 1804 the seat of the French Academy, where many great French artists—from Ingres and David to Balthus—found inspiration; it has gardens famous for their Roman style. Head north on Viale del Museo Borghese to reach the Casino Borghese, which houses the magnificent **Museo e Galleria Borghese ❹**. Here, the palace is as stupendous—wait until you see the frescoed ceilings—as the Berninis and Titians on view. Once you've viewed Cardinal Scipione's collections, take time to enjoy the vast park. On the right, as you leave the casino, you can continue along Viale dell'Uccelliera to Rome's once-forlorn zoo, which has been transformed into a "biopark." Alternatively, turn left (south) onto Viale dei Pupazzi and head toward Piazza dei Cavalli Marini, with its sea-horse fountain. Continue straight ahead on Viale dei Pupazzi or turn right: either way you'll come upon the **Piazza di Siena ❺**, a grassy hippodrome shaded by tall pines. At the northwest end of Piazza di Siena, turn left onto Viale Canonica and you'll come to the entrance of the delightful Giardino del Lago (Lake Garden).

If you want to take in one or both of the other museums on this walk, head northwest from the Giardino del Lago to Piazzale Paolina Borghese, at the head of a broad, monumental staircase that descends to Viale della Belle Arti and the **Galleria Nazionale d'Arte Moderna ❻** (National Gallery of Modern Art). About ¼ km (⅛ mi) northwest on Viale delle Belle Arti is the **Museo Etrusco di Villa Giulia ❼** (Etruscan Museum). The entrance is at the far end of the building, on Piazza di Villa Giulia. Returning to the staircase, climb it to enter Villa Borghese again. Follow Via Bernadotte to Piazza del Fiocco and turn left onto Viale La Guardia, named for the celebrated New York mayor.

At circular Piazza delle Canestre head west on Viale delle Magnolie. A bridge over heavily trafficked Viale del Muro Torto leads to the **Pincio** ❽ gardens. After admiring its layout from the Pincio terrace, which offers one of Rome's finest panoramas, descend the ramps and stairs to the famous **Piazza del Popolo** ❾ and **Porta del Popolo** ❿. Stop in at the church of **Santa Maria del Popolo** ⓫ to see the art treasures inside, including two paintings by Caravaggio. The paired churches of **Santa Maria in Montesanto** ⓬ and **Santa Maria dei Miracoli** ⓭ were part of a grand project initiated in the 1500s under several popes who urbanized this triangular area, previously sparsely inhabited. Take Via di Ripetta, the most westerly of the three streets fanning out from Piazza del Popolo. On the left you pass the San Giacomo Hospital, and on the right is the horseshoe-shape, Neoclassical building of the Academy of Fine Arts, usually covered with not-so-fine student graffiti. Famed for its moving sculpted reliefs, the **Ara Pacis Augustae** ⓮ (Altar of Augustan Peace)—the most distinctive monument created to honor Emperor Augustus—and the Mausoleo di Augusto are on huge Piazza Augusto Imperatore, newly renovated and redesigned by American architect Richard Meier.

TIMING   This is a fair-weather walk, much of it in Villa Borghese park. The walk alone takes about three hours, plus two hours for a visit to the Galleria Borghese. Advance reservations are usually mandatory for your visit to the Galleria. In addition to the Galleria Borghese, the walk includes two other major museums. If you intend to do justice to all three, it's advisable to skip the two on Viale delle Belle Arti during this walk, saving them for another day (or days). Both the Museo Etrusco di Villa Giulia and the Galleria Nazionale d'Arte Moderna are easily accessible from Via Flaminia. They are about 1 km (½ mi) from Piazza del Popolo. Tram 19 stops in front of both museums, and Tram 225, which runs along Via Flaminia, stops at Piazza delle Belle Arti, about ⅔ km (⅕ mi) from Villa Giulia's entrance. Allow about an hour each for visits to the Museo Etrusco di Villa Giulia and the Galleria Nazionale d'Arte Moderna.

## What to See

★ ⓮ **Ara Pacis Augustae** (Altar of Augustan Peace). One of the most vibrant monuments of the imperial age, this altar was erected in 13 BC to celebrate the Pax Romana, the era of peace ushered in by Augustus's military victories. It's covered with spectacular and moving relief sculptures showing the procession of the Roman imperial family. Notice the poignant presence of several forlorn children; historians now believe they attest to the ambition of Augustus's notorious wife, the Empress Livia, who succeeded in having her son, Tiberius, ascend to the throne by dispatching his family rivals with poison, leaving a slew of orphans in her wake. Next to it is the imposing bulk of the marble-clad **Mausoleo di Augusto,** built by the emperor for himself and his family. Like the emperor Hadrian's tomb across the Tiber, it was transformed into a fortress during the Middle Ages. For decades, the altar, set on the northwest cor-

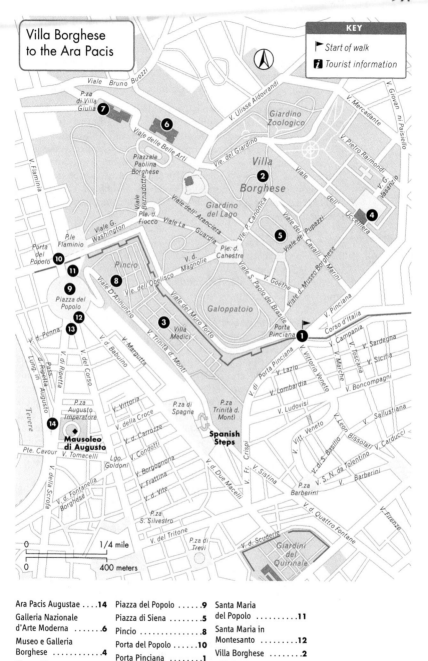

## Villa Borghese to the Ara Pacis

**KEY**

▶ Start of walk

🛈 Tourist information

ner of Piazza Augusto Imperatore, was housed in a tin shed widely criticized for its ugliness. A new pavilion designed by the eminent American architect Richard Meier is being constructed in its place and the altar has been closed for restoration while a new museum to house it is being built. A new opening is scheduled for 2006 or 2007. ⊠ *Via Ripetta, Piazza di Spagna* ⊕ *romabeniculturali.it/arapacis* ⊗ *Closed for restoration.*

**❻ Galleria Nazionale d'Arte Moderna** (National Gallery of Modern Art). This massive white Beaux Arts building looks anything but modern, yet it contains one of Italy's leading collections of 19th- and 20th-century works. It's primarily dedicated to the history of Italian modernism, examining the movement's development over the last two centuries, but crowd-pleasers Degas, Monet, Courbet, Van Gogh, and Cézanne put in appearances along with an outstanding Dadaist collection. ⊠ *Via delle Belle Arti 131, Villa Borghese* ☎ *06/322981* ⊡ *€6.50* ⊗ *Tues.–Sun. 8:30–7:30; later in summer.*

need a
break?

The **Caffè delle Arti** (⊠ Via Gramsci 73, Villa Borghese ☎ 06/ 32651236), attached to the Galleria d'Arte Moderna, has a pretty terrace and is a favorite all-day rendezvous for Romans and visitors to Villa Borghese park and its museums. This is the place to break up your walk with a gelato or lunch.

**❹ Museo e Galleria Borghese.** A pleasure place created by Cardinal Scipione Borghese, this magnificent building was erected as a showcase for his fabulous antiquities collection. The Casino Borghese, as the building is known, was built in 1613 partly to house the cardinal's rich collections of painting and sculpture and partly to provide an elegant venue for summer parties and musical evenings. Today, it's a monument to Roman 17th-century interior decoration at its most extravagant: room after room opulently adorned with porphyry and alabaster and topped with vast ceiling frescoes make for an eye-popping spectacle unequaled in Rome. With the passage of time, the building has become less celebrated than the collections housed inside, which includes one of the finest collections of Baroque sculpture anywhere.

Fodor'sChoice
★

Like the gardens, the casino and its collections have undergone many changes since the 17th century. Camillo Borghese, the husband of Napoléon's sister Pauline, was responsible for most of them. He sold off a substantial number of the paintings to Napoléon and swapped 200 of the classical sculptures for an estate in Piedmont, in northern Italy, also courtesy of Napoléon. These paintings and sculptures are all still in the Louvre in Paris. At the end of the 19th century a later member of the family, Francesco Borghese, replaced some of the gaps in the collections and also transferred to the casino the remaining works of art housed in Palazzo Borghese. In 1902 the casino, its contents, and the park were sold to the Italian government.

The most famous work in the collection is Canova's Neoclassical sculpture of Pauline Borghese. It's technically known as *Venus Victrix,* but there has never been any doubt as to its real subject. Pauline reclines on a Roman sofa, bare-bosomed, her hips swathed in classical drapery, the very model of haughty detachment and sly come-hither. Camillo Borghese seems to have been remarkably unconcerned that his wife had posed for this erotic masterpiece. Pauline, on the other hand, is known to have been shocked that her husband took such evident pleasure in showing off the work to guests. This coyness seems all the more curious given the reply Pauline is supposed to have made to a lady who asked her how she could have posed for the sculpture: "Oh, but the studio was heated." Much to the dismay of Canova, after Camillo and Pauline's divorce, the statue was locked away for many years, though the artist was occasionally allowed to show it to a handpicked few. This he would do at night by the light of a single candle.

The next two rooms hold two key early Baroque sculptures: Bernini's *David* and *Apollo and Daphne*. Both illustrate Bernini's extraordinary technical facility. Both also demonstrate the Baroque desire to invest sculpture with a living quality, to transform inert marble into living flesh. Whereas Renaissance sculptors wanted to capture the idealized beauty of the human form that they had discovered in ancient Greek and Roman sculptures, Baroque sculptors such as Bernini wanted movement and drama as well, capturing not an essence but an instant, infused with theatricality and emotion. The *Apollo and Daphne* shows the moment when, to escape the pursuing Apollo, Daphne is turned into a laurel tree. Leaves and twigs sprout from her fingertips as she stretches agonizingly away from Apollo, who instinctively recoils in terror and amazement. This is the stuff that makes the Baroque exciting. There are more Berninis to see in the collection, notably a very uncharacteristic work, a large unfinished figure called *Verità*, or Truth. Bernini had started work on this brooding figure after the death of his principal patron, Pope Urban VIII. It was meant to form part of a work titled *Truth Revealed by Time*. His successor as pope, Innocent X, had little love for the ebullient Urban, and, as was the way in Rome, this meant that Bernini, too, was excluded from the new pope's favors. However, Bernini's towering genius was such that it gained him the patronage of the new pope with almost indecent haste.

The Caravaggio Room holds works by this hotheaded genius who died of malaria at age 37. The disquieting *Sick Bacchus* and charming *Boy with a Basket of Fruit* are naturalistic early works, bright and fresh compared with a dark *Madonna* and the *David and Goliath,* in which Goliath is believed to be a self-portrait of the artist.

In the Pinacoteca (Picture Gallery) on the first floor of the casino, three Raphaels, a Botticelli, and a Pinturicchio are only a few of the paintings that the cardinal chose for his collection, which includes an incisive Cranach *Venus* and a shadowy Del Sarto *Madonna*. Probably the most famous painting in the gallery is Titian's allegorical *Sacred and Profane Love*, with a nude figure representing sacred love. Admission is by reserved ticket. Visitors are admitted in two-hour shifts 9 AM to 5 PM, and, to be on the safe side (since prime time slots in peak season can sell out days in advance), you can reserve by phone or through www.

ticketeria.it (note you need to collect your reserved ticket at the museum ticket office a half-hour before your entrance). In practice, however, when it's not busy you can go to the museum before the next entrance appointment and buy a ticket to be let in then. ⊠ *Piazza Scipione Borghese 5, off Via Pinciana, Villa Borghese* ☎ *06/8413979 information, 06/ 32810 reservations* ⊕ *www.galleriaborghese.it* ⌨ *€10.50 (including €2 reservation fee); audio guide or English tour €5* ⊙ *Tues.–Sun. 9–7, with sessions on the hour beginning every two hours.*

**❼ Museo Etrusco di Villa Giulia** (Etruscan Museum of Villa Giulia). The world's outstanding collection of Etruscan art and artifacts is housed in Villa Giulia, built around 1551 for Pope Julius III (hence its name). Among the team called in to plan and construct the villa were Michelangelo and his fellow Florentine Vasari. Most of the actual work, however, was done by Vignola and Ammannati. The villa's nymphaeum—or sunken sculpture garden—is a superb example of a refined late-Renaissance setting for princely pleasures. No one knows precisely where the Etruscans originated. Many scholars maintain that they came from Asia Minor, appearing in Italy about 2000 BC, and creating a civilization that was a dazzling prelude to the ancient Romans. Unfortunately, the exhibitions here are as dry as their subject matter—hundreds of glass vitrines stuffed with objects. Even so, you'll find that even the tiniest gold earrings and brooches and the humblest bronze household implements display marvelous workmanship and inventiveness. Among the most striking pieces are the terra-cotta statues, such as the *Apollo of Veio* and the serenely beautiful *Sarcophagus of the Wedded Couple.* ⊠ *Piazzale Villa Giulia 9, Villa Borghese* ☎ *06/3226571* ⊕ *www.beniculturali.it* ⌨ *€4* ⊙ *Tues.–Sun. 8:30–7:30.*

**❾ Piazza del Popolo.** With its obelisk and twin churches, this immense square is a famed Rome landmark. It owes its current appearance to architect Giuseppe Valadier, who designed it about 1820, also laying out the terraced approach to the Pincio and the Pincio's gardens. It marks what was for centuries the northern entrance to the city, where all roads from the north converge and where visitors, many of them pilgrims, would get their first impression of the Eternal City. The desire to make this entrance to Rome something special had been a pet project of popes and their architects over three centuries. The piazza takes its name from the 15th-century church of Santa Maria del Popolo, huddled on the right side of the Porta del Popolo, or city gate. In the late 17th century, the twin churches of Santa Maria in Montesanto (on the left as you face them) and Santa Maria dei Miracoli (on the right) were added to the piazza at the point where Via del Babuino, Via del Corso, and Via di Ripetta converge. The piazza has always served as a meeting place, crowded with fashionable carriages and carnival revelers in the past. It's now a pedestrian zone and serves as a magnet for the fashionable young and old at its café tables. At election time, it's the scene of huge political rallies, and on New Year's Eve Rome stages a mammoth alfresco party in the piazza. ⊠ *Junction of Via del Babuino, Via del Corso, and Via di Ripetta.*

**need a break?**

A café that has never gone out of style, **Rosati** (⊠ Piazza del Popolo 5 ☎ 06/3225859) is a rendezvous of literati, artists, and actors. There's a sidewalk café, a tearoom, and an upstairs dining room for a more upscale lunch. Off Piazza del Popolo on Via di Ripetta you'll find places where you can stop for sustenance. **Cose Fritte** (⊠ Via di Ripetta 3) specializes in rice croquettes, batter-fried vegetables, and other tasty snacks to take out. **PizzaRé** (⊠ Via di Ripetta 14 ☎ 06/3211468) offers a wide choice of toppings for pizza cooked in a wood-burning oven. **Buccone** (⊠ Via di Ripetta 19 ☎ 06/3612154) is a wineshop serving light snacks at lunchtime and wine by the glass all day long.

**⑤ Piazza di Siena.** Set within the Villa Borghese park, this piazza—actually an 18th-century reproduction of an ancient Roman amphitheater—was built for the Borghese family's games and named after the Tuscan city from which the family originated. In May, the arena hosts an international horse show. ⊠ *Viale Canonica at Via dei Pupazzi, Villa Borghese.*

**⑧ Pincio** (Pincian Hill). Redolent of the yesteryear days of Henry James and Edith Wharton, the Pincio gardens have always been a favorite spot for strolling. Grand Tour-ists, fashion-plates, even a pope or two would head here to see and be seen among the beau monde of Rome. Today, the Pincio terrace remains a favorite spot to cool off overheated locals. Their rather formal, early-19th-century style contrasts with the far more elaborate terraced gardens of Lucullus that once adorned the site. Lucullus, the Roman gourmand, held lush banquets here that were legendary. Pathways are lined with white marble busts of Italian heroes and artists. Along with the similar busts on the Gianicolo (Janiculum Hill), their noses have been victims of vandalism. Depending on the date of the last nose-knocking wave, you'll see the Pincio's busts forlornly noseless or in the throes of obvious plastic surgery.

The Pincian Hill is one of the seven hills of ancient Rome, and they are still separated from the southwest corner of Villa Borghese by a stretch of ancient walls. From the balustraded Pincio terrace you can look down at Piazza del Popolo and beyond, surveying much of Rome. Across the Tiber, Via Cola di Rienzo goes through the Prati district toward the heights of Monte Mario. That low, brownish building on top of the hill is the Rome Hilton. Off to the left are Castel Sant'Angelo and the dome of St. Peter's Basilica. In the foreground is the curve of the Tiber, embracing Old Rome, where the low-slung dome of the Pantheon emerges from a sea of russet-tile rooftops and graceful cupolas. Southeast of the Pincio terrace is the **Casina Valadier,** a magnificently decorated templelike Neoclassic building perennially due for renovation and reopening as a restaurant. ⊠ *Piazzale Napoleone I and Viale dell'Obelisco, Villa Borghese.*

**⑩ Porta del Popolo** (City Gate). The medieval gate in the Aurelian walls was replaced in 1561 by the current one, which was further embellished by Bernini in 1655 for the much-heralded arrival of Queen Christina of

Sweden, who had abdicated her throne to become a Roman Catholic. ⊠ *Piazza del Popolo and Piazzale Flaminio, Villa Borghese.*

► ❶ **Porta Pinciana** (Pincian Gate). Framed by two squat, circular towers, the gate was constructed in the 6th century. Here you can see just how well the Aurelian walls have been preserved and imagine hordes of Visigoths trying to break through them. Sturdy as the walls look, they couldn't always keep out the barbarians: Rome was sacked three times during the 5th century alone. ⊠ *Piazzale Basile, junction Via Veneto and Corso d'Italia, Villa Borghese.*

❸ **Santa Maria dei Miracoli.** A twin to Santa Maria in Montesanto, this church was built in the 1670s by Carlo Fontana as an elegant frame for the entrance to Via del Corso from Piazza del Popolo. ⊠ *Via del Corso 528, Piazza del Popolo* ☏ *06/3610250* ☉ *Daily 6–1 and 4–7:30.*

★ ❶ **Santa Maria del Popolo.** Standing inconspicuously in a corner of the vast Piazza del Popolo, this church often goes unnoticed, but the treasures inside make it a must for art lovers, as they include an entire chapel designed by Raphael and one adorned with striking Caravaggio masterpieces. Bramante enlarged the apse of the church, which had been rebuilt in the 15th century on the site of a much older place of worship. Inside, in the first chapel on the right, you'll see some frescoes by Pinturicchio from the mid-15th century; the adjacent **Cybo Chapel** is a 17th-century exercise in marble decoration. Heading to the second chapel on the left, you'll see Raphael's famous **Chigi Chapel,** built around 1513 and commissioned by the banker Agostino Chigi (who also had the artist decorate his home across the Tiber, the Villa Farnesina). Raphael provided the cartoons for the vault mosaic—showing God the Father in benediction—and the designs for the statues of Jonah and Elijah in the Chigi Chapel. More than a century later, Bernini added the oval medallions on the tombs and the statues of Daniel and Habakkuk, when, in the mid-17th century another Chigi, Pope Alexander VII, commissioned him to restore and decorate the building.

The organ case of Bernini in the right transept bears the Della Rovere family oak tree, part of the Chigi family's coat of arms. The **choir,** with vault frescoes by Pinturicchio, contains the handsome tombs of Ascanio Sforza and Girolamo delle Rovere, both designed by Andrea Sansovino. The best is for last: The **Cerasi Chapel,** to the left of the high altar on the side walls, has two Caravaggios, both key early-Baroque works that show how modern 17th-century art can be. Compare their earthy realism and harshly dramatic lighting with the much more restrained and classically "pure" *Assumption of the Virgin* by Caravaggio's contemporary and rival, Annibale Carracci; it hangs over the altar of the chapel. ⊠ *Piazza del Popolo 12, near Porta Pinciana* ☏ *06/3610836* ☉ *Daily 7–noon and 4–7.*

❶ **Santa Maria in Montesanto.** One of the two bookend churches on the eastern side of Piazza del Popolo, this edifice was built by Carlo Fontana, supervised by his brilliant teacher, Bernini (who may even have designed the saints' statues topping the facade). ⊠ *Via del Babuino 197, Piazza del Popolo* ☏ *06/3610594.*

🕐 ❷ **Villa Borghese.** Rome's "Central Park," the Villa Borghese was originally part of the pleasure gardens laid out in the early 17th century by Cardinal Scipione Borghese, a worldly and cultivated cleric and nephew of Pope Paul V. The word "villa" was used to mean suburban estate, of the type developed by the ancient Romans and adopted by Renaissance nobles. Today's gardens bear little resemblance to the originals. Not only do they cover a much smaller area—by 1630, the perimeter wall was almost 5 km (3 mi) long—but they have also been almost entirely remodeled. This occurred at the end of the 18th century, when a Scottish painter, Jacob More, was employed to transform them into the style of the "cunningly natural" park so popular in 18th-century England. Until that time, the park was probably the finest example of an Italian-style garden in the entire country.

In contrast to the formal and rigidly symmetrical gardens of 17th-century France—those at Versailles are the best example—these Italian gardens had no overall symmetrical plan. Rather, they consisted of a series of small, interlinked formal gardens attached by paths and divided by meticulously trimmed hedges. Flowers—the Romans were particularly fond of tulips—statues, ponds, and small enclosures for animals (the more exotic the better; lions and peacocks were favorites) were scattered artfully around. Here, the cardinal and his friends strolled and discussed poetry, music, painting, and philosophy. Today the area immediately in front of the casino and the sunken open-air "dining room," a small stone pavilion close to the low wall along the Via di Porta Pinciana side of the park, are all that remain from the cardinal's original grounds. Now the gardens are studded with neoclassical temples and statuary added to suit early-19th-century tastes.

In addition to the gloriously restored Galleria Borghese museum, the highlights of the park are Piazza di Siena, a graceful amphitheater; and the botanical garden on Via Canonica, where there is a pretty little lake, a neoclassical faux–Temple of Aesculapius (a favorite photo-op), and a café under the trees. The park has bike, in-line skating, and electric scooter rental concessions and a children's movie theater (showing films for adults in the evening). ✉ *Main entrances at Porta Pinciana, the Pincio, Piazzale Flaminio (Piazza del Popolo), Viale delle Belle Arti, and Via Mercadante* ⊕ *http://www.romabeniculturali.it/villeparchi/.*

★ ❸ **Villa Medici.** Purchased by Napoléon and today the home of the French Academy, the Villa Medici, otherwise closed to the public, stages prestigious art exhibits and music festivals, advertised on posters around its gates. The gardens are occasionally open for guided tours on Sunday mornings; call the academy directly or check with the tourist office for details. A tour here is very special, as you walk in the footsteps of Velázquez, Fragonard, and Ingres, who all worked at the academy. This is also the only way you can see the incredibly picturesque garden facade, which is studded with Mannerist and Rococo sculpted reliefs and overlooks a loggia with a beautiful fountain devoted to Mercury. ✉ *Viale Trinità dei Monti, Piazza di Spagna* ☎ *06/69921653.*

# ACROSS THE TIBER:
# THE GHETTO, TIBER ISLAND & TRASTEVERE

Sometimes futilely resisting the tides of change, Rome has several little communities that have staunchly defended their authenticity over the centuries; this tour takes in two of the oldest. The old Ghetto, on the banks of the Tiber, is a neighborhood that has proudly retained its Jewish heritage. Right up to the end of the 19th century, this really was a ghetto, its dark buildings clinging to the sides of ancient ruins for support. Next to it is the charming Tiberina island, and beyond, Trastevere. Despite creeping gentrification, Trastevere remains about the most tightly knit community in Rome, its inhabitants proudly proclaiming descent—whether real or imagined—from the ancient Romans. As far back as the Roman Republic, Trastevere had a large foreign colony. Jews who came to Rome also settled here in the 2nd century BC. Raphael's model and mistress, the dark-eyed Fornarina (literally, "the baker's daughter"), is believed to have been a Trasteverina. The artist reportedly took time off from painting the Vatican Stanze and the *Galatea* in Villa Farnesina to romance—and perhaps marry—the winsome girl.

Literally translated, Trastevere means "across the Tiber"; the Trasteverini have always been proud and combative, a breed apart. In the Middle Ages, Trastevere wasn't considered part of Rome, and the "foreigners" who populated its maze of alleys and piazzas fought bitterly to obtain recognition for the neighborhood as a *rione*, or official district of the city. In the 14th century the Trasteverini won out and became full-fledged Romans. Since then, though, they have stoutly maintained their separate identity. They may be hard to find at first amid the gentrification, but the real Trasteverini are still here, hearty and uninhibited, and justly galled by the immense popularity of their neighborhood among the invading hordes. Trastevere is still romantic and evocative, with crumbling medieval buildings lining sunny piazzas and laundry strung out over narrow, cobbled streets. Come nighttime, though, the trappings of trendiness are everywhere: countless boutiques, cafés, pizzerias, music clubs, and discos draw lively crowds, especially on weekends. For Romans and foreigners alike, Piazza Santa Maria in Trastevere is the center of the action, a sort of outdoor living room, open to all comers. The Gianicolo (Janiculum Hill) affords an overview of the neighborhood below and a marvelous vista of the entire city and the Castelli Romani.

*Numbers in the text and margin correspond to points of interest on the Trastevere and the Jewish Ghetto map.*

a good walk

Piazza Venezia is the starting point for touring the ancient ghetto quarter of the city. From the piazza, walk to the base of the Campidoglio, take Via del Teatro Marcello, and turn right across the street onto Via Montanara and enter Piazza Campitelli, with its Baroque church and fountain. Take Via dei Funari at the northwest end of the piazza and follow it into Piazza Mattei, where one of Rome's loveliest fountains, the 16th-century **Fontana delle Tartarughe** ❶ ▶ (Fountain of the Turtles), is tucked away. A few steps down Via Caetani, off the north side of Piazza Mattei, you'll find a doorway into the public part of the old **Palazzo Mattei** ②, well worth a peek for its time-stained sculpture-rich courtyard and staircase.

From Piazza Mattei go south on Via della Reginella onto Via Portico d'Ottavia, heart of the Jewish Ghetto. On the buildings, medieval inscriptions, ancient friezes, and half-buried classical columns attest to the venerable history of this area, a lively commercial quarter of old buildings and palaces. Visit at dusk in the summertime for the flavor of an old Roman neighborhood. Tables and chairs are set outside doorways as evening falls, and friends and neighbors gather to enjoy an alfresco card game or chat.

After the church of **Sant'Angelo in Pescheria** ③, set within the remaining columns of the Portico d'Ottavia, you come to the **Teatro di Marcello** ④ (Theater of Marcellus) on the left side of Via Portico d'Ottavia and the **Sinagoga** ⑤ (Synagogue) on the right. Cross the oldest bridge in the city, Ponte Fabricio, built in 62 BC, onto the **Isola Tiberina** ⑥ (Tiber Island); then cross Ponte Cestio and head into Trastevere.

Begin your exploration of Trastevere at **Piazza in Piscinula** ⑦. (You'll need a detailed street map to make your way around this intricate maze of winding side streets.) Explore the little streets and piazzas around the piazza. This was the site of Trastevere's port, Ripa Grande, the largest in 17th-century Rome; it was destroyed early in the 20th century to make way for the modern embankments. Via del Porto gives you a fine view of the Aventine Hill across the Tiber. Piazza dei Mercanti is especially noted for its colorful, if somewhat touristy, restaurants.

Take Via dell'Arco dei Tolomei, one of the city's most charming byways, and cross Via dei Salumi, where the sausage makers stored their goods, onto tiny Vicolo dell'Atleta. It was in this minuscule alley, in 1849, that excavators discovered the statue *Apoxyomenos* (the athlete holding a *strigil*, or scraper) that is now in the Vatican Museums. Turn left onto Via dei Genovesi, then right into the piazza in front of the church of **Santa Cecilia in Trastevere** ⑧. Behind Santa Cecilia in Trastevere, on Via Anicia, the **Chiostro San Giovanni dei Genovesi** ⑨ is open on Tuesday and Thursday afternoons. Several blocks down Via Anicia at **San Francesco a Ripa** ⑩ is a famous Bernini sculpture of the Blessed Ludovica Albertoni. Go west on Via San Francesco a Ripa to Viale Trastevere. Take a detour east on Viale Trastevere to see the 13th-century mosaic pavements in the church of **San Crisogono** ⑪ on Piazza Sonnino. On the adjacent Piazza Belli the medieval Torre degli Anguillara (Anguillara Tower) is a restored fortified residence dating from the Middle Ages. Piazza Belli is named for the top-hatted 19th-century dialect poet Giuseppi Belli, whose bronze statue watches jauntily over the square.

Follow Via San Francesco a Ripa or Via della Lungaretta west to the very heart of Trastevere. Piazza San Cosimato hosts the neighborhood's busy outdoor marketplace on weekday mornings, but **Piazza Santa Maria in Trastevere** ⑫ is the place where the neighborhood is at its best, embellished with the glimmering mosaics on the church of **Santa Maria in Trastevere** ⑬ and with an octagonal fountain, as well as inviting cafés. Some people feel Santa Maria is Rome's most spectacular church—its grand nave lined with towering ancient Roman columns and altar surrounded by gilded mosaics created a majesty that even Hadrian would have been impressed with. Sit at the back of the church and see if you agree.

Via Fonte dell'Olio, on the north side of the piazza, leads to Piazza dei Renzi. Bear right onto Via della Pelliccia or Vicolo dei Renzi to Via del Moro and then proceed to Piazza Trilussa. Ponte Sisto links this part of Trastevere with Old Rome, across the Tiber. The bridge was built in the 15th century by Pope Sixtus IV to expedite commercial traffic in view of the upcoming Holy Year of 1475. On the north side of Piazza Trilussa stands a monument to the beloved, racy dialect poet Trilussa. Both Via Benedetta and Via S. Dorotea lead north to Porta Settimiana (from here Via della Lungara heads straight down toward the Vatican). At the end of Via Corsini, off Via della Lungara, is the **Orto Botanico** ⑭ (Botanical Garden).

Walk north on Via della Lungara to visit **Villa Farnesina** ⑮—famed for its Raphael and Sodoma frescoes—on the right, and, opposite, the section of the Galleria Nazionale d'Arte Antica, which is housed in the grand **Palazzo Corsini** ⑯, once home to Queen Christina of Sweden. Return to Porta Settimiana, and turn right onto Via Garibaldi, which climbs to the Gianicolo. Continue up Via Garibaldi to the church of **San Pietro in Montorio** ⑰ to see Bramante's architectural gem, the Tempietto, housed in the cloister. Stairs provide shortcuts up and down the Gianicolo from various points in Trastevere; they save a lot of walking. As you continue your ascent of the Gianicolo, you come upon the huge **Fontana dell'Acqua Paola** ⑱, an early-17th-century creation with a vast pool that can be tempting on a hot day. The fountain is near the entrance to the park at the summit of the **Gianicolo** ⑲ (Janiculum Hill). Take in the views and then, if you're tired or pressed for time, ride Bus 870 north toward Corso Vittorio Emanuele, across the Tiber. You'll pass a curious lighthouse, a gift of the Argentines in recognition of Garibaldi's efforts on behalf of their independence.

TIMING This walk could take from four to five hours, but it's easily broken up into two parts—the Ghetto and Isola Tiberina, and Trastevere and the Gianicolo—the first taking about an hour, and the second three to four hours, allowing time for detours into Trastevere's interesting shops and eating places. If you time your visit to Santa Cecilia in Trastevere for Tuesday or Thursday morning between 10 and noon, you can see a famous fresco. If it's not a clear day, end your walk at San Pietro in Montorio; the vistas are the rewards for the effort of making your way to the top of the Gianicolo, so save this part of the walk for a day when visibility is good.

## What to See

⑨ **Chiostro San Giovanni dei Genovesi.** You have to ring for the custodian, who will show you the 15th-century cloister of San Giovanni dei Genovesi, an example of the serene Renaissance architectural harmony often found in Florence and rarely in Rome. In fact, it's attributed to Florentine architect Bacio Pontelli. ✉ *Via Anicia 12, Trastevere* ☎ *Do-*

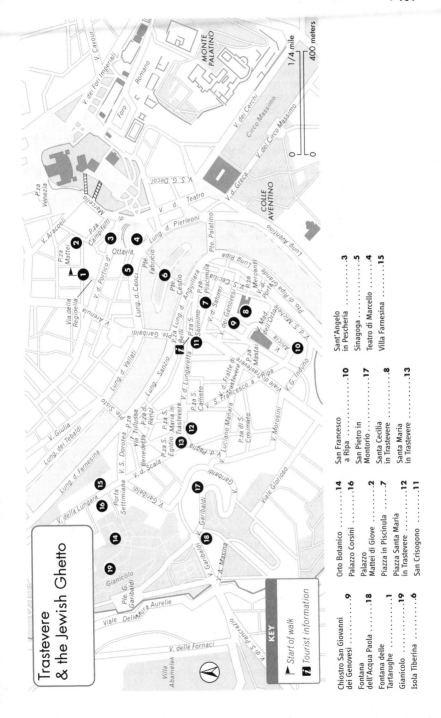

# Trastevere & the Jewish Ghetto

**KEY**

► Start of walk

ℹ Tourist information

*nation expected* ⊙ *May–Sept., Tues. and Thurs. 3–6; Oct.–Apr., Tues. and Thurs. 2–4.*

⓲ **Fontana dell'Acqua Paola.** With a facade inspired by ancient Rome's triumphal arches and worthy of an important church, this 17th-century fountain was commissioned by Pope Paul V to celebrate his renovation of Trajan's 1st-century AD aqueduct. This fountain has a namesake in the large but less imposing fountain that is the centerpiece in Piazza Trilussa, which was moved across the river from Via Giulia in 1898 when the Tiber's embankments were constructed. It, too, was built by Paul V. ⊠ *Via Garibaldi, Trastevere.*

▶ ❶ **Fontana delle Tartarughe** (Fountain of the Turtles). Set in venerable Piazza Mattei, this 16th-century fountain is Rome's most charming, designed by Giacomo della Porta in 1581 and sculpted by Taddeo Landini. The focus of the fountain is four bronze boys, each grasping a dolphin that spouts water into marble shells. Bronze turtles held in the boys' hands drink from the upper basin. The turtles are thought to have been added in the 17th century by Bernini. ⊠ *Piazza Mattei, Ghetto.*

🕲 ⓳ **Gianicolo** (Janiculum Hill). The Gianicolo is famous for splendid views of the city, a noontime cannon, statues of Giuseppe and Anita Garibaldi (Garibaldi was the guiding spirit behind the unification of Italy in the 19th century; Anita was his long-suffering wife), and, like on the Pincio, noseless and bedaubed busts. At the plaza here there's a daily free **puppet show** (⊙ Weekdays 4–7, weekends 10:30–1 and 4–7) in Italian. ⊠ *Via Garibaldi and Passeggiata del Gianicolo, Trastevere.*

★ ❻ **Isola Tiberina** (Tiber Island). Home to a restaurant or two, a famous hospital, a medieval church, and an ancient Roman ship prow sculpted in stone, the Tiberina is one of Rome's most charming nooks. The main landmark of this little island in the Tiber River is the hospital of **Fatebenefratelli** (literally, "Do good, brothers"); though a city hospital, it belongs to the Franciscan Order. It continues a tradition that began in 291 BC when a temple to Aesculapius, with annexed infirmary, was erected here. Aesculapius—Asclepius to the Greeks—was the ancient god of healing and the son of the god Apollo. His symbol was the snake. The Romans adopted him as their god of healing in 293 BC during a terrible plague. A ship was sent to Epidaurus in Greece—heart of the cult of Aesculapius and a sort of Greek Lourdes—to obtain a statue of the god. As the ship sailed back up the Tiber, a great serpent was seen escaping from it and swimming to the island. This was taken as a sign that a temple to Aesculapius should be built here. Here the sick would come to bathe in the island's spring waters and to sleep in the temple, hoping that Aesculapius would visit them in their dreams to cure them. There's no trace of the temple now, but the island has been associated with medicine ever since—the current hospital was built on the site of a medieval hospital.

On the other end of the island is the church of **San Bartolomeo,** built at the end of the 10th century by the Holy Roman Emperor Otto III. Restorations and rebuilding down through the years have left precious little of Otto's original church. It's thought, however, that the small wellhead on the chancel steps—the steps leading to the choir—is original and that it stands on the site of the spring in the temple.

Seasonally, when the Tiber is in flood, the level of the river rises to within a few yards of the level of the piazza, and the island is half submerged. If the waters are low, descend the steps from the piazza and explore the embankment, where Romans like to stroll on fair days and take the sun while listening to the rushing waters of the rapids. In imperial times, Romans sheathed the entire island with marble to make it look like a ship, with the prow pointed downstream. Look for the few remnants of the travertine facing, with a figure of Aesculapius, on the downstream end opposite the left bank. ⊠ *Ponte Fabricio, Lungotevere dei Pierleoni to Via Ponte Quattro Capi; Ponte Cestio, Lungotevere degli Anguillara to Piazza San Bartolomeo all'Isola, Ghetto.*

☼ **⑭ Orto Botanico** (Botanical Garden). Behind Palazzo Corsini is an attractive oasis of greenery that was once part of the palace's extensive grounds. The garden is known for an impressive collection of orchids, ferns, and cacti, but it's also just a peaceful, green park where kids can run and play. Don't miss the **garden for the blind,** with a variety of flowers and plants with strong aromas or unusual to the touch. ⊠ *Largo Cristina di Svezia at end of Via Corsini, Trastevere* ☎ *06/6864193* ☛ *€2.50* ☼ *Mon.–Sat. 9–7.*

**⑯ Palazzo Corsini.** A refined example of Baroque style, the palace houses part of the 16th- and 17th-century sections of the collection of the Galleria Nazionale d'Arte Antica and is across the road from the Villa Farnesina. Among the most famous paintings in this large, dark collection are Guido Reni's *Beatrice Cenci* and Caravaggio's *St. John the Baptist.* Stop in, if only to climb the 17th-century stone staircase, itself a drama of architectural shadows and sculptural voids. ⊠ *Via della Lungara 10, Trastevere* ☎ *06/68802323* ⊕ *www.galleriaborghese.it* ☛ *€4* ☼ *Tues.–Sun. 8:30–1:30.*

**② Palazzo Mattei di Giove.** Astonishingly Roman and opulently Baroque, the arcaded, multi-story courtyard of this palazzo is a masterpiece of late-16th-century style. Designed by Carlo Maderno, it is a veritable panoply of sculpted emperor busts, heroic statues, sculpted reliefs, and Paleo-Christian epigrams, all collected by Marchese Asdrubale Mattei. Have your Nikon ready. The ground floor of the palazzo is home to the Centro Italiano di Studio Americani (Center for American Studies). ⊠ *Via Michelangelo Caetani 32, Ghetto.*

Fodor'sChoice
★

**⑦ Piazza in Piscinula.** The square takes its name from some ancient Roman baths on the site (*piscina* means "pool"). The tiny church of **San Benedetto** on the piazza is the smallest church in the city and, despite its 18th-century facade, is much older than it looks, probably dating back to the 4th century AD. Opposite is the medieval **Casa dei Mattei** (Mattei House). Rich and powerful, the Mattei family lived here until the 16th century, when, after a series of murders on the premises, they decided to move out of the district entirely, crossing the river to build their magnificent palace in the Ghetto. ⊠ *Via della Lungaretta, Piazza della Gensola, Via in Piscinula, and Via Lungarina, Trastevere.*

★ ⊕ ⑫ **Piazza Santa Maria in Trastevere.** At the very heart of the Trastevere *rione* (district) is this beautiful piazza, with its elegant raised fountain and sidewalk cafés, a sort of outdoor living room, open to all comers. The showpiece is the 12th-century church of Santa Maria in Trastevere. The striking mosaics on the church's facade—which add light and color to the piazza especially at night when they are spotlit—are believed to represent the Wise and Foolish Virgins. Through innumerable generations, this piazza has seen the comings and goings of tourists and travelers, intellectuals and artists, who lounge on the steps of the fountain or eat lunch at an outdoor table at Sabatini's. Here the paths of Trastevere's residents intersect repeatedly during the day; they pause, gathering in clusters to talk animatedly in the broad accent of Rome or in a score of foreign languages. At night, it's the center of Trastevere's action, with street festivals, musicians, and gamboling dogs vying for attention from the throngs of people taking the evening air. ⊠ *Via della Lungaretta, Via della Paglia, and Via San Cosimato, Trastevere.*

⑪ **San Crisogono.** Eagles and dragons, symbols of the Borghese family, crown the portico of this pretty church, an early Christian basilica that was done over in the Middle Ages and again in the 17th century. The medieval bell tower can best be seen from the little piazza flanking the church or from the other side of Viale Trastevere. San Crisogono is the religious focus of a lively festival honoring Trastevere's patron, the Madonna of Noantri, with a procession on July 15. ⊠ *Piazza Sonnino 44, Trastevere* ☎ *06/5818225.*

> **need a break?** The specialty is in the name of the **Casa del Tramezzino** (House of Sandwiches; ⊠ Viale Trastevere 81 ☎ No phone), which offers a tantalizing variety of choices, Roman- and mom-style, on white bread with the crusts cut off. Try Roman classics like tuna with artichoke hearts, or spinach with mozzarella. Counter service only.

★ ⑩ **San Francesco a Ripa.** Set at one end of Trastevere, this Baroque church attached to a 13th-century Franciscan monastery is noted for one of Bernini's last works, a statue of Blessed Ludovica Albertoni. This is perhaps Bernini's most hallucinatory sculpture, a dramatically lighted figure ecstastic at the prospect of entering heaven as she expires on her deathbed. She clutches her breast as a symbol, art historians have recently deciphered, of the "milk of human kindness" and Christian *caritas* (charity). ⊠ *Piazza San Francesco d'Assisi 88, Trastevere* ☎ *06/5819020* ☉ *Daily 7–noon and 4–7.*

★ ⑰ **San Pietro in Montorio.** Built by order of Ferdinand and Isabella of Spain in 1481 near the spot where, tradition says, St. Peter was crucified, this church is a handsome and dignified edifice. It contains a number of well-known works, including the *Flagellation* in the first chapel on the right, painted by the Venetian Sebastiano del Piombo from a design by Michelangelo, and *St. Francis in Ecstasy,* in the next-to-last chapel on the left, in which Bernini made one of his earliest experiments with concealed lighting effects.

However, the most famous work here is the circular **Tempietto** (Little Temple) in the monastery cloister next door. This sober little building—though tiny, holding only 10 people, it's actually a church in its own right—is one of the key Renaissance buildings in Rome. It was designed by Bramante, the original architect of the new St. Peter's Basilica, in 1502 and represents one of the earliest and most successful attempts to reproduce an entirely classical building with the lessons of ancient Greek and Roman architecture fully evident. The basic design was derived from a circular temple on the grounds of the emperor Hadrian's great villa at Tivoli outside Rome. ⊠ *Piazza San Pietro in Montorio 2 (Via Garibaldi); entrance to cloister and Tempietto at portal next to church, Trastevere* ☎ *06/5813940* ☼ *Daily 9–noon and 4–6; Tempietto, Oct.–Mar., daily 9:30–12:30 and 2–4; Apr.–Sept., daily 4–6.*

**⑧ Santa Cecilia in Trastevere.** The aristocratic St. Cecilia, patron saint of music, is commemorated here. One of ancient Rome's most celebrated early Christian martyrs, she was put to a supernaturally long death by the emperor Diocletian around the year AD 300. After an abortive attempt to suffocate her in the baths of her own house (a favorite means of quietly disposing of aristocrats in Roman days), she was brought before the executioner. But not even three blows of the executioner's sword could dispatch the young girl. She lingered for several days, converting others to the Christian cause, before finally dying. A striking white marble statue of the saint languishing in martyrdom, her head half-severed, lies below the main altar. If you time your visit to the church for Tuesday or Thursday morning between 10 and noon, you can enter the cloistered convent to see what remains of Pietro Cavallini's powerful and rich fresco *Last Judgment,* dating from 1293. It's the only major fresco in existence known to have been painted by Cavallini, a forerunner of Giotto. ⊠ *Piazza Santa Cecilia in Trastevere 22* ☎ *05/5899289* 🎟 *Frescoes €2* ☼ *Daily 9:30–12:30 and 3:45–6:30.*

**⑬ Santa Maria in Trastevere.** Originally built sometime before the 4th century, this is certainly one of the oldest churches in the city, and one of the grandest, too. With a nave framed by a processional of two rows of gigantic columns taken from ancient Roman temples and an altar studded with gilded mosaics, this is an interior that often produces involuntary gasps from unsuspecting visitors. Although there are larger naves in Rome, none seems so majestic, as it's bathed in a mellow glow from the 12th- and 13th-century mosaics and overhead gilding. Supposedly the first church in Rome to have been dedicated to the Virgin Mary, the church was rebuilt in the 12th century, and the portico, which was added in the 19th century, seems to focus attention on the 800-year-old mosaics on the facade, which represent the parable of the Wise and Foolish Virgins. The piazza is enhanced by their aura, especially at night, when the front of the church and its bell tower are illuminated. In the interior's mosaics, look for the representation of the *Life of the Virgin* and note the little building labeled "Taberna Meritoria" just under the figure of the Virgin in the Nativity scene, with a stream of oil flowing from it. It recalls the legend that on the day Christ was born, a stream of pure oil flowed from the earth on the site of the piazza, signifying the coming of

**Fodor'sChoice**
★

the grace of God. Off the north side of the piazza, there's a little street called Via delle Fonte dell'Olio in honor of this miracle. ⊠ *Piazza Santa Maria in Trastevere* ☎ *06/5819443* ⊘ *Daily 9–noon and 4–9.*

**❸ Sant'Angelo in Pescheria.** A landmark of the Ghetto district, this church was built right into the ruins of the ancient Roman Portico d'Ottavia, whose few surviving columns now frame it. The huge porticoed enclosure, named by Augustus in honor of his sister Octavia, was 390 feet wide and 433 feet long. It encompassed two temples, a meeting hall, and a library and served as a kind of grandiose entrance foyer for the adjacent Teatro di Marcello. The ruins of the portico became Rome's *pescheria* (fish market) during the Middle Ages. A stone plaque on a pillar, a relic of that time, admonishes in Latin that the head of any fish surpassing the length of the plaque was to be cut off "up to the first fin" and given to the city fathers or else the vendor was to pay a fine of 10 gold florins. The heads were used to make fish soup and were considered a great delicacy. The church is not usually open to the public, but ring the bell in back and the friendly priest may let you have a look. ⊠ *Via Tribuna di Campitelli 6, Ghetto* ☎ *06/68801819.*

**need a break?**    Stop in at the bakery **Dolceroma** (⊠ Via Portico d'Ottavia 20/b, Ghetto ☎ 06/6892196) to indulge in American and Austrian baked treats. **Franco e Cristina** (⊠ Via Portico d'Ottavia 5, Ghetto) is a stand-up pizza joint with the thinnest, crispiest pizza in town.

**❺ Sinagoga** (Synagogue). This big, aluminum-roof synagogue is the city's largest temple and a Roman landmark. It contains a museum of precious ritual objects and other exhibits documenting the history of Rome's Jewish community. Until the 13th century the Jews were esteemed citizens of Rome. Among them were the bankers and physicians to the popes, who had themselves given permission for the construction of synagogues. But later popes of the Renaissance and Counter-Reformation revoked this tolerance, confining the Jews to the Ghetto and imposing a series of restrictions, some of which were enforced as late as 1870. The main synagogue was built in 1904; earlier, five smaller synagogues for communities of different national origin had existed on nearby Piazza delle Cinque Scole. ⊠ *Lungotevere Cenci 15, Ghetto* ☎ *06/68400661* ⚏ *€6* ⊘ *Oct.–Apr., Mon.–Thurs. 9–5, Apr.–Oct., Mon.–Thurs. 9–8; all year Fri. 9–2, Sun. 9–noon, closed Jewish holidays.*

**❹ Teatro di Marcello** (Theater of Marcellus). With its time-worn hulk looking like something taken from a Piranesi print, hardly recognizable as a theater today, this place was begun by Julius Caesar and completed by the emperor Augustus in AD 13. It was Rome's first permanent building dedicated to theater, and it held 20,000 spectators. Like other Roman monuments, it was transformed into a fortress during the Middle Ages. Later, during the Renaissance, it was converted into a residence by the Savelli, one of the city's noble families. The small archaeological zone is used as a summer venue for open-air classical music and lyrical concerts. ⊠ *Via del Teatro di Marcello, Ghetto* ☎ *06/87131590 for concert information* ⊕ *www.tempietto.it.*

★ ⑮ **Villa Farnesina.** Money was no object to extravagant host Agostino Chigi, a banker from Siena who financed many a papal project. His munificence is evident in this elegant villa, built for him about 1511. He was especially proud of the delicate fresco decorations in the airy loggias, now glassed in to protect their artistic treasures. When Raphael could steal a little time from his work on the Vatican Stanze, he came over to execute some of the frescoes himself, notably a luminous *Galatea*. In his villa, host Agostino entertained the popes and princes of 16th-century Rome. He delighted in impressing his guests at alfresco suppers held in riverside pavilions by having his servants clear the table by casting the precious silver and gold dinnerware into the Tiber. His extravagance was not quite so boundless as he wished to make it appear, however: he had nets unfurled a foot or two under the water's surface to catch the valuable ware.

In the **Loggia of Psyche** on the ground floor, Giulio Romano and others worked from Raphael's designs. Raphael's lovely *Galatea* is in the adjacent room. On the floor above you can see the trompe l'oeil effects in the aptly named **Hall of Perspectives** by Peruzzi. Agostino Chigi's bedroom, next door, was frescoed by Il Sodoma with scenes from the life of Alexander the Great, notably the *Wedding of Alexander and Roxanne,* which is considered to be the artist's best work. The palace also houses the **Gabinetto Nazionale delle Stampe,** a treasure-house of old prints and drawings. When the Tiber embankments were built in 1879, the remains of a classical villa were discovered under the Farnesina gardens, and their decorations are now in the Museo Nazionale Romano's collections in Palazzo Massimo alle Terme. ⊠ *Via della Lungara 230, Trastevere* ☎ *06/68027268* ⊕ *www.lincei.it* ⊠ *€5* ☉ *Mon.–Sat. and 1st Sun. of month 9–1.*

# A JOURNEY BACK:
# THE AVENTINO TO ST. PAUL'S

A rush of silence all but drowns out the street's traffic when you enter the nave of Santa Maria in Cosmedin, just one of the many sights that hauntingly capture the poetry of medieval Rome on this tour. But we also skip over the centuries here, beginning with a pair of ancient Rome's prettiest temples (set side by side, no less) and hurtling on to Testaccio, the city's newly emerging "Left Bank" neighborhood. Much of the area covered, however, is on the **Aventino,** the Aventine Hill, one of the seven hills on which the city was founded, which enjoys a serenity hard to find elsewhere in Rome. It's one of the city's quietest and greenest neighborhoods, an island on which ancient churches and gardens rise above streams of heavy traffic and the daily hubbub in the Trastevere and Testaccio neighborhoods below. The approach from the Circus Maximus is worthy of the Aventine's august atmosphere. On the Aventine are a number of Rome's oldest and least-visited churches as well as one of the city's most surprising delights: the keyhole in the gate to the garden of the Knights of Malta. Beyond lies Testaccio, with traditional and inexpensive restaurants and an animated after-hours scene, and the Piramide di Caio Cestio, one of

Rome's most distinctive and idiosyncratic landmarks: it's a tomb, built by an ancient Roman with more than half an eye on posterity. Not far away is one of the greatest pilgrimage churches in Italy, the medieval basilica of San Paolo fuori le Mura (St. Paul's Outside the Walls).

*Numbers in the text and margin correspond to points of interest on the Aventino to St. Paul's map.*

**a good walk**

Start your walk at the southern end of Via del Teatro Marcello at the little church of **San Nicola in Carcere** ❶ ▶. Follow Via Petroselli south, passing the Casa dei Crescenzi (Crescenzi House), on your right. This is one of only a handful of medieval houses in Rome to have survived almost intact. The inscription on its facade announces that the house was built by Nicolò di Crescenzio, and that in building it he wished—and you must at least admire his ambition—to re-create the glory of ancient Rome. To this end he incorporated various classical fragments in the facade. Far more important are the two small temples in front of you on Piazza Bocca della Verità, both more than 2,000 years old and remarkably well preserved for their age. The rectangular **Tempio della Fortuna Virilis** ❷ and the circular **Tempio di Vesta** ❸ (also known as the Temple of Hercules) were both built about 100 BC. Piazza della Bocca della Verità was the site of ancient Rome's cattle market; across the street is the picturesque church of **Santa Maria in Cosmedin** ❹, famous for the Bocca della Verità (Mouth of Truth) sculpture.

Next, head up the Aventine Hill. Take care crossing broad Via della Greca—where cars pick up speed—and walk along the street, turning into the first street on the right, Clivo dei Publici. This skirts Valle Murcia, the city's rose garden, open in May and June. Where Clivo dei Publici veers off to the left, continue on Via di Santa Sabina. You'll see the church of Santa Sabina ahead, but just before you reach it, you can take a turn around the delightful walled park, known as the Giardino degli Aranci, famous for its orange trees and wonderful view of the Tiber and St. Peter's Basilica (regrettably, women alone should take extra care here, as the quiet streets around Giardino degli Aranci have been known to attract the occasional seamy character, and episodes of harassment have been reported). Three of the Aventine's main attractions are lined up, one after another, on the right side of Via di Santa Sabina: the churches of **Santa Sabina** ❺—an early Christian landmark—and **Sant'Alessio** ❻, and the famous keyhole on **Piazza Cavalieri di Malta** ❼, the Square of the Knights of Malta. Via di Sant'Anselmo winds through the district's quiet residential streets. Cross busy Viale Aventino at Piazza Albania and climb the so-called Piccolo Aventino (Little Aventine) on Via di San Saba to the medieval church of **San Saba** ❽.

To explore the Testaccio neighborhood, return to Viale Aventino and head west, cutting across the park to Via Marmorata. The neighborhood has plain early 1900s housing, a down-to-earth working-class atmosphere, plenty of good trattorias where you can find traditional Roman food—and, of course, Monte Testaccio, a grassy knoll about 150 feet high. What makes this otherwise unremarkable-looking hill special is the fact that it's made from pottery shards—pieces of amphorae, large jars used in ancient times to transport oil, wheat, wine, and other goods. What began as a dump for the broken earthenware jars seemed in time to have taken on a life of its own, until by the Middle Ages the hill, growing even larger, had become a place of pilgrimage. Now clusters of converted warehouses around its base set the latest trends in Roman nightlife. Make your way to Piazza Testaccio, the marketplace, and prettier Piazza di Santa Maria Liberatrice. There are some quintessential Roman trattorias along Via Marmorata and near the Mattatoio, the former slaughterhouse.

Viale Aventino and Via Marmorata converge at **Porta San Paolo** ⑨, one of the ancient city gates in the 3rd-century AD Aurelian walls. You can't miss the big white **Piramide di Caio Cestio** ⑩. Behind it is the **Cimetero degli Inglesi** ⑪ (English Cemetery), final resting place of Keats and other foreign notables. To reach the Church of **San Paolo fuori le Mura** ⑫, literally St. Paul's Outside the Walls, take a taxi or Metro line B (it's the second stop in the Laurentina direction) or Bus 23. The **Centrale Montemartini** ⑬, where classical sculpture is juxtaposed with 20th-century machinery, lies in the same direction.

TIMING The walk takes about 3½ hours, allowing 10–15 minutes for each church and the Protestant cemetery; 30 minutes for the visit to San Paolo fuori le Mura; and 40 minutes to see the ancient sculpture in the Centrale Montemartini on Via Ostiense.

### What to See

⑬ **Centrale Montemartini.** The 1912 Montemartini power plant serves as an unusual setting for the display of antique classical sculpture. Life-size statues are juxtaposed with the plant's massive machinery. Many of the sculptures have never been on permanent public display before. Discovered throughout the city, they span the early Republican through the late imperial periods. In addition to the sculptures, there's a large mosaic of a hunting scene that once made up the floor of an imperial residence. ⊠ *Viale Ostiense 106, Aventino* ☎ *06/39967800* ⊡ *€4.20* ◷ *Tues.–Sun. 9:30–7.*

★ ⑪ **Cimetero degli Inglesi** (English Cemetery). A relentlessly picturesque cemetery reminiscent of a country churchyard, this was intended for non-Catholics. A pilgrimage shrine for lovers of literature, this is where you'll find the tomb of John Keats, who tragically died in Rome after succumbing to consumption at age 25 in 1821. The stone is famously inscribed with "Here lies one whose name was writ in water" (the poet said no dates or name should appear). Nearby is the place where Shelley's heart was buried, as well the tombs of Italian communist Antonio Gramsci and beat poet Gregory Corso. The cemetery is set behind the Piramide, a stone pyramid built in 12 BC at the order of the Roman *praetor* (senior magistrate) who was buried here and is about a 20-minute walk south from the Arch of Constantine along Via San Gregorio and Viale Aventino. ⊠ *Via Caio Cestio 6, Aventino* ☎ *06/5741900* ⊕ *www.protestantcemetery.it* ◷ *Mon.–Sat. 9–5, ring bell for cemetery custodian.*

⑦ **Piazza dei Cavalieri di Malta.** Peek through the keyhole of the **Priorio di Malta**, the walled compound of the Knights of Malta and you'll get a

Aventino
to St. Paul's

KEY

▶ *Start of walk*

surprising eyeful: a picture-perfect view of the dome of St. Peter's Basil-ica, far across the city. The Order of the Knights of Malta is the world's oldest and most exclusive order of chivalry, founded in the Holy Land during the Crusades. Though nominally tenders of the sick in those early days, a role that has since become the order's raison d'être, the knights amassed huge tracts of land in the Middle East and established them-selves as a fearsome mercenary force. From 1530 they were based on the Mediterranean island of Malta, having been expelled from another Mediterranean stronghold, Rhodes, by the Turks in 1522. In 1798 Napoléon expelled them from Malta, and in 1834 they established themselves in Rome, with headquarters on Via Condotti. The com-pound here is the headquarters of the Italian branch of the order. The square itself, and the church and gardens inside the compound, were designed around 1765 by Piranesi, 18th-century Rome's foremost en-graver—you have him to thank for the view. The gardens can be viewed only by appointment. ⊠ *Via Santa Sabina and Via Porta Lavernale, Aventino* ☎ *06/6758–1234.*

**⑩ Piramide di Caio Cestio.** An immensely wealthy praetor in imperial Rome, Gaius Cestius, had this monumental tomb built for himself in the form of a 120-foot-tall pyramid in 12 BC. Though little else is known about him, he clearly had a taste for grandeur and money to burn. The struc-ture was completed in just over a month, an extraordinary feat even for the ancient Romans. On the site of the pyramid is a cat colony run by the famous Roman *gattare* (cat ladies). They look after and try to find homes for some 300 of Rome's thousands of strays. They also give free tours of the graveyard, the pyramid, and their cat shelter on Saturday afternoon. ⊠ *Piazzale Ostiense, Aventino.*

**⑨ Porta San Paolo** (St. Paul's Gate). This gate marked the beginning of the Via Ostiense, the city's vital overland link with the port city of Ostia, 16 km (10 mi) away. Porta San Paolo, one of some 13 gates in the Au-relian walls, defended Rome's vital market area, including the Empo-rium—the riverside docks and warehouses through which supplies brought in by barge were funneled into the city. ⊠ *Viale Piramide Ces-tia, Via Marmorata, and Via Ostiense, Aventino.*

**▶ ❶ San Nicola in Carcere.** The exterior of this church illustrates to perfec-tion the Roman habit of building and rebuilding ancient sites, incor-porating parts of existing buildings in new buildings, adding to them, and then adding to them again. The church stands on the site of a tem-ple built around 250 BC; some of the temple's columns are visible to the right of the church as you face it, beside the remains of the medieval campanile, or bell tower. The facade, dating from the mid-16th century, is thought to have been designed by Giacomo della Porta, the architect who completed the dome of St. Peter's Basilica after Michelangelo's death. ⊠ *Via Teatro di Marcello 46, Ghetto* ☎ *06/68307198.*

**⑫ San Paolo fuori le Mura** (St. Paul's Outside the Walls). For all the drea-riness of its location—and, indeed, for all of its exterior's dullness (19th-century British writer Augustus Hare said the church looked like "a very ugly railway station")—St. Paul's is one of the most historic and important churches in Rome, second in size only to St. Peter's Basilica and one of the city's four pilgrimage churches, along with St. Peter's, San Giovanni in Laterano, and Santa Maria Maggiore.

Built in the 4th century AD by Constantine over the site where St. Paul had been buried, St. Paul's was then rebuilt and considerably enlarged about a century later. At the time it was the largest church in Europe, but its location outside the city walls left it especially vulnerable to attack, and it was sacked by the rampaging Saracens in 846. Although fortified in the 9th century, the church gradually declined in importance, especially as the surrounding marshland became malarial swamps. Sheep wandered through the basilica, undisturbed by the few remaining monks. This sorry state of affairs came to a sudden end in the middle of the 11th century with the arrival of a new abbot, Hildebrandt. He restored the building, recruited new monks, and made St. Paul's a revered center of pilgrimage once more. And so it remained until July 1823, when a fire burned the church to the ground. All that remained, apart from a few mosaics, the sculptured ciborium (tabernacle), and other decorations, were the cloisters. Although the rebuilt St. Paul's has a sort of monumental grandeur, with its columns stretching up the dusky nave and its 19th-century mosaics glinting dully, it's only in the cloisters that you get a real sense of what must have been the magnificence of the original building. ⊠ *Piazzale San Paolo, Via Ostiense 190, Testaccio* ☎ *06/5410341* ⊘ *Daily 7–6; cloister 9–1 and 3–6.*

**⑨ San Saba.** A medieval church with an almost rustic interior and Cosmatesque mosaic pavement, San Saba harbors a hodgepodge of ancient marble pieces and, on the aisle on the left-hand side of the church, a curious fresco cycle painted by an unknown 13th-century artist. The most famous scene shows three young girls lying naked on a bed. Unlikely as it may seem, this is actually an illustration of the good works of St. Nicholas—the girls are naked because their impoverished father (at right) sees no future for them but prostitution. Outside the window, however, St. Nick is about to save the day, by tossing a bag of gold coins in the window to keep the family from a life of shame. ⊠ *Piazza Gianlorenzo Bernini 20, Via San Saba, Aventino* ☎ *06/5743352* ⊘ *Daily 7–noon and 4–6.*

**⑥ Sant'Alessio.** The church's entrance and Romanesque bell tower are on a medieval courtyard. As a whole, the church is the result of reconstructions and restorations over the centuries. Look for the curious marble sculpture at the head of the left nave commemorating St. Alexis, son of a wealthy patrician family in early Christian times. ⊠ *Via Sant'Alessio 23, Aventino* ☎ *06/5743446* ⊘ *Daily 8:30–6:30, until 7 in summer.*

**④ Santa Maria in Cosmedin.** Though this is one of Rome's oldest churches, with a haunting, almost exotic interior, it plays second fiddle to the renowned artifact installed in the church portico, on the left as you enter. The **Bocca della Verità** (Mouth of Truth) is in reality nothing more than an ancient drain cover, unearthed during the Middle Ages. Legend has it, however, that the teeth will clamp down on a liar's hand, and to tell a lie with your hand in the fearsome mouth is to risk losing it. Hordes

FodorśChoice
★

of tourists line up to take the test every day, cameras in hand to bring the proof to the folks back home.

Few churches, inside or out, are as picturesque as this one. The church was built in the 6th century for the city's burgeoning Greek population. Heavily restored at the end of the 19th century, it has the typical basilica form, but it also has an altar screen, an element characteristic of Eastern churches. It stands across from the **Piazza della Bocca della Verità**, originally the location of the Forum Boarium, ancient Rome's cattle market, and later the site of public executions. ⊠ *Piazza Santa Maria in Cosmedin, Aventino* ☎ *06/6781419* ⊗ *Daily 9–5, until 7 or 8 May–Sept.*

❺ **Santa Sabina.** This early Christian basilica demonstrates the severe simplicity common to churches of its era. Later decorations have been peeled away, leaving the essential form as Rome's Christians knew it in the 5th century. Once the church was bright with mosaics and frescoes, now lost. The beautifully carved and preserved wooden doors are the oldest of their kind in existence; they, too, date from the 5th century. ⊠ *Piazza Pietro d'Illiria 1, Via di Santa Sabina, Aventino* ☎ *06/57941* ⊗ *Daily 6:30–12:30 and 4–6, until 7 May–Sept.*

★ ❷ **Tempio della Fortuna Virilis.** A picture-perfect, if dollhouse-size, Roman temple, this rectangular edifice from the 2nd century BC is built in the Greek style, as was the norm in Rome's early years. It owes its fine state of preservation, considering its venerable age, to the fact that it was consecrated and used as a Christian church. ⊠ *Piazza Bocca della Verità, Aventino.*

★ ❸ **Tempio di Vesta.** Long called the Temple of Vesta because of its similarity in shape to the building of that name in the Roman Forum, it's now recognized as a temple to Hercules Victor. All but one of the 20 Corinthian columns of this evocative ruin remain intact. Like its next-door neighbor, the Tempio della Fortuna Virilis, it was built in the 2nd century BC. ⊠ *Piazza Bocca della Verità, Aventino.*

# HIDDEN CORNERS: THE CELIAN HILL TO THE BATHS OF CARACALLA

Like the Aventino, the **Celio** (Celian Hill) seems aloof from the bustle of central Rome. On the slopes of the hill, paths and narrow streets wind through a public park and past walled gardens. Here are some of Rome's earliest churches, such as Santa Maria in Domnica, Santo Stefano Rotondo, and Santi Quattro Coronati, whose medieval poetry is almost palpable. Close by are the Terme di Caracalla, towering ruins of what must have been a spectacular bathing complex, though it does take some imagination to picture what they might have looked like in their prime. In contrast to the busier and noisier districts of the city, the Celio is pervaded by a quiet charm that encourages relaxation and reflection about some of the elements that make Rome so special: the grandeur of antiquity, the mystic power of religion, and the gentle blessings of nature.

*Numbers in the text and margin correspond to points of interest on the Celio and the Baths of Caracalla map.*

Start at the Arco di Costantino—right by the Colosseum—and walk south along Via di San Gregorio. To your right, on the slopes of the Palatine Hill, are all that remains of the great aqueduct built by the consul Appius Claudius in about 300 BC. At the end of Via di San Gregorio, climb the shallow flight of stairs to visit the grandly Baroque church of **San Gregorio Magno ❶** ▶. Then head up the hill on the Clivo di Scauro to the ancient church of **Santi Giovanni e Paolo ❷**. The Clivo—an ascending road which passes under the Romanesque arches of the church—was described by noted author Georgina Masson as one of the few spots in Rome that a medieval pilgrim would easily recognize (if there are no cars parked there, that is). Opposite the church is the gated entrance to private television studios. Just up from there is a tiny door in the wall that opens onto a corner of Villa Celimontana, a park largely unknown to visitors. The gate is sometimes locked; if so, try another entrance on Via San Paolo della Croce just around the corner. Keep to the left as you wander through the park to reach the main entrance on Via della Navicella, where there's a whimsical fountain topped with a Renaissance model in marble of an ancient Roman ship, in front of the church of **Santa Maria in Domnica ❸**. This little church packs lavish decoration, including some vibrant mosaics, into a small space. Opposite, the round church of **Santo Stefano Rotondo ❹** is unusual for its circular plan, beam ceiling, and horrifying paintings of martyrdoms.

Then head north into the large Piazza Celimontana. Passing the entrance to the military hospital, continue straight ahead into Via Celimontana. Turn right onto Via San Giovanni in Laterano, the route of papal processions between the basilicas of San Giovanni in Laterano and St. Peter's. The famous church of **San Clemente ❺** is sandwiched between Via San Giovanni in Laterano and Via Labicana. The 12th-century church is built on the site of an earilier church and even more ancient Roman buildings. From San Clemente walk uphill on Via Santi Quattro Coronati to the 12th-century church of **Santi Quattro Coronati ❻**, part of a fortified abbey that provided refuge to early popes and emperors. Next, retrace your steps, returning to Piazza Celimontana. From Via della Navicella, follow Via Druso to huge Piazza Numa Pompilio, a busy crossroads. On the northwest side of the piazza, the little church of **Santi Nereo e Achilleo ❼** is worth a visit. The tall brick ruins of the **Terme di Caracalla ❽** (Baths of Caracalla) dominate this side of the piazza. The entrance to the baths is at the northwest end.

TIMING The walk takes about 2½ hours, allowing about 10 minutes in each church. Save an additional 45 minutes for a visit to San Clemente's subterranean levels, and about one hour to explore the Terme di Caracalla.

## What to See

❺ **San Clemente.** One of the most impressive archaeological sites in Rome, San Clemente is a 12th-century church built on top of a 4th-century church, which in turn was built over a 2nd-century pagan temple to the god Mithras. Little of the temple remains, but the 4th-century church

Fodor'sChoice
★

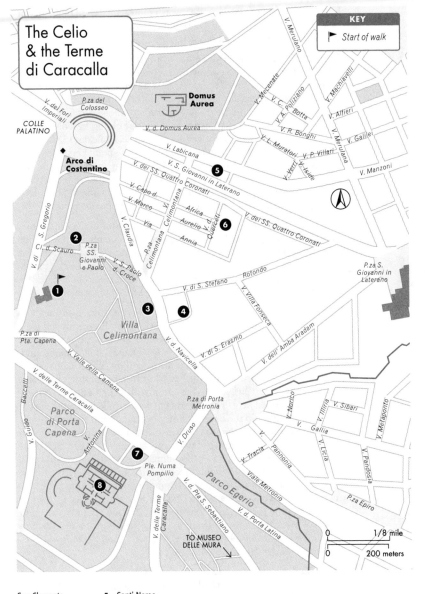

The Celio & the Terme di Caracalla

KEY
▶ *Start of walk*

Domus Aurea

P.za del Colosseo

COLLE PALATINO

V. del Fori Imperiali

**Arco di Costantino**

V. d. Domus Aurea

V. Merulano

V. Mercenate

V. C. Poliziano

V. A. Botta

V. R. Bonghi

V. L. Muratori

V. P. Villari

V. Verri

V. Isíde

V. Alfieri

V. Galilei

V. Merulana

V. Manzoni

V. Labicana

V. S. Giovanni in Laterano **5**

V. del SS. Quattro Coronati

V. Capo d.

V. Marco

Via

Celimontana

Celimontana

Africa

Aurelio

V. d. Querceti **6**

Annia

V. del SS. Quattro Coronati

V. di S. Gregorio

Cl. di d. Scauro

V. di

**2** P.za SS. Giovanni e Paolo

V. Claudia

V. S. Paolo d. Croce

P.za SS.

**3**

**4**

V. di S. Stefano Rotondo

V. Villa Fonseca

P.za S. Giovanni in Laterano

*Villa Celimontana*

V. d. Navicella

V. di S. Erasmo

V. dell' Amba Aradam

P.za di Pta. Capena

V. Valle delle Camene

V. delle Terme Caracalla

Baccelli

*Parco di Porta Capena*

V. Guido

V. Antonina

**7**

P.za di Porta Metronia

V. Druso

V. Narico

V. Tiflia

V. A. Gallia

V. Sibari

V. Metaponto

V. Tracia

V. Pannonia

Viale Metronio

V. Licia

V. Pandosia

P.za Epiro

*Ple. Numa Pompilio*

**8**

*Parco Egerio*

V. delle Terme Caracalla

V. di Pta S. Sebastiano

V. d. Porta Latina

TO MUSEO DELLE MURA

0 ———— 1/8 mile
0 ———— 200 meters

is largely intact, perhaps because it wasn't unearthed until the 19th century. (It was discovered by Irish Dominican monks; members of the order still live in the adjacent monastery.)

The upper church, which you enter from street level, holds a beautiful early-12th-century mosaic showing a cross on a gold background, surrounded by swirling green acanthus leaves, teeming with little scenes of everyday life. The marble choir screens, salvaged from the 4th-century church, are decorated with early Christian symbols: doves, vines, and fish. In the left nave is the Castiglioni chapel, holding frescoes painted around 1400 by the Florentine artist Masolino da Panicale (1383–1440), a key figure in the introduction of realism and one-point perspective into Renaissance painting. Note the large Crucifixion and scenes from the lives of Sts. Catherine, Ambrose, and Christopher, plus an Annunciation (over the entrance). Before you leave the upper church, take a look at the pretty cloister—evening concerts are held here in summer.

From the right nave, stairs lead down to the remains of the 4th-century church, which was active until 1084, when it was damaged beyond repair during a siege of the area by the Norman prince Robert Guiscard. The vestibule is decorated with marble fragments found during the excavations (which are still under way), and in the nave are colorful 11th-century frescoes depicting stories from the life of St. Clement.

From the left nave follow the signs to the Mythraeum, a shrine dedicated to the god Mithras, whose cult spread from Persia and gained a hold in Rome during the 2nd and 3rd centuries AD. Mithras was believed to have been born in a cave and was thus worshipped in underground, cavernous chambers, where initiates into the all-male cult would share a meal while reclining on stone couches. Most such pagan shrines in Rome were destroyed by Christians, who often built churches over their remains, as happened here. The Mithraeum was installed sometime in the 2nd or 3rd century in the basement of a Roman *domus* (house). Corridors lead to other of the house's chambers, partly decorated with stucco and frescoes. Proceed through the domus basement, cross a very narrow alley, and enter an adjacent building, the oldest known structure on the property. It was possibly once a mint, gutted by Nero's fire in AD 64 and rebuilt as a courtyard surrounded by small rooms. The herringbone brickwork of the floors and the waterproof plaster seem to indicate that the rooms were used as a depot. Following the signs will bring you back to the lower church. ⊠ *Via San Giovanni in Laterano 108, Colosseo* ☎ *06/70451018* ⊠ *€3* ⊗ *Mon.–Sat. 9–noon and 3–6, Sun. and holidays 10–12:30 and 3–6.*

▶ ❶ **San Gregorio Magno.** Set amid the greenery of the Celian Hill, this church wears its Baroque facade proudly. Dedicated to St. Gregory the Great (who served as pope 590–604), it was built about 750 by Pope Gregory II to commemorate his predecessor and namesake. It was from the monastery on this site that Pope Gregory the Great dispatched St. Augustine to Britain in 596 to convert the heathens there. The church of San Gregorio itself has the appearance of a typical Baroque structure, the result of remodeling in the 17th and 18th centuries. But you can still see what's said to be the stone slab on which the pious Gregory the Great slept; it's in the far right-hand chapel. Outside are three chapels. The right chapel is dedicated to Gregory's mother, St. Sylvia, and contains a Guido Reni fresco of the *Concert of Angels*. The one on the left contains the simple table at which Gregory fed 12 poor men every day. According to legend, one day an angel joined them as the 13th diner. The chapel in the center, dedicated to St. Andrew, contains two monumental frescoes showing scenes from the saint's life. They were painted at the beginning of the 17th century by Domenichino (*The Flagellation of St. Andrew*) and Guido Reni (*The Execution of St. Andrew*). It's a striking juxtaposition of the sturdy, if sometimes stiff, classicism of Domenichino with the more flamboyant and heroic Baroque manner of Guido Reni. ⊠ *Piazza San Gregorio, Colosseo* ☎ *06/7008827* ⊘ *Daily 8–12:30 and 1:30–7.*

**❸ Santa Maria in Domnica.** This early Christian structure was built over the house of a Roman martyr, St. Cyriaca, about whom little seems to be known other than that she was wealthy. The vibrantly colored 9th-century mosaics in the apse behind the altar are worth seeing. Notice the handkerchief carried by the Virgin Mary: it's a *mappa*, a fashionable accoutrement in 9th-century Byzantium. ⊠ *Via della Navicella 10, Colosseo* ☎ *06/7001519* ⊘ *Daily 9–noon and 3:30–6:30.*

**❷ Santi Giovanni e Paolo.** Perched up the incline of the Clivus di Scauro—

Fodor'sChoice ★ a magical time-machine of a street where the dial seems to be stuck somewhere in the 13th century—Santi Giovanni e Paolo is an image that would tempt most landscape painters. Landmarked by one of Rome's finest Romanesque belltowers, it looms over on a poetic piazza. But the most notable thing about this church is what lies beneath it: a whole block of ancient buildings. The site's detailed English signage explains the development of what was originally a group of simple houses and taverns. By the 2nd century AD they had been taken over by wealthier owners, who installed private thermal baths, fountains, and frescoes. On these grounds in 362, St. John and St. Paul (not the apostles, but high-ranking patricians) were executed by Julian the Apostate, a successor of Constantine who attempted to restore paganism in Rome.

A basilica erected on the spot was, like San Clemente, destroyed in 1084 by attacking Normans. Its half-buried columns, near the current church entrance, are visible through misty glass. The current church has its origins at the start of the 12th century, but the interior dates mostly from the 17th century and later. The lovely, incongruous chandeliers are a hand-me-down from New York's Waldorf Astoria hotel, a gift arranged by the late Archbishop Francis Spellman of New York, whose titular church this was. Spellman also initiated the excavations here in 1949. ⊠ *Piazza Santi Giovanni e Paolo 13, Colosseo* ☎ *06/772711* ⊘ *Daily 9–11 and 3:30–6.*

**❼ Santi Nereo e Achilleo.** One of Rome's oldest churches, probably dating from the 4th century, Sts. Nereus and Achilleus has accumulated treasures such as 8th-century mosaics, a medieval pulpit on a multicolor marble base from the Terme di Caracalla, a 13th-century mosaic choir, and a fine, 16th-century episcopal—or bishop's—throne. ⊠ *Viale* *delle Terme di Caracalla 28, Aventino* ☎ *06/5757996* ☼ *Apr.–Oct., Sat.–Thurs. 10–noon and 4–6.*

**❻** **Santi Quattro Coronati.** One of the magical cul-de-sacs in Rome where
Fodor'sChoice history seems to be holding its breath, this church is strongly embued
★ with the sanctity of the Romanesque era. Marvelously redolent of the
Middle Ages, this is one of the most unusual and unexpected corners
of Rome, a quiet citadel that has resisted the tide of time and traffic flowing below its ramparts. The church honors the Four Crowned Saints—
the four brothers Seveus, Severinus, Carpophorus, and Victorius, all
Roman officials who were whipped to death for their faith by emperor
Diocletian (284-305). The original 9th-century church was twice as
large as the current one. The abbey was partially destroyed during the
Normans' sack of Rome about 1085, but it was reconstructed about 30
years later. This explains the inordinate size of the apse in relation to
the small nave. Don't miss the **cloister,** with its well-tended gardens and
12th-century fountain. The entrance is the door in the left nave; ring
the bell if it's not open.

There's another medieval gem hidden away off the courtyard at the
church entrance: the **Chapel of San Silvestro.** (Enter the door marked
MONACHE AGOSTINIANE and ring the bell at the left for the nun; she will
pass the key to the chapel through the wheel beside the grille.) The chapel
has remained, for the most part, as it was when consecrated in 1246, decorated with marbles and frescoes. These tell the story of the Christian emperor Constantine's recovery from leprosy thanks to Pope Sylvester I. Note,
too, the delightful *Last Judgment* fresco above the door, in which the angel
on the left neatly rolls up sky and stars like a backdrop, signaling the end
of the world. When you leave, lock the door and return the key to the
nun. A donation is appropriate. ⊠ *Via Santi Quattro Coronati 20,
Colosseo* ☎ *06/70475427* ☼ *Church and chapel daily 9:30–noon and
3:30–6; cloister 9:30–noon and 4:30–6; ring bell to visit at other times.*

**❹** **Santo Stefano Rotondo.** This 5th-century church was inspired perhaps by
the design of the church of the Holy Sepulchre in Jerusalem. Its unusual
round plan and timbered ceiling set it apart from most other Roman
churches. The vast barnlike space has walls aplenty, and most of them
are covered with frescoes that lovingly depict the most gory martyrdoms
of Catholic saints. You've been warned: these are not for the faint-hearted.
⊠ *Via Santo Stefano Rotondo 7, Colosseo* ☎ *06/421191* ☼ *Tues.–Sat.
9–1 and 1:50–4:20, Mon. 1:50–4:20, 2nd Sun. of month 9–noon.*

★ ♻ **❽** **Terme di Caracalla** (Baths of Caracalla). Although not the largest in ancient Rome, these public baths seem to have been by far the most opulent. Begun in AD 206 by the emperor Septimius Severus and completed
by his son, Caracalla, they could accommodate 1,600 bathers at a time.
Taking a bath was a long and complex process, which is eminently un-
derstandable if you see it as a social activity first and foremost. Remember,
too, that for all their sophistication, the Romans didn't have soap. You
began in the *sudatoria,* a series of small rooms resembling saunas.
Here you sat and sweated. From these you moved to the *calidarium,* a
large circular room that was humid rather than simply hot. This was

where the actual business of washing went on. You used a *strigil,* or scraper, to get the dirt off; if you were rich, your slave did this for you. Next you moved to the *tepidarium,* a warmish room, the purpose of which was to allow you to begin gradually to cool down. Finally, you splashed around in the *frigidarium,* the only actual "bath" in the place, in essence a shallow swimming pool filled with cold water. The rich might like to complete the process with a brisk rubdown with a scented towel. It was not unusual for a member of the opposite sex to perform this favor for you (the baths were open to men and women, though the times when they could use them were different). There was a nominal admission fee, often waived by officials and emperors wishing to curry favor with the plebeians.

For the Romans, the baths were much more than places to wash. Although providing bathing facilities was their main purpose, there were also recital halls, art galleries, and libraries to improve the mind, and massage and exercise rooms as well as sports grounds to improve the body, in addition to halls and gardens just for talking and strolling. Even the smallest public baths had at least some of these amenities, and in the capital of the Roman Empire, they were provided on a lavish scale. Their functioning depended on the slaves who cared for the clients, checking their robes, rubbing them down, and seeing to their needs. Under the magnificent marble pavement of the stately halls, other slaves toiled in a warren of tiny rooms and passages, stoking the fires that heated the water. ⊠ *Via delle Terme di Caracalla 52, Aventino* ☎ *06/39967700* ⊕ *www. pierreci.it* ⬛ *€5* ☉ *Tues.–Sun. 9–1 hour before sunset, Mon. 9–2.*

# HISTORIC KALEIDOSCOPE: MONTI TO SAN GIOVANNI IN LATERANO

In ancient times, the Suburra (the present-day Monti neighborhood) was one of Rome's most populous areas. A dark, warrenlike sector of multistory dwellings, it was the cramped home of a substantial portion of ancient Rome's more than 1 million citizens in the 1st century AD, a notorious slum that lived by its own rules (or lack of them—many of the gladiators that fought in the nearby Colosseum lived here). So infamous were the Suburra's mean streets that it's thought that the great fire of AD 64, which all but destroyed the neighborhood, may have been intentionally set to clear out the area for better-planned and more hygienic dwellings. A high stone wall separating the Suburra from the Imperial Fora acted as a barrier, keeping the flames from endangering Rome's most august monuments.

The neighborhood is clearly different from the Old Rome area to the west. Here you'll find the stamp of a much more remote past. The Colosseum's marble-clad walls loom at the end of narrow, shadowy streets with Latin-sounding names: Panisperna, Baccina, Fagutale. Other walls, built for the Caesars, shore up medieval towers; streets dip and climb, hugging the curves of two of the seven hills on which Romulus founded his city. Amid the hints of antiquity, several great churches of the Christian era stand out like islands, connected by broad avenues. The newer streets—laid out by the popes and, later, by city planners at the time of Italy's unification—slice through the meandering byways, providing more direct and navigable routes for pilgrims and commerce. The majestic Santa Maria Maggiore, its interior gleaming with gold from the New World, and San Giovanni in Laterano, with its grand, echoing vastness, are among the oldest of the city's churches, though restored and remodeled through the centuries. They are also major pilgrimage sites, the focus of Holy Year rites for Roman Catholics, and a magnet for anyone interested in art and architecture. Another attraction is the smaller, hard-to-find church of San Pietro in Vincoli, with its hidden treasure—Michelangelo's statue of *Moses*.

*Numbers in the text and in the margin correspond to numbers on the Monti and San Giovanni in Laterano map.*

**a good walk**

Start at the Colosseum and walk up the stairs through the Metro station to reach Largo Agnesi, a scenic overlook with views of the Colosseum and the columns of the Tempio di Venere e Roma. Facing away from the Colosseum, walk right, then turn left on Via Fagutale, which runs along and above the sunken main road. Turn right at Via della Polveriera, then left at Via Eudosiana to reach the piazza that's home to the church of **San Pietro in Vincoli ❶ ↱**, where Michelangelo's *Moses* attracts throngs of tourists. Walk down the staircase, called Salita dei Borgia, passing under Torre Borgia, home of the notorious Vannozza, mistress of Borgia pope Alexander VI.

Return to Via Cavour, turning right onto it and heading northeast (or take the quieter Via Urbana, which runs parallel). Make a brief detour to the left (west) to see the noted early Christian mosaics in the church of **Santa Pudenziana ❷**, especially the giganitic apse mosaic that portrays Christ teaching the apostles, a magnificent remnant of 5th-century culture. Both Via Urbana and Via Cavour lead straight to Piazza dell'Esquilino and the sweeping staircase at the rear of **Santa Maria Maggiore ❸**, one of the four great pilgrimage churches of Rome. Walk around the enormous church to Piazza Santa Maria Maggiore, taking a moment to admire the full effect of facade, loggia, and bell tower. Narrow Via di Santa Prassede, which is at the southwest corner of the piazza, leads to the little church of **Santa Prassede ❹**, whose Chapel of St. Zenone mosaics are among the most beautiful in Italy, especially the figures of four angels hovering in the blue vault. Returning to Via Merulana, you reach Largo Brancaccio. On your right is the large **Museo Nazionale d'Arte Orientale ❺**, Rome's main collection of art and artifacts from the East and Middle East. The area between Via Merulana and Stazione Termini, to the east, with Piazza Vittorio as its fulcrum, is as multiethnic as Rome gets. Asian, Indian, and African grocery stores and restaurants abound.

Via Merulana was laid out as a pilgrimage route in the 1500s and runs as straight as an arrow between the basilicas of Santa Maria Maggiore and **San Giovanni in Laterano ❻**, the immense cathedral of Rome. Attached to the north flank of the church is the **Palazzo Apostolico Lateranense ❼**. The shrine of the **Scala Santa ❽** (Holy Staircase) is in the churchlike edifice diagonally across from the Lateran Palace. Turn south into **Piazza San Giovanni in Laterano** ❾. On the square is the octagonal **Battistero** ❿ (Baptistry).

From Piazza di Porta San Giovanni and the ancient city walls, follow Viale Carlo Felice east to the church of **Santa Croce in Gerusalemme** ⓫. To the left of the church is the **Museo Nazionale degli Strumenti Musicali** ⓬ (National Museum of Musical Instruments). Then you can head back to San Giovanni's Metro stop and bus lines, or continue northeast to see **Porta Maggiore** ⓭ (Main Gate), a part of the Acqua Claudia aqueduct.

TIMING   The walk takes about four hours, including visits to the basilicas. They're open through lunch hour, but if you want to see Michelangelo's *Moses* in San Pietro in Vincoli, you have to get there before 12:30 or after 3:30. Santa Pudenziana and Santa Prassede also close from about noon to 3 or 4. Allow an additional 30 minutes for a visit to the Museo d'Arte Orientale and 20–30 minutes for a cursory look at the Museo Nazionale degli Strumenti Musicali.

## What to See

❿ **Battistero** (Baptistry). Though much altered through the centuries, the Baptistry of San Giovanni is the forerunner of all such buildings where baptisms take place, a ritual of key importance in the Christian faith. It was built by Constantine in the 4th century and enlarged by Pope Sixtus III about 100 years later. It stands on the site of the baths attached to the home of Constantine's second wife, Fausta, who, emperor's wife or not, was suffocated in the hot room of the baths after having falsely accused Constantine's son by his first wife of having tried to rape her. This exceedingly unpleasant death is an example of one of the accepted Roman methods of dealing with members of the ruling classes who were implicated in scandals of this type. Of the four chapels arranged around the walls of the baptistry, the most interesting is the first on the right as you enter. It has a set of ancient bronze doors whose hinges send out a musical sound when the doors are opened and closed. They probably came from the Terme di Caracalla. Notice also the splendid porphyry columns that support the entire structure, typical of the Romans' love of luxurious and exotic materials. ⊠ *Piazza San Giovanni in Laterano, San Giovanni* ⊙ *Daily 9–1 and 3–1 hr before sunset.*

❺ **Museo Nazionale d'Arte Orientale** (National Museum of Oriental Art). The museum's extensive collection of Middle Eastern and East Asian art is being continually enriched by the finds of Italian archaeological expeditions. Italian archaeologists have been in on some of the most important finds of recent decades, such as Ebla in Syria. ⊠ *Via Merulana 248, Colosseo* ☎ *06/4874415* ⊠ *€4* ⊙ *Mon., Wed., Fri., Sat. 9–2; Tues., Thurs., Sun. 9–7; closed 1st and 3rd Mon. of month.*

⓬ **Museo Nazionale degli Strumenti Musicali** (National Museum of Musical Instruments). Just behind Santa Croce is this museum housing a sizable collection of instruments from prehistory to the present, arranged by type, including folk instruments, mechanical instruments, a 16th-century clavichord, and the richly carved 17th-century Barberini Harp. ⊠ *Pi-*

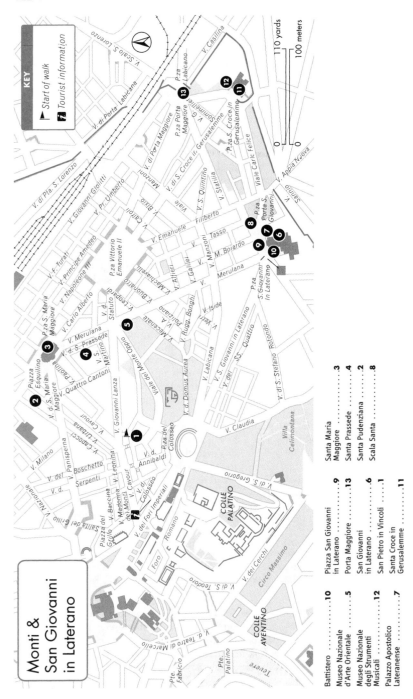

Monti &
San Giovanni
in Laterano

KEY

▲ Start of walk

🚹 Tourist information

110 yards

100 meters

*azza Santa Croce in Gerusalemme 9/a, San Giovanni* ☎ *06/7014796*
🎟 *€2* 🕐 *Tues.–Sun. 8:30–7:30.*

**❼ Palazzo Apostolico Lateranense.** The building flanking the basilica of San
Giovanni was the popes' official residence until their exile to Avignon
in the south of France in the 14th century. The current palace was built
by Domenico Fontana in 1586. Still technically part of the Vatican, it
now houses the offices of the Rome Diocese and the Vatican Historical
Museum. On the (required) tour you'll see the historic Papal Apartment,
with antique furnishings, medieval sculptures, and Renaissance tapestries,
and the Sala della Conciliazione, with a magnificent 16th-century carved
and painted wood ceiling. ✉ *Entrance outside at atrium of San Gio-*
*vanni in Laterano, San Giovanni* ☎ *06/69886386* 🎟 *€4* 🕐 *Sat. tours*
*at 9:30, 11, and 12:15; 1st Sun. of month tours at 8:45 and 1.*

**❾ Piazza San Giovanni in Laterano.** At the center of this square stands
Rome's oldest and tallest obelisk, which originally stood in front of the
Temple of Ammon in Thebes, Egypt, in the 15th century BC. It was brought
to Rome by Constantine in AD 357 to stand in the Circus Maximus and
finally was set up here in 1588. Adjoining the square is the rambling
city hospital of San Giovanni, founded in the Middle Ages as a kind of
infirmary for Rome's poor and pilgrims. ✉ *Via Merulana at Via Amba*
*Aradam, San Giovanni.*

**★ ⓭ Porta Maggiore** (Main Gate). The massive 1st-century AD monument is
not only a *porta* (city gate) but also part of the Acqua Claudia aqueduct. It gives you an idea of the grand scale of ancient Roman public
works. On the Piazzale Labicano side of the portal, to the east, is the
curious **Baker's Tomb**, erected in the 1st century BC by a prosperous baker.
Look closely—the tomb is decorated with stone ovens and charming friezes
with scenes of the deceased's trade. ✉ *Junction of Via Eleniana, Via di*
*Porta Maggiore, and Via Casilina, San Giovanni.*

**❻ San Giovanni in Laterano.** This is Rome's cathedral; it's here that the pope
officiates in his capacity as bishop of Rome. The towering facade dates
from 1736 and was modeled on that of St. Peter's Basilica. The 15 colossal statues (Christ, John the Baptist, John the Evangelist, and the 12 Apostles of the church) look out on the sea of dreary suburbs that have spread
from Porta San Giovanni to the lower slopes of the Alban Hills. San Giovanni was founded in the 4th century on land donated by the emperor
Constantine, who had obtained it from the wealthy patrician family of
the Laterani. Vandals, earthquakes, and fire damaged the original and
successive constructions. Finally, in 1646, Pope Innocent X commissioned
Borromini to rebuild the church, and it's Borromini's rather cool, tense
Baroque interior that you see today.

Under the portico on the left stands an ancient statue of Constantine.
Another link with Rome's past is the central portal's ancient bronze doors,
brought here from the Curia building in the Forum. Inside, little is left
of the early decorations. The fragment of a fresco on the first pillar in
the double aisle on the right depicts Pope Boniface VIII proclaiming the
first Holy Year in 1300; it's attributed to the 14th-century Florentine
painter Giotto. The mosaic in the apse was reconstructed from a 12th-

# San Giovanni in Laterano

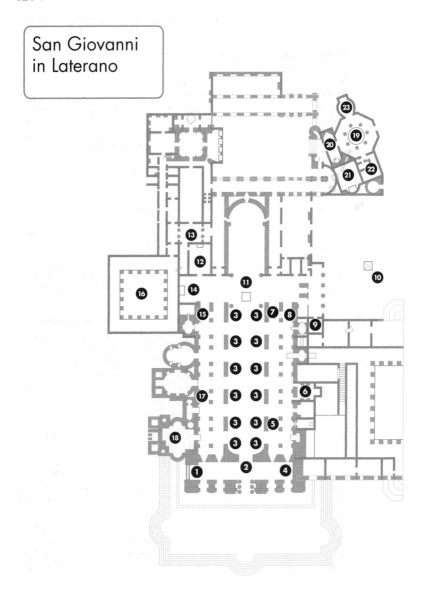

century original by Torriti, the same Franciscan friar who executed the apse mosaic in Santa Maria Maggiore. The papal altar at the center of the church contains a wooden table believed to have been used by St. Peter to celebrate the Eucharist. The altar's rich Gothic tabernacle dates from 1367 and, somewhat gruesomely, contains what are believed to be the heads of Sts. Peter and Paul. You shouldn't miss the church **cloister**, with its twin columns encrusted with 13th-century Cosmatesque mosaics by the Vassallettos, a father-and-son team. Enter the cloister from the last chapel at the end of the left aisle. ⊠ *Piazza di Porta San Giovanni* ☎ *06/69886433* ◳ *Cloister €2.50* ۞ *Basilica daily 7–6, until 7 May–Sept.; cloister daily 9–½ hr before church closing.*

⮞ ★ ❶ **San Pietro in Vincoli.** What has put this otherwise unprepossessing church on the map is the monumental statue of Moses carved by Michelangelo in the early 16th century for the never-completed tomb of his patron, Pope Julius II, which was to include dozens of statues and stand nearly 40 feet tall when installed in St. Peter's Basilica. Only three statues—*Moses* and the two that flank it here, *Leah* and *Rachel*—had been completed when Julius died. His successor as pope, from a rival family, had other plans for Michelangelo, and Julius's tomb was abandoned unfinished. The fierce power of this remarkable sculpture dominates its setting. People say that you can see the sculptor's profile in the lock of Moses' beard right under his lip, and that the pope's profile is also there somewhere. But don't let the search distract you from the overall effect of this marvelously energetic work. As for the rest of the church, St. Peter, after whom the church is named, takes second billing to Moses. What are reputed to be the chains *(vincoli)* that bound St. Peter during his imprisonment by the Romans in Jerusalem are in a bronze and crystal urn under the main altar. Other treasures in the church include a 7th-century mosaic of St. Sebastian, in front of the second altar to the left of the main altar, and, by the door, the tomb of the Pollaiuolo brothers, two lesser 15th-century Florentine artists. ⊠ *Piazza San Pietro in Vincoli, Colosseo* ☎ *06/4882865* ۞ *Daily 7–12:30 and 3:30–6, until 7 May–Sept.*

⓫ **Santa Croce in Gerusalemme.** Like Santa Maria Maggiore and San Giovanni in Laterano, the outward appearance of this church doesn't give away its ancient origins. The Romanesque bell tower off to one side was put up in the 12th century, the facade was rebuilt in the 18th century, and the interior was extensively remodeled in the 17th and 18th centuries. But the church foundations were once part of the 4th-century AD palace of St. Helena, mother of the emperor Constantine. She was an indefatigable collector of holy relics, and her most precious discovery was fragments of the Holy Cross—the cross on which Christ was crucified—which she had unearthed during one of many forays through the Holy Land. The relics of the cross are in the modern chapel at the end of the left aisle. The chapel dedicated to St. Helena, in the lower level of the building, was redecorated in the 15th century with a dazzling gold-and-blue version of an earlier mosaic. ⊠ *Piazza Santa Croce in Gerusalemme, San Giovanni* ☎ *06/7014769* ۞ *Daily 7–7.*

❸ **Santa Maria Maggiore.** The exterior of the church, from the broad sweep of steps on Via Cavour to the more elaborate facade on Piazza Santa Maria

## Santa Maria Maggiore

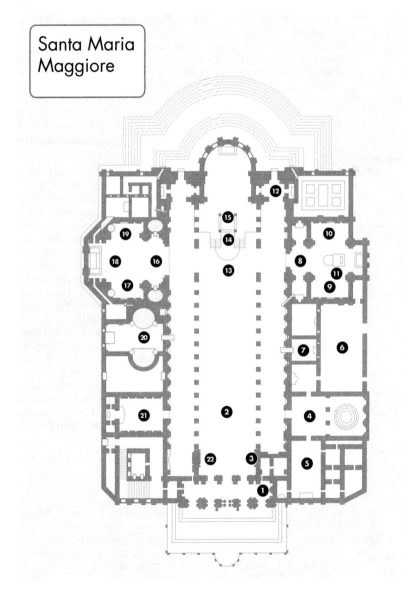

Maggiore, is that of a gracefully curving 18th-century building, a fine example of the Baroque architecture of the period. But in fact Santa Maria Maggiore is one of the oldest churches in Rome, built around 440 by Pope Sixtus III. One of the four great pilgrimage churches of Rome, it's by far the most complete example of an early Christian basilica in the city—one of the immense, hall-like structures derived from ancient Roman civic buildings and divided into thirds by two great rows of columns marching up the nave. The other six major basilicas in Rome—San Giovanni in Laterano and St. Peter's Basilica are the most famous—have been entirely transformed, or even rebuilt. Paradoxically, the major reason why this church is such a striking example of early Christian design is that the same man who built the incongruous exteriors about 1740—Ferdinando Fuga—also conscientiously restored the interior, throwing out later additions and, crucially, replacing a number of the great columns.

Every August 5, a special mass in Santa Maria Maggiore's Cappella Sistina commemorates the miracle that led to the founding of the basilica: the Virgin Mary appeared in a dream to Pope Liberio and ordered him to build a church in her honor on the spot where snow would fall on the night of August 5 (an event about as likely in a Roman August as snow in the Sahara). The Madonna of the Snows is celebrated with a shower of white rose petals from the ceiling.

Precious 5th-century mosaics high on the nave walls and on the triumphal arch in front of the main altar are splendid testimony to the basilica's venerable age. Those along the nave show 36 scenes from the Old Testament (unfortunately, they are hard to see clearly without binoculars), and those on the arch illustrate the Annunciation and the Youth of Christ. The majestic mosaic in the apse was created by a Franciscan monk named Torriti in 1275. The resplendent carved wood ceiling dates from the early 16th century; it's supposed to have been gilded with the first gold brought from the New World. The inlaid marble pavement (called Cosmatesque after the family of master artisans who developed the technique) in the central nave is even older, dating from the 12th century.

The **Cappella Sistina** (Sistine Chapel), which opens onto the right-hand nave, was created by architect Domenico Fontana for Pope Sixtus V in 1585. Elaborately and heavily decorated with precious marbles "liberated" from the monuments of ancient Rome, the chapel includes a lower level in which some 13th-century sculptures by Arnolfo da Cambio are all that's left of what was once the incredibly richly endowed chapel of the *presepio* (Christmas crèche), looted during the Sack of Rome in 1527. Directly opposite, on the other side of the church, stands the **Cappella Paolina** (Pauline Chapel), a rich Baroque setting for the tombs of the Borghese popes Paul V—who commissioned the chapel in 1611 with the declared intention of outdoing Sixtus's chapel across the nave—and Clement VIII. The *Madonna* above its altar is a precious Byzantine image painted perhaps as early as the 8th century. The **Cappella Sforza** (Sforza Chapel) next door was designed by Michelangelo and completed by della Porta (the same partnership that was responsible for the dome of St. Peter's Basilica). ⊠ *Piazza Santa Maria Maggiore, Termini* ☎ *06/4814287* ⊙ *Daily 7–7.*

**④ Santa Prassede.** This small and inconspicuous 9th-century church is
Fodor'sChoice   known above all for the exquisite little **Cappella di San Zenone,** just to
★   the left of the entrance. It gleams with vivid mosaics that reflect their
Byzantine inspiration. Though much less classical and naturalistic than
the earlier mosaics of Santa Pudenziana, they are no less splendid and
the composition of four angels hovering on the sky-blue vault is one of
the masterstrokes of Byzantine art. Note the square halo over the head
of Theodora, mother of St. Pasquale I, the pope who built this church.
It indicates that she was still alive when she was depicted by the artist.
The chapel also contains one curious relic: a miniature pillar, supposedly part of the column at which Christ was flogged during the Passion.
It was brought to Rome in the 13th century. Next to the entrance to the
chapel is an early work of Bernini, a bust of Bishop Santoni, executed
when the sculptor was in his midteens. Over the main altar, the magnificent mosaics on the arch and apse are also in rigid Byzantine style;
in them Pope Pasquale I wears the square halo of the living and holds
a model of his church. ⊠ *Via di Santa Prassede 9/a, Termini* ☎ *06/
4882456* ◷ *Daily 7:30–noon and 4–6:30.*

**② Santa Pudenziana.** Outside of Ravenna, Rome has some of the most op-
Fodor'sChoice   ulent mosaics in Italy and this church has one of the most striking ex-
★   amples. Commissioned during the papacy of Innocent I, its late 4th-century
apse mosaic represents Christ Teaching the Apostles and sits high on the
wall perched above a Baroque altarpiece surrounded by a bevy of florid
18th-century paintings. Not only is it the largest early Christian apse mosaic extant (although tiny compared to the now-lost example of nearby
San Giovanni in Laterano), it is remarkable for its iconography. At the
center sits Christ Enthroned, looking a bit like a Roman emperor, presiding over a chorus line of saints all wearing togas in best Roman senator fashion. Each saint faces the spectator, literally rubs shoulders with
his companion (unlike earlier hieratic styles where each figure is isolated),
and bears an individualized expression, although the latter may be due
to a 17th-century restoration. Above the figures and a landscape that sym-
bolizes the Heavenly Jerusalem floats the signs of the four evangelists in
a blue sky flecked with an orange sunset, all done in thousands of
tesserae. This extraordinary composition seems a sort of paleo-Christian
forerunner of Raphael's *School of Athens* in the Vatican.

To either side of Christ, Sts. Praxedes and Pudentia hold wreaths over
the heads of Sts. Peter and Paul. These two women were actually daughters of the Roman senator Pudens (probably the one mentioned in 2 Tim
4:21), whose family befriended both apostles. During the persecutions
of Nero, both sisters collected the blood of many martyrs and then suffered the same fate. Pudentia transformed her house into a church, but
this namesake church was constructed over a 2nd century bath house.
Beyond the sheer beauty of the mosaic work, the size, rich detail, and
number of figures make this both the last gasp of ancient Roman art
and one of the first monuments of early Christianity. ⊠ *Via Urbana 160,
Termini* ☎ *06/4814622* ◷ *Mon.–Sat. 8–6:30.*

**⑧ Scala Santa.** A 16th-century building encloses the Holy Steps, which tradition holds to be the staircase from Pilate's palace in Jerusalem, brought

to Rome by St. Helena, mother of the emperor Constantine. Wood protects the 28 marble steps worn smooth by the knees of pilgrims through the centuries. There are two other staircases that you can ascend to see the **Sancta Sanctorum,** the private chapel of the popes. The chapel is richly decorated with well-preserved Cosmatesque mosaics and a famous painting of Jesus, claimed to have been painted by angels. ⊠ *Piazza San Giovanni in Laterano, San Giovanni* ☎ *06/69886433* ⊘ *Apr.–Oct., daily 6:15–12:15 and 3:30–7; Nov.–Mar., daily 3:30–6.*

# QUO VADIS?:
# THE CATACOMBS & THE APPIAN WAY

In the swelling tide of urban development, a greenbelt of pastures and villas along **Via Appia Antica** has survived as an evocative remnant of the Roman *campagna* (countryside). Strewn with classical ruins and dotted with grazing sheep, the Via Appia (Appian Way) stirs images of chariots and legionnaires returning from imperial conquests, of barrel-shape Roman carts transporting produce from the farms of Campania to the south, and of tearful families mourning at the tombs of their dead. Though time and vandals have taken their toll on the tombs along the Via Appia, what remains of them gives you an idea of how Rome's important families made sure that their ancestors, and the family name, would be remembered by posterity. Known as the "Queen of Roads," the Via Appia was completed in 312 BC by Appius Claudius, who also built Rome's first aqueduct. He had it laid out to connect Rome with settlements in the south, in the direction of Naples: it was later extended to Brindisi, the port on the Adriatic. The dark, gloomy catacombs, the underground cemeteries that early Christians turned into places of worship, contrast with the fresh air, lush greenery, and classical ruins along the ancient road.

The catacombs aren't Rome's oldest cemeteries. Even before Christianity reached Rome, those citizens who couldn't afford a fine funeral monument along one of the consular roads were either cremated or buried in necropoli outside the city gates. An imperial law prohibited burial within the city—except for deified emperors. During the 1st and 2nd centuries AD, Rome's Christians were buried together with their pagan brothers in these common burial grounds. Because of Rome's booming population, burials, including Christian ones, soon required more space. Christians then began to build cemeteries of their own, in which they performed their religious rites. With the approval of the city fathers, they dug their cemeteries in the hilly slopes that lined the consular roads, usually on private land that the owner—often a Christian himself—granted for this purpose. As the need for space became more pressing, the cemeteries were extended in a series of galleries, often on two or more levels.

The general belief that the catacombs served as secret hiding places for the Christians during the persecutions that broke out during early Christian times is romantic but unrealistic. The catacombs were well known to the Romans. Between persecutions, the bodies of the martyrs who had fallen under the sword or had met death by fire, water, or wild beasts were interred in the catacombs. Their remains were given a place of honor,

and their presence conferred great prestige on the underground cemetery in which they lay, attracting a stream of devout pilgrims.

You'll see a great variety of tombs and decorations here. They range from
a simple rectangular niche in the wall that was closed by bricks or marble slabs, to a sarcophagus carved out of the wall and surmounted by
a niche, to a freestanding sarcophagus in terra-cotta, marble, or lead.
Off some of the galleries you'll see rooms lined with niches, where
members of the same family or community were buried. Later, when
space became scarce, tombs were dug in the pavement. Each tomb was
distinguished by a particular mark or sign so that the deceased's relatives could recognize it among the rows of niches. Sometimes this was
an object, such as a coin or oil lamp; sometimes it was an inscription.
The wealthier families called in painters to decorate their tombs with
frescoes and ordered sculptured sarcophagi from artisans' workshops.

After AD 313, when Constantine's edict put an end to the persecutions
and granted full privileges to the Christians, the construction of the catacombs flourished; they were increasingly frequented by those who
wished to honor their own dead and to venerate the tombs of the early
martyrs. In the Dark Ages, invading armies made a habit of showing
up at the gates of the city, devastating the countryside, and plundering
from the living and the dead. During the same period this part of the
Campagna Romana became a malaria-infested wasteland, so the popes
prudently decreed that the remains of the martyrs be removed from the
catacombs and laid to rest in the relative security of Rome's churches.
With the loss of these holy relics and the appearance of the first cemeteries within the city walls, the catacombs fell into disuse and were abandoned and forgotten, with the sole exception of the Catacombe di San
Sebastiano. The interest of 19th-century archaeologists and 20th- and
21st-century tourists has brought the catacombs back to life.

*Numbers in the text and margin correspond to points of interest on the
Catacombs and Via Appia Antica map.*

**a good
walk**

The initial stretch of the Via Appia Antica is not pedestrian-friendly—
there is fast, heavy traffic and no sidewalk all the way from Porta San
Sebastiano to the Catacombe di San Callisto. Also, the gardens and villas along this stretch are hidden behind walls, so there's really not much
to see, except for the little church of **Domine Quo Vadis?** ➊ ▶, a short
way beyond Porta San Sebastiano. The church commemorates the legendary spot where Christ appeared to St. Peter.

To reach the catacombs and the prettier stretch of the Via Appia Antica, take Bus 218 (which starts from San Giovanni in Laterano) at the
stop near Porta San Sebastiano; the bus route follows Via Ardeatina,
parallel to Via Appia Antica. You can get off at the stop nearer to the
**Catacombe di San Callisto** ➋, or at Via San Sebastiano, which you take
to reach **Catacombe di San Sebastiano** ➌. Alternately, to start farther down
the road, take Metro line A to Colli Albani and Bus 660 to the tomb of
Cecilia Metella. A slightly more expensive, but hassle-free option is to
take Bus 110 from Piazza Venezia; the small, air-conditioned buses

allow you to hop on and off as you please. They run every hour from the stop to the left of the San Marco church.

Visit the catacomb of your choice; then walk south on Via Appia Antica. Opposite San Sebastiano are some Jewish catacombs, not open to the public. Also on the left are the ruins of the round Mausoleo di Romolo, built by Emperor Maxentius as a tomb for his son Romulus, and the entrance to the **Circo di Massenzio** ❹ (Circus of Maxentius). Continue south to the famous ancient tomb, **Tomba di Cecilia Metella** ❺, which marks the beginning of the most interesting and evocative stretch of Via Appia, lined with vine-covered tombs and fragments of statuary. Cypresses and umbrella pines stand guard over the ruined sepulchres, and the occasional tracts of ancient paving stones are the same ones trod by Roman legions returning in triumph from southern conquests. In some stretches you can see the ruts worn in them by ironclad cart wheels. Along the road are inconspicuous gateways to exclusive villas, residences of a lucky few.

Walk as far as you like along the road, but keep in mind that you have to retrace your steps to return to the bus stop. Among the more curious tombs here is a huge mass that seems balanced on a slender stem, and another tall mound on which a little house was built in a later age. You pass ruins of ancient villas, and to the left you can see the arches of an aqueduct.

TIMING    Weather is a determining factor, as the walk is almost entirely outdoors. There are no sidewalks along Via Appia Antica, so you'll be walking mainly on beaten earth. Give a thought to carrying a picnic lunch, or plan to dine at one of the pleasant restaurants near the catacombs. The walk takes about two hours, plus an hour for a visit to one of the catacombs, but allow extra time for the round-trip by bus, because service runs only once an hour.

## What to See

★ ❷ **Catacombe di San Callisto** (Catacombs of St. Calixtus). Burial place of many popes of the 3rd century, this is the oldest and among the most important and best-preserved underground cemeteries. One of the (English-speaking) friars who act as custodians of the catacomb will guide you through its crypts and galleries, some of which are adorned with early Christian frescoes. Watch out for any wrong turns here: this is a five-story catacomb! ⊠ *Via Appia Antica 110, Via Appia Antica* ☎ *06/ 51301580* 🖾 *€5* ☽ *Thurs.–Tues. 8:30–12:30 and 2:30–5.*

❸ **Catacombe di San Sebastiano** (Catacombs of St. Sebastian). The 4th-century church was named after the saint who was buried in the catacomb, which burrows underground on four different levels. This was the only early Christian cemetery to remain accessible during the Middle Ages, and it was from here that the term "catacomb" is derived—it's in a spot where the road dips into a hollow, known to the Romans as *catacumbas* (Greek for "near the hollow"). The Romans used the name to refer to the cemetery that had existed here since the 2nd century BC, and it came to be applied to all the underground cemeteries discovered in Rome in later centuries. ⊠ *Via Appia Antica 136* ☎ *06/7850350* 🖾 *€5* ☽ *Mid-Nov.–mid-Oct., Mon.–Sat. 8:30–noon and 2:30–5:30.*

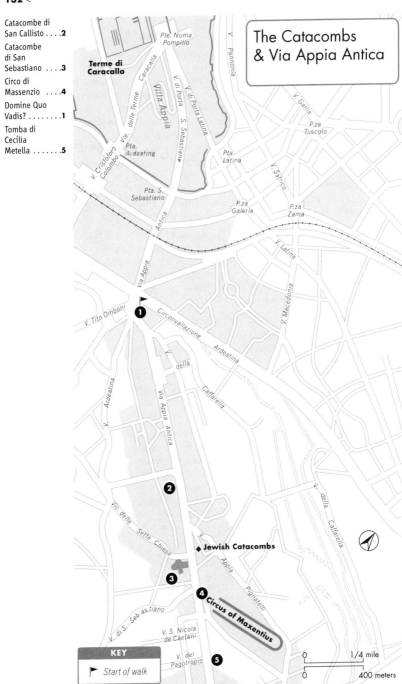

The Catacombs
& Via Appia Antica

**❹ Circo di Massenzio.** The ruins of the Circus of Maxentius, built in AD 309, give you an idea of what the Roman circuses looked like. You can see the towers at the entrance; the *spina,* the wall that divided it down the center; and the vaults that supported the tiers of seating for the spectators. The obelisk now in Piazza Navona was found here. The adjacent **Mausoleo di Romolo** is a huge tomb built by the emperor for his son Romulus, who died young. The tomb and circus were on the grounds of the emperor's villa, much of which is yet to be excavated. ☒ *Via Appia Antica 153* ☏*06/820771* ☒*€3* ☉ *Oct.–Mar., Tues.–Sun. 9–5; Apr.–Sept., Tues.–Sun. 9–7.*

▶ **❶ Domine Quo Vadis?** (Church of Lord, Where Goest Thou?). This church was built on the spot where tradition says Christ appeared to St. Peter as the apostle was fleeing Rome and persuaded him to return and face martyrdom. A paving stone in the church bears an imprint said to have been made by the feet of Christ. ☒ *Via Appia Antica at Via Ardeatina* ☏ *06/5120441* ☉ *Daily 7–6:30.*

**❺ Tomba di Cecilia Metella.** For centuries, sightseers have flocked to this famous landmark, one of the most complete surviving tombs of ancient Rome. One of the many round mausolea that once lined the Appian Way, this tumulus-shape tomb is a smaller version of the Mausoleum of Augustus, but impressive nonetheless. It was the burial place of a Roman noblewoman, wife of the son of Crassus, one of Julius Caesar's rivals and known as the richest man in the Roman empire. The original decoration includes a frieze of bulls' skulls near the top. The travertine stone walls were made higher and the medieval-style crenellations added when the tomb was transformed into a fortress by the Caetani family in the 14th century. An adjacent chamber houses a small museum of the area's geological phases. Beyond the tomb are other ancient ruins, including the tumuli tombs of the Horatii and the Curiatti and the Villa dei Quintilli, once one of Rome's most lavish estates and confiscated from the owners by the Emperor Commodus. ☒ *Via Appia Antica 162* ☏*06/39967700* ☒ *€2* ☉ *Tues.–Sat. 9–1 hr before sunset, Sun. and Mon. 9–2.*

Fodor'sChoice
★

**off the beaten path**

**DIO PADRE MISERICORDIOSO** – Richard Meier's brand-new church of "Merciful God the Father," planted amid decrepit housing projects in Rome's far-flung periphery, shakes up the neighborhood as much as if it were a just-landed spaceship. Three great curved walls rise through the structure like billowing sails, supporting glass walls that fill the church with light meant to evoke the presence of the divine. It's like no other church in Rome, and probably a must for architecture buffs, but be forewarned—it's way, way off the beaten path. To get here, plan ninety minutes each way from the center on public transportation, an hour if you have a car. ☒ *Via Francesco Togliatti, Tor Tre Teste* ☏ *06/2315833* ⊕ *www.diopadremisericordioso.it* ☉ *Daily 7–12:30 and 3:30–7:30* ☞ *Take Metro A to Subaugusta, Bus 451 13 stops to Togliatti (ask driver), then Bus 556 for 7 stops, or consult www.atac.roma.it for route information.*

# Where to Eat

**WORD OF MOUTH**

Of course, the gnocchi is not be missed, but I could eat it everyday—and I almost did!

—Len

Eat at a late hour if you want to be with the locals. After dinner we like to spend time walking to seek out a place for the next night.

—patrick

I love the potato pizza at Dar Poeta: delicious and a lovely carb overload!

—SeaUrchin

Eat a lot of gelati. Eat more gelati. Have I mentioned gelati?

—DWeller

By Dana
Klitzberg

**SINCE ANCIENT TIMES ROME** has been known for grand banquets, and though the days of Caesar's imperial triclinium and the Saturnalia feasts are long past, dining out is still a favorite Roman pastime. But even the city's *buongustaii* (gourmands) will be the first to tell you that Rome is distinguished more by a positive attitude toward food than by a multitude of world-class restaurants. Here, in this Eternal(ly Culinarily Conservative) City, simple yet joyously traditional cuisine still reigns supreme. Most chefs prefer to follow the mantra of freshness over fuss, simplicity of flavor and preparation over complex cooking methods, and sauces that veil, more than reveal, the flavors of land and sea. In Rome it's always the old reliables that apply, the recipes time-tested by centuries of mammas that still manage to put meat on your bones and smiles on your faces. The payoff, of course, means that you will enjoy a lot of seriously *deliciozo* dining.

So when Romans keep on ordering the old standbys, it's easy to understand why. And we're talking about some *very* old standbys: at Al Pompiere, you can dine on a beef-and-citron stew that comes from an ancient recipe of Apicius, probably the first celebrity chef (to Emperor Tiberius) and cookbook author of the Western world. Today, Rome's cooks excel at what has taken hundreds, sometimes thousands, of years to perfect. This is why the basic trattoria menu is more or less the same wherever you go. And it's the reason even top Roman chefs—Angelo Troiani at Il Convivio and Agata Parisella at Agata e Romeo, for example—feature their versions of simple classics like pasta *all'amatriciana* (pasta with a tomato, Roman bacon, chili pepper, and pecorino cheese sauce—sometimes with onion, although that's an issue of debate). To a great extent, Rome is deliciously still a town where the most frequent response to "what are you in the mood to eat?" is pizza or pasta.

Still, if you're hunting for newer-than-now nouvelle developments, things are slowly changing. Talented young chefs are exploring new culinary frontiers, as witness these tongue-tingling temptations: potato gnocchi with sea urchin sauce, artichoke strudel, and "Nasdaq" tagliolini with lobster (the dollar-green pasta is made with curaçao liqueur). Of course, there's grumbling about the number of chefs who, in a clumsy effort to be *"nuovo,"* simply end up tossing together a laundry-list of ingredients (avocado, canned corn, strawberries, and tuna fish do not a composed salad make). In these cases, collision rather than fusion is the sad result.

But most Romans are not going to allow a lot of newfangled food to get the best of them. When they go out to eat, they expect to "eat local"—that is, traditional Roman. Even *bollito* from Bologna or cuttlefish risotto from Venice are regarded as "foreign" food. That noted, Rome *is* the capital city, and the influx of "immigrants" from other regions of the country is enough to ensure there are more variations on the Italian theme here than you'd find anywhere else in the country. Sicilian, Tuscan, Pugliese, Bolognese, Marchegiano, Sardinian, and northern Italian regional cuisines are all represented. And, reflecting the increasingly cosmopolitan nature of the city, you'll find a growing number of good-quality international food outposts here as well, particularly Japanese, Indian, and Ethiopian.

Oddly enough for a nation that prides itself on *bella figura* ("looking good"), you'll soon lose count of the *trattorias* and *osterias* that have walls lined with cheap reproductions of Raphael's cherubic angels or soccer posters. Most Romans don't care about the fanfare of decor. Then again, why should they? After all, this is a city where you can lunch in the gorgeous garden of Da Romolo, the erstwhile Casa di Fornarina, the old haunt of Raphael himself. Or sit outside on a glorious piazza and dine in a "virtual" Baroque painting. Back inside, unfortunately, you may have to overlook garish lighting that illuminates your pallid skin and every wrinkle you never knew you had. Or the lack of music (except for the occasional schmaltzy Mina tune) and harried service. Or the fact that there never seem to be enough menus to go around.

But if you can get past this, if you can look beyond the trappings, as Romans do, you can eat like an emperor—or at least a well-fed member of the Roman working class—for very little money. Then, the camaraderie and friendships and conversations that arise are just a bonus; it's not unusual to share wine with neighbors, or have a forkful of pasta offered to you by the older gent sitting on his own at the next table (he probably eats here three times a week). In the end, you'll discover there's immeasurable joy in allowing someone to *fare una scarpetta* (literally "make a little shoe," meaning to sop up sauce with a piece of bread) in your pasta bowl, if only for the satisfied grin on the person's face while doing it.

## Aventino & Testaccio

These two neighboring zones stand in great contrast to each other. The Aventine Hill is a primarily residential area peppered by private villas. Testaccio is Rome's original working class neighborhood, now shared by the old "Romani di Roma" and hip young Italians taking over loft spaces and digs around Monte Testaccio, now Rome's largest area for clubs and nonstop nightlife.

**$–$$$$** ✕ **Checchino dal 1887.** Literally carved out of a hill of ancient shards of amphorae, Checchino remains the perfect example of a classic, family-run Roman restaurant. Here, you can find the great traditional dishes of Rome prepared with care and presented without fanfare or decoration. Although these are a far cry from elegant, the atmosphere is another story, being more traditional-upscale, with wooden tables and chairs swathed in creamy linens, reserved service, and one of the best wine cellars in the region. Though the slaughterhouses of this quarter, Testaccio, are long gone, an echo of their past existence lives on in the restaurant's soul food. Butchers long ago had to make do with what remained after they'd sold the better parts of meat to paying customers, so a cuisine based on this "quinto quarto" (fifth quarter)—mostly offal and other less-traditionally appealing cuts—was born. *Trippa* (tripe), *testina* (head cheese), *pajata* (intestine with the mother's milk still inside), *zampa* (trotter), and *coratella* (sweetbreads and heart of beef) are all still on the menu for die-

Until relatively recently, there was a distinct hierarchy delineated by the names of Rome's eating places. A *ristorante* was typically elegant and expensive; a *trattoria* served more traditional, home-style fare in an atmosphere to match; an *osteria* was even more casual, essentially a wine bar and gathering spot that also served food, and where originally patrons came to drink and brought their own food! The terms still exist but the distinction has blurred considerably. An osteria in the center of town can be far fancier (and pricier) than a ristorante across the street.

**2**

In a Roman sit-down restaurant, whether a ristorante, trattoria, or osteria, you're generally expected to order at least a two-course meal, such as a *primo* (first course) and a *secondo* (second course, which is really a "main course" in English parlance) or a *contorno* (vegetable side); an antipasto (starter) followed by a primo or secondo; or a secondo and a *dolce* (dessert). In an *enoteca* (wine bar) or pizzeria, it's common to order just one dish. Most pizzerias offer more than pizza, and there's no harm in skipping the pizza altogether. The handiest places for a snack between sights are bars, cafés, and pizza *al taglio* (by the slice) shops. Bars are places for a quick coffee and a sandwich, rather than drinking establishments. A café (*caffè* in Italian) is a bar but usually with more seating. If you place your order at the counter, ask if you can sit down: some places charge considerably more for table service. Often you'll pay a cashier first, then give your *scontrino* (receipt) to the person at the counter who fills your order. Note: a law prohibiting smoking in restaurants, bars, and enclosed public spaces was put into effect in January 2005. The result? Alfresco dining even more popular than ever.

## Mealtimes & Closures

Breakfast (*la colazione*) is usually served from 7 to 10:30, lunch (*il pranzo*) from 12:30 to 2:30, dinner (*la cena*) from 7:30 to 11. Peak times are around 1:30 for lunch and 9 for dinner. Within these confines, though, one of the joys of a meal in Rome is that most restaurants will not rush you out. Accordingly, service is often more relaxed than speedy, and the *conto* (bill) will not be brought until you ask for it.

Enoteche are sometimes open in the morning and late afternoon for snacks. Most pizzerias open at 8 PM and close around midnight–1 AM. Most bars and cafés are open from 7 AM to 8–9 PM. Almost all restaurants close one day a week (in most cases Sunday or Monday) and for at least two weeks in August. The city is zoned, however, so that there are always some restaurants in each zone that remain open, to avoid tourists (and residents) getting stuck without any options whatsoever.

## Reservations & Dress

Reservations are always a good idea in restaurants and trattorias, especially on weekends. We mention them in reviews only when they're essential or not accepted. We mention dress only when men are required to wear a jacket or a jacket and tie. Keep in mind that Italian men never wear shorts in a restaurant or enoteca, and infrequently wear sneakers or running shoes, no matter how humble. The same "rules" apply to ladies' casual shorts, running shoes, and plastic sandals. Shorts are acceptable in pizzerias and cafés.

## Prices & Tipping

All prices include tax. Restaurant menu prices include service *(servizio)* unless indicated otherwise on the menu. It's customary to leave a small tip (from a euro to 10% of the bill) in appreciation of good service. Tips are always given in cash. Most restaurants have a "cover" charge, usually listed on the menu as *"pane e coperto."* It should be modest (€1–€2.50 per person) except at the most expensive restaurants. Some restaurants instead charge for bread, which should be brought to you (and paid for) only if you order it. When in doubt, ask about the servizio, pane, and coperto policy upon ordering. The price of fish dishes is often given by weight (before cooking); the price on the menu will be for 100 grams, not for the whole fish. An average fish portion is about 350 grams.

| WHAT IT COSTS in euros | | | | | |
|---|---|---|---|---|---|
| | **$$$$** | **$$$** | **$$** | **$** | **¢** |
| AT DINNER | over €22 | €17–€22 | €12–€17 | €7–€12 | under €7 |

Prices are per person for a second course *(secondo piatto)*—the Italian "main course."

hard Roman purists. For the less adventuresome, house specialties include *coda alla vaccinara* (stewed oxtail), a popular Roman dish, and *abbacchio alla cacciatora* (braised milk-fed lamb) with seasonal vegetables. Head here for a taste of old Rome, but note that Checchino is really beginning to show its age. ✉ *Via di Monte Testaccio 30* ☎ *06/5746318* ☱ *AE, DC, MC, V* ⊙ *Closed Sun., Mon., and Aug.*

**$–$$$** ✕ **Perilli.** Testaccio has long been considered one of Rome's most authentic neighborhoods—the "Romani di Roma" (families with at least six generations here) are often from this part of town—although nowadays it can seem all discos and funky restaurants. But the old Testaccio remains, in the very local Testaccio food market and places like this one, which dates from 1911, and has the decor to prove it. There's the seasonal antipasto table, offering Roman specialties like Roman artichokes and *puntarelle* (curled chicory stems in a garlicky vinaigrette based on lots of lemon and anchovy). There are the waiters, the sort who retire after having worked 45 years in the same establishment, wearing crooked bow ties. They're just a little bit too hurried—until, that is, you order classics like pasta *all'amatriciana* and carbonara, which they relish tossing in a big bowl tableside. This is also the place to try rigatoni *con pajata* (with calves' intestines)—if you're into that sort of thing. Second plates are for carnivores only, with classic Roman preparations like oven-roasted lamb with potatoes and chicken stewed with peppers and tomatoes. The house wine is a golden nectar from the Castelli Romani. ✉ *Via Marmorata 39, Testaccio* ☎ *06/5742415* ☱ *AE, DC, MC, V* ⊙ *Closed Wed.*

**$** ✕ **Osteria ai Mercati.** Testaccio has always had its fair share of down-to-earth, family-owned trattorias. They cater mostly to locals and Romans who are "in the know" about where to get honest food at decent prices. Osteria ai Mercati may be newer than most but it feels like an old fit. When in the working-class heart of Rome, eat as the Romans do: simply and heartily. Start with a basic bruschetta—toasted bread rubbed with garlic and drenched in good quality olive oil and salt, the definition of Italian simplicity (and the original garlic bread)—and add different toppings as you fancy: fresh, sweet tomato and basil, or maybe smoked salmon and arugula. For primi, the potato-stuffed ravioli and *ciecamariti* (literally "blind the husbands," pasta in a spicy tomato sauce) are excellent. And yes, go on and order a second course (which is really your third, but who's counting—you're in Italy!), like pork with porcini mushrooms and chestnuts, a country-style delight in cooler weather. After a panna-cotta dessert, you may wonder: *How do they eat like this all the time?* Experience the solution, Italian-style: *digestivo*. Try a *limoncello* for a sweet-tart finish, or an *amaro* (bitter liqueur) for its supposed medicinal combination of herbs. ⊠ *Piazza del Gazometro 1, Testaccio* ☎ *06/5743091* ⊟ *AE, DC, MC, V* ⊘ *Closed 2 wks in mid-Aug. No lunch weekends.*

## Campo de' Fiori

In the heart of Old Rome, the Campo de' Fiori square itself is historic food market by day, lively restaurant and bar scene by night, and offers the perfect mix of Romans young and old, tourists, and students. It seems that everyone in central Rome, no matter what their plans, stops by the Campo and surrounding blocks at some point in their evening out.

★ $$–$$$$  ✕ **Evangelista.** It's almost as if this restaurant, so subtle in its quiet grace, is in seclusion. It seems to be tucked away, so close to the busy Lungotevere (the street that runs the length of the Tiber River) and yet it keeps such a low profile even locals have difficulty stumbling upon it. That it's only open for the dinner trade adds to this elusiveness. Everybody, however, seems to know and love its *carciofi al mattone* (roasted artichokes pressed flat between two hot bricks); this fame is well deserved, as the artichoke comes out crispy and delicious, looking almost like a perfectly seared vegetable carpaccio. Pastas are excellent—with fresh fava beans, pecorino cheese, and mint in spring—as are the homemade potato gnocchi, light and fluffy as they should be, but rarely are elsewhere, and unadorned in a vegetable ragout with a touch of saffron—a great first course. Then feast on roast pork loin with juniper berries in winter, swordfish with Marsala, mint, and pistachio in summer. The arched white ceilings, tasteful paintings hung on the walls, Persian rugs, and flowered curtains lend an air of comfortable elegance, like a tastefully understated restaurant in the country. ⊠ *Via delle Zoccolette 11/a, Campo de' Fiori* ☎ *06/6875810* ⊟ *MC, V* ⊘ *Closed Sun. and Aug. No lunch.*

★ $$–$$$$  ✕ **Hosteria del Pesce.** If you can get through the crowds of politicians, soccer players, and film and TV personalities waiting for their tables, you'll see that the entrance to this restaurant looks like an upscale *pescheria* (fish market), which is a good indicator of what awaits you inside: seafood from Terracina, on the coast south of Rome, beautiful enough to display like aquatic jewels. The space, all hardwood floors, subtle lighting, and walls in royal blue and chili-pepper red, buzzes with energy. And Poseidon's treasures are all here: Mediterranean sea bass, turbot, gilthead bream, swordfish, as well as huge iced bowls of mussels and clams geysering out shots of their briny water. Other top choices are the *gambero rosso* (Italian red shrimp), baby calamari the size of a thumbnail, and the *arragosta* (local spiny lobster). The freshness of this seafood can best be appreciated with a large assortment of *crudi,* a raw seafood platter, but the warm dishes are also winners, particularly sautéed shrimp with cherry tomatoes, monkfish with olives, and a lip-smacking cappellini with lobster. For a sweet ending, the ubiquitous molten chocolate cake is done justice here, although you could also make like a local and order the *sgroppino,* a refreshing digestif of lemon sorbet with prosecco and vodka. ⊠ *Via di Monserrato 32* ☎ *06/6865617* ⌖ *Reservations essential* ⊟ *AE, DC, MC, V* ⊗ *Closed Sun. and 2 wks in Aug. No lunch.*

**$$–$$$** ✕ **Albistrò.** Just a hop, skip, and a jump from Piazza Farnese, this small, surprisingly affordable restaurant turns out both classic Italian dishes and more varied, modern offerings. Its internal courtyard and relaxed atmosphere make this little gem an oasis of calm in this bustling, historic area of the city (although the harried service can sometimes kill the "buzz of tranquillity").The small menu changes often, but you can always find interesting risottos, such as pumpkin with bits of almond cookies, and tasty second courses such as guinea fowl with chestnuts. One of the owners is from Switzerland, so be on the lookout for such regional specialties as *pavé,* a semolina pudding with fresh strawberries. You can also taste this "border" influence with northern-tinged dishes like a *sformatino,* a puddinglike soufflé of zucchini and speck (a northern Italian smoked prosciutto). The Swiss may be considered the neutral party in European politics, but here the flavors they add to the mix are anything but. ⊠ *Via dei Banchi Vecchi 140/a, Campo de' Fiori* ☎ *06/6865274* ⊟ *AE, DC, MC, V* ⊗ *Closed Wed. and 3 wks in July and Aug. No lunch Mon.–Sat.*

**$$–$$$** ✕ **Monserrato.** In a high-rent area dense with design stores, antique shops, and jewelers, this simple spot is just a few steps from elegant Piazza Farnese and yet happily devoid of throngs of tourists. Monserrato's signature dishes are its fish specials: carpaccio *di pesce spada* (swordfish carpaccio, served with lemon and arugula), *insalatina di seppie* (cuttlefish salad), *bigoli con gamberi e asparagi* (homemade pasta with shrimp and asparagus), and grilled fish that are simple but very satisfying. There's also a nice antipasto assortment so you can eat your share of veggies as well. Select a nice white from the Italo-centric wine list and when the weather heats up, you can enjoy it all with a breeze at umbrella-covered tables on the small, adjacent piazza. ⊠ *Via di Monserrato 96* ☎ *06/6873386* ⊟ *AE, MC, V* ⊗ *Closed 2 wks in Aug., 1 wk at Christmas.*

**$$–$$$** ✕ **Roscioli.** What used to be a fairly run-of-the-mill alimentari, owned by the Roscioli family (and owners of the famous *forno,* or bread bakery, around the corner), is now much, much more. Since December 2002, this food shop has beckoned with a selection of top-quality comestibles just as pleasing to the eye as it is to the palate: whole prosciuttos, wild Alaskan smoked salmon, fresh regional cheeses, a dizzying array of wines, and the best prosciutti (including those not of Italian origin, like the Spanish Bellota Iberica and Pata Negra varieties, at about $100 per pound). But hidden within this sleek, slate-and-chrome interior is a restaurant. That you'll get top-quality cheese and salami, oil, vinegar, and bread is a given, but it's worth expanding beyond what's in the display case to try menu items like a homemade pasta with duck prosciutto, or the potato gnocchi with a sea urchin sauce, both original uses of fairly esoteric (but steadfastly Italian) ingredients. Whatever you choose, all dishes are made to be paired with one of the 800 wines on offer (and if you book ahead, you can reserve a table in the cozy wine cellar beneath the dining room). ⊠ *Via dei Giubbonari 21/22* ☎ *06/6875287* ⊕ *www. rosciolifinefood.com* ⊟ *AE, DC, MC, V* ⊘ *Closed Sun.*

**$$**
**Fodor'sChoice**
**★**
✕ **Ditirambo.** Don't let the country-kitchen ambience fool you. At this little spot off Campo de' Fiori, the constantly changing selection of off-beat takes on Italian classics is a step beyond ordinary Roman fare. Many offer kudos to this establishment for being *anti*-establishment—the place is usually packed with diners who appreciate the adventuresome kitchen *and* the location near the ever-bustling Campo market (although you may overhear complaints about the often decidedly brusque service). Antipasti can be delicious, like a basic top-quality plate of prosciutto and buffalo-milk mozzarella, or an octopus salad on a puree of white beans (though it lacked salt), or tasteless, like a plate of overcooked asparagus that were no longer even green. Secondi like flavorful steaks with balsamic vinegar, and fish cooked *al cartoccio* (cooked in paper or foil) with herbs and vegetables remain simple but satisfying. But people really love this place for dishes like the Calabrian eggplant "meatballs" or the hearty spaghetti-of-sorts with sheep's milk cheese and sweet red onions. ⊠ *Piazza della Cancelleria 74, Campo de' Fiori* ☎ *06/ 6871626* ⊟ *AE, MC, V* ⊘ *Closed Aug. No lunch Mon.*

**$-$$**
✕ **Trattoria Moderna.** When this restaurant opened in 2003, the general opinion was "not *another* trattoria redux"—but this is more than just a high-design space with a lowbrow, traditional menu. The space is, in fact, modern—airy, with high ceilings, and done in shades of beige and gray. An oversize chalk board displays daily specials, such as a delicious chickpea and *baccalà* (salt cod) soup. The food runs toward the traditional but with a twist, like a pasta *all'amatriciana* with kosher beef instead of the requisite *guanciale* (cured pork jowl) or the take on pasta *alla Norma* with an eggplant pureé and ricotta cheese. Main courses are more creative, as well as more hit-or-miss. The jumbo shrimp in a cognac sauce with couscous was tasty, but the scant four shrimp a drawback. The sliced veal with potatoes and prosciutto was a mix reminiscent of something a home cook might throw together on a lazy Sunday night. And the turkey "parmesan" with tomatoes and buffalo milk mozzarella was overcooked, though a good idea. "A" for effort, with a friendly serving staff and very reasonable prices, and an extra bonus is the outdoor seating—a few tables surrounded by greenery, off the lovely, cobblestone street. ⊠ *Vicolo dei Chiodaroli 16* ⊕ *www.trattoriamoderna. it* ☎ *06/68803423* ⊟ *AE, DC, MC, V.*

**$**
✕ **Da Sergio.** Every neighborhood has at least one "old school" Roman trattoria and, for the Campo de' Fiori area, Da Sergio is it. The central

location and friendly service make this a popular spot for refueling after several *aperitivi* in the nearby piazza (that is, if you're willing to wait for a table). Once you're seated, the red-and-white-check paper table-covering, the bright lights, the '50s kitsch, and the stuffed boar's head on the wall remind you that you're smack in the middle of the genuine article. So please, if you must ask for a menu (the waiters generally recite the limited selection *a voce,* out loud), then try not to chuckle at the translations in English. Go for the delicious version of pasta *all'amatriciana,* or the generous helping of gnocchi with a tomato sauce and lots of Parmesan cheese, served, as tradition dictates, on Thursday. There's a nice selection of seasonal vegetable antipasti and *contorni*(side dishes), as well as high-quality beef, served in preparations ranging from *straccetti con rughetta* (thinly sliced sautéed beef with arugula) to a meaty fillet. ⊠ *Vicolo delle Grotte 27* ☎ *06/6864293* ▤ *DC, MC, V* ◯ *Closed Sun. and 2 wks in Aug.*

¢ ✕ **Filetti di Baccalà.** For years, Filetti di Baccalà has been serving just that—battered, deep-fried fillets of salt cod—and not much else. The Roman specialty doesn't require much accompaniment—in fact, as fish-and-chips in London is often served in newspaper, here the cod is served wrapped in plain paper to absorb the oil. You'll find no-frills starters such as *bruschette al pomodoro* (garlic-rubbed toast topped with fresh tomatoes and olive oil), sautéed zucchini, and, in winter months, the cod is served alongside *puntarelle,* chicory stems topped with a delicious anchovy-garlic-lemon vinaigrette. And the location, down the street from Campo de' Fiori in a little piazza in front of the beautiful Santa Barbara church, begs you to eat at one of the outdoor tables when the weather allows. The atmosphere, in or out, is always convivial and very casual—just the way Romans like it. Long operating hours allow those hungry enough and still on U.S. time to eat as early (how gauche!) as 6 PM. ⊠ *Largo dei Librari 88, Campo de' Fiori* ☎ *06/6864018* ▤ *No credit cards* ◯ *Closed Sun. and Aug. No lunch.*

## Colosseo

★ $$$–$$$$     ✕ **San Teodoro.** The atmosphere: far removed from the madding crowds. The setting: an enclosed piazza, walls covered in ivy, in the Palatine hill area of Rome, nestled by the Roman Forum and Monte Caprino, the hillside park adjacent to the Campidoglio. The specialty: refined Roman cuisine, featuring tastes of Roman Jewish fare and specializing in seafood. With (mostly) courteous service and an interesting menu, San Teodoro is the perfect choice for those who want more than a trattoria, but don't want to go for an all-out, break-the-bank Michelin star meal. In spring and summer there's a lovely outdoor deck with umbrellas and candlelight (the candle holders, star-of-David shaped, reflect the restaurant's proximity to the Jewish ghetto), and in cooler months, the bright rooms decorated with contemporary art offer an extremely pleasant dining option. The menu includes classic fried artichokes (among the best in the city), homemade ravioli *con cipolla di Tropea* (filled with red onion and tossed in balsamic vinegar—an exquisite combination for fans of *agrodolce,* or sweet with tart flavors), and the Roman classic rigatoni *all'amatriciana.* Everything down to the last bite (make your dessert choice the chocolate medley) is a pleasure. ✉ *Via dei Fienili 50, Colosseo* ☎ *06/6780933* ▭ *AE, DC, MC, V* ۞ *Closed Sun.*

**$–$$** ✕ **Ai Tre Scalini.** Over the past couple of years, the Celio—the area of the Celian Hill—has experienced a resurgence, with the opening of a few upper-level hotels and a handful of better restaurants. Rising housing costs in other *centro storico* (historic center) zones have provided a miniboom in apartment rentals in the area, too, and these new residents need places to eat, drink, and be merry. One of these high-quality restaurants, near the Colosseum, is Ai Tre Scalini, and a welcome surprise it is. Sit outside in warm weather, but if it gets too hot, the naturally cool rooms on the lower level are fantastically refreshing. Sample chef Angelo Annarumi's playful salmon roulades with ricotta cheese and pink grapefruit, or the unusual radicchio and cheese-stuffed *zagnolotti* (small ravioli) in a delicious lobster sauce. A wide variety of second courses, from *orata in crosta di patate con vongole* (gilthead bream topped with crunchy potatoes and sprinkled with tasty baby clams) to simple beef with rosemary, are all served with flair. ✉ *Via SS. Quattro 30, Colosseo* ☎ *06/7096309* ▭ *AE, DC, MC, V* ۞ *Closed Mon. and 10 days in Sept.*

## The Ghetto

This is the historic Jewish quarter of Rome, still home to Rome's largest synagogue and a string of eateries and shops, famed for their ageless Roman Jewish fare.

★ **$$$–$$$$** ✕ **Piperno.** *The* place to go for Rome's extraordinary *carciofi alla giudia* (fried whole artichokes), Piperno has been in business for more than a century. The location, up a tiny hill in a piazza tucked away behind the palazzi of the Jewish Ghetto, lends the restaurant a rarefied air. It's a popular location for Sunday brunch, old-school Roman style, which basically means it serves hearty Roman fare at lunchtime, much to the joy of hungry multigenerational local family groups. Meals are served in three small wood-panel dining rooms and at a handful of tables outdoors by seasoned waiters decked in jackets and bow ties, exhibiting a reserve unusual for Romans in the service industry. Try *pasta e ceci* (a thick soup of pasta tubes and chickpeas), *fiori di zucca ripieni e fritti* (fried stuffed zucchini flowers), and *filetti di baccalà* (fillet of cod)—the display of fresh local fish is enticing enough to lure diners to try offerings from sea instead of land. ✉ *Monte dei Cenci 9, Ghetto* ☎ *06/68806629* ▭ *AE, DC, MC, V* ۞ *Closed Mon. and Aug. No dinner Sun.*

**$$–$$$** ✕ **La Taverna Degli Amici.** This restaurant, on an idyllic ivy-draped piazza tucked away in the Jewish Ghetto, has what is considered one of the most delightful dining settings in Rome. The outdoor tables under big white umbrellas are a hot ticket, understandably, but even in autumn and winter, this "Tavern of Friends" is warm and inviting, with distinctive green-and-white-check table linens, wood accents, candles, and a happy vibe. The clientele comprises sophisticated Italians and international businesspeople with a sprinkling of expats. Generally the menu features high-quality versions of Roman and Roman-Jewish classics. The *amatriciana* and *cacio e pepe* pastas are delicious, as are various antipasti (stuffed zucchini flowers, eggplant meatballs, artichokes, and other vegetarian-

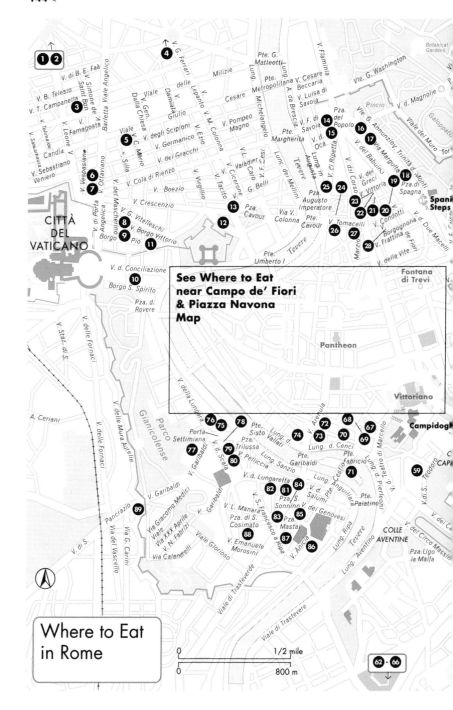

Where to Eat
in Rome

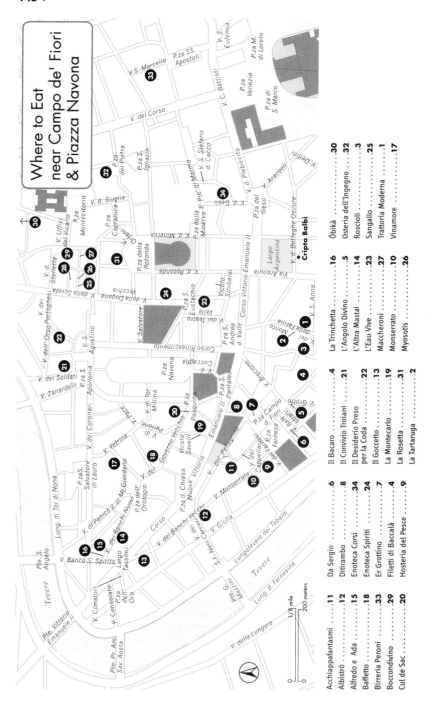

# Where to Eat near Campo de' Fiori & Piazza Navona

Cripta Balbi

Acchiappafantasmi .....11
Albistrò .........12
Alfredo e Ada .........15
Baffetto .........18
Birreria Peroni .........33
Boccondivino .........29
Cul de Sac .........20

Da Sergio .........6
Ditirambo .........8
Enoteca Corsi .........34
Enoteca Spiriti .........24
Er Grottino .........7
Filetti di Baccalà .........4
Hosteria del Pesce .........9

Il Bacaro .........4
Il Convivio Troiani .........21
Il Desiderio Preso
per la Coda .........22
Il Goccetto .........13
La Montecarlo .........19
La Rosetta .........31
La Tartaruga .........2

La Trinchetta .........16
L'Angolo Divino .........5
L'Altra Mastai .........14
L'Eau Vive .........23
Maccheroni .........27
Monserrato .........10
Myosotis .........26

Obikà .........30
Osteria dell'Ingegno .....32
Roscioli .........3
Sangallo .........25
Trattoria Moderna .........1
Vinamore .........17

1/8 mile
200 meters

friendly delights). The *secondi* courses continue the friendly feast with well-executed beef fillets with rosemary, roasted sea bream with potatoes, and a veal chop, pounded extra-thin, breaded and fried and topped with chopped cherry tomatoes and arugula. A selection from the unusual dessert list is a special treat here; try the cinnamon mousse. The wine list is edited and the markup substantial, but hey, what's a few extra euros among *amici?* ⊠ *Piazza Margana 36* ☎ *06/69920637* ⊟ *AE, MC, V* ⊗ *Closed Fri. and 2 wks in Aug.*

**$$–$$$** ✕ **Sora Lella.** The namesake of this restaurant was the zaftig sister of a supersize Roman film star—character actor, really—beloved by locals. The sister became a bit of a pop-culture phenom and TV star herself, and after her death in 1993 her son opened this trattoria as a tribute to his mother, serving up Roman cooking without the kitsch one might expect, considering the pedigree. It's on Tiber Island, sharing this tiny spit of land in the river with the oldest hospital in Rome and little else. Two small, charming dining rooms are lined with wood paneling and wine bottles, and although prices are higher than your average trattoria, so is the quality of the food. Daily specials are written on the chalkboard; you'll usually find homey meatballs, *pasta e fagioli* (a thick soup of short pasta and beans), and *maialino all'antica roma* (suckling pig with prunes, pine nuts, and raisins). Leave room for the quintessential Roman ricotta cake. ⊠ *Via Ponte Quattro Capi 16, Ghetto* ☎06/6861601 ⊟*AE, DC, MC, V* ⊗ *Closed Sun. and Aug.*

**$** ✕ **Al Pompiere.** The entrance on a narrow side street leads you up a charming staircase and into the main dining room of this neighborhood favorite. The windows from the dining room look out over Piazza delle Cinque Scole, one of the oldest squares in the Jewish Ghetto, and although the room itself is fairly spare, the wood-beam ceilings soar overhead and give you the impression of dining in an old palazzo in another century. Still, Al Pompiere manages to keep its informal feel, which has changed very little over the years. Its Roman dishes, such as fried zucchini flowers, battered salt cod, and gnocchi, are all consistently good and served without fanfare on white dishes with a simple border. The traditional *coda alla vaccinara* (stewed oxtail with celery and tomato) is here, too. But there are some nice, historic touches like a beef-and-citron stew that comes from an ancient Roman recipe of Apicius. There was a terrible fire in a shop below the restaurant in late 2004, but the restaurant was soon back in business, the only remaining evidence being the scorch marks below the windows on the piazza. But the irony here is as thick as the kitchen's tomato sauce: *Al Pompiere* means "the fireman." ⊠ *Via Santa Maria dei Calderari 38, Ghetto* ☎06/6868377 ⊟*AE, MC, V* ⊗ *Closed Sun. and Aug.*

# Parioli

A 10-minute cab ride from the city center, up Via Veneto and across Villa Borghese, Parioli is the posh, verdant neighborhood of the Eternal City. It's more residential than most areas and seems to have more Smart cars per square meter than any other *quartiere* of Rome.

**$$–$$$** ✕ **Al Ceppo.** The well-heeled, the business-minded, and those of more refined palate frequent this outpost of tranquillity owned by Cristina, a local of Le Marche, the region north of Rome that borders the Adriatic. There's a palpable feminine air to the place—in the luxe fabrics and flowers, the ornate oil paintings—and Cristina and her daughter dote on their customers as you'd wish a sophisticated Italian *mamma* would, spoiling them with an ample selection of classic Italian dishes prepared with a creative flair. There's always a selection of dishes from their native region, such as *olive ascolane* (large green olives, stuffed with seasoned ground meat, breaded, and fried), various pasta dishes, and succulent roast lamb. Other temptations include the pasta (made fresh every day), a beautiful display of seafood fresh from the Adriatic, and a wide selection of meats and vegetables all ready to be grilled in the fireplace in the front room. ⊠ *Via Panama 2, Parioli* ☎ *06/8419696* 🖃 *AE, DC, MC, V* ☻ *Closed Mon. and 2 wks in Aug.*

**$$–$$$** ✕ **Duke's.** So you'd prefer not to look at another plate of pasta for a good long time—but still, you'd rather not hit the Hard Rock Cafe. Well, Duke's may be the ticket. It dubs itself a California-style restaurant and bar, although the California rolls have tuna and carrot in them and they've added a flourish of fresh mint leaves to the Caesar salad. The truth is, once you look at Duke's menu after a stretch of Italian-only bingeing, you may actually want it *all*. Perhaps a nice, juicy beef fillet, served as what Americans refer to as an *entrée* (that is, a main course with side dishes on the same plate, something difficult to come by in Italy). There's always the finishing touch of the molten chocolate cake, or even a nice warm apple pie served with gelato (well, we are in Rome, let's not forget). The decor is, in fact, Malibu-beachhouse-minimalist, the outdoor patio out back in the summer consummately SoCal chic. And up front, opening out onto the street, all the beautiful *Pariolini* (people from Parioli, read: plenty of unnatural blondes) are huddled around the bar, sipping frozen cocktails, the whir of blenders and the music blaring in the background. If you squint, you could really be in California. ⊠ *Viale Parioli 200* ☎ *06/80662455* 🖃 *AE, MC, V* ☻ *Closed Sat. and 1 wk in Aug.*

**$–$$** ✕ **Trattoria Fauro.** Berlusconi is the richest head-of-state in the free world, but that doesn't mean he can't appreciate a good dining bargain. His party, the Italian right wing, in fact, has used this spot as headquarters during elections, proving this point. Fish is especially strong here—owner Franco Zambelli buys daily from the renowned fish market in the coastal town of Fiumicino. And although seafood is notoriously expensive in Rome, Franco is, shall we say, fair. Highlights from the menu include roasted octopus with fresh herbs (a southern Italian specialty), a fantastic house *crostino* (fatty bacon and shrimp on a slab of toasted bread), and sea bass with wild fennel. But the best thing to do is to toss the menu aside and place your appetite in Franco's hands. He knows all about the freshest catch (or hunt) of the day and how it's best prepared. ⊠ *Via R. Fauro 44, Parioli* ☎ *06/8083301* 🍴 *Reservations essential* 🖃 *No credit cards* ☻ *Closed Sun.*

## Piazza di Spagna

Though a hustling business and shopping district during the day, this area tends to empty out a bit at night, but retains a concentration of restaurants and wine bars in the area's luxury hotels and a few fabled restaurants.

**$$$$** ✕ **Caffé Romano dell'Hotel d'Inghilterra.** One of Rome's most soigné hotels, the d'Inghliterra used to house the chicest dining spot, a veritable neoclassic salon swagged with Empire fabrics right out of an Ingres painting. Sadly, it has now been replaced with this rather standard-issue symphony in beige marbles, beechwood walls, and Tuscan columns. Shoppers will stifle their yawns, however, because this oasis is set right in the middle of the busy Piazza di Spagna shopping district. You can tell that jet-setters like this spot—it's got an *orario continuato,* or nonstop opening hours, from 10 AM on, so snacking or having a late lunch is a possibility here; and second, the menu features dishes from around the world, rather a rarity in Rome. Best bets include steamed prawns with an artichoke flan; the ravioli *con fave, cipolotti, e salsa d'agnello* (with fava beans, green onions, and lamb); the elegant lobster salad with avocado; and a Middle Eastern *mezze* (snack) plate. There's also lovely outdoor seating for a good half of the calendar year (Romans love their dining *al fresco*), and tables are close together, so plan on having eavesdropping neighbors . . . or eavesdropping on yours. ⊠ *Via Bocca di Leone 14, Piazza di Spagna* ☎ *06/699811* ⊟ *AE, DC, MC, V.*

★ **$$$$** ✕ **El Toulà.** One of Rome's more celebrated outposts of luxe, El Toulà has the warm, welcoming comforts of a 19th-century country house: white walls, antique furniture in dark wood, framed prints, vaulted ceilings, and Venetian-style lampshades. All the refined touches are here, with beautiful table linens, heavy silver serving dishes, and spectacular fruit and flower arrangements to soothe the eye. It's the kind of place both seasoned Italians and visitors frequent, to enjoy a multicourse meal in an elegant setting where you may wish to, and can, linger for hours in comfort (or in the cozy bar off the entrance). Along with the usual suspects of high-roller choices (caviar and blini), the chef offers a menu rich with contemporary interpretations of Italian classics, as well as those special El Toulà dishes that come with a Venetian slant (the mother restaurant is in Treviso). This means delicious, expertly prepared risottos (served in the Venetian, more soupy style) and a nod to the various sea creatures of the Adriatic coast and Venetian lagoon. Note that jacket and tie are required November through February. ⊠ *Via della Lupa 29/b, Piazza di Spagna* ☎ *06/6873750* ⊕ *www.toula.it/* ⌕ *Reservations essential* ⊟ *AE, DC, MC, V* ⊙ *Closed Sun. and Aug. No lunch Mon. and Sat.*

**$$–$$$$** ✕ **Dal Bolognese.** The darling of the media, film, and fashion communities (yes, that was Scorsese . . . and Valentino, you're looking tan!), this classic restaurant on Piazza del Popolo is not only an "in-crowd" dinner destination but makes a convenient shopping-spree lunch spot. The expansive pedestrian piazza offers prime people-watching real estate, and tables inside are perfectly spaced for table hopping and lots of two-cheek kissing. As the name promises, the cooking adheres to the hearty tradition of Bologna. Start with a plate of buttery, sweet *San Daniele*

*Fodor's*Choice
★

# CloseUp

## LA CUCINA ROMANA

**H**EARTY, UNFLINCHING, AND **PROUD,** la cucina romana originates from all of the various geographic and cultural influences that influenced the city for more than 2,000 years.

This has led to an emphasis on meat, since Rome's Testaccio area was once a central zone for the butcher trade in this part of the country, resulting in some tongue-tingling "soul food"—making ubiquitous such delights as guanciale (cured pork jowl) in Roman pastas, as well as meat dishes like abbacchio (baby lamb) and porchetta (roast pork).

From this grew the famed (or notorious) old-school Roman dishes of the quinto quarto, or "fifth quarter": offal and throw-away parts that remained after the butchers had sold the best cuts to paying customers.

This gave birth to coda alla vaccinara (oxtail stewed with celery and tomatoes), pasta with pajata (baby lamb or calf intestines with the mother's milk still inside), coratella (a mix of lamb innards including heart), and trippa alla romana (tripe boiled in a savory tomato sauce).

But Roman cuisine takes as much from the sea as it does from the land, as the Mediterranean—Ostia and Fiumicino being the closest towns—is only 25 km (15 mi) from the city center.

A variety of fish, including sea bass, turbot, and gilthead bream, is served in local restaurants, cooked simply in the oven, on the grill, or baked in a salt crust. And crustaceans, from gamberetti (baby shrimp) to scampi (langoustines) to spiny lobster are served alongside a family of calamari, cuttlefish, octopus, and small and large versions of everything in between.

And the produce! Heading to an outdoor market anywhere in the city will educate you on exactly what is in season at the moment, and what the bounties of Italy, and particularly the Lazio region (where Rome is located) have to offer.

Rome has always loved its greens, whether it's chicory or spinach or arugula, or dandelion, beet, or broccoli greens. Not to mention beans (string, fava, and broad, to name a few), as well as squash, zucchini, pumpkin, broccoli, and agretti, a staunchly Roman green that resembles sturdy chives but tastes more like spinach—ask for it outside of Rome and vendors will look at you as if you come from another planet.

Speaking of outside of Rome, the most delicious strawberries (and teeny, fragrant wild strawberries) of the region come from Nemi, a hill town in the Castelli Romani outside of the city.

Rome in summer has an abundance of stone fruits and seasonal treats (fresh plums, apricots, and figs are nothing like their dried counterparts and the difference must be tasted to be believed), and great citrus in cooler months, like the sweet-tasting, beautiful blood oranges arriving daily from Sicily, which are often fresh-squeezed and served in tall glasses at Roman cafés.

For the complete scoop on la cucina romana, see "Feasting at Rome's Table" in the Understanding Rome chapter.

prosciutto with melon, then move on to the traditional egg pastas of Emilia-Romagna, with delicious homemade tortellini *in brodo* (in broth)—the ultimate central Italian comfort food—and fresh pastas in creamy sauces. Second plates include the famous Bolognese *bollito misto,* a steaming tray of an assortment of boiled meats (some recognizable, some indecipherable) served with a tangy, herby green sauce. Among the desserts, try the *dolce della mamma* (a concoction of gelato, zabaglione, and chocolate sauce) and the fruit-shape gelato. And get ready for your close-up. ⊠ *Piazza del Popolo 1, Piazza di Spagna* ☎ *06/ 3611426* ⊟ *AE, DC, MC, V* ⊗ *Closed Mon. and Aug.*

**\$\$–\$\$\$**  ✕ **Al 34.** It can be hard to find a place to eat near Piazza di Spagna without spending outrageous sums, but Al 34 has been a popular mid-range favorite for many years. Inside the narrow interior, the walls are dressed in a deep tomato-red, and adorned with modern artwork. The ceilings soar, reminding us of the rich history of this part of town that continues to this day with the opulent boutiques of nearby Via Condotti. Dive into rich dishes like salmon and caviar fettucine, lobster risotto, or the chef's famous pasta with a creamy pumpkin sauce. And if you're feeling a bit more like a home-cooked meal, try the carbonara pasta. The restaurant is open at lunch (perfect for shoppers), and there are two seatings for dinner, at 7:30 and 9:30. ⊠ *Via Mario de' Fiori 34, Piazza di Spagna* ☎ *06/6795091* ⌕ *Reservations essential* ⊟ *AE, DC, MC, V* ⊗ *Closed Mon.*

**\$\$–\$\$\$**  ✕ **La Penna d'Oca.** Owner Francesco Tola transformed an old osteria into one of the most interesting restaurants in the area near Piazza del Popolo. Harking back to his Sardinian seaside roots, he has created a menu dedicated primarily to fish. Marinated red mullet and rockfish are delicate starters. Homemade gnocchi with shrimp and radicchio in a butter-and-sage sauce are unusually light. Roast *sarago,* a hard-to-find Mediterranean fish, served with artichokes and potatoes, is a favorite, as is the succulent lobster and the mixed seafood grill, featuring the best of the catch of the day. The soufflés are delicious for a sweet ending (note that they need to be ordered at the beginning of the meal), and the desserts in general have a southern Italian slant. The decor is simple and streamlined, with comfortable seating and an atmosphere conducive to concentrating on the clean flavors of your meal. ⊠ *Via della Penna 53, Piazza di Spagna* ☎ *06/3202898* ⊟ *AE, DC, MC, V* ⊗ *Closed Sun. and Aug. 10–31. No lunch Sat.*

**\$\$–\$\$\$**  ✕ **Nino.** A favorite among international journalists and fashionistas, Nino
**Fodor'sChoice**  has been casting its spell for many decades and remains one of the most
★  dependable restaurants in the historic center. Nino sticks to the classics, in food and adorbale decor (yellow walls, dark-wood paneling, a plethora of framed prints), as well as in its waiters (dapper old gentlemen in bow ties and white jackets)—the ambience is both cultured and cozy. Much of what you find on the menu here, as well as at the antipasto table, are Roman staples with a Tuscan slant. To start, try a selection from the fine antipasto spread, or go for the Tuscan cured meats or warm *crostini* (toasts) spread with liver pâté. Move on to pappardelle *al lepre* (with a rich hare sauce) or the juicy grilled beef, another succulent delicacy from our Tuscan friends in the Val di Chiana, home of the prized Chi-

anina beef herd. Simple sweets, such as *castagnaccio,* a chestnut dessert, are all worth the extra calories. Nino's location near Piazza di Spagna makes it an excellent choice for lunch after a morning of shopping. ⊠ *Via Borgognona 11, Piazza di Spagna* ☎ *06/6786752* ▤ *AE, DC, MC, V* ☉ *Closed Sun. and Aug.*

**$–$$$** ✕ **'Gusto.** There's an urban-loft feel to this trendy two-story space, a bit like Pottery Barn exploded in Piazza Agusto Imperatore (the name of the restaurant is a play on this location and the Italian word for taste/flavor). The owners of this mega-operation should be proud, as they've revived a piazza that had seen better days. Since the late '90s it's been packed with check-shirted businessmen at lunch and a young, vibrant crowd in the evenings, paving the way for other restaurants to open up on the square while Rome awaits the opening of Richard Meier's remodeled Ara Pacis pavilion alongside the piazza. The ground floor contains a buzzing pizzeria-etc., while upstairs is the more upscale restaurant, where a Mediterranean-meets-Asia menu results in some real misses (eggplant and chickpea strudel with sesame-goat cheese sauce, anyone?). We prefer the casual-but-hopping vibe of the ground-floor wine bar in the back, where a rotating selection of wines by the glass and bottle are served up alongside a vast array of cheeses, salami, and bread products. And for the kitchen enthusiast, the 'Gusto "complex" includes a store, selling everything from cookware to cookwear. ⊠ *Piazza Augusto Imperatore 9, Piazza di Spagna* ☎ *06/3226273* ▤ *AE, MC, V* ☉ *Closed Mon.*

**$–$$$** ✕ **ReCafé.** Here in a soaring space in the center of the city, we have another nod to perhaps the greatest Neapolitan contribution to Italian cuisine (at least on a popularity scale): pizza. And it's not just another hole in the wall. There's an upstairs space, cathedral-like in proportion, with a funky chandelier and minimalist furniture, and there's a downstairs room with the look of a sleek sound-studio, where diners relax on deep grape leather banquettes at dark-wood tables piled high with fried starters, pizzas, and salads. There's also a vast outside piazza set with tables plus the alfresco zone up front. Here is where the ReCafé *aperitivo* happens, with countless tanned brunettes in suits and skirts convening after office hours to flirt and catch up socially. On the menu, there are antipasti in true Naples style: either fried (*pizzette,* minipizzas stuffed with buffalo mozzarella, cherry tomatoes, and eggplant—*delicioso!*) or from the sea (stewed octopus with local black olives), and local mozzarella figures importantly as well. They serve a decent fillet of beef, sausages, and chicken breast all hot off the grill, but the real reason to come here is the pizza. It's fresh, well-made, and thicker than the typical Roman pizza—but you knew that. ⊠ *Piazza Augusto Imperatore 36* ☎ *06/68134730* ▤ *AE, DC, MC, V* ☉ *Closed 2 wks in Aug.*

**$–$$** ✕ **Margutta Vegetariano.** Parallel to posh Via del Babuino, Via Margutta has long been known as *the* street where artists have their studios in Rome. It's also on this quiet but colorful street, covered in ivy and full of beautiful old palazzi and garages-cum-glass-paned workspaces, that Gregory Peck's character lived in *Roman Holiday.* How fitting, then, that the rare Italian vegetarian restaurant, with changing displays of modern art, sits on the far end of this gallery-lined street closest to Piazza del Popolo. Here it takes on a chic and cosmopolitan air, where you'll find meat-free versions of classic Mediterranean dishes as well as more daring tofu concoctions. ⊠ *Via Margutta 118, Piazza di Spagna* ☎ *06/32650577* ⊟ *AE, DC, MC, V.*

¢–$$  ✕ **Osteria della Frezza.** You can get regular osteria fare and service at this member of the 'Gusto restaurant empire (which dominates the surrounding block) . . . but why would you? The beauty of this newish spot (opened in 2003) is what makes it *different* from any other trattoria in town: its adaptation of the idea of *cichetti,* a sort of Italian tapas that originated in the venerable bars of Venice. As wandering from bar to bar, over bridges and along canals (and getting lost along the way) is part of the fun of a night out in *La Serenissima,* so this Venetian idea has now been adapted to the Roman lifestyle. Here in the Eternal City, one meets friends for drinks, one eats, one lingers, and Osteria della Frezza is the perfect place to do just that. Head to the bar area (the only place cichetti service is available) and, for between one and four euros, sample pretty much anything on the regular osteria menu in a snack-sized portion, including the pastas and secondi—an easy way to sample without "committing" to any one dish. Many will want to begin by choosing from the incredible selection of 400 cheeses in the basement cellar, then from the various *fritti* (fried items), moving onto pastas such as sheep's milk and pepper spaghetti. Small portions of the secondi, like baby lamb chops with potatoes, can be disappointingly plain, but the *polpettine in sugo* (meatballs in tomato sauce) bring to mind the best dish of that Italian grandmother everyone longs to have in their kitchen. And the miniportions make you feel as if you're behaving, even if in the end you finish off the whole plate. ⊠ *Via della Frezza 16* ☎ *06/3226273* ⊟ *AE, DC, MC, V.*

$  ✕ **GiNa.** "Homey minimalism" isn't a contradiction at this whitewashed café with a modern edge. The block seats and sleek booths, the single flowers in Mason jars, white chandeliers, and multiplicity of mirrors, make this small but multilevel space a tiny gem tucked away on the street leading from Piazza di Spagna up to Villa Borghese. With a menu ranging from various bruschette to interesting mixed salads, sandwiches, and pastas (the pesto *trofie,* or short pasta twists, with cherry tomatoes is a fresh-tasting delicious choice), to American-style desserts, this is the perfect spot for a light lunch, an aperitivo, or a light dinner that won't break the bank in this high-end neighborhood. The sundaes here are special, with artisanal gelato and all the trimmings that you don't normally find in the gelaterias. Also available are fully stocked gourmet picnic baskets, complete with checked tablecloth, to pick up on the way to the Villa Borghese. For a relaxed Saturday evening, join the young, friendly owners for live jazz from 9:30 to midnight. ⊠ *Via San Sebastianello 7A* ☎ *06/6780251* ⊟ *AE, MC, V* ☉ *Closed Sun. and Aug.*

## Piazza Navona–Pantheon

With scenic piazzas ready made for socializing, this is one of the most central and densely-packed areas of the city for eating, drinking, and basic revelry. But it's the serpentine back streets where you'll find some hidden gems of Roman gustatory style.

**$$$$**
Fodor'sChoice
★
✕ **Il Convivio Troiani.** In a tiny, nondescript *vicolo* where the Tiber bends north of Piazza Navona, the three Troiani brothers—Angelo in the kitchen, and brothers Giuseppe and Massimo presiding over the dining room and wine cellar—have quietly been redefining the experience of Italian eclectic *alta cucina* for many years. There are three separate dining rooms: one has walls covered in terra cotta–color frescoes, one is hung with dark, classical oil paintings, while the main room is alight with a juxtaposition of old and new, with eggshell damask table linens, figurine candleholders, and silky drapes, but with very spare, modern light fixtures. And one could say that the food matches the decor, or vice versa. Antipasti include a "roast beef" of tuna fillet laquered with chestnut honey, rosemary, red peppercorns, and ginger served with a green apple salad, while an update on the Roman-style (braised) artichoke comes served not in a pool of oil as is traditional, but on a *velouté* of sole and leeks. Pasta dishes like a delicious, restrained but flavorful version of *vermicelli bucati all'amatriciana* (thick, hollow spaghetti with a tomato, Roman bacon, and onion sauce) satisfy the classicists, while a squid ink risotto with baby cuttlefish, sea asparagus, lemongrass, and basil sates the appetites of those with dreams of *fantasia*. Main courses include a fabulous version of a cold-weather pigeon dish for which Il Convivio is famous (at last check, it was a bay leaf–scented pigeon "in casserole" with a blood orange sauce and a potato tartlet). The pastry chef serves up inventive sweets like a ricotta-and-cherry cheesecake with almond *granita* (ice) or a chocolate-hazelnut mousse served with the seemingly bizarre addition of radicchio from Treviso and aged balsamic vinegar (somehow, it works). This is classic Roman food but face-lifted for the 21st century. Service is attentive without being overbearing, and all the right touches are there, from the homemade bread and petits-fours that respectively open and close the meal, to the ministools for women's purses and the automatic everything on hand in the restrooms. The tasting menu, which changes weekly, is a great deal at €85 (excluding wine) for those who want to go for all out. ✉ *Vicolo dei Soldati 31, Piazza Navona* ☎ *06/6869432* ⊕ *www.ilconviviotroiani.com* ⚑ *Reservations essential* ▤ *AE, DC, MC, V* ☺ *Closed Sun. and 1 wk in Aug. No lunch Mon.*

★ **$$$$**
✕ **L'Altra Mastai.** The setting is elegant, the food delicious, and the service ultra-attentive. Executive chef Fabio Baldassare (former sous-chef to La Pergola's legendary Heinz Beck) turns out beautiful Mediterranean dishes at this recent (2003) entry onto Rome's fine-dining scene. Pastas are flavored with a delicate hand (thin Roman broccoli ravioli in a truffle-scented sauce); secondi, such as sea bass with tomatoes and olives, taste of the sea and sun, while swordfish with cauliflower emulsion in a Beluga caviar and *salsa all'arancia* (orange sauce) balance earthy, salty, and tart tastes beautifully. Still, the portions on each course range from restrained to quibbling. Desserts, however, are exquisitely prepared and presented (if ever you were to order a variation on chocolate anywhere, order it here!). Homemade bread, *assagini* (little nibbles) and courteous service help ease the wait between courses, which seems longer when business is slow. The chef also runs the casual wine bar across the street where light bites and a few pastas and salads are served

at reasonable prices. ⊠ *Via G. Giraud 53* ☎ *06/68301296* ⊟ *AE, DC, MC, V* ⊘ *Closed Sun., Mon., and Aug.*

$$$$  ✕ **La Rosetta.** Chef-owner Massimo Riccioli took the nets and fishing gear off the walls of his parents' trattoria to create what is widely known as *the* place to go in Rome for first-rate seafood. It's not often that in a place this intimate and popular—set in the shadow of the Pantheon—that the chef-owner will (occasionally) take your order, recommending his best dishes of the day and the wine he feels will best complement them. But beware: the staff may be friendly and the fish may be of high quality, but the preparation is generally very simple, and the prices can be numbingly high. The dining room is small (although those who feel constrained in the space should take a peek in the kitchen!) but elegant and warm. Start with the justifiably well-known selection of marinated seafood appetizers, like carpaccios of fresh, translucent fish drizzled with high-quality olive oil, sprinkled with sea salt and perhaps a fresh herb. Each of these offerings has it own clear and distinct flavor. Pastas tend to mix shellfish, or are prepared *in bianco* (usually with a touch of oil, white wine, and lemon). Simple dishes such as the classic *zuppa di pesce* (fish soup) or perfectly grilled fish and crustaceans deserve star billing under the title of secondi—and command star prices. ⊠ *Via della Rosetta 9, Piazza Navona* ☎ *06/6861002* ⌖ *Reservations essential* ⊟ *AE, DC, MC, V* ⊘ *Closed Sun. and Aug. No lunch Sat.–Wed.*

★ $$–$$$$  ✕ **Sangallo.** Small and intimate, this low-key restaurant snuggled between Piazza Navona and the Pantheon is an outpost of high-quality seafood in the tradition of Anzio, the coastal town south of Rome from which the owner hails. He still picks out the fish himself, and he views dinner as something meant to last all night. You won't argue as you sit in the tranquil pastel-hued dining room lined with colorful (but not jarring) oil paintings. The menu has some sophisticated touches, such as oysters tartare, snapper with foie gras, and a truffle-theme fixed-price menu. The pastas, made with toothsome Gragnano pasta, beckon from their pristine white dishes. There are precious few tables in the tiny dining room, so make sure to book ahead. ⊠ *Vicolo della Vaccarella 11/a, Piazza Navona* ☎ *06/6865549* ⌖ *Reservations essential* ⊟ *AE, DC, MC, V* ⊘ *Closed Sun., 1 wk in Jan., and 2 wks in Aug. No lunch Mon.*

$$–$$$$  ✕ **Myosotis.** Although overshadowed by trendier spots surrounding it, this restaurant of the *classico* ilk is not to be overlooked. It does look a bit stodgy from the outside, but it's easy to get beyond the stern-looking business types and stiff first dates in the front dining room. The recently expanded space is brighter, fresher, with parquet floors, creamy table linens, and walls sponge-painted the color of fresh *fettucine*. Starters include a very open-minded selection of cured meats, including the famed *pata negra* Iberian prosciutto (which trumps the Parma variety, although few Italians will admit this). If you prefer soup, a whitefish, fava bean, and chicory version was a study in bittersweet flavors. Second dishes range from a hearty veal chop *alla milanese* (breaded and pan-fried) to a delicate but flavorful fresh catch of the day, served in a garlic, olive oil, and tomato broth. Desserts like the chocolate mousse in chocolate-raspberry sauce are a perfect end to a very satisfying meal elegant in its simplicity. But

the highlight of the meal, beyond the food, is the care with which the food is described by the waiters and the great pride they take in making sure you dine well here. ⊠ *Via della Vaccarella 3/5, Piazza Navona* ☎ *06/6865554* ▱ *AE, DC, MC, V* ☉ *Closed Sun. No lunch Mon.*

**$$–$$$** ✕ **Boccondivino.** This is a funky spot near the Pantheon and various government offices, where the Italian notion of the *bella figura* (looking good, particularly to others) is as much at work as *mangiando bene* (eating well). The four pillars around which the structure is built are ancient Roman, but when you walk through the 16th-century door, it's clear that Boccondivino (which means "divine mouthful") is all about the here-and-now, with the animal-print chairs and glass-fronted dining room, dramatic lighting and marble floors, and eclectic modern artwork on the walls. The outdoor seating in the intimate piazzetta out front is a great summer spot. The €18 prix-fixe lunch menu is a terrific deal for a lunch meeting, but wait, this is also the perfect place for a dinner date. Start, perhaps, with a citrus-marinated salmon served with peppery Roman arugula, then move on to (or split) the delicious angler fish ravioli made elegant by a *salsa di fiori di zucca* (pumpkin flower sauce). Then go for a secondo—the seared duck breast is all gamey goodness, while the fillet of turbot stuffed with foie gras is an innovative coupling. ⊠ *Piazza Campo Marzio 6* ☎ *06/68308626* ▱ *AE, DC, MC, V* ☉ *Closed Sun. and 3 wks in Aug.*

**★ $$–$$$** ✕ **Osteria dell'Ingegno.** This casual but trendy spot is a great place to enjoy a glass of wine or a meal in the city center. It sits in Piazza della Pietra, the site of the equivalent of the old Roman stock market, and you gaze out onto towering ancient Corinthian columns that make you feel very, uh, *recent* in the grand scheme of things. No matter, the cheery, modern decor—walls hung with colorful paintings by local artists, lots of glass—and hip young waiters will bring you back to the present day. So, too, will the simple but innovative menu. Go for the tasty duck breast with a raspberry-balsamic sauce. ⊠ *Piazza di Pietra 45, Piazza Navona* ☎ *06/6780662* ⚐ *Reservations essential* ▱ *AE, DC, MC, V* ☉ *Closed Sun. and 2 wks in Aug.*

**$$** ✕ **Il Bacaro.** With a handful of choice tables set outside against an ivy-draped wall, this tiny candlelighted spot not far from the Pantheon makes for an ideal romantic evening *in coppia* (as a couple). Inside, the warm ambience makes it equally suited for close friends and convivial conversation over well-prepared, simple dishes. Marinated fish or beef carpaccio are fine starters, while pastas—like *orecchiette* (little ear-shape pasta) with broccoli and sausage, a dish that *lip*-smacks of Puglia—are strong. As a bonus, the thoughtful kitchen helps its clients avoid picking at each other's plates, as it offers up side dishes of all the pastas ordered among those at the table. The choice main courses are mostly meat—the beef fillet with balsamic vinegar or a London broil–style marinaded in olive oil and rosemary are winners, all unpretentious but satisfying. ⊠ *Via degli Spagnoli 27, Piazza Navona* ☎ *06/6864110* ⚐ *Reservations essential* ▱ *DC, MC, V* ☉ *Closed Sun. and 1 wk in Aug. No lunch Sat.*

**$–$$** ✕ **Alfredo e Ada.** There's no place like home, and you'll feel like you're back there from the moment you squeeze into a table at this hole-in-the-wall just across the river from Castel Sant'Angelo. There's no menu, just plate after plate of whatever the owners think you should try, from hearty, classic pastas to *involtini di vitello* (savory veal rolls with tomato) and homemade sausage. Everything seems to contain meat and/or tomatoes, but that was the way Romans ate back in the good old days—in the 1940s, actually, when the trattoria opened. Sit back, relax, and let Ada regale you with stories of old, and allow her to spoil you like only a real *nonna* (grandmother) would, plying you with cookies and wine until you feel you might burst. ✉ *Via dei Banchi Nuovi 14, Vatican* ☎ *06/6878842* ▭ *No credit cards* ⊘ *Closed weekends.*

**$–$$** ✕ **Il Desiderio Preso per la Coda.** The name means "desire grabbed by the tail" and is surely in the running for the most original restaurant name in Rome. Tucked behind Piazza Navona, the walls of this modern-ish eatery are adorned with contemporary art, some of which was done by the wife of one of the owners. Service in this austerely lighted and furnished space can range from knowledgeable to frigid, but often the food can make up for it. The small menu changes often and has a Tuscan slant and includes such dishes as *pappa al pomodoro* (a Tuscan bread and tomato soup), fig risotto, and *polpettone* (meat loaf), the perfect comfort food. ✉ *Vicolo della Palomba 23, Piazza Navona* ☎ *06/68307522* ▭ *AE, DC, MC, V* ⊘ *Closed Mon. and Aug. No lunch.*

★ **$–$$** ✕ **L'Eau Vive.** Now here's an experience you can find only in Rome, home of the Vatican: for three decades this restaurant has been run by a society of French missionary nuns. That it happens to serve decent classic French food is a plus, but it's the "experience" that brings people here more often than not. A serene, soothing place, the upstairs rooms have gorgeous frescoes adding to the churchlike tranquillity. Soft devotional music plays as the smiling sisters speedily bring plate after plate of classic, hearty, and rich dishes. Of course, it's well known that the French and Italians have an ongoing rivalry, culinary and otherwise, which actually stems more from the similarities than the differences between the two cultures. So how refreshing to choose from classic French fare such as foie gras and steak *au poivre* (steak with peppercorns). The nuns take a brief pause from serving before dessert to sing "Ave Maria"—a moment of unexpected but inspiring music in which everyone is welcome to join. You'll savor the food more knowing that all proceeds go to charity. ✉ *Via Monterone 85, Piazza Navona* ☎ *06/68801095* ▭ *AE, DC, MC, V* ⊘ *Closed Sun. and Aug.*

**$–$$** ✕ **Maccheroni.** This boisterous, convivial trattoria north of the Pantheon makes for a fun evening out. The decor is basic: white walls with wooden shelves lined with wine bottles, blocky wooden tables covered in white butcher paper—but there's an "open" kitchen (with even the dishwashers in plain view of the diners) and an airy feel that attracts a young clientele as well as visiting celebrities. The menu sticks to Roman basics such as simple pasta with fresh tomatoes and basil or rigatoni *alla gricia* (with bacon, sheep's-milk cheese, and black pepper). The specialty pasta, *trofie* (short pasta twists) with a black truffle sauce, inspires you to lick your plate. Probably the best choice on the menu is the *tagliata con rughetta*, a juicy, two-inch-thick steak sliced thinly and served on arugula. ✉ *Piazza delle Coppelle 44, Piazza Navona* ☎ *06/68307895* ▭ *AE, MC, V.*

**$–$$** ✕ **Ōbikā.** If you've ever wanted to take in a "mozzarella bar," here's your chance. Indeed, the owners of this new restaurant-bar (its name is

Neapolitan for "here it is") are to be commended for trying something original while remaining within the confines of the Italian tradition. Mozzarella is featured here much like sushi bars showcase fresh fish—even the decor is modern Japanese minimalism-meets-ancient Roman grandeur. Mozzarella cheese, in all its varieties, is the focus of the dishes: there's the familiar cow's milk, the delectable water buffalo milk varieties from the Campagnia region, and the sinfully rich *burrata* from Puglia (a fresh cow's milk mozzarella encasing a creamy center of unspun mozzarella curds and fresh cream). They're all served with various accompanying cured meats, vegetables, sauces, and breads. An outdoor deck just opened for the summer is a great plus for dining alfresco. ✉ *Piazza di Firenze, at Via dei Prefetti* ☎ *06/6832630* ▭ *AE, DC, MC, V.*

$  ✕ **Birreria Peroni.** With its long wooden tables, hard-back booths, and free-flowing beer, this casual restaurant seems to belong more to the genre of Munich beer hall than popular Roman hangout. But let's remember that to the north, way north, of Rome, lies a part of Italy in which the people speak as much German as they do Italian, where the wines they drink are Reislings and Gewurtztraminer, and the simple food seems more *tedesco* than *italiano*. It's from this place that Birreria Peroni draws its inspiration, and the goulash or the many sausage specialties—with sauerkraut and potatoes, of course—certainly provide a nice respite from pasta and tomato sauce. The place gets packed at lunch with nearby office workers and members of Parliament, but dinnertime is more relaxed. ✉ *Via di San Marcello 19, Piazza Navona* ☎ *06/6795310* ▭ *AE, DC, MC, V* ☺ *Closed Sun. and Aug. No lunch Sat.*

## Termini & Monti

Termini has long been known as the "sketchy" area around the train station. It's now the city's main ethnic neighborhoods, and as such offers several interesting choices for cuisine other than typical Italian fare. Monti was a sleepy residential 'hood neighboring Termini, but has of late turned into a newly chic area with lots of cute boutiques, wine bars, and restaurants.

$$$–$$$$  ✕ **Agata e Romeo.** For the perfect marriage (pun intended) of fine dining, **Fodor's**Choice  creative cuisine, and rustic Roman tradition, the husband-and-wife team ★  of Agata Parisella and Romeo Caraccio is the top. The couple runs one of Rome's best-loved restaurants. Chef Agata is a well-known figure on the Italian restaurant scene, and she's both guest cooking instructor and author of a cookbook on Italian olive oils and vinegars. More importantly, she was perhaps the first chef in the capital city to put a gourmet spin on Roman ingredients and preparations, elevating dishes of the common folk to new levels, wherein familiar staples like *coda alla vaccinara* (stewed oxtail with celery) were transformed into a rich oxtail ragout with celery root, both as a puree and as shoestring fries. Her signature style is both simple and elegant, perhaps best seen in her *sformato di formaggio di fossa* (a soufflé-tart of sheep's cheese aged in special caves) with a pear sauce and Acacia honey—a perfect balance between sweet and sharp. Pastas are more traditional, with *paccheri di Gragnano* (special oversize ziti of top quality, originating near Naples) *all'amatriciana*, as well as a risotto with

# ARTICHOKES & CHEESECAKE

**A**S ROME CLAIMS THE OLDEST CONTINUOUS JEWISH POPULATION in Europe, so Roman cuisine has been influenced by this 2,000-year-old legacy. Obviously, keeping kosher figures heavily into what Roman Jews have always eaten, while keeping the Sabbath and not being able to work (which includes cooking) from sundown Friday to sundown Saturday gave rise to many of the dishes in the Roman Jewish repertoire that are prepared ahead, sometimes marinated, and served at room temperature. But probably most influential is the use of ingredients that Jews favored (and thus shunned by the Catholic majority over the centuries), including eggplant, pumpkin, fennel, and that most Roman of vegetables, carciofi, the big, round bulb artichokes. We see them fried, alla giudea (Jewish style), braised (Roman style), and tossed with fresh fettucine. We see a lot of

baccalà, or salt cod, as well as bottarga, pressed, cured mullet or tuna roe, which is considered a delicacy. And when you see the pairing of raisins and pine nuts in Roman food, this is a holdover from the love of agrodolce, or sweet-and-sour, brought to the Italian continent from Sicily and originally from by Jews who fled Spain during the Inquisition. Perhaps the most beloved dessert that Roman Jews have given to Roman cuisine is the ricotta cheesecake. At the famous corner bakery in the Ghetto, it's served spiked with either chocolate chips or cherries, and is almost always sold out by closing time.

asparagus, quail egg, crunchy prosciutto, and parmesan shavings. The baccalà secondo, here of top quality Icelandic salted codfish prepared four ways to show its versatility, is a case study in Agata's remodeling of a typically Roman favorite. And the desserts! Any of the chocolate offerings are to die for, and the famous *millefoglie di Agata* (Agata's Napoléon) is a winner. Husband Romeo presides over the dining room and delights in the selection of good wine and pairing it with food. The prices here are steep, yes, and at €125 the tasting menu can induce facial ticks. But for those who appreciate extremely high-quality ingredients, homemade salami and breads, an incredible wine cellar and warm service—all done with simplicity and clarity of purpose—dining here is a real treat. ⊠ *Via Carlo Alberto 45, Termini* ☎ *06/4466115* ▭ *AE, DC, MC, V* ⊙ *Closed weekends, 2 wks in July, and 2 wks in Aug.*

**$$–$$$$** ✕ **Monte Caruso.** The regional delicacies of certain areas of Italy are grossly underrepresented in Rome, and for this, Monte Caruso is a standout, as its menu focuses on food from Lucania, an area of Italy divided between the southern regions of Basilicata and Calabria. Homemade pastas have strange-sounding names, such as *cautarogni* (large cavatelli with Sicilian broccoli) and *cauzuni* (enormous ricotta-stuffed ravioli), but the dishes are generally simple and hearty. ⊠ *Via Farini 12, Termini* ☎ *06/ 483549* 🖃 *AE, MC, V* ⊗ *Closed Sun. and Aug. No lunch Mon.*

**$–$$** ✕ **Trattoria Monti.** Not far from Santa Maria Maggiore and one of the most dependable, moderately priced trattorias in the city, Monti favors the cuisine of the Marches, an area to the northeast of Rome and poised to perhaps become "The Next Big Thing" in Italy. There are very few places specializing in this humble fare considering there are more *marchegiani* here in Rome than in the whole region of Le Marche. The fare served up by the Camerucci family is hearty and simple, represented by various roasted meats and game and a selection of generally vegetarian timbales and soufflés that change seasonally. The region's rabbit dishes are much loved, and here the *timballo di coniglio con patate* (rabbit casserole with potatoes) is no exception. ⊠ *Via di San Vito 13, Termini* ☎ *06/4466573* 🖃 *AE, DC, MC, V* ⊗ *Closed Sun., Mon., Aug., and 1 wk each at Christmas and Easter.*

**¢** ✕ **Africa.** Ethiopia was the closest thing Italy ever had to a "colony" at one point so, as a result, what Indian food is to London, so Ethiopian/ Eritrean is to Rome. Exotica includes meat stews, yogurt-based breakfasts, and utensil-free dining. ⊠ *Via Gaeta 26, Termini* ☎ *06/4941077* 🖃 *No credit cards* ⊗ *Closed Mon.*

## Trastevere

The mix of old-school Romans, local artists, and expats in this area makes for a very bohemian, Greenwich Village vibe. It's known for its vast selection of affordable pizzerias, trattorias, and birrerias/wine bars. Still, its hip factor has brought in young restaurateurs and bar owners to perk up this slice of picturesque Roman life across the Tiber from the city center.

**$$–$$$** ✕ **Antico Arco.** Founded by three friends with a passion for wine and
**Fodor's**Choice fine food, Antico Arco attracts foodies from Rome and beyond with its
★ culinary inventiveness and high style. The location is a bit removed from the city setting, up on top of the Janiculum hill, right near the Villa Pamphili park. But its charming setting, in a precious little villa, makes for a homey ambience that's difficult to come by elsewhere in the city. There's a substantial bar at which you can enjoy an aperitivo while you wait for a table, but do book ahead, as this place gets packed with its fans from the nearby American Academy and staff of the American University of Rome. Seating upstairs is cozy, particularly in winter; you feel as if you're dining in a friend's lovely attic. The menu changes with the season, but you may find such delights as *flan di taleggio con salsa di funghi* (a taleggio cheese flan with mushroom sauce), or a *carré d'agnello* (rack of lamb) with foie gras sauce and pears in port wine. The chocolate soufflé with a molten chocolate center, is justly famous among chocoholics all over the city. ⊠ *Piazzale Aurelio 7, Trastevere* ☎ *06/ 5815274* 🐟 *Reservations essential* 🖃 *AE, DC, MC, V* ⊗ *Closed Sun. and 2 wks in Aug. No lunch.*

**$$–$$$** ✕ **Ferrara.** What used to be a well-stocked *enoteca* (wine bar) with a few nibbles has become what locals now know as the "Ferrara block": the enoteca has expanded to become a full-fledged restaurant, a wine

# WITH CHILDREN?

I N RESTAURANTS AND TRATTORIAS *you may find a high chair or a cushion for the child to sit on, but there's rarely a children's menu. Order a mezza porzione (half portion) of any dish, or ask the waiter for a porzione da bambino (child's portion) or pasta in bianca (pasta with butter or olive oil), Italian children's favorite. Though spaghetti and meatballs are not found on menus (ever!), approximations to it, such as spaghetti al pomodoro (with tomato sauce) are*

*suitable substitutions. Italian children are fond of spaghetti with Parmesan, and even if it's not on the menu, most chefs will be happy to prepare it. Pizza offers a familiar treat. Generally, children will feel welcomed at casual establishments such as trattorias, but only exceptionally well-behaved children should go to higher-end restaurants.*

bar, and a gastronomic boutique taking over a good section of one of the area's most famous streets, Via del Moro. The renovations have resulted in an airy, modernist destination, with incredibly comfy high-back chairs mixed in with smaller colorfully tiled enoteca tables. Service can be iffy to slow, and, in the end, the results coming out of the kitchen are less consistent than the space is gorgeous. A fine starter is the ricotta and herb-stuffed zucchini flowers sprinkled with crispy pancetta, or perhaps the *zuppa di moscardini,* a lightly spicy tomato broth with baby octopus and croutons. Primi include a risotto of the day and a rigatoni with a *coda alla vaccinara* (stewed oxtail) sauce. And seconds range from seared tuna in a sesame seed crust to roast pork with prunes. But true to its enoteca roots, it's the wine selection that impresses here. It calls itself a wine bar, but Ferrara's menu makes it a bona fide restaurant with a *carta dei vini* the length of a short novel. ⊠ *Piazza Trilussa 41, Trastevere* ☎ *06/58333920* ⌖ *Reservations essential* ☰ *AE, DC, MC, V.*

**$$–$$$**
**Fodor'sChoice**
★
✕ **Romolo.** Nowhere else do the lingering rays of the setting Roman sun seem more inviting than within the tavern garden of this charming Trastevere haunt—reputedly the onetime home of Raphael's lady love, La Fornarina. Generations of Romans and tourists have enjoyed its romantic courtyard, where, in the evening, you might be serenaded by strolling musicians. The cuisine won't win any awards but is appropriately Roman and tasty enough; specialties include *mozzarella alla fornarina* (deep-friend mozzarella with ham and anchovies). Alternatively, try one of the new vegetarian pastas featuring carciofi artichokes or radicchio. ⊠ *Via di Porta Settimiana 8, Trastevere* ☎ *06/5818284* ☰ *AE, MC, V* ☉ *Closed Mon. and Aug. 2–23.*

**$$–$$$**
✕ **Spirito di Vino.** At this restaurant on the less-traveled side of Viale Trastevere, diners can enjoy an evening of historic and culinary interest. The restaurant itself was rebuilt on the site of a 12th-century Jewish synagogue, and as such, the spot is rich with history—several ancient sculp-

tures, now in the Vatican and Capitoline museums, were unearthed in the basement. The food ranges from inventive (delicious minimeatballs seasoned with coriander) to traditional (spaghetti with cacio cheese and pepper), to historical (braised pork shoulder with apples and leeks, following an ancient Roman recipe). The dining room is welcoming and refined, with brick-red walls and dark-wood details. The proud owner is happy to explain every dish on the menu (in English to boot), and he even offers a post-dinner tour of the wine cellar—and that basement. ⊠ *Via dei Genovesi 31* ☎ *06/5896689* ⊟ *AE, MC, V* ⊘ *Closed Sun. and 2 wks in Aug.*

**$–$$$** ╳ **Paris.** On a small square just off Piazza Santa Maria in Trastevere, Paris (named after a former owner) has a reassuring, understated ambience, without the hokey flamboyance of many eateries in this neighborhood. It's been a Trastevere landmark for years, a favorite for classic Roman cuisine, particularly those dishes of Jewish Roman origin. It's a notch above your average trattoria or Jewish Roman joint, both in terms of price and level of elegance. The waiters are classically decked in creamy tuxedo jackets and black bow ties, and serve the clientele with reverence and wit (a difficult combo to come by these days). The decorating sticks to the classic Roman *ristorante* motif: curtains and ruffles, linens, and wall sconces. Of course, the lights are much too bright—which is why, in warm weather, the outdoor tables are the ones to snag. ⊠ *Piazza San Calisto 7/a, Trastevere* ☎ *06/5815378* ⊟ *AE, DC, MC, V* ⊘ *Closed Mon. and 3 wks in Aug. No dinner Sun.*

**$–$$$** ╳ **Sicilia al Tappo.** A relatively new and good Sicilian spot, this spot has a menu that offers a taste of the south—a welcome respite from the usual Roman fare in Trastevere. The owner, from the northeast Sicilian port town of Messina, emphasizes the seafood with which he grew up, not to mention the fresh salads and fried goodies that make true Sicilian food so beloved by connoisseurs of Italian regional fare. Pastas include the Sicilian favorite pasta *alla Norma*, so-named for the Normans who once conquered the Mediterranean island. Main courses include a thin swordfish fillet with a *salmoriglio* sauce of parsley, oregano, garlic, lemon, and olive oil. Desserts include many *sorbetti* and ice creams (said to have been invented with the Sicilian snow from Mount Etna). The rooms are filled with colorful Sicilian porcelain—tiles on the walls and tables, as well as bowls and sculptures in every available nook—although the black-and-white photos on the walls strike a jarring note. ⊠ *Via Garibaldi 68* ☎ *06/58335490* ⊟ *MC, V* ⊘ *Closed Mon.*

**$–$$** ╳ **Da Fabrizio della Malva.** At this unassuming trattoria down the street from Piazza Trilussa, Fabrizio has turned this space into the seafood-focused sibling to his carnivores' heaven, Da Fabrizio, around the corner. Although meat and fish get equal billing on this menu, and the fillet of Danish beef is delicious, it's the briny temptations you'll succumb to. Appetizers like sea scallops gratinéed with bread crumbs in a squid-ink sauce are plump, juicy, and an unusual, welcome preparation. Or try the mixed selection of *pesce crudo* (raw seafood), which could include sea bass carpaccio, scampi, salmon marinated in citrus with pink peppercorns, and octopus salad. Pastas range from the traditional, including a great version of spaghetti with mussels, to the *strozzapreti* (literally, "priest stranglers") with clams, broccoli, and a healthy dose of garlic. The outdoor dining area, with a vine-covered trellis overhead, is a lovely spot to spend an evening before heading for a nightcap in one of Trastevere's many watering holes. ⊠ *Piazza San Giovanni della Malva 14/b, Trastevere* ☎ *06/ 5816646* 🚫 *AE, DC, MC, V* ⊘ *Closed Mon. and 2 wks in Aug.*

$ ✕ **Alle Fratte di Trastevere.** Here you can find staple Roman trattoria fare as well as dishes with a Neapolitan slant. This means that *spaghetti alla carbonara* (with chopped bacon, eggs, and cheese) shares the menu with the likes of penne *alla Sorrentina* (with tomato, basil, and fresh mozzarella), as well as a delicious pressed octopus carpaccio (cooked, no worries!) on a bed of arugula with olive oil and a squeeze of lemon. For starters, the bruschette here are exemplary; it's a very simple antipasto that most places get wrong. As for secondi, you can again look south and to the sea for a mixed seafood pasta or a grilled sea bass with oven-roasted potatoes, or go for the meat with a fillet *al pepe verde* (fillet cooked with green peppercorns in a brandy cream sauce). There are pizzas as well, so there's something for everyone. Service is always with a smile, with boisterous owner Francesco, his American wife, and their trusted waiter Peppe making you feel at home. The *dopo cena* (after dinner) digestives flow freely. ⊠ *Via delle Fratte di Trastevere 49/50* ☎ *06/ 5835775* 🚫 *AE, DC, MC, V* ⊘ *Closed Wed. and 2 wks in Aug.*

$ ✕ **Jaipur.** Named after the pink city in India, this restaurant meets the standards of the most discerning Londoners, who know a thing or two about their curries. Here, in this large space just off the main Viale Trastevere, you'll find a vast, high-ceilinged dining room decked in retina-burning yellow with festive Indian decorations on the huge walls (there's also dining outside when the weather calls for it). Portions are small but made for sharing, so go ahead and get a variety of dishes to "divide and conquer." ⊠ *Via di San Francesco a Ripa 56* ☎ *06/5803992* 🚫 *MC, V* ⊘ *Closed Mon.*

# Vatican

Another area that's busy with industry by day, and residential and quiet at night. As a result, many restaurants are local, frequented by clientele of the *zona*. Several spots are worth the trip across town for a good meal in a relaxing atmosphere.

$$$–$$$$ ✕ **La Veranda dell'Hotel Columbus.** Deciding where to sit at La Veranda is not easy, since both the shady courtyard, torch-lit at night, and the frescoed dining room are among Rome's most spectacular settings. The restaurant is part of the historic Palazzo Della Rovere, a 15th-century structure with a lovely internal courtyard and lots of authentic touches of the Italian aristocracy left in place throughout the hotel. While La Veranda has classic Roman cuisine on tap, the kitchen offers nice, refreshing twists on the familiar with an innovative use of spices and herbs, such as their *fiori di zucca con mazzancolle e salsa allo yogurt* (zucchini flowers stuffed with prawns in a yogurt sauce). The chickpea ravioli with a spicy tomato sauce is unusual, and fresh sea bass fillets with a saffron sauce and fresh peas give a subtle jolt to the taste buds. The chef also offers "historical" dishes, such as a 17th-century recipe for sea bream, baked in an almond

crust. Call ahead, especially on Saturday, because the hotel often hosts weddings, which close the restaurant. ✉ *Borgo Santo Spirito 73, Vatican* ☎ *06/6872973* ✍ *Reservations essential* 🖃 *AE, DC, MC, V.*

★ $$–$$$$ ✕ **Cesare.** An old standby in the residential area near the Vatican known as Prati, Cesare is a willing slave to tradition. The refrigerated display of fresh fish of the day is a tipoff of what's on offer. Classic fish dishes, such as fresh marinated anchovies and sardines (a world apart from their salt-packed sad cousins sold in the United States), mixed seafood salad dressed in a lemon citronette, and smoked swordfish, quell those seafood cravings. Homemade pasta with meat sauce is the primo to get, and *saltimbocca* (thinly sliced veal with prosciutto and sage) or the thick Florentine steaks are the ultimate meat-lover's dishes. As with any other real Roman restaurant, gnocchi are served on Thursday and pasta with chickpeas on Friday. The look of the place is quite clubby, and the menu's tendency towards stick-to-the-ribs comfort food make it a great place to go in the autumn and winter, when the cooler weather ushers in dishes featuring truffles, game, porcini mushrooms, and hearty bean soups. ✉ *Via Crescenzio 13, Vatican* ☎ *06/6861227* 🖃 *AE, DC, MC, V* ☉ *Closed Mon., Aug., and Easter wk. No dinner Sun.*

★ $$–$$$$ ✕ **Il Simposio di Costantini.** At perhaps the most upscale wine bar in town, decorated with wrought-iron vines, wood paneling, and velvet, you can choose from about 30 wines. You can sit at the bar and sip and chat with the owners about the latest vintages, or why you prefer pinot nero to merlot (*alla* "Sideways"). But now that they're serving food at this enoteca-turned-restaurant, why not come for a full meal? Especially when the food is appropriately *raffinato* (refined): marinated and smoked fish, composed salads, top-quality salami and other cured meats (classical and wild), as well as the hard-to-come-by terrines and pâtés. There are plenty of dishes with classic Roman leanings, like the artichoke dish prepared three ways—Roman style, Jewish style, and in a soufflé of sorts. Main courses like a delicious roast lamb, a fillet with foie gras, or game (like pigeon, in season) round out the meal and compliment the obviously excellent wine selection (particularly the vast offering of top-notch reds). The restaurant boasts 80 assorted cheeses, so with your fragrant slices, savor a nice glass of dessert wine. Ask, and trust, your server. ✉ *Piazza Cavour 16, Vatican* ☎ *06/3211502* 🖃 *AE, DC, MC, V* ☉ *Closed Sun. and last 2 wks of Aug. No lunch Sat.*

$$$ ✕ **Osteria dell'Angelo.** At this boisterous and authentic eatery, the mandatory prix-fixe menu at dinner is not a ploy to attract tourists; it's just great food at a great price—even the house wine is included. The decor consists of photos of rugby players and boxers, the two sports about which Angelo is almost as passionate as he is about food. If you go in a group, ask for family-style portions and try a bit of everything they bring out. From mixed antipasti of vegetables, beans, cured meats, and bruschetta to spaghetti *cacio e pepe* and sautéed veal with mushrooms, it's all Roman and it's all good. For dinner, reservations are a must. ✉ *Via G. Bettolo 24, near St. Peter's Basilica Metro stop, Vatican* ☎ *06/3729470* 🖃 *No credit cards* ☉ *Closed Sun., Aug., and Christmas wk. No lunch Wed., Thurs., and Sat.–Mon.*

**$–$$$** ✕ **Da Benito e Gilberto.** Commonly known as "da Benito," this fish restaurant opened in 1976 with Benito and his son Gilberto at the helm. Ever since, despite its appearance of a tourist trap in an area full of them, this restaurant has come to be known as a great seafood spot not far from the Vatican that strikes a nice balance between refinement and a welcoming homeyness. It's small (only 30 seats) with lots of friendly photos lining the walls. Wooden chairs and tables covered in yellow linens keep the setting low-key, which allows diners to concentrate on the simple, classic seafood. As at most seafood establishments, the quality of their primary ingredients can best be tasted in their large assortment of raw offerings. Winners include their fettuccine with lobster, *bombolotti* (half-rigatoni) with zucchini and little langoustines, or traditional fish fry. ⊠ *Via del Falco 19, Vatican* ☎ *06/6867769* ▤ *AE, DC, MC, V* ☺ *Closed Sun., Mon., and Aug.*

★ **$$** ✕ **Taverna Angelica.** The area surrounding St. Peter's Basilica isn't known for culinary excellence, but Taverna Angelica is an exception. Its tiny size (just 20 seats) allows the chef to concentrate on each individual dish, and the results are impressive. The menu is creative without being pretentious. Dishes such as warm octopus salad on a bed of warm mashed potatoes with a basil-parsley pesto drizzle are more about taste than presentation. The chickpeas with a fondue of pecorino cheese provided an interesting pairing that worked nicely, and the lentil soup with pigeon breast brought hunter's cuisine to a new level. And the breast of duck in balsamic vinegar was exquisitely executed. It may be difficult to find, on a section of the street that's set back and almost subterranean, but it's worth searching out. The candlelighted dining room, tasteful decor, and excellent service are all icing on the cake. ⊠ *Piazza A. Capponi 6, Vatican* ☎ *06/6874514* ⚖ *Reservations essential* ▤ *AE, V.*

**$–$$** ✕ **Dal Toscano.** An open wood-fired grill and classic dishes such as *ribollita* (a thick bread and vegetable soup) and *pici* (fresh, thick pasta with wild hare sauce) are the draw at this great family-run Tuscan trattoria near the Vatican. The cuts of beef visible at the entrance tell you right away that the house special is the prized *bistecca alla fiorentina*— a thick grilled steak left rare in the middle and seared on the outside, with its rub of gutsy Tuscan olive oil and sea salt forming a delicious crust to keep in the natural juices of the beef. Seating outside on the sidewalk in warm weather is a nice touch and gives you the sensation of being at a summer block party in the center of a small town in Tuscany. ⊠ *Via Germanico 58, Vatican* ☎ *06/39725717* ▤ *DC, MC, V* ☺ *Closed Mon., Aug., and 2 wks in Dec.*

**¢–$** ✕ **Tre Pupazzi.** The "three puppets," after which the trattoria is named, are the worn stone figures on a fragment of an ancient sarcophagus that embellishes a building on this byway near the Vatican. Little has changed here since the place was built in 1625, and the restaurant upholds a tradition of good food, courteous service, and reasonable prices. The menu offers classic Roman and Abruzzese trattoria fare, including fettuccine and abbacchio, plus pizzas at lunchtime, a rarity in Rome. The restaurant opens early, at noon for lunch and 7 for dinner. ⊠ *Borgo Pio 183, at Via dei Tre Pupazzi, Vatican* ☎ *06/68803220* ▤ *AE, DC, MC, V* ☺ *Closed Sun. and Aug.*

## Via Appia Antica

The ancient road leading out of (or into) Rome gives you the feeling of being outside of the city and allows you to lose track of what century it is. The restaurants in this setting aid this by setting up dining areas outdoors by torchlight and in antico locations. Still, beware of the tourist traps.

**$–$$$** ✕ **L'Archeologia.** In this farmhouse just beyond the catacombs, you dine indoors beside the fireplace in cool weather or in the garden under age-old vines in summer. The atmosphere is friendly and intimate. Specialties include fettuccine *al finocchio salvatico* (with wild fennel), abbacchio alla scottadito, and fresh seafood. But remember that the food here is secondary: you're there, and you're paying for the view and the setting more than any culinary adventure or excellence with the classics. ⊠ *Via Appia Antica 139* ☎ *06/7880494* 🖃 *AE, MC, V* ⊗ *Closed Tues.*

**$–$$$** ✕ **Ristorante Cecilia Metella.** From the entrance on Via Appia Antica, almost opposite the catacombs, you walk uphill to a low-lying but sprawling construction designed for wedding feasts and banquets. There's a large terrace shaded by vines for outdoor dining. Although obviously geared to larger groups, Cecilia Metella also gives individuals and small groups good service and traditional Roman cuisine. The specialties are the *scrigno alla Cecilia* (baked green noodles) and *pollo al Nerone* (chicken à la Nero—flambéed, of course). ⊠ *Via Appia Antica 125, Via Appia Antica* ☎ *06/5136743* ⊕ *www.ceciliametella.it/* 🖃 *AE, DC, MC, V* ⊗ *Closed Mon. and last 2 wks in Aug.*

## Via Veneto

What was once the center of the Roman Dolce Vita set of the '50's and '60's is mostly a tourist-friendly area of hotels and shops. Still, some classic restaurants are going strong and a new interest in revitalizing the area has brought in some hip new hotels and dining spots.

**$$$$** ✕ **La Terrazza dell'Eden.** Spectacular is the only word to describe the
**Fodor's**Choice   rooftop setting from the Hotel Eden, where all of Roma Divina seems
★   to be lying at your feet. The restaurant of the superluxe Hotel Eden, this aerie has wraparound windows to frame the grand vistas (too bad, the room's ceiling is so low). Enhancing the heady high is the lambinage of the decor, all soothing beiges and grays, with plenty of mirrors for all those makeup checks by Hollywood starlets. Happily, the food is nearly as lofty as the views. Chef Adriano Cavagnini is still in his early thirties, but he aims high as his crispy breast of quail with parma ham, lentils, and apples tatin, or "Casonelli" pasta filled with pumpkin and almond biscuits, or Barbera Maccheroncini with duck ragout and wild mushrooms, or chocolate mousse with crispy bananas and walnut ravioli prove. If you're a wine enthusiast, ask the maître d' to let you view the restaurant's showcase cellar. And don't forget the "Bar La Terraza," where you can sip, if not fully taste, "the high life" with an outdoor terrace to boot. ⊠ *Hotel Eden, Via Ludovisi 49, Via Veneto* ☎ *06/47812752* 🖎 *Reservations essential* 🏛 *Jacket and tie* 🖃 *AE, DC, MC, V.*

★ **$$$-$$$$** ✕ **Papá Baccus.** Italo Cipriani takes his meat as seriously as any Tuscan. He uses real Chianina beef, the prized breed from the Val di Chiana traditionally used for the house-specialty, the *bistecca alla fiorentina*, a thick grilled steak served on the bone and rare in the center. Cipriani brings many ingredients from his hometown on the border of Emilia-Romagna and Tuscany. Try the sweet and delicate prosciutto from Pratomagno or the *ribollita*, a traditional bread-based minestrone soup. Tuscans are nicknamed "the bean eaters," and after a taste of the *fagioli zolfini* (tender white beans), you'll understand why. The welcome is warm, the service excellent. The pale yellow walls and the colorful paintings on them lend a cheery touch to the two dining rooms, and the glass of prosecco (gratis) starts the meal on the right foot. ⊠ *Via Toscana 36, Via Veneto* ☎ *06/42742808* ⊟ *AE, DC, MC, V* ☉ *Closed Sun. and 2 wks in Aug. No lunch Sat.*

**$$$** ✕ **Moma.** Almost a sister in spirit to the Hotel Aleph, a new favorite of the design trendoisie located across the street, Moma is modern, moody, and very "concept." The design palette looks to nature, with dark-wood tables, subtle lighting, dark comfy leather chairs, and a soothing palette of gray on the geometric-patterned walls. The menu has hits and misses, and attempts to raise the nouvelle bar in Rome——foie gras *millefoglie* with apple slices and cider vinegar geleé, anyone? Seared scallops, plump and sweet, were a find, seared and served with steamed potato slices and raspberry vinegar. A mixed plate of raw fish allowed the fresh seafood to shine, although it desperately needed some salt and olive oil. The rigatoni *all'amatriciana* were tasty. And the main plate of Argentinian rib eye with balsamic vinegar was delicious, although the potatoes on the side, specifically billed as *croccante* (crispy) were soggy. There are several basic desserts, of which the molten chocolate cake (again, we know, we know) is probably the best, with pear sorbetto and chocolate sauce. ⊠ *Via San Basilio 42/43* ☎ *06/42011798* ⊟ *AE, DC, MC, V* ☉ *Closed Sun. and 2 wks in Aug.*

**$$-$$$** ✕ **Tullio.** Just off Piazza Barberini sits this Tuscan-accented upscale trattoria known for years among the international business set as well as the entertainment industry. The decor is basic wood paneling and white linens, with the requisite older—and often grumpy—waiters. The menu is heavy on Tuscan classics such as *ribollita* (a bread-based minestrone soup), white beans, and the famed *bistecca alla fiorentina*, a carnivore's dream. Meat dishes other than beef, such as lamb and veal, are also dependably good. The homemade pappardelle *al cinghiale* (wide, flat noodles in a tomato and wild boar sauce) are delectable. And fresh seafood is also offered in abundance, as well as a few key Roman dishes and greens like *brocoletti,* sauteéd to perfection with garlic and olive oil. The wine list favors robust Tuscan reds and thick wallets. ⊠ *Via San Nicola da Tolentino, near Piazza Barberini, Termini* ☎ *06/4745560* ⊟ *AE, DC, MC, V* ☉ *Closed Sun. and Aug.*

## Beyond the City Center

You'll find some fine options in Rome's outlaying areas—from the famed *alta cucina* of La Pergola at the Rome Hilton to the spots popping up in San Lorenzo, the counterculture and student quarter just a short cab ride east of the Stazione Termini.

**$$$$**    ✕ **La Pergola.** For decades, everyone made a pilgrimage to the city sub-
Fodor'sChoice    urbs and the Cavalieri Hilton, perched high atop Monte Mari, to feast
★    on the creations of Heinz Beck, "the best chef in Rome." These days,
of course, he has some serious competition, but the effort to get out here
is still richly rewarded. The setting is grand: La Pergola's rooftop setting offers a commanding view of the city; trompe-l'oeil ceilings and handsome wood paneling combine with low lighting to create an intimate
atmosphere; the quality of the table settings lets you know you're being
fussed over. Once seated in your plush chairs (of which there are only
60, so reservations are recommended well in advance), one of your many
waiters will present you with menus—food, wine, and water (you read
correctly). The German Wunder-chef's *alta cucina* still means great
haute cuisine—this may be the only restaurant in Rome to charge 35
euros for a tomato salad, but most everything will prove to be the best
version of the dish you've ever tasted. Lobster is oh-so-lightly poached,
and melt-in-your-mouth lamb in a veggie-accented jus is deceptively simple but earthy and perfect. Ditto the scallops served with black truffle,
each coin-sized mollusk and truffle thinly sliced and meticulously fanned
across the plate. Each course comes with a flourish of sauces or extra
touches that makes it an event in its own right, while the cheese cart is
well-explained by knowledgeable servers. And the dessert course is extravagant, including tiny petits-fours and treats tucked away in small
drawers that make up the serving "cabinet." The wine list is as thrilling
as one might expect with the financial backing of the Hilton and their
investment in one of the top wine cellars in Italy; still, markup is steep
so choose wisely. ⊠ *Cavalieri Hilton, Via Cadlolo 101, Monte Mario*
☎ *06/3509221* ⌂ *Reservations essential* 🏛 *Jacket and tie* ▤ *AE, DC,*
*MC, V* ☉ *Closed Sun. and Mon. and 2 wks in Dec. No lunch.*

★ **$–$$$**    ✕ **Siciliainbocca.** The owners, both natives of the beautiful island of Sicily,
decided to open up Siciliainbocca after years of frustration at not finding
decent renditions of the food for which their home region is so renowned.
As a result, the pasta *alla norma* (with eggplant, tomato sauce, and aged
ricotta cheese) here is one of the best versions in Rome. Try specialties
such as caponata (a sweet-and-sour veggie ratatouille heavy on the egg-
plant), or risotto *ai profumi di Sicilia* (with lemon, orange, mozzarella,
and zucchini). Proof of the emphasis on the island's fishing industry's spoils
is the delicious grilled swordfish, shrimp, and squid. Even in the dead of
winter, Siciliainbocca's yellow walls and brightly colored ceramic plates
make you feel as if you're in sunny Palermo or Taormina, and there's out-
door seating in summer to add to this illusion. ⊠ *Via E. Faà di Bruno*
*26, Vatican* ☎ *06/37358400* ▤ *AE, DC, MC, V* ☉ *Closed Sun.*

★ **$$**    ✕ **Uno e Bino.** The setting is as simple as can be, with wooden tables and
chairs on a stone floor with little more than a few shelves of wine bot-
tles lining the walls for decor. But here, you want to concentrate and use
all the senses to experience what you're putting on your palate. Gi-
ampaolo Gravina's restaurant in this artsy corner of the San Lorenzo neighborhood is popular with Romans from all over town. He works the dining
room, offering suggestions from an impressive wine list, and his sister
Gloria is in the kitchen turning out inventive cuisine inspired by the family's Umbrian and Sicilian roots. Dishes such as octopus salad with as-

paragus and carrots, and spaghetti with swordfish, tomatoes, and capers are specialties. The parmesan soufflé is a study in lightness and silky-salty. And the perfectly prepared pigeon will satisfy even the most critical foodie on an autumn night. Desserts are delicious and upscale-simple as well, making this small establishment one of the top dining deals—and pleasurable meals—in Rome. ⊠ *Via degli Equi 58, San Lorenzo* ☎ *06/ 4460702* ⊟ *AE, DC, MC, V* ☒ *Closed Mon. and Aug. No lunch.*

**$–$$** ✗ **Da Franco ar Vicoletto.** In the heart of the city's student-filled San Lorenzo district, Da Franco ar Vicoletto is one of Rome's few affordable fish restaurants. The prix-fixe menu is always more or less the same: an appetizer of sautéed mussels or clams; a choice of seafood lasagna, spaghetti with clams, or pasta with beans and shellfish (a seemingly strange combination that succeeds heroically); and then grilled, roasted, and fried fish. It's the kind of place best visited in a group—the more people at your table, the more food that pours out of the kitchen. ⊠ *Via dei Falisci 1/b, San Lorenzo* ☎ *06/4957675* ⊟ *No credit cards* ☒ *Closed Mon. and 3 wks in Aug.*

**$–$$** ✗ **Il Dito e la Luna.** One of the first places to mark the "revival" of sorts that the San Lorenzo neighborhod has undergone over the past six years, this is the place to go for updated Sicilian fare. The decor is warm and simple. Pasta *con le sarde* (with fresh sardines, bread crumbs, pine nuts, and orange peel), a headlining dish in the Sicilian repertoire, is excellent. The dishes made with eggplant—one of Sicily's staple ingredients—shouldn't be missed, either. More creative dishes include rabbit with prunes and lamb chops with a sharp cheese sauce. Wines tend towards the up-and-coming Sicilian winemakers, worth trying while they're still reasonably priced and still little-known (at least outside Italy). Cannoli are the real thing here: light, airy, and filled with delicious sweet ricotta and chocolate chips. ⊠ *Via dei Sabelli 51, San Lorenzo* ☎ *06/ 4940726* ⊟ *No credit cards* ☒ *Closed Sun. and 2 wks in Aug. No lunch.*

**$–$$** ✗ **Tram Tram.** Across the streetcar tracks not far from the main Stazione Termini, this bustling trattoria is usually snugly packed with hungry Romans. The name refers to its proximity to the tram tracks, but could also describe its size, as it's narrow-narrow and often stuffed to the rafters-rafters. In warmer weather, there's a "side car" of tables enclosed along the sidewalk. But regardless of your seating arrangement, you eat well here. The focus of the food is Puglian, where the cook hails from (the heel of the boot of the Italian peninsula), and emphasizes both seafood and lots of vegetables, often with pastas of very particular shapes. Fish is a good bet here; try homemade *orecchiette*, a pasta specialty with clams and broccoli. ⊠ *Via dei Reti 44/46, San Lorenzo* ☎ *06/490416* ⊟ *AE, DC, MC, V* ☒ *Closed Mon. and 1 wk in mid-Aug.*

**$** ✗ **Cannavota.** On the square next to San Giovanni in Laterano, this place has a large and faithful following and has fed generations of neighborhood families over the years. Everything about it says old-school Roman tratt—the wood-beam ceilings and wood-paneled walls, hung with photos from past decades (dig those '70s duds and thick mustaches on the groovy diners!), paintings, and a random mish-mash of knickknacks that say this place has been here a long while. The food is as good as any trattoria might serve, sometimes better, and the service is warm and welcoming.

Seafood seems to dominate, but carnivores are satisfied also. Try one of the pastas with seafood sauce—fettuccine with scampi, or wide pappardelle noodles with a mixed seafood ragu. Seconds range from fresh grilled fish to a veal chop. And the prices here are of *una volta* (another time), as the most expensive thing on the menu, more or less, is 13 euros. ⊠ *Piazza San Giovanni in Laterano 20, San Giovanni* ☎ *06/77205007* ☰ *AE, DC, MC, V* ☺ *Closed Wed. and 3 wks in Aug.*

**$** ✕ **Da Gianni.** About a 20-minute walk from St. Peter's Basilica, this tiny trattoria is well worth the stroll. Also known as "Cacio e Pepe," Da Gianni turns out exclusively Roman food of high quality. Although there are no antipasti on offer, heaping plates of *tonnarelli cacio e pepe* (long pasta with sheep's cheese and pepper), tonnarelli alla carbonara, *polpettone,* and fried anchovies are simple and satisfying main courses. Sit outside at folding wooden tables and check out the area's film and television crowd as they talk on their cell phones. ⊠ *Via G. Avezzana 11, Vatican* ☎ *06/3217268* ☰ *No credit cards* ☺ *Closed Sun. and Aug. No dinner Sat.*

**¢–$** ✕ **Pommidoro.** Mamma's in the kitchen and the rest of the family greets, serves, and keeps you happy and well fed at this trattoria popular with artists, filmmakers, and actors. It's near Rome's main university in the San Lorenzo neighborhood. The menu sticks pretty much to the standards of Roman trattorias, but the focus here is on all things grilled—meats and game birds and even grill-friendly seafood, like calamari. But you can also expect classic home-style *cucina,* since that's what the Romans always return to. You can dine semi-outside in warm weather, as there's a seating area in the piazza enclosed by plastic roll-up walls and surrounded by shrubs. Your best bet is to ask for a table where the crowd is thickest, as that ensures you the most attentive service and a central view of all goings-on. ⊠ *Piazza dei Sanniti 44, San Lorenzo* ☎ *06/4452692* ☰ *AE, DC, MC, V* ☺ *Closed Sun. and Aug.*

# Enoteche

It was not so long ago that wine in Rome (and other towns) was strictly local; you didn't have to walk far to find an osteria, where you could buy wine straight from the barrel or sit down to drink and nibble a bit, chat, or play cards. The tradition continues today, as many Roman wineshops are also open as *enoteche* (wine bars). The folding chairs and rickety tables have given way to designer interiors and chic ambience. Enormous barrels of Frascati have been replaced by shelves lined with hundreds of bottles from all over the country, representing the best in Italian wine making. Behind the bar you can find a serious wine enthusiast—maybe even a sommelier—with several bottles open to be tasted by the glass. And the food has changed, too. There are usually carefully selected cheeses and cured meats, and a short menu of simple dishes and desserts, making a stop in an enoteca an appealing alternative to a three-course restaurant meal.

## Campo de' Fiori

**★ $$** ✕ **La Tartaruga.** This wine bar feels like a small, elegant restaurant. The food matches the atmosphere, and offerings include risotto with asparagus,

# MENU BASICS

**R**OMAN COOKING IS SIMPLE. *Meat and fish are most often roasted, baked, or grilled. Many traditional recipes are based on innards, but you won't find much of that on the menu in restaurants in the center of town, with the exception of* trippa alla romana *(tripe stewed in tomatoes).*

*The typical Roman fresh pasta is* fettuccine, *golden egg noodles at their best when laced with ragu, a rich tomato and meat sauce.* Spaghetti alla carbonara *is tossed with a sauce of egg yolk, chunks of* guanciale *(cured pork cheek—truly Roman) or* pancetta *(salt-cured bacon),* pecorino Romano *cheese, and lots of freshly ground black pepper.*

*Pasta all'amatriciana has a sauce of tomato,* guanciale, *and (sometimes) onion. Potato* gnocchi, *served with a tomato sauce and a dusting of Parmesan or pecorino, are a Roman favorite for Thursday dinner.*

*The best meat on the menu is often* abbacchio, *milk-fed lamb. Legs of lamb are usually roasted with rosemary and potatoes, and the chops are grilled* alla scottadito *(literally "burn your finger," for small chops eaten with your fingers hot off the grill).* Saltimbocca alla romana *(veal with prosciutto and sage) is another tried-and-true local specialty.*

*Most Mediterranean fish are light yet flavorful, among them* spigola *(sea bass),* orata *(gilthead bream), and* rombo

*(turbot). Romans swoon for batter-fried* baccalà *(salt cod), at its best light and flaky. Seasonal vegetables are usually available, although they may not be listed on the menu.* Cicoria *and* spinaci ripassati *(fried chicory and spinach) are favorite side dishes among Romans and should satisfy your daily quota of greens.*

*Many restaurants make a specialty of the* fritto misto *(literally "mixed fried") consisting of whatever vegetables are in season. Rome is famous for* carciofi *(artichokes)—the season runs from November to April—traditionally prepared* alla romana *(stuffed with garlic and mint and braised in oil) or* alla giudia *(fried whole, making each petal crisp).*

*Local cheeses are made from sheep's milk; the best-known is the aged, sharp* pecorino Romano. *Fresh ricotta is a treat all on its own, and finds its way into a number of dishes, including desserts—look for* torta di ricotta, *the Roman answer to cheesecake.*

*Typical wines of Rome are from the Castelli Romani, the towns in the hills to the southeast: Frascati, Colli Albani, Marino, and Velletri. Restaurants usually have you choose between bottled waters, either* gassata *(sparkling) or* liscia *(not).*

*vitello tonnato* (veal in a cold tuna sauce), and an excellent selection of cheeses and cold meats from all over Italy. ✉ *Via del Monte della Farina 53, Campo de' Fiori* ☎ *06/6869473* 🖃 *AE, DC, MC, V* ☾ *Closed Mon. and Aug.*

$-$$ ✕ **Il Goccetto.** Sergio Ceccarelli, one of Rome's most knowledgeable wine store owners, is more than willing to help perplexed customers.

Choose from about 20 wines by the glass or from hundreds of bottles stocked on the wood shelves. Then curb your hunger with a wide selection of cheeses from all over Italy, marinated vegetables, and meats from the famed Falorni *salumificio* (meat curer) in Tuscany. Il Goccetto's location near Campo de' Fiori and its cool, quiet interior make it a welcome rest stop after sightseeing or a perfect place to sip an *aperitivo* (predinner drink) before a meal at one of the neighborhood's many restaurants. ⊠ *Via dei Banchi Vecchi 14, Campo de' Fiori* ☎06/6864268 ➌*AE, MC, V* ✆ *Closed Sun. and last 3 wks in Aug.*

¢–$ ✕ **L'Angolo Divino.** There's something about this cozy wine bar that feels as if it's in a small university town instead of a bustling metropolis. Serene blue-green walls lined with wood shelves of wines from around the Italian peninsula add to the warm atmosphere. Smoked fish, cured meats, cheeses, and salads make a nice lunch or light dinner, and the kitchen stays open until the wee hours. Ask about tasting evenings dedicated to single grape varieties or regions. ⊠ *Via dei Balestrari 12, Campo de' Fiori* ☎ *06/6864413* ➌*MC, V* ✆ *Closed 1 wk in Aug. No dinner Mon.*

### Colosseo

¢–$ ✕ **Cavour 313.** Wine bars are popping up all over the city, but Cavour
FodorśChoice 313 has been around much longer than most. With a tight seating area
★ in the front of the place, your best bet is to head to the large space in the rear, which is divided into sections with "booths" that give this bar a rustic feel, halfway to a beer hall. Open for lunch and dinner, it serves an excellent variety of cured meats, cheeses, and salads. Choose from about 25 wines by the glass or uncork a bottle (there are more than 1,200) and stay a while. ⊠ *Via Cavour 313, Colosseo* ☎ *06/6785496* ➌*AE, DC, MC, V* ✆ *Closed Aug. No lunch weekends. No dinner Sun. June 15–Sept.*

### Jewish Ghetto

$–$$ ✕ **Vinando.** Of all of the city's neighborhoods, finding a new place in the winding backstreets of the old Jewish Ghetto can feel the most rewarding, as it gives the immediate sensation of discovering a hidden secret. This latest venture, from the people behind Taverna degli Amici across the piazza, shares a lot of the same menu items as its parent restaurant: artichokes, classic pastas, well-executed standard Roman *secondi*. But the emphasis here is on the wine, representing most of Italy's 20 regions, with some hard-to-find labels. The dining room is cozy, and the enoteca and wine bar up front are adorably *nuovo* rustic. ⊠ *Piazza Margana 23* ☎ *06/69200741* ➌*AE, MC, V.*

¢–$ ✕ **La Bottega del Vino di Anacleto Bleve.** This cozy wineshop sells bottles to take away throughout the day and early evening but, at lunchtime only, Anacleto Bleve and his sons set out tables to serve locals who pack the place. The owners make the rounds, proposing the latest cheese they have procured from the farthest reaches of Italy. Instead of a menu, there's Mamma at the counter with a good selection of mixed salads, smoked fish, and sliced meats, as well as a few soups and *sformati* (thick flans). You point, and she serves it up. There are always wines to drink by the glass, or you can choose from the several hundred bottles on the shelves

# REFUELING THE ROMAN WAY

**S**TAGGERING UNDER THE WEIGHT of a succession of three-course meals, you may ask yourself, how do the Romans eat so much, twice a day, every day? The answer is, they don't.

If you want to do as the Romans do, try lunch at a tavola calda (literally, hot table), a cross between a café and a cafeteria where you'll find fresh food in manageable portions.

There's usually a selection of freshly prepared pastas, cooked vegetables such as bietola all'agro (cooked beet greens with lemon) and roast potatoes, and sometimes meat or fish.

Go to the counter to order an assortment and quantity that suits your appetite, and pay by the plate, usually about €5 plus drinks. Tavole calde aren't hard to find, particularly in the city center, often marked with TAVOLA CALDA or SELF-SERVICE signs.

The other ubiquitous options for a light lunch or between-meal snack are pizza al taglio (by the slice) shops, bars, and enoteche (wine bars). At bars throughout Italy, coffee is the primary beverage served (drinking establishments are commonly known as pubs or American bars); at them you can curb your appetite with a panino (a simple sandwich) or tramezzino (sandwich on untoasted white bread, usually heavy on the mayonnaise).

Enoteche vary widely in the sophistication and variety of food available. You can count on cheese and cured meats at the very least.

---

that surround you. ⊠ *Via Santa Maria del Pianto 9/a, Ghetto* ☎ *06/6865970* ⊟ *AE, DC, MC, V* ☺ *Closed Sun. and Mon. No dinner.*

## Piazza di Spagna

**$$–$$$** ✕ **Il Brillo Parlante.** Il Brillo Parlante's location near Piazza del Popolo makes it convenient for lunch or dinner after a bit of shopping in the Via del Corso area. Choose from 20 wines by the glass at the bar or eat downstairs in one of several wood-panel rooms. The menu is extensive for a wine bar; choose from cured meats, *crostini* (toasted bread with various toppings such as pâté or prosciutto), pastas, grilled meats, and even pizzas. ⊠ *Via della Fontanella 15, Piazza di Spagna* ☎ *06/3243334* ⊟ *AE, DC, MC, V* ☺ *Closed Mon. and 1 wk in mid-Aug.*

**$** ✕ **Enoteca Severini.** It's more of a hole-in-the-wall than an actual wine bar, but if you want authenticity, come to Enoteca Severini. Each day, the eccentric owner opens up a few bottles on the counter for customers to sip. It's tiny and strange, yet charming and very, very Roman. ⊠ *Via Bocca del Leone 44/a, Piazza di Spagna* ☎ *06/6786031* ⊟ *MC, V* ☺ *Closed Sat.*

**$** ✕ **L'Enoteca Antica di Via della Croce.** This wine bar is always crowded, and for good reason. It's long on personality: colorful ceramic-tile tables are always filled with locals and foreigners, as is the half-moon-shape bar where you can order from the large selection of salumi and cheeses on offer. Peruse the chalkboard highlighting the special wines by-the-glass for that day to accompany your nibbles. There's waiter service at the tables in back and out front on the bustling Via della Croce, where people-watching is in high gear. ⊠ *Via della Croce 76/b, Piazza di Spagna* ☎ *06/6790896* ▭ *AE, DC, MC, V* ⊙ *Closed 2 wks in Aug.*

## Piazza Navona

**$–$$**  ✕ **La Trinchetta.** A Lilliputian-size bar close to the Tiber, this comes with a relatively large dining menu, well-chosen wine list, and faithful clientele. Choose from a vast array of unusual cured meats, terrines, rare cheeses, vegetable tarts, and simple desserts. A large selection of wines by the glass impresses, but it's the grappas that offer a point of departure for this establishment. Walls lined with various bottles made from a vast assortment of grape varietals allows customers to experiment. ⊠ *Via dei Banchi Nuovi 4, Piazza Navona* ☎ *06/68300133* ▭ *AE, MC, V* ⊙ *Closed last 2 wks in Aug. No lunch Sun.*

**$**  ✕ **Cul de Sac.** This popular wine bar near Piazza Navona is among the city's oldest enoteche and offers a book-length selection of wines from Italy, France, the Americas, and elsewhere. Food is eclectic, ranging from a huge assortment of Italian meats and cheeses (try the delicious *lonza,* cured pork loin, or *speck,* a northern Italian smoked prosciutto) to various Mediterranean dishes, including delicious baba ghanoush, a tasty Greek salad, and a spectacular wild boar pâté. Outside tables get crowded fast, so arrive early, or come late, as they serve until about 1 AM. ⊠ *Piazza Pasquino 73, Piazza Navona* ☎ *06/68801094* ⌘ *Reservations not accepted* ▭ *MC, V* ⊙ *No lunch Mon.*

**$**  ✕ **Vinamore.** The name of this small wine bar tucked behind Piazza Navona means, aptly enough, "wine love," and wine is the main focus here, paired with simple dishes of cured meats, cheeses, and salads. Tasting classes are available, and although the owners have yet to offer them in English, some things need no translation. ⊠ *Via Monte Giordano 63, Piazza Navona* ☎ *06/68300159* ▭ *AE, MC, V* ⊙ *Closed Aug. No lunch Mon.*

**¢–$**  ✕ **Enoteca Corsi.** Very convenient to the historic center for lunch or an afternoon break, this little hole-in-the-wall looks like it missed the revolution; prices and decor are *come una volta* (like once upon a time) when the shop sold—as the sign says—wine and oil. The genuinely dated feel of the place has its charm: you can still get wine here by the liter, or choose from a good variety of fairly priced alternatives in bottles. The place is packed at lunch, when a few specials—classic pastas and some second dishes like veal roast with peas—are offered. ⊠ *Via del Gesù 88, Piazza Venezia* ☎ *06/6790821* ▭ *AE, DC, MC, V* ⊙ *Closed Sun. No dinner.*

**¢–$**  ✕ **Enoteca Spiriti.** Around the corner from the Pantheon, this modern wine bar looks out onto a gorgeous little piazza, lined with old buildings in dark stone covered in ivy (a look inside the lit rooms after dark reveals beautiful wood-beamed ceilings). The prime times here are during *aperitivo* hour(s) before dinner, and post-sup for a drink or two. At lunch there's always a pasta and soup selection, as well as fish and meat specials of the day. Dinner is lighter, focusing on cured meats and cheeses. ⊠ *Via Sant'Eustachio 5, Pantheon* ☎ *06/6833691* ⊟ *MC, V* ⊘ *Closed Sun. and Aug. No lunch Sat.*

## Termini

**$$–$$$$** ✕ **Coriolano.** It's off the tourist path (near Porta Pia), but a visit here is rewarded with quintessential Italian cucina—and that means market-fresh ingredients, especially seafood, light homemade pastas, and choice olive oil. The tables in the small antiques-filled dining room are set with immaculate white linen, sparkling crystal, and silver. Seafood dishes vary, but *tagliolini all'aragosta* (thin noodles with lobster sauce) is the house specialty; also consider the seasonal porcini mushrooms (a secret recipe). The wine list is predominantly Italian but includes some French and California choices. ⊠ *Via Ancona 14, Termini* ☎ *06/44249863* ⊟ *AE, DC, MC, V* ⊘ *Closed Aug.*

**$–$$$** ✕ **Bistro.** The atmosphere here is both airy and intimate; high, pale yellow arched ceilings, immense gilded mirrors, rich oak paneling, and an original wrought-iron bar counter are all true to the art nouveau style. Chef Emanuele Vizzini serves fusion dishes such as *fettuccine al Cabernet con scampi* (red-wine fettuccine with scampi and vegetables) and Nasdaq tagliolini with lobster (the dollar-green pasta is made with curaçao liqueur). The sommelier has selected 300 labels (12 available by the glass) of lesser-known, high-quality wines. ⊠ *Via Palestro 40, Termini* ☎ *06/44702868* ⊟ *AE, DC, MC, V* ⊘ *No lunch Sun.*

**$–$$$** ✕ **Trimani Il Winebar.** This is a handy address for diners in a town where most restaurants don't open before 8 PM. Trimani operates nonstop from 11 AM to 12:30 AM and serves hot food at lunch and dinner. Decor is minimalist, and the second floor provides a subdued, candlelighted space to sip wine. There's always a choice of a soup and pasta plates, as well as second courses and *torte salate* (savory tarts). Around the corner is a wineshop, one of the oldest in Rome, of the same name. Call about wine tastings and classes (in Italian). ⊠ *Via Cernaia 37/b, Termini* ☎ *06/4469630* ⊟ *AE, DC, MC, V* ⊘ *Closed Sun. and 2 wks in Aug.*

## Trastevere

**$–$$$** ✕ **Il Cantiniere di Santa Dorotea.** With 35 wines by the glass, Santa Dorotea is a great place to meet for a drink after dinner, especially since it stays open until 2 AM. But with such wine-bar fare available as radicchio soup, *piadine* (a specialty from Emilia-Romagna, where the owner hails from, flat bread stuffed with ham, cheese, and vegetables and then grilled), cured meats, salads, and cheeses, you can have a satisfying meal here as well. ⊠ *Via di Santa Dorotea 9, Trastevere* ☎ *06/5819025* ⊟ *AE, DC, MC, V* ⊘ *Closed Sun. and Aug.*

**¢–$** ✕ **Enoteca Trastevere.** Most wine bars in Rome seem to share the same interior decorator and this one is no exception, with its dark-wood tables, chairs, and shelves lined with bottles of Italian wines. Rome's enoteca menu consultant is a busy person as well; the usual crostini, cheeses, cured meats, and salads are all here. But what sets this wine bar apart from others is its central location with a large outdoor seating space and big, white umbrellas. Its large selection of organic wine is another selling point, as well as its rich selection of grappas, distilled liquors, and *amari* (Italian bitter herbal digestives). The reasonable prices and friendly service round out the pleasant experience. ⊠ *Via della Lungaretta 86* ☎ *06/5885659* ⊟ *AE, MC, V* ⊘ *Closed 3 wks in Jan.*

**Vatican**

**$–$$** ✕ **Del Frate.** This impressive wine bar, adjacent to one of Rome's noted wineshops, matches sleek and modern decor with creative cuisine and three dozen wines available by the glass. The house specialty is marinated meat and fish, and you can also get cheeses, smoked meats, and composed salads. For dessert, dip into the chocolate fondue. ⊠ *Via degli Scipioni 118, Vatican* ☎ *06/3236437* ⊟ *AE, MC, V* ⊘ *Closed 3 wks in Aug.*

# Pizzerias

Don't leave Rome without sitting down to a Roman pizza in a pizzeria. Yes, pizza may have been invented somewhere else, but in Rome you can hardly walk a block without passing it in one form or another. Look for a place with a *forno a legna* (wood-burning oven), a must for a good thin-crust, plate-size Roman pizza. You can also find places that prefer to serve a thicker-crust, Neapolitan style pizza ("alta"). With either option, tradition is the rule: don't look for pineapple or barbecued chicken among your topping options, nor should you ask for *peperoni* and expect a salami—in Italian, it means (sweet) pepper. Instead, expect crispy pizzas with sauce and cheese that are a cut above anything you've had elsewhere. Standard models are the *margherita* (tomato, mozzarella, and basil), *napoletana* (tomato, mozzarella, and anchovy), and *capricciosa* (tomato, mozzarella, prosciutto, artichokes, olives, and a hard-boiled egg), but most pizzerias have a long list of additional options, including tasty *mozzarella di bufala* (buffalo-milk mozzarella). Many small shops specialize in pizza *al taglio* (by the slice), priced by the *etto* (100 grams, about ¼ pound), according to the kind of topping (or endless combinations thereof) from which to choose. Most pizzerias are open only for dinner, usually from 8 PM to midnight. The wine at a pizzeria is worth skipping; Italians drink beer with pizza. There are often other things to order on a pizzeria menu, including standard starters like bruschetta (grilled bread, usually topped with chopped fresh tomato, basil, garlic, and olive oil), crostini (toasts with toppings and usually melted mozzarella), and *fritti* (deep-fried finger foods) such as *olive ascolane* (breaded green olives with a meat stuffing) and *supplì* (rice and tomato-sauce balls with mozzarella centers). Here are a few good by-the-slice pizzeria choices:

**Il Forno di Campo de' Fiori** (⊠ Campo de' Fiori ☎ 06/68806662 ⊘ Closed Sun.) makes excellent pizza bianca and rossa all day. Due to its popularity, the pizza is always running out, and just as constantly, they're carrying in another meter of it, fresh from the oven. Behind Piazza Navona, **Lo Zozzone** (⊠ Via del Teattro Pace 32 ☎ 06/68808575 ⊘ Closed Sun. and Aug.) makes wood-fired pizza bianca. Fillings are spread out along the bar—everything from ham and turkey and *mortadella* (the original thinly sliced bologna)—so just point and choose to make a fantastic sandwich. **Panificio Renella** (⊠ Via del Moro 15–16, Trastevere ☎ 06/5817265) is Trastevere's best bet for bakery pizza and is one of the few places open on Sunday; lines throughout the day are a testament to its pizza makers' bravura. The pizza with cooked prosciutto, mozzarella, and rosemary is delicious. **Pizza alla Pala** (⊠ Via del Pellegrino 11, Campo de' Fiori ☎ 06/6865083 ☉ Closed Sun.) has thick-crust pizza with multiple toppings; try it *ai porcini* (with mushrooms) or *piccante con pomodorini e prezzemolo* (with chilis, cherry tomatoes, and parsley). **Pizzeria Vecchio Borgo** (⊠ Borgo Pio 27/a, Vatican ☎06/68806355 ☉Closed Sun. and Sat. afternoon in summer) churns out piping-hot pizzas; try the *boscaiola,* with sausage, mushrooms, and mozzarella, or *la bomba,* a truly explosive concoction with chili peppers. **Zí Fenizia** (⊠ Via Santa Maria del Pianto 65, Ghetto ☎ 06/6896976 ☉ Closed Sat. No dinner Fri.) makes kosher pizza in the Jewish Ghetto— don't expect cheese on that pizza but lots of delicious vegetables and crumbled kosher beef sausage.

## Aventine & Testaccio

¢–$  ✕ **Acqua e Farina?** Not quite a pizzeria, trendy Acqua e Farina? sticks close to its name, which translates as "water and flour." The menu offers takeoffs on pizza, such as *strufolini,* cylinders of pizza dough stuffed with mozzarella, anchovies, and zucchini flowers, or smoked provolone, mushrooms, and prosciutto. Try other shapes and fillings to create a fun meal. ⊠ *Piazza O. Giustiniani 2, Testaccio* ☎ *06/5741382* ⊟ *AE, MC, V* ☉ *No lunch.*

★ ¢–$  ✕ **Remo.** Expect a wait at this perennial favorite in Testaccio frequented by students and neighborhood locals. You won't find tablecloths or other nonessentials, just classic Roman pizza and boisterous conversation. ⊠*Piazza Santa Maria Liberatrice 44, Testaccio* ☎ *06/5746270* ⊟ *No credit cards* ☉ *Closed Sun., Aug., and Christmas wk. No lunch.*

## Campo de' Fiori

★ $–$$  ✕ **Acchiappafantasmi.** This popular pizzeria near Campo de' Fiori offers pizza—and much more. In addition to the traditional margherita and capricciosa, you'll find a spicy pizza with chili peppers and hot salami and their prizewinning version with buffalo mozzarella and cherry tomatoes, shaped like a ghost (a theme throughout, hence the name, which means "Ghostbusters"). Appetizers are just as delicious—as well as the traditional fried goodies the menu includes a variety of items not standard to pizzerias, such as a spinach salad with bacon, mushrooms, and walnuts. And true to the owners' Calabrian roots, they offer spicy homemade *'nduja,* a spreadable sausage comprised of pork and chili pepper at a ratio of 50-50—not for the weak of constitution! ⊠ *Via dei Cappellari 66, Campo de' Fiori* ☎ *06/6873462* ⊟ *AE, D, MC, V* ☉ *Closed Tues. except in summer.*

$  ✕ **Er Grottino.** Among the many pizzerias and restaurants lining the Campo de' Fiori, Er Grottino is the best choice for crispy Roman pizza. No strange combinations here, just classics such as mushroom, ham, or vegetable. Obviously, the location is truly prime real estate. The service is friendly, and it's open for lunch. ⊠ *Campo de' Fiori 32* ☎ *06/ 68803618* ⊟ *AE, DC, MC, V* ☉ *Closed Tues. and Aug. 8–31.*

### Colosseo

¢–$ ✕ **Alle Carrette.** Tucked around the corner from the Forum on a tiny side street, Alle Carrette is easy to miss. Hunt it down for tasty Roman pizzas and the usual starters such as bruschetta and supplì. It's one of the best pizzerias in the touristy area around the ruins. ⊠ *Vicolo delle Carrette 14, Colosseo* ☎ *06/6792770* ▭ *MC, V.*

### Parioli

¢–$ ✕ **La Maremma.** La Maremma has been one of the biggest draws in Parioli for years, and its popularity has spawned a second outpost, closer to Via Veneto. Pizzas are available Roman style with a thin crust, or Neapolitan style, thicker and more filling. Outside tables can be had year-round, thanks to heaters that warm the terrace in winter. ⊠ *Viale Parioli 93/c* ☎ *06/8086002* ⊠ *Via Alessandria 119/d, Via Veneto* ☎ *06/8554002* ▭ *MC, V* ⊗ *Closed Mon. and Aug. No lunch.*

### Piazza di Spagna

¢–$ ✕ **Il Leoncino.** Lines out the door on weekends attest to the popularity of this fluorescent-lighted pizzeria in the otherwise big-ticket neighborhood around Piazza di Spagna. This is one of the few pizzerias open for lunch as well as dinner. ⊠ *Via del Leoncino 28, Piazza di Spagna* ☎ *06/6876306* ▭ *No credit cards* ⊗ *Closed Sun. and Aug.*

### Piazza Navona

$ ✕ **La Montecarlo.** Run by the niece of the owner of the pizzeria Baffetto, La Montecarlo has a similar menu and is almost as popular as its relative around the corner. Pizzas are super-thin and a little burned around the edges—the sign of a good wood-burning oven. It's one of few pizzerias open for both lunch and dinner. ⊠ *Vicolo Savelli 13, Piazza Navona* ☎ *06/6861877* ▭ *No credit cards* ⊗ *Closed 2 wks in mid-Aug. and Mon. Nov.–Apr.*

¢–$ ✕ **Baffetto.** Down a cobblestone street not far from Piazza Navona, this is Rome's most popular pizzeria and a summer favorite for street-side dining. The plain interior is mostly given over to the ovens, but there's another room with more paper-covered tables. Outdoor tables (enclosed and heated in winter) provide much-needed additional seating. Turnover is fast and lingering is not encouraged. ⊠ *Via del Governo Vecchio 114, Piazza Navona* ☎ *06/6861617* ▭ *No credit cards* ⊗ *Closed Aug. No lunch.*

### Termini

$ ✕ **La Soffitta.** You pay a little more, but hey, it's imported. This is Rome's hottest spot for classic Neapolitan pizza (thick, though crunchy on the bottom, rather than paper thin and crispy like the Roman kind) and one of the few *pizzerie* in town certified by the True Neapolitan Pizza Association. Desserts are brought in daily from Naples. ⊠ *Via dei Villini 1/e, Termini* ☎ *06/4404642* ▭ *AE, DC, MC, V* ⊗ *Closed Aug. 10–31. No lunch.*

¢–$ ✕ **La Gallina Bianca.** This pizzeria's location right down the road from Termini station makes it a perfect place for a welcome-to-Rome meal. A bright, noisy locale, La Gallina Bianca attracts a young crowd and serves classic thin-crust pizzas. Try the "full-moon" specialty, perfect for cheese lovers, with ricotta, Parmesan, mozzarella, ham, and tomato. There are other menu items available from the trattoria menu for those who may be trying to stick to a more Atkins-friendly diet. ✉ *Via A. Rosmini 5, Termini* ☎ *06/4743777* 🖃 *AE, MC, V* ⊙ *Closed Aug.*

¢ ✕ **Pizzeria L'Economica.** The name translates as "cheap pizzeria," but you can get more than you pay for at this authentic Roman pizza joint. On the edge of the funky San Lorenzo neighborhood, L'Economica is a hit with local students who head here for, first and foremost, good pizza on a tight budget. ✉ *Via Tiburtina 48, San Lorenzo* ☎ *No phone* 🖃 *No credit cards* ⊙ *No lunch.*

### Trastevere

¢–$ ✕ **Da Ivo.** Never *not* busy, this place opens early and closes late, and in-between the pizzeria is packed with locals, some tourists, and sports fans who know they can watch the Roma soccer team play on big TVs, in good company. The selection of pizzas is large, and there's a trattoria menu available to boot. A coveted streetside table is a great spot from which to view Trastevere's people parade. ✉ *Via di San Francesco a Ripa 158* ☎ *06/5817082* 🖃 *AE, DC, MC, V* ⊙ *Closed Tues. and 2 wks in Jan.*

¢–$ ✕ **Dar Poeta.** Romans drive across town for great pizza from this neighborhood institution on a small street in Trastevere. Maybe it's the
Fodor'sChoice dough—it's made from a secret blend of flours that's reputed to be eas-
★ ier to digest than the competition. They offer both thin-crust pizza and a thick-crust ("alta") Neapolitan-style pizza with any of the given toppings. For dessert, there's a ridiculously good calzone with Nutella chocolate-hazelnut spread and ricotta cheese, so save some room. Service from the owners and friendly servers is smile-inducing. ✉ *Vicolo del Bologna 45, Trastevere* ☎ *06/5880516* 🖃 *AE, DC, MC, V* ⊙ *No lunch.*

¢ ✕ **Panattoni.** Nicknamed "the mortuary" for its marble-slab tables, Panattoni is actually about as lively as you can get. Packed every night, it serves crisp pizzas as well as a variety of tasty bean dishes. The fried starters here, like a nice *baccalà* (deep-fried codfish), are light and tasty. Panattoni stays open past midnight, convenient for a late meal after the theater or a late movie nearby. ✉ *Viale Trastevere 53–57* ☎ *06/5800919* 🖃 *No credit cards* ⊙ *Closed Wed. and 2 wks in mid-Aug. No lunch.*

### Vatican

¢–$ ✕ **L'Isola della Pizza.** Right near the Vatican Metro stop, the "Island of Pizza" is also known for its copious antipasti. Simply ask for the house appetizers, and a waiter will swoop down with numerous plates of salad, seafood, bruschetta, prosciutto, crispy pizza bianca, and supplì. Though it's all too easy to fill up on these fun starters, the pizza is dependably good, and meat lovers can get a decent steak. ✉ *Via degli Scipioni 47, Vatican* ☎ *06/39733483* 🖃 *AE, MC, V* ⊙ *Closed Sun., Aug., and Christmas wk. No lunch.*

### San Lorenzo

¢–$ ✕ **Formula 1.** Posters of Formula 1 cars and drivers past and present attest to the owner's love for auto racing. The atmosphere is casual and friendly and draws students from the nearby university as well as pizza lovers from all over the city. Its location in the trendy San Lorenzo neighborhood makes it a convenient stop for dinner before checking out some of the area's bars. ✉ *Via degli Equi 13, San Lorenzo* ☎ *06/4453866* 🖃 *No credit cards* ⊙ *Closed Sun. and Aug. No lunch.*

## Cafés

Although Rome may not boast the grand cafés of Paris or Vienna, it does have hundreds of small places on pleasant side streets and piazzas to while away the time. Many have tons of personality and are quite friendly to lingering patrons, whether with friends, a laptop, a book, or your dog. The coffee is routinely of high quality. Locals usually stop in for a quickie at the bar, where prices are much lower than for the same drink taken at the table.

★ Pricey **Antico Caffè Greco** (⊠ Via dei Condotti 86, Piazza di Spagna ☎ 06/6791700) is a national landmark; its red-velvet chairs and marble tables have hosted the likes of Byron, Shelley, Keats, Goethe, and Casanova. Located in the middle of shopping madness on the upscale Via Condotti, this place is indeed filled with tourists, but there are some locals who love to breathe the air of history within these dark-wood walls.

Fodor'sChoice Coming at off-hours is your best bet to glimpse authenticity. **Caffè**
★ **Sant'Eustachio** (⊠ P. Sant'Eustachio 82, Piazza Navona ☎ 06/6861309), traditionally frequented by Rome's literati, has what is generally considered Rome's best cup of coffee. Just walking into the blue-and-yellow spot, the smell of freshly ground beans wafts over you, letting you know that this is *the* place. Servers purposely hidden behind a huge espresso machine vigorously mix the sugar and coffee for you to protect their "secret method" for the perfectly prepared cup. (If you want your *caffè* without sugar here, ask for it *amaro*.) Don't miss the *gran*
★ *caffè*, a secret concoction unlike anything else in the city. **Tazza d'Oro** (⊠ Via degli Orfani, Pantheon ☎ 06/5835869) has many admirers who contend it serves the city's best cup of coffee. The hot chocolate in winter, all thick and gooey goodness, is a treat. And in warm weather, the coffee granita is the perfect cooling alternative to a regular espresso.

You can sit yourself down and watch the world go by at **Rosati** (⊠ Piazza del Popolo 5, Piazza di Spagna ☎ 06/3225859), where tourists and locals have met for decades to sip and be seen. This is one of the closest "institution"-like places that Rome has in its café culture. With its sidewalk tables taking in Santa Maria della Pace's adorable piazza, **Caffè della Pace** (⊠ Via della Pace 3, Piazza Navona ☎ 06/6861216) has long been the haunt of Rome's *beau monde*. Set on a quiet street near Piazza Navona, it also has two rooms filled with old-world personality (also see Bars in the Nightlife chapter). Just around the corner from Caffè della Pace, **Bar del Fico** (⊠ Piazza del Fico 28, Piazza Navona ☎ 06/6865205) is another spot to see and be seen. During the day it's a humble, tranquil bar where locals go for a coffee underneath the fig tree. By night, the indoor and outdoor tables are packed, the music blasts, and the young and beautiful come here to meet before and after dinner. **Caffè Teichner** (⊠ Piazza San Lorenzo in Lucina 15–18, Piazza di Spagna ☎ 06/6871683), just off the Corso, is a relatively pricey establishment on a lively piazza. It offers all the basic nibbles (tramezzini, panini) of most bars, but with the patronage of true Roman residents. **Bar Notegen** (⊠ Via del Babuino 159, Piazza di Spagna ☎ 06/3200855) sits on one of Rome's most fashionable streets among the designer boutiques near the Spanish Steps—one of few places to stop and refuel (all day long) on this stretch where the real estate is dedicated to material goods instead of edibles. For a taste of Brussels, check out the Belgian chain **Le Pain Quotidien** (✉ Via Tomacelli 24–25, Piazza di Spagna ☎ 06/68807727); order the fresh bread, brought to the table with a selection of sweet spreads flavored with chocolate or chestnut.

**Cafe Renault** (✉ Via Nazionale 183, Piazza di Trevi ☎ 06/47824966), on one of Rome's main shopping streets, is a big, popular café that serves a large selection of food. It used to be the Renault car dealership, hence the name, and with a space this vast (especially in the center of Rome), it retains this look. On Via Vittorio Veneto, Rome's hippest street in the 1950s and 1960s, you'll find the **Café de Paris** (✉ Via Veneto 90, Via Veneto ☎ 06/4885284), which is also a *pasticceria* (pastry shop) and *gelateria* (gelato shop). It's got plenty of tables in one of the glassed-in outdoor seating areas that line this via, although the glory of its *La Dolce Vita* heyday is long gone. Bring a book to **Bar Taruga** (✉ Piazza Mattei 8, Ghetto ☎ 06/6892299), in one of Rome's loveliest piazzas in the Jewish Ghetto, and curl up in one of the mismatched armchairs or sofas with a cappuccino or hot tea. The atmosphere is quirky, like the owner (who banned smoking in his bar well before the national law went into effect), and who can be very grumpy. But the location is fabulous and the Renaissance-era turtle fountain out front can mesmerize. **Bar Vezio** (✉ Via de' Delfini 23, Ghetto ☎ 06/6786036) is a tiny bar decorated with posters, slogans, banners, and photos from last century's socialist movements. As you walk toward Viale di Trastevere, you'll discover the small and wonderfully down-at-the-heels **Bar San Calisto** (✉ Piazza San Calisto 4, Trastevere ☎ 06/5895678), immensely popular with the old local community and expat crowd, but largely unfrequented by tourists. The surrounding piazza and its cars and scooters become the playground of the patrons (ranging from ragged street dwellers to local hipsters). The drinks are cheap, cheap, cheap but a little-known fact: the hot chocolate and chocolate gelato are some of the best in town. In Trastevere, **Ombre Rosse** (✉ Piazza Sant'Egidio 12, Trastevere ☎ 06/5884155) is a relaxed café that attracts a very mixed clientele. It's good for a morning cappuccino, an afternoon tea, or an evening glass of wine. And local *Trasteverini* (Trastevere residents) rub elbows with English-speaking locals and German and French tourists. The sandwiches, soups, and salads are a half-notch above your average café offerings. **Caffè della Scala** (✉ Via della Scala 4, Trastevere ☎ 06/5803610) is a mellow locale with old photos of jazz artists lining the walls. The decor is French-Moroccan-brothel-meets-Louisiana-piano-bar, but the clientele is mixed Roman and expat. As is so often the case, the outdoor tables are the ones to snag.

## Gelaterie

For many travelers, the first taste of *gelato*—Italian ice cream—is one of the most memorable moments of their Italian trip. Almost a cross between regular American ice cream and soft serve, gelato's texture is lighter and fluffier than hard ice cream because of the process by which it's whipped when freezing. Though you won't find the more byzantine concoctions of the States (toffee pecan, double chocolate-chip brownie, Chunky Monkey, and so on), the flavors offered—hazelnut and *straciatella* (chocolate chip), to name just two of a hundred artisanal, or handmade, choices—often put American ice creams in the shade. Along with the listings here, you can find a number of gelaterias in Via di Tor Millina, a street off the west side of Piazza Navona, where there are also a couple of good places for frozen yogurt and delicious *frullati*—shakes made with milk, crushed ice, and fruit of your choosing.

**Il Gelato di San Crispino** (⊠ Via della Panetteria 54, Piazza di Trevi ☎ 06/6793924 ⊘ Closed Tues.) makes perhaps the most celebrated gelato in all of Italy, without artificial colors or flavors. It's worth crossing town for—nobody else creates flavors this pure. To preserve the "integrity" of the flavor, the ice cream is only served in paper cups. For years **Giolitti** (⊠ Via degli Uffici del Vicario 40, Pantheon ☎ 06/6991243) was considered the best gelateria in Rome, and it's still worth a stop if you're near the Pantheon. **Della Palma** (⊠ Via della Maddalena 20/23, Pantheon ☎ 06/68806752) is close to the Pantheon on a street just north of the Piazza della Rotonda. It serves 100 flavors of gelato, and for sheer gaudy display and range of choice it's a must. Immediately beside the Pantheon is **Cremeria Monteforte** (⊠ Via della Rotonda 22, Pantheon ☎06/6867720), which has won several awards for its flavors. Also worth trying is its chocolate sorbetto—it's an icier version of the gelato without the dairy (instead ask for whipped cream on top). **Fiocco di Neve** (⊠ Via del Pantheon 51, Pantheon ☎ No phone ⊘ Closed Sun.) has excellent *granita di caffè* (coffee ice slush) as well as gelato. The chocolate chip and After Eight (mint chocolate chip) flavors are delicious. **Fonte della Salute** (⊠ Viale Trastevere ☎ 06/5897471 ⊘ Closed 4 wks at Christmas) serves about 50 flavors, as well as a wide variety of frozen yogurt. Its location on the corner of Viale Trastevere affords it a seating area that most gelaterias don't offer, so it's a nice place to stop and take a break.

**Gelateria alla Scala** (⊠ Via della Scala 51, Trastevere ☎ 06/5813174 ⊘ Closed Dec. and Jan.) is a tiny place, but don't let the size fool you. It does a good business offering artisanal gelato prepared in small batches, so when one flavor runs out on any given day, its finished. **Cremeria Ottaviani** (⊠ Via Leone IV 83/85, Vatican ☎ 06/37514774 ⊘ Closed Wed.) is an old-fashioned gelateria with an excellent granita di caffè. On Prati's main shopping street, **Pellacchia** (⊠ Via Cola di Rienzo 3–5, Vatican ☎ 06/3210807 ⊘ Closed Mon.) is a classic *artigianale* (homemade) ice-cream parlor that has been going since the 1920s. **Al Settimo Gelo** (⊠ Via Vodice 21/a, Vatican ☎ 06/3725567), in Prati, has been getting rave reviews for both classic flavors and newfangled inventions. Inventive flavors, such as cardamom and chestnut, wow locals and gelato fans from all over Rome. West of Prati, on the hill of Monte Mario, **Lo Zodiaco** (⊠ Viale del Parco Mellini 90, Stadio Olimpico ☎ 06/35496640) is perhaps more remarkable for the city vista than for the ice cream. To the north of the city center in the wealthy district of Parioli, **Caffè Parnaso** (⊠ Piazza delle Muse 22, Parioli ☎ 06/8079741), as the name suggests, doubles as a café and pasticceria.

## Pasticcerie

Romans are not known for having a sweet tooth, and there are few pastry shops in town that distinguish themselves with particularly good ex-

# COOKING THE ITALIAN WAY

VISITORS TO ITALY, once they return home, always have the same complaint: the food never tastes as good here as it does over there. And while you can't perfectly reproduce a delicious Italian tomato, you can acquire the tools to reproduce the authentic dishes you ate during your stay in Italy. Blu Aubergine (☎ 39/347/260746 ⊕ www.bluaubergine.com), a culinary venture started by New York-trained professional chef and critic Dana Klitzberg, offers private cooking classes in her own home in the heart of Rome. Each class begins with a trip to the nearby Campo de' Fiori market, so you can learn how to spot great primary ingredients—half the battle in Italian cuisine. The group returns to Dana's kitchen to prepare a multi-course meal (everything from classic Roman cuisine to the Tastes of Tuscany, Sicily, Venice—whatever you fancy), which you then enjoy for lunch.with accompanying wines, of course! Private chef and catering services, for those who may be renting an apartment or villa within a few hours of Rome, are also highly popular.

amples of the few regional desserts that Italy boasts. One exception is the **Forno del Ghetto** (⊠ Via del Portico d'Ottavia 2, Ghetto ☎ 06/6878637 ⊙ Closed Fri. evening, Sat., and Jewish holidays). You might not expect a Jewish bakery in Rome, but this hole-in-the-wall—no sign, no tables, just a take-out counter—is an institution, preserving a tradition of Italian Jewish sweets that cannot be found anywhere else. Some call it the "burnt bakery" as most of the smattering of sweets they sell often has a browned edge or top. But you won't mind that so much when you taste the ricotta cake (with sour-cherry jam or chocolate chips): it's unforgettable. **Josephine's Bakery** (⊠ Piazza del Paradiso 56/57, Camp de'Fiori ☎ 06/6871065 ⊕ www.josephinesbakery.com ⊙ Closed Sun. and Mon. morning) opened in March 2005 and is run by a delightful English woman who found a love of baking and cake decorating after leaving the television production biz. As such, this is the place in the city center to find Anglo-American sweets like cupcakes and brownies, carrot cake, and chocolate cake. They do cakes to order for special events, with lots of whimsical designs. At **Dolceroma** (⊠ Via del Portico d'Ottavia 20/b, Ghetto ☎ 06/6892196 ⊙ Closed Mon. and 4 wks in July and Aug.), in the Jewish Ghetto, the apple strudel and Sacher torte may not be Italian, but Romans flock here just the same. A good bet for both Italian and foreign delights is **Dolci & Doni** (⊠ Via delle Carrozze 85, Piazza di Spagna ☎ 06/6782913), where a wide range of goodies is served in a precious, refined atmosphere. In the center, off Corso Vittorio, **La Deliziosa** (⊠ Vicolo Savelli 50, Piazza Navona ☎ 06/68803155 ⊙ Closed Mon.) serves fantastic ricotta cakes and a mean *bigné di San Giuseppe*, a cream-filled fried delight available around St. Joseph's Day in March.

# Where to Stay

3

**WORD OF MOUTH**

A hotel room is where you go to change clothes and sleep–and everything else is frosting on the cake. So if your room doesn't meet your expectations . . . you are STILL in ROME! Drown your disappointment in gelato!

—viajero2

If you have a hotel room with a view of the Pantheon, it's like you are living among the ancients.

—DonnieD

Keep in mind that it is not hard to get around Rome and if you do not get your preferred hotel location you still will be able to easily see the main sights.

—samber

www.fodors.com/forums

By Valerie
Hamilton

**IT'S THE CLICK OF YOUR HEELS ON INLAID MARBLE,** the whisper of 600-count Frette sheets, the murmured *"buongiorno"* of a coat-tailed porter bowing low as you pass. It's a rustic attic room with wood-beam ceilings, a wrought-iron balcony for your morning cappuccino, a white umbrella on a roof terrace, a 400-year-old palazzo with Casanova's name in the guest book. Maybe it's the birdsong warbling into your room as you swing open French windows to a sun-kissed view of the Colosseum, a time-worn piazza, a flower-filled marketplace. Whatever your Roman holiday hotel fantasy, Audrey Hepburn couldn't have had it better. Dolce Vita, here you come.

If you're prepared to hock grandma's ring to finance your Roman hotel stay, keep dreaming. If not, read on.

Hotels in Rome are something like the Sistine Chapel: at the top, they're heaven, but at the lower end, they can feel more like *purgatorio*. Palatial settings, cloud-nine comfort, and high standards of service can be taken for granted in Rome's top establishments. But in other categories, especially moderate and inexpensive, standards vary considerably. That's a nice way of saying that very often, Rome's budget hotels are not up to the standards of space, comfort, quiet, and service that are taken for granted in the United States: think tiny rooms, lumpy beds, and anemic air-conditioning. Essentially you get what you pay for. Luxury hotels like the Eden, the Hassler, and the Hotel de Russie are justly renowned for sybaritic comfort: postcard views over Roman rooftops, white linen and silver at a groaning-table breakfast buffet, and the fluffiest, thirstiest, softest towels since cotton was king. Can you hear the angels singing? At the other end of the scale, many of the family-run pensions near Termini station and elsewhere suffer from too little space, too much noise, and chronic, some say fatal, lack of homeyness. For some travelers, tacky linens and linoleum floors are their own small circle of hell.

Happily, the good news is that if you're flexible there are happy mediums aplenty. The Abruzzi is cheap and spartan—but has knockout views of the Pantheon. The Campo de' Fiori has no elevator and tiny rooms—but a roof terrace where you'll want to spend the whole morning. The Panda is a walkup in a residential building, but a stone's throw from the Spanish Steps, and its little jewels of rooms are done up with frescoes and plaster statuary, a Roman fantasy in miniature.

Before you choose your hotel, prioritize. If a picturesque location is your main concern, stay in one of the small hotels around Piazza Navona or Campo de' Fiori. If luxury is, head for Via Veneto, where price-quality ratios are high and some hotels have swimming pools. Most of Rome's good budget hotels are concentrated around Termini train station, but you'll have to use public transportation to get to the historic part of town. There are obvious advantages to staying in a hotel within easy walking distance of the main sights, particularly because parts of downtown Rome are closed to traffic and are blessedly quieter than they once were. Here, no matter how inexpensive these lodgings may be, they give their guests one priceless perk: a sense of being in the heart of history.

## Aventino

Leafy residential streets, quiet nights, and fresh hilltop breezes are some of the perks of staying in this well-heeled (and relatively unhistoric) neighborhood. Hotels take full advantage of the extra space and the sylvan setting, most with gardens or courtyards where you can enjoy alfresco R & R far from the madding crowds. Bear in mind that public transportation is somewhat limited up here, and allow a half-hour by foot to major sights.

**$$** ⊞ **Domus Aventina.** Set next to a municipal rose garden, not far from the Temple to Mithras and the House of Aquila and Priscilla (where St. Peter touched down), this friendly little hotel is right in the heart of the historic Aventine. The 17th-century facade has been so restored it almost looks modern—ditto for the inside, where guest rooms have standard modern decors. Still, set around an ancient cloister, they make for tranquil islands of tranquillity. Half the rooms have balconies. ⊠ *Via di Santa Prisca 11/b, Aventino, 00153* ☎ *06/5746135* 🖷 *06/57300044* ⊕ *www.domusaventina.com* ⥱ *26 rooms* ⚲ *Free parking* ⊟ *AE, DC, MC, V* ¶Oⵏ *BP.*

★ **$$** ⊞ **Hotel San Anselmo.** Birdsongs emanating from the tree-lined avenues tell you the San Anselmo is as much a retreat as a hotel. It's far from the bustle of the city center, perched on top of the Aventine Hill in a residential neighborhood. And what a residence: glowing in archetypal Roman cantelope-hue stone, this full-scale 19th-century villa still has some Stil Liberty (the Italian form of Art Nouveau) gracenotes, including the scrollwork gates that greet you. Inside, the lobby and adjacent "tearoom" are stuffed with a quirky mix of gilded mirrors, plate-glass windows, and a riot of Italianate Rococo chairs and sofas. Sophia Loren, in her early days, would feel right at home. Others will find the best features here are the verdant garden and terrace bar. Guest rooms are period in flavor, complete with huge armoires, old-fashioned painted headboards, and Empire-style drapes and chandeliers. All in all, the San Anselmo is *molto* charming. ⊠ *Piazza San Anselmo 2, Aventino, 00153* ☎ *06/5745231* 🖷 *06/5783604* ⊕ *www.aventinohotels.com* ⥱ *45 rooms* ⚲ *Bar* ⊟ *AE, DC, MC, V* ¶Oⵏ *BP.*

★ **$$** ⊞ **Villa San Pio.** Like its sister hotel, the San Anslemo, this option goes for decor alla Romana—florid, seductive, and lush. Fabulous marble inlays are everywhere here, from the spacious lobby to the brand-new bathrooms, a feast for the eyes that gives the impression that this old-fashioned hotel is much swankier than it is. Spacious gardens and vine-covered terraces are perfect for breakfast, evening cocktails, or reading in the afternoon, and the neighborhood is quiet and peaceful. Many rooms have Jacuzzi tubs, and although beds are not all the newest, overall it's very comfortable, and within pleasant walking distance of the historic center. ⊠ *Via Santa Melania 19, Aventino, 00153* ☎ *06/5783214* 🖷 *06/5783604* ⊕ *www.aventinohotels.com* ⥱ *78 rooms* ⚲ *Restaurant, minibars, cable TV, hot tub, 2 bars, free parking* ⊟ *AE, DC, MC, V* ¶Oⵏ *BP.*

**$** ⊞ **Santa Prisca.** The Fascist-era architecture lends this place a rather institutional air (in fact, it's owned by an order of nuns), but it's comfortable and tastefully decorated. Rooms are spacious, and those on the third floor have French windows; some have small balconies. There's

## Facilities

At the end of each hotel review, we mention whether or not the hotel's room rate includes breakfast: BP (Breakfast Plan) indicates those that do, EP (European Plan) indicates those that do not. Needless to say, the most expensive hotels have all the amenities you would expect at top levels and rates, with full services, spacious lounges, bars, restaurants, and some fitness facilities. Mid-range hotels may have minibars and in-room safes and double glazing to keep out street noise. Budget hotels will have private bathrooms and in-room direct-dial telephone and TV, and most will have air-conditioning. In less expensive places, you may have to pay extra for air-conditioning, and the shower may be the drain-in-the-floor type that hovers over the toilet. In the very cheapest hotels you may have to share a bathroom and do without an elevator. Always inquire about air-conditioning when booking a room for summer. Rooms in high-end hotels are soundproof, but noise may be a problem in less expensive hotels anywhere in the city. Ask for an inside room if you're a light sleeper, but don't be surprised if it's on a dark courtyard.

**3**

## Reservations

It's always wise to book in advance, even if only a few days ahead. There's never a period when the city's hotels are predictably empty, though July and August and late January to February are relatively slack months. Inquire about special rates at all times. If you do arrive without reservations, try **HR** (Hotel Reservation service; ☎ 06/6991000), with desks at Leonardo da Vinci Airport and Termini Station (an English-speaking operator is available daily 7 AM–10 PM). Municipal Information kiosks throughout the city can also help you find accommodations free of charge. **CTS** (✉ Via Andrea di Vesalio 6, northeast of Termini Station ☎ 06/441111 ✉ Via Genova 16 ☎ 06/4620431), a student travel agency, can help find rooms.

You can book via e-mail or by telephoning and then following up with a letter or fax confirmation. You may be asked to send a deposit; get a statement from the hotel about its refund policy before releasing your credit card number or mailing a money order. Insist on a written confirmation from the hotel stating the duration of your stay, room rate, any extras, and location and type of room. When corresponding with hotels, remember that mail in Italy can be exasperatingly slow; telephone, fax, and e-mail are more effective.

## Prices

Rates are inclusive of service, but it's customary to tip porters, waiters, maids, and concierges.

| WHAT IT COSTS In euros | | | | |
| --- | --- | --- | --- | --- |
| | $$$$ | $$$ | $$ | $ | ¢ |
| FOR 2 PEOPLE | over €300 | €225–€300 | €150–€225 | €75–€150 | under €75 |

Prices are for a standard double room in high season.

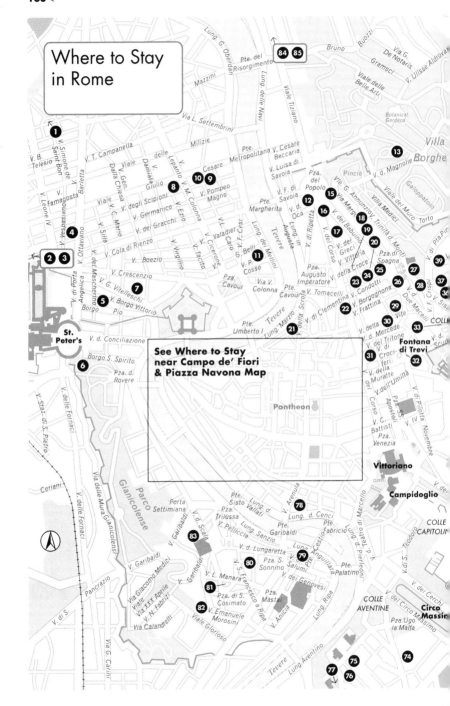

Where to Stay
in Rome

See Where to Stay
near Campo de' Fiori
& Piazza Navona Map

| | |
|---|---|
| Via Pietro Raimondi | **86** |
| Museo Borghese | **14** |
| V. Po | **45** |
| Porta Pinciana | |
| Corso d'Italia | **43** **44** |
| V. Piemonte | **42** |
| V. Veneto | **41** |
| V. Bissolati | **46** |
| V. Sallustiana | **48** |
| V. Goito | **49** **50** **51** **52** **53** |
| V. Montebello | |
| **58** **59** **56** **57** **54** **55** |
| **34** | |
| Quirinale / Quattro Fontane | **60** **61** |
| V. Nazionale | **62** **63** |
| Stazione Termini | |
| **64** | |
| **66** **67** **65** | |
| **68** | |
| COLLE VIMINALE | **69** |
| Domus Aurea | |
| COLLE ESQUILINO | |
| **2** | |
| COLLE PALATINO | |
| Colosseo | |
| **73** | S. Quattro |
| COLLE CELIO | |
| Terme di Caracalla | |
| S. Giovanni in Laterano | |

0 — 1/2 mile
0 — 800 meters

|  |  |  |  |
|---|---|---|---|
| Adler | **59** | Italia | **62** |
| Alexandra | **36** | Julia | **33** |
| Alimandi | **3** | La Residenza | **40** |
| Aleph | **46** | Locarno | **12** |
| Alpi | **49** | Lord Byron | **13** |
| Amalia | **4** | Majestic | **38** |
| Aphrodite | **55** | Marcella Royal | **48** |
| Arenula | **78** | Margutta | **17** |
| Art Deco | **50** | Marriott Grand Hotel Flora | **43** |
| Atlante Star | **7** | Mascagni | **56** |
| Barberini | **35** | Mecenate Palace Hotel | **65** |
| Britannia | **61** | Miami | **60** |
| Carmel | **83** | Montreal | **67** |
| Carriage | **24** | Morgana | **64** |
| Casa di Santa Francesca Romana | **79** | Nerva | **70** |
| Castello della Castelluccia | **84** | Nuovo Hotel Quattro Fontane | **35** |
| Cavalieri Hilton | **1** | Panda | **19** |
| Celio | **73** | Parco dei Principi | **14** |
| Cisterna | **80** | Pensione Suisse | **28** |
| Condotti | **20** | Regina Baglioni | **41** |
| D'Este | **68** | Residenza Cellini | **58** |
| Dei Borgognoni | **30** | Residenza Paolo VI | **6** |
| Des Artistes | **51** | Richmond | **72** |
| D'Inghilterra | **22** | Romae | **52** |
| Domus Aventina | **74** | San Carlo | **23** |
| Doria | **67** | San Giuseppe della Montagna | **2** |
| Duca d'Alba | **69** | Sant'Anna | **5** |
| Duke | **86** | Santa Prisca | **76** |
| Eden | **39** | Scalinata di Spagna | **26** |
| Empire Palace Hotel | **47** | Trastevere | **81** |
| Exedra | **57** | Trevi | **32** |
| Farnese | **9** | Tritone | **31** |
| Forum | **71** | Valadier | **16** |
| Fraterna Domus | **21** | Venezia | **53** |
| Gerber | **8** | Victoria | **44** |
| Giuliana | **63** | Villa Glori | **85** |
| Giulio Cesare | **10** | Villa delle Rose | **54** |
| Hassler | **27** | Villa San Pio | **77** |
| Homs | **29** | Westin Excelsior | **42** |
| Hotel Art | **18** | | |
| Hotel dei Mellini | **11** | | |
| Hotel de Russie | **15** | | |
| Hotel San Anselmo | **75** | | |
| Hotel Santa Maria di Trastevere | **83** | | |
| Hotel Villa Borghese | **45** | | |
| Imperiale | **37** | | |
| Inn at the Spanish Steps | **25** | | |

also an ample terrace. The extensive grounds offer plenty of parking. ⊠ *Largo M. Gelsomini 25, Aventino, 00153* ☎ *06/5750009* 🖷 *06/ 5746658* ⊕ *www.hotelsantaprisca.it* ⟿ *49 rooms, 1 suite* ⚷ *Restaurant, cable TV, bar, laundry service, free parking, no-smoking rooms* ⊟ *AE, DC, MC, V* ⑩ *BP.*

## Campo de' Fiori

You're in the heart of gorgeously beautiful Vecchia Roma (Old Rome) here—a neighborhood that spreads out from two of the most colorful squares in town, Campo de' Fiori and Piazza Farnese, and not far from the city's most elegant residential address, Via Giulia. That noted, many hotels here are refurbished (or not) medieval tenements, with small rooms and precipitous stairs, so it's probably not the place to come looking for sybaritic luxury.

**$$$$**
**Fodor's Choice**
★

**Ponte Sisto.** With one of the prettiest patio-courtyards in Rome (Europe?), this hotel offers its own blissful definition of *Pax Romana*. Peace, indeed, will be yours sitting in this enchanting spot, shadowed by gigantic palm-trees, set with tables, and adorned with pink and white flowers, all surrounded by the suavely ochre walls of the hotel, which was renovated in 2001 from a palazzo built by the noble Venetian Palottini family. Some rooms overlook the garden of the historic Palazzo Spada. Inside is more peace, thanks to the sleek decors, replete with cherry wood accents, recessed lighting, and luminous marble floors. Guest rooms are cool cocoons, bathrooms can be lavishly modern, and there's a handy bar and restaurant. The location is an award-winner—just off the Ponte Sisto, the pedestrian bridge that connects the Campo de' Fiori area with Trastevere (whose trattorias and bars are thus just a delightful jaunt away), and a second from Via Giulia, Rome's prettiest street. ⊠ *Via dei Pettinari 64, Campo de' Fiori, 00186* ☎ *06/686310* 🖷 *06/68301712* ⊕ *www. hotelpontesisto.it* ⟿ *103 rooms* ⚷ *Restaurant, in-room safes, minibars, cable TV, bar* ⊟ *AE, DC, MC, V* ⑩ *BP.*

**$$–$$$**

**Tiziano.** Smack dab in the middle of everything, this charismatic choice allows you to enjoy the buzz of today—outside, the Corso Vittorio Emanuele is teeming with shoppers and tourists—as well as the charm of yesteryear, since this was once the grand Palazzo Pacelli back in the 18th century. Inside, a cool, quiet marble lobby is a haven of calm. On the second floor—the old *piano nobile*—you'll find guest rooms with some of the loftiest ceilings in Rome, all extrovertedly done with Roman cornices, bold color schemes, French windows, parquet floors, and "modern" furnishings. Some rooms have adorable balconies, set over church cupolas. No question—this is an ideally located base for sampling the historic Campo de' Fiori and Piazza Navona districts. ⊠ *Corso Vittorio Emanuele II 110, Campo de' Fiori, 00186* ☎ *06/6865019* 🖷 *06/6865019* ⊕ *www.tizianohotel.it* ⟿ *51 rooms* ⚷ *Restaurant, inroom safes, minibars, cable TV, bar, laundry service, concierge, parking (fee), no-smoking rooms* ⊟ *AE, DC, MC, V* ⑩ *BP.*

**★ $$**

**Casa di Santa Brigida.** Obviously, the sisters of Santa Brigida offer their guests some very special things: insider tickets to papal audiences, a house that overlooks the magnificent Piazza Farnese (where one of Michelan-

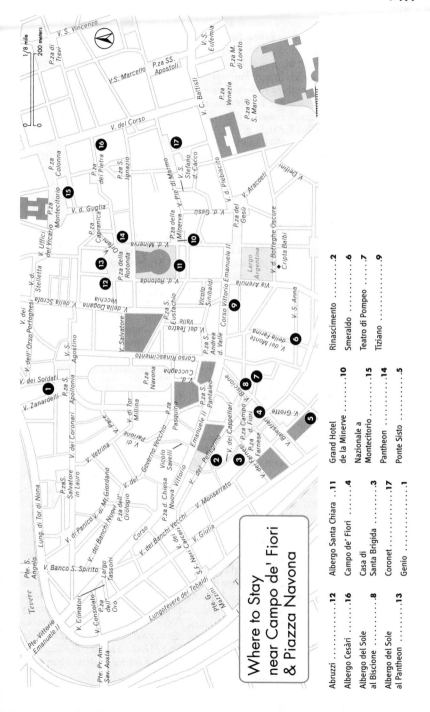

# Where to Stay near Campo de' Fiori & Piazza Navona

Abruzzi . . . . . . . . . . . .**12**

Albergo Cesàri . . . . . . .**16**

Albergo del Sole
al Biscione . . . . . . . . . .**8**

Albergo del Sole
al Pantheon . . . . . . . . .**13**

Albergo Santa Chiara . .**11**

Campo de' Fiori . . . . . . .**4**

Casa di
Santa Brigida . . . . . . . . .**3**

Coronet . . . . . . . . . . . .**17**

Genio . . . . . . . . . . . . . . .**1**

Grand Hotel
de la Minerve . . . . . . . .**10**

Nazionale a
Montecitorio . . . . . . . . .**15**

Pantheon . . . . . . . . . . . .**14**

Ponte Sisto . . . . . . . . . . .**5**

Rinascimento . . . . . . . . .**2**

Smeraldo . . . . . . . . . . . .**6**

Teatro di Pompeo . . . . . .**7**

Tiziano . . . . . . . . . . . . . .**9**

gelo's buildings surveys all), and a most enviable location in the heart of Old Baroque Rome. But you have to remember this is part of the Convent of St. Bridget, so guest rooms are simple (and serene—no TV), the nuns don't bend over backward to get you ice for your soda (presumably they have more important things on their minds), and the breakfasts are nothing to write home about. Still, the atmosphere is redolent (antiques dot the bedrooms), there's a lovely roof terrace overlooking the Palazzo Farnese, a fine chapel and library, and the Brigidine sisters are known for their gentle manner (they wear a distinctive habit and veil with a caplike headband). Little wonder you need to book well in advance here. Inquire about meal plans here. Note that the address is that of the church of Santa Brigida, but the guesthouse entrance is around the corner at Via Monserrato 54. ⊠ *Piazza Farnese 96, Campo de' Fiori, 00186* ☎ *06/68892497* 🖷 *06/68891573* ⊕ *www.brigadine. org* ⇌ *24 rooms* ⊟ *AE, DC, MC, V* ⦿ *BP.*

**$$** 🖭 **Hotel Rinascimento.** In an old palazzo in the heart of the Campo de' Fiori district, this small hotel has an ideal address for exploring the atmospheric alleyways of the old city. Atmospheric, however, this hotel is not. Lots of white walls, a simple "Art Nouveau" glass-panel bar, and low-key lighting make the reception area a bit lugubrious. However, the owners are charming and always helpful; their English is a bit hit-or-miss, so it helps to know a few key phrases in Italian or have a phrase book handy. Upstairs, the 19 smallish rooms are neat and pleasant, with terra-cotta floors, wood-beam ceilings, padded headboards, and framed lithographs. ⊠ *Via del Pellegrino 122, Campo de' Fiori, 00186* ☎ *06/6874813* 🖷 *06/6833518* ⊕ *www.hotelrinascimento.com* ⇌ *19 rooms* ⚭ *Restaurant, bar, cable TV, in-room safes, parking (fee)* ⊟ *AE, DC, MC, V* ⦿ *BP.*

**$$** 🖭 **Teatro di Pompeo.** Where else can you breakfast under the ancient stone vaults of Pompey's Theater, historic site of Julius Caesar's assassination? At this intimate and refined little hotel in the heart of Old Rome you are part of that history; at night, you sleep under restored beamed ceilings that date from the days of Michelangelo. Rooms are simple but tasteful, with terra-cotta floors and old-fashioned beds. Book well in advance. ⊠ *Largo del Pallaro 8, Campo de' Fiori, 00186* ☎ *06/68300170* 🖷 *06/68805531* ⊕ *www.hotelteatrodipompeo.it/* ⇌ *13 rooms* ⚭ *In-room safes, minibars, cable TV, bar, laundry service* ⊟ *AE, DC, MC, V* ⦿ *BP.*

**★ $** 🖭 **Albergo del Sole al Biscione.** Built on the ruins of the ancient Theater of Pompey, in the very heart of the timeless Campo de' Fiori area, this little gem has one of the quaintest multilevel terraces in old Rome; stunning views are guaranteed, with center stage taken by the great dome of Santa Andrea della Valle. Don't be put off by the hotel's neon-ish sign out front—the atmosphere inside is cozy, with open-beam ceilings and old-fashioned furnishings. Modern comforts include an elevator. Rooms are set out in simple pensione style, featuring early-20th-century wardrobes and veneer bed frames. Don't confuse this with the famous Albergo del Sole al Pantheon hotel. ⊠ *Via del Biscione 76, Campo de' Fiori, 00186* ☎ *06/68806873* 🖷 *06/6893787* ⊕ *www.solealbiscione. it* ⇌ *58 rooms, 26 with bath* ⚭ *Cable TV, parking (fee); no a/c in some rooms* ⊟ *No credit cards* ⦿ *EP.*

★ **$** ⊞ **Campo de' Fiori.** Frescoes, exposed brickwork, and picturesque effects throughout this little hotel could well be the work of a set designer. There's an aura of romanticism in the decoration, with the layout making the most of limited space. Though a few rooms are so compact they're almost claustrophobic, the decor reminds you that you're in the heart of Rome. There's no elevator, but the climb to the roof terrace rewards you with a marvelous view. ⊠ *Via del Biscione 6, Campo de' Fiori, 00186* ☎ *06/68806865* 🖷 *06/6876003* ⊕ *www.hotelcampodefiori.it* 🛏 *28 rooms, 10 with bath* ♢ *Minibars* ▤ *MC, V* ◯ *BP.*

**$** ⊞ **Smeraldo.** The emerald-green marble entrance and other touches of marble throughout are only the beginning of what sets this bargain hotel apart from the rest. There are two terraces, air-conditioning, cable TV in every room, and a bar. The rooms are fresh and immaculate, and some have private balconies. A handy location near Piazza Navona and Campo de' Fiori makes it ideal for taking in all the action. ⊠ *Via dei Chiodaroli 9, Campo de' Fiori, 00186* ☎ *06/6892121* 🖷 *06/68805495* ⊕ *www.smeraldoroma.com* 🛏 *50 rooms* ♢ *Cable TV, bar* ▤ *AE, DC, MC, V* ◯ *EP.*

**Fodor's**Choice
★

## Colosseum & the Campitelli (Forum) Area

When Nero fiddled, this neighborhood burned—the lowlands around the Colosseum and the Forum were the Suburra, the Imperial City's most notorious slum. There's nary a trace of evildoing now, and narrow alleys are quaint rather than sinister. This is a fine base for the sights of the ancient city, but area eating and drinking establishments can have a touch of the tourist trap. Waking up to views of the Forum, maybe you won't mind.

**$$–$$$$** ⊞ **Forum.** Wrapped around a medieval belltower, this hotel comes into its own for the traveler, or should we say diner, with tired feet. The panorama of the spotlighted Roman Forum from the hotel's landmark Roof-Garden restaurant is a view that you cannot get enough of. A long-time favorite, this converted 18th-century convent remains a fine middle-of-the-road choice. Everyone praises its special setting, on one side of the Fori Imperiali, with a cinematic view of ancient Rome across the avenue (remember you can drink all this in also at the rooftop bar). The hotel itself is considerably less exciting. The decor is traditional in the extreme, with the requisite gold wall sconces, walnut paneling, red-velvet armchairs, and Asian carpets painting the usual lobby picture. Upstairs, the guest rooms are similarly lowkey, although comfortable in the extreme; suites offer velvety fabrics and some antiques. Bathrooms have been restyled using antique tiles. Little on the restaurant menu can compete with the view—if you get the view (many tables are not ringside, so to speak). ⊠ *Via Tor de' Conti 25–30, Colosseo, 00184* ☎ *06/6792446* 🖷 *06/6786479* ⊕ *www.hotelforumrome.com* 🛏 *80 rooms* ♢ *Restaurant, in-room safes, cable TV, bar, laundry service, parking (fee), no-smoking rooms* ▤ *AE, DC, MC, V* ◯ *BP.*

**$$–$$$** ⊞ **Celio.** Yes, the Colosseum is two blocks away, but the special ambience of this hotel is provided by its Celian Hill setting. Many poetic, often overlooked marvels, such as the haunting Santi Quattro Coronati church, the time-capsuled Piazza Santi Giovanni e Paolo, and the verdant slopes of the Villa Celimontana park, are just a stroll away. Not far is Nero's Golden House but lest you lose track of modern times, this hotel offers free Wi-Fi access and a rooftop gym. A cute historical note is the decor of the guest rooms, all small but sumptuously frescoed with "faux" paintings in styles ranging from Pompeiian to Renaissance. French windows and elegant marble bathrooms (some with Jacuzzis) are other nice touches. But the hidden-corner-of-Rome locale may be the trump card. ⊠ *Via dei Santissimi Quattro 35/c, Colosseo, 00184* ☎ *06/70495333* 🖷 *06/7096377* ⊕ *www.hotelcelio.com* 🛏 *18 rooms, 2 suites* ⚗ *Restaurant, bar, in-room safes, Wi Fi, minibars, cable TV, bar, laundry service, parking (fee), no-smoking rooms* ⊟ *AE, DC, MC, V* ⦿ *CP.*

**$$** ⊞ **Nerva.** History is truly on your doorstep at this charming hotel. The cobbled, narrow street is flanked by ruins of breathtaking splendor, and the Forum is only a short walk away. The hotel itself is clean and well-run, and rooms are soundproofed and air-conditioned, if a bit small. ⊠ *Via Tor de Conti 3, Colosseo, 00184* ☎ *06/6781835* 🖷 *06/6793764* ⊕ *www.hotelnerva.com* 🛏 *19 rooms* ⚗ *Restaurant, bar* ⊟ *AE, DC, MC, V* ⦿ *CP.*

**★ $$** ⊞ **Richmond.** Right at the beginning of Via Cavour, this charming little hotel is ideally situated for visits to the Forum, the Colosseum, and all the major sights of ancient Rome. Several cafés downstairs are just right for breakfast, or head up to the attractive rooftop terrace and take in the panoramic views. The decor is highlighted with tasteful, classical touches, and the modern rooms feature hand-painted frescoes. The staff is helpful and multilingual. ⊠ *Largo Corrado Ricci 36, Colosseo, 00184* ☎ *06/69941256* 🖷 *06/69941454* 🛏 *13 rooms* ⚗ *Bar, in-room safes, cable TV, no smoking rooms, laundry service, parking (fee)* ⊟ *AE, D, DC, MC, V* ⦿ *BP.*

**$–$$** ⊞ **Duca d'Alba.** Marble accents and reproductions of ancient paintings recall ancient Rome in this elegant, small hotel near the Colosseum. More modern is the residential neighborhood, the Suburra, once rather louche but now coming up in the world. The tasteful neoclassical-style decor includes custom-designed furnishings and marble bathrooms. Some rooms have recently been made over to a more modern style. Breakfast consists of an ample buffet. With its attentive staff and reasonable rates, Duca d'Alba is a good value. ⊠ *Via Leonina 14, Colosseo, 00184* ☎ *06/484471* 🖷 *06/4884840* ⊕ *www.hotelducadalba.com* 🛏 *26 rooms, 1 suite* ⚗ *In-room data ports, in-room safes, some kitchenettes, minibars, cable TV, bar, laundry service, parking (fee), no-smoking rooms* ⊟ *AE, DC, MC, V* ⦿ *BP.*

# Il Ghetto

The impossibly narrow alleyways and deep quiet of most of this small quarter make it easy to imagine its bohemian-chic condos as the teeming tenements they once were. There are few cafés and restaurants here, but the neighborhood is so small and central that it's just a few minutes' walk out to busy Largo Argentina, where choice is wider.

**$** ⊞ **Arenula.** Standing on an age-worn byway off central Via Arenula, on the edge of the quaint Ghetto neighborhood and just across the Tiber from Trastevere, this hotel is a superb bargain by Rome standards. With an imposingly elegant stone exterior, this hotel welcomes you with a luminous and cheerful all-white interior. Guest rooms are simple in decor but have pale-wood furnishings and gleaming bathrooms, as well as double-glaze windows and air-conditioning (in summer only; ask when you reserve). Two of the rooms accommodate four beds. Of course, you can't have everything, so that the graceful oval staircase of white marble and wrought iron in the lobby cues you that there is no elevator. Those guests with rooms on the fourth floor better be in good shape! ⊠ *Via Santa Maria dei Calderari 47, off Via Arenula, Ghetto, 00186* ☎ *06/6879454* 🖷 *06/6896188* ⊕ *www.hotelarenula.com* ⤴ *50 rooms* ⚲ *Cable TV; no a/c in some rooms* ⊟ *AE, DC, MC, V* ⦿ *BP.*

## The Spanish Steps

Central Rome's most fashionable neighborhood is packed with hotels, mostly suiting the style and budget of patrons of the local shops—Gucci, Prada, Hermès—although there are a few less expensive choices that book up far in advance. Absolutely central for shopping, café-ing, and eating out, it's the best location for enjoying Rome's pleasures. Don't try to drive here.

**$$$$**   🏨 **D'Inghilterra.** Lizst, Mendelssohn, Hans Christian Andersen, Mark
**Fodor's**Choice Twain, Hemingway, and now you? Ever since it opened its doors in 1845,
★ the d'Inghilterra has welcomed Rome's most discerning tourists—indeed, it was named to honor all those Brits who once colonized the Spanish Steps district back in the Grand Tour era. Today the hotel's 19th-century elegance has been transposed to the 21st. Down the block from the former pied-à-terre of poet Robert Browning, across the street from the couture salon of Principessa Galitzine, and set on a potted-palm cobblestone stretch of posh Via Bocca di Leone, this "albergo" is like a charming sepia photograph come to life. With a marvelous residential feel and a staff that is as warm as the surroundings are velvety, this hotel has lots going for it. Even a pedigree: it started life as the guesthouse of the fabulously rich Prince Torlonia (whose palazzo was across the way). The lobby is a jewel—tiny, unassuming, like a sentry box against the hustle and bustle outside the front door. In fact, you're in the heart of the shopping district here, so traffic noises can intrude even the double-pane windows (the best rooms here overlook a quiet, plant-covered terrace). Upstairs, some guest rooms are so full of carpets, gilt-framed mirrors, and cozy bergères, you may not care about the snug dimensions. No matter: guests like to repair to the public salons on the first floor, including the Bar, which is James Bond–suave. Happily, the breakfast cellar is still aswirl with trompe-l'oeil frescoes. ⊠ *Via Bocca di Leone 14, Piazza di Spagna, 00187* ☎ *06/69981* 🖷 *06/69922243* ⊕ *www. royaldemeure.com* ⤴ *77 rooms, 20 suites* ⚲ *Restaurant, in-room safes, minibars, cable TV, bar, laundry service, parking (fee), no-smoking rooms* ⊟ *AE, DC, MC, V* ⦿ *EP.*

**$$$$**   🏨 **Hassler.** As an inscription in marble at the adjacent Santa Trinità con-
**Fodor's**Choice vent announces, *Non est in tota laetior Urbe locus*, there's no more de-
★ lightful place in all the world. Well, that does explain why this famous

hotel was built to take advantage of the spectacular view from the peak of one of Rome's seven hills. Here, in villas atop the Pincian Hill, Poussin, Piranesi, Ingres, and Berlioz once enjoyed having all Rome at their feet. Today, movie stars and millionaires do the same by staying at this hotel, which sits just to the right of the church atop the Spanish Steps. The outside may be fairly unmellifluous—the Swiss Wirth family rebuilt the hotel exterior in 1939—but the guest rooms are certainly among the world's most beautiful and opulent. If you're not willing to pay V.I.P prices, of course, you get more standard-issue rooms at the rear of the hotel (and the lowest priced of these are overpriced for what you get elsewhere), but many are soigné and some come with views of the Villa Medici park. Better, the hotel has become a Disneyland of elegant bars, restaurants, and retreats. The Rooftop Restaurant (which guests use for the breakfast buffet) is world-famous for its view (ask for the plan that points out the monuments along the skyline) if not for its food; the Hassler Bar was where Princess Diana savored one of the hotel's "Veruschkas" (pomegranate juice, vodka, and champagne); the Palm Court Garden, which becomes the hotel bar in summer, is a riot of flowers; and the new Salone Eva is a stunning homage to 19th-century style, with enough tufted velvets, satin drapes, embroidered pillows, red banquettes, and passementerie to please even Valentino. ⊠ *Piazza Trinità dei Monti 6, Piazza di Spagna, 00187* ☎ *06/699340* 🖷 *06/69941607* ⊕ *www.hotelhasslerroma.com* ⇘ *85 rooms, 13 suites* ♨ *Restaurant, in-room safes, in-room data ports, minibars, cable TV, gym, hair salon, bar, laundry service, concierge, 3 meeting rooms, parking (fee), no-smoking rooms* ▭ *AE, DC, MC, V* ⫶◯⫶ *EP.*

★ **$$$$** 🏨 **Hotel de Russie.** A favorite for highlifers, this "buzz"-y hotel is set in a 19th-century historic hotel, which once counted Russian princes among its guests. Later Picasso and Cocteau leaned out the windows to pick oranges from the trees on its courtyard terrace, a garden spectacular that climbs the Pincian Hill and remains one of the most gorgeous spots in Rome. Out front, Piazza del Popolo is a few steps away. Restored to full-luxe status in 2002 by famed hotelier Sir Rocco Forte, this hotel is a sleek posherie done up in chic Italian contemporary style. Granted, there are the stray velvet hunting-lodge sofa and the Murano chandeliers, but most of the furnishings are mod, minimalistic, and (yawn) interchangeable with any contempo hotel from Tribeca to Temple Bar. The furniture is Donghia-style, the colors are gray and grayer, and you've seen it all before. Well, the bathrooms do have Roman mosaic motifs. But the best thing here is that many rooms overlook that amazing garden courtyard (but not all—beware of those that overlook side streets), which everyone can enjoy with an outdoor table in the hotel's swank Le Jardin de Russie restaurant (which has plenty of tables indoors). High rollers will opt for the suites with panoramic terraces and a long spell in the hotel's spa facility, which glows with a bluer-than-blue pool. ⊠ *Via del Babuino 9, Piazza di Spagna, 00187* ☎ *06/328881* 🖷 *06/32888888* ⊕ *www.roccofortehotels.com* ⇘ *94 rooms, 31 suites* ♨ *Restaurant, in-room safes, minibars, cable TV, health club, hair salon, spa, in-room data ports, bar, 5 meeting rooms, parking (fee), laundry service, no-smoking rooms* ▭ *AE, DC, MC, V* ⫶◯⫶ *EP.*

**$$$–$$$$** 🏨 **Dei Borgognoni.** This quietly chic hotel is on a byway in the heart of the smart shopping district near Piazza San Silvestro. The centuries-old palazzo building has been remodeled to provide spacious lounges, a glassed-in garden courtyard, and stylishly furnished rooms that are cleverly arranged to create an illusion of space, though they are actually petite. Some rooms have balconies or terraces on the interior court. Just ask for free use of the hotels' bicycles. ✉ *Via del Bufalo 126, Piazza di Spagna, 00187* ☎ *06/69941505* 🖷 *06/69941501* ⊕ *www.hotelborgognoni.it* 📞 *51 rooms* ♿ *In-room safes, minibars, cable TV, bar, laundry service, concierge, business services, parking (fee), no-smoking rooms* ⊟ *AE, D, DC, MC, V* �📋 *BP.*

**$$$–$$$$** 🏨 **Hotel Art.** The Art does its best to bring Rome into the 21st century, with a dedication to contemporary (you guessed it) art and design that is brand-new in this eternal city. Just the place for an Italian *Vogue* fashion shoot (or the next Austin Powers movie?), the public areas are spacious and spectacular, with smooth concrete and high white arches contrasting starkly with glossy neo-'60s furnishings. You'll think you've wandered into a SoHo art gallery in the lobby, which then opens up to the glossy white reception area. The jewel is the Crystal Bar, set in an old chapel, with gilded panels in Raphaelesque style and topped off with a glittering chandelier. Guest rooms, color-coordinated, inexplicably, with hallways, are a more standard upper-middle contemporary style, with sleek wood headboards, crowd-pleasing puffy white comforters, and plug-in data ports. ✉ *Via Margutta 56, 00187* ☎ *06/328711* 🖷 *06/36003995* ⊕ *www.hotelart.it* 📞 *44 rooms, 2 suites* ♿ *Restaurant, in-room safes, minibars, cable TV, in-room data ports, bar, laundry service, no-smoking rooms* ⊟ *AE, DC, MC, V* �📋 *BP.*

**$$$–$$$$** 🏨 **The Inn at the Spanish Steps.** Small and exclusive, this luxury place fits right into the neighborhood, and you'll fit right in with your bags from Gucci and Prada, just down the street. Set on Rome's glamorous Via Condotti, it's ideally located for shop-till-you-droppers, but it's not all consumer glitz—the hotel occupies the upper floors of a centuries-old town house it shares with Casanova's old haunt, Antico Caffè Greco. The rooms are *Architectural Digest*–worthy, if on the slender side in dimension. All junior suites, they are handsomely decorated with damask fabrics, antiques, and a great sense of style. The simpler rooms glow with ochre walls and framed paintings, while the grander ones are jewelboxes complete with frescoed ceilings and elegantly striped walls. For the full blow-out, repair to the annex in a penthouse a few doors down on the piazza. It has it all, from plasma televisions to a full-time butler, and prices to match. ✉ *Via Condotti 85, Piazza di Spagna, 00187* ☎ *06/69925657* 🖷 *06/6786470* ⊕ *www.atspanishsteps.com* 📞 *22 rooms, 3 suites* ♿ *In-room safes, minibars, cable TV, bar, laundry service, airport shuttle, no-smoking rooms* ⊟ *AE, DC, MC, V* �📋 *BP.*

**$$$–$$$$**
**Fodor'sChoice**
**★**
🏨 **Scalinata di Spagna.** An old-fashioned pensione that has hosted generations of romantics, this tiny hotel is booked solid for months—even years—ahead. Its location at the very top of the Spanish Steps, inconspicuous little entrance, and quiet, sunny charm add up to the feeling of your own pied-à-terre in the city's most glamorous neighborhood. Guest rooms have been renovated in a thoroughly chic manner, with high-style

floral fabrics and Empire-style sofas. Of course, the rooms most in demand are those overlooking the Spanish Steps, but even if you don't land one of those few, you can repair to the hotel's exquisite roof garden, where you can have breakfast with Rome at your feet. Thoughtful amenities—from in-room Internet access to a breakfast service until noon—help make you feel at home. ⊠ *Piazza Trinità dei Monti 17, Piazza di Spagna, 00187* ☎ *06/6793006* 🖷 *06/69940598* ⊕ *www.hotelscalinata.com* 🛏 *16 rooms* & *In-room safes, minibars, laundry service, Internet, parking (fee), no-smoking rooms* ☰ *AE, D, MC, V* ❍| *BP.*

$$–$$$$  🏨 **Valadier.** Oh, if these walls could talk. Once a convent, later a house of ill repute, this palazzo has seen it all. Not a trace remains of either incarnation, and today it's a hotel known for comfortable rooms with marble and travertine bathrooms and a fine location, just off Piazza del Popolo and a few minutes' walk from the Spanish Steps. As for decor, it's traditional hotel luxe, with a lot of polished surfaces, mirrors, and shiny lights, so don't expect any time-burnished patina. However, the view from the rooftop terrace restaurant, taking in a panorama of domes and cupolas, is enchanting. ⊠ *Via della Fontanella 15, Piazza di Spagna, 00187* ☎ *06/3611998* 🖷 *06/3201558* ⊕ *www.hotelvaladier. com* 🛏 *60 rooms* & *2 restaurants, in-room safes, minibars, cable TV, piano bar, no-smoking rooms* ☰ *AE, DC, MC, V* ❍| *EP.*

$$–$$$$  🏨 **Locarno.** The sort of place that inspired a movie (Bernard Weber's 1978
**Fodor's**Choice  *Hotel Locarno*, to be exact), this has been a longtime choice for art afi-
★  cionados and people in the cinema. But everyone will appreciate this hotel's fin de siècle charm, intimate feel, and central location off Piazza del Popolo. Exquisite wallpaper and fabric prints are coordinated in the rooms, and some rooms have antiques—the grandest room looks like an art director's take on a Medici bedroom. Everything is lovingly supervised by the owners, a mother-daughter duo. The buffet breakfast is ample, there's bar service on the panoramic roof garden, and complimentary bicycles are available if you feel like braving the traffic. A newly renovated annex is done in art deco style. ⊠ *Via della Penna 22, Piazza di Spagna, 00186* ☎ *06/3610841* 🖷 *06/3215249* ⊕ *www. hotellocarno.com* 🛏 *63 rooms, 3 suites* & *In-room data ports, in-room safes, minibars, cable TV, bar, laundry service, parking(fee), no-smoking rooms* ☰ *AE, DC, MC, V* ❍| *BP.*

★ $$–$$$  🏨 **Condotti.** As its name suggests, this small hotel is two blocks from Rome's premier shopping street, Via Condotti (that is, not on it), and one block from the Spanish Steps. The emphasis here is on peace and comfort, created by surprisingly elegant period furnishings and a relatively quiet location. All rooms are soundproof, and many enjoy views of the rooftops of Rome. Walnut furniture and gilt-edge mirrors raise the rent, with rich fabrics used for the curtains and bedspreads. Each room has its own temperature control, a rarity in Rome. ⊠ *Via Mario de'Fiori 37, Piazza di Spagna, 00187* ☎ *06/6794661* 🖷 *06/6790457* ⊕ *www.hotelcondotti.com* 🛏 *16 rooms, 2 suites* & *Minibars, cable TV, bar, laundry service* ☰ *AE, DC, MC, V* ❍| *CP.*

$$–$$$  🏨 **Tritone.** A hundred yards from the Fontana di Trevi, the Tritone is within easy walking distance of virtually every important site in the historic center. The flip side is that you're on one of Rome's busiest thor-

oughfares, so noise can be an issue, though high-quality soundproofing helps keep the din down. Rooms have modern decor with wall-to-wall carpeting, plasma-screen satellite TV, and spacious travertine bathrooms. A buffet breakfast can be taken in the roof garden, with panoramic views of the Eternal City. ⊠ *Via del Tritone 210, Piazza di Trevi, 00187* ☎ *06/69922575* 🖶 *06/6782624* ⊕ *www.tritonehotel.com* 🖙 *43 rooms* ⚘ *In-room safes, minibars, cable TV, bar, laundry service, parking (fee), no smoking rooms* ▤ *AE, DC, MC, V* ⧧ *BP.*

**$$** 🏨 **Carriage.** The Carriage's *centralissima* location is its main appeal: it's two blocks from the Spanish Steps, in the heart of Rome, set on one of the historic center's quietest and most elegant streets. The decor of subdued Baroque accents, richly colored wallpaper, and antique reproductions lends a touch of elegance. Some furniture has seen better days, and rooms can be pint-size, but several have small terraces. A roof garden adds to the appeal. ⊠ *Via delle Carrozze 36, Piazza di Spagna, 00187* ☎ *06/6990124* 🖶 *06/6788279* ⊕ *www.hotelcarriage.net* 🖙 *24 rooms, 3 suites* ▤ *AE, DC, MC, V* ⧧ *BP.*

**$$** 🏨 **Homs.** At this midsize hotel, on a quiet street in the heart of the historic center, two rooftop terraces provide fine views of the whole area; the larger terrace is suitable for breakfast year-round. Although room furnishings are a bit plain overall, beautiful antiques accent strategic spots for an air that's a cut above average. Rome's most complete English-language bookshop, the Anglo-American, is directly across the street. ⊠ *Via della Vite 71–72, Piazza di Spagna, 00187* ☎ *06/6792976* 🖶 *06/6780482* 🖙 *48 rooms* ⚘ *Bar, parking (fee)* ▤ *AE, DC, MC, V* ⧧ *BP.*

**$$** 🏨 **San Carlo.** Marble accents are everywhere at this refurbished hotel, with an overall effect that's refined and decidedly classical. Rooms are bright and comfortable, and some have their own terraces with rooftop views. A top-floor terrace is ideal for having breakfast or taking the sun throughout the day. ⊠ *Via delle Carrozze 93, Piazza di Spagna, 00187* ☎ *06/6784548* 🖶 *06/69941197* ⊕ *www.hotelsancarloroma.com* 🖙 *56 rooms, 2 suites* ⚘ *Cable TV, bar, laundry service, no-smoking rooms* ▤ *AE, DC, MC, V* ⧧ *CP.*

**$$** 🏨 **Trevi.** Location, location, location: this delightful place is tucked away down one of Old Rome's quaintest alleys. The smallish rooms are bright and clean, and a few of the larger ones have antique furniture and wooden ceilings with massive beams. There's an arborlike roof-garden restaurant where you can eat marvelous pasta. ⊠ *Vicolo del Babbuccio 20, Piazza di Spagna, 00187* ☎ *06/6789563* 🖶 *06/69941407* ⊕ *www.gruppotrevi.it/trevi/index.htm* 🖙 *29 rooms* ⚘ *Restaurant, parking (fee)* ▤ *AE, DC, MC, V* ⧧ *BP.*

**$–$$** 🏨 **Margutta.** For location, good value, and friendly owner-managers, the Margutta is outstanding. The lobby and halls in this small hotel are unassuming, but rooms are a pleasant surprise, with a clean and airy look, attractive wrought-iron bedsteads, and modern baths. Three of the rooms on the top floor have private terraces. Though it's in an old building, there's an elevator. The location is on a quiet side street between the Spanish Steps and Piazza del Popolo. ⊠ *Via Laurina 34, Piazza di Spagna, 00187* ☎ *06/3223674* 🖶 *06/3200395* ⊕ *www.hotelmargutta. it* 🖙 *24 rooms* ▤ *AE, DC, MC, V* ⧧ *BP.*

$ ⊞ **Hotel Suisse.** Long known (and beloved) as the Pensione Suisse, this old standby of the budgeteer set recently got a makeover into hotel status (all rooms now enjoy their own bath). The biggest plus about this place is its address: the Via Gregoriana, the picturesque street that debouches into the top of the Spanish Steps and one of Rome's more fabled streets (the painter Ingres and the author Hans Christian Andersen used to live a few doors up the block). Set in a somewhat unprepossing apartment building, the hotel itself is sweet and serviceable, with rooms on an array of floors. If possible, opt for the ones facing the back—blissfully quiet even though you're in the thick of things. ⊠ *Via Gregoriana 54, Via Veneto, 00187* ☎ *06/6783649* 🖷 *06/6781258* ⊕ *www. hotelsuisserome.com* ⇱ *12 rooms* ⚲ *Air-conditioning in 7 rooms only* ⊟ *MC, V* ⦿❘ *BP.*

$ ⊞ **Panda.** One of the best deals in Rome, the Panda is particularly remarkable given that the neighborhood is Via della Croce, one of Piazza di Spagna's chic shopping streets. Guest rooms are outfitted in terracotta and wrought iron; they're smallish, but quiet, thanks to double-glaze windows, and spotlessly clean. Pay even less by sharing a bath—in low season, you may have it to yourself anyway. ⊠ *Via della Croce 35, Piazza di Spagna, 00187* ☎ *06/6780179* 🖷 *06/69942151* ⊕ *www. hotelpanda.it* ⇱ *20 rooms, 14 with bath* ⚲ *No room TVs, no minibars* ⊟ *AE, MC, V* ⦿❘ *EP* ⦿❘ *EP.*

FodorśChoice
★

# Piazza Navona

Encompassing the area around and between spectacular Piazza Navona and the Pantheon to the east, this is an upscale, and equally picturesque, alternative to Campo de' Fiori just to the south. There's a range of places to stay here, from frayed-at-the-edges *pensioni* to top-of-the line historic hotels, all housed in the 17th- and 18th-century buildings that make up this part of Rome. Much of the area is pedestrian-only, with a lively mix of restaurants and nightlife.

★ $$$$ ⊞ **Grand Hotel de la Minerve.** The Minerve is the stylish reincarnation of the hostelry that occupied this 17th-century palazzo for hundreds of years, hosting literati from Stendhal to Sartre and de Beauvoir along with a bevy of crowned (and uncrowned—Carlotta, the deposed Empress of Mexico resided here for a while) heads. It sports one of Rome's to-die-for locations: on the famous piazza with Bernini's elephant obelisk, and just a few feet from the Pantheon and the church of Santa Maria sopra Minerva. Inside, a zillion-dollar renovation nearly gutted the building. What emerged was a vast and sleek lobby (complete with 19th-century statues and some rather gaudy stained glass), big banquet facilities, the lush La Cesta restaurant, and guest rooms aswim in Italian modern furnishings. Readers love the staff here, and no one can resist the lavish roof terrace. Open for summer dining in fair weather, it almost allows you to touch the dome of Hadrian's famous temple. ⊠ *Piazza della Minerva 69, Pantheon, 00186* ☎ *06/695201* 🖷 *06/6794165* ⊕ *http://grand-hoteldelaminerve.it/* ⇱ *119 rooms, 16 suites* ⚲ *Restaurant, in-room safes, minibars, cable TV, gym, piano bar, laundry service, no-smoking rooms* ⊟ *AE, DC, MC, V* ⦿❘ *EP.*

$$$$ ⊞ **Nazionale.** Given its prime location adjacent to the Parliament, this 16th-century palazzo has been the venue for any number of momentous meetings of Italy's top politicos. In keeping with its national importance, it offers every traditional service and modern comfort: refined but comfortable guest rooms, a bar, a restaurant, meeting rooms, and first-class staff. The second-floor penthouse suite offers a private terrace and amazing views. ⊠ *Piazza Montecitorio 131, Pantheon, 00186* ☎ *06/695001* 🖷 *06/6786677* ⊕ *www.nazionaleroma.it* ☞ *92 rooms, 3 suites* ⚒ *Restaurant, in-room safes, minibars, cable TV, bar, laundry service, concierge, meeting rooms, parking (fee)* ⊟ *AE, DC, MC, V* ⊚ *BP.*

$$$$ ⊞ **Pantheon.** The Pantheon is a superb place to stay right next door to the monument of the same name. The lobby is the very epitome of a Roman hotel lobby—a warm, cozy, yet opulent setting that comes replete with Stil Liberty stained glass, sumptuous wood paneling, a Renaissance beamed ceiling, and a massive and glorious chandelier. A print of one of Rome's obelisks on the door welcomes you to your room, where you'll find antique walnut furniture, fresh flowers, and more woodbeam ceilings. ⊠ *Via dei Pastini 131, Pantheon, 00186* ☎ *06/6787746* 🖷 *06/6787755* ⊕ *www.hotelpantheon.com* ☞ *20 rooms, 1 suite* ⚒ *Bar* ⊟ *AE, DC, MC, V* ⊚ *EP.*

$$$–$$$$ ⊞ **Albergo del Sole al Pantheon.** Grandly sited directly opposite the immortal portico of the Pantheon, this place is in the running as a candidate for the world's oldest hotel. Welcoming the great ever since it opened in 1467, it has hosted Frederick III, Ariosto, Cagliostro, and Pietro Mascagni (who came here to celebrate the opening night of his opera, *Cavalleria Rusticana*). Over the years, travelers have accepted the rather cramped quarters in exchange for the location on this historic square (and now the indignity of being perched next to a McDonalds). Needless to say, the hotel has been renovated many times over and most vestiges of the distant past are long gone. The good news is that the refurbishment has been done in high style: artfully placed columns, Rococo windows, Renaissance-style beds, high ceilings, and terra-cotta floors all lend a certain authenticity to your stay. Obviously, specify if you want a room with a view over the Pantheon; with it, you'll also get the din of the piazza's gorgeous café scene, but double-glaze windows work their magic. ⊠ *Piazza della Rotonda 63, Pantheon, 00186* ☎ *06/6780441* 🖷 *06/69940689* ⊕ *www.hotelsolealpantheon.com* ☞ *25 rooms* ⚒ *In-room safes, minibars, cable TV, bar, laundry service* ⊟ *AE, DC, MC, V* ⊚ *BP.*

$$ ⊞ **Abruzzi.** Rarely do magnificent views of world-famous ancient monuments come with such a relatively gentle price tag. From the windows of this old-fashioned little establishment, the Pantheon is literally in your face. Unfortunately the facilities also recall a Rome of yesteryear: sink in the room, bathroom down the hall (some higher-price rooms have a private bath). But the rooms are clean and the beds comfortable. To make your reservation, you have to send a signed traveler's check with the name of the hotel on it. ⊠ *Piazza della Rotonda 69, Pantheon, 00186* ☎ *06/6792021* 🖷 *06/69788076* ⊕ *www.hotelabruzzi.it* ☞ *26 rooms, 15 with bath* ⚒ *In-room safes, minibars, cable TV; no a/c in some rooms* ⊟ *AE, MC, V* ⊚ *BP.*

$$ ⌧ **Albergo Cesàri.** The exterior of this intimate hotel on a traffic-free street is as it was when Stendhal stayed here in the 1800s. Inside, the hotel has been renovated and there's no patina left from the days when Garibaldi and Gregorovius were guests, yet most rooms are sweetly embellished with old prints of Rome and soft-green drapes and bedspreads, creating an air of comfort and serenity. Furniture is new, yet traditionally styled. Bathrooms are done in smart two-tone blue marble. ⊠ *Via di Pietra 89a, Pantheon, 00186* ☎ *06/6749701* 🖨 *06/67497030* ⊕ *www. albergocesari.it* ↘ *47 rooms* ⚬ *Cable TV, in-room safes, bar, laundry service, parking (fee)* ⊟ *AE, DC, MC, V* ⑩ *BP.*

★ $$ ⌧ **Albergo Santa Chiara.** With its white shutters and pretty canteloupe-hue stone, this hotel is comprised of three historic buildings set behind the Pantheon. It's been in the same family for 200 years, and the personal attention shows in meticulously decorated and maintained lounges and rooms. The lobby is *alla Romana*—an all white affair; it's elegantly accented with a Venetian chandelier, a stucco statue, a gilded Baroque mirror, and a walnut concierge desk. Upstairs, the pricier rooms are most fetching, with stylish yet comfortable furniture. Each room has built-in oak headboards, a marble-top desk, and a travertine bath. Double-glaze windows are handy for those rooms that look out over the Piazza della Minerva. There are three apartments, for two to five people, with full kitchens. ⊠ *Via Santa Chiara 21, Pantheon, 00186* ☎ *06/6872979* 🖨 *06/6873144* ⊕ *www.albergosantachiara.com* ↘ *97 rooms, 4 suites, 3 apartments* ⚬ *Some kitchenettes, minibars, cable TV, in-room safes, bar, laundry service* ⊟ *AE, DC, MC, V* ⑩ *BP.*

$–$$ ⌧ **Coronet.** This small hotel occupies part of a floor in one wing of the vast and regal Palazzo Doria Pamphilj; seven interior rooms overlook the family's lovely private garden court. Don't expect palatial ambience, but antique-style molding in the carpeted halls and beam ceilings in several rooms do lend a historic air. The good-size rooms have oldish baths, some very small; some rooms share a bathroom. Several rooms can accommodate three or four beds. While this place seems to have several things going for it, some readers on Fodor's Rants & Raves web site forum beg to differ. ⊠ *Piazza Grazioli 5, Piazza Venezia, 00186* ☎ *06/6792341* 🖨 *06/69922705* ⊕ *www.hotelcoronet.com* ↘ *13 rooms, 10 with bath* ⚬ *No a/c, no minibars* ⊟ *AE, MC, V* ⑩ *EP.*

$–$$ ⌧ **Genio.** Rooms at the top of this medium-size hotel, just at the ancient entrance to Piazza Navona, have terraces and citywide views. There's also a roof terrace for all, where you can have breakfast. Modeled along classic Roman lines, the lobby, public areas, and rooms are cozy. Rooms are decorated in warm colors and have parquet floors and a harmonious mix of modern and antique reproduction furnishings. ⊠ *Via G. Zanardelli 28, Piazza Navona, 00186* ☎ *06/6832191* 🖨 *06/68307246* ↘ *60 rooms* ⚬ *Bar, parking (fee)* ⊟ *AE, DC, MC, V* ⑩ *BP.*

$ ⌧ **Fraterna Domus.** Italy is famous for its "bed and blessings" accommodations—simple rooms set in convents or monasteries. Here's a bargain option on a byway near Piazza Navona. Run by nuns who do not wear religious habits, this guesthouse is comprised of spartan rooms, but they have all the essentials, including small private bathrooms (some simply have a showerhead perched above the toilet). The room rate includes breakfast, but a meal plan is available for dinners, which are hearty and inexpensive. Curfew here is 11 PM. ⊠ *Vicolo del Leonetto 16, Piazza Navona, 00186* ☎ *06/68802727* 🖷 *06/6832691* 📞 *20 rooms* ♿ *No a/c in some rooms, no room TVs* 🖃 *No credit cards* ¶⊙¶ *BP.*

## Termini

The wide, busy streets around Rome's central train station feel much more urban than the rest of the city center. Traffic is heavier, 19th-century buildings are taller, and the overall feeling is gray and commercial—not the Rome of travel brochure fantasies. But the hotel density here is the highest in the city, and you're assured of finding a room in a pinch. Although most travelers choose this neighborhood because it's cheap, there are a surprising number of top-end hotels here as well, and if you're looking for a luxurious room, the price-quality ratio here is better than in swankier parts of town.

**$$$$** 🏨 **Empire Palace Hotel.** The word palace here is no exaggeration—this hotel was once the stately residence of a noble Venetian family. Today the spacious marble-floor lobby and sitting areas are decorated with works by contemporary artists, and the guest rooms are luxurious, with antique furniture, thoughtful accessories, and fine paintings on the walls. The hotel's popular restaurant, Aureliano, is a reason in itself to stay—after a trip through the renowned wine list, you may not feel like walking far from this somewhat out-of-the-way location. ⊠ *Via Aureliana 39, Termini, 00187* ☎ *06/421281* 🖷 *06/42128400* ⊕ *www.empirepalacehotel.com* 📞 *113 rooms* ♿ *Restaurant, in-room safes, minibars, cable TV, gym, bar, laundry service, concierge, parking (fee), no-smoking rooms* 🖃 *AE, DC, MC, V* ¶⊙¶ *EP.*

**$$$$** 🏨 **Exedra.** If Rome's semi-stodgy hotel scene has an It-Girl, it's the Exedra. Hardly a travel column unfolds without a mention of it, celebs vie for face time, and it's the hostess of the moment for out-of-town high rollers and Roman big spenders alike. Unlike its naughty younger brother the Aleph, the Exedra is a model of neoclassical respectability, all gilt-framed mirrors and fresh flowers, but there's a glint of cutting edge in the paparazzi-inspired (and inspiring) Tazio brasserie. Rooms are predictably luscious in an uptown way, with silky linens and handsome nouveau-colonial bedsteads, and many face the spectacular fountain in the piazza outside. Why stay here, rather than at the umpteen other expensively elegant hotels in central Rome? You can think about it while you lounge by the rooftop swimming pool. ⊠ *Piazza della Repubblica 47, 00185* ☎ *06/489381* 🖷 *06/48938000* ⊕ *www.exedra.boscolohotels.com* 📞 *238 rooms, 9 suites* ♿ *2 restaurants, bar, in-room safe, high-speed internet, minibar, cable TV, fitness center, spa, rooftop pool, concierge, meeting rooms, non-smoking rooms* 🖃 *AE, DC, MC, V* ¶⊙¶ *EP.*

**$$–$$$$** 🏨 **Mascagni.** Outside is one of Rome's busiest, most central streets, but not a sound filters into the interior of this elegant establishment, where windows and even doors are soundproof. The lobby is fetchingly accented by two statues of goddesses, while an Empire-style sofa and Baroque mirror set a stylish tone. In guest rooms, pretty damask curtains, high ceilings, and new, firm beds are a pleasure. The intimate lounges and charming bar—very cozy and pretty with its floral fabric and wood bar—follow the same decorating scheme, as does the breakfast room, where a generous buffet is laid in the morning, complete with free newspapers. Discounted rates can be a good deal, so be sure to ask. The friendly, creative management is always coming up with new offers, including the "Family Perfect" room, which includes a Playstation, a DVD player with Disney movies, and wooden blocks for small children to play with. ⊠ *Via Vittorio Emanuele Orlando 90, Termini, 00185* ☎ *06/48904040* 🖷 *06/4817637* 🌐 *www.hotelmascagni.com* 🖎 *40 rooms* ♿ *In-room safes, minibars, cable TV, bar, laundry service, concierge, business services, parking (fee), no-smoking rooms* ▤ *AE, DC, MC, V* ⟍◉⟋ *BP.*

**$$$** 🖾 **Art Deco.** The name says it all: the decor at this hotel is attuned to the streamlined moderne sensibilities of the 1920s, with whimsical accents in (patently new) Art Deco paintings and antiques. Set in a rather pretty early-20th-century building, the hotel offers some modern amenities, including whirlpool baths. Set in a residential neighborhood just a few minutes' walk from Termini Station, it's handy to public transport (which you'll need to get to the center of Rome). ⊠ *Via Palestro 19, Termini, 00185* ☎ *06/4457588* 🖷 *06/4441483* 🌐 *www.travel.it/roma/ artdeco* 🖎 *68 rooms* ♿ *Restaurant, in-room safes, cable TV, hot tub, bar, laundry service, no-smoking rooms* ▤ *AE, DC, MC, V* ⟍◉⟋ *BP.*

**$$-$$$**
FodorsChoice
★ 🖾 **Britannia.** Set in a very regal white villa, smartly fitted out with black shutters (and a not so smart neon sign), this is a very enticing option. The attention to detail is evident in every corner, from the frescoed halls to the breakfast room. Downstairs, public rooms have somewhat crass allusions to Empire 19th-century style. But upstairs, guest rooms, each with an individual layout, feel like rooms in a grand private home, furnished with luxury fabrics and original artwork, as well as handsome marble bathrooms. One has a wall lined with photos, another has a bed with a tondo painting of a rose hovering above it. Others cosset with sweet 19th-century style moldings. The caring management provides such amenities as English-language dailies and local weather reports delivered to your room each morning. A light-filled rooftop suite opens onto a private terrace. ⊠ *Via Napoli 64, Termini, 00184* ☎ *06/4883153* 🖷 *06/ 48986316* 🌐 *www.hotelbritannia.it* 🖎 *32 rooms, 1 suite* ♿ *In-room safes, in-room data ports, minibars, cable TV, bar, laundry service, free parking* ▤ *AE, DC, MC, V* ⟍◉⟋ *BP.*

★ **$$-$$$** 🖾 **Residenza Cellini.** Fresh flowers in the foyer help make this small, family-run residence feel like a gracious home. The lobby's glossy parquet floors, elegant door moldings, and handsome wood Empire-style desk and chairs make a sweet impression. Traditionally furnished guest rooms have king-size beds, padded headboards, and Persian-style rugs. There are only six rooms, so you're guaranteed personal attention from the eager-to-please staff. This is yet another hotel that is somewhat distant from the historic heart of Rome, but the Stazione Termini is very close and has all the transportation links you could wish for. ⊠ *Via Modena 5, Termini, 00184* ☎ *06/47825204* 🖷 *06/47881806* 🌐 *www. residenzacellini.it* 🖎 *6 rooms* ♿ *In-room safes, minibars, cable TV, in-room data ports, laundry service, parking (fee), no-smoking rooms* ▤ *AE, D, DC, MC, V* ⟍◉⟋ *BP.*

**$–$$$** ☐ **Mecenate Palace Hotel.** Named after ancient Rome's most important patron of the arts, who lived at this location more than 2,000 years ago, the Mecenate is situated on top of the Esquiline, one of Rome's seven hills. From the rooftop terrace there's a marvelous view of the bell tower of Santa Maria Maggiore. The rooms are in two adjacent buildings, and the lobby has been renovated to a facsimile of its original fin de siècle style. However, some guest rooms are fairly generic in tone, so if you stay here splurge for the best. In winter months, special room rates apply. ⊠ *Via Carlo Alberto 3, Termini, 00185* ☎ *06/44702024* 📠 *06/ 4461354* ⊕ *www.mecenatepalace.com* 🛏 *59 rooms, 3 suites* ⚿ *In-room safes, minibars, cable TV, bar, laundry service, concierge, parking (fee), no-smoking rooms* ☰ *AE, DC, MC, V* ⦿ *BP.*

**$$** ☐ **D'Este.** The decor in this distinguished 19th-century hotel tries to evoke turn-of-the-20th-century comfort, with brass bedsteads and lamps as well as dark-wood period furniture. Rooms are quiet, light, and spacious; many can accommodate families. The attentive owner-manager likes to have fresh flowers in the halls and sees that everything works. He encourages inquiries about special rates, particularly during the slack summer months. The location is within hailing distance of Santa Maria Maggiore and close to Termini Station. (You can arrange to be picked up there, free of charge, by the hotel car.) ⊠ *Via Carlo Alberto 4/b, Termini, 00184* ☎ *06/4465607* 📠 *06/4465601* ⊕ *www.hotel-deste.com* 🛏 *37 rooms* ⚿ *Restaurant, minibars, cable TV, bar, laundry service, concierge, free parking, no-smoking rooms* ☰ *AE, DC, MC, V* ⦿ *BP.*

**$$** ☐ **Hotel Venezia.** It's unusual to find a low-price hotel in Rome that's this *pretty*—16th-century wood tables and sideboards are set off by cozy matching armchairs, and tapestries give the public areas the feel of an elegant country house (in miniature). Guest rooms are somewhat simpler but still a cut above other hotels in this price range. It's a few blocks from the frantic Stazione Termini, making it convenient to public transportation. ⊠ *Via Varese 18, Termini, 00185* ☎ *06/4457101* 📠 *06/4957687* ⊕ *www. hotelvenezia.com* 🛏 *60 rooms* ⚿ *In-room safes, minibars, cable TV, laundry service, no-smoking rooms* ☰ *AE, D, MC, V* ⦿ *BP.*

**$$** ☐ **Marcella Royal.** A midsize hotel with the feel of a smaller, more intimate establishment, the Marcella is 10 minutes from Via Veneto and Termini Station. Here you can do your sightseeing from the roof terrace, taking in the view while you breakfast. Many rooms also have good views, and they are all furnished with flair, using tasteful color schemes, floral prints, and mirrored walls, echoing the elegant winter-garden decor of the lounges and bar. The spacious suites are ideal for families. ⊠ *Via Flavia 106, Termini, 00187* ☎ *06/42014591* 📠 *06/4815832* ⊕ *www.marcellaroyalhotel.com* 🛏 *73 rooms, 2 suites* ⚿ *Cable TV, bar, parking (fee)* ☰ *AE, DC, MC, V* ⦿ *BP.*

**$–$$** ☐ **Alpi.** The sweeping marble entrance here is cool and welcoming; it
Fodor'sChoice sets the tone for the rest of this reasonably priced hotel. What sets it
★ apart is the feeling of space—high ceilings with elegant chandeliers, white walls, and marble or parquet floors lend an elegance unusual for the price. Some of the bedrooms have antique furniture, and all are most tastefully decorated, although beds are old-fashioned. There are slightly formal lounges and a cozier bar downstairs, as well as a respectable restau-

rant. ⊠ *Via Castelfidardo 84, Termini, 00185* ☎ *06/4441235* 🖨 *06/4441257* ⊕ *www.hotelalpi.com* ⤴ *48 rooms* ⚘ *Restaurant, in-room safes, minibars, cable TV, bar, laundry service, parking (fee), no-smoking rooms* ⊟ *AE, DC, MC, V* ⧉ *BP.*

★ **$–$$** 🖼 **Des Artistes.** The three personable Riccioni brothers have transformed their hotel into the best in the neighborhood in its price range. It's bedecked with paintings and handsome furnishings in mahogany, and rooms are decorated in attractive fabrics. Marble baths are smallish but luxurious for this price, with hair dryers and towel warmers. Des Artistes hasn't forgotten its roots, though: there's also a "hostel" floor with 11 simpler rooms for travelers on a budget. Book well ahead. As for location, this is somewhat on the fringe, being several blocks (in the wrong direction) from Stazione Termini. ⊠ *Via Villafranca 20, Termini, 00185* ☎ *06/4454365* 🖨 *06/4462368* ⊕ *www.hoteldesartistes.com* ⤴ *40 rooms, 27 with bath* ⚘ *In-room data ports, in-room safes, minibars, cable TV, bar, concierge, parking (fee); no smoking* ⊟ *AE, DC, MC, V* ⧉ *BP.*

**$–$$** 🖼 **Doria.** A convenient location and reasonable rates are the advantages of this small hotel. Space is ingeniously exploited, from the minuscule elevator to the nicely furnished but smallish rooms. Newly renovated, the rooms all now feature soundproof windows. One of the hotel's most attractive features is the roof garden—again, not very large, but fine for enjoying an alfresco breakfast and a pleasant view. The Doria has a clone, the Hotel Amalfi, across the street, with the same amenities and some larger rooms with three beds. ⊠ *Via Merulana 4, Termini, 00185* ☎ *06/4465888* 🖨 *06/4465889* ⤴ *20 rooms* ⚘ *Cable TV, in-room safes, bar* ⊟ *AE, DC, MC, V* ⧉ *EP.*

**$–$$** 🖼 **Giuliana.** A friendly family operates this small, cozy residence with pride. The decor is unprepossessing, with 1960s modern furniture but guest rooms are large (if sparely furnished) and the tiled baths are shiny clean. Make sure to specify bath or shower when you make your reservation; it's one or the other. ⊠ *Via A. Depretis 70, Termini, 00184* ☎ *06/4880795* 🖨 *06/4824287* ⊕ *www.hotelgiuliana.com* ⤴ *11 rooms* ⚘ *In-room safes, minibars, cable TV, bar, parking (fee), no-smoking rooms; no a/c in some rooms* ⊟ *AE, MC, V* ⧉ *BP.*

**$–$$** 🖼 **Miami.** Rooms at this low-key hotel, in a dignified 19th-century building on Rome's busy Via Nazionale, are soundproof and tastefully styled with coordinated curtains, bedspreads, and wallpaper. The location, on main bus lines and near Termini Station and the Metro, is very central for sightseeing and shopping, although it's not ideal for eating out. Winter rates from November through February are a good bargain. Rooms on the courtyard are quieter. ⊠ *Via Nazionale 230, Termini, 00184* ☎ *06/4817180* 🖨 *06/484562* ⊕ *www.hotelmiami.com* ⤴ *42 rooms, 4 suites* ⚘ *Minibars, in-room safes, cable TV, bar, laundry service, parking (fee)* ⊟ *AE, D, DC, MC, V* ⧉ *BP.*

**$–$$** 🖼 **Montreal.** A good choice for budget travelers, this hotel is on a central avenue across the square from Santa Maria Maggiore, three blocks from Stazione Termini. The modest Montreal occupies three floors of an older building and has been totally renovated and offers fresh-looking, though small, rooms. The owner-managers are pleasant and helpful, and the neighborhood has plenty of reasonably priced restaurants.

✉ *Via Carlo Alberto 4, Termini, 00185* ☎ *06/4457797* 🖷 *06/4465522* 🌐 *www.hotelmontrealroma.com* 🛏 *30 rooms* ⚙ *In-room safes, mini-bars, cable TV, bar, laundry service, parking (fee), no-smoking rooms* 🖃 *AE, DC, MC, V* ⏧ *BP.*

★ **$–$$** 🖾 **Morgana.** Step into the richly marbled lobby and lounges done up in tartan wallpapers, antiquarian mezzotints, and framed landscape paintings and experience an elegance rare at this price level. Among Rome's lower-price hotels, the Morgana is relatively large, with 108 rooms. What that means here is a wide choice of amenities—four different categories of rooms, with corresponding prices, offer a chance to mix and match: modern or antique furniture, Jacuzzi tub or data port, or both. Ask and you shall receive—but no matter which guest room you land, you'll have few complaints about the decor, which is chic and charming in most instances. You would never use those adjectives to describe the immediate neighborhood—just a block removed from Stazione Termini—but you can't have everything. ✉ *Via Filippo Turati 33, Termini, 00185* ☎ *06/4467230* 🖷 *06/4469142* 🌐 *www.hotelmorgana.com* 🛏 *108 rooms* ⚙ *In-room safes, minibars, cable TV, bar, laundry service, concierge, no-smoking rooms* 🖃 *AE, DC, MC, V* ⏧ *BP.*

**$–$$** 🖾 **Villa delle Rose.** Although just two blocks away from the hustle and bustle of Termini Stazione, this is a comfortable retreat. The entrance is grand, set within a 19th-century palazzo with a rusticated base. Guest rooms here are a little old-fashioned, with simple furnishings dressed up by table lamps and faux-Persian rugs over the wall-to-wall carpeting, but the lobby is elegant. Have breakfast or tea in the small garden, blooming with bougainvillea, roses, and jasmine. ✉ *Via Vicenza 5, Termini, 00185* ☎ *06/4451795* 🖷 *06/4451639* 🌐 *www.villadellerose.it* 🛏 *39 rooms* ⚙ *Cable TV, bar, laundry service, free parking* 🖃 *AE, DC, MC, V* ⏧ *BP.*

**$** 🖾 **Adler.** This tiny pensione run by the same family for more than three decades provides a comfortable stay on a quiet street near the main station for a very good price. Ideal for families, Adler has six spacious rooms that sleep three, four, or five, as well as a single and a double. Rooms are basic, but impeccably clean. Worn but cozy chairs line the lobby, and in summer breakfast can be taken on the leafy courtyard balcony. ✉ *Via Modena 5, Termini, 00184* ☎ *06/484466* 🖷 *06/4880940* 🛏 *8 rooms* ⚙ *Bar, no-smoking rooms* 🖃 *AE, D, DC, MC, V* ⏧ *BP.*

**$** 🖾 **Aphrodite.** Given a recent design makeover, this hotel offers plenty of panache for the money. The mod, minimalist reception area strikes an elegant note (a little offkey since the immediate area here is right next door to Termini Station). Guest rooms are clean and friendly, adorned with colorful prints. Some rooms are on the spartan side, but the overall feel is fresh and modern. White walls and curtains lend a peaceful, almost monastic quality to the place. You can't beat it for value. ✉ *Via Marsala 90, Termini, 00185* ☎ *06/491096* 🖷 *06/491579* 🌐 *www.accommodationinrome.com/* 🛏 *40 rooms* ⚙ *Bar* 🖃 *AE, DC, MC, V* ⏧ *BP.*

**¢–$** 🖾 **Italia.** It looks and feels like a classic pension: low-budget with a lot of heart. A block off the very trafficky Via Nazionale, this friendly, family-run hotel offers inexpensive rooms with big windows, desks, parquet floors, and baths with faux-marble tiles, but the rooms aren't really the point. The price is, and it's made all the more tempting by a generous buffet breakfast and thoughtful touches like an ice machine and free wireless internet access. Ask for even lower midsummer rates. ⊠ *Via Venezia 18, Termini, 00184* ☎ *06/4828355* 🖷 *06/4745550* ⊕ *www.hotelitaliaroma.com* 🖃 *31 rooms* ⚐ *In-room safes, cable TV, bar, parking (fee), no smoking rooms* 🚭 *AE, MC, V* ⦿ *BP.*

¢–$ 🏨 **Romae.** In the better part of the Termini Station neighborhood, the Romae has the advantages of a strategic location—it's within walking distance of many sights, and handy to bus and subway lines. The pictures of Rome in the small lobby and breakfast room, the luminous white walls and light-wood furniture in the rooms, and the bright little baths all have a fresh look. Amenities such as satellite TV, in-room safe, and hair dryer are unusual for a hotel of this price. There are special rates and services for families. Some of the cheapest rooms in Rome can be found in the Romae's adjacent B&B facility—a pretty good deal at a €100 room rate. ⊠ *Via Palestro 49, Termini, 00185* ☎ *06/4463554* 🖷 *06/4463914* ⊕ *www.hotelromae.com* 🖃 *40 rooms* ⚐ *Restaurant, in-room safes, minibars, cable TV, bar, Internet, parking (fee), no-smoking rooms; no a/c in some rooms* 🚭 *AE, DC, MC, V* ⦿ *BP.*

# Trastevere

Once Raphael's Rome, this has been transformed from artist's haven to working-class ghetto to, currently, the home base of many of Rome's expats and exchange students. Hotels, squeezed into the neighborhood's former denizens' very modest buildings, tend toward the budget pension, although a few mid-range hotels set in stylishly-converted convents have sprung up in the last few years.

$$ 🏨 **Hotel Santa Maria di Trastevere.** A Trastevere treasure, this may be one

FodorśChoice of Rome's newer hotels but has a pedigree going back four centuries.

★ In parts ivy-covered, mansard-roofed, and rosy-brick-red, this erstwhile Renaissance-era convent has been transformed by Paolo and Valentina Vetere into a true charmer. Surrounded by towering tenements, the complex is centered around a monastic porticoed courtyard, oh-so-prettily set with orange trees—a lovely place for breakfast. The guest rooms are sweet and simple: a mix of brick walls, "cotto" tile floors, modern oak furniture, and stylishly floral bedspreds and curtains. Best of all, the location is *buonissimo*—just a few blocks from the Tiber and its *isola.* ⊠ *Vicolo del Piede 2, Trastevere, 00153* ☎ *06/5894626* 🖷 *06/5894815* ⊕ *www.htlsantamaria.com* 🖃 *20 rooms* ⚐ *In-room safes, minibars, cable TV* 🚭 *AE, MC, V* ⦿ *BP.*

★ $ 🏨 **Casa di Santa Francesca Romana.** Not far from some of the sweetest nooks and crannies of medieval Trastevere, this former monastery (once the Palazzo dei Ponziani) was built to honor the 15th-century St. Francesca Romana. A large complex, the hotel is centered around an impressive ochre-colored courtyard, set with potted trees and tables. Guest rooms are standard-issue and these cool white walls, tile floors, simple desks, and simpler desks won't win any design-awards. But for the money, this is a fabulous location and spectacular buy, made even attractive if you want to opt for the half- or full-board options available.

⊠ *Via dei Vasceillari 61, Trastevere, 00153* ☎ *06/5812125* 🖷 *06/5882408* ⊕ *http://web.tiscali.it/sfromana/* ⇆ *31 rooms, 4 suites* ♿ *Library; no room TVs.* ⊟ *MC, V* ⏹ *BP.*

$ 🏨 **Cisterna.** On a quiet street in the very heart of medieval Trastevere, this basic but comfortable hotel is ideally located for getting to know Rome's most authentic neighborhood, a favorite of artists and bohemians for decades. Beamed ceilings add a rustic touch, and there's a marble terrace-garden with a classical fountain. One room, number 40, has its own private terrace. ⊠ *Via della Cisterna 7–9, Trastevere, 00153* ☎ *06/5881852* 🖷 *06/65810091* ⇆ *18 rooms* ♿ *Cable TV* ⊟ *DC, MC, V* ⏹ *EP.*

$ 🏨 **Trastevere.** This tiny hotel captures the villagelike charm of the Trastevere district. The entrance hall features a mural of the famous Piazza di Santa Maria, a block away, and hand-painted Art Nouveau wall designs add a touch of graciousness throughout. Open medieval brickwork and a few antiques here and there complete the mood. Most rooms face Piazza San Cosimato, where there's an outdoor food market every morning except Sunday. ⊠ *Via Luciano Manara 24–25, Trastevere, 00153* ☎ *06/5814713* 🖷 *06/5881016* ⊕ *www.hoteltrastevere.net* ⇆ *19 rooms* ⊟ *AE, DC, MC, V* ⏹ *BP.*

¢–$ 🏨 **Carmel.** Rome's only kosher hotel sits across the Tiber from the main synagogue. Although its room furnishings are spartan, the staff is very friendly and there's a charming vine-covered terrace. There are two kitchens for use by guests keeping kosher, and prepared kosher meals can be arranged. Breakfast is offered in the snack bar next door. ⊠ *Via Goffredo Mameli 11, Trastevere, 00153* ☎ *06/5809921* 🖷 *06/5818853* ⊕ *www.hotelcarmel.it* ⇆ *10 rooms, 8 with bath, 1 suite* ♿ *In-room safes, parking (fee), no-smoking rooms* ⊟ *MC, V* ⏹ *EP.*

## Vatican

Although you won't be able to stay in Vatican City itself, the neighborhoods to the east of the city state host a wide range of hotels, from pilgrim-simple to cardinal-luxe. The Borgo, directly outside the Vatican walls, has medieval charm, but can be overrun by tourists. A ten-minute walk to the north lie residential streets and many of the hotels listed below, with a local flair and still within easy striking distance of St. Peter's.

$$–$$$$ 🏨 **Atlante Star.** The lush rooftop-terrace garden café and the Les Etoiles (the Stars) restaurant of this comfortable hotel near St. Peter's have a knockout view of the basilica and the rest of Rome. In a distinguished 19th-century building, the guest rooms are attractively decorated with striped silks and prints for an old-world atmosphere; many bathrooms have hot tubs. The friendly family management is attentive to guests' needs and takes pride in offering extra-virgin olive oil from its own trees in the country. A sister hotel, the **Atlante Garden**, just around the corner, has larger rooms at slightly lower rates. Just ask and the Atlante Star will pick you up at Fiumicino airport for free. ⊠ *Via Vitelleschi 34, Vatican, 00193* ☎ *06/6873233* 🖷 *06/6872300* ⊕ *www.atlantehotels.com* ⇆ *70 rooms, 15 suites* ♿ *Restaurant, in-room safes, minibars, cable TV, bar, laundry service, concierge, parking (fee), no-smoking rooms* ⊟ *AE, DC, MC, V* ⏹ *BP.*

**$$$** ⊞ **Giulio Cesare.** An aristocratic town house in the residential Prati district, the Giulio Cesare is a 10-minute walk across the Tiber from Piazza del Popolo—while close to the Vatican, it's rather far from the *centro istorico* and this probably means taxis to get back here late at night. It's beautifully run, with a friendly staff and a quietly luxurious air. The rooms are elegantly furnished, with chandeliers, thick rugs, floor-length drapes, and rich damasks in soft colors. Public rooms have Oriental carpets, old prints and paintings, marble fireplaces, and a grand piano. The buffet breakfast is a veritable banquet. ⊠ *Via degli Scipioni 287, Vatican, 00192* ☎ *06/3210751* 🖨 *06/3215129* ⊕ *www.venere.it/roma/giuliocesare* ⇝ *90 rooms* ⚬ *Bar, parking (fee)* ⊟ *AE, DC, MC, V* ⫴◎⫴ *BP.*

★ **$$$** ⊞ **Hotel Dei Mellini.** On the west bank of the Tiber between the Spanish Steps and St. Peter's Basilica, a three-minute stroll from Piazza del Popolo, this place has class to match its setting. The luxurious reception rooms are a welcome haven for weary sightseers, as antique prints and fresh flowers give warmth to the light-filled rooms. Guest rooms are sleek and sumptuous; grand drapes, wood-grain headboards, marble-top sinks, elegant chairs, and framed photos all make for ankle-deep luxury. Marble bathrooms complete the pampered feel. Free parking is available nearby. ⊠ *Via Muzio Clementi 81, Vatican, 00193* ☎*06/324771* 🖨 *06/32477801* ⊕ *www.hotelmellini.com* ⇝ *80 rooms* ⚬ *Restaurant, in-room safes, minibars, cable TV, bar, laundry service, no-smoking rooms* ⊟ *AE, DC, MC, V* ⫴◎⫴ *EP.*

**$$–$$$** ⊞ **Farnese.** Polished walnut antiques, linen sheets, and the occasional
FodorsChoice painted ceiling—it's all in the details here. An early-20th-century man-
★ sion, the Farnese is carefully authentic, preserving a polished Belle Epoque elegance that sits well with its well-traveled clientele. Add to this a comfortable sitting room you'll actually want to use and a roof garden with a view. It's also near the Metro and within walking distance of St. Peter's. ⊠ *Via Alessandro Farnese 30, Vatican, 00192* ☎ *06/ 3212553* 🖨 *06/3215129* ⇝ *23 rooms* ⚬ *Minibars, cable TV, bar, laundry service, concierge, free parking* ⊟ *AE, DC, MC, V* ⫴◎⫴ *EP.*

**$$–$$$** ⊞ **Residenza Paolo VI.** Set in a former monastery that is still an extrater-
FodorsChoice ritorial part of the Vatican and magnificently abutting Bernini's colon-
★ nade of St. Peter's Square, the Paolo VI (pronounced Paolo Sesto, Italian for Pope Paul VI) is unbeatably close to St. Peter's. Replete with a stone terrace that directly overlooks Bernini's 17th-century porticoes, this hotel enjoys one of the most spectacular perches in Rome. As for the decor, guest rooms are luxurious and comfortable and amazingly quiet. Within breathing distance of the residence of Benedict XVI, it's not surprising that the management here is devoutly Catholic, as you may gather from the framed portraits of the pope on the front desk and the daily prayer slipped under your door in lieu of a newspaper. But heaven can wait once you settle into your breakfast buffet on the wonderful roof terrace and drink in the view of Michelangelo's great dome. ⊠ *Via Paolo VI 29, Vatican, 00193* ☎ *06/68134108* 🖨 *06/6867428* ⊕ *www.residenzapaolovi. com* ⇝ *29 rooms* ⚬ *In-room safes, minibars, cable TV, bar, laundry service, parking (fee), no-smoking rooms* ⊟ *AE, D, MC, V* ⫴◎⫴ *BP.*

**$–$$** ⊞ **Amalia.** Handy to St. Peter's, the Vatican, and the Cola di Rienzo shopping district, this small hotel is crisp and smart with striped bedspreads and freshly painted walls. On several floors of a 19th-century building, its rooms are spacious for Rome, and marble bathrooms gleam (hair dryers included). The Ottaviano stop of Metro line A is a block away. ⊠ *Via Germanico 66, Vatican, 00192* ☎*06/39723356* ⌨*06/39723365* ⊕*www. hotelamalia.com* ↩ *31 rooms, 26 with bath, 1 suite* ♿ *In-room safes, minibars, laundry service, parking (fee), no-smoking rooms; no a/c in some rooms* ☰ *AE, DC, MC, V* ⧉ *BP.*

★ **$–$$** 🖼 **Sant'Anna.** In the picturesque old Borgo neighborhood in the shadow of St. Peter's, this fashionable small hotel has exceedingly stylish ample bedrooms with new wood-beam ceilings, designer fabrics, and comfy beds. The frescoes in the vaulted breakfast room and fountain in the courtyard add an individual touch. The marvelously decorated and spacious attic rooms have tiny terraces. ⊠ *Borgo Pio 133, Vatican, 00193* ☎ *06/68801602* ⌨ *06/68308717* ⊕ *www.hotelsantanna.com* ↩ *20 rooms* ♿ *Minibars, cable TV, in-room data ports, in-room safes, laundry service, parking (fee), no-smoking rooms* ☰ *AE, DC, MC, V* ⧉ *BP.*

**$** 🖼 **Alimandi.** On a side street a block from the Vatican Museums, this family-operated hotel offers excellent value in a neighborhood with moderately priced shops and restaurants. A spiffy lobby and ample lounges, a tavern, terraces, and roof gardens are some of the perks, as is an exercise room equipped with step machines and a treadmill. Rooms are spacious and well-furnished; many can accommodate extra beds. Needless to say the location here is quite far away from Rome's historic center. ⊠ *Via Tunisi 8, Vatican, 00192* ☎ *06/39723948* ⌨ *06/39723943* ⊕ *www.alimandi.it/* ↩ *35 rooms* ♿ *In-room safes, cable TV, gym, bar, free parking, no-smoking rooms* ☰ *AE, DC, MC, V* ⧉ *EP.*

**$** 🖼 **Gerber.** On a quiet side street eight blocks from the Vatican and across the river from Piazza del Popolo, this intimate, unpretentious hotel offers genuinely friendly service. Immaculately maintained throughout, it features a garden and sun terrace for breakfast or a relaxed moment. Simple rooms have pleasant, neutral-tone modern furnishings. ⊠ *Via degli Scipioni 241, Vatican, 00192* ☎ *06/3221001* ⌨ *06/3217048* ⊕ *www.hotelgerber.it* ↩ *23 rooms* ♿ *Minibars, cable TV, in-room safes, bar, parking (fee), laundry service* ☰ *AE, DC, MC, V* ⧉ *BP.*

**¢** 🖼 **San Giuseppe della Montagna.** This convent is just outside the Vatican walls, near the entrance to the Vatican Museums. Some of the guest rooms have three beds, and all have private bathrooms. There's no curfew; guests are given keys. ⊠ *Viale Vaticano 87, Vatican, 00165* ☎ *06/39723807* ⌨ *06/39721048* ↩ *15 rooms* ♿ *No a/c, no room TVs* ☰ *No credit cards* ⧉ *CP.*

## Via Veneto

If you're looking for Fellini's glamorous boulevard, packed with movie stars and the paparazzi who stalk them, you're about forty years too late. But Via Veneto retains a stately elegance, and a wide choice of large luxury hotels, that make it the clear choice for many business travelers. The American Embassy is here, and it's convenient to Villa Borghese, the Spanish Steps, and Rome's subway—Barberini station is at the bottom of the uphill-winding (and rather steep) street.

**$$$$** ⊞ **Barberini.** Here you can find about all you could ask for in a Rome hotel: charm, taste, and the good fortune to look out onto one of the best museums in town, Palazzo Barberini. The marble-floor lobby is light and welcoming, and upstairs each room is furnished with fixtures designed exclusively for the hotel. The breakfast buffet (not included in the price of the room) on the rooftop is in a league of its own: fresh, delicious, and copious. The creative management often has special deals for dinners, theater tickets, and the like on offer, so make sure to ask. ✉ *Via Rasella 3, Via Veneto, 00187* ☎ *06/4814993* 🖷 *06/4815211* ⊕ *www.hotelbarberini.com* ⇗ *31 rooms, 4 suites* ♿ *In-room safes, minibars, cable TV, bar, laundry service, parking (fee), no-smoking rooms* ⊟ *AE, DC, MC, V* ⍟*I BP.*

★ **$$$$** ⊞ **Eden.** Once the preferred haunt of Hemingway, Ingrid Bergman, and Fellini, this superlative hotel combines dashing elegance and stunning vistas of Rome with the warmth of Italian hospitality. Set atop a oh-my-weary-feet hill near the Villa Borghese (and a bit out of the historic center for serious sightseers), this hotel was opened in the late 19th century and quickly became famous for its balcony views and Roman splendor. After a multimillion dollar restoration in the 1990s by Lord Forte, you'll now dive deep here into the whoooooossh of luxury, with antiques, sumptuous Italian fabrics, linen sheets, and marble baths competing for your attention. Even the most basic room here is elegantly designed (which is as it should be if your basic double room goes for some 700 euros). Banquette window seats, rich mahogany furniture, soaring ceilings, Napoléon-Trois sofas are just some of the allurements here. Topping it all off, literally, is one of Rome's most fabled "food-with-a-view" restaurants, La Terrazza dell'Eden, whose perch offers views that are truly panaromantic (the restaurant may offer food that is 25 euros per blink but you can enjoy almost the same vistas for the price of a Campari on the rooftop bar—remember to dress up all the same). ✉ *Via Ludovisi 49, Via Veneto, 00187* ☎ *06/478121* 🖷 *06/4821584* ⊕ *www.hotel-eden.it* ⇗ *108 rooms, 13 suites* ♿ *Restaurant, in-room safes, minibars, cable TV, gym, bar, laundry service, concierge, parking (fee), no-smoking rooms* ⊟ *AE, DC, MC, V* ⍟*I EP.*

**$$$$** ⊞ **Majestic.** Mirroring the famous curve of Via Veneto, this was built as Rome's first luxury hotel in 1889, and it's still preening with luxurious furnishings, spacious, light-filled rooms, up-to-date accessories, and white marble bathrooms. There are authentic antiques in the public rooms, and the excellent restaurant looks like a Victorian conservatory. If that's not enough *dolce vita* for you (a scene from the famed Fellini film was set outside the hotel), some suites have whirlpool baths. The Ninfa grill-café on street level is a good spot to watch the Italian rich and famous watch each other. ✉ *Via Veneto 50, 00187* ☎ *06/421441* 🖷 *06/4880984* ⊕ *www. hotelmajestic.com* ⇗ *85 rooms, 13 suites* ♿ *2 restaurants, in-room data ports, in-room safes, minibars, cable TV, bar, laundry service, concierge, parking (fee), no-smoking rooms* ⊟ *AE, DC, MC, V* ⍟*I EP.*

**$$$$** ⊞ **Regina Baglioni.** A former playground of kings and poets, the Regina Baglioni is sumptuously decorated in neoclassical style and enjoys a commanding location on Via Veneto, handy to the street's dolce vita cafés and the Villa Borghese. The lobby is royal in its elegance, replete with chandeliers, grand staircases, red carpets, and gigantic statues. The guest rooms continue the palatial theme in their appointments, with Oriental carpets, luxury brocades, wall silks, and period antiques. Le Grazie restaurant is notable for its fine cuisine and equally fine table settings. The seventh-floor suites enjoy superb views of the Eternal City. ⊠ *Via Veneto 72, 00187* ☎ *06/421111* ⊟ *06/42012130* ⊕ *www.baglionihotels.com* ⤳ *123 rooms, 7 suites* ⟂ *Restaurant, in-room safes, minibars, cable TV, bar, laundry service, concierge, parking (fee)* ▤ *AE, DC, MC, V* ⑩ *EP.*

**$$$$** ⊞ **Westin Excelsior.** Ablaze with lights at night, this seven-layer-cake hotel is topped off by its famous corner cupola, a landmark nearly as famous as the American Embassy palazzo sitting next door. Once a herding pen for princes and maharajahs, the Excelsior today is the hotel of choice for visiting diplomats, celebrities, and, well, American business conferences. But it remains of the breed of Via Veneto old-fashioned hotels that really put the luxe in deluxe: every corner is lavished with mirrors, moldings, Oriental rugs, crystal chandeliers, and huge, baroque floral arrangements. Guest rooms have elegant drapery, marble baths, top-quality linens, and big, firm beds. While traditional, refined, and luxurious, the cheaper rooms here don't really offer a lot of bang for the buck, so spring for the better ones, or settle elsewhere. The hotel has an array of restaurants and bar, none more famous than Doney's—once the epicenter of Fellini's paparazzi—which is now being restored and is due to open in late 2005. ⊠ *Via Veneto 125, 00187* ☎ *06/47081* ⊟ *06/4826205* ⊕ *www.westin.com/excelsiorrome* ⤳ *286 rooms, 35 suites* ⟂ *Restaurant, in-room safes, minibars, cable TV, indoor pool, gym, bar, laundry service, concierge, no-smoking rooms* ▤ *AE, DC, MC, V* ⑩ *EP.*

**$$$–$$$$** ⊞ **Aleph.** Wondering where the beautiful people are? Look no further
**Fodor's**Choice than the Aleph, the most unfalteringly fashionable of Rome's new class
★ of design hotels. The just-this-side-of-kitsch theme here is Dante's Divine Comedy, and you can walk the line between heaven and hell through the Angelo bar, the red-red-red Sin restaurant, and Paradise spa. The shiny blood-red-and-black color scheme looks great with your sunglasses, darling, but guest rooms are thankfully less threatening, in subdued neutral tones with wood furniture, made galleryesque by giant black-and-white photos of Rome. As many will guess, this hotel was über-designed by Adam Tihany (who also did the honors at Rome's Exedra). His relentless, in-your-face decors throw everything into the mix, from Shogun suits to his signature red twigs to shirred silk lamps. Happily, he likes to poke fun at himself (clothes hooks shaped like devil's horns; tiny TVs set in the bathroom floors in front of your toilet), and earnestly cool staff notwithstanding, the Aleph doesn't take itself as seriously as might be feared. When old Rome feels, well, old—this is something new. ⊠ *Via San Basilio 15, 00187* ☎ *06/422901* ⊟ *06/42290000* ⊕ *www.boscolohotels. com* ⤳ *94 rooms, 2 suites* ⟂ *Restaurant, bar, in-room safes, minibars, cable TV, spa, laundry service, no-smoking rooms* ⑩ *EP.*

**$$–$$$$** ⊞ **Imperiale.** Inside a handsome stone palazzo on Via Veneto, polished parquet floors, airy fabrics, and light-color walls set a gracious tone. The guest rooms are decorated in a classical style that's in keeping with the building itself. The spacious dining room serves first-class cuisine, and there's a covered gazebo restaurant on Via Veneto. ⊠ *Via Veneto*

*24, 00185* ☎ *06/4826351* 🖨 *06/4742583* 🛏 *96 rooms, 2 suites* ♨ *2 restaurants, minibars, in-room safes, cable TV, bar, concierge, parking (fee), no-smoking rooms* ☰ *AE, DC, MC, V* ⦿ *BP.*

**$$$** 🏨 **Marriott Grand Hotel Flora.** This handsome hotel, at the top of Via Veneto next to the Villa Borghese park, is something of a beacon on the Rome landscape, not least because it's painted deep pink. Opinions may differ about the color choice, but there's little doubt that Grand Hotel Flora's standard of excellence is among the highest in the city. No expense has been spared in decorating the rooms and suites. Each one is unique, and carefully chosen antiques grace them all; the bathrooms are the last word in ablution chic. There's a lovely roof-garden restaurant on the seventh floor and a large conference hall. ⊠ *Via Veneto 191, 00187* ☎ *06/489929* 🖨 *06/4820359* ⊕ *www.marriotthotels.com* 🛏 *127 rooms, 24 suites* ♨ *2 restaurants, in-room safes, minibars, cable TV, bar, laundry service, concierge, business services, free parking* ☰ *AE, DC, MC, V* ⦿ *EP.*

**$$$** 🏨 **Victoria.** Oriental rugs, oil paintings, and fresh flowers are scattered throughout the lobbies, and guest rooms, while heavy on traditional-style wallpapers, are well furnished with armchairs and other amenities. American businesspeople, who prize the hotel's personalized service, restful atmosphere, and elegantly designed restaurant and bar, are frequent guests. Some upper rooms and the roof terrace overlook the majestic pines of the Villa Borghese. ⊠ *Via Campania 41, Via Veneto, 00187* ☎ *06/473931* 🖨 *06/4871890* ⊕ *www.hotelvictoriaroma.com* 🛏 *110 rooms* ♨ *Restaurant, in-room safes, minibars, cable TV, bar, meeting rooms* ☰ *AE, DC, MC, V* ⦿ *EP.*

**$$–$$$** 🏨 **Alexandra.** An unassuming establishment with an old-fashioned feel, the Alexandra has been run by the same family for nearly a century. On brassy Via Veneto, its modest demeanor is something of an anomaly. The reception rooms here look as though they've remained untouched since King Vittorio Emanuele II's time, but the bedrooms are airy and spotlessly clean. Breakfast is served in a sunny conservatory. All in all, it's a great bargain for the pricey Via Veneto district. ⊠ *Via Veneto 18, 00187* ☎ *06/4881943* 🖨 *06/4871804* 🛏 *60 rooms* ♨ *Restaurant, minibars, cable TV, laundry service, parking (fee), no-smoking rooms* ☰ *AE, DC, MC, V* ⦿ *BP.*

**$$** 🏨 **Julia.** Tucked away behind Piazza Barberini down a sinuous cobbled lane, this small establishment welcomes you with a reception area that is surprisingly modern and straightforward. The guest rooms are more traditional, although they're short on character. However, they're marvelously spacious and clean. Guests have access to free, wireless, high-speed Internet. ⊠ *Via Rasella 29, Via Veneto, 00187* ☎ *06/4881637* 🖨 *06/4817044* ⊕ *www.hoteljulia.it* 🛏 *33 rooms, 30 with bath, 2 suites* ♨ *In-room safes, bar, laundry service, no-smoking rooms* ☰ *AE, DC, MC, V* ⦿ *BP.*

**★ $$** 🏨 **La Residenza.** Mainly Americans frequent this cozy hotel in a converted town house near Via Veneto. Rooms are basic, comfortable, and tasteful (although single rooms are windowless), but the real charm of the hotel is found in its bar, terrace, and lounges (smoking and no-smoking) adorned with warm wallpaper and love seats that invite you to make yourself at home. Rates include a generous American-style buffet breakfast and an in-house movie every night. ⊠ *Via Emilia 22, Via Veneto, 00187* ☎ *06/4880789* 🖷 *06/485721* ⊕ *www.thegiannettihotelsgroup. com* ⬥ *28 rooms* ⚬ *In-room safes, minibars, cable TV, bar, laundry service* ▤ *AE, MC, V* ⊙ *BP.*

$$ ▦ **Nuovo Hotel Quattro Fontane.** The opulence and glory of ancient Rome have inspired the decoration at this peaceful hotel. The reception hall's draped curtains, suits of armor, and banquet-hall ceilings leave you in a very evocative state of mind. The bedrooms are understated by comparison, and the dining room has a monastic simplicity about it that acts as a nice contrast. ⊠ *Via 4 Fontane, Via Veneto, 00184* ☎ *06/ 4884480* 🖷 *06/4814936* ⬥ *36 rooms* ⚬ *Restaurant, bar, business services* ▤ *AE, DC, MC, V* ⊙ *BP.*

## Beyond the City Center

★ $$$$ ▦ **Castello della Castelluccia.** Ten miles from the hustle and bustle of Rome's city center, this beautifully renovated 12th-century castle is an oasis of calm set in a small wooded park. The original structure has been preserved intact, complete with crumbling watchtower (now a three-level suite); all that's missing is a medieval knight clinking down the echoing stone halls. Guest rooms are luxuriously appointed, with inlaid-wood antiques and four-poster beds; a few have marble fireplaces, and two have giant, tiled hot-tub alcoves. There's shuttle bus service to central Rome. ⊠ *Via Carlo Cavino, Località La Castelluccia, 00123* ☎ *06/ 30207041* 🖷 *06/30207110* ⊕ *www.lacastelluccia.com* ⬥ *18 rooms, 6 suites* ⚬ *Restaurant, room service, in-room data ports, minibars, cable TV, pool, spa, horseback riding, bar, laundry service, meeting room, free parking, some pets allowed* ▤ *AE, D, MC, V* ⊙ *BP.*

$$$$ ▦ **Cavalieri Hilton.** Though the Cavalieri is outside the city center, distance has its advantages, one of them being the magnificent view over Rome (ask for a room facing the city), and another, that elusive element of more central Roman hotels: space. Occupying a vast area atop modern Rome's highest hill, this oasis of good taste often feels more like a resort than a city hotel. Central to its appeal, particularly in summer, is a terraced garden that spreads out from an Olympic-size pool and smart poolside restaurant and café; legions of white-clothed cushioned lounge chairs are scattered throughout the greenery, so there's always a place to sun yourself. Inside, spacious rooms, often with large balconies, are done up in striped damask, puffy armchairs, and such Hiltonesque amenities as a "pillow menu"—get comfy, princess. If you can tear yourself away, the city center is just a 15-minute complimentary shuttle bus ride away. The strawberry on top: La Pergola restaurant (see the Dining chapter) is renowned as one of Rome's very best. ⊠ *Via Cadlolo 101, Monte Mario, 00136* ☎ *06/35091* 🖷 *06/35092241* ⊕ *www.cavalieri-hilton.com* ⬥ *357 rooms, 17 suites* ⚬ *2 restaurants, tennis court, 2 pools (1 indoor), health club, hair salon, spa, bar* ▤ *AE, DC, MC, V* ⊙ *EP.*

$$$$ ▦ **Parco dei Principi.** The 1960s-era facade of this large, seven-story hotel contrasts with the turn-of-the-20th-century Italian court decor, and the extensive botanical garden, right on the border of the exclusive Parioli district and the Villa Borghese park, adds an outdoorsy touch. The result is a combination of traditional elegance and contemporary pleasure:

picture windows in every room with views over an ocean of green, sur-mounted by St. Peter's dome; a wonderful free-form swimming pool; a piano bar with stained glass and carved walnut appointments; and chamber music in the garden. ✉ *Via G. Frescobaldi 5, Parioli, 00198* ☎ *06/854421* 🖷 *06/8845014* ⊕ *www.parcodeiprincipi.com* 🛏 *160 rooms, 20 suites ⚒ 3 restaurants, pool, health club, bar, piano bar, business services, parking (fee)* ▭ *AE, DC, MC, V* ⟊ *BP.*

**$$$–$$$$**   🏨 **Duke Hotel.** This luxurious establishment is in the heart of the chic Parioli district. The Villa Glori and Villa Borghese parks flank it, creating the feel of a country club in the midst of the city. Beautiful furniture and the building's original features have been skillfully thrown into relief by plain, off-white walls and light-filled rooms. There's a free shuttle bus to the city center. ✉ *Via Archimede 69, Parioli, 00197* ☎ *06/367221* 🖷 *06/36004104* ⊕ *www.thedukehotel.com* 🛏 *64 rooms, 14 suites ⚒ Restaurant, in-room safes, minibars, in-room data ports, bar, laundry service, concierge, business services, 3 meeting rooms, parking (fee), no-smoking rooms* ▭ *AE, D, DC, MC, V* ⟊ *BP.*

**$$$–$$$$**   🏨 **Lord Byron.** Once the top hangout for Rome's 1990s wheeler-dealers and yacht-brokers, currently the retreat for Berlusconi's courtiers, the Lord Byron has been a byword for decadent chic for some time. When this villa first opened (with a rather overrestored exterior) it was Rome's first boutique hotel and still retains much of that jewel-like charm inside. Hanging on the elegant white walls, a painted bevy of Divinely Deco beauties eye you as you enter the intimate public salons, where sidetables are adorned with objets d'art and art books. This is a private world where carpets are deep and diamonds are big, so you won't have too much fun here if you don't find cheek-kissing second nature. The downstairs bar—a magnificent piece of cabinetry—is a conversation piece. Nearby is the new Sapori restaurant, whose in-house French chef earns consistently high marks. Upstairs, modern and antique styles combine to create highly polished opulence in the guest rooms. Surrounded by the twittering of birds in the posh and pricey Parioli district, the Lord Byron feels like a small country hotel, or better, a small country manor where you are the lord. ✉ *Via G. de Notaris 5, Parioli, 00197* ☎ *06/3220404* 🖷 *06/3220405* ⊕ *www.lordbyronhotel.com* 🛏 *23 rooms, 9 suites ⚒ Restaurant, in-room safes, minibars, cable TV, bar, lounge, laundry service, concierge, parking (fee), no-smoking rooms* ▭ *AE, DC, MC, V* ⟊ *BP.*

**$$**   🏨 **Hotel Villa Borghese.** There's a reason why this place is such a great value: it's a little farther out of the city center than comparable hotels. Having said that, it overlooks Villa Borghese, the city's most famous park, and all the wonderful Borghese museums are just a short walk away. Antique furniture and paintings ranging from modern to classical are found throughout; the walls are predominantly white, giving the hotel a light, airy feel. Avoid the bedrooms that have a bathroom built into a "box" inside the room itself; make sure yours is truly en suite. ✉ *Via Pinciana 31, Parioli, 00198* ☎ *06/85300919* 🖷 *06/8414100* 🛏 *32 rooms ⚒ Bar* ▭ *AE, DC, MC, V* ⟊ *BP.*

**$–$$**   🏨 **Villa Glori.** This unassuming midsize hotel is a bit off the beaten path, but the neighborhood has lots of charm and it's only a 10-minute tram ride to the historic center. It's on a quiet cul-de-sac that, together with the next private street over, is called *piccola Londra* (little London) for its architectural style that's unique in all of Rome. The interior is pleasant: clean and homey, with furnishings in blond wood and beige leather, with a Jacuzzi or oversize shower in every room. There's an American-style buffet breakfast. ⊠ *Viale del Vignola 28, Parioli, 00196* ☎ *06/3227658* 🖷 *06/3219495* ⊕ *www.villaglori.it* 🛏 *52 rooms* ⚫ *In-room safes, cable TV, bar, laundry service, parking (fee), no-smoking rooms* ⊟ *AE, DC, MC, V* ⌶◉⌶ *BP.*

## Residence Hotels

If you want the independence offered by an apartment, consider staying in a residence hotel. Residence hotels have fully equipped kitchens and offer linens, laundry, and cleaning services. Most are available for monthly rentals; costs for an apartment for two range from about €1,300 for a week to €2,600 per month.

**$–$$$** 🖬 **Residence Aldrovandi.** Red-carpet treatment indeed: a sweeping marble staircase makes the entryway of this lobby feel like a very elegant mansion. In fact, it's a former women's college in the swish Parioli district, now renovated to small apartments with old-fashioned furnishings, including functional kitchens, and wonderful views over Villa Borghese. A concierge and maids take care of organizing your life and cleaning it up, but where you'll really feel like a Roman high roller is next door, at the Hotel Aldrovandi, where Residence guests can use the pool. ⊠ *Via U. Aldrovandi 11, Parioli, 00197* ☎ *06/3221430* 🖷 *06/3222181* ⊕ *www.aldrovandiresidence.it* 🛏 *41 apartments* ⚫ *In-room safes, kitchens, cable TV, laundry service* ⊟ *AE, DC, MC, V.*

**$–$$$** 🖬 **Residence Ripetta.** This is the most central of all of Rome's residence hotels, a renovated Baroque convent near Piazza del Popolo. Compact apartments are furnished in smart contemporary style that takes advantage of the original 17th-century structure, and there are meeting facilities for business travelers. The courtyard is lovely, but even better is the roof terrace, where you can sit under umbrellas to rest and relax away from the hustle and bustle outside. ⊠ *Via di Ripetta 231, Piazza di Spagna, 00186* ☎ *06/3231144* 🖷 *06/3203959* ⊕ *www.ripetta.it* 🛏 *69 apartments* ⚫ *Kitchens, cable TV, concierge, minibars, meeting rooms, parking (fee)* ⊟ *AE, DC, MC, V.*

**$$** 🖬 **Palazzo al Velabro.** One of Rome's best-kept secrets, Palazzo al Velabro offers refined comfort right in the heart of the Boario Forum, adjacent to the Arch of Janus. Suites, named after Roman emperors, gods and kings, are outfitted with Italian-modern dining and living areas, with touches of marble and framed prints to remind you you're in Rome. The minimum stay here is seven nights. ⊠ *Via del Velabro 16, Ghetto, 00186* ☎ *06/6792758* 🖷 *06/6793790* ⊕ *www.velabro.it* 🛏 *34 apartments* ⚫ *Kitchens, cable TV, free parking, no smoking rooms, laundry service* ⊟ *AE, DC, MC, V* ⌶◉⌶ *EP.*

Fodor'sChoice
★

# Nightlife & the Arts

**4**

Updated by
Dana Klitzberg

**AS THE FAMOUS ITALIAN FILM DIRECTOR FEDERICO FELLINI** showed us over and over again, Roman nightlife has been setting trends since time immemorial—and being a native son, he would know. *Fellini Satyricon* focused on those Lucullan all-night banquets (and some more naughty entertainments) of the days of the emperors; *La Dolce Vita* immortalized the nightclubs and *paparazzi* of the city's Hollywood-on-the-Tiber era. Many people, however, know that Rome, the city, is entertainment enough. It's piazzas, fountains, and delicately colored *palazzi* make impressive backdrops for the living theater of the vivacious city, with a *fortissimo* of motor vehicles. It has learned to make the most of its spectacular cityscape, transforming its most beautiful places into settings for the performing arts, outdoors in summer and in splendid palaces and churches in winter. When performances are held at such locations as Villa Celimontana, Piazza Trinità dei Monti, the Baths of Caracalla, or the church of Sant'Ignazio, the venue often steals the show. Of all the performing arts, music is what Rome does best to entertain people until the wee hours, whether it be opera or jazz or disco. Theater, and especially the cinema, is a big draw, particularly for Italian-language speakers. But the way most Romans (and visitors) spend an enjoyable evening is late-night café-sitting in a trendy or traditional spot, in gorgeous piazzas, watching the colorful crowds parade by—it's great fun, even if you don't speak the language. Little wonder Fellini made people-watching into an art form in his famous films.

# THE ARTS

In the decades leading up to the 2000 Jubilee celebrations it was accurate to say that Romans took their culture rather distractedly, but after left-leaning mayor Francesco Rutelli took office in the early 1990s, the arts have been promoted and sponsored like never before. Rutelli's successor, Walter Veltroni, has continued to support the trend. In 2002 Rome gained a new concert hall, designed by world-famous Italian architect Renzo Piano. It offers what the city long lacked: a high-tech, high-capacity venue for hosting international orchestras, musicians, and vocalists. Beyond the formal surroundings of the Parco della Musica complex, most of Rome's cultural offerings happen in smaller venues peppered throughout the city; some of them are staged at outdoor venues during the warmer months. (For all outdoor events in the evening, it's wise to bring a jacket or sweater and something to cover your legs—Roman nights can be cool). Events generally are poorly publicized; keep your eyes peeled for the various posters pasted on walls, columns, and scaffolding around the city, as these announce many of the bigger events in town. Reading listings in newspapers and specialized publications helps as well.

The most comprehensive listings of what's going on in the city (movies, museum exhibitions, concerts, sporting and cultural events) are in the weekly *roma c'è* booklet, which comes out every Wednesday. It has a short English-language section at the back. *Time Out Rome* is a monthly publication that gives comprehensive event schedules as well as editors' picks; listings are mainly in Italian (with a small summary in English) but are easy to decipher. Schedules of events are also published in the daily newspapers, in the *Trovaroma* Thursday supplement of *La Repubblica* newspaper, in the *Guest in Rome* booklet distributed free at many hotel desks, and in fliers available at Azienda di Promozione Turistica di Roma (APT) offices and city tourist information kiosks. A biweekly English-language periodical, *Wanted in Rome,* available at many newsstands, has good coverage of events in the arts. Look for posters outside churches announcing free concerts and recitals of religious music. The RomaEuropa Festival, which runs from September to the end of November, is a multivenue avant-garde performing-arts program (see ⊕ www.romaeuropa.net for more details). For a schedule of the outdoor concerts, movies (some in English), and other cultural events that make up the rich and varied Estate Romana festival, ask for information at a tourist office or log on to ⊕ www.estateromana.it.

Depending on the venue, concert tickets can cost between €7 and €50, and as much as several hundred euro for an exclusive, sold-out event. Often, you can find seating that is nonreserved (identified in Italian as *posti non numerati*). Inquire about this when you buy the tickets; you may have to arrive early to get a good seat. Procure opera and concert tickets in advance at the box office, or try just before the performance. **Roman Reference** (✉ Via de' Capocci 94, Santa Maria Maggiore ☎ 06/48903612 ⊕ www.romanreference.com) is basically a business that organizes short-term apartment rentals but is also happy to provide many types of personalized services for tourists, including online ticket reservations for events in Rome and other parts of Italy. Tickets for major events are usually handled by **Orbis** (✉ Piazza Esquilino 37, Santa Maria Maggiore ☎ 06/4744776), a multipurpose ticket agency. **Hello Ticket** (☎ 06/47825710), in the "Ala Mazzoniana" section of Termini train station, sells tickets for concerts and theater events. **Box Office** (✉ Viale Giulio Cesare 88, Prati ☎ 06/37500375) sells concert tickets from Monday to Saturday.

## Dance

One cultural category in which Rome *doesn't* excel is dance. Throughout the year, there are some small dance companies, both from within Italy and from abroad, that give performances in various theaters, but it seems most of the headlining companies prefer Milan, Florence, Bologna, Cremona, Naples—almost anywhere but Rome. If you keep a diligent watch on the key venues, however, you can find some performances to satisfy your longing for live dance. The **Rome Opera Ballet** gives regular performances at its home base, Teatro dell'Opera, although despite aging ballet mistress Carla Fracci at its helm, the company is not up to the caliber of other urban ballet companies around the world. Still, they perform many of the classics, sometimes with leading international guest stars. In summer, performances move to outdoor venues like the lovely Baths of Caracalla. Most of its performances are at **Teatro dell'-Opera** (✉ Piazza Beniamino Gigli 8, Termini ☎ 06/481601, 06/48160255 tickets). **Teatro Olimpico** (✉ Piazza Gentile da Fabriano 17, Stadio Olimpico ☎ 06/3265991) is the venue for contemporary dance companies, visiting international ballet companies, and touring Broaday shows (like

*Stomp*). From June to August, the gardens of the **Museo Nazionale degli Strumenti Musicali** (✉ Piazza di Santa Croce in Gerusalemme 9/a, San Giovanni ☎ 06/70300048) are the setting of a festival of classical and contemporary dance—with great variety and relatively high standards.

## Film

Rome has dozens of movie houses that screen international films, but beware: Italians will proudly tell you that they have the best dubbing artists in the world, but that's because it seems they dub more films here than in any other country! If you want to see an English-language movie, or a non-Italian movie, it will almost never be subtitled. Look for "V.O." in a movie listing, which means *versione originale* (original version) indicating that the film will be shown in its original language. For programs and show times for films, see the entertainment pages of daily newspapers, *roma c'è,* or Rome's English-language publications. Or check on line at (⊕ www.trovacinema.it) for all the films playing around the city. Tickets range in price from €4.50 for matinees and some weekdays up to €8 for weekend evenings. The high-tech and comfort-

★ able **Metropolitan** (✉ Via del Corso 7, Piazza di Spagna ☎ 06/32600500) is refurbished and has four screens. It dedicates one of its screens to English-language films from September to June. It's also right near Piazza del Popolo, which makes it good for post-shopping entertainment. Here you can prebook with a credit card and pick up your tickets from machines inside the cinema. **Warner Village Moderno** (✉ Piazza della Repubblica 45–46, Termini ☎ 06/47779202), which is well located and easily accessible, has five screens. One screen shows English-language films. The **Alcazar** (✉ Via Merry del Val 14, Trastevere ☎ 06/5880099) has movies in their original language with Italian subtitles on Monday only (although even then it requires checking to make sure the film, in its original version, has in fact arrived). The **Nuovo Olimpia** (✉ Via in Lucina 16/b, Piazza di Spagna ☎ 06/6861068) is just off Via del Corso, and features classic and current films often in their original language. Wednesday night tickets are half-price. In mid-September many of Rome's movie theaters take part in the **Da Venezia a Roma festival** (⊕ www.agisanec.lazio.it), which shows all the films just shown at the Venice film festival, often in their original versions. Lucky visitors in past seasons were able to see films like *Memento* and *Lost in Translation* a good 6–18 months before they became indie sensations in the U.S. Check out the local press or the Web site for more details.

## Fine Arts

Rome is not a city known for innovative exhibitions; the churches and permanent collections in its many museums are the star artistic attractions. Nonetheless, the **Palazzo delle Esposizioni** (✉ Via Nazionale 194, Termini ☎ 06/48941230 ⊕ www.palazzoesposizioni.it) often stages worthwhile shows. It's closed for restoration work until late 2005. The **Chiostro del Bramante** (✉ Via della Pace 5, Piazza Navona ☎06/68809098, 06/68809035 tickets ⊕ www.chiostrodelbramante.it) is a beautiful smaller venue attached to the evocative church and cloister of Santa Maria della Pace, which was renovated and transformed into a cultural center and hosts some of the most interesting shows in town. Past shows in this impressive space designed by Bramante, Renaissance architect of St. Peter's, have included Jean-Michel Basquiat, Giacomo Balla, and Keith Haring. The **Acquario Romano** (⊠ Piazza M. Fanti 47, near Stazione Termini ☎ 06/4468616) is a restored 19th-century aquarium open to the public for special shows and concerts. Academic institutions such as the **British School** (⊠ Via Gramsci 61, Parioli ☎ 06/478141) often host special exhibitions and free lectures by visiting professors. The **American Academy** (⊠ Via Angelo Masina 5, on the Janiculum Hill, Trastevere ☎ 06/58461 ⊕ www.aarome.org) has shows and lectures by internationally renowned artists, architects, writers, and photographers, as well as by scholars in residence. The **MACRO** (⊠ Via Reggio Emilia 54, Piazza Fiume ☎ 06/67107900) is a redesigned city-owned gallery in a former brewery, and it's definitely worth a look for its funky design, its own collection of contemporary art, and for its exhibitions.

# Music

## Classical

Since 2002 Rome finally has had its very own state-of-the art auditorium a 10-minute tram ride north of Piazza del Popolo—the Parco della Musica (or Music Park), splashed over the pages of glossy magazines everywhere. However, if you prefer smaller or quirkier venues, Rome does not disappoint. Classical music concerts take place at numerous places throughout the city, and you're likely to see memorable performances in smaller halls and churches, often for free. This is true particularly at Christmas and Easter, especially busy concert seasons in Rome. Some churches that frequently host concerts are Sant'Ivo alla Sapienza, San Francesco a Ripa, and San Paolo entro le Mura. But one of the charming things about Rome is that, with all the little side streets tucked behind quiet piazzas, not to mention the nearly 1,000 churches throughout the Eternal City, it's quite easy to stumble upon a choir rehearsing, or a chorus performing for just a few churchgoers. Sometimes all it takes is some wandering around, and serendipitous luck, to trip over a memorable concert experience.

**Fodor's**Choice ★ Designed by famed architect Renzo Piano, the **Auditorium-Parco della Musica** (⊠ Viale Pietro de Coubertin 30, Flaminio ☎ 06/80241, 06/68801044 information and tickets ⊕ www.musicaperroma.it) features three halls with nearly perfect acoustics—this may have something to do with the fact that their shapes are like giant turtle shells (*Condé Nast Traveler* nicely described them as "armadillo-like"). The auditoria—there's also a large courtyard to be used for major performances—host major classical, jazz, and pop concerts, not to mention dance troups and cultural festivals. Acts range from The Manhattan Transfer, Norah Jones, and Diana Ross to local-turned-national pop talent Alex Britti, to major chamber ensembles—even a cultural Thai festival featuring music, crafts, massage, and culinary demonstrations. A major concert series is organized year-round by the **Accademia di Santa Cecilia** (Concert hall and box office ⊠ Via della Conciliazione 4, San Pietro ☎ 06/68801044), featuring Rome's Orchestra dell'Accademia di Santa Cecilia and frequent guest soloists. The orchestra also performs at the Auditorium-Parco della Musica. The Accademia Filarmonica Romana concerts are performed at the **Teatro Olimpico** (✉ Piazza Gentile da Fabriano 17, Flaminio ☎ 06/3265991, 06/3201752 information). The internationally respected **Oratorio del Gonfalone** (✉ Via del Gonfalone 32/a, Campo de' Fiori ☎ 06/6875952) series focuses on Baroque music ★ in an exquisite setting. **Il Tempietto** (✉ Area Archeologica del Palatino, Cortile di San Teodoro, Via di San Teodoro 7, Circo Massimo ☎ 06/87131590) organizes music festivals and concerts throughout the year. Depending on the venue, tickets run from about €10 to €30.

From June to August, the courtyard of the Basilica di San Clemente hosts the **New Opera Festival** (☎ 340/0880077 ⊕ www.newoperafestivaldiroma. com), an Italo-American project to raise money for young musicians, with a varied program that often includes the likes of Mozart, Handel, Verdi, and Puccini. The Renaissance-era **Chiostro del Bramante** (✉ Vicolo della Pace 2, Piazza Navona ☎ 06/68809098) has a summer concert series. The **Orto Botanico** (✉ Largo Cristina di Svezia 23/a, Trastevere ☎ 06/6868441), off Via della Lungara in Trastevere, has a summer concert series with a beautiful, verdant backdrop. Look for posters outside churches announcing free concerts, particularly at the church of **Sant'Ignazio** (✉ Piazza Sant'Ignazio, Pantheon ☎ 06/6794560), which often hosts concerts in a spectacularly frescoed setting.

## Rock, Pop & Jazz

Local and smaller-act rock, pop, and jazz concerts are frequent in Rome, although big-name acts come through less frequently—almost exclusively during warmer weather, although even these performances may not be well advertised. Some locales are outside the city center, and sometimes as far as Tivoli, so it's worth asking about transportation *before* you buy your tickets. The **Estate Romana** (Roman Summer) program, organized by the local and regional governments, has been growing every year (corresponding with the increasing number of Romans who stay in town during July and August). The program now includes a diverse offering of well-publicized and well-organized cultural events, most set outdoors and all free or reasonably priced. Events spread from the center of town to the periphery and run from early June to early September. They include music of every sort, as well as outdoor cinema, theater, and other events, such as book fairs and guided tours of some of Rome's monuments by night. Mayor Veltroni has really made the push for important music acts to give free concerts, and the crowds at these gigs prove that music is, in fact, an international language. James Taylor recently gave a heartfelt free performance in lovely Piazza del Popolo, and the summers of 2003 and 2004 saw record crowds fill the Via dei Fori Imperiali, from Piazza Venezia down to the stage in front of a brightly lighted Colosseum, for free concerts by no less than Paul McCartney and Simon & Garfunkel, respectively. And where Roman emperors once watched chariot races, Quincy Jones organized his benefit fundraiser concert in May 2004, featuring acts from around the world, including headliners Alicia Keyes and Carlos Santana, playing day-into-night in the Circus Maximus. Beyond music, many events are, of course, in Italian, but what follows is a selection of some that are of interest to English-speaking visitors.

Tickets for larger musical performances are usually sold by **Orbis** (✉ Piazza Esquilino 37, Santa Maria Maggiore ☎ 06/4744776). **Messaggerie Musicali** (✉ Via del Corso 473, Piazza di Spagna ☎ 06/684401) is a huge and central store that sells music, DVDs, books, and concert tickets.

FodorśChoice
★ **Caracalla Festival** (✉ Viale delle Terme di Caracalla, Circo Massimo ☎ 06/68801044 ⊕ www.santacecilia.it) is the summer season (July) of the Accademia Nazionale di Santa Cecilia. The venue is the much-loved Baths of Caracalla, but fear of damage to the site has led local authorities to limit the performances to small crowds (and left the summer opera series without a home). In addition to classical music from the Orchestra di Santa Cecilia, the program typically includes jazz, folk groups, and soloists.

**Fiesta!** (✉ Ippodromo delle Capannelle, Via Appia Nuova 1245 ☎ 06/71299855 ⊕ www.fiesta.it) is 90,000 square meters of world music and culture with a dominant Latin American component, and is very popular among young Italians. The event includes more than 4,000 hours of live Latin and Caribbean music, as well as jazz and blues stars of international stature every summer, along with exhibits related to Latin American culture, dozens of shops and stands selling food and goods from all over the world, and four outdoor dance floors. Events run in the evenings from mid-June through August, and admission is €8.

★ **Jazz & Image** (✉ Villa Celimontana, Piazza della Navicella, San Giovanni ☎ 06/5897807) is the longest-running jazz festival in Europe. From mid-June to early September it brings a program of everything from contemporary electronic and acid jazz to earlier, more classic styles, on the lawns of the restored baroque Villa Celimontana, on the Caelium hill adjacent to the Colosseum. Admission is typically €8.

FodorśChoice
★ **Roma Incontra il Mondo** (✉ Laghetto di Villa Ada, Via di Ponte Salario, Villa Ada ⊕ www.villaada.it) has grown in a few short years to become one of Europe's most impressive world-music festivals. Live music most evenings from late June to early August starts at 10 PM, followed by dancing until 2 AM. Stands sell handmade goods from around the world and Italian, Arab, and African food.

★ **RomaEstate al Foro Italico** (✉ Viale delle Olimpiadi, Stadio Olimpico ☎ 06/3238288 ⊕ www.romaestate.net) takes place from early June to mid-August, every day from 10 AM to 2 AM (last admission midnight). This complex built by Mussolini was the site of the Olympic Games in 1960, and since the early '90s has been one of Rome's main summer event venues, with 200 live concerts, and a fitness area that includes a swimming pool and Spinning and bodybuilding facilities. There's a roller park, food stands, and a playground, too. Admission is €6, though some concerts—Alanis Morissette, for example—cost considerably more. Concerts usually start at 9 PM.

## Opera

Opera buffs know that the best performances and most exquisite surroundings for opera are to be found at Milan's La Scala, Venice's newly reconstructed La Fenice, and at Verona's Arena (outdoor ampitheater). But

# OPERA ALFRESCO

Roman nightlife moves outdoors in summertime, and that goes not only for pubs and discos but for higher culture as well. Open-air opera is a venerable Italian tradition that has staged a comeback. Competing opera companies commandeer church courtyards, ancient villas, and soccer stadiums for performances that range from student-run mom-and-poperas to full-scale extravaganzas. The quality of performances is generally quite high, even if small productions often resort to school-play scenery and folding chairs to cut costs. Tickets run from about €15 to €40. The more sophisticated productions may be listed in newspapers and magazines such as roma c'e and Wanted in Rome, but your best sources for information are old-fashioned posters plastered all over the city, advertising classics such as Tosca and La Traviata.

Rome is Italy's capital, and so although its opera company does not have the renown of the aforementioned landmarks, it has a healthy following. Rome's opera season runs from November or December to May, and performances are staged in the **Teatro dell'Opera** (✉ Piazza Beniamino Gigli 8, Termini ☎06/481601, 06/48160255 tickets ⊕www.operaroma.it). Tickets go on sale at the beginning of the season; the box office (Piazza Beniamino Gigli 1) is open from 9 to 5 from Tuesday to Saturday and Sunday mornings until 1:30 PM. Prices range from about €16 to €80 for regular performances; they can cost much more for special events, such as an opening night or the appearance of an internationally acclaimed guest singer.

After the summer opera season was evicted from the ruins of the ancient **Terme di Caracalla,** the debate over a permanent open-air venue continues. The city's **Olympic Stadium** (✉ Stadio Olimpico, Foro Italico, Stadio Olimpico) has been summer opera's home in recent years, and temporary venues such as the Piazza del Popolo have also been used. Call the **Teatro dell'Opera** (☎ 06/48160255 ⊕ www.operaroma.it) for tickets and information.

## Theater

Rome is home to many small-scale acting troupes, both Italian and English-speaking. And since Cinecittà—one of the world's largest film studios—has seen a renewed popularity (Scorsese's *Gangs of New York, Ocean's Twelve,* and HBO/BBC Production's series *Rome,* to name a few recent projects), Rome has again, in recent years, become Hollywood-on-the-Tiber. As such, the city teems with a healthy collection of actors who work onstage when they're not onscreen. Rome's official theater is the **Teatro di Argentina** (✉ Largo Argentina, Campo de' Fiori ☎ 06/68804601), but it has mostly plays in Italian, although it does feature some dance performances from time to time. It's larger and more beautiful inside (all burgundy velvet and crystal chandeliers) than the outside of the theater would suggest. The **India theater** (⊠ Via Pierantoni 6, Lungotevere dei Papareschi, Testaccio ☎ 06/68804601) is a former soap factory that is home to some productions in English. Expect industrial, funky surroundings—and not the most comfortable seating. The English Theatre of Rome mounts original plays in English once a week at **Arte del Teatro** (⊠ Via Urbana 107, Santa Maria Maggiore ☎ 06/4885608). For a comedic look at Roman history, in English, with a backdrop that's "the real deal," check out the **Miracle Players** (⊕ www.miracleplayers.org) during the summer months. Every Tuesday and Friday at sunset, they give a Monty Python-esque original show in the Roman Forum.

# NIGHTLIFE

*La Dolce Vita* notwithstanding, Rome's nightlife is decidedly more lively for locals and "insiders" who know whose palms to grease and when to go where. Still, discos, live-music spots, and late-night bars do exist for denizens and tourists alike. The "in" places, especially the discos, change like the flavor of the month and may fade into oblivion after a brief season of popularity. The best sources for an up-to-date list of late-night spots and of who's playing what at the music clubs are the weekly entertainment guides, *roma c'è* and *Trovaroma*. If you'd prefer to see where the night takes you, hubs of after-dark activity are the area between Piazza Navona and the Pantheon, the Campo de' Fiori, Trastevere, and Testaccio. The Spanish Steps are strictly for tourists.

Now that smoking has been banned in all public indoor areas in Italy (that's right, it's actually happened), Roman aversion to clean air has initiated a thinning of crowds in bars and clubs. Still, Romans love to *"fare un salotto nella strada"* (that is, to turn the street into one's living room), and warmer weather brings hibernating smokers—and crowds of garrulous Romans in general—back into the streets, piazzas, and the locales that line them. In summer, many bars and discos close to beat the heat (although some simply relocate to the beach, where many Romans spend their summer nights). The city-sponsored **Estate Romana** (Roman summer) festival takes over, lighting up hot city nights with concerts, bars, and discos, all in the open air. The summer of 2004 saw the return to the *Roman Holiday* days of dancing and drinking along the Tiber River, with bars and open-air markets selling everything from sarongs to mojitos, under the stars.

## Bars

There's a bar for every taste in Rome. One at a better hotel will offer elegant surroundings and soft music, with drinks mixed by an expert *barista* (bartender). Customers found at such a place are usually a mix of Italians and foreigners, and prices are usually steep. Then there's a spate of informal cafés and wine bars catering to an eclectic crowd faithfully observing the Roman ritual of the evening aperitif between 6:30 and 10. There are always the plethora of quaintly named English and Irish pubs, complete with Guinness, darts, and soccer on the TV—a staple in European cities. Italians love them even though they're seldom the real McCoy, and tourists and foreign students flock to them as they offer a bit of the familiar. But perhaps the most radical change in the (slowly evolving) bar scene in Rome has been the handful of more sophisticated wine bars or so-called lounge bars that have become trendy. Many of them feature modern interior design and variations on the martini and could be in Anywhere Urban, Planet Earth. But a few have managed to marry worldly sophistication with Roman flavor, and these are the places that have a future on the nocturnal map of the Eternal City.

## Cafés & Wine Bars

★ Hipsterious celebrities and literati hang out at **Antico Caffè della Pace** (✉ Via della Pace 5, Piazza Navona ☎ 06/6861216), known to all as Bar della Pace, a turn-of-the-20th-century-style café near Piazza Navona. The atmosphere ranges from relaxed to electric, and while indoor tables are cozy in winter, the outdoor tables by the ivy-covered walls are prime real estate after dark—the view is of the enchanting *piazzatina* (tiny piazza) of Santa Maria della Pace, an urban masterstroke by Baroque architect Pietro da Cortona. A cult coffeehouse with an upscale pizzeria annex next door, La Pace has steep prices, and service can be infuriatingly distracted.

Once a modest neighborhood coffee bar, **Bar del Fico** (✉ Piazza del Fico 27, Piazza Navona ☎ 06/6865205) is now a popular rendezvous for locals and artists who prefer the earthy to the intellectual; watch out for huge crowds on weekend and summer nights.

**L'Enoteca Antica di Via della Croce** (✉ Via della Croce 76/b, Piazza di Spagna ☎ 06/6790896) is a rustic wine bar occupying historic quarters on a corner near the Spanish Steps. The menu offers a nice selection of cheeses and salumi, perfect for a snack or a light lunch. On summer evenings the outdoor tables become prize people-watching spots.

★ **Cul de Sac** (✉ Piazza Pasquino 73, Piazza Navona ☎ 06/68801094) crams a counter and two rows of wooden tables into a small space (with sidewalk tables as well) where you can sample myriad wines and lots of imaginative food delicacies, including a huge list of Italian cheeses and cured meats, along with non-Italian offerings like Greek salads and baba ghanoush. It's a popular place and you can't book a table, so come early or late if you don't want to wait.

**Sloppy Sam's** (✉ Campo de' Fiori 10 ☎ 06/68802637) is an American-run outpost, popular with a young, carefree crowd and plenty of American and U.K. expats and students. There's also outdoor seating on one of Rome's busiest squares, and a light food menu, including big *panini* (sandwiches on toasted bread) and nachos.

★ **Société Lutéce** (✉ Piazza Montevecchio 17, Piazza Navona ☎ 06/68301472) is the Roman outpost of the Turin original. The clientele is a mix of Rome's scruffy-chic, young and old, and the vibe is energized while still managing to be laid-back. The crowd spills out onto the tiny square outside the cramped quarters (the red, white, and blue decor leans toward Gallic '70s clubhouse). And the owners know how to host a party for the locals, offering a vast assortment of nibbles for aperitivo hours(s).

**Stardust** (✉ Vicolo de' Renzi 4, Trastevere ☎ 06/58320875) is a neighborhood institution. It's a tiny locale catering to an eclectic mix of local denizens, Italian actors and musicians, and expats. Brunch is served on Sundays from noon to 5 PM; otherwise, the place doesn't fill up until midnight.

With the resources of the huge Trimani wineshop behind it, the sophisticated two-level **Trimani Il Winebar** (✉ Via Cernaia 37/b, Termini ☎ 06/4469630) has an abundance of good wine and tasty food to go with it, taken either at the counter or at tables inside or out. It's closed on Sunday. You never know who you'll find at **Vineria Reggio** (✉ Campo de' Fiori 15 ☎ 06/68803268), referred to simply as "Vineria." The crowd ranges from aging beatnik poets to smartly turned-out young executives, reflecting the heterogeneous character of this colorful market square.

### Elegant Bars

Sophisticated, and for a trendier set, is the new **BarBar** (✉ Via Crescenzio 18, Prati ☎ 06/68308435), a cavernous and modern lounge bar that plays good music and has a cigar room. The crowd is thirties-to-forties. **Crudo** (✉ Via Degli Specchi 6 ☎ 06/6838989), is a spacious, modern, New York–style lounge serving well-made cocktails and *crudo* (raw) nibbles such as sushi and carpaccio. The main room is the airy lounge, all mod leather chairs and sofas in gray, white, and red, with a video projected on one large wall throughout the evening. A restaurant here also serves "raw" dinners as well. **Fluid** (✉ Via del Governo Vecchio 46/47, Piazza Navona ☎ 06/6832361) serves up drinks surrounded by rushing water-streamed walls to young, cool patrons seated on glowing "ice-cube" chairs.

Fodor's Choice ★ **Le Bain** (✉ Via delle Botteghe Oscure 32/a, Piazza Venezia ☎ 06/6865673) is a refined and striking cocktail bar and restaurant in a 16th-century palazzo. Formerly a disco, it's been refurbished, and now the restaurant is perfect for an intimate meal for two or for small groups of friends. The cuisine is creative and quite good.

Fodor's Choice ★ **Rooftop Bar of the Hotel Raphael** (✉ Largo Febo 2, Piazza Navona ☎ 06/682831) is one of the more fabled bars of Rome, noted for its perch overlooking the campaniles and palazzi of the Piazza Navona, a block away. No matter that the fancy hotel may be notorious for its snooty staff—it's worth risking the chill to bask in the beauty here.

Situated on a lovely, narrow piazza, **Salotto 42** (✉ Piazza di Pietra 42, Pantheon ☎ 06/6785804) is open from morning until late in the evening. The cozy-sleek room (high-backed velvet chairs, zebra-print rug, chandeliers) reflects the owners' Roman-New York-Swedish pedigree as it moves from daylight bar with smorgasboard to cocktail design den complete with art books and local sophisticates.

★ Off the lobby of Rome's newest addition to the grand hotel scene, **Tazio** (✉ Hotel Exedra, Piazza della Repubblica 47, Termini ☎ 06/489381), named after the original Italian *paparazzo* (celebrity photographer), is an Adam Tihany-designed champagne bar. If the inside is '80s in feel, with red, black, and white lacquer everything and crystal chandeliers, the outside seating area is simple and modern and allows those swilling bubbly (the bar has a vast assortment) to watch the people parade in one of Rome's most beautifully refurbished piazzas.

### Pubs

The wood-panel walls and fireplace provide a cozy mood at **Artù** (✉ Largo F. Biondi 5, off Piazza Santa Maria, Trastevere ☎ 06/5880398), a popular hangout with an ample selection of beer, wine, and tasty snacks and bar food.

**Birreria Marconi** (✉ Via di Santa Prassede 9/c, Santa Maria Maggiore ☎ 06/486636), more a beer hall than a pub, occupies a corner overlooking Santa Maria Maggiore and has tables outdoors. Young Italians flock here for pizza and beer.

**Antica Birreria** (✉ Via di San Marcello 19, Piazza Venezia ☎ 06/6795310) is an Stil Liberty (Art Nouveau)–era beer hall near Piazza Venezia. Expect filling canteen-style meals and big steins of German beer. This place is cheap but good. Avoid the lunch rush.

**Fiddler's Elbow** (✉ Via dell'Olmata 43, Santa Maria Maggiore ☎ 06/4872110) is the oldest Irish pub in Rome, and its scruffy authenticity shows up the fancier usurpers that have opened all over town. Singing is encouraged.

**Trinity College** (✉ Via del Collegio Romano 6, Piazza Venezia ☎ 06/6786472) has two floors of traditional pub trappings, with an old-school look and convivial music and drinking until 2 AM, with Italian snacks all day and British-style brunch on Sunday from noon to 4.

**Victoria House** (✉ Via Gesù e Maria 18, Piazza di Spagna ☎ 06/3201698). Off Via del Corso, a stone's throw from Piazza del Popolo, this was the first of the English pubs and is still considered one of the best. It has an authentic, run-down, slightly tea-color air, and a good range of beer.

## Discos & Nightclubs

Most dance clubs open about 10:30 PM, but they really warm up only after midnight. They usually charge a cover of around €10 to €20, which sometimes also includes the first drink. Subsequent drinks cost about €10. Some clubs also open on weekend afternoons for the under-16s. Many relocate to the beach in the summer, so when it's warm it's best to call ahead to confirm details.

**Alibi** (✉ Via di Monte Testaccio 40 ☎ 06/5743448), one of the most famous gay discos in town, has lost a bit of its luster in recent years. It's a rambling space with a terrace facing Monte Testaccio that's open for dancing in the summer. Straights head here, too, but the crowd is predominantly gay men. Events here are often organized by the **Circolo Mario Mieli** (☎ 06/5413985 ⊕ www.mariomieli.org), a gay advocacy group.

The glitzy haunt of movers and shakers from the worlds of politics, commerce, and showbiz, **Bella Blu** (✉ Via Luciani 21, Parioli ☎ 06/3230490) is in one of Rome's poshest residential districts. It's a supper club, with disco dancing and a piano bar. Wear suit and tie.

The stark, postindustrial style leaves plenty of room for young rockers to enjoy themselves at **Black Out** (✉ Via Saturnia 18, San Giovanni ☎ 06/70496791), and there's a separate "off-music" room for chilling out. Under various names and guises, this disco has hosted generations of Roman youth.

The Roman nightlifers have already discovered **Cabala** (✉ Via dei Soldati 23, Piazza Navona ☎ 06/68301192). This multilevel disco–piano bar in a gorgeous palazzo by the river is uncomfortably packed on weekends. Being a professional soccer player or a model will help you get past the doorman.

In trendy Testaccio, **Caffè Latino** (✉ Via di Monte Testaccio 96, Testaccio ☎ 06/57288556) attracts a thirtyish crowd with dancing, an occasional live music performance, and a separate music-video room and bar. **Gilda** (✉ Via Mario de' Fiori 97, Piazza di Spagna ☎ 06/6784838) is the place to spot famous Italian actors and politicians. This nightspot near the Spanish Steps has a piano bar as well as a restaurant and dance floors with live and disco music. Jackets are required.

Showbiz and sports personalities have no trouble getting past the doorman at **Jackie O'** (✉ Via Boncompagni 11, Via Veneto ☎ 06/42885457), but common mortals are advised to call in advance; this old-school disco, famous decades ago, is again glamorous, but now it's often taken over for PR events. There's a restaurant, piano bar, and disco—all dressy. The piano bar is open daily. The disco is closed Sunday and Monday.

From the owners of LeBain comes the disco-lounge **La Maison** (✉ Vicolo dei Granari 4, Piazza Navona ☎ 06/6833312). Bedecked in purple velvet and crystal chandeliers, there are two distinct spaces—one usually a V.I.P. area, the other a dance floor, with a DJ dishing up the latest dance tunes. Expect a lot of cheek kissing and "beautiful people."

In the Trieste district, **Piper** (✉ Via Tagliamento 9, Parioli ☎ 06/8414459), one of Rome's first discos, is still somewhat hot, drawing a young, often gay, clientele. It has dance music, live groups, pop videos, and a dance floor surrounded by many intimate seating areas. Piper is open only weekends.

**Qube** (✉ Via di Portonaccio 212, San Lorenzo ☎ 06/4385445), open only Thursday through Saturday, is Rome's biggest underground disco, a veritable sea of young bodies dancing until they drop. Friday night hosts the Muccassassina—at one time Rome's most famous and transgressive gay event. It has paid a price for its fame, and is now more straight than gay.

★ **Supper Club** (✉ Via dei Nari 14, Pantheon ☎ 06/68807207) is not only a place for dinner-in-recline, but also a trendy club where DJs and live entertainment draw a sexy crowd to the various rooms, most lined with big white beds and fluffy pillows (no shoes, please), complete with roaming masseurs. Monday nights feature a laid-back hip-hop party organized by a former L.A. club promoter.

★ **Testaccio Village** (✉ Via di Monte Testaccio ☎ 06/57288333) is the hippest element of the Estate Romana festival. Running from June to September, it's a temporary "village" with various pavilions where you can get drinks and food and two areas where you can enjoy both live and recorded ethnic music. From July to September it transforms into the "Gay Village" and attracts a hedonistic, mixed gay and straight crowd that dances and smoulders all night long.

## Music Clubs

Jazz, folk, pop, and Latin-music clubs are flourishing in Rome, particularly in the Trastevere and more workaday Testaccio neighborhoods. Jazz clubs are especially popular at the moment, with local talent sometimes joined by visiting musicians from other countries. For admission, many clubs require that you buy a membership card (usually about €5–€10, which may or may not include one drink).

★ **Alexanderplatz** (✉ Via Ostia 9, Vatican ☎ 06/39742171), Rome's most important live jazz and blues club, consistently books the best of Italian and international performers. Near the Vatican, it has both a bar and a restaurant. Reservations are a good idea.

**Big Mama** (✉ Vicolo San Francesco a Ripa 18, Trastevere ☎06/5812551), a small club, is a Roman institution for live music, including jazz, blues, rhythm and blues, African, and rock. There's a bar, and snacks are available. It's closed Monday.

**Classico Village** (✉ Via Libetta 3, Ostiense ☎ 06/57288857), a multicultural space in a converted factory near the Ostiense train station, hosts an eclectic mix of theater and performance art, as well as live electronic and ethnic dance music. Call first to see what's on. Friday night is usually gay, with one communal dance floor plus separate dance rooms for men and for women.

Near Castel Sant'Angelo, **Fonclea** (✉ Via Crescenzio 82/a, Prati ☎ 06/6896302) is a cellar with a publike atmosphere, a no-smoking policy, and live music every night of the week—from jazz to Latin American to rhythm and blues, depending on who's in town. The kitchen serves Italian and Mexican food.

In the heart of the after-hours scene near Piazza Navona, little **Il Locale** (✉ Vicolo del Fico 3, Piazza Navona ☎ 06/6879075) is jammed with a lively, young, genuinely music-loving crowd that likes to listen to what's new in rock from both sides of the Atlantic, live or recorded.

Near the Vatican, **Mississippi Jazz Club** (✉ Borgo Angelico 18/a, Vatican ☎ 06/68806348) is a historic jazz club, with live performances by American and other international groups on Friday and Saturday.

Latin rhythms are the specialty at **No Stress Brasil** (✉ Via degli Stradivari 35, Trastevere ☎ 06/5813249), which has live music with a Brazilian orchestra from Tuesday to Saturday. Monday is karaoke night, and Sunday is restaurant-only.

**Fodor's**Choice ★ An unexpected haven of good taste and live music in an uninspiring area is **La Palma Club** (✉ Via Giuseppe Mirri 35, Tiburtino ☎ 06/43599029). Despite its out-of-the-way location, La Palma has become synonymous with quality, the newest and most interesting in jazz and ethnic sounds, and its ability to woo some of the classiest names on the international music scene.

**The Place** (✉ Via Alberico II 27–29, Vatican ☎ 06/68307137) is a recent addition to the Rome music scene, and it has serious intentions. On offer is a mixture of live funk, Latin, and jazz sounds accompanied by excellent fusion cuisine.

# Shopping

**WORD OF MOUTH**

Ooh, romance! Perhaps you could buy your sweetheart an Italian handbag (Furla maybe, or if you are really flush, Fendi or D & G) and then fill it with surprises for that evening. For example, tickets to the Rome opera. Or a corkscrew for the bottle of wine you will purchase to drink on the Spanish Steps after dinner (don't forget plastic cups!). Or a print of a romantic restaurant (and then take her to that restaurant for dinner after the opera). Or a plastic replica of one of the city's famous monuments and then stroll by it at night, making sure to have someone take your picture together there.

—nnolen

By Margaret
Stenhouse

**TO SHOP OR NOT TO SHOP IN ROME?** For people who put Valentino, Bulgari, and Fendi right up there with the Forum, the Capitoline Museum, and the Baths of Caracalla, there has never been any doubt. After all, visiting shopaholics have always thought a trip to Rome incomplete without a visit to Gucci (so much so that Romans long considered it more of an American shop). Today, things may have changed—after all, the famous double-Gs can now be found in boutiques around the world—but nearly everybody still loves to satisfy their acquisitional desires in the Eternal City. This is not only because you find so many of the world's most famous designers and finest craftspeople here but also because shopping and sightseeing are hard to separate from one another. Many stores occupy scenic locations in beautiful squares, often enough next to Renaissance monuments and Baroque fountains. Where else can you try on a pair of jeans in the same noble *palazzo* where Napoléon's mother lived until her death in 1836, or purchase an 18th-century engraving of Bernini's Piazza Navona fountain from a shop located just a few feet away from its plashing waters?

Shopping in Rome can be a thrilling experience even when your pocketbook calls for mere window gazing. The Italian flair for transforming display windows into whimsical theatrical tableaus makes ordinary window-shopping an aesthetic experience. So even if you're not buying, it's worth a stroll through the Piazza di Spagna or along the Via Bocca dei Leone to take in the window displays and the spectacle of Romans on the hunt for that perfect pair of shoes. When you explore the fashion golden triangle that fans down from the Spanish Steps, you'll find that you don't have to spend a single euro to have fun. The atmosphere is almost carnival-like. Street vendors hawk fake Vuittons and fresh coconuts or chestnuts (depending on the season) on almost every corner as shoppers stroll happily from store to store, or stop to sip a cappuccino at one of the many sidewalk cafés that crowd the narrow streets. An oasis sheltered from the grandeur of classical Rome, this area is a network of pedestrianized streets, with people, not cars, given the right of way (although every now and then an Alfa Romeo roars through the forbidden zone to an operatic chorus of oaths).

The best known of Rome's gilded shopping throughfares is the Via Condotti, and for good reason. This is Rome's "shopping mall"—one lined with Bulgari diamonds, Pratesi linens, and Bises silks. Rome has been perfecting luxury ever since the days of the Caesars, so it's little wonder that this is the city that gave us the timelessly elegant Gucci "moccasin" loafer, Fendi bag, and the Valentino dress Jackie O wore when she became Mrs. Onassis. Spend any serious time around here and, sooner or later, you too will probably be seduced into handing over some of your hard-earned euros to the Eternal City's merchants. The good news is that although a Valentino ensemble can certainly set his *gran signoras* back many thousands of euros, glam girls can happily find similar Roman taste and styling at more affordable prices around town. Boutique fashions may be slightly less expensive in Rome than in the United States, although since the euro was introduced, Romans have seen many of their favorite stores mark up prices by as much as 50%. If you're a bargain shopper, know that the notice PREZZI FISSI (fixed prices) means just that: in shops displaying this sign it's a waste of time to bargain unless you're buying a sizable quantity of goods or a particularly costly object. Always bargain, however, at outdoor markets (except food markets) and when buying from street vendors.

With a history spanning millenia, it's no surprise that the city has many shops that are historic monuments in their own right. The Antica Erboristeria Romana has been dispensing herbal remedies since 1783 and still has the original painted wooden ceiling. The Pesci Pharmacy by the Trevi Fountain dates back to 1552. Roman ladies have been buying Parma violet cologne at the Profumeria Materozzoli since 1870. Schostal on the Via del Corso has supplied shirts, complete with spare collars and cuffs, to discerning Roman men for more than a century. Giorgi e Febbi, on the Pantheon Square, are still selling fabrics in the same cramped premises in the hotel where Mascagni stayed when his *Cavalleria Rusticana* premiered at the Rome Opera House. A large number of smaller shops are family businesses, run with pride by members of the same family for three or more generations. In stores like these, the owner will be there to serve you personally, like the gracious, silver-haired lady in the Venier & Colombo lingerie shop, or the Buccone brothers in their historic wine bar, who will gladly show you their antique ice cabinet and lovingly polished old silver cash register.

Although Rome, like everywhere else, has not escaped the invasion of cheap, mass-produced articles and clothes imported from the Far East, you'll see that Italian handicraft traditions are still very much alive. The largest concentration of craftspeople is clustered in the areas around the Pantheon and Campo de Fiori, where you can watch silversmiths, antique furniture restorers, decorators, shirtmakers, and jewelers working away at their craft. Most are pleased to show you their skills and explain their techniques. For some of the best fun, explore the mazes of narrow little side streets, where you find small, specialized boutiques and workshops. Here, away from the traffic and crowds, life still runs at a leisurely pace, so don't be surprised if you come across places with handwritten signs dangling from the door handle saying: "Gone for a coffee. Back in five minutes."

Whether out for something fancy or funky, be sure to explore stores and sights together—as a unique, all-encompassing experience. Rome is fortissimo when it comes to antiques shops, but when you trawl for treasures along Via Margutta and Via del Babuino, pay hommage to Federico Fellini's former home, peek in the luxurious *giardino* of the Hotel de Russie, and have lunch at the Museum-Atelier Canova, where the great 18th-century sculptor once worked. Fashion-firsters will head instead to the San Lorenzo district—Rome's new "Left Bank"—and its hipsterish boutiques favored by Italian movie and TV stars. Whatever area you head to you'll be sure to find an amazing *caleidoscopio* of perfect gifts, from a 19th-century Roman micro-mosaic snuff box to a Colosseum crafted out of chocolate to a bottle of the Elixir dell'Amore (love potion) you'll find at Ai Monasteri. Crafted by monks, its recipe dates back to the 16th century and if you don't feel like coughing up €50 for a

**5**

## Opening Hours

Traditional shopping hours are from 9 or 9:30 to 1 PM and from 3:30 or 4 to 7 or 7:30 PM—or 8 in summer. However, most shops in the historic center stay open all day, including Sunday. With the exception of food stores, most stores also close on Monday morning from September to mid-June and Saturday afternoon from mid-June through August.

## Sizing It Up

Italian sizes are not uniform, so always try on clothing before buying, and measure gift items. Children's sizes are all over the place, and though they usually go by age, sizes are calibrated to Italian children. (Average size-per-age standards vary from country to country.) Check washing instruction labels on all garments (often in English as well as Italian); many are not washable, and those that are may not be preshrunk. Glove sizes are universal. In any case, remember that Italian stores generally will *not* give refunds and often cannot exchange goods because of limited stock.

## Counterfeits

The Prada, Gucci, Fendi, and Vuitton bags sold by sidewalk vendors are fakes. An underground network organizes the illegal manufacture, distribution, and sale of these seemingly perfect counterfeits of stylish status symbols. Both manufacturers and vendors are always one jump ahead of the police. If an incredibly good buy in a name-brand product of any kind is proposed to you, examine the goods carefully. Reliable stores sell at the prices indicated by the manufacturers—so any enormous discount is suspect.

## Duty-Free Shopping

Value-added tax (IVA) is 20% on clothing and luxury goods, but it's already included in the amount on the price tag of consumer goods. If you're not a resident of the European Union, you may be eligible, under certain conditions, for a refund of this tax on goods purchased here—Tax-Free for Tourists V.A.T. tax refunds are available at most large stores for purchases of more than €155.

## Shipping

Whenever possible, it's preferable to take your purchases with you: otherwise there's always a risk of delays and things going missing. *Never* put anything of value in your suitcase. Carry it as hand baggage. If the goods are bulky or you're unable to take them with you for some reason, make sure that the shop is accustomed to handling shipping and exportation formalities and that your purchases will be insured against loss or damage. It's wise when shipping to pay with a credit card.

## Sales

*Saldi* (end-of-season sales) can mean real bargains in clothing and accessories. The main sale periods are January 6 through February and late July to mid-September. Most stores adopt a no-exchange, no-return policy for sale goods. At other times of year, a *liquidazione* sign indicates a close-out sale, but take a hard look at the goods; they may be bottom-of-the-barrel.

bottle, you can always try the shop's Elixir of Happiness, a bargain—if it works—at €12.50.

## Shopping Districts

### Cola di Rienzo

Between Piazza del Popolo and the Vatican, this broad avenue is lined with upscale shops that many Romans prefer to those around Piazza di Spagna because the wide sidewalks and big display windows make shopping easier. The area is frequented mostly by locals. Clothing, housewares, gourmet foods, books, and, of course, shoes and bags, along with a Coin department store—Cola di Rienzo has it all, in a medium-to-high price range in the stores. Street-corner stands, on the other hand, deal in bargain shoes, clothing, and glassware. Near the Vatican at the west end of the avenue, off Piazza Risorgimento, a score of shops sell religious souvenirs, many of them on Via di Porta Angelica. This area is a short walk from the center of town, as well as from the Metro stop Lepanto on line A; you can also take Bus 30, 70, 224, or 913.

### Piazza Navona, Campo de' Fiori & Pantheon

The narrow byways and gracious piazzas of Old Rome draw shoppers who are looking for something different. Via del Governo Vecchio is the place to browse for vintage evening dresses, wedding hats, and accessories of yesteryear. The web of twisting lanes and intersections around Campo de Fiori and the Pantheon are home to a great number of Rome's skilled artisans. Piazza Navona is a fulcrum for street artists, who set up their easels and offer to paint your portrait or sell you watercolor views of Rome. True to its origins as a Roman circus, the piazza also has toy stores stocked with enormous stuffed animals. The historic center is full of fascinating antiques shops that attract casual browers as well as serious collectors. The most prestigious antiques dealers are concentrated in Via Margutta and Via del Babuino, where objects for sale tend to be rarer and prices higher, as well as Via dei Coronari, which holds a traditional torchlighted antiques fair in spring and autumn. Romans shop on Via dei Giubbonari, right off the Campo de' Fiori piazza, for funky young fashions and household linens. Although Old Rome is quite central, you can take any bus to Corso Vittorio Emanuele II to get here, including the popular number 40 and 64 buses.

### Piazza Colonna & Piazza Barberini

The palatial pink marble Galleria Alberto Sordi at Piazza Colonna is Rome's most elegant shopping mall. This is the best place to take a coffee break and enjoy a bit of people-watching under the soaring Stil Liberty glass roof. The Gallery's two corridors are filled with elegant boutiques, such as Emporio Armani, Trussardi, the Richard Ginori china shop, and Adriana V. Campanile's his-and-hers shoe shops. La Feltrinelli book and music store occupies the central part of the building. The Rinascente department store is just across the road and the Trevi Fountain, submerged in a maze of little streets with small souvenir and specialty shops, is a five-minute-walk away. The busy thoroughfare of Via del Tritone, with a variety of shops offering medium-price clothing, shoes, and leather apparel, leads straight uphill toward Piazza

Rome is an absolute treasure-trove for the antiques lover, with dozens of shops filled with, as Edith Wharton once put it, "all those fragile and elaborate trifles that the irony of fate preserves when brick and marble crumble." Going on the Roman antiques trail is one of the most fascinating ways to experience lesser known aspects of this ancient city. Via Margutta, lined with the cavelike premises of some of Italy's most prestigious antiques dealers and art galleries, is less than five-minutes' walk away from the bustle of Piazza di Spagna, but it could be in another world. Strung along the foot of the wooded Pincio hill, the street has all the air of a slumbering, forgotten village, with its 18th-century town houses, shady courtyards, and walled gardens.

**5**

For more than three centuries, this was the heart of Rome's artists' colony, as the little fountain decorated with a palette and paint brushes (which you'll find on your right hand side about a third of the way along Via Margutta) testifies. Nowadays, however, high rents have forced most of the artists out and their studios have been taken over by families of eminent Roman antiques dealers, like Cocozza, Vangelli, and Di Castro, who have been in the business for generations and are true experts in their field.

To get to Via Margutta, go to Via del Babuino, which leads off from the left-hand side of Piazza di Spagna. The first street on your right is Vicolo Alibert, where you can stop off at the Alinari photo and prints gallery-store. Angelo Di Castro is near, at No. 20. Turning left into Via Margutta, you'll find an almost bewildering choice of antiques shops and art galleries strung out on both sides of this narrow, pedestrianized street. Of special interest, however, are the Cocozza shops, at No. 52 and No. 67, with prestigious pieces of 17th- and 18th-century Italian furniture and marble busts; Il Quadrifoglio at No. 47, with 18th-century Venetian painted cabinets; Galleria Eliodoro at No. 69, with rare objets d'art; Piergabriele Vangelli at No. 35, a specialist in Italian 18th-century antiques; and, at No. 67, Stampa Perera, founded in 1911, for rare prints, lithographs, and drawings. As a break from the antiques scene, you can visit the many art galleries, like Il Saggiatore, at No. 83/b and Il Mondo dell'Arte, which exhibits 20th-century contemporary works. Sculptress Vittoria Cusatelli has her studio at No. 94, where her charming terra-cotta figures of children and animals can be found. The Cascialli goldsmith's workshop is at No. 8/b. Stop by and watch Gilberto, the third generation Cascialli, at work. At the far end of the street, Maurizio Grossi's marble emporium sells inlaid tabletops and copies of old Roman busts at No. 109, right next door to the former home of *La Dolce Vita* movie director, Federico Fellini.

Via Margutta terminates at the Margutta Arcade, a welcoming little shopping center grouped round a courtyard. The eleven shops inside include Chic & Chocolate, where owner Rosanna Sozio will treat you to a freshly brewed cup of delicious hot chocolate. On the second floor you'll find the jeweler Scortecci, with unique pieces inspired by Southern Italian Baroque architecture, and the showroom of up-and-coming stylist, Vittoriana. Going through the arcade, you come out at Via del Babuino, beside the super-deluxe Hotel de Russie. Its enchanting "Secret Garden" makes it a favorite with visiting movie celebrities.

Via del Babuino is as busy as Via Margutta is quiet. Walking back toward the Spanish Steps, you'll find other prominent antiques dealers of international repute, like Apolloni, at No. 133; Megna at No. 148; and Galleria Benucci at No. 151, set between fashion boutiques and shoe stores. The street's focal point is the time-weathered statue of the "baboon" (actually a satyr) that gave it its name. Right next to the baboon is the Museum Atelier Canova-Tadolini, where the great 18th-century Neoclassical sculptor (and his favorite pupil) worked. The old studios have been perfectly preserved, complete with the plaster-cast models, some unfinished works, and the tools used by the artists. Inside the museum, there's also a coffee bar and restaurant. What better place to stop and have lunch?

---

Barberini. One of Italy's most prestigious tailors and purveyors of classy men's ready-to-wear is Brioni, on Via Barberini. Branching off Piazza Barberini, Via Veneto, the street once famous for *la dolce vita,* is lined with elegant cafés and high-price boutiques and shoe stores, as well as newsstands selling a large selection of English-language newspapers and magazines. You can walk or take the Metro (line A) to Piazza Barberini, or any of a number of buses, including 116.

### Piazza di Spagna

The most elegant and expensive shops are concentrated in the area fanning out westward from the foot of the Spanish Steps. Via Condotti and Via Borgognona are lined with the boutiques of some of the leading names in high fashion: Armani, Versace, Prada, Mila Schön, and Gianfranco Ferré. Valentino has boutiques on Via Condotti and Via Bocca di Leone and Fendi has a whole palazzo on Largo Goldoni, at the bottom of Via Condotti. From the bottom of the Spanish Steps and off to the right are Via Margutta and Via del Babuino, with their many art galleries and antiques shops, interspersed with trendy designer boutiques. Intersecting the top-price shopping streets are a number of others, such as Via del Corso, Via Frattina, and Via del Gambero, which are lined with specialty shops and boutiques of all kinds where goods are more competitively priced. To get to this area, walk to take the Metro (line A) to Spagna.

### Via del Corso

Running right through the heart of Rome, this congested thoroughfare attracts droves of Romans and tourists who overflow the narrow sidewalks onto the street, dodging taxis and buses. Crowds are elbow-to-elbow in front of display windows full of clothing and accessories. Young Rome comes here for jeans and inexpensive, trendy wear, some of which is sold in the 17th- and 18th-century mansions that line the street. At the Piazza Venezia end, for example, Stefanel has a sales outlet in the former Bonaparte palace. In the chic area of Piazza San Lorenzo in Lucina, smart and expensive specialty shops, such as the Profumeria Materozzoli, a 19th-century landmark, cater to the people who live in the patrician palaces in the area. Piazza della Fontanella Borghese, flanking the palace once inhabited by the uninhibited Paolina Borghese, who posed nude for Canova, has a picturesque street market of permanent stalls selling prints and old books. If you don't feel like walking—though this area is very central—take Bus 62, 63, 117, 199, or 492 to get here.

## Via Nazionale

With a few notable exceptions, the merchandise available along this wide thoroughfare near Stazione Termini tends to be of the cheap and cheerful variety. A host of shoe shops and off-the-rack clothing stores offer mainly youthful styles in what's fashionable this season. There are, however, some good luggage and leatherwear stores, where prices are sometimes better than in the historic center. Some more upmarket stores, such as Max Mara, Frett, and Furla, also have branches here. Via Nazionale runs down into Via IV Novembre, where Ta Matete, Rome's most exclusive art gallery and book store, opened in early 2005. At Ta Matete you can purchase the magnificent art books and art magazines published by Franco Maria Ricci. All the buses stop here, including the 40 and 64, as does the Metro (line A) to Repubblica.

### Trastevere

Trastevere is just across the river from Via Giulia and the historic center—so it's easily accessible by foot—but it seems worlds away. It's loud, colorful, and staunchly separate, and feels like a large, rambling village in Rome. Although its popularity with tourists at all hours of the day and night means that some of the stores have adopted an aggressive manner of selling regardless of quality, it remains a perfect area to check out smaller arts and crafts stores, with artisans from shoemakers to *liutai* (makers of stringed instruments) still working in front of your eyes. Look up Dermit O'Connell, owner of the Almost Corner Bookshop in Via del Moro 45, who will be happy to chat and give you a resident's insight into life in Rome. If you don't feel like walking across the Ponte Sisto bridge to get here, take Tram 8 from Largo Argentina three stops.

### San Lorenzo

San Lorenzo is probably Rome's most up-and-coming area. Bombed during the last war, it was hastily rebuilt to house a destitute working-class population. It therefore has none of the charm of old Rome, but, as compensation, it hums with vitality and life—especially after sunset, when the myriad bars, pubs, pizzerie, and ethnic restaurants open up to welcome young Romans out for a good time. Cheap rents and the proximity of Rome's La Sapienza university have attracted a large number of students as well as struggling unknown artists and craftspeople. Recently, some Italian showbiz personalities have moved in, giving this somewhat grubby, down-at-the-heels part of Rome a touch of glamour and prestige. The smart dress boutique, L'Anatra all'Arancia, with its captivating window displays, stands out on the busy Via Tiburtina, which dissects the district. If you like avant-garde art, visit the 16 artists' studios in the old Cerere pasta factory on Via degli Ausoni to view the work of budding talents. San Lorenzo is a 10-minute walk from Termini Station, through some of Rome's less attractive streets. Otherwise, take the 71 bus from the station.

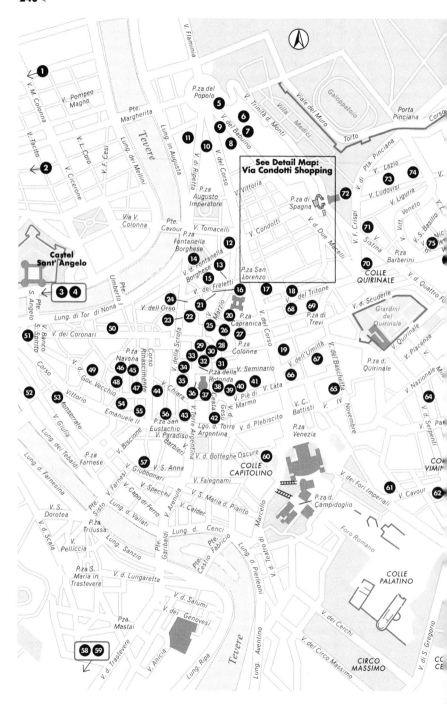

Rome
Shopping

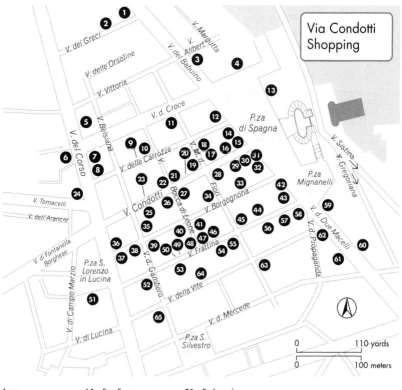

Via Condotti
Shopping

## Department Stores

Rome has few department stores. The classiest are the two Rinascente stores and the three main Coin stores. These outposts have welcome desks, multilingual guides, and tax-free refund desks. They're open all day and on Sunday, too.

Rome's handiest shopping mall is the **Forum** (⊠ Stazione Temini ⊕ www.romatermini.it), which is set in one part of Rome's modernistic Termini station. There are more than 100 shops (some of which stay open late in the evening), includding: Coronel Tapiocca for sports and outdoors wear; Intimissimi for outrageous colorful underwear; Carina Bijoux, a brand new chain of costume jewellery and fashion accessories; Optimissimo, with a choice of over 3000 super stylish sunglasses by top Italian designers; as well as old worldwide favorites like United Colors of Benetton.

**Coin** (⊠ Via Cola di Rienzo 173, Vatican ☎ 06/36004298 ⊠ Piazzale Appio 7, San Giovanni ☎06/7080020 ⊠ Via Mantova 1/b, Piazza Fiume ☎ 06/8416279) has upscale merchandise arranged in well-spaced displays. The clothing ranges from classic and dressy to casual chic, with good separates and sportswear departments for men and women. The downstairs housewares department usually has a good stock of Italian ceramic ware and innovative home furnishings and tableware.

**La Rinascente** (⊠ Piazza Colonna, Piazza di Spagna ☎06/6797691 ⊠ Piazza Fiume ☎06/8841231) is Rome's best-known department store, and the early 1900s building at Piazza Colonna provides a fine showcase for five floors of clothing and accessories. Perfumes and cosmetics share the main floor with handbags, costume jewelry, fun hats, and beautiful silk scarves. Upstairs are mainstream styles—both casual and dressy—for men, women, and children. Their Piazza Fiume location has more floor space and a wider range of goods, including a housewares department.

### Budget

The low- to moderately priced Oviesse and Upim chains have fair- to middle-quality goods and at their stores located throughout Rome you can pick up cheap, off-the-rack clothing, bathing suits, underwear, scarves, and various accessories. They also carry toiletries, some makeup ranges and first-aid needs. Most Oviesse and Upim stores have invaluable while-you-wait shoe-repair counters. There's a large central Upim store in Piazza Santa Maria Maggiore, and an Oviesse store on Viale Trastevere 62/64.

## Markets

### Flea Markets

Open-air markets are a regular feature in Roman life. They're usually noisy and overcrowded and you may have to elbow your way in to the most popular stalls. Prices are cheaper than in shops, but you may have to bargain. Look for good buys in discontinued clothes and shoes. Weekly or monthly secondhand and antiques markets can yield interesting finds. Watch out for pickpockets and tricksters inviting you to play their card games: they always win the bets!

Rome's biggest flea market is on Sunday morning at **Porta Portese** (⊠ Via Portuense and adjacent streets between Porta Portese and Via Ettore Rolli, Trastevere) and offers practically everything. Romans come to search for anything from a crystal drop for their chandelier, or a spare part for an old bike. A large section of this sprawling market is given over to new and secondhand clothing, where—if you're lucky—you may pick up a like-new cashmere sweater or genuine designer jeans for a song. If you don't like crowds, stay away, especially in summer when it gets unbearably hot. Though not strictly a flea market, the outdoor stalls at **Via Sannio** (⊠ Near basilica San Giovanni in Laterano, San Giovanni), open weekdays 8–2 and Saturday 8–5, is where you'll find bargains on used clothing and army surplus. Also expect great deals on shoes—you can buy good-quality name-brand shoes that have been used in shop window displays. There are a number of monthly or weekly markets selling bric-a-brac, arts and crafts, old comics, and secondhand laces and linen. Dates vary, so you should phone to check first. One of the most picturesque is **Ponte Milvio Antiques Market** (⊠ On the banks of the Tiber between Ponte Milvio and Ponte Duca d'Aosta, Flaminia ☎ 06/9077312), an antiques and collector's market, with stands set up on the river bank beside the old stone bridge marking the spot where the Roman emperor Constantine won the battle that subsequently heralded in the Christian era. Cycling paths along the embankment can turn this into a pleasant day's outing. This is held on the first weekend of every month. **Soffitta sotto i Portici** (⊠ Piazza Augusto Imperatore, Piazza di Spagna ☎ 06/36005345) has more than 100 stands to pick among. This market is held every second Sunday of the month from 10 AM to sunset. **Garage Sale** (⊠ Via Flaminia 60 ☎ 06/5880517) is a chic flea market where you find all kinds of high-class junk, including costume jewelry and vintage clothes. This is held every Sunday from 10 to 7. **Mercatino Piazza Verdi** (⊠ Piazza Verdi, Parioli ☎ 06/8552773) in Rome's upper crust neighborhood has quality crafts, rare old books, collectors' pieces, bric-a-brac, and food items. Look for it every fourth Sunday of the month.

### Food Markets

Still shadowed by the massive 16th-century Orsini palazzo and a statue of the famed philosopher Giordano Bruno, who was burned at the stake
★ here on accusations of heresy in 1600, the **Campo de' Fiori** (near Piazza Navona) is Rome's oldest food market, situated just south of Rome's Renaissance/Baroque quarter and the Piazza Farnese. Too wide to be called picturesque, the market is nevertheless a favorite photo-op, due to the *ombrelloni* (canvas umbrellas) food stands, which proffer everything from cheese to fish. You have to look hard to find the interesting regional foodstuffs, such as Colle Romani strawberries or chestnuts. At one end, flower stands serve to remind us that Emperor Pompey's legendary theater-temple garden used to stand here, still alluded to in the square's name. Two other big and colorful food markets are **Mercato Trionfale** (on Via Andrea Doria in the Prati neighborhood, north of the Vatican), and **Nuovo Mercato Esquilino** (in a former barracks with its main entrance on Via Filippo Turati, between Via Mamiani and Via G. Pepe), the last strongly influenced by the various ethnic groups that have settled in the Esquiline area not far from the station. There are smaller outdoor markets in every

neighborhood. All outdoor markets are open Monday to Saturday from early morning to about 2; some markets (among them Trionfale and Piazza dell'Unita, on Via Cola di Rienzo) are open all day.

# Specialty Shops

### Antiques & Prints

Rome is one of Italy's happiest hunting grounds for antiques and bric-a-brac. Here you'll find streets lined with shops groaning with gilded Rococo tables, charming Grand Tour memorabilia, fetching 17th-century *veduti* (view) engravings, and curios, perhaps even Lord Byron's snuff spoon. Antiques, yes; antiquities, no. Ancient Grecian statues and Roman busts are now virtually unmarketable, due to difficulties in obtaining export permits. Although most dealers specialize in objets d'art from the Renaissance to Art Deco, objects from the 1950s and 1960s are beginning to enter the picture as the antiques of tomorrow. Via dei Coronari is Rome's traditional center of antiques. The many shops lining this Renaissance artery that once took pilgrims to St. Peter's deal mainly in Victoriana and Art Deco. But Rome's most prestigious and upmarket dealers are mainly concentrated around Via del Babuino and Via Margutta. Serious collectors should head to those locales.

**Alinari** (✉ Via Alibert 16/a, Piazza di Spagna ☎ 06/6792923) is Italy's equivalent of the Bettman Archive and celebrated the firm's 150th anniversary in 2002. Founded in Florence as the Fratelli Alinari, this trio of brothers made their name with beautiful sepia collotypes of famous Italian landmarks, soon prized as souvenirs by 19th-century Grand Tour-ists. In this gallery-store you can browse through early photographs of Rome, art and photography books, and high-quality lithographs, made with the traditional collotype process, of which Alinari are the last, proud custodians.

**Ex Libris** (✉ Via dell'Umiltà, Fontana di Trevi ☎ 06/6791540) is listed as one of Rome's historic shops. It's lined from floor to ceiling with towering wooden bookshelves full of rare editions, prints, and antique maps.

**Galleria Benucci** (✉ Via del Babuino 151–153, Piazza di Spagna ☎ 06/36002190) is a showcase of prestigious carved and gilded late Baroque and Empire period furniture, culled from the noble houses of Italy. The mirrors, gilt frames, marble busts, and inlaid tables on display all reflect an era when opulence was unashamedly indulged in and admired.

**Galleria Biagiarelli** (✉ Piazza Capranica 97, Pantheon ☎ 06/6784987) has a superb setting—the former chapel of the Renaissance Palazzo Capranica. Carlo Maria Biagiarelli is Rome's leading antiques dealer in 18th- and 19th-century Russian icons. He has also a large collection of Eastern European antique china figurines and English watercolors.

**Nardecchia** (✉ Piazza Navona 25 ☎ 06/6869318) always showcases some of its large selection of beautiful prints of Rome in its display window right in front of the famous Bernini Fountain of the Four Rivers. The view, combined with soft classical background music, makes a visit to this store an especially pleasant experience.

**Noce Begnigni Olivieri** (✉ Via della Scrofa 20, Pantheon ☎ 06/6861837) enjoys Christmas morning *every* morning—the shop specializes in 18th-

and 19th-century Neapolitan Christmas cribs and handmade crêche figures. Rococo Baby Jesus figurines, carved wooden camels, and historic blackamoor figurines are all superb examples of craftsmanship and prized by obsessed collectors. The figures may be small but the prices are not. **Quattrocolo** (✉ Via della Scrofa 54, Pantheon ☎ 06/68801367) is a historic shop dating back to 1938 that showcases exquisite antique micromosaic jewelry (a craft that was perfected in Rome), 18th- and 19th-century cameos, and beautiful engraved stones.

**Tanca** (✉ Salita dei Crescenzi 12, Pantheon ☎ 06/6875272) is a well-known Rome dealer in 20th-century table ornaments, lamps, candlesticks, and prints  You can hunt through piles and boxes in one of the three rather cluttered rooms; in another are vitrines full of Art Nouveau jewelry, old silver, and objets d'art.

## Bookstores

Almost all of Rome's big bookstores have a few shelves of English-language books, and the newsstands on Via Veneto also sell paperbacks in English, but the broadest selections are available in the specialized English-language stores listed below.

**Almost Corner Bookstore** (✉ Via del Moro 45,, Trastevere ☎ 06/5836942) is a well-loved meeting point for English speaking residents and visitors to the lively Trastevere district. Owner Dermit O'Connell is on the spot with a warm Irish welcome and plenty of advice on the latest and greatest books.

**Anglo-American Book Co.** (✉ Via della Vite 102, Piazza di Spagna ☎ 06/6795222) carries a wide selection of current fiction, cookery, history, and children's books, as well as reference and scientific works. It also handles special orders. If you want to give an Italian friend a subscription to an English-language magazine, this is the place to arrange it.

**Il Mare International Bookshop** (✉ Via di Ripetta 239, Piazza del Popolo ☎ 06/3612091) is a joy for anyone who has a passion for the sea. The spacious, well laid-out premises offer a wide selection of books on ships, sailing, and travel in general, in English as well as Italian. It also sells maps, barometers, and some navigational equipment for small boats and yachts.

**La Feltrinelli** (✉ Galleria Alberto Sordi 33, Piazza Colonna, Piazza di Spagna ☎ 06/69755001 ✉ Via V.E. Orlando 84, Termini ☎ 06/4827878) is Rome's most important bookstore chain. The Piazza Colonna flagship branch has a stunning situation in the heart of the pink marble halls of the 19th-century Galleria Alberto Sordi (newly commemorated after one of Italy's most popular screen stars). Lifts and escalators make its three floors easily accessible. The second floor stocks a wide selection of books on art, architecture, and photography, some in English. The music department on the third floor is equipped with ear-phones, so customers can listen to the recordings of their choice. There are also seating areas and a café where you can relax.

**Mel Bookstore** (✉ Via Nazionale 254–255, Termini ☎ 06/4485405) fills two floors of an appealingly spacious Art Deco interior, with videos, a small but interesting selection of secondhand books and CDs, many English-language paperbacks, catalogs of current and recent art exhibitions in Rome, and a café upstairs that serves salads and snack lunches.

**Mondadori Fontana di Trevi** (✉ Via San Vincenzo 10 ☎ 06/6976501) is a peaceful haven with a small English-language book department placed near their comfortable lounge bar on the ground floor. An escalator takes you up to the top floor where they stock a wide selection of computer software and accessories, printers, mobile phones, and digital cameras. Mondadori remains one of the most prestigious Italian publishers, noted for their select fiction and fabulous coffee-table art books.

Fodor'sChoice **Ta Matete** (✉ Via Quattro Novembre 140, Quirinale ☎ 06/6791107) is
★ Rome's most stylish art gallery and bookstore, the showcase of the famous FMR publisher and ART'E' group. Franco Maria Ricci's magnificent art books and monthly magazines are collector's pieces. Many are limited editions, hand-bound, with top-quality illustrations and texts written by leading art critics and writers: in other words, books to cherish.

**The Lion Bookshop** (✉ Via dei Greci 33/36, Piazza di Spagna ☎ 06/32654007) was Rome's first English-language bookstore, established in 1947. The owners invite you to browse through the large selection of fiction, children's books, cookery, and books on Italy. They also have a café where they serve American cakes, cookies, and bagels.

## Ceramics & Crafts

Italy has always been known for its wonderful craftmanship in the decorative arts. In Rome, you can find many skilled artisans carrying on the traditions of the past, as well as innovative artists creating new and exciting objects and works of art.

**Archeo Roma** (✉ Largo del Teatro Valle 5, Piazza Navona ☎ 06/6877590) is a modern curio shop where you can find unusual mementos like reproduction Etruscan and Roman jewelry, replicas of Roman helmets and armor, as well as handcrafted ceramic urns, marble busts of emperors, and bronze statuettes to grace the mantelpiece.

**Arte del Vetro Natolli Murano** (✉ Corso Rinascimento 72, Pantheon ☎ 06/68301170) immerses you into the magnificent ambience of a Doge's palace, with shimmering, multicolor Venetian chandeliers, goblets, mirrors, and glass sculptures—note the pair of lifesize parrots with red tails that grace the entrance. The Natolli lines produce handcrafted glassworks in the noblest Murano tradition, many of them produced as limited-number collector's pieces.

**Canova** (✉ Via della Conciliazione 4f, Vatican ☎ 06/68806373) stands out among the religious souvenir shops lining the street leading up to St. Peter's. It stocks high-quality crafts, such as angels and crib figures with hand-sewn robes, alabaster copies of famous sculptures, woven tapestry pictures, and pictography reproductions on canvas or plaster. Don't expect these items to be cheap.

**Ceramica Italiana** (✉ Piazza Sant'Andrea della Valle 1, Pantheon ☎ 06/6874819) is a small, exclusive showroom with the cream of Italian ceramics. If you have a mansion, you may fancy the pair of crouching lions to grace the foot of your staircase, or the 5-foot high ceramic fountain featuring a gleaming white nymph. There are also exclusive smaller pieces, such as hand-decorated plates, cachepots, and table centerpieces.

**Ceramica Sarti** (✉ Via Santa Dorotea 21, Trastevere ☎ 06/5882079) features the work of Domenico and his daughter Lavinia, both skilled potters, who transform clay into beautiful and useful lamps, wall lights, bowls, baskets, and cachepots.

**Chiurato** (✉ Via Due Macelli 61, Piazza di Spagna ☎ 06/6780914) is a good place to come if you want unusual souvenirs that are also useful. This welcoming little shop is crammed full of household items, like colorful espresso coffee pots and cups, amusing clocks and fruit bowls, and table centerpieces of dried flowers, leaves, or pasta compositions set in perspex, all made in Italy.

**Galleria Savelli** (✉ Via Paolo VI, 27-29, Vatican ☎ 06/68307017) is a favorite with tour guides who bring their groups here to shop for religious souvenirs. However, it's worth a visit to view the collection of those famous 18th- and 19th-century micro-mosaics and—better yet—to watch artists demonstrate this ancient craft. Not only can you buy the mosaic boxes and jewelry on display, you can commission your own design.

**Il Giardino di Domenico Persiani** (✉ Via Torino 92, Termini ☎ 06/4883886) is a delightful little garden with hundreds of terra-cotta objects laid out under the branches of a gnarled oak. Choose from myriad old Roman reproduction vases, masks, and statuettes of gods and goddesses and pots to decorate your home and garden.

★ **INOR** (✉ Via della Stelletta 23, Pantheon ☎ 06/6878579) is a top-of-the-line silver and china store occupying the *piano nobile* of the 16th-century Palazzo Drago. Displays of magnificent silverware created by famous silversmiths like Pampaloni of Florence and Bellotto of Padua are laid out under the painted ceilings of the lofty salons. There are also dinner services by Richard Ginori and other leading manufacturers, as well as smaller gift items and jewelry.

**Le 4 Stagioni** (✉ Via dell'Umiltà 30/b, Fontana di Trevi ☎ 06/69941029) stocks a colorful selection of traditional Italian pottery from well-known manufacturers like Capodimonte, Vietri, Deruta, Caltagirone, and Faenza. If you're looking for something *alla Romana*, opt for the brown glazed pots with a lacy white border and charming flower basket wall ornaments, made in the Rome area.

**Le Terre di AT** (✉ Via degli Ausoni 13, San Lorenzo ☎ 06/491748) is a little pottery in the heart of the working-class district that is tipped to become Rome's "Left Bank." Angela Torcivia works on the premises and gives a new, ethnic-inspired twist to her work. Contemporary bowls, vases, and mugs in bright colors, ceramic jewelry, and necklaces plated with gold and platinum make up this truly exquisite selection.

★ **Rob'Art** (✉ Piazza di Pietra 32–33, Pantheon ☎ 06/69380484) is a showcase of Italian ceramics and glass from all the most famous Italian producers. A succession of rooms takes you through shelves full of Moor's-head cachepots from Caltagirone, Capodimonte floral compositions, Tuscan apothecary vases, and Murano glass plates and jewelry. Prices range from moderate to high.

## Clothing

CHILDREN'S
CLOTHING
Shopping in Rome for the little ones can be a delight—even children's clothes have designer labels. But keep three things in mind. One, are the garments easy to care for? The prettiest things may not be washable, and cottons are not necessarily preshrunk. Two, are they practical? Features such as gripper-fastened leg openings and neck openings are

not widely adopted in children's fashions here. Three, will they fit? Sizes are totally different from U.S. children's sizes, so take measurements before you leave home and bring along your tape measure, or get a good size-conversion chart.

★ **I Vippini** (⊠ Via Fontanella di Borghese 65 ☎ 06/68803754) lives up to its name ("Little V.I.P.s") with beautiful, exclusive fashionwear for boys and girls aged up to 10. Hand-embroidered party dresses and matching shoes will ensure that your little girl will be the belle of any ball.

**La Cicogna** (⊠ Via Frattina 138, Piazza di Spagna ☎ 06/6791912 ⊠ Via Cola di Rienzo 268, Vatican ☎ 06/6896557), a nationwide chain, has several stores in Rome. Each is like a small department store, with clothing, shoes, carriages, baby supplies, and so forth, for children—from infants to age 14. There's a maternity-wear department, too.

**Pùre Pùre** (⊠ Via Frattina 111 ☎ 06/6794555) is set up to look like a kiddies' playground, with toddler dummies frolicking around in the window. Inside, they stock cute, with-it clothes for fashion-conscious under-tens, designed by Cavalli Angels, Pinko Pallino, Miss Blumarine, Simonetta, and other famous Italian brand names.

**Quadrifoglio** (⊠ Via delle Colonelle 10, Pantheon ☎ 06/6784917) is a discount shop stocking discontinued brand name clothes for under-tens. If you don't feel like stumping up the large sums required to kit your kid out in this season's designer gear, this is the place for you.

**Rachele** (⊠ Vicolo del Bollo 6–7, Campo de' Fiori ☎ 06/6864975) is a small, charming shop tucked down a side alley not far from the Campo de' Fiori piazza. The clothes are all handmade, from high-quality fabrics. Items in stock are for children up to age 6; clothes are made to order for children up to 12.

HIGH-FASHION
BOUTIQUES

**Dolce & Gabbana** (⊠ Piazza di Spagna 93 ☎ 06/69380870) is the Rome outpost of these celebrated Italian designers, long favored by Madonna, glamazons, and supermodels everywhere. While considered a little long in the tooth by some fashionistas, the two boys still define bravura Italian style. Armani may be Milan and cool, but D & G remain hot and southern, and their legion of fans wouldn't have it any other way. Though their style—brocade cutouts on jeans, jeweled Sicilian bustiers, and tasseled taffeta skirts—is High Baroque, their boutique is mod and minimalist, with a giant screen set into stainless steel paneled walls. The white linoleum floor, long glass counters, and rhythmic background music all add to the atmosphere.

★ **Fendi** (⊠ Largo Carlo Goldoni 419–421, Piazza di Spagna ☎ 06/696661 ⊠ Via Borgognona 36–40, Piazza di Spagna ☎ 06/696661) is still going strong after two decades of headling-grabbing styles. So much so that the Fendi sisters have consolidated their empire and crowned it with a new "Palazzo Fendi," the erstwhile aristocratic Palazzo Boncompagni, which reigns over the square on Via del Corso at the very bottom of Via Condotti. One of the great Roman names, legendary for its bags and furs, Fendi has been beloved by fashionistas ever since "Mamma" Fendi opened her doors in the 1920s. In 1963 she moved her little fur shop to Via Borgognona, which was unfashionable until the skillful team of Mamma and her five daughters began to attract such a following that everybody else decided they wanted to be there, too. Legend has it that Mamma always knew just what her customers wanted. Her secret: She hid behind a screen in the shop and wrote down everything her customers said. Another mark of Mamma's genius is that she hired Karl Lagerfeld to design the Fendi furs in 1975, when he was just beginning his career. His furs—ripped, dyed, and sculpted—became famed for their ingenuity. The old Via Borgognona store now just has men's wear.

**Giorgio Armani** (✉ Via Condotti 77, Piazza di Spagna ☎ 06/6991460) is a Milanese designer through and through—cool, sleek, and minimalist. Originally a men's tailor, he literally reinvented the structure of tailoring and his suits have always been amazingly light and effortless to wear. When he began designing for women in the 1970s, the softness and femininity of his tailoring was a revelation. Worn by starlets and executives, he remains the epitome of understated (and un-Roman) elegance.

**Krizia** (✉ Piazza di Spagna 87 ☎ 06/6793772) tempts you with a video screen showing her models sweeping regally down the catwalk. Inside, white walls and an elegant, minimalist setting is a perfect foil for her distinctively cut ready-to-wear line.

★ **Laura Biagiotti** (✉ Via Borgognona 43, Piazza di Spagna ☎ 06/6791205) is synonymous with soft, ultra-feminine clothes, often in white, cream, or neutral colors. Her spacious boutique attracts women who wish to project a calm, self-assured image.

**Missoni** (✉ Piazza di Spagna 78 ☎ 06/6792555) means knitwear, for both men and women, in designs known for their original patterns and use of color. They became so famous in the 1970s they had to struggle to cast off that decade's tacky aura, which they have succeeded in doing, as many new fashion fans attest. The reflection of the Spanish Steps in the tall store windows adds a magical touch.

FodorśChoice
★ **Patrizia Pepe** (✉ Via Frattina 1 Piazza di Spagna ☎ 06/6784698) is one of the dynamic new generation of Italian designers. Her trendy, low-slung jeans and beaded tops in subtle shades are a hit with Italian women on the fast track.

★ **Prada** (✉ Via Condotti 92/95, Piazza di Spagna ☎ 06/6790897), as a brand, has become an international status symbol, favored by celebs like Demi Moore and cherished by those who like its quirky, anti-glamour outlook. On the ground floor you'll find handbags, sunglasses, and the cosmetics line. A roomy lift wafts you upstairs to a series of thickly carpeted rooms where a flock of discreet and willing assistants are waiting to help you in your choice of dresses, shoes, lingerie, and fashion accessories.

**T'Store Trussardi** (✉ Via del Corso 477–478, Piazza di Spagna ☎ 06/3226055), a flawlessly chic line that originates in Milan, here spotlights its jeans and sport collections for men and women. For a casual look, take your pick among the jackets, pants, and knitwear with the characteristic greyhound logo. You'll also find accessories, perfume, and jewelry.

FodorśChoice
★ **Valentino Donna** (✉ Via Condotti 13, Piazza di Spagna ☎ 06/6795862 ✉ Via del Babuino 61 ☎ 06/36001906) remains the epitome of ultra-elegant luxury. In the 1960s, Valentino put Rome on the fashion map big-time, knocking Dior and Balenciaga off their elevated Paris perches in the process. Still the darling of the château and luxury yacht set, Val

has learned to hop to a hip new beat and has won the hearts of a new generation of fashion divas, thanks to his crisp, clean dresses, suits, and separates for day, fairy-princess gowns for night. Although he tearfully "retired" two years ago, he still rules his kingdom from his palazzo on Piazza Mignanelli. At his main Via Condotti store, a plush red carpet leads upstairs to the gilded salons where off-duty celebs can make their purchases in complete privacy. Of course, prices are stratospheric, but these can be investments that will pay off over seasons of wear. Valentino's second and more informal boutique, carrying both his "R.E.D." and "Roma" lines, is on Via del Babuino. The men's boutique is around the corner at Via Bocca di Leone 15.

**Versace** (✉ Via Bocca di Leone 26–27, Piazza di Spagna ☎ 06/6780521 ✉ Via Borgognona 24–25 ☎ 06/6795037) occupies the ground floor of a noble palazzo with wrought-iron gratings on the windows and a mosaic pavement. You can find sandals, handbags, and sunglasses, in addition to clothes, all in that out-there, leopard-print glamour so beloved by paparazzi. The men's collections can be found at Via Borgognona.

KNITWEAR **Albertina** (✉ Via Lazio 20, Via Veneto ☎ 06/4885876) elevates women's knitwear to high fashion, imparting line and substance to creations (for women) that never go out of style. Coats, jackets, dresses, pants, and tops are made in exclusive wool, silk, or blended yarns.

**Taro** (✉ Via della Scrofa 50, Pantheon ☎ 06/6896476) produces handmade knitwear in unusual yarns, designed by owners Marisa Pignataro and Enrico Natoli. The selection includes shawls, loose sleeveless jackets, and pants, with an ample, easy-to-wear line. The prices are in keeping with the quality.

**Yarn Textile Art** (✉ Via dei Banchi Nuovi 1, Vatican ☎ 06/68135765) offers exclusive knitted, woven, and crocheted garments, made by Rita Miliani and designed by her daughter, Elisabetta. In their little shop-cum-laboratory you'll also find small, handmade items like cushion covers, slippers, and crocheted flower brooches.

LEATHER CLOTHING Leather clothing for men and women is a good buy in Italy, where skins were first cut and tailored to make high-fashion garments. Go to the area around Via dei Due Macelli and Via del Tritone, near Piazza di Spagna, where several large leather stores are grouped more or less together. In Rome you'll also find small workshops where jackets, skirts, and coats can be made to measure.

**Renard** (✉ Via dei Due Macelli 53, Piazza di Spagna ☎ 06/6797004) is a leather boutique, displaying a selection of styles made exclusively in Italy. Their elegant jackets and suits in soft, pastel suede are a real temptation. Next door, at No. 50, they have their outlet shop, with discontinued stock at reduced prices.

**Skin** (✉ Via dei Due Macelli 87, Piazza di Spagna ☎ 06/69940590) has just about anything you could want in leather—in any color, too. House styles are classic models of suits, skirts, jackets, and pantsuits. They also show high-fashion styles by Missoni and other designers.

**Suede and Skin** (✉ Via Francesco Crispi 69, Piazza di Spagna ☎ 06/ 6782793) is a Florentine leather factory, with this small sales outlet in Rome. There's a good selection of jackets, belts, and bags at very reasonable prices. The shop will also do alterations for you, if required.

**Very Pel** (✉ Via Cavour 174, Colosseo ☎ 06/4817640) is a small shop with a workroom on the premises. Domenico Scorza and his wife Gina make the jackets, skirts, and pants in leather and suede on the spot and will alter any models to suit you. Prices are lower than at the fancier leather boutiques.

**Viroel** (✉ Via del Tritone 76, Piazza di Trevi ☎ 06/42014643) occupies an entire corner of the busy intersection with Via Francesco Crispi. Much of the merchandise, including handbags and belts, is on display, making choosing easy. Styles in leather suits and jackets for men and women tend to be fairly classic.

MEN'S CLOTHING
Fodor'sChoice
★

**Brioni** (✉ Via Barberini 79, Via Veneto ☎ 06/484517) has long dressed Roman princes and American billionaires, with tailors who could cut a suit the way Michelangelo could carve a block of marble. Back when, Rome was the center of men's haberdashery and this outpost is one of the last great relics of that era. The setting is suitably grand—complete with marble staircase, giant chandelier, and nearly 600 square meters of impeccably made suits and overcoats, sumptuous leather jackets, silk ties in exclusive designs, and pullovers in finest cashmeres.

**Eddy Monetty** (✉ Via Condotti 63/a, Piazza di Spagna ☎ 06/6783794) has the British look that Italians love, with Burberry a big seller. There are plenty of Italian labels to choose from, too—Malo, Brunello Cucinelli, and Etro are just a few. Nothing here comes cheap.

**Ermenegildo Zegna** (✉ Via Borgognona 7/e, Piazza di Spagna ☎ 06/6789143), of the unpronounceable name, is one of Italy's finest manufacturers of men's clothing, with fans like actors Jude Law and Diego Luna. The classic ready-to-wear line is made of the firm's premier fabrics (the Zegna family has been legendary for their fabrics for more than a century). Zegna has also developed innovative materials for rain jackets and outerwear.

**Grima' S** (✉ Via del Gambero 11/a, Piazza di Spagna ☎ 06/6784423) is a store that has an old-world charm, with its retro wooden counter and display shelves. Styles are classic: smart as well as casual (and prices are reasonable). The man who prefers a more conservative style of dressing will feel at home here.

**Il Portone** (✉ Via delle Carrozze 71, Piazza di Spagna ☎ 06/6793355) embodies a tradition in custom shirt making. For decades, a man was a fashion nobody if he didn't have a few Portone shirts in his closet, identifiable by their cut and signature stripes. The store also carries nightshirts and underwear.

**Osvaldo Testa** (✉ Via Frattina 42–43, Piazza di Spagna ☎ 06/6790660) is a byword for quality, stocking everything the well-dressed businessman could require. The fine Italian labels carried include Loro Piana and Cerrutti. If your suitcase has been lost, this is the place to come for everything from boxers to suits to shoes.

**Schostal** (✉ Via del Corso 158, Piazza di Spagna ☎ 06/6791240) has been serving the gentlemen of Rome since 1870 and still preserves a genteel air. The fine-quality shirts come with spare collars and cuffs. You can also buy ultraclassic underwear, handkerchiefs, and pure wool sweaters.

MEN'S &
WOMEN'S
CLOTHING

**Battistoni** (✉ Via Condotti 60–61/a, Piazza di Spagna ☎ 06/6976111) is a name that has been associated with smart, conservative style for generations. Classic Battistoni jackets, suits, shoes, and accessories are staples in the wardrobes of Rome's elegant set.

**Davide Cenci** (✉ Via Campo Marzio 1–7, Pantheon ☎ 06/6990681) is a Roman classic for high-quality clothing and accessories for every occasion, from a sailboat party to a formal wedding. Trench coats, cashmeres, and beautifully tailored ready-to-wear, all strictly made in Italy, are Cenci specialties.

**Degli Effetti** (✉ Piazza Capranica 93 and 79, Pantheon ☎ 06/6790202) has cutting-edge fashion for men and women, in separate stores on opposite sides of the piazza. The women's store carries cool, contemporary names, including Martin Margiela, Dries Van Noten, and John Galliano.

★ **Ilcuoiocucitoamano** (✉ Via di S. Ignazio 38, Pantheon ☎ 06/6795119) actually translates as "leather sewn by hand." This little boutique tucked away in a side street produces an amazing variety of handcrafted clothes and accessories. Antonio Ferretti makes his exclusive bags from top-quality leather tanned in Tuscany, while Maria Rita Tegolini designs knitted tops, dresses, and two-piece outfits in bold and striking colors. For men, there are waistcoats, ties, and jumpers. They will also make to order.

Fodor'sChoice
★

**L'Anatra all'Arancia** (✉ Via Tiburtina 103/109, San Lorenzo ☎ 06/4456293) has the locals in this bustling working class district agog at its window displays of flowing silk scarves, Campers shoes, fresh and innovative designer clothes, teeny-weeny bikinis, and zany underwear. Owner Donatella Baroni believes in fashion being fun. Their men's shop is across the road at No. 130, where you can find pure linen shirts and trousers in unusual colors for young, trendy men. The clientele includes Italian TV and stage personalities who live in the area.

**Tombolini** (✉ Via della Maddalena 31/38, Pantheon ☎ 06/69200342) is a spacious department store with a wide range of good-quality, comfortably classic clothes, all produced in their own factory in the Marches region of Italy.

TEENS' CLOTHING

**Fiorucci** (✉ Via Nazionale 236, Termini ☎ 06/4883175) displays its signature angels on T-shirts, which tend to delight adolescents (and some aggressively youthful women). Downstairs are feminine dresses, skirts, and blouses by Fiorucci, Kenzo, Gaultier Soleil, Kookai, and D&G. Upstairs are kitschy shoes, gadgets, and T-shirts by Indian Rose and Miss Sixty. Clothes are hip but affordable.

**Monica** (✉ Via dei Chiavari 25, Campo dé Fiori ☎ 06/6861406) is a jumble of hipsterious fashion and accessories, designed and made in Italy. Beyond the crocheted hats, bright striped jumpers, and chunky shawls, teenage girls will love rummaging around the counters and shelves, crammed with skimpy tops, sequined bags, silk handbags, and cloth tote bags.

**Replay** (✉ Via della Rotonda 25, Pantheon ☎ 06/6833073) is a typical example of young Italians' passion for American trends. All these jeans and T-shirts with American sports teams blazoned on the front are actually made in Italy, with that little extra touch of Italian style that transforms sloppy hip into casual chic. Background music of the latest hits adds to the way-cool atmosphere. Prices are moderate.

VINTAGE CLOTHING   In Rome you can create your personal version of the Boho (Bohemian Chic) look by rummaging through the discarded fashion articles of various epochs, which are showcased in the vintage clothes shops around Piazza Navona and in the Monti area off Via Nazionale.

★ **Le Gallinelle** (⊠ Via del Boschetto 76, Termini ☎ 06/4881017) is a tiny boutique in a former butcher's shop—hence the large metal hooks. Owner Wilma Silvestri transforms vintage, ethnic, and contemporary fabrics into inspired retro clothing with a modern edge. She also sells vintage accessories and garments. Prices are fairly reasonable.

**Mado** (⊠ Via del Governo Vecchio 89/a, Piazza Navona ☎ 06/6875028) is like a trunk in your grandmother's attic. You'll probably find Mado sitting on the sofa in her shop, sewing little bags to put her Lea Stein brooches in. Admire her collection of vintage Japanese kimonos displayed on the wall, then take in her big selection of retro evening gowns.

**Vestiti Usati Cinzia** (⊠ Via del Governo Vecchio 45, Piazza Navona ☎ 06/6832945) has mainly 1960s and '70s styles—including lots of jeans, leather jackets, shoes, and evening dresses. A glass cabinet contains more precious items, like Mary Quant sunglasses.

WOMEN'S CLOTHING   **Arsenale** (⊠ Via del Governo Vecchio 64, Piazza Navona ☎ 06/6861380) has a sleek layout and a low-key elegance that stand out, even in Rome.
★ The dimly lighted interior and soft background music all combine to create a soft, intimate atmosphere. Roman designer Patrizia Pieroni creates clothes to match with muted colors drawn from nature, sleek, uncluttered lines, and touches of glamor from beaded scrollwork or embroidery.

**Discount dell'Alta Moda** (⊠ Via Agostino Depretis 87/88, Termini ☎ 06/47825672) is a bargain hunter's paradise. This shop near the city's opera house sells brand names like Prada, Gucci, Fendi, Max Mara, Moschino, and D & G at 50% discount. You can find both casual and formal wear, as well as designer shoes, bags, costume jewelry, jeans, and sunglasses.

**Elena Mirò** (⊠ Via Frattina 11–12, Piazza di Spagna ☎ 06/6784367 ⊠ Via Nazionale 197, Termini ☎ 06/4823881) is an attractive shop with a selection of stylish casual and dressy wear in larger women's sizes. The fabrics and colors reflect fashion trends.

**Galassia** (⊠ Via Frattina 20–21, Piazza di Spagna ☎ 06/6797896) has expensive, extreme, and extravagant women's styles by Gaultier, Westwood, Miyake, and Demeulemeister. The funky hats, feather boas, and flashy costume jewelry strikingly contrast with the shop's austere gray walls and black floor.

**Le Tartarughe** (⊠ Via Piè di Marmo 17, Pantheon ☎ 06/6792240) makes a subtle fashion statement with its selection of versatile, easy-to-wear and easy-to-pack styles for normal sizes (not models). Many of the clothes are done in knit fabrics, all designed in-house.

**Luisa Spagnoli** (⊠ Via del Tritone 30, Piazza di Trevi ☎ 06/69922769 ⊠ Via Veneto 130 ☎ 06/42011281 ⊠ Via Frattina 84/b, Piazza di Spagna ☎ 06/6991706) is an internationally known name for women's classic jersey suits, but these have largely been phased out in favor of a more up-to-date, mix-and-match range. It's worth looking at Spagnoli's evening and formal wear in ultra-feminine chiffons and satins.

★ **Maga Morgana** (✉ Via del Governo Vecchio 27, Piazza Navona ☎ 06/ 6879995 ✉ Via del Governo Vecchio 98, Piazza Navona ☎ 06/ 6878085) is a family business where everyone's nimble fingers contribute to produce the highly original, hippy-chic clothes and accessories. Designer Luciana Iannace creates lavishly ornate party dresses and bridal outfits. Her son Marco makes the vegetable-dyed knitwear and tops, while twin brother Fabio fashions the original sculptures you can see in both shops.

**Mariella Burani** (✉ Via Bocca di Leone 28, Piazza di Spagna ☎ 06/ 6790630) has classic chic with judiciously used high-fashion overtones. These clothes are ever-wearable and never boring.

★ **Victory** (✉ Via S. Francesco a Ripa 19, Trastevere ☎ 06/5812437) spotlights youthful, lighthearted styles created by lesser known Italian stylists, such as Rose D, Nina, Alessandrini, and Dondup, that are all made for flaunting. A menswear version of the store is at Piazza San Calisto 10 in Trastevere.

## Cosmetics–Perfume

**Antica Erboristeria Romana** (✉ Via Torre Argentina 15, Pantheon ☎ 06/ 6879493 ⊕ www.anticaerboristeriaromana.com) is a historic shop with the atmosphere of yesteryears. It dates from 1783 and still has the original painted wood-panel ceiling and wooden dressers to store the herbs. The friendly staff will advise you on time-honored herbal remedies and beauty products.

**Bottega Verde** (✉ Via del Babuino 51/A ☎ 06/3218162) has its own line of cosmetics and beauty products made in Pienza, Tuscany (only natural ingredients are used, with no animal testing). The daffodil yellow floor and green display shelves have a fresh, cheerful look that reflects the company's philosophy. Prices are very reasonable.

**Castelli** (✉ Via Frattina 54, Piazza di Spagna ☎ 06/6790339, 06/6780066 beauty salon ✉ Via Condotti 22, Piazza di Spagna ☎ 06/6790998 ✉ Via Oslavia 5, Vatican ☎ 06/3728312) is a perfumed paradise offering everything imaginable in the way of beauty aids, cosmetics, and hair accessories, plus a dazzling selection of high-quality costume jewelry. Writer James Joyce started his masterpiece *Ulysses* in what is now the Castelli beauty salon at Via Frattina 52, where Rome's high society ladies still go for treatments and pampering.

Fodor'sChoice **Profumeria Materozzoli** (✉ Piazza San Lorenzo, Lucina 5, Piazza di
★ Spagna ☎ 06/68892686) dates from 1870, but has modernized its interior to display its vast range of high-quality toiletries and perfumes, including the classic Parma violets line, Crabtree & Evelyn, and Kiehl face, hair, and body products. The shop is on the ground floor of the aristocratic Palazzo Fiano, where workmen digging out the foundations discovered Augustus' Altar of Peace, the Ara Pacis, in 1568.

## Fabrics

Italy is famous for silks and woolens. The country is one of the world's major textile manufacturers, so the choice is vast. You can find some real bargains when *scampoli* (remnants) are on sale. A good place for these are the unflashy but well-stocked stores on Via delle Botteghe Oscure, just off Piazza Venezia.

**Fratelli Bassetti** (✉ Corso Vittorio Emanuele II 73, Piazza Venezia ☎ 06/6892326) has a vast collection of world-famous Italian silks and fashion fabrics on several floors of a rambling palazzo.

★ **Giorgi e Febbi** (✉ Piazza Rotonda 60–62, Pantheon ☎ 06/6791649) has been fabric heaven since 1784. Chic decorators—including those who worked for Agnelli and Onassis—flock here to find the shop usually stacked from floor to ceiling with bales of upholstery material and curtain fabrics, some of which are produced in the company mill in Sicily. Look for intricate jacquards and brocades in muted Italian colors, antique Indian Tree of Life bedspreads, pure-cotton strips for awnings and garden chairs, plus a wide selection of silk cords and various trimmings.

## Food, Wine & Delicacies

★ **Ai Monasteri** (✉ Corso del Rinascimento 72, Piazza Navona ☎ 06/68802783 ⊕ www.monasteri.it) has dark-wood paneling, choirlike alcoves, and painted angels. Here you'll find traditional products made by Italy's diligent friars and monks. The herbal decoctions, liqueurs, beauty aids, and toiletries are all explained in English, as well as Italian. The recipe for its Elixir dell'Amore (love potion) is centuries old, or opt for a bottle of its always popular Elixir of Happiness. There are myriad products, ranging from bath-oils specially formulated to protect your sun tan, colognes for children, quince-apple jams, Royal Jelly honeys, barola grappas, and a wide array of skin treatments.

**Angelini** (✉ Via del Viminale 62, Termini ☎ 06/4881028) dates from 1880 and is the last of Rome's traditional old wine shops where you can buy local Castelli wine from the tap. It's open in the evening until midnight and since it's so near the Opera House you may well find singers or members of the orchestra in buying a drink after the performance. The shop also has a huge collection of miniature liqueur bottles for collectors and hand-blown bottles of grappa in curious shapes.

**Buccone** (✉ Via di Ripetta 19, Piazza del Popolo ☎ 06/3612154) is a landmark 1800s wineshop inside the former coach-house of the noble town house. Its 10 layers of shelves are packed with quality wines and spirits ranging in price from a few euros to hundreds of euros for rare vintages. The old ambience has been preserved with the original beamed ceiling and an antique till and ice compartment. You can also buy sweets, biscuits, and packaged candy; light lunches are available every day and dinner at weekends.

**Castroni** (✉ Via Cola di Rienzo 196, Vatican ☎ 06/6874383) has a broad and aromatic range of food products from all over the world. This is where members of foreign countries come to find specialties from home, but you'll also find plenty of Italian goodies. The coffee alone is worth the visit.

★ **Chic & Chocolate** (✉ Margutta Arcade, Via Margutta 3, Piazza di Spagna ☎ 06/89927614) is a welcoming little shop selling a wide variety of crafts, as well as top-quality chocolate that is certified as suitable for diabetics. Little chocolate reproductions of Roman monuments make nice novelty gifts, but don't overlook the unusual glasses, plates, costume jewelry, and bags.

**Enoteca al Parlamento** (✉ Via dei Prefetti 15, Pantheon ☎ 06/6873446 ⊕ www.enotecaalparlamento.it) is an Aladdin's cave of gastronomic treasures. The tantalizing smell of truffles from the snack counter, where a sommelier waits to organize your wine-tasting session, is enough alone to lure you in. This is one of the city's traditional wineshops and its proximity to Montecitorio, the Italian Parliament building, makes it a favorite with journalists and politicos who stop in for wine by the glass. The Enoteca will show you their most prized possessions: bottles of the Brunello di Montalcino vintages 1891 and 1925, strictly not for sale.

**Moriondo e Gariglio** (✉ Via Piè di Marmo 21, Pantheon ☎ 06/6990856) makes its own handmade chocolates on the premises. Do what the Italians do: drop in and buy just one to try before making your selection. The shop makes up beautiful gift boxes to your specification.

**Trimani** (✉ Via Goito 20, Termini ☎ 06/4469661), the oldest and one of the best-stocked wine dealers in Rome, also has a broad selection of regional Italian delicacies.

Fodor'sChoice ★ **Volpetti** (✉ Via Marmorata 47, Testaccio ☎ 06/5742352), a Roman institution, sells the best cured meats and a score of different salami. You'll also find a vast selection of cheeses, genuine buffalo-milk mozzarella (much tastier that the more common cow's milk version), and variegated pasta colored with tomatoes, spinach, or squid ink.

## Handbags & Luggage

Really good bags—the classic kind that you can carry for years—are not inexpensive. Almost all the leading fashion houses have their own line of bags, but there are also hundreds of small, lesser known companies producing bags of good quality that are gentler on the pocketbook.

**A. Testoni** (✉ Via Condotti 80, Piazza di Spagna ☎ 06/6788944) makes hyper-refined handmade shoes and bags for men and women. Their soft, calfskin sneakers and matching messenger bags all carry the fire-embossed "T" brand mark. Their limited-edition "Turtle bag," made with interlaced strips of leather, is tipped to become a collector's item.

★ **Bracciolini** (✉ Via Mario De' Fiori 73, Piazza di Spagna ☎ 06/6785750) is a new and highly innovative Florentine stylist. The bags are authentic works of art, with fun bags shaped like little gold taxis or Santa Fe stagecoaches. The delightful beach bags have picture postcard scenes of Italian resorts made of brightly colored appliquéd leather: very expensive, but to treasure.

**Fabris al Pantheon** (✉ Via Degli Orfani 87, Pantheon ☎ 06/6795603) is a three-story shop just behind the Pantheon, with a vast choice of bags and luggage to suit all tastes. Most of the designs are in quiet good taste and of good quality.

**Furla** (✉ Piazza di Spagna 22 ☎ 06/69200363) has 13 shops in Rome alone. Its flagship store to the left of the Spanish Steps has been entirely refurbished in 2005 to make it even more inviting. Be prepared to fight your way through crowds of Japanese tourists, all anxious to possess one of the delectable bags, wallets, or watch straps in ice-cream colors.

**Gherardini** (✉ Via Belsiana 48/b, Piazza di Spagna ☎ 06/6795501) has taken over a deconsecrated church and transformed it into a showplace for their label, which is known for its casual, easy-to-carry bags in leather and logo-stamped synthetic material. It has leather totes and colorful bags, and a line of soft luggage.

★ **Gucci** (✉ Via Condotti 8, Piazza di Spagna ☎ 06/6790405) still has groups of eager customers lined up at the door waiting for a chance to get at its legendary shoes, wallets, luggage, and—thanks to Tom Ford (who has since moved on, but never mind)—chicer-than-thou clothing. It all began back in 1906, when Guccio Gucci (hence the double-G trademark) began to reproduce saddles and luggage for the very rich. During the 1920s and 1930s, the shop's reputation grew, but it took serendipity to make Gucci a household word. During World War II leather was scarce, so Gucci developed a line of luggage in sturdy canvas, printed with the double-G design and trimmed with woven red-and-green webbing. With that fashion history was made. The Gucci moccasin was a more deliberate design, but its popularity is just as great. With the Tom Ford era of the 1990s, Gucci exploded onto the clothing scene and its designs are now as coveted as any signature. Although prices should be ostensibly lower in Italy, there's no such thing as a Gucci bargain. Gucci means expensive the world over.

**Mandarina Duck** (✉ Via dei Due Macelli 59, Piazza di Spagna ☎ 06/6786414) makes soft bags and luggage in durable synthetic fabrics, with the Mandarina Duck logo trim. Eminently practical in form and design (they can be folded up and slipped in a suitcase, and their capacity seems limitless), the bags are a boon to travelers.

★ **Volterra** (✉ Via Barberini 102, Via Veneto ☎ 06/4819315) has one of the widest and best selections of handbags from top Italian stylists and manufacturers, and prices are competitive. The styles run the gamut from the elegant bag for an evening at the opera to practical daytime hold-alls to trendier options for a night on the town.

### Hats, Gloves & Ties

**Borsalino Boutique** (✉ Piazza del Popolo 20, Piazza di Spagna ☎ 06/32650838) is the home of the famous trilby-style hat that well-dressed men have worn on and off for three generations and is now coming back again into fashion. There are also women's hats in signature styles—dressy or informal, and always stylish. The store also carries a line of shirts and ties.

**Di Cori** (✉ Piazza di Spagna 53 ☎ 06/6784439) packs a lot of gloves into a tiny space, offering every type in every color imaginable. There are also some scarves and ties.

**Roxy** (✉ Via Frattina 115, Piazza di Spagna ☎ 06/6796691 ✉ Via Barberini 112, Via Veneto ☎ 06/4883931) has the best selection of moderately priced ties to be found in Rome. The selection is bewilderingly large, and the stores are tiny and usually packed with customers.

**Sermoneta** (✉ Piazza di Spagna 61 ☎ 06/6791960) allures with its stacks of gloves in rainbow hues, all displayed under red, cone-shape lights that create a cozy, intimate atmosphere in this small boutique.

**Tie Shop** (✉ Via Campo Marzio 11, Pantheon ☎ 06/6892485) sells its own brand of gloves and scarves, made in Milan and Bologna. Prices are a little higher than in other glove shops, but styles are more varied. You can also find luxury items like leather gloves with cashmere linings.

### Jewelry

**Agua** (✉ Via della Vite 57, Piazza di Spagna ☎ 06/69380699) is the brainchild of a group of four young Roman designers, who make striking chunky jewelry, mostly in silver with semi-precious stones, amber, and pearls. Their enormous rings will never go unnoticed.

**Art Privé** (⊠ Via Leonina 8, Termini ☎ 06/47826347) is a small, brightly lighted little shop, where Tiziana Salzano designs charming jewelry sets and individual pieces inspired by nature—flowers and butterflies are favorite themes.

**Buccellati** (⊠ Via Condotti 31, Piazza di Spagna ☎ 06/6790329) is a tradition-rich Florentine jewelry house renowned for elaborately worked silver pieces and nostalgic jewelry recalling the days of grand décolletés and tiaras.

**Bulgari** (⊠ Via Condotti 10, Piazza di Spagna ☎ 06/6793876) is to Rome what Tiffany's is to New York and Cartier is to Paris. Every capital city has its great jeweler, and Bulgari is Rome's, with a list of customers that range from Queen Juliana of the Netherlands to Nicole Kidman (well, at least she donned one of their necklaces to the Oscars). In the middle of the 19th century, the great-grandfather of the current Bulgari brothers began working with silver in his native Greece. He later moved to Rome, where, with his son, he started perfecting a style that used Byzantine-style gold and cabochon precious stones. They moved to the Via Condotti in 1910. By the 1960s, prices had become so astronomical they made even Elizabeth Taylor and Richard Burton blanch, but if you gather your courage and step through the velvet-curtained door into the marble-pillared room, you could splurge on a Bulgari pen to sign your checks—it will cost the same as a pair of top designer shoes.

**Creazioni D'Arte Diego Percossi Papi** (⊠ Via Sant'Eustachio 16, Pantheon ☎ 06/68801466) has his tiny atelier in the former mews of the ancient Sant'Eustachio church. This master jeweler makes to order individual cloisonné pieces with precious stones, pearls, and fired enamels.

*Fodor'sChoice* ★ **Gioielli in Movimento** (⊠ Via della Stelletta 22/b, Pantheon ☎ 06/6867431) draws customers like Andie McDowell, hooked on Carlo Cardena's ingenious jewelry designs. Carlo's "Twice as Nice" earrings, which can be transformed from fan-shape clips into elegant drops, were Uno Erre's best selling earrings between 1990 and 1998. His latest "Up and Down" pendant, which can be worn two different ways, is set to become another hit.

## Lingerie & Linens

**Blunauta** (⊠ Piazza di Spagna 35 ☎ 06/6780110) belongs to the Greco family of Rome, who were among the first Italian stylists to have their designs manufactured in China. You can find pure silk underwear, blouses, and nightwear at very affordable prices.

**Brighenti** (⊠ Via Frattina 7–8, Piazza di Spagna ☎ 06/6791484) looks like what it is—a traditional Roman shop of a gentler era, with a marble floor and a huge crystal chandelier suspended overhead. Elegant silk negligees, with lavish lace trimmings, are displayed downstairs. Go upstairs for swim suits and underwear.

★ **Cesari** (⊠ Via del Babuino 195, Piazza di Spagna ☎ 06/3613456) is where Italian brides traditionally buy their trousseaux. The frilly, seductive lingerie, high-quality household linens, and sumptuous decorator fabrics are a dream for old-fashioned girls of all ages. There's also a selection of less expensive items, including aprons, beach towels, and place mats.

**Emy Funaro** (✉ Piazza di Spagna 79 ☎ 06/69922267) attracts women who are looking for innovative, exciting designs in underwear and bathing suits, by stylists like R. Cavalli, Andres Sarda, Versace, and D&G. You can also find trendy leisure suits to cut a dash at the gym.

**Frette** (✉ Piazza di Spagna 11 ☎ 06/6790673 ✉ Via Nazionale 80, Termini ☎ 06/4882641) has luxurious, fluffy towel sets and coordinated bathrobes, as well as pure cotton, silk, and linen sheets and pillow cases, all in pastel shades and subdued patterns for homemakers who prefer a restful atmosphere. Nightwear ranges from filmy negligees to flannel dressing-gowns.

**La Perla** (✉ Via Condotti 78, Piazza di Spagna ☎ 06/69941934) has glamorous lingerie and lacy underwear for women, as well as stylish beachwear.

**Marisa Padovan** (✉ Via delle Carrozze 81, Piazza di Spagna ☎ 06/6793946) is the place for exclusive, and sometimes extravagant, lingerie and bathing suits, trimmed with rhinestones or feathers, all designed in the Padovan atelier.

**Rossatti** (✉ Piazza di Spagna 52 ☎ 06/6790016) is charmingly old-fashioned, with the green paint gently flaking off its antique wooden counter and cabinets. It keeps old-fashioned hours as well, with a long lunch break. In compensation, it stocks hand-embroidered tablecloths and bedlinen, monogrammed towels, nightdresses, and lacy hankies at moderate prices.

**Tebro** (✉ Via dei Prefetti 46–54, Pantheon ☎ 06/6873441), dating to 1867, is a large, classic Roman establishment with a long-standing reputation for quality and courtesy. This is where the well-heeled Roman shops for lingerie and household linens.

**Venier e Colombo** (✉ Via Frattina 79, Piazza di Spagna ☎ 06/6787705) is one of Rome's most historic shops. You'll find a breathtaking selection of lace-trimmed lingerie and linens, as well as exquisite christening robes for babies and hand-embroidered lavender bags.

## Music & Videos

Most video stores have a section with English and American movies in the original language, sometimes with Italian subtitles.

**Blockbuster** (✉ Via Barberini 3, Via Veneto ☎ 06/4871666) has invaded Italy. This is just one of an army of stores in Rome stocked with a mega selection of videos and DVDs.

**Messagerie Musicali** (✉ Via del Corso 472, Piazza di Spagna ☎ 06/684401) has central Rome's largest selections of tapes and CDs. It has a video and book department and sells sheet music and musical instruments, too.

**Ricordi Media Stores** (✉ Via Giulio Cesare 88, Vatican ☎ 06/37351589) can provide any kind of music imaginable on tape or CD, from Italy's golden oldies to the latest on worldwide charts.

**Rinascita** (✉ Via delle Botteghe Oscure 1–5, Piazza Venezia ☎ 06/69922436) is a bookshop and music store next door to each other with a distinctly socialist slant in the former, and an ethnic and world music accent in the latter.

## Shoes

Rome's shoe stores seem to be as numerous as the *motorini* (mopeds) buzzing around downtown. They range from custom-made-shoe boutiques to stores with huge displays of every model imaginable for men, women, and children. Most Italian shoes are made to a single, average width; if you need a narrower shoe, you may have to try on many before you find the right fit. Valleverde and Melluso brands make wider, softer shoes for men and women.

**AVC** (⊠ Via Frattina 141, Piazza di Spagna ☎ 06/6790891) is the showcase for Adriana V. Campanile's glamorous creations. Eye-catching designs and relatively contained prices make her a special favorite with young Italians. The men's shop is inside the Galleria Colonna.

**Ballin** (⊠ Via Sistina 14, Piazza di Spagna ☎ 06/4819681) is ultrafeminine and ornate—these shoes are made in Venice and often come with matching bags. Ballins are for special occasions—with price tags to match.

**Bruno Magli** (⊠ Via Condotti 6, Piazza di Spagna ☎ 06/6793587) has classy shoes at fairly high prices. Magli shoes are considered so comfortable that they are the preferred choice of many airline stewardesses.

**Charles** (⊠ Via del Corso 109–110, Piazza di Spagna ☎ 06/6792345) shows a host of styles in big display windows, offering practically all of the top-quality shoe labels, from Rossi to Rossetti. The store is clearly geared to tourists, but Romans come, too, for the wide selection and competitive prices.

**Fausto Santini** (⊠ Via Frattina 120, Piazza di Spagna ☎ 06/6784114) gives a hint of extravagance in minimally decorated, all-white show windows displaying surprising shoes that fashion mavens love. Santini's footwear for men and women is bright, colorful, and trendy, sporting unusual forms, especially in heels. Coordinated bags and wallets add to the fun. Past collections at half-price are available at Via Cavour 106, Colosseo.

**Ferragamo Uomo** (⊠ Via Condotti 65, Piazza di Spagna ☎ 06/6781130) shows classic styles in shoes for men, handcrafted in fine leather and in fabric for more sporty models.

**Fratelli Rossetti** (⊠ Via Borgognona 5/a, Piazza di Spagna ☎ 06/6782676) combines classic quality and good looks in men's and women's shoes with the telling detail that puts them high in fashion.

**Louis Big Shoes** (⊠ Via Cavour 309 ☎ 06/6791677) specializes in shoes for men and women with bigger than average feet. Sizes range from 12 to 22 for men and from 7 to 13 for women. Don't be put off by the unprepossessing outward appearance of this little store near the Roman Forum. Inside, owner Luigi Catemario has a range of fashionable styles and elegant handmade shoes, as well as sports models and sneakers.

**Mada Shoes** (⊠ Via della Croce 57, Piazza di Spagna ☎ 06/6798660) has a selection of classic, conservative shoe styles for women with attractive details that make them distinctive.

**Pollini** (⊠ Via Frattina 22–24, Piazza di Spagna ☎ 06/6798360) is a his-and-hers store, divided down the middle into narrow, separate shops. Pollini styles for both sexes are classic and exceedingly well crafted, with relatively high prices.

★ **Sorè** (⊠ Piazza di Trevi 97, Colosseo ☎ 06/6793206) is a hot favorite with both Italians and foreigners because of its selection of high-fashion shoes at very affordable prices. Its location overlooking the Trevi Fountain means there's a waterfall of customers going in and out, but sales staff are efficient and able to cope.

**Superga** (⊠ Via della Maddalena 30/a, Pantheon ☎ 06/6868737) sells those timeless sneakers that every Italian wears at some point, in classic white or—yum—in a rainbow of colors. There's also a line of sportswear for men and women.

FodorśChoice **Tod's** (⊠ Via Fontanella di Borghese 56a/c, Piazza di Spagna ☎ 06/
★ 68210066) has become hyperfashionable, *again*. They occupy the ground floor in the celebrated 16th-century Palazzo Ruspoli. Today, Tod's shoes are considered a "must" by every well-dressed Italian, which says a lot in a land famed for its fine shoes!

## Stationery

★ **Il Papiro** (⊠ Via del Pantheon 50 ☎ 06/6795597) is a treasure trove of hand-decorated boxes and notebooks, made with the marbleized technique developed in the 18th century. This Florentine company also makes its own high-quality printed stationery and cards, as well as wrapping paper featuring Roman monuments (just the thing to wrap your gift in).

FodorśChoice **Pineider** (⊠ Via di Fontanella Borghese 22, Piazza di Spagna ☎ 06/
★ 6878369) is where Rome's aristocratic families have their wedding invitations engraved and their stationery personalized. For stationery and desk accessories, hand-tooled in the best Florentine leather, it has no equal. The second shop in Via dei Due Macelli stocks briefcases and office notepaper.

## Toys

**Al Sogno** (⊠ Piazza Navona 53 ☎ 06/6864198) greets you with a life-size stuffed bear in the doorway. It sets the tone for this rather eccentric shop that sells collectible dolls, puppets, masks, stuffed animals, and an assortment of curios.

★ **Bartolucci** (⊠ Via dei Pastini 98, Pantheon ☎ 06/69190894) attracts shoppers with a life-size Pinocchio pedaling furiously on a wooden bike. Inside is a shop that would have warmed Gepetto's heart. All the toys, animal pendulum clocks, bookends, and bedside lamps are made of wood by the Bartolucci family, who live in a tiny village in the Marche region. You can even buy a child-size vintage car entirely made of wood, including the wheels.

**Bertè** (⊠ Piazza Navona 107–111 ☎ 06/6875011) is a toy shop of the good, old-fashioned kind, packed with the kind of toys you or even your parents played with, such as meccano, Legos, train sets, and doll's prams. You'll find a vast selection of dolls and unusual stuffed animals.

**La Città del Sole** (⊠ Via della Scrofa 65, Pantheon ☎ 06/68803805) is the progressive parent's ideal store, chock-full of educational toys for all ages—even for adults (puzzles, tricks, and gadgets). Shelves and floor space are crammed with toys (in safe plastics and in wood) and with games, puzzles, and children's books, mainly in Italian.

# Side Trips from Rome

## 6

## WORD OF MOUTH

Caught the local bus up to Tivoli and went to the Villa d'Este. What a treat! The villa itself has been turned into a sculpture museum, but most of the frescoes remain in very good condition. The real surprise were the beautiful gardens and fountains! It was just as I had always expected an Italian Renaissance garden to look. The fountains were spectacular and just overwhelming! I noticed that everyone was walking around with smiles.

—dayle

At ancient Ostia, we could almost see the Roman soldiers clip-clopping down the cobblestones on horses, the heavy gates swinging open for them.

—kswl

Updated by
Margaret
Stenhouse

**ALL ROADS MAY LEAD TO ROME,** but today's sightseers should take a cue from imperial emperors and Renaissance popes and head *fuori porta*—"beyond the gates." Here in the province known as Lazio, those privileged people built spectacular palaces and patrician villas, in hopes of exchanging the capitol's overheated air for a breath of refreshing country air. So why not follow their lead and head to the hills? In addition to rewarding you with a break from city sightseeing, a tour of Lazio's varied delights can immeasurably broaden your understanding of the Roman Empire and its legacy.

One of Italy's most fascinating but least known regions, Lazio is set between the Mediterranean Sea to the west and the Apennine mountain ridge to the east, with the forests, hills, and lakes of Tuscia to the north. The area not only has an astounding variety of scenery but, befitting the former playground of princes and prelates, offers a spectacular harvest of sights: great Roman ruins like Emperor Hadrian's villa and Ostia Antica, called the "Pompeii" of Rome; the palatial estates of Frascati, Bagnaia, and Tivoli, whose Villa d'Este has the most spectacular fountains in Europe; medieval castles, villages, and churches full of forgotten works of art. If it weren't so obscured by the glare and fame of nearby Rome, Latium (as it was called by the ancient Romans) would still be one of Italy's star attractions.

East of Rome lie some of the region's leading sites, which could be combined with sightseeing along a route that loops through hills where ancient Romans built their summer resorts. At Tivoli, Hadrian's Villa reveals the scale of individual imperial Roman egos—an emperor's dream come true, it was the personal creation of the scholarly ruler, who, with all the resources of the known world at his command, filled his vast retreat with structures inspired by ancient monuments that had impressed him during his world travels. Moving on to Tivoli's Villa d'Este, you can see how a worldly cardinal diverted a river so that he could create a garden stunningly set with hundreds of fountains, demonstrating that the arrival of the Renaissance did not diminish the bent of the ruling classes for self-aggrandizement. Eastward, at Palestrina, the magnificent ancient Roman sanctuary to the Goddess of Good Fortune has been the inspiration for many modern buildings with like pretensions of grandeur, including the Monument to Vittorio Emanuele II in Rome's Piazza Venezia. At Subiaco, St. Benedict founded the hermitage that gave rise to Western monasticism.

Less than 24 km (15 mi) south of Rome, the famous Castelli Romani are clustered amidst the Alban hills. Surrounded by acres of rolling fields and vineyards, the picturesque little Castelli towns and villages each have a strong sense of identity, with their own exclusive dialects, customs, gastronomic specialties and feast days. Reigning queen of all the Castelli is Frascati, renowned for its wine and its 16th- and 17th-century noble estates, while Castelgandolfo is where the Pope has his summer retreat. But all the 12 Castelli towns (so-called because of the medieval fortresses that crown their highest points) merit a visit. Public transport from Rome is good, if not deluxe, and most of the Rome travel agencies will organize day trips. Hiring a car, however, is probably the best way to tour the area and enjoy the breathtaking scenery around the two crater lakes of Albano and Nemi.

One of the easiest excursions from the capital takes you west 25 km (15½ mi) to the sea, where tall pines stand among the well-preserved ruins of Ostia Antica, ancient Rome's main port and an archaeological site that rivals Pompeii. A visit to Ostia Antica tells you more about the way the ancient Romans lived than the Roman Forum does. (And it brings home just how close Islamic troops came to overrunning Rome, as they would have if their fleet had not been defeated off Ostia in 849.)

Venture deep into the countryside north of Rome to Viterbo, where you can find an intact medieval core and historic traces of its days as a papal stronghold, interspersed with all the trappings of modern industry. Close by, the gardens of Villa Lante at Bagnaia and Palazzo Farnese at Caprarola give an inkling of how Renaissance cardinals took a break from their duties at the papal court. And at Bomarzo a 16th-century prince created one of the first theme parks in Europe.

*Numbers in the margin correspond to numbers on the Side Trips from Rome and Ostia Antica maps.*

## Exploring

Although organized tours from the capital only go to the most famous sights, like Tivoli and Ostia Antica, all the places we have listed can easily be reached by public transport for a day's outing. You may find, however, that there's so much to see that you prefer a longer stay. The hotels we have listed have been chosen both for character and comfort, and are conveniently placed to allow you to explore the surrounding area.

### About the Restaurants & Hotels

Meal prices are generally comparable with similar standard restaurants in Rome. Romans love to dine out, so weekends tend to attract large numbers from the capital. Although good-class hotels abound in resort areas like the Castelli Romani and Sperlonga, they're less readily available in more industrialized zones like Viterbo and Palestrina, where accommodations cater more to commercial travelers than to tourists. The hotels we have chosen offer a high standard of service and are also full of character, reflecting the true atmosphere of the Roman countryside.

| WHAT IT COSTS in euros | | | | |
|---|---|---|---|---|
| | $$$$ | $$$ | $$ | $ | ¢ |
| RESTAURANTS | over €22 | €17–€22 | €12–€17 | €7–€12 | under €7 |
| HOTELS | over €210 | €160–€210 | €110–€160 | €60–€110 | under €60 |

Restaurant prices are per person for a main course *(secondo piatto)*. Hotel prices are for two people in a standard double room in high season, including tax and service.

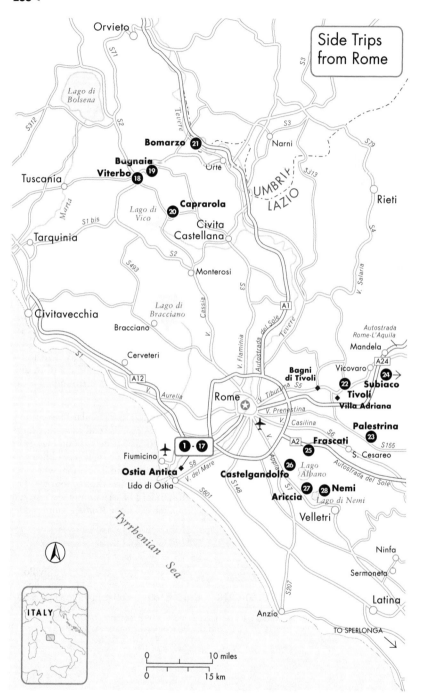

Side Trips
from Rome

Orvieto

*Lago di
Bolsena*

Tuscania

**Bomarzo** 21

Narni

**Bugnaia** 19
**Viterbo** 18

Orte

UMBRIA
LAZIO

Rieti

*Lago di
Vico*

20 **Caprarola**

Civita
Castellana

Tarquinia

Monterosi

*Lago di
Bracciano*

Civitavecchia

Bracciano

Cerveteri

A12

*Autostrada
Rome–L'Aquila*

Mandela

Vicovaro

A24

24 →

**Bagni
di Tivoli** 22

**Subiaco**

**Tivoli**
**Villa Adriana**

Rome

**Palestrina**

23

**Frascati**

25

S. Cesareo

Fiumicino

1 – 17

**Ostia Antica**

Lido di Ostia

26 **Castelgandolfo**

*Lago
Albano*

27 28 **Nemi**

**Ariccia**

*Lago di Nemi*

Velletri

*Tyrrhenian Sea*

Ninfa

Sermoneta

Latina

ITALY

Anzio

TO SPERLONGA ↘

0          10 miles

0          15 km

# OSTIA ANTICA

Set 25 km (15½) mi from the capital, Ostia Antica, Rome's ancient port on the Tiber estuary, is not quite as famous as Pompeii, but in many ways, gives an even more vivid idea of what life was like 2,000 years ago. Founded around the 4th century BC, Ostia served as Rome's harbor for several centuries until the Tiber changed course, leaving the town high and dry. Walking along its paved streets shaded by umbrella pines conjures up a poignant picture of life as it was back when. There are remarkably "modern" buildings, such as the *suburra* (apartment houses with balconies), the firemen's barracks, and the great market square of the various corporations, with their trademarks etched into the white mosaic pavement. It's easy to imagine this busy port thronged with people from all the corners of the Roman empire, and ships plying in and out with their merchandise. Eventually, the power of Rome crumbled, the Tiber silted up and the harbor was abandoned. Barbarians and mosquitoes (once frequent in central Italy's low-lying marshy areas) did the rest. Ostia Antica slumbered under the sand and mud until the beginning of the last century, when excavations began.

Fair weather and good walking shoes are essential when touring the ruined city today. One of the most pleasant ways to get to Ostia Antica is by boat: daily services sail down the Tiber from Rome. In summer, torchlighted theater or dance performances are often held in the terraced Roman theater. A visit to the excavations and adjoining museum takes at least two to three hours.

**Fodor's**Choice  **Ostia Antica** was inhabited by a cosmopolitan population of rich busi-
★  nessmen, wily merchants, sailors, slaves, and their respective families. The great *horrea* (warehouses) were built in the 2nd century AD to handle huge shipments of grain from Africa; the *insulae* (forerunners of the modern apartment building) provided housing for the growing population. Under the combined assaults of the barbarians and the *Anopheles* mosquito, and after the Tiber changed course, the port was eventually abandoned. Tidal mud and windblown sand covered the city, which lay buried until the beginning of the 20th century. Now the **Scavi di Ostia Antica** (Ostia Antica excavations) have been extensively excavated and are well maintained.

Before exploring Ostia Antica's ruins, it's worthwhile to take a detour to stroll around the quaint medieval *borgo* (old town) and visit the im-
▶ ❶ posing **Castello della Rovere.** This is the distinctive castle, easily spotted as you come off the footbridge from the train station, built by Pope Julius II when he was the cardinal bishop of Ostia in 1483. Its triangular form is unusual for military architecture. Inside are (badly faded) frescoes, believed to be by Michelangelo's pupil Baldassare Peruzzi.

❷ The **Porta Romana,** one of the city's three gates, is where you'll enter the Ostia Antica excavations. It opens onto the Decumanus Maximus, which is the main thoroughfare and crosses the city from end to end.

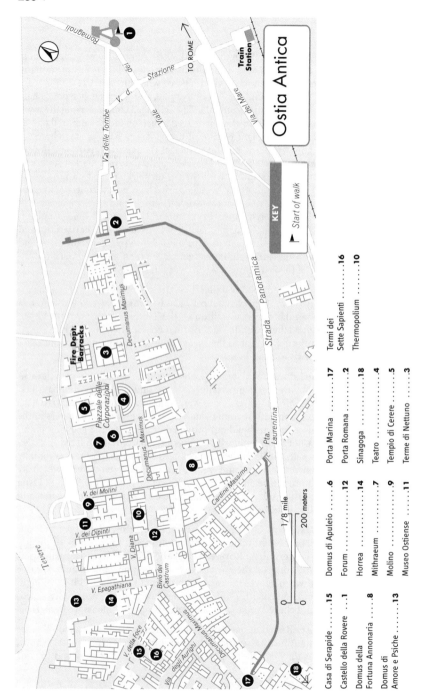

# Ostia Antica

To your right, a staircase leads to a platform—the remains of the upper

❸ floor of the **Terme di Nettuno** (Baths of Neptune)—from which you get a good view of the black-and-white mosaic pavements representing a marine scene with Neptune and Amphitrite. Directly behind the baths are the barracks of the fire department, which played an important role in a town whose warehouses were generally full of valuable goods and foodstuffs.

❹ On the north side of the Decumanus Maximus is the beautiful **Teatro** (Theater), built by Agrippa, remodeled by Septimius Severus in the 2nd century AD, and finally restored by the Rome City Council in the 20th century. In the vast Piazzale delle Corporazioni, where organizations sim-

❺ ilar to trade guilds had their offices, is the **Tempio di Cerere** (Temple of Ceres), which is only appropriate for a town dealing in grain imports—Ceres, who gave her name to cereal, was the goddess of agriculture. You

❻ can visit the **Domus di Apuleio** (House of Apuleius), built in Pompeian style, which meant lower to the ground and with fewer windows than

❼ was characteristic of Ostia. Next door, the **Mithraeum** has balconies and a hall decorated with symbols of the cult of Mithras. This male-only religion, imported from Persia, was especially popular with legionnaires.

❽ On Via Semita dei Cippi, just off Via dei Molini, the **Domus della Fortuna Annonaria** (House of Fortuna Annonaria) is the richly decorated former residence of a wealthy Ostian, which displays the skill of the mosaic artists of the period. One of the rooms opens onto a secluded garden.

❾ On Via dei Molini you can see a **molino** (mill), where grain for the warehouses next door was ground with stones that are still here. Along Via

❿ di Diana you come upon a **thermopolium** (bar) with a marble counter and a fresco depicting the fruit and foodstuffs that were sold here. At

⓫ the end of Via dei Dipinti is the **Museo Ostiense** (Ostia Museum), open the same hours as the Scavi (but enter at least a half hour before closing time), which displays sarcophagi, massive marble columns, and statuary too large to be shown anywhere else, including a beautiful figure of Mithras slaying the bull, which was taken from the underground Mithraeum.

⓬ The **Forum,** on the south side of Decumanus Maximus, holds the monumental remains of the city's most important temple, dedicated to Jupiter, Juno, and Minerva; other ruins of baths; a basilica (which in Roman times was a secular hall of justice); and smaller temples.

⓭ West of Via Epagathiana, the **Domus di Amore e Psiche** (House of Cupid and Psyche), a residence, was named for a statue found there (now on display in the museum); you can see what remains of a large pool in an enclosed garden decorated with marble and mosaic motifs. Even in ancient times a premium was placed on water views: the house faces the shore, which would have been only about ⅓ km (⅕ mi) away. Via

⓮ Epagathiana leads toward the Tiber, where there are large **horrea** (warehouses), which were erected during the 2nd century AD to store the enormous amounts of grain imported into Rome during that period, the height of the empire.

**⑮**    The **Casa di Serapide** (House of Serapis) on Via della Foce is a 2nd-century multilevel dwelling; another apartment building stands one street over
**⑯**    on Via degli Aurighi. Nearby, the **Termi dei Sette Sapienti** (Baths of the Seven Wise Men) are named after a group of bawdy frescoes found there.

**⑰**    The **Porta Marina** leads to what used to be the seashore. About 300 meters (1,000 feet) to the south of the Porta Marina are the ruins of the
**⑱**    **sinagoga** (synagogue), one of the oldest in the Western world.

⊠ *Via dei Romagnoli 717* ☎ *06/56358099* ⊕ *www.itnw.roma.it/ostia/ scavi* 🎫 *€4, includes admission to Museo Ostiense* ⊙ *Tues.–Sun. 9–1 hr before sunset.*

### Where to Eat

**$–$$$**   ✕ **Cipriani.** In a side street in the little medieval borgo near the excavations, this atmospheric small trattoria, with wooden beamed ceilings and frescoed walls, specializes in typical Roman cuisine. ⊠ *Via del Forno 11* ☎ *06/56359560* ▤ *AE, DC, MC, V* ⊙ *Closed Mon.*

## Ostia Antica A to Z

*To research prices, get advice from other travelers, and book travel arrangements, visit www.fodors.com.*

#### CAR TRAVEL
Follow Via del Mare southwest, which leads directly from Rome to Ostia (a 30- to 40-minute trip). It's best to avoid weekends in summer when Romans head for the beach and traffic can be heavy.

#### TRAIN TRAVEL
Regular train service links the Ostia Antica station with Rome's Piramide Metro line B station, near Porta San Paolo. Exit the Metro and go to the adjacent station called Ostia Lido. The ride takes about 35 minutes. Trains depart every half hour throughout the day.
🚃 **Cotral** ☎ 800/150008 ⊕ www.cotralspa.it

#### BOAT TRAVEL
Two boat companies operate regular services to Ostia Antica. Both leave from Ponte Marconi (Marconi Bridge) in Rome. The trip down the Tiber takes 2 hours and 15 minutes.

**Battelli di Roma** ☎ 06/6789361 ⊕ www.battellidiroma.it. Departures: Friday, Saturday, Sunday at 9:15, return trip from Ostia Antica: 1:30. Tickets: €10.

**Battelli "Invincibili 1" and "Love Boat"** ☎ 06/56304094 ⊕ www.gitesultevere.com. Daily departures at 10 AM. Tickets: €12 (booking essential).

# TUSCIA

The Viterbo region, north of the capital, is rich in history embodied in cameo scenes of dark medieval stone, dappled light on wooded paths, and magnificent country estates where Renaissance cardinals and princes came to enjoy their leisure. From Viterbo to Caprarola and Villa Lante, this region has a concentration of first-rate attractions—with the surprising Renaissance theme park at Bomarzo thrown in for good measure. The city of Viterbo, which overshadowed Rome as a center of papal power for a short time during the Middle Ages, is in the heart of Tuscia, the modern name for the Etruscan domain of Etruria, a landscape of dramatic beauty punctuated by thickly forested hills and deep, rocky gorges. The farmland east of Viterbo conceals small quarries of the dark, volcanic *peperino* stone used in the walls, as well as in portals and monumental fireplaces, of so many buildings here. Lake Bolsena, Europe's fifth largest volcanic lake, contains the island of Bisentina, where St. Francis of Assisi lived for a time in a cave. Boat trips go there in summer. The smaller Lake Vico is also of volcanic origin. The sulfur springs that still bubble up in Viterbo's spas were used by the ancient Romans.

Two of the greatest estates of late-Renaissance Italy are here: Bagnaia's Villa Lante's gardens, fountains, and waterfalls are a connoisseur's delight and sent Edith Wharton into ecstasy; and the huge 16th-century palace and gardens designed for the Farnese family at Caprarola is a triumph of Mannerist architecture. Both were the work of the virtuoso architect Giacomo Barozzi (circa 1535–circa 1584), known as Vignola, who later worked with Michelangelo on St. Peter's. He even rearranged the little town of Caprarola to enhance the palazzo's setting.

The ideal way to explore this region is by car, with Bomarzo as your first stop. By train, you would start at Viterbo, then get to Bagnaia by local bus. If you're traveling by train and/or bus, you'll have to check schedules carefully, and you may have to allow for an overnight if you want to see all four attractions.

## Viterbo

🔞 *104 km (64 mi) north of Rome.*

For a brief moment in the 13th century, Viterbo was the center of Christendom, when it became the seat of the papal court. The magnificent papal palace, in the heart of the San Pellegrino medieval quarter, witnessed five conclaves, including one that dragged on for two years and eight months while squabbling cardinals tried to make up their minds. The old buildings inside the 12th-century walls, whose windows are brightened with geraniums, are made of peperino, the local dark gray stone, contrasted here and there with the golden tufa rock of walls and towers. Peperino is also used in the characteristic medieval exterior staircases seen throughout the old town. In the 20th century, Viterbo blossomed into a regional commercial center, and much of the modern city is busy and industrial. The result is an intriguing mix of old and new, with daily life in the old part carried on in a setting that has remained practically unchanged over the centuries. The city is also a renowned spa center with natural hot springs just outside of town.

The Gothic **Palazzo Papale** (Papal Palace) was built in the 13th century for popes to use as a retreat from the city. At that time Rome was a notoriously unhealthful place, ridden with malaria and plague and rampaging factions of rival barons. In 1271 the palace was the scene of a novel type of rebellion. A conclave held here to elect Clement IV's successor had been trailing on for months. The people of Viterbo were exasperated by the delay, especially because custom decreed they were responsible for the cardinals' board and lodging for the duration of the conclave. So they tore the roof off the great hall where the cardinals were meeting, and put them on bread and water. Sure enough, a new pope—Gregory X—was soon elected. Inquire at the nearby Curia to see the Hall of the Conclave. ⊠ *Piazza San Lorenzo* ☎ *0761/341716.*

The facade and interior of Viterbo's cathedral, **Chiesa di San Lorenzo,** date from the Middle Ages. A small museum adjoins the cathedral. ⊠ *Piazza San Lorenzo* ☎ *0761/309623* ☉ *Daily 8–12:30 and 3:30–7.*

★ The medieval district of **San Pellegrino** is one of the best preserved of any in Italy. It has charming vistas of arches, vaults, towers, exterior staircases, worn wooden doors on great iron hinges, and tiny hanging gardens. You pass many antiques shops as you explore the little squares and byways. The **Fontana Grande** in the piazza of the same name is the largest and most extravagant of Viterbo's authentic Gothic fountains. ⊠ *Via San Pellegrino.*

☾ Viterbo has been a spa town for centuries, and the **Terme dei Papi** continues the tradition. This excellent spa offers the usual rundown of health and beauty treatments, but with an Etruscan twist: try a facial with local volcanic mud, or a steam bath in an ancient cave, where hot mineral water direct from the Bullicam spring splashes down a waterfall to a pool under your feet. The Terme dei Papi's main draw, however, is the *terme* (baths) themselves: a 100,000-square-foot outdoor limestone pool of Viterbo's famous naturally hot water, which pours in on the shallow end (which is much hotter) at 59°C (138°F)++CE: The degree symbol doesn't appear in hard copy; appears as infinity symbol, but command looks correct. How to fix?++ and intoxicates with its sulfurous odor. Floats and deck chairs are for rent, but bring your own bathrobe and towel, unless you're staying at the hotel. ⊠ *Strada Bagni 12, Viterbo* ☎ *0761/3501* ⊕ *www.termedeipapi.it* 🔳 *€15* ☉ *Pool Wed.–Mon. 9–7 PM, spa daily 9–6.*

### Where to Stay & Eat

★ $$$$ ✕ **Enoteca La Torre.** One of the best wine cellars in Italy takes center stage at the elegant Enoteca La Torre. It's also a temple to good eating: in addition to an ever-changing menu, there are lists for cheeses, mineral waters, oils, and vinegars. Chestnut fritters and rabbit stew are unusual delicacies, but whatever you choose will be local, traditional, and of the highest quality. The Enoteca's epic wine list includes a complex matrix of ratings from Italy's foremost wine reviewers. ⊠ *Via della Torre 5* ☎ *0761/226467* ▤ *AE, DC, MC, V* ☉ *Closed Sun.*

★ $–$$ ✕ **Tre Re.** Viterbo's oldest restaurant—and one of the most ancient in Italy—has been operating in the city's historic center since 1622. A gregarious buzz of Viterbese businesspeople and families fills the small wood-paneled, white-walled room to overflowing at lunchtime, as diners enjoy the truest versions of such Lazio specialties as *acquacotta viterbese* (literally "cooked water," a hearty vegetable and hot-pepper soup that was the ancient sustenance of shepherds and stockmen). ⊠ *Via Macel Gattesco 3* ☎ *0761/304619* ▤ *AE, MC, V* ☉ *Closed Thurs.*

**$$–$$$**  🏨 **Hotel Niccolò V.** This upscale, airy hotel is connected to Viterbo's mineral baths and spa at Terme dei Papi. Although the Niccolò, 5 km (3 mi) from the center of town, is certainly the most convenient lodging to the baths, the complex is also a surreal mix of doctors in scrubs, half-naked bathers, and hotel guests wandering through an enormous maze-like lobby. In the guest rooms, though, marble baths and wooden floors give an air of country-house elegance. A sumptuous breakfast buffet is offered in a wood-beamed gallery overlooking a small garden. Hotel guests are allowed free use of the outdoor and indoor pools. ✉ *Strada Bagni 12, 01100* ☎ *0761/350555* 📠 *0761/350273* ⊕ *www.termedeipapi.it* ⤶ *20 rooms, 3 suites* ♿ *Restaurant, in-room safes, minibars, pool, bar, meeting rooms* ☐ *AE, DC, MC, V.*

## Bagnaia

⑲ *5 km (3 mi) east of Viterbo.*

The village of Bagnaia, 5 km (3 mi) east of Viterbo, is the site of 16th-century cardinal Alessandro Montalto's summer retreat. Small twin res-

Fodor'sChoice idences are but an excuse for the hillside gardens—the **Villa Lante**—that

★ surround them, designed by Vignola for a member of the papal court. The park is a terraced extravaganza, which relies on a panoply of stonework pools and fountains and cut hedges—a highly regimented view of nature that would find its ultimate influence in the parterres and "green geometries" of Versailles. On the lowest terrace a delightful Italian garden has a centerpiece Fountain of the Moors fed by water channeled down the hillside. On another higher terrace a stream of water runs down a *catena d'acqua,* or water chain, designed by Vignola to resemble the leg of a crayfish (*gambara*—a reference to cardinal Giovanni Gambara who was the first to expand the garden complex). This watercourse then flows along a long stone table where the cardinal liked to entertain his friends alfresco, chilling wine in the running water. That's only one of the most evident and innocent of the whimsical water games that were devised for the cardinal. The symmetry of the formal gardens contrasts with the wild, untamed park adjacent to it, reflecting the paradoxes of nature and artifice that are the theme of this famous pleasure garden. In the 17th century the garden passed into the hands of the princely Rovere family and is now maintained by the state. ✉ *Via G. Baroni 71* ☎ *0761/288008* 🎟 *Park free, gardens and residences €2* ⊙ *Tues.–Sun. 8:30–7:30.*

## Caprarola

⑳ *19 km (12 mi) south of Viterbo.*

The wealthy and powerful Farnese family took over this sleepy village in the 1500s and endowed it with a palace that rivals the great residences

Fodor'sChoice of Rome. The magnificent 16th-century **Palazzo Farnese** started life as

★ a fortress, which explains the unusual pentagonal structure, built with former watchtowers on each corner. Cardinal Alessandro Farnese, the grandson of Pope Paul III, commissioned Vignola to transform his family's austere keep into a residence that would serve as a showplace where he could dazzle guests. One of the most impressive features is the spiral Grand Stairway connecting the Portal of Honors with the cardinal's domain on the *piano nobile*—a magnificent span that was wide enough for His Eminence to ride his horse right up to his bedchamber. Although there aren't many furnishings (true to Renaissance fashion), the staircase walls and all the palace rooms are covered with frescoes painted by the leading Mannerist artists of the day, one of whom was Taddeo Zuccero. The surrounding park contains many of the elements of a typical Renaissance garden, with formal shrubbery and paths, rows of sculpted herms, and cascades and fountains where the Farnese court could dine in the cool of the evening, listening to the refreshing sound of running water. ⊠ *Via Nicolai* ☎ *0761/646052* 🎫 *€2* ☉ *Tues.–Sun. 9–1 hr before sunset.*

## Bomarzo

**㉑**   *15 km (9 mi) east of Viterbo.*

🐾   The eerie 16th-century **Parco dei Mostri** (Monster Park) is populated by weird and fantastic sculptures of mythical creatures and fantastic monsters. The story goes that the eccentric Prince Vicino Orsini created this strange park in 1552 for the amusement of a mysterious lady he was in love with. The overgrown state of the garden adds to the wild effect, with a stone elephant peeping out of a tangle of creepers, an enormous turtle with a moss-covered shell, and a gigantic ogre whose gaping mouth leads into a dark cave. Harry Potter might even feel at home. Children love it, and there are photo ops galore. ⊠ *1½ km (1 mi) west of town* ☎ *0761/924666* 🎫 *€8* ☉ *Daily 8:30–1 hr before sunset.*

## Viterbo, Bagnaia, Caprarola & Bomarzo A to Z

### BUS TRAVEL

There's a frequent COTRAL bus service for Viterbo, departing from the Saxa Rubra stop of the Ferrovie COTRAL train. The so-called "diretta" (direct) bus takes about 75 minutes. Buses from Viterbo go to Bomarzo every two hours, starting at 9:20. The last bus back leaves Bomarzo at 6:45 PM. Bagnaia (Villa Lante) can also be reached from Viterbo by local city bus. For Caprarola, COTRAL buses leave from the Saxa Rubra station, Rome. From Viterbo, there are three bus services in the morning and three in the afternoon.

🚍 **APT Viterbo** ⊠ Via Romiti ☎ 0761/304795. **COTRAL** ⊠ Piazzale Flaminio ☎ 800/150008 ⊕ www.cotralspa.it.

### CAR TRAVEL

Head out of Rome on the A1 autostrada, exiting at Attigliano. Bomarzo is only 3 km (2 mi) from the autostrada. The trip takes one hour.

### TOURS

For Viterbo, authorized guides are available through the APT office ( ⇨ Visitor Information).

**TRAIN TRAVEL**
There's a fast mainline train service from Rome to Viterbo, which takes an hour and 40 minutes. For schedules and information, contact Trenitalia.
🚩 **Trenitalia** ☎ 166/105050 ⊕ www.trenitalia.it.

**VISITOR INFORMATION**
🚩 **APT Viterbo** ✉ Via Ascenzi 4 ☎ 0761/325992 ⊕ www.tusciainforma.it/viterbo (in English).

# TIVOLI, PALESTRINA & SUBIACO

Tivoli is a five-star draw, its attractions being its two villas—an ancient one in which Hadrian reproduced the most beautiful monuments in the then-known world, and a Renaissance one, in which cardinal Ippolito d'Este put a river to work for his delight. Unfortunately, the road from Rome to Tivoli passes through miles of uninspiring industrial areas with chaotic traffic. Grit your teeth and persevere. It'll be worth it. In the heart of this gritty shell lie two pearls that are rightly world famous. You'll know you're close to Tivoli when you see vast quarries of travertine marble and smell the sulfurous vapors of the little spa, Bagni di Tivoli. Both sites in Tivoli are outdoors and entail walking.

With a car, you can continue your loop through the mountains east of Rome, taking in two very different sights that are both focused on religion. The ancient pagan sanctuary at Palestrina is set on the slopes of Mount Ginestro, from which it commands a sweeping view of the green plain and distant mountains. Subiaco, the cradle of Western monasticism, is tucked away in the mountains above Tivoli and Palestrina. Unless you start out very early and have lots of energy, plan an overnight stop along the way if you want to take in all three.

## Tivoli

**㉒** *36 km (22 mi) east of Rome.*

In ancient times, just about anybody who was anybody had a villa in Tivoli, including Crassius, Trajan, Hadrian, Horace, and Catullus. Tivoli fell into obscurity in the medieval era until the Renaissance, when popes and cardinals came back to the town and built villas showy enough to rival those of their extravagant predecessors. Nowadays Tivoli is small but vibrant, with winding streets and views over the surrounding countryside, including the deep Aniene river gorge, which runs right through the center of town, and comes replete with a romantically sited bridge, cascading waterfalls, and two jewels of ancient Roman architecture that crown its cliffs—the round **Temple of Vesta** and the ruins of the rectangular **Sanctuary of the Sibyl,** probably built earlier. These can be picturesquely viewed across the gorge from the park of the **Villa Gregoriana** park, named for Pope Gregory XVI, who saved Tivoli from chronic river damage by diverting the river through a tunnel, weakening its flow. An unexpected (but not unappreciated) side effect was the creation of the **Grande Cascata** (Grand Cascade), which shoots a huge jet of water into the valley below. The Villa Gregoriana is at Largo Sant'Angelo (from the Largo Garibaldi bus stop, follow V. Pacifici—it changes name six times—and veer left on V. Roma to the Largo). There's a small admission charge to the park, which affords a sweaty, steep hike down to the river, so you may prefer to repair to the Antico Ristorante Sibilla, set right by the Temple of Vesta. From its dining terrace, you can drink in one of the most memorably romantic landscape views in Italy, one especially prized by 19th-century painters.

Fodor'sChoice ★ The astonishingly grand 2nd-century AD **Villa Adriana** (Hadrian's Villa), 6 km (4 mi) south of Tivoli, was an emperor's theme park, an exclusive retreat below the ancient settlement of Tibur where the marvels of the classical world were reproduced for a ruler's pleasure. Hadrian, who succeeded Trajan as emperor in AD 117, was a man of genius and intellectual curiosity, fascinated by the accomplishments of the Hellenistic world. From AD 125 to 134, architects, laborers, and artists worked on the villa, periodically spurred on by the emperor himself when he returned from another voyage full of ideas for even more daring constructions (he also gets credit for Rome's Pantheon). After his death, the fortunes of his villa declined. It was sacked by barbarians and Romans alike; many of his statues and decorations ended up in the Musei Vaticani, but the expansive ruins are nonetheless compelling.

It's not the single elements but the peaceful and harmonious effect of the whole that makes Hadrian's Villa such a treat. The vast estate is a fascinating succession of baths, theaters, temples, libraries, guest pavilions, nymphaeums, and open-air gymnasiums. The most famous "sight" in the Villa is the Canopus, an artificial valley with a long pool modeled after an Egyptian canal on the Nile, surrounded by colonnades and sculptures. Hadrian did not live long enough to enjoy his creation. He fell ill and retired to Baia near Naples, where he died in AD 138. Oleanders, pines, and cypresses growing among the ruins heighten the visual impact. A visit here should take about two hours, more if you like to savor antiquity slowly. Remember that it can get very hot in summer; try to visit early or in the afternoon. In the summer months, you may be able to view these spectacular ruins by night, where clever lighting effects show them up in all their haunting beauty. Times vary, year by year, so visitors should check up first with the local tourist office (0774/311249). Maps are issued free with the audio guides (€4) at the ticket office. From Tivoli, you can get a bus (going to Rebibbia) which stops at Villa Adriana, departing every two hours between 5.15 AM and 9 PM. ⊠ *Bivio di Villa Adriana, off Via Tiburtina, 6 km (4 mi) southwest of Tivoli* ☎ *0774/382733* 🎟 *€6.50, €8.50 when special exhibitions are running* ☉ *Daily 9–1 hr before sunset.*

★ Right in the center of Tivoli, **Villa d'Este,** created by cardinal Ippolito d'Este in the 16th century, was the most amazing pleasure garden of its day and still stuns visitors with its beauty. Inspired by the recent excavation of Villa Adriana and a devotee of the Renaissance celebration of human ingenuity over nature, Este (1509–72) paid architect Pirro Ligorrio an astronomical sum to create a mythical garden with water as its artistic centerpiece. To console himself for his seesawing fortunes in the political intrigues of his time (he happened to be cousin to Pope Alexander VI), he had his builders tear down part of a Franciscan monastery to clear the site, then divert the Aniene River to water the garden and feed the fountains—and what fountains: big, small, noisy, quiet, rushing, running, and combining to create a late-Renaissance, proto Busby Berkeley masterpiece in which sunlight, shade, water, gardens, and carved stone create an unforgettable experience. There are fountains of all shapes and sizes, from the tiny cascades that line the stone staircases leading down to the fish ponds at the bottom of the garden to the massive organ fountain that once played music. To this day, several hundred fountains cascade, shoot skyward, imitate bird songs, and simulate rain. Ancient cypress trees provide shade along the pathways. There's also a café on the upper terrace leading from the palace entrance, where you can sit and admire the view. Allow at least an hour for this visit (although you may want to spend the entire day) and bear in mind that you'll be climbing a lot of stairs. On some weekends in summer, "Villa d'Este at Night" allows you to tour the gardens and gape at all the fountains spotlighted to spectacular effect; show hours are from 9 to midnight (for annual dates, see the Web site). ⊠ *Piazza Trento 1* ☎ *0774/312070* ⊕ *www.villadestetivoli.info* 🖾 *€6.50, €10 at night* ☉ *Tues.–Sun. 9–1 hr before sunset.*

## Where to Stay & Eat

**$$$–$$$$**

**Fodor'sChoice**

★

✕**Antico Ristorante Sibilla.** This famed restaurant should be included among the sights of Tivoli. Built in 1730 beside the circular Roman Temple of Vesta and the Sanctuary of the Sibyl, the terrace garden has a spectacular view over the deep gorge of the Aniene river, with the thundering waters of the great waterfall in the background. The guest list reads like a visitor's book at Buckingham Palace. Marble plaques on the walls list the famous and the royals who have come here to dine over two and a half centuries. In decades gone by, the tour buses arrived and the food suffered. Today, however, food, wine, and service standards are high, as befits the sublime setting. ⊠ *Via della Sibilla 50* ☎*0774/335281* ☐*AE, DC, MC, V* ☉ *Closed Mon.*

**$$$**

🏨 **Hotel Torre S. Angelo** Set in a grand, rambling structure topped off with a soaring medieval tower, this deluxe hotel is 1 km (½ mi) from Tivoli. Standing on a hill with a magnificent view over the Aniene Falls and the Temple of the Sibyl, it's surrounded by olive groves. The building's history stretches back 2,000 years—erected in AD 600 on the ruins of the Roman poet Catullus's villa, it was a monastery for many centuries until it became the summer residence of the Princes Massimo in 1700. Restructured as a hotel in 1994, its rooms come with Jacuzzi, minibar, air-conditioning, safe, and satellite TV. Guest rooms have been (too?) glossily renovated, with Empire-style chairs and traditional wallpapers, but comfort is supreme. The garden has a swimming pool and there's a golf course 20 minutes away. The elegant restaurant serves Italian and international cuisine. Half- or full-board plans are available. ⊠ *Via Quintilio Varo, 00019* ☎*0774/332533* 🖷*0774/ 332533* ⊕ *www.hoteltorresangelo.it/* ⌨ *25 rooms, 10 suites* ⚭ *Restaurant, minibars, in-room safes, cable TV, pool* ☐ *AE, DC, MC, V.*

**$**

✕🏨 **Adriano.** At the entrance to Hadrian's Villa, this restaurant-inn is a handy place to have lunch before heading up the hill to Villa d'Este—or a good base for the night before or after exploring. The restaurant is Italian with a sophisticated touch, as in risotto *ai fiori di zucchine* (with zucchini flowers) or grilled porcini mushrooms in season. The atmosphere is relaxing, especially at outdoor tables in summer. The Adriano's 10 rooms are casually elegant and immaculately kept. ⊠ *Via di Villa Adriana 194* ☎ *0774/382235* 📠 *0774/535122* ↩ *10 rooms* ⚐ *Restaurant, tennis courts, bar; no smoking* ▤ *AE, DC, MC, V* ☉ *No dinner Sun.*

# Palestrina

**㉓** *27 km (17 mi) south of Tivoli on S636, 37 km (23 mi) east of Rome along Via Prenestina.*

Palestrina is surprisingly little known outside Italy, except to students of ancient history and music lovers. Its most famous native son, Giovanni Pierluigi da Palestrina, born here in 1525, is the greatest composer of the Renaissance period. His house, now the **Fondazione Giovanni Pierluigi da Palestrina,** in the heart of the old town is now a museum containing a collection of 6,000 music manuscripts and volumes dating back to the 16th century. ⊠ *Vicolo Pierluigi* ☎ *06/9538083* 💶 *€5* ☉ *Wed.–Sun. 10–12.*

Of course, Palestrina was a celebrated cult center long before the composer's day. Ancient Praeneste (modern Palestrina) flourished much earlier than Rome. It was the site of the **Temple of Fortune Primigenia,** which dates from the 2nd century BC. This was one of the largest, richest, most frequented temple complexes in all antiquity—people came from far and wide to consult its famous oracle. In modern times, no one had any idea of the extent of the complex until World War II bombings exposed ancient foundations occupying huge artificial terraces stretching from the upper part of the town as far downhill as its central *duomo* (cathedral) along the slopes of Monte Ginestro.

Large arches and terraces scale the hillside up to the imposing **Palazzo Barberini,** built in the 17th century along the semicircular lines of the ancient temple. It's now a museum containing material found on the site, dating from throughout the classical period. This well-labeled collection of Etruscan bronzes, pottery, and terra-cotta statuary as well as Roman artifacts takes second place to the chief attraction, a 1st-century BC mosaic representing the Nile in flood with innumerable details. It alone is worth the trip to Palestrina. But there's more: a model of the temple as it was in ancient times, which will help you appreciate the immensity of the original construction. ⊠ *Museo Nazionale Archeologico, Palazzo Barberini* ☎ *06/9538100* 💶 *€4* ☉ *Daily 9–8; archaeological zone of temple daily 9–1 hr before sunset.*

## Where to Eat

**$$–$$$** ✕ **Il Piscarello.** Tucked away at the bottom of a steep side road, this elegant restaurant comes as a bit of a surprise. The yellow damask table linen and deep gold curtains give the spacious dining room a warm and sunny look, and there's a trim patio overlooking the garden for alfresco dining in good weather. Specialties on the menu include black-and-white truffles, *porcini* mushrooms, seafood, and fish. ⊠ *Via del Piscarello 2* ☎ *06/9574326* ▤ *AE, MC, V* ☉ *Closed Mon.*

## Subiaco

**24** *54 km (33 mi) east of Rome.*

Tucked in among wooded mountains in the deep and narrow valley of the Aniene River, which empties into the Tiber in Rome, Subiaco is a modern town built over World War II rubble. It's chiefly known (aside from being the birthplace of actress Gina Lollobrigida, whose family name is common in these parts) as the site of the monastery where St. Benedict devised his rule of communal religious life in the 6th century, founding the order that was so important in transmitting learning through the ages. Even earlier, the place was a refuge of Nero, who built a villa here to rival that of Hadrian at Tivoli, damming the river to create three lakes and a series of waterfalls. The road to the monastery passes the ruins of the emperor's villa. Besides the sights below, located outside town, Subiaco has some sights in town, including frescoes by Il Sodoma in the 14th-century church of San Francesco and a fortified abbey, which contains the frescoed apartments of Pius VI, who was abbot of Subiaco before he became pope.

**Convento di Santa Scolastica,** between Subiaco and St. Benedict's hermitage on the mountainside, is the only hermitage founded by St. Benedict to have survived the Lombard invasion of Italy in the 9th century. It has three cloisters extant; the oldest dates from the end of the 12th century. The library contains precious volumes; this was also the site of the first print shop in Italy, set up in 1464. ⊹ *Road to Jenne and Vallepietra, 2½ km (1½ mi) east of Subiaco* ⊠ *Free* ⊙ *Daily 9–12:30, 3:30–7.*

The 6th-century **Monastero di San Benedetto** is a landmark of Western monasticism. It was built over the grotto where the saint lived and meditated. Clinging to the cliff on nine great arches, it has resisted assaults for almost 900 years. Over the little wooden veranda at the entrance, a Latin inscription wishes PEACE TO THOSE WHO ENTER. The upper church is covered with frescoes by Umbrian and Sienese artists of the 14th century. In front of the main altar, a stairway leads to the lower church, carved out of the rock, with another stairway leading down to the grotto where Benedict lived as a hermit for three years. The frescoes here are even earlier than those above; look for the portrait of St. Francis of Assisi, painted from life in 1210, in the **Cappella di San Gregorio** (Chapel of St. Gregory), and for the oldest fresco in the monastery, in the **Grotta dei Pastori** (Shepherds' Grotto). ⊠ *Subiaco* ☎ *0774/85039* ⊠ *Free* ⊙ *Daily 9–12:30 and 3–6.*

### Where to Stay & Eat

$ ✗⊞ **Miramonti.** This small hotel and its restaurant, La Botte di Bacco ($–$$; closed Wednesday), are on the road between Subiaco and Monte Livata. The restaurant is homey and cordial; specialties include the inviting gnocchi *al radicchio e tartufo* (with radicchio and black truffles) and *bistecca di cinghiale* (wild boar steak). Adequate for an overnight, the rooms are simply furnished but comfortable. ⊠ *Viale Giovanni XXIII 4* ☎ *0774/825029* ⇨ *11 rooms* ⌂ *Restaurant, bar* ▭ *DC, MC, V.*

## Tivoli, Palestrina & Subiaco A to Z

### BUS TRAVEL

COTRAL buses leave Rome for Tivoli every 15 minutes from the terminal at the Ponte Mammolo stop on Metro line B. The ride takes about one hour. There's a shuttle bus service from Tivoli main square to Hadrian's Villa. From Rome to Palestrina, take the COTRAL bus from Anagnina on Metro line A or Rebibbia on Metro line B. From Rome to Subiaco, take the COTRAL bus from the Rebibbia stop on Metro B; buses leave every 40 minutes. The circuitous trip takes one hour and 45 minutes.
🚍 **COTRAL** ☎ 800/150008.

### CAR TRAVEL

For Tivoli, take the Rome–L'Aquila autostrada (A24). To get to Palestrina directly from Rome, you can follow the old Roman Via Prenestina. This can be heavily congested, so an alternative route is the Autostrada del Sole (A2) to the Valmontone exit and then to the 55/a Pedemontana 11 road. The trip will take at least an hour, depending on traffic. To go to Palestrina from Tivoli, take the Via Maremmana, then the Via Prenestina. From Rome to Subiaco, take the S155 east for about 40 km (25 mi) and the S411 for 25 km (15½ mi); the trip takes about 90 minutes.

From Tivoli to Palestrina, follow signs for Via Prenestina and Palestrina. To get to Subiaco from either Tivoli or Palestrina, take the autostrada for L'Aquila (A24) to the Vicovaro-Mandela exit, then follow the local road to Subiaco.

### TOURS

All major tour companies, like Appian Line, Vastours, and Carrani organize trips to Tivoli and its Villa d'Este and Hadrian's Villa.
🚍 **Vastours** ☎ 06/4814246 ⊕ www.vastours.it/roma.htm. **Appian Line** ☎ 06/487861 ⊕ www.appianline.it. **Carrani Tours** ☎ 06/4742501 ⊕ www.carrani.com. **APT(Rome Tourist Information Office)** ☎ 06/36004399 ⊕ www.aptprovroma.it/.

### TRAIN TRAVEL

Local trains connect Rome's Tiburtina station with Tivoli in about 30 minutes and there's a shuttle bus service from the station to the town center and Villa d'Este. For Palestrina, take a train to Zagarola, where there's a COTRAL shuttle bus service to the center of Palestrina. The total journey takes about 40 minutes.
🚍 **Trenitalia** ☎ 166/105050 ⊕ www.trenitalia.it.

### VISITOR INFORMATION

🚍 **Palestrina** ✉ Piazza della Cortina ☎ 06/9538100. **Subiaco** ✉ Via Cadorna 59 ☎ 0774/822013. **Tivoli** ✉ Largo Garibaldi ☎ 0774/334522 ⊕ www.tivoli.it/turismo.htm.

# THE CASTELLI ROMANI

The "castelli" aren't really castles, as their name would seem to imply. They're little towns that are scattered on the slopes of the Alban Hills near Rome. And the Alban hills aren't really hills, but extinct volcanoes.

There were castles here in the Middle Ages, however, when each of these towns, fiefs of rival Roman lords, had its own fortress to defend it. Some centuries later, the area became given over to villas and retreats, notably the pope's summer residence at Castelgandolfo, and the 17th- and 18th-century villas that transformed Frascati into the Beverly Hills of Rome. Arrayed around the rim of an extinct volcano that encloses two crater lakes, the string of picturesque towns of the Castelli Romani are today surrounded by vineyards, olive groves, and chestnut woods—no wonder overheated Romans have always loved to escape here.

Ever since Roman times, the Castelli towns have been renowned for their wine. In the narrow, medieval alleyways of the oldest parts, you can still find old-fashioned hostelries where the locals sit on wooden benches, quaffing the golden nectar straight from the barrel. Following the mapped-out Castelli Wine Route around the numerous vineyards and wine cellars is a more sophisticated alternative. Exclusive local gastronomic specialties include the bread of Genzano, baked in traditional wood-fired ovens, the *porchetta* of Ariccia, and the *pupi* biscuits of Frascati, shaped like women or mermaids with three or more breasts (an allusion to ancient fertility goddesses). Each town has its own feasts and saints days, celebrated with costumed processions and colorful events. Some are quite spectacular, like Marino's annual Wine Festival in October, where the town's fountains flow with wine, or the Flower Festival of Genzano in June, when an entire street is carpeted with millions of flower petals, arranged in elaborate patterns.

## Frascati

**㉕** *21 km (13 mi) southwest of Subiaco, 20 km (12 mi) south of Rome.*

Frascati was the chosen sylvan retreat of prelates and princes, who built magnificent villas on the sun-drenched slopes overlooking the Roman plain. The most spectacular of these is **Villa Aldobrandini,** which dominates Frascati's main square from the top of its steeply sloped park. Built in the late 16th century and adorned with frescoes by the Zuccari brothers and the Cavalier d'Arpino, the hulking villa is still privately owned by the Princes Aldobrandini. However, its park is a marvel of Baroque fountains and majestic box-shaded avenues and you can go and see the magnificent Water Theater that Cardinal Pietro Aldobrandini, Pope Clement VIII's favorite nephew, built to impress his guests, thinking nothing of diverting the water supply that served the entire area in order to make his fountains play. The gigantic central figure of Atlas holding up the world is believed to represent the Pope. You can also see another Water Theater in the grounds of nearby Villa Torlonia, which is now a public park. Visitors to this villa must apply for a permit from local Azienda Turismo Frascati first, located at Piazza Marconi 1 ⊠ *Via Cardinale Massaia* ☎ *06/9420331 (tourist office)* ⬛ *Free* ☉ *Mon.–Fri. 9–1, 3–6.*

Villa Aldobrandini looks across Piazza Marconi to the Belvedere terrace, a sort of outdoor parlor for the town. This is a favorite gathering place for young and old alike, especially on summer evenings when the lights of Rome can be seen twinkling in the distance. It's worth taking a stroll through Frascati's lively old center. Via Battisti, leading from the Belvedere, takes you into Piazza S. Pietro with the imposing gray-and-white **Cathedral**. Inside is the cenotaph of Prince Charles Edward, last of the Scottish Stuart dynasty, who tried unsuccessfully to regain the British crown, and died an exile in Rome in 1788. A little arcade beside the monumental fountain at the back of the piazza leads into Market Square, where the smell of fresh baking will entice you into the Purificato family bakery to see the traditional *pupi* biscuits, modeled on old pagan fertility symbols.

Take your pick from the cafés and trattorias fronting the central Piazzale Marconi, or do as the locals do—buy fruit from the market gallery at Piazza del Mercato, then get a huge slice of *porchetta* (roast suckling pig) from one of the stalls, a hunk of *casareccio* bread, and a few *ciambelline frascatane* (ring-shape cookies made with wine), and take your picnic to any one of the numerous local *cantine* (homey wine bars), and settle in for some sips of tasty, inexpensive vino.

## Where to Stay & Eat

★ **$$$-$$$$** ✕ **Al Fico Vecchio.** This is a historic coaching inn, dating back to the 16th century, situated on an old Roman road a couple of miles outside Frascati. It has a charming garden, shaded by the branches of the old fig tree that gave it its name. The dining room has been tastefully renovated, preserving many of the characteristic antique features. The menu offers a wide choice of local dishes. Not to be confused with the Nuovo Fico just up the road. ⊠ *Via Anagnini 257* ☎ *06/945–9261* ▭ *AE, DC, MC.*

★ **$$$$** ⌂ **Park Hotel Villa Grazioli.** One of Frascati's famous noble residences, this elegant patrician villa, halfway between Frascati and Grottaferrata, is now converted into a first class hotel. Built in 1580 and modeled after Rome's Villa Farnesina, the house was owned over the centuries by the regal Borghese and Odelscalchi families, and was nearly destroyed by bombs in World War II. Happily, the vast reception rooms on the *piano nobile*—covered with frescoes of landscapes, mythological figures, and garden scenes by eminent 17th-century painters—survived mostly unscathed. The showpiece remains the South Gallery, frescoed by Giovanni Paolo Pannini in a swirl of trompe-l'oeil scenes, a masterpiece of Baroque decorative art. The drama ends when you get to the guest rooms, which are standard-issue, white-wall salons with traditional furniture; rooms found in the adjacent rustic-style Limonaia lodge have lovely wood-beam ceilings. The hotel is surrounded by a vast park, with swimming pool, hanging gardens, and a panoramic terrace. The cherry on top is the luxurious Acquaviva restaurant, where you can enjoy half- or full-board plans. The hotel's air-conditioning is tops, too. ⊠ *Via Umberto Pavoni 19, Grottaferrata 00046* ☎ *06/9454001* 🖷 *06/9413506* ⊕ *www.villagrazioli.com* ⌦ *56 rooms, 2 suites* ⌂ *Restaurants, minibars, cable TV, in-room safes, pool* ▭ *AE, DC, MC, V.*

# Castelgandolfo

**㉖** *8 km (12 mi) southwest of Frascati, 25 km (15 mi) south of Rome.*

This little town is well known as the Pope's summer retreat. It was the Barberini pope Urban VIII who first headed here, eager to escape the malarial miasmas that afflicted summertime Rome; before long, the city's princely families also set up country estates around here. The 17th-century **Villa Pontifica** has a superb position overlooking Lake Albano and is set in one of the most gorgeous gardens in Italy; unfortunately, neither the house nor the park are open to the public (although crowds are admitted into the inner courtyard for papal audiences). On the little square in front of the palace there's a fountain by Bernini, who also designed the nearby Church of San Tommaso da Villanova, which has works by Pietro da Cortona. The village has a number of interesting craft workshops and food purveyors, in addition to the souvenir shops on the square. On the horizon, the silver astronomical dome belonging to the Specola Vaticana observatory—one of the first in Europe—where the scientific Pope Gregory XIII indulged his interest in stargazing, is visible for miles around.

To the right of the papal palace, a walled road leads down to the lakeside, 300 feet below. The **lakeside lido** is lined with restaurants, ice-cream parlors, and cafés and is a favorite spot with Roman families. No motorized craft are allowed on the lake, but you can rent paddle boats and kayaks. The waters are full of seafowl, such as swans and herons, and nature trails are mapped out along both ends of the shore. All along the central part there are bathing establishments where you can rent deck chairs, or stop to eat a plate of freshly prepared pasta or a gigantic Roman sandwich at one of the little snack bars under the oaks and alder trees. There's also a small, permanent fairground for children.

## Where to Eat

★ **$$$–$$$$** ✕ **Antico Ristorante Pagnanelli.** One of most refined restaurants in the Castelli Romani, this has been in the same family since 1882—the present generation, Aurelio Pagnanelli and Jane, his Australian wife, with the help of their four sons, have lovingly restored this old railway inn perched high above Lake Albano. The dining room windows open onto a breathtaking view across the lake to the conical peak of Monte Cavo. In winter a log fire blazes in a corner; in summer dine out on the flower-filled terrace. Many of the dishes are prepared with produce from the family's own farm. The wine cellar, carved out of the living tufa rock, boasts more than 3,000 labels. ✉ *Via Gramsci 4* ☎ *06/9360004* ▭ *AE, DC, MC, V* ✪ *Closed Tues.*

# Ariccia

➋➐ *8 km (13 mi) southwest of Castelgandolfo, 26 km (17 mi) south of Rome.*

Ariccia is a gem of Baroque town planning. When millionaire banker Agostino Chigi became Pope Alexander VII, he commissioned Gian Lorenzo Bernini to redesign his country estate to make it worthy of his new station. Bernini consequently restructured not only the existing 16th-century palace, but also the town gates, the main square with its loggias and graceful twin fountains, and the round church of **Santa Maria dell'Assunzione** (the dome is said to be modeled on the Pantheon). The rest of the village coiled around the apse of the church down into the valley below. Strangely, Ariccia's splendid heritage has been largely forgotten in the 20th century, and yet it was once one of the highlights of every artist and writer's Grand Tour. Corot, Ibsen, Turner, Longfellow, and Hans Christian Andersen all came to stay at the Martorelli Inn on the main square (next to the pharmacy, but only open for rare temporary exhibitions; inside are some lovely 19th-century frescoed rooms).

★ **Palazzo Chigi** is a rare example of a Baroque residence whose original furniture, paintings, drapes, and decorations are still mostly intact. The Italian film director Lucchino Visconti shot most of the internal scenes of the film *The Leopard* inside the villa. The rooms contain intricately carved pieces of 17th-century furniture, like the Pharmacy designed by Carlo Fontana and Bernini's splendid consoles, as well as textiles and costumes from the 16th to the 20th century. See the Room of Beauties, lined with paintings of the loveliest ladies of the day, and the Nuns' Room, with portraits of 10 Chigi sisters, all of whom took the veil. The park stretching behind the palace is a wild wood, the last remnant of the ancient Latium forest, where herds of deer still graze under the trees. ⊠ *Piazza di Corte 14* ☎ *06/9330053* ⊕ *www.palazzochigiariccia.it/* ⊡ *€7* ⊗ *Guided tours only: weekends every hr 10:30–7, Tues.–Fri. at 11, 4, 5:30.*

A visit to Ariccia is not complete without tasting the local gastronomic specialty: *porchetta,* the delicious roast whole pig stuffed with herbs. The shops on the Piazza di Corte will make up a sandwich for you, or you can do what the Romans do: take a seat at one of the *fraschette* wine cellars that serve cheese, cold cuts, pickles and olives, and sometimes a plate of pasta. Conditions are rather rough and ready: you sit on a wooden bench at a trestle table covered over with simple white paper, but there's no better place to make friends and maybe join in a singsong.

### Where to Eat

$ ✕ **La Locanda del Brigante Gasparone.** The first of the string of *fraschette* (informal hostelries) you find clustered under the Galloro bridge, on the right-hand side of Palazzo Chigi, this locanda has seats either inside or outside under an awning—a fine place to enjoy simple, robust pasta dishes, washed down with a carafe of local Castelli wine. ⊠ *Via Borgo S. Rocco 7* ☎ *06/9333100* ⊟ *No credit cards* ⊗ *Closed Wed.*

# Nemi

❷❽ *4 km (10 mi) west of Ariccia, 34 km (21 mi) south of Rome.*

Nemi is the smallest and prettiest village of the Castelli Romani. Perched on a spur of rock 600 feet above the small crater lake of the same name, it has an eagle's-nest view over the rolling Roman countryside as far as the coast some 18 km (29 mi) away. The one main street, Corso Vittorio Emanuele, takes you to the baronial Castello Ruspoli (private, now owned by a businessma), with its 11th-century watch tower, and the quaint little Piazza Umberto 1, lined with outdoor cafés serving the tiny wood-strawberries harvested from the crater bowl. If you continue on through the arch that joins the castle to the former stables, you come to the entrance of the dramatically landscaped public gardens, which curve steeply down to the panoramic **Belvedere** terrace. If you enjoy walking, you can follow the road past the garden entrance and go all the way down to the bottom of the crater.

Nemi may be small in size, but it has a long and fascinating history. In Roman times there was an important sanctuary to the moon goddess Diana on the lakeside, which drew thousands of pilgrims from all over the Roman empire. In the 1930s, the Italian government drained the lake in order to recover two magnificent ceremonial ships, loaded with sculptures, bronzes, and art treasures, that had lain submerged for 2,000 years. Unfortunately, the ships were burned during World War II. The state-of-the-art **Museo delle Navi Romani** (Roman Ship Museum) on the lake shore, which was built to house them, has scale models and photographs of the complex recovery operation, as well as some finds from the sanctuary. ⊠ *Via del Tempio di Diana 9* ☎ *06/9398040* ▭ *€2* ☉ *Daily, 9–6:30.*

## Where to Eat

$$ ✕ **Specchio di Diana.** Situated halfway down the main street is Nemi's most historic inn—Byron reputedly stayed here when visiting the area. A wine bar and café are on street level while the restaurant proper on the second floor offers marvelous views, especially at sunset. Pizzas are popular, but don't neglect Nemi's regional specialties: *fettucine al sugo di lepre* (fettucine with hare sauce), roast *porcini* mushrooms, and the little wood-strawberries with whipped cream. ⊠ *Corso Vittorio Emanuele 13* ☎ *06/9368805* ▭ *AE, MC, V.*

# The Castelli Romani A to Z

### BUS TRAVEL

COTRAL buses run frequent services to the various Castelli towns from the Anagnina Metro A terminal (on Rome outskirts at the end of the Metro A line and easily accessible from metro A stations in city center). The journey takes from 50 minutes to an hour, depending on your destination. To get to Nemi, take the bus to Genzano, where a bus leaves for Nemi every two hours. If this isn't convenient, you can get a taxi or, if you feel energetic, walk the 5 km (3 mi) around the lake.
🔧 **COTRAL** ☎ 800/150008 ⊕ www.cotralspa.it

### CAR TRAVEL

To get to Frascati, take the Via Tuscolano, which branches off the Via Appia Nuova just after St. John Lateran in Rome. For Castelgandolfo, follow the Appia Nuova to Albano and branch off at the signs for Castelgandolfo. To get to Ariccia, carry on straight through Albano. The same road takes you on to Genzano and Nemi. Since distances are not great, you can plan a circular tour.

### TRAIN TRAVEL

Hourly train services leaving from Rome's Termini Station connect Frascati and Castelgandolfo-Albano. Both trips take just under an hour, partly on single-line tracks running through fields and vineyards. Buses from Albano connect with Ariccia and Nemi.
🔧 **Trenitalia** ☎ 800/431784 ⊕ www.trenitalia.it

### VISITOR INFORMATION

🔧 **APT Frascati** ⊠ Piazza G. Marconi 1 ☎ 06/9324081 ⊕ www.frascati2000.it. **APT Provincia di Roma** ⊠ Via XX Settembre 26 ☎ 06/421381 ⊕ www.aptprovroma.it. **Castelli Wine Route** ⊕ www.stradadeivinideicastelliromani.it.

# UNDERSTANDING ROME

**F**OR THE LOVER OF ART, Rome remains the richest city in the world, its accumulated treasures inexhaustible despite centuries of plundering and decay. The epic time span of its art and architecture is immediately apparent when you arrive at Termini train station: although still under the daring modern sweep of the station's curving forecourt roof (finished in 1950), you can see to the right imposing fragments of the first city walls (of the 4th century BC, but traditionally ascribed to the 6th-century BC King Servius Tullius), and a walk across the piazza leads to Michelangelo's brilliant adaptation for Christian use in the 1560s of the last of the great imperial Roman baths (finished by Diocletian in AD 306). In fact, the idlest stroll in town offers a succession of subtle or dramatic pleasures for the eye.

Given Rome's reputation as an artistic center and source of inspiration, it is surprising, but significant, that it has almost never had a native school of art. Most of the distinguished works to be seen are imports, copies, or the work of outsiders in the service of kings, consuls, emperors, or popes.

## Etruscan & Greek Influences

The story of the earliest Roman art is that of domination by the neighboring Etruscans (and, through them, by the colonizing Greeks). The first great temple—that of Jupiter, Juno, and Minerva on the Campidoglio—was built for the last of the ancient kings, Tarquin the Proud, by "workmen summoned from every part of Etruria," among them the first named artist to work in Rome, sculptor Vulca from Veii. Only the blocks of the temple's base survive—a large portion came to light in 1998 under the pavement of Palazzo Caffarelli, on the Campidoglio— but its lively, colored terra-cotta ornament can be judged from the grinning faces on antefixes preserved in museums, especially in the Etruscan Museum in Villa Giulia.

From the Etruscans, the Romans adopted the habit of making graven images of their gods and probably also of casting statues in bronze. (There are reports of bronzes made at the time of the first Etruscan kings, but among the earliest and most numerous to survive are renderings of the Capitoline Wolf—vigilantly offering her teats to the infants Romulus and Remus—and these are of later date.) Etruscan, too, was the practice that prevailed throughout antiquity of setting up commemorative portrait statues in public—of kings and of women but, principally, of military heroes. The victorious Republican Spurius Carvilius used the enemy armor he captured in 293 BC to have a giant figure of Jupiter made; and, from the filings left over, a statue of himself was cast—one of the many precursors to the splendid marble Augustus now in the Vatican. In 158 BC the Forum had become so crowded with portrait statues that the consuls removed those that had not been authorized.

Portraits were also commonly made for family reasons. Wax masks of the dead (which could be worn by the living so that a man's ancestors could be present at his funeral), along with triumphal spoils, might be displayed on the lintels of the family house. Portraits were frequent also on the later marble coffins, or sarcophagi, in which even freed slaves might be buried. Although neither sarcophagi nor portraits were invented by the Romans, their eventual mastery of portraiture is legendary; the early bronze bust of *Brutus* on the Campidoglio is a noble example.

Elegance was in general a marked feature of early Roman taste. But the expulsion of the Etruscans and the kings, and the expansion in the last centuries BC of the republican state that was to dominate Italy and eventually the whole Mediterranean, brought with them a massive influx into the capital city of foreign booty; not just captured weapons but captured works of art, carried in the triumphal processions of returning generals along with paintings of their exploits and set up later as public ornaments. "Prior to this," says Pliny, "Rome knew nothing of these exquisite and refined things . . . rather it was full of barbaric weapons and bloody spoils; and though it was garlanded with memorials and trophies of triumphs there was no sight which was joyful to refined spectators." As the old-fashioned Cato is reported to have said, "Now I hear far too many people praising and marveling at the ornaments of Corinth and Athens, and laughing at our terra-cotta antefixes of the Roman gods."

Rome was thus exposed to a much more direct contact with Greek art, and the new conquests brought Greek artists and materials as well as finished works. Temples retained some traditional Etruscan features in plan but began to look more Greek, such as those in Largo Argentina or the 2nd-century BC Temple of Fortuna Virilis by the Tiber, built of rough local tufa and travertine. The nearby circular Temple of Vesta (originally the Temple of Hercules, as an inscription discovered in the 20th century has shown), which dates from the 3rd century, is made of the more "luxurious" material of marble. Not all old-style macho Romans welcomed this. When Lucius Crassus used foreign marble for his house on the Palatine, he was dubbed the "Palatine Venus." The great orator Cicero was not unusual in collecting examples of Greek art for his villa (a practice he called "my voluptuous pleasure"). Similarly, public art galleries were set up. Masterpieces of Greek sculpture were indeed in such demand that war booty did not suffice, and many works were mechanically copied by the "pointing" process (invented by the Greeks and now used for the first time on a large scale)—so many in fact that a great proportion of the surviving antique statues in Rome's museums, even the Belvedere Apollo in the Vatican, are Roman copies or adaptations of Greek originals.

Art in Republican Rome was not entirely the consequence of plunder or imported labor. There were some exceptional native artists, principally in the more socially acceptable field of painting, in which a noble, Fabius Pictor, worked as early as the 4th century BC and later emperors such as Nero and Hadrian are reported to have excelled. Mural painting is also a genre in which one can speak of a distinctively Roman contribution. Compared with Pompeii, however, sadly little ancient painting or interior decoration survives in Rome, particularly from the early period. A noteworthy find, made in 1998, is a large bird's-eye view of a city that may be Rome itself, painted in Nero's time on a wall of the emperor's fabulous Domus Aurea (Golden House). There are some very fine examples of 1st-century BC painting and stucco—the charming landscape garden of Livia's villa and the "picture gallery" decor of the Farnesina House—in the Museo Nazionale Romano in Palazzo Massimo alle Terme and on the Palatine.

## The Art of the Empire

The transition from a republican to an imperial form of government in the late 1st century BC was achieved gradually, by stealth as well as force. Julius Caesar and Augustus used public art as propaganda to buttress their positions; they undertook major building projects, leading to the famous claim that Augustus "found Rome brick and left it marble." Marble had of course been introduced earlier, but the forum Augustus built contains a greater variety of foreign colored marbles imported from the subject provinces of the Mediterranean than had been used before. Similarly, he was responsible for the introduction to Rome of the first Egyptian obelisks, which came to be a distinctive part of the city scene. (The one at Montecitorio was originally used as a giant sundial.)

The triple-bayed triumphal arch built for him in the Foro Romano (whose fragments helped to build St. Peter's) also prefigures a characteristically Roman form, but Augustus's patronage was not overwhelmingly self-promoting. He was responsible for, but did not give his name to, the Theater of Marcellus and other buildings. He built a temple in honor of the deified Julius Caesar, but he would not allow temples to be dedicated to himself unless they were also dedicated to Rome. The most attractive and best-preserved monument from his day is the Ara Pacis (Altar of Augustan Peace), reconstructed near his mausoleum in the 20th century. Its sophisticated carving is interesting as a revival of classical Greek style, though the use of historical imagery, with its portrait scenes, allegories, and episodes from the early history of the city, is characteristically Roman.

Augustus's successors were not so circumspect. Whereas Tiberius followed in his footsteps and left little personal mark on the city, and Claudius busied himself more with practical matters such as the aqueducts (most imposingly represented by the Porta Maggiore), Caligula and Nero were notorious megalomaniacs—Nero wanted to rename the city Neropolis. Many of Nero's public buildings—the Circus and the first great public baths—and the city planning undertaken after the great fire of AD 64 benefited the city as a whole, but the most extensive project of his reign was the enormous Domus Aurea he built for himself, an engineering marvel set in parklike surroundings. When it was finished he said he was "at last beginning to live like a human being." The revolving ivory ceilings of the dining rooms are gone, but its dark ruins are still brightened by the paintings of the fastidious Famulus, who always wore a toga as he painted.

The succeeding Flavian emperors (Vespasian, Titus, and Domitian) erased many traces of Nero's work. Nero's Colossus (a 115-foot gilt statue of him) was converted into an image of the sun, and an amphitheater was built by Vespasian nearby on the site of the Domus Aurea's ornamental lake. This was the Colosseum, most famous of all Rome's buildings and scene of the grisly spectacles with which all classes of Rome were kept amused. It's also a distinguished piece of engineering, embodying another of the comparatively few architectural forms invented by the Romans—the amphitheater.

The Flavians were not themselves against self-advertisement. They continued to use the triumphal arch as a billboard to boast of their victories and assert their divinity (a notable survivor is the Arch of Titus, where the emperor is carried to heaven by an eagle), and the style of their sculpture was more robust and confidently ornamental than ever before.

Under the Spaniard Trajan (AD 98–117) the empire reached its widest extent. He was the last to add to the series of Imperial Fora. (The adjacent market is still fairly intact.) The largest forum to date, his was financed by the booty from his campaigns against the Dacians in what is modern-day Romania. Trajan's exploits are immortalized in the continuous sculpted narrative spiraling around the innovative 120-foot column that still dominates the area.

Trajan's ward Hadrian (117–138)—the first bearded emperor, a keen hunter, singer, and devotee of the arts, and nicknamed "the little Greek"—was perhaps less concerned with his own fame, but no less active in embellishing the city. He was responsible for the rebuilding of the Pantheon, a masterpiece of mathematical proportion and the only surviving structure that demonstrates the spectacular impression created by the Romans' increasing use of colored marble from the imperial provinces. (Most of the marble from the other ancient buildings, like the great baths, has long since been stripped off and now adorns the churches and palaces of Christian Rome.) Hadrian was an enthusiastic builder and frequenter of public baths, which, besides offering exercise and hygiene for the body, pleased the eye with their marble and mosaic decorations and their collections of sculpture. They also nourished the mind with the literature kept in their libraries.

Having made plans for the most elaborate mausoleum in the city (which was later converted into Castel Sant'Angelo), Hadrian spent his last years almost exclusively at his sumptuous villa at Tivoli, a few miles outside the city. This complex is notable both for the variety and beauty of its experimental architecture, with its references to famous sites in the Hellenistic world, and for the classical Greek Revival sculpture that has been found here.

## Constantine & the Coming of Christianity

The Greek tradition dominated most Roman art until the time of Hadrian, but with his successors other ideals emerged, the change being particularly evident in the differing styles of the two sculpted panels of the base of the column of Anoninus Pius (circa 161), now in the Vatican; in the Arch of Septimius Severus (203); and, later, in the magnificent, if highly eclectic, Arch of Constantine (circa 315). On this latter arch, reliefs and statues from earlier monuments of Trajan, Hadrian, and Marcus Aurelius are juxtaposed, perhaps deliberately, with Constantinian reliefs, which are striking in their formality, severity, frontality, and, it must be said, crudity. The first two of these characteristics are often connected with the increasing absolutism of the Imperial Court.

The age of Constantine was a great turning point in the history of Rome and its art. The city was no longer the center of the empire (Diocletian had spent most of his time in Italy in Milan) and was not safe from external attack (as Aurelian had judged in 270, when he began building the massive walls that still ring the city). Constantine himself is famous for having founded the "New Rome" of Constantinople (previously named Byzantium and now known as Istanbul) in 330, but he did have a notable effect on the old city. Primarily this involved the discreet promotion, with imperial backing, of his adopted religion, Christianity, and the building of impressive churches for Christian worship and the privilege of burial. But this did not mean immediately abandoning all the old values, and indeed one of his principal achievements as emperor was the completion of what is now the dominant structure in the Forum, the Basilica, which had been begun by, and retains the name of, his rival, Maxentius. In its apse was placed for veneration a gigantic seated figure of the emperor, whose scale can be judged from the fragments of head, hand, and foot in the courtyard of Palazzo dei Conservatori on the Campidoglio.

For his Christian churches Constantine adopted a form that had long served a variety of functions in Roman secular life and was to remain a standard church design for hundreds of years: the colonnaded basilica, with a flat roof and semicircular apse—a barnlike structure with two rows of pillars down its length and one rounded end. The principal ones, San Giovanni in Laterano and old St. Peter's, were on a massive scale, but it's worth noting that Constantine's churches were rather plain externally and placed on the outskirts of the city on imperial property. They were not assertively imposed on Rome's civic and religious heart.

San Giovanni in Laterano and St. Peter's have since been remodeled or rebuilt, but a Constantinian interior, though smaller in scale and circular in plan, may be seen at Santa Costanza, the mausoleum built for the emperor's daughter, who was buried in an awe-inspiring imperial porphyry sarcophagus, now in the Vatican. Here the artistic continuity between pagan and Christian Rome is neatly exemplified. The column capitals are not all of the same type and, like so much of the building material used for subsequent churches, were clearly taken from earlier buildings, whereas the grape-crushing putti in the mosaics (and on the sarcophagus) had long been popular as a Bacchic motif and were now adopted by Christians as an allusion to the Eucharist.

No paintings survive in the early Christian basilicas, but paintings can be seen in the many catacombs, such as those of Sant'Agnese, near Santa Costanza. (The catacombs had been used for Christian burials not from fear of persecution or as hiding places but because land for burial was expensive.) In these paintings, too, you see a similar transfer of pagan forms to Christian uses.

After Constantine, no emperor returned to reside permanently in Rome, and the next century saw a struggle by the early Church to assert itself in the face of old, established pagan power. Churches were built closer to the center, such as the original San Marco, near the Campidoglio, and the impressively Roman authority of Christian imagery can be seen in the apse mosaics of Santa Pudenziana (circa 400), where the Apostles wear togas.

### The Centuries of Decline

By 408 imperial edicts had forbidden the use of pagan temples, or any other place, for pagan worship (though it was not until 609 that the Pantheon became the first pagan temple to be used as a Christian church). The sack of Rome in 410 by the Visigoths, the first major military disaster for the city in 1,000 years, was traumatic but did not prevent the emergence of the Church as the unrivaled heir to the grand cultural dominance exercised previously by the now-absent emperor. This is visibly expressed in the large 5th-century churches of Santa Maria Maggiore—where the well-preserved mosaics on the triumphal arch show the Virgin Mary as an empress with a jeweled crown—and Santa Sabina, restored in the 1930s as the most graceful and perfect example of an early Christian basilica, its 20 Corinthian columns taken from classical buildings.

But the centuries of decline had already begun. The city was sacked again—by the Vandals in 455—and taken over by the Goths. When Gregory the Great became pope in 590, Rome had been for years a mere outpost of Byzantium, its population shrunk and its urban fabric reduced to a skeleton by decades of war and natural disasters. The Byzantine commander, when cornered in Hadrian's mausoleum, had repelled besieging Goths by having its statues smashed and the pieces catapulted at them. The erection of new churches had not entirely stopped: in the 520s the city prefect's audience hall in the Forum was converted into the church of Santi Cosma e Damiano and given mosaics in the more formal and abstract Byzantine style—and the administration of the city increasingly fell into the hands of the Church. But the future was bleak.

In the eight turbulent centuries that followed, the city's prosperity—and art—depended on the patchy success with which the pope could maintain his claim to temporal and spiritual power in the "Western" world, keeping the marauding Lombards, Saracens, and Normans at bay and the population of Rome in order. A major revival was signaled in 800, when the German emperor Charlemagne, who saw himself as a new Constantine, acknowledged the supreme authority of the pope in the West by receiving his crown from Leo III in St. Peter's. Impressive new basilicas such as San Prassede were built and, not surprisingly, given Charlemagne's revivalist ideology, their form and mosaic decoration owed more to the art of Constantine's early church in Rome than to contemporary Byzantium.

But the revival was short-lived, not to be matched until the early 12th century, which saw a crop of new churches. In basic form they are almost monotonously traditional basilicas, innocent of developments taking place elsewhere in Europe, but they have attractive extras: tall brick bell towers (Santa Maria in Trastevere); cool colonnaded cloisters (Santi Quattro Coronati) and porticoes (San Lorenzo fuori le Mura); and lavish ancient marble fittings and pavements of the kind the Cosmati family were to specialize in, as well as mosaics (San Clemente). At San Clemente in particular, the charming still-life details and lush acanthus scrolls of the mosaics show a renewed interest in the pagan ingredients of early Christian art. But these ingredients had long been absorbed into Christian culture, and the examples of purely pagan art that survived had, to judge from pilgrim guidebooks, acquired superstitious, magical connotations—like the ancient marble mask installed in the portico of Santa Maria in Cosmedin, reputed to bite the hands of liars.

But development in Rome suddenly ground to a halt when the popes moved to Avignon in 1309, and for 100 years the city became a backwater. Petrarch lamented the state of "widowed Rome": cows wandered in the Forum, and the only artistic event of note was the building of the massive stairs up to Aracoeli, part of the populist Cola di Rienzo's fantasy of reviving the ancient Roman Republic on the Campidoglio.

## Restoration & Renewal

The schism caused by the move of the popes to Avignon ended with the emergence of Martin V, a Roman, as undisputed pope (1417–31). He began the long process of restoration and renewal that, over the next three centuries, eventually resulted in spectacular and successful attempts to rival and surpass the achievements of the ancients.

To begin with, this involved the restoration of civil order and much repair work, but Martin V and his successors lived at a time of artistic resurgence in the rest of Italy, particularly in Florence, and they were able to import distinguished talent from outside. The great Florentine painter Masaccio came to Rome in the 1420s; his colleague Masolino's attractive frescoes survive at San Clemente as the first example of the new, more naturalistic style in painting with its mathematical perspective; other Florentines—Donatello and Filarete—produced idiosyncratic but impressive sculpture for St. Peter's.

All these artists were stimulated by what they could see of ancient Rome, and their patrons by what they could read of its literature. In particular, Nicholas V (1447–55) was a classical scholar and, convinced that the only way of impressing the authority of the Church on the illiterate masses was by means of "outstanding sights . . . great buildings . . . and divine monuments," he produced an ambitious plan of building and decoration for Rome in general and the Vatican in particular, doubtless with the help of his friend and fellow scholar, the artist Alberti.

His successor, Pius II (1458–64), remarked that if the projects "had been completed, they would have yielded to none of the ancient emperors in magnificence," but little progress was in fact made. A rare exception was the decoration of the chapel of Nicholas V in the 1440s by Fra Angelico, with, for him, extraordinarily monumental frescoes. More substantial results were achieved by the Franciscan Sixtus IV (1471–84), who built a new bridge across the Tiber—only two had survived from antiquity, at the island and at Castel Sant'Angelo—and a large up-to-date hospital (Santo Spirito) near the Vatican, both designed to accommodate the pilgrims who flocked to Rome in Jubilee years.

Churches, such as Santa Maria del Popolo, and palaces for cardinals, such as the enormous Cancelleria, were begun in new styles that paid increasing if still limited attention to ancient example. Property development was encouraged by new legislation. Although he was something of a philistine in his artistic taste, Sixtus did choose to import such outsiders as Botticelli and Perugino to decorate his large new chapel in the Vatican and tried to organize painters in Rome by setting up a guild. Although he was not especially interested in classical culture, and, like all the popes of his period, continued to use the ancient ruins as quarries, he performed an important service by setting up on the Campidoglio the first modern public museum of antique sculpture.

## Raphael & Michelangelo at the Service of the Popes

Such at this point was the enthusiasm for excavated antique sculpture that Sixtus's nephew Julius II (1503–13) was quickly able to stock the sculpture garden that he in turn set up in the Vatican Belvedere with the choicest pieces, such as the Laocoön group, dug up in 1506. And it's partly because of the presence in Rome of these rediscovered and revalued treasures that the artists he employed, notably Raphael and Michelangelo, were inspired to evolve their grand styles of painting and sculpture, which is fair to think of as specifically Roman, even though their art owed so much to Florence.

They must also have been responding to the imperial vision of their employer, the aggressive warrior-pope, who, in his determined efforts to continue his uncle's policy for the city, ordered the demolition of Constantine's St. Peter's, to be replaced by an audacious structure planned by his architect, Bramante (nicknamed the Wrecker), which would, in scale and design, have "placed the dome of the Pantheon on the vaults of the Temple of Peace." Julius followed the lead of previous popes in commissioning Raphael to paint dramatic works of propaganda in the Stanza of Heliodorus in the Vatican, but he also evoked antiquity in the murals of his castle at Ostia, which compared him to Trajan. On his return from an expedition in 1507, a copy of the Arch of Constantine, depicting a history of his own exploits, was erected at the Vatican. Michelangelo's decoration of the Sistine Chapel ceiling, with its grand ensemble of sculptural figures, medallions, and reliefs, is clearly an imaginative exercise in this imperial genre, and his original design for the pope's tomb (which is in San Pietro in Vincoli) "surpassed every ancient and imperial tomb ever made . . . in its beauty and magnificence, wealth of ornament and richness," according to Vasari.

The luxury-loving Medici pope, Leo X (1513–21), who followed, asked Raphael to decorate the largest room in the papal apartments with scenes from the life of Constantine, but he also borrowed jokes from Augustus and is reported to have said, "Since God has given us the papacy, let us enjoy it." There is plenty to enjoy in the long private loggia that Raphael and his pupils decorated next door, where tiny scenes from the Bible are overwhelmed by hundreds of painted and stucco images, mimicking ancient cameos and the kind of ancient fantasy painting to be seen in what had become the grottoes of Nero's Domus Aurea when it was rediscovered in the 1480s. Hence was born the name "grotesque" for the style of painting that was to become enormously popular in Roman and, with the spread of engravings, European interior decorations in subsequent years. It was also used in Raphael's saucy decoration of the nearby (but not visitable) bathroom of Cardinal Bibbiena and on a grand scale in the imposing, unfinished Villa Madama, designed by Raphael for Leo's cousin. This is hard to visit, too, but other attractive villas of the day exist—the Farnesina, also decorated by Raphael, and the later Villa Giulia.

Villa Madama was a conscious re-creation of the ancient Roman villa as described by Pliny, and contemporary palaces tried to re-create the ancient-Roman house with its atrium and courtyards, as described by the Roman architect Vitruvius. Palazzo Farnese, finished by Michelangelo, is a stunning example, and Peruzzi's Palazzo Massimo is on a smaller scale but no less impressive. The courtyards of Palazzo Massimo alle Colonne and Palazzo Mattei also show how contemporaries displayed their prize antique sculptures—by setting them in the wall as decorations. Many less wealthy Romans imitated this fashion by having monochrome sculpturelike frescoes on their facades. A lonely survivor is Palazzo Ricci in Via di Monserrato.

In 1527 the fun had to stop when German soldiers sacked the city, causing an exodus of artists (with further diffusion of their ideas) and, it's often believed, a change of heart in the city's art. Certainly Michelangelo's *Last Judgment* in the Sistine Chapel is a tremendous warning to the wicked, though artists such as Salviati and Perino del Vaga continued to paint in exuberant and witty style, for example at Castel Sant'Angelo.

The Church did attempt to reform itself from inside, however, and among the churches built for the new religious orders after the Council of Trent (1545–63) were the Gesù for the Jesuits, originally rather severe inside, and the Chiesa Nuova for the Oratorians, one of the many churches to be influenced by the design of the Gesù, with a broad nave for preaching to large congregations. Here, St. Philip Neri, the founder of the Oratorians, was frequently found in a state of ecstasy in front of the painting of the Visitation by Barocci, his (and many others') favorite artist.

## Spiritual Intensity & Civic-Minded Architecture

Spiritual excitement and intensity, theatrically presented, were to become dominant themes in the next century's art—most obviously in Bernini's chapel in Santa Maria della Vittoria, where members of the Cornaro family look out from their boxes at an ethereal vision of the ecstasy of St. Teresa, bathed in light, the whole executed in splendid ancient and modern marbles and other materials. Not all artists, though, looked so resolutely to heaven, and the most brilliant and influential painter in the period after Barocci was the passionate criminal Caravaggio, whose dramatically illuminated and con-

troversial work ranged from homosexual pornography for clerics to profound but distinctly earthy religious subjects—notice the obtrusively dirty feet of the adoring peasant in his St. Agostino altarpiece. Other distinguished painters of the day were more traditional—indeed, Annibale Carracci and his relatives pioneered a revival and extension of the styles of Raphael and Michelangelo, notably the opulent Galleria in Palazzo Farnese (circa 1600). Their work can be compared to (and contrasted with) that of Caravaggio in Santa Maria del Popolo.

Humble details such as Caravaggio's dirty feet may have moved the lower orders, but art was still effectively commanded by popes and cardinals: if Julius II's artistic propaganda had been grandiose, it was almost eclipsed by the whopping stories put out for the 17th-century Church. In painting this means, among others, the extraordinary achievements of Pietro da Cortona, who extended the powerful language of Michelangelo's decorations with a Venetian fluency and sense of color in his exaltation of the Barberini family on the ceiling of their palace's salone. But the most spectacularly theatrical effects were created in public architecture, both on a large scale in Bernini's piazza for St. Peter's, for example, where hundreds of huge travertine columns provide encircling porticoes, and on a smaller scale in innumerable projects such as Pietro da Cortona's brilliant scenographic setting for Santa Maria della Pace. Perhaps the most gifted and inventive of these architects was Borromini, a difficult (and in the end suicidal) person who did not get the biggest commissions. But his San Carlo and Sant'Ivo show how he could convert a restricted site into a tight ensemble of exhilarating power.

Although this architecture was designed to impress, attempts were also afoot to make the city more comfortable. Bernini's porticoes not only broadcast the fame of Alexander VII but protected pilgrims from rain and sun. From the 16th century on, popes had striven to create straighter, wider streets, making it easier to visit the principal basilicas and speeding the progress of carriages. They also restored some of the ancient Roman aqueducts. The latter provided increasingly necessary water for the populace and supplied the impressive sculpted fountains that, from Bernini's Fontana dei Quattro Fiumi in Piazza Navona to Salvi's Fontana di Trevi, continue to delight and refresh the populace.

The Fontana di Trevi, the Spanish Steps, and Galilei's facade for San Giovanni in Laterano were among the last great spectacles of the late 17th and early 18th centuries. The artistic importance of 18th-century Rome lay not so much in what was done for the city as in what the city did for its many visitors. These were now the foreign artists studying the history paintings of Raphael and the religious works of Michelangelo in Rome's academies and the grand tourists, rather than the pilgrims of old. Piranesi's prints, fighting a magnificent rear-guard action for the grandeur of Rome against the growing popularity of a different—more purely Greek—view of antiquity, provided souvenirs for them; Batoni elegantly painted their portraits; and most of Canova's cool poetic sculptures were produced for export. The most distinguished building commissioned by the Vatican in this period was a museum—the Museo Pio-Clementino.

## Secular Modernity

The power of the popes, and the city's art, continued to decline in importance in the 19th century as Rome emerged as the secular capital of the modern Italian state. Large but creaking and empty edifices were erected to its ideals—the monument to King Vittorio Emanuele and the Palace of Justice. The city was besieged by suburbs, and the river embanked to cope with flooding and traffic, but it survived remarkably well even the ambitions of Mussolini. His attempts to re-create something of the glory of the Roman Empire produced monotonous boulevards through the Forum and at St. Peter's, spoiling the effect of Bernini's piazza. But his grandiosity also gave birth to the striking architecture of the suburb of EUR (Esposizione Universale di Roma).

Nor, in modern times, has Rome been an international center of the musical and theatrical arts, though ancient theaters and triumphal arches testify to the early Roman love of spectacle—even emperors performed and sang. Nero, who made his operatic debut with a group of sycophants in Naples, put his stage clothes on and sang (not fiddled) to a select audience while Rome burned. Opera lovers can recapture something of this experience at open-air performances of Verdi's *Aida,* traditionally staged each summer with great gusto.

At the summer-long, outdoor, multiscreen movie festival you can see what gives Rome its claim to modern preeminence in the arts—the cinema. Successive generations of filmmakers working in the city and at Cinecittà (Italy's largest production studio) since World War II—Rossellini, Pasolini, and Fellini—have created an enduring art, perceptively chronicling and imaginatively exploring the inside and the outside of modern life and particularly, and most endearingly, of Roman society.

As for the future, Rome is definitely striding forward. Everyone is talking about the dramatic, post-millenial architecturural statements dotting the "new" city: Renzo Piano's Parco della Musica, Richard Meier's Tor Tere Teste Jubilee church, Zaha Hadid's Natianal Museum of Art of the XXI Century (MAXXI), and Rem Koolhaas Mercati Generali market are just a few of the projects that are ushering Rome into the 21st century in a big way.

—Roger Jones

# FEASTING AT ROME'S TABLES

N ITALY, COOKERY IS CIVILIZATION. In the days of the Roman legions, pundits used to say *"Ubi Roma ibi allium"* (Where there are Romans, there is garlic). Ever since the days of the Caesars, Italian chefs have taken one of life's sensory pleasures and made it into an art, and today's travelers can feast on an incredible array of culinary delights. Of course, Italian food has come a long way since the days when Horace, the great poet of ancient Rome, feasted on lamprey boiled in five-year-old wine, the liver of a goose fattened on figs, and apples picked by the light of the waning moon. But not that long: although nouvelle cusine has made inroads in Rome, it only proffers the new by revamping the simple, rustic, centuries-old forms of *cucina rustica* so beloved by Romans.

There is no single Italian cuisine. The dishes most commonly identified around the world as "Italian" food are actually a mix of different regional specialties. Lasagna and tortellini come from Bologna, veal cutlet and creamy risotto from Milan, pasta *e fagioli* (pasta and bean soup) and tiramisu from Venice, pizza and spaghetti with tomato sauce from Naples. Rome, too, has its very own culinary specialties, drawn from a tradition that goes back to the days when ancient Romans bought their groceries in the brand-new market that Emperor Hadrian had built. Yet Roman cooking seems to have had few ambassadors abroad.

Strangely enough, even in Rome genuine Roman cooking can be difficult to find. Restaurants and trattorias often serve the cooking of other regions and other countries, catering to an increasingly heterogeneous population. The "Romans of Rome," a distinction that can be claimed only by those who have seven generations of Rome-born ancestors, are outnumbered by the "new" Romans—Italians from other regions and foreign residents, including immigrants from Asia, Africa, and Eastern Europe.

Authentic Roman cooking is based on local ingredients, many of which are at their best only at certain times of year—milk-fed lamb, glorious globe artichokes from the sandy coastal plains, fresh vegetables from the farms of the Campagna Romana, as the countryside around Rome has been called since the time of the Caesars. Now, thanks to technology and imports from distant lands, most ingredients are available year-round, but die-hard Roman cooks know there's no substitute for the real thing—food that nature has made ready for eating, not for traveling.

Simple, hearty, and redolent of herbs, genuine Roman cooking comprises the economical dishes of the carters, shopkeepers, and artisans of Old Rome along with the refined and elaborate specialties concocted in the kitchens of popes, emperors, and kings. In the 1st century Juvenal wrote of dining on "a kid from the Agro Tiburtino, tenderest of the flock, who had not yet tasted grass and had more milk than blood in its veins." Martial, writing in the same era, sings the praises of the "lettuce, leeks, mint and dandelion greens, joys of the garden" brought to him by a farmer's wife. True to Roman tradition, he includes in his menu a baby lamb, "saved from the wolf's cruel jaws" only to meet a similar fate on Martial's table.

Celery, the indispensable ingredient of today's oxtail stew and bean soup, was covered with honey in ancient Rome and served as a dessert. Fish has also been a Roman choice through the centuries. In Trajan's time, slaves selected their master's favorite fish live from large tanks in the market, choosing between fresh- and saltwater varieties. At the entrance to the church of Sant'Angelo, at Portico d'Ottavia in the Ghetto, site of the old fish market, a curious plaque with a Latin inscription warns that the head of any fish surpassing the length of the plaque is to be cut off "up to the first fin" and given to the Conservators of the Capitol under pain of a fine of 10 gold florins. The heads were used to make a superb soup and were considered a great delicacy.

Eating habits have changed rapidly in Rome over the past few decades. Breakfasts are still sketchy: people usually start their day with a cappuccino and *cornetto* (croissant) at a neighborhood bar. Then, when midmorning hunger pangs strike, they go to the nearest bakery for a square of crisp pizza *all'olio*, also known as pizza *bianca* (baked pizza dough, salt, and olive oil) hot from the oven. Romans love to eat it slathered with fresh ricotta cheese or dotted with sliced fresh figs. Pizza recurs throughout the day as a snack or quick meal; you can find it in bakeries and from morning to evening in the ubiquitous pizza *rustica* places where you can buy squares of crusty pizza with all kinds of toppings to take out or eat standing up. Pizzerias keep restaurant hours and serve classic round pizzas that are made to order and served at your table. Pizzerias also offer *bruschetta* (toasted garlic bread, often topped with sliced tomatoes) and *crostini* (rounds of toasted bread topped with grilled mozzarella and prosciutto or anchovies).

On their coffee breaks Romans have an espresso. Like all Italians they consider the cappuccino, half coffee and half frothy milk, strictly a morning drink, like *caffè latte* (much more milk than coffee)—they would never order it after a meal. If they want their coffee diluted, they'll ask for *caffè lungo,* made with a little more water, or *caffè macchiato* (espresso with a splash of steamed milk). Many bars serve what they call *caffè americano,* a cup of American-style coffee. Caffè Hag is the best-known brand of decaffeinated coffee. *Caffè freddo* has little in common with iced coffee; it's more like coffee syrup and is served

cold but not iced. *Granità di caffè* is frozen coffee slush that is sweetened and usually served with whipped cream. *Thè freddo* is presweetened tea served cold but not iced. It may be served *alla pesca* (with peach flavoring) or *al limone* (with lemon flavoring). Ice is something the Italians use little of, other than in a granità. Except in top hotels and restaurants, if you ask for ice in Rome you're likely to get only a few small pieces served on the side. It's for your own good, the Italians would say; iced drinks are harmful, as they upset the all-important digestion and can cause collapse. It's not easy to get a really cold beer, either. But you can try: ask for whatever you want *molto freddo* (very cold), and emphasize the molto!

\* \* \*

I N THEORY, the main midday meal consists of several courses. However, problems of time and distance have forced Rome's working population to accept the idea of a light lunch, especially since offices and even stores have done away with the three-hour lunch break. As a result more and more places have sprung up in the city where you can find one-course meals, salads, and such, with table or cafeteria-style service. Some restaurants also offer lunch menus.

A classic full Roman meal starts with an antipasto (hors d'oeuvre). In its simplest form, antipasto usually consists of a few slices of salami and prosciutto with olives and pickled vegetables and a butter curl (butter isn't served with bread anywhere in Italy, except in the most tourist-conscious places). A summertime delicacy is *melone* (chilled melon) or *fichi* (fresh figs) with prosciutto. *Antipasto di mare* is a seafood salad, usually already dressed with a citronette or vinaigrette sauce. Some restaurants are famed for their antipasto tables. This poses the question of how to order. As a rule of thumb, consider the antipasto the equivalent of one course. Throughout Italy pasta or soup is considered a first course; that's why these dishes are called *primi* (first). A normal meal would include a *primo* and a *secondo* (a main meat or seafood course). A basic restaurant or trattoria meal thus consists of two courses, with antipasto, vegetables and/or salad, and dessert as individually priced options. To have only the antipasto is to snub the kitchen and to cut into the proprietor's cost-profit ratio. If you want to do as the Romans do, have one other course before or after the antipasto, perhaps a pasta or a second course or even a vegetable (a *carciofo,* or artichoke, nicely substitutes for a first or main course).

Though you'll find all sorts of primi on the menu, from the tortellini of the Emilia Romagna region to the risotto of northern Italy, remember that the truly Roman pasta is fettuccine: light golden ribbons of egg pasta cooked al dente and served with a savory meat sauce (*al ragù*) or *alla papalina,* in a delicate sauce of butter, ham, and mushrooms (sometimes with peas, too). Fettuccine may also be served with seasonal vegetables such as artichokes and porcini mushrooms.

You'll hear several versions of the origin of spaghetti *alla carbonara,* served piping hot with raw egg, chunks of *guanciale* (unsmoked bacon), and lots of freshly ground black pepper. The one holding that the flecks of pepper evoke the image of a carbonara (one of the sturdy women who sold coal on the streets of Old Rome) is as good as any. Another Roman favorite is pasta *all'amatriciana,* served with a sauce of tomato, guanciale, and a bit of hot chili pepper, with a generous dusting of pecorino (sheep's-milk cheese). Pasta *alla gricia,* dressed with hot oil, guanciale, and plenty of black pepper, also is typically Roman, though it's not found on many menus. For an utterly simple and delicious summer dish, try pasta *alla checcha,* steaming hot pasta that is tossed with fresh, uncooked chopped tomatoes, garlic, olive oil, and basil. *Giovedì gnocchi* (Thursday gnocchi) is a weekly tradition in Roman restaurants and trattorias. Gnocchi are tiny dumplings of semolina or potatoes, served as a first course with tomato sauce and lots of cheese.

The truly Roman soup is *stracciatella,* steaming chicken broth with a beaten egg stirred into it together with Parmigiano cheese and a dash of nutmeg. The egg cooks as it's carried to the table.

Among the second courses, *abbacchio,* the baby lamb mentioned by Martial, is a classic choice. Spring is the best time for this dish. It's either roasted or served *al scottadito*—that is, grilled in the form of tiny chops that may burn your fingers (scotta dito) as you pick them up, a practice quite acceptable here.

\* \* \*

O N THE MENU, in addition to the usual *bistecca* (steak; with the exception of Tuscan meat, beef tends to be tough) and *cotoletta* (cutlet), you'll probably find *saltimbocca alla romana* (tender veal cutlets with sage and prosciutto) and *straccetti* (paper-thin slices of beef sautéed in oil). *Involtini* are little meat rolls, and *polpette* are meatballs. *Pollo alla diavola,* grilled chicken with a touch of lemon, is a simple main course. Many varieties of seafood are offered, from scampi (large shrimp) to *dentice* or *orata* (types of bream) and *rombo* (turbot). Though seafood dishes are generally more expensive, they are in great demand, so many Rome restaurants make seafood a specialty. "He's a baccalà" the Romans say, meaning that a person is stupid, perhaps unjustly maligning the *baccalà,* or codfish, which they otherwise esteem, especially in the form of crunchy hot fillets fried in batter.

The Roman way with innards is a story in itself. Centuries ago the men who cleaned and tanned the hides of the animals butchered in Rome were given the animals' innards to take home as a bonus. Ingenious housewives used these humble ingredients to create numerous dishes that have become staples of authentic Roman cooking. The most famous is *coda alla vaccinara*, oxtail simmered for hours in a tomato and celery stew. *Trippa* (tripe) is another favorite and a tradition on Saturday. *Coratella* (sautéed lamb's innards) and *pagliata* (baby lamb's intestines, usually served with rigatoni pasta) are still specialties of the restaurants and trattorias of Testaccio, where the slaughterhouses used to be. *Fritto misto alla romana* consists of batter-fried tidbits of artichokes or zucchini, ricotta, apples, brains, and sweetbreads. Roman trattorias may also serve *fagioli con le cotiche*, beans with pork rind.

Green vegetables are good in Rome. You'll see them on open-air market stalls in the morning and in the gastronomic still lifes that greet you in restaurants. Order *piselli e prosciutto* (peas and ham) in the spring, green salads, and *cipolline in agrodolce* (baby onions in a sweet-sour sauce), and by all means try *puntarelle*, a truly Roman specialty, a variety of tender chickory curled in ice water and served with a garlicky anchovy dressing. It's usually available only in winter and spring.

The queen of Roman vegetables is the *carciofo romanesco* (globe artichoke), grown mainly in the iron-rich fields of the coastal plain north of Rome. It's particularly delicate when prepared *alla giudia*, the Jewish way, just as it originated in the kitchens of the Ghetto. Tender young artichokes are deep-fried and opened out to take the form of a flower, with each petal crisp and light enough to melt in your mouth. Carciofo *alla romana* is sautéed whole with garlic and parsley or mint.

As in most of Italy, Romans like to finish off their meal with fresh fruit or *macedonia* (fruit cup). Tiramisu is popular, as is *panna cotta*, milk custard that may be served with berries. Gelato (ice cream) is

usually available and may be served *affogato* (literally, "drowned," with whiskey). *Torta di ricotta* is the Roman version of cheesecake, made with ricotta. The local cheeses are mild caciotta and sharp, hard pecorino. You may be offered a liqueur by your host, and it will probably be *limoncello*, the popular sweet lemon liqueur.

The ideal accompaniment to Roman food is the wine produced in the nearby hill towns known as the Castelli Romani and in the wineries around Lake Bolsena, a bit farther afield. Among the Castelli Romani wines, Frascati is a dry, fruity white; when it's good it's very, very good, but too often the stuff served in carafes as Frascati is a poor substitute for the real thing. When in doubt, ask for a bottled wine. Colli Albani is quite similar to Frascati. Lanuvio is dry, golden-yellow, and rather robust. Marino may be either dry (*secco*) or slightly sweet (*abboccato*); it can be either white or red. Velletri also produces a dry white and a red that ranges in color from pale to ruby red. The dry white Est Est Est of Montefiascone, on Lake Bolsena, turns up on Roman tables, as do some unpretentious but good whites from Capena and Cerveteri and whites and reds from Vignanello, near Viterbo.

Not many Romans indulge in the full banquet anymore, except on special occasions, mainly family get-togethers. But Romans do consider eating an essential component of traditional conviviality. With fast-food chains encroaching and the pace of life quickening, they defend their sociable and relaxed lifestyle by seizing every opportunity to gather in noisy family groups to enjoy good food and wine and congenial company.

—Barbara Walsh Angelillo

# BOOKS & MOVIES

## Books

Italian history, art, and culture have been examined in countless English-language books. Their profusion is a testament both to the wonders of Italy and to the challenge of defining what exactly "Italian" is. *The Italians,* by Luigi Barzini, dates from 1964 but remains a valuable effort toward this end; its lively analysis of the national character is both enlightening and frustrating in ways that make reading it a genuinely Italian experience. More recent musings on Italian life include *Italian Days* by Barbara Grizzuti Harrison and *That Fine Italian Hand* by Paul Hofman, for many years *New York Times* bureau chief in Rome. *The New Italians* by Charles Richards is a well-researched overview of modern Italy's society and psyche by a British journalist.

For an introduction to Rome, *City of the Soul* by William Murray is a good place to start: its brief, personal musings make for a lucid and surprisingly comprehensive overview of the city. *A Thousand Bells at Noon* by G. Franco Romagnoli is an entertaining collection of anecdotes that captures the character of Rome as seen through the eyes of a prodigal son. Eleanor Clark's *Rome and a Villa* is a passionate evocation of the city as it was in the mid-20th century. *Inside Rome,* from Phaidon Press, is a picture book that gives you a tantalizing peek into the sumptuous palaces, galleries, private homes, athletic clubs, and even historic coffeehouses of the eternal city.

Some of literature's icons have written movingly about Italy—Henry James's perceptive *Italian Hours* and Edith Wharton's *Italian Backgrounds* and *Italian Villas and Their Gardens* are prime examples. Stendhal, Goethe, and Dickens are among the luminaries excerpted in the collection *Italy in Mind,* edited by Alice Leccese Powers.

For historical background, try Christopher Hibbert's *Rome: The Biography of a City,* which manages to be at once erudite and readable. James Lees-Milne's *Roman Mornings* tells the history of the city through an examination of eight of its most significant buildings. For in-depth classical history, there's nothing quite like Edward Gibbon's *Decline and Fall of the Roman Empire,* an 18th century masterpiece (available in abridged form) that has withstood the test of time. An enlightening, though sometimes slow-going, study of the complexities of Italy's recent history is offered in two books by Paul Ginsborg, *A History of Contemporary Italy: Society and Politics 1943–1988* and *Italy and Its Discontents.*

Aficionados of Rome's artistic treasures will find Georgina Masson's *Companion Guide to Rome* a must. A comprehensive introduction to Italian art is Frederick Hartt's *History of Italian Renaissance Art*; Peter and Linda Murray's *The Art of the Renaissance* is a useful handbook. Consult Giorgio Vasari's *Lives of the Artists* and the *Autobiography of Benvenuto Cellini* for eyewitness accounts of Renaissance Italy.

For lively historical fiction, pick up *I Claudius* and *Claudius the God* by Robert Graves, available in a single edition. Irving Stone's *The Agony and the Ecstasy* relates a fictionalized version of the life of Michelangelo. Rome's inhabitants are portrayed during and after World War II in *History: A Novel,* by Elsa Morante. Some of modern Italy's best literature has been set in Rome: try Carlo Emilio Gadda's *Quer Pasticciaccio Brutto de Via Merulana,* Pier Paolo Pasolini's *Ragazzi di Vita,* Gabriele D'Annunzio's *Il Piacere,* and Alberto Moravia's *Donna di Roma,* all of which can be found in English translation. For lovers of detective fiction, Michael Dibdin's *A Long Finish* is an enjoyable case for his irascible Roman detective Aurelio Zen.

## Movies

Set in a Rome that was recovering from World War II, Roberto Rossellini's *Rome, Open City* (1946) and Vittorio De Sica's *Shoeshine* (1946) and *The Bicycle Thief* (1948) are classics of the postwar cinema's neorealism. The delightful *Roman Holiday* (1953) won Audrey Hepburn an Oscar. Federico Fellini's *La Dolce Vita* (1961) gave its name to an era. Fellini's *Roma* (1972) is the director's exuberant paean to the city. Much of Pier Paolo Pasolini's work is set in the slums of Rome, including *Mamma Roma* (1962), and *Accattone* (1961). Nanni Moretti has earned a cult following here and across Europe with films such as *Caro Diario, Ecce Bombo,* and *Sogni D'Oro,* all of which are set wholly or partly in his native Rome. Peter Greenaway's *Belly of an Architect* (1987), Bernardo Bertolucci's *The Besieged* (1998), and Anthony Minghella's *The Talented Mr. Ripley* (1999) all benefited from Rome's incomparable cityscape.

# ROME AT A GLANCE: A CHRONOLOGY

ca. 1000 BC  Etruscans settle in central Italy.

753  Legendary founding of Rome by Romulus.

600  Latin script develops. Rome becomes urban center.

510  Last of the Etruscan kings—Tarquin the Proud—expelled from Rome; Republic founded, headed by two annually elected consuls. First Temple of Jupiter on the Capitol built.

471  First plebeian magistrate is elected.

390  Rome sacked by Celts.

380  Servian wall built to defend city.

312  Appius Claudius begins construction of the Via Appia and Acqua Appia, Rome's first aqueduct.

280–75  War against Pyrrhus, King of Epirus.

260–41  First Punic War: Rome struggles with Carthage in North Africa for control of central Mediterranean; gains Sicily.

250  Rome completes conquest of Italy.

220  Flaminian Way between Rome and Rimini completed.

219–02  Second Punic War: Hannibal invades Italy and destroys Roman army in 216; Scipio Africanus carries war back to Spain and to Carthage; in 206, Rome gains control of Spain; in 203, Hannibal defeated by Scipio.

168  Rome begins colonization of Greece and defeats Macedonia.

149–46  Third Punic War: Carthage is laid waste for good.

146  Rome completes conquest of Greece.

133  Rome rules entire Mediterranean basin except for Egypt.

102–01  Gaius Marius defeats Germanic tribes invading from north.

86  Civil war: Sulla defeats Marius.

82  Sulla becomes dictator of Rome.

71  Slaves revolt under Spartacus.

66–63  Pompey colonizes Syria and Palestine.

49  Gallic War: Julius Caesar defeats Gaul.

47–45  Civil War: Julius Caesar becomes ruler of Rome.

46  Julian calendar introduced.

44  Julius Caesar assassinated.

31  Octavian (later Augustus) defeats Antony and Cleopatra in the battle of Actium and becomes sole ruler of Rome.

27  Octavian becomes Emperor Augustus: Imperial Age begins. Augustan Age (31 BC–AD 14) is celebrated in the works of Virgil (70 BC–AD 19), Ovid (43 BC–AD 17), Livy (59 BC–AD 17), and Horace (65 BC–AD 27).

AD 42  Building of harbor at Ostia Antica begins.

43  Emperor Claudius (AD 41–54) invades Britain.

50  Population of Rome reaches 1 million; city is largest in world.

64  Rome burns; Nero (54–68) begins rebuilding city.

79  Emperor Titus (79–81) completes Colosseum.

90–120  Silver age of Latin literature: Tacitus (circa 55–120), Juvenal (circa 55–140), Martial (circa 38–102).

98–117  Emperor Trajan builds the Baths of Trajan and the Mercati Traianei.

100  Roman army reaches peak, with 300,000 soldiers.

116  Conquest of Mesopotamia.

117  Roman Empire at its apex.

125  Emperor Hadrian (117–138) rebuilds Pantheon and begins construction of his mausoleum (now Castel Sant'Angelo).

161–80  Rule of Marcus Aurelius, philosopher-emperor.

165  Smallpox ravages empire.

211–17  Rule of psychopath Caracalla; he begins Terme di Caracalla.

284–305  Rule of Diocletian; empire divided between West and East.

312–37  Rule of Constantine; reunites empire but transfers capital to Byzantium (later renamed Constantinople, today known as Istanbul).

313  Edict of Milan recognizes Christianity; Constantine begins construction of St. Peter's and San Giovanni in Laterano basilicas.

370  Huns appear in Europe.

380  Christianity made state religion.

406  Vandals lay waste to Gaul and Spain.

410  Visigoths under Alaric invade Italy and take Rome; Western Empire collapses.

452  Huns invade northern Italy.

455  Rome sacked by Vandals.

488  Ostrogoths invade Italy; in 493 Theodoric proclaimed ruler of Gothic Kingdom of Italy.

536–40  Justinian, Byzantine emperor, invades Italy.

553  Italy reincorporated into Roman Empire.

570 Lombards gain control of Rome.

590–604 Pope Gregory the Great reinforces power of papacy.

609 Pantheon consecrated as a church.

610 Eastern Empire separated from Rome for good and continues (until 1453) as Byzantine Empire.

800 Charlemagne crowned Holy Roman Emperor in Rome.

1073 Gregory VII elected pope; his rule sees start of struggle for supremacy between papacy and Germanic Holy Roman Empire. Rome sinks into stagnation and ruin for five centuries.

1309 Papacy moves to Avignon in southern France.

1347 Cola di Rienzo, adventurer and dreamer, tries to restore the Roman Republic; he is hanged six months later.

1377 Pope returns to Rome; Gregory XI makes Vatican the papal residence.

ca. 1500 Renaissance spreads to Rome—still little more than a malarial ruin—chiefly in persons of Bramante (1444–1514), Michelangelo (1475–1564), and Raphael (1483–1520).

1503–13 Reign of Pope Julius II; begins rebuilding St. Peter's and commissions Raphael to decorate his *stanze* (apartments) and Michelangelo to paint the Sistine Chapel.

1527 Sack of Rome: confidence of High Renaissance evaporates as troops of Holy Roman Empire ravage city.

1534 Michelangelo begins *Last Judgment* in Sistine Chapel.

1546 Michelangelo commissioned to complete rebuilding of St. Peter's.

1568 Church of the Gesù begun.

1595 Annibale Carracci begins painting *salone* of Palazzo Farnese, ushering in Baroque Age. Architects Bernini (1598–1680) and Borromini (1599–1667) build churches, palaces, and fountains, largely under ecclesiastical patronage, transforming face of Rome. Leading painters include Caravaggio (1571–1610), Guido Reni (1575–1642), and Pietro da Cortona (1596–1669).

1626 St. Peter's completed.

1656–67 St. Peter's Square built.

1735 Spanish Steps laid out.

1797 Napoléon captures Rome and proclaims a new republic; Pope Pius VI expelled from city.

1808 Pope Pius VII prisoner in Quirinale.

1814 Pope Pius VII reinstated as ruler of Rome.

1870 Italian nationalists storm Rome and make it capital of united Italy; in protest, pope withdraws into voluntary confinement in Vatican.

1885  Monument to Vittorio Emanuele II begun (completed 1911).

1922  Fascists under Mussolini march on Rome.

1929  Lateran Treaty establishes formal relations between pope and state; Via dei Fiori Imperiali begun (completed 1933).

1936  Via della Conciliazione begun (completed 1950).

1944  Rome liberated from German occupation.

1957  Treaty of Rome establishes European Economic Community.

1960  Rome hosts Olympic Games.

1962  Pope John XXIII convenes the Second Vatican Council, culmination of his efforts to promote ecumenism and give new vitality to the Roman Catholic Church.

1978  Pope John Paul II, first Polish pope, elected. Extremist political activity in Italy reaches climax with kidnapping and murder of Premier Aldo Moro.

1981  Attempted assassination of Pope John Paul II. Cleaning of Michelangelo's frescoes on ceiling of Sistine Chapel in Vatican begins.

1990  Cleaning of Sistine Chapel ceiling completed. Work begins on cleaning Michelangelo's *Last Judgment* on wall over altar. Italian government passes so-called Law for Rome Capital, allotting funds and energy to a wave of major urban projects, including conservation and infrastructure.

1991  Rome's first mosque opens.

1997  Countdown toward replacement of the lira with the euro, the new European currency, begins, with the lira due to be phased out entirely by 2002. A copy of the statue of Roman emperor Marcus Aurelius is mounted on the pedestal of the original on the Campidoglio as a symbol of Rome's historic grandeur.

1998  Public works and restorations in preparation for the Jubilee year 2000 throughout Rome. Several 1st-century AD frescoes discovered in excavations of Nero's Domus Aurea on the Colle Oppio, including one cityscape that is the first of its kind ever found.

1999  Restoration work in the Sistine Chapel finally completed to universal acclaim.

2000  The Jubilee of the third millennium proclaimed by Pope John Paul II. Millions of pilgrims flock to the Eternal City.

2002  After more than 2,000 years Italy gives up its monetary independence: the lira becomes obsolete and the new currency of all the European Community, the euro, is introduced.

2005  Benedict XVI is elected pope in April 2005.

# ITALIAN VOCABULARY

| English | Italian | Pronunciation |
|---------|---------|---------------|

## Basics

| English | Italian | Pronunciation |
|---------|---------|---------------|
| Yes/no | Sí/No | see/no |
| Please | Per favore | pear fa-**vo**-ray |
| Yes, please | Sí grazie | see **grah**-tsee-ay |
| Thank you | Grazie | **grah**-tsee-ay |
| You're welcome | Prego | **pray**-go |
| Excuse me, sorry | Scusi | **skoo**-zee |
| Sorry! | Mi dispiace! | mee dis-spee-**ah**-chay |
| Good morning/ afternoon | Buongiorno | bwohn-**jor**-no |
| Good evening | Buona sera | **bwoh**-na **say**-ra |
| Good-bye | Arrivederci | a-ree-vah-**dare**-chee |
| Mr. (Sir) | Signore | see-**nyo**-ray |
| Mrs. (Ma'am) | Signora | see-**nyo**-ra |
| Miss | Signorina | see-nyo-**ree**-na |
| Pleased to meet you | Piacere | pee-ah-**chair**-ray |
| How are you? | Come sta? | **ko**-may **stah** |
| Very well, thanks | Bene, grazie | **ben**-ay **grah**-tsee-ay |
| And you? | E lei? | ay **lay**-ee |
| Hello (phone) | Pronto? | **proan**-to |

## Numbers

| English | Italian | Pronunciation |
|---------|---------|---------------|
| one | uno | **oo**-no |
| two | due | **doo**-ay |
| three | tre | tray |
| four | quattro | **kwah**-tro |
| five | cinque | **cheen**-kway |
| six | sei | say |
| seven | sette | **set**-ay |
| eight | otto | **oh**-to |
| nine | nove | **no**-vay |
| ten | dieci | dee-**eh**-chee |
| eleven | undici | **oon**-dee-chee |
| twelve | dodici | **doe**-dee-chee |
| thirteen | tredici | **tray**-dee-chee |

| | | |
|---|---|---|
| fourteen | quattordici | kwa-**tore**-dee-chee |
| fifteen | quindici | **kwin**-dee-chee |
| sixteen | sedici | **say**-dee-chee |
| seventeen | diciassette | dee-cha-**set**-ay |
| eighteen | diciotto | dee-**cho**-to |
| nineteen | diciannove | dee-cha-**no**-vay |
| twenty | venti | **vain**-tee |
| twenty-one | ventuno | vain-**too**-no |
| twenty-two | ventidue | vain-tee-**doo**-ay |
| thirty | trenta | **train**-ta |
| forty | quaranta | kwa-**rahn**-ta |
| fifty | cinquanta | cheen-**kwahn**-ta |
| sixty | sessanta | seh-**sahn**-ta |
| seventy | settanta | seh-**tahn**-ta |
| eighty | ottanta | o-**tahn**-ta |
| ninety | novanta | no-**vahn**-ta |
| one hundred | cento | **chen**-to |
| one thousand | mille | **mee**-lay |
| ten thousand | diecimila | dee-eh-chee-**mee**-la |

## Useful Phrases

| | | |
|---|---|---|
| Do you speak English? | Parla inglese? | **par**-la een-**glay**-zay |
| I don't speak Italian | Non parlo italiano | non **par**-lo ee-tal-**yah**-no |
| I don't understand | Non capisco | non ka-**peess**-ko |
| Can you please repeat? | Può ripetere? | pwo ree-**pet**-ay-ray |
| Slowly! | Lentamente! | **len**-ta-men-tay |
| I don't know | Non lo so | non lo **so** |
| I'm American/ British | Sono americano(a) | **so**-no a-may-ree-**kah**-no(a) |
| | Sono inglese | **so**-no een-**glay**-zay |
| What's your name? | Come si chiama? | **ko**-may see kee-**ah**-ma |
| My name is . . . | Mi chiamo . . . | mee kee-**ah**-mo |
| What time is it? | Che ore sono? | kay **o**-ray **so**-no |
| How? | Come? | **ko**-may |
| When? | Quando? | **kwan**-doe |
| Yesterday/today/ tomorrow | Ieri/oggi/domani | **yer**-ee/**o**-jee/ do-**mah**-nee |

| | | |
|---|---|---|
| This morning/ afternoon | Stamattina/Oggi pomeriggio | sta-ma-**tee**-na/**o**-jee po-mer-**ee**-jo |
| Tonight | Stasera | sta-**ser**-a |
| What? | Che cosa? | kay **ko**-za |
| What is it? | Che cos'è? | kay ko-**zay** |
| Why? | Perché? | pear-**kay** |
| Who? | Chi? | kee |
| Where is . . . | Dov'è . . . | doe-**veh** |
| the bus stop? | la fermata dell'autobus? | la fer-**mah**-ta del ow-toc-**booss** |
| the train station? | la stazione? | la sta-tsee-**oh**-nay |
| the subway station? | la metropolitana? | la may-tro-po-lee-**tah**-na |
| the terminal? | il terminale? | eel ter-mee-**nah**-lay |
| the post office? | l'ufficio postale? | loo-**fee**-cho po-**stah**-lay |
| the bank? | la banca? | la **bahn**-ka |
| the . . . hotel? | l'hotel . . .? | lo-**tel** |
| the store? | il negozio? | eel nay-**go**-tsee-o |
| the cashier? | la cassa? | la **kah**-sa |
| the . . . museum? | il museo . . .? | eel moo-**zay**-o |
| the hospital? | l'ospedale? | lo-spay-**dah**-lay |
| the first-aid station? | il pronto soccorso? | eel **pron**-to so-**kor**-so |
| the elevator? | l'ascensore? | la-shen-**so**-ray |
| a telephone? | un telefono? | oon tay-**lay**-fo-no |
| Where are the restrooms? | Dov'è il bagno? | do-**vay** eel **bahn**-yo |
| Here/there | Qui/là | kwee/la |
| Left/right | A sinistra/a destra | a see-**neess**-tra/ a **des**-tra |
| Straight ahead | Avanti dritto | a-**vahn**-tee **dree**-to |
| Is it near/far? | È vicino/lontano? | ay vee-**chee**-no/ lon-**tah**-no |
| I'd like . . . | Vorrei . . . | vo-**ray** |
| a room | una camera | **oo**-na **kah**-may-ra |
| the key | la chiave | la kee-**ah**-vay |
| a newspaper | un giornale | oon jor-**nah**-lay |
| a stamp | un francobollo | oon frahn-ko-**bo**-lo |
| I'd like to buy . . . | Vorrei comprare . . . | vo-**ray** kom-**prah**-ray |
| a cigar | un sigaro | oon see-**gah**-ro |
| cigarettes | delle sigarette | **day**-lay see-ga-**ret**-ay |
| some matches | dei fiammiferi | **day**-ee **fee**-ah-**mee**-fer-ee |
| some soap | una saponetta | **oo**-na sa-po-**net**-a |
| a city plan | una pianta della città | **oo**-na **pyahn**-ta **day**-la chee-**tah** |

| | | |
|---|---|---|
| a road map of . . . | una carta stradale di . . . | **oo**-na **cart**-a stra-**dah**-lay dee |
| a country map | una carta geografica | **oo**-na **cart**-a jay-o-**grah**-fee-ka |
| a magazine | una rivista | **oo**-na ree-**veess**-ta |
| envelopes | delle buste | **day**-lay **booss**-tay |
| writing paper | della carta da lettere | **day**-la **cart**-a da **let**-air-ay |
| a postcard | una cartolina | **oo**-na car-toe-**lee**-na |
| a guidebook | una guida turistica | **oo**-na **gwee**-da too-**reess**-tee-ka |
| How much is it? | Quanto costa? | **kwahn**-toe **coast**-a |
| It's expensive/cheap | È caro/economico | ay **car**-o/ay-ko-**no**-mee-ko |
| A little/a lot | Poco/tanto | **po**-ko/**tahn**-to |
| More/less | Più/meno | pee-**oo**/**may**-no |
| Enough/too (much) | Abbastanza/troppo | a-bas-**tahn**-sa/**tro**-po |
| I am sick | Sto male | sto **mah**-lay |
| Call a doctor | Chiama un dottore | kee-**ah**-mah oon doe-**toe**-ray |
| Help! | Aiuto! | a-**yoo**-toe |
| Stop! | Alt! | ahlt |
| Fire! | Al fuoco! | ahl **fwo**-ko |
| Caution/Look out! | Attenzione! | a-ten-**syon**-ay |

## Dining Out

| | | |
|---|---|---|
| A bottle of . . . | Una bottiglia di . . . | **oo**-na bo-**tee**-lee-ah dee |
| A cup of . . . | Una tazza di . . . | **oo**-na **tah**-tsa dee |
| A glass of . . . | Un bicchiere di . . . | oon bee-key-**air**-ay dee |
| Bill/check | Il conto | eel **cone**-toe |
| Bread | Il pane | eel **pah**-nay |
| Breakfast | La prima colazione | la **pree**-ma ko-la-**tsee**-oh-nay |
| Cocktail/aperitif | L'aperitivo | la-pay-ree-**tee**-vo |
| Dinner | La cena | la **chen**-a |
| Fixed-price menu | Menù a prezzo fisso | may-**noo** a **pret**-so **fee**-so |
| Fork | La forchetta | la for-**ket**-a |
| I am diabetic | Ho il diabete | o eel dee-a-**bay**-tay |
| I am vegetarian | Sono vegetariano/a | **so**-no vay-jay-ta-ree-**ah**-no/a |
| I'd like . . . | Vorrei . . . | vo-**ray** |

| | | |
|---|---|---|
| I'd like to order | Vorrei ordinare | vo-**ray** or-dee-**nah**-ray |
| Is service included? | Il servizio è incluso? | eel ser-**vee**-tzee-o ay een-**kloo**-zo |
| It's good/bad | È buono/cattivo | ay **bwo**-no/ka-**tee**-vo |
| It's hot/cold | È caldo/freddo | ay **kahl**-doe/**fred**-o |
| Knife | Il coltello | eel kol-**tel**-o |
| Lunch | Il pranzo | eel **prahnt**-so |
| Menu | Il menù | eel may-**noo** |
| Napkin | Il tovagliolo | eel toe-va-lee-**oh**-lo |
| Please give me . . . | Mi dia . . . | mee **dee**-a |
| Salt | Il sale | eel **sah**-lay |
| Spoon | Il cucchiaio | eel koo-kee-**ah**-yo |
| Sugar | Lo zucchero | lo **tsoo**-ker-o |
| Waiter/Waitress | Cameriere/ cameriera | ka-mare-**yer**-ay/ ka-mare-**yer**-a |
| Wine list | La lista dei vini | la **lee**-sta **day**-ee **vee**-nee |

# MENU GUIDE

| English | Italian |
|---|---|
| Set menu | Menù a prezzo fisso |
| Dish of the day | Piatto del giorno |
| Specialty of the house | Specialità della casa |
| Local specialties | Specialità locali |
| Extra charge | Extra . . . |
| In season | Di stagione |
| Cover charge/Service charge | Coperto/Servizio |

## Breakfast

| | |
|---|---|
| Butter | Burro |
| Croissant | Cornetto |
| Eggs | Uova |
| Honey | Miele |
| Jam/Marmalade | Marmellata |
| Roll | Panino |
| Toast | Pane tostato |

## Starters

| | |
|---|---|
| Assorted cold cuts | Affettati misti |
| Assorted seafood | Antipasto di pesce |
| Assorted appetizers | Antipasto misto |
| Toasted rounds of bread, fried or toasted in oil | Crostini/Crostoni |
| Diced-potato and vegetable salad with mayonnaise | Insalata russa |
| Eggplant parmigiana | Melanzane alla parmigiana |
| Fried mozzarella sandwich | Mozzarella in carrozza |
| Ham and melon | Prosciutto e melone |
| Cooked sausages and cured meats | Salumi cotti |
| Filled pastry shells | Vol-au-vents |

## Soups

| | |
|---|---|
| "Angel hair," thin noodle soup | Capelli d'angelo |
| Cream of . . . | Crema di . . . |
| Pasta-and-bean soup | Pasta e fagioli |
| Egg-drop and Parmesan cheese soup | Stracciatella |

## Pasta, Rice, and Pizza

| | |
|---|---|
| Filled pasta | Agnolotti/ravioli/tortellini |
| Potato dumplings | Gnocchi |

| | |
|---|---|
| Semolina dumplings | Gnocchi alla romana |
| Pasta | Pasta |
| *with four cheeses* | *al quattro formaggi* |
| *with basil/cheese/pine nuts/ garlic sauce* | *al pesto* |
| *with tomato-based meat sauce* | *al ragù* |
| *with tomato sauce* | *al sugo* or *al pomodoro* |
| *with butter* | *in bianco* or *al burro* |
| *with egg, Parmesan cheese, and pepper* | *alla carbonara* |
| *green (spinach-based) pasta* | *verde* |
| Rice | Riso |
| Rice dish | Risotto |
| *with mushrooms* | *ai funghi* |
| *with saffron* | *alla milanese* |
| Noodles | Tagliatelle |
| Pizza | Pizza |
| Pizza with seafood, cheese, artichokes, and ham in four different sections | Pizza quattro stagioni |
| Pizza with tomato and mozzarella | Pizza margherita |
| Pizza with oil, garlic, and oregano | Pizza marinara |

## Fish and Seafood

| | |
|---|---|
| Anchovies | Acciughe |
| Bass | Persico |
| Carp | Carpa |
| Clams | Vongole |
| Cod | Merluzzo |
| Crab | Granchio |
| Eel | Anguilla |
| Lobster | Aragosta |
| Mackerel | Sgombro |
| Mullet | Triglia |
| Mussels | Cozze |
| Octopus | Polpo |
| Oysters | Ostriche |
| Pike | Luccio |
| Prawns | Gamberoni |
| Salmon | Salmone |
| Shrimp | Scampi |
| Shrimps | Gamberetti |
| Sole | Sogliola |
| Squid | Calamari |
| Swordfish | Pescespada |

| | |
|---|---|
| Trout | Trota |
| Tuna | Tonno |

## Methods of Preparation

| | |
|---|---|
| Baked | Al forno |
| Cold, with vinegar sauce | In carpione |
| Fish stew | Zuppa di pesce |
| Fried | Fritto |
| Grilled (usually charcoal) | Alla griglia |
| Seafood salad | In insalata |
| Smoked | Affumicato |
| Stuffed | Ripieno |

## Meat

| | |
|---|---|
| Boar | Cinghiale |
| Brain | Cervella |
| Braised meat with wine | Brasato |
| Chop | Costoletta |
| Duck | Anatra |
| Lamb | Agnello |
| Baby lamb | Abbacchio |
| Liver | Fegato |
| Pheasant | Fagiano |
| Pork roast | Arista |
| Rabbit | Coniglio |
| Steak | Bistecca |
| Sliced raw steak with sauce | Carpaccio |
| Mixed boiled meat | Bollito misto |

## Methods of Preparation

| | |
|---|---|
| Battered with eggs and crumbs and fried | . . . alla milanese |
| Grilled | . . . ai ferri |
| Grilled (usually charcoal) | . . . alla griglia |
| Raw, with lemon/egg sauce | . . . alla tartara |
| Roasted | . . . arrosto |
| Very rare | . . . al sangue |
| Well done | . . . ben cotta |
| With ham and cheese | . . . alla valdostana |
| With Parmesan cheese and tomatoes | . . . alla parmigiana |

## Vegetables

| | |
|---|---|
| Artichokes | Carciofi |
| Asparagus | Asparagi |
| Beans | Fagioli |

| | |
|---|---|
| Brussels sprouts | Cavolini di Bruxelles |
| Cabbage | Cavolo |
| Carrots | Carote |
| Cauliflower | Cavolfiore |
| Cucumber | Cetriolo |
| Eggplants | Melanzane |
| Green beans | Fagiolini |
| Leeks | Porri |
| Lentils | Lenticchie |
| Lettuce | Lattuga |
| Mushrooms | Funghi |
| Onions | Cipolle |
| Peas | Piselli |
| Peppers | Peperoni |
| Potatoes | Patate |
| *Roasted potatoes* | *Patate arroste* |
| *Boiled potatoes* | *Patate bollite* |
| *Fried potatoes* | *Patate fritte* |
| *Small, roasted potatoes* | *Patatine novelle* |
| *Mashed potatoes* | *Purè di patate* |
| Radishes | Rapanelli |
| Salad | Insalata |
| *vegetable* | *mista* |
| *green* | *verde* |
| Spinach | Spinaci |
| Tomatoes | Pomodori |
| Zucchini | Zucchini |

## Sauces, Herbs, and Spices

| | |
|---|---|
| Basil | Basilico |
| Bay leaf | Lauro |
| Chervil | Cerfoglio |
| Dill | Aneto |
| Garlic | Aglio |
| Hot dip with anchovies (for vegetables) | Bagna cauda |
| Marjoram | Maggiorana |
| Mayonnaise | Maionese |
| Mustard | Mostarda *or* senape |
| Oil | Olio |
| Parsley-based sauce | Salsa verde |
| Pepper | Pepe |
| Rosemary | Rosmarino |
| Tartar sauce | Salsa tartara |
| Vinegar | Aceto |
| White sauce | Besciamella |

## Cheeses

| | |
|---|---|
| *Fresh:* | Caprino fresco |
| | Mascarpone |
| | Mozzarella |
| | Ricotta |
| *Mild:* | Caciotta |
| | Caprino |
| | Fontina |
| | Grana |
| | Provola |
| | Provolone dolce |
| | Robiola |
| | Scamorza |
| *Sharp:* | Asiago |
| | Gorgonzola |
| | Groviera |
| | Pecorino |
| | Provolone piccante |
| | Taleggio |
| | Toma |

## Fruits and Nuts

| | |
|---|---|
| Almonds | Mandorle |
| Apple | Mela |
| Apricot | Albicocca |
| Blackberries | More |
| Black currant | Ribes nero |
| Blueberries | Mirtilli |
| Cherries | Ciliege |
| Chestnuts | Castagne |
| Coconut | Noce di cocco |
| Dates | Datteri |
| Figs | Fichi |
| Green grapes | Uva bianca |
| Black grapes | Uva nera |
| Grapefruit | Pompelmo |
| Hazelnuts | Nocciole |
| Lemon | Limone |
| Melon | Melone |
| Nectarine | Nocepesca |
| Orange | Arancia |
| Pear | Pera |
| Peach | Pesca |
| Pineapple | Ananas |
| Plum | Prugna/Susina |
| Prune | Prugna secca |

| | |
|---|---|
| Raisins | Uva passa |
| Raspberries | Lamponi |
| Red currant | Ribes |
| Strawberries | Fragole |
| Tangerine | Mandarino |
| Walnuts | Noci |
| Watermelon | Anguria/Cocomero |
| Dried fruit | Frutta secca |
| Fresh fruit | Frutta fresca |
| Fruit salad | Macedonia di frutta |

## Desserts

| | |
|---|---|
| Custard filed pastry, with candied fruit | Cannoli |
| Ricotta filled pastry shells with sugar glaze | Cannoli alla siciliana |
| Ice cream with candied fruit | Cassata |
| Ricotta filed cake with sugar glaze | Cassata siciliana |
| Chocolate | Cioccolato |
| Cup of ice cream | Coppa gelato |
| Caramel custard | Crème caramel |
| Pie | Crostata |
| Fruit pie | Crostata di frutta |
| Ice cream | Gelato |
| Flaked pastry | Millefoglie |
| Chestnuts and whipped-cream cake | Montebianco |
| Whipped cream | Panna montata |
| Pastries | Paste |
| Sherbet | Sorbetto |
| Chocolate-coated ice cream | Tartufo |
| Fruit tart | Torta di frutta |
| Apple tart | Torta di mele |
| Ice-cream cake | Torta gelata |
| Vanilla | Vaniglia |
| Egg-based cream with sugar and Marsala wine | Zabaione |
| Ice-cream filled cake | Zuccotto |

## Alcoholic Drinks

| | |
|---|---|
| On the rocks | Con ghiaccio |
| Straight | Liscio |
| With soda | Con seltz |
| | |
| Beer | Birra |
| *light/dark* | *chiara/scura* |

| | |
|---|---|
| Bitter cordial | Amaro |
| Brandy | Cognac |
| Cordial | Liquore |
| Aniseed cordial | Sambuca |
| Martini | Cocktail Martini |
| Port | Porto |
| Vermouth | Vermut/Martini |
| Wine | Vino |
| *blush* | *rosé* |
| *dry* | *secco* |
| *full-bodied* | *corposo* |
| *light* | *leggero* |
| *red* | *rosso* |
| *sparkling* | *spumante* |
| *sweet* | *dolce* |
| *very dry* | *brut* |
| *white* | *bianco* |
| Light wine | Vinello |
| | |
| Bottle | Bottiglia |
| Carafe | Caraffa |
| Flask | Fiasco |

## Nonalcoholic Drinks

| | |
|---|---|
| Mineral water | Acqua minerale |
| *carbonated* | *gassata* |
| *still* | *non gassata* |
| Tap water | Acqua naturale |
| Tonic water | Acqua tonica |
| | |
| Coffee with steamed milk | Cappuccino |
| Espresso | Caffè espresso |
| *with milk* | *macchiato* |
| *decaffeinated* | *decaffeinato* |
| *lighter espresso* | *lungo* |
| *with cordial* | *corretto* |
| Fruit juice | Succo di frutta |
| Lemonade | Limonata |
| Milk | Latte |
| Orangeade | Aranciata |
| Tea | Tè |
| *with milk/lemon* | *col latte/col limone* |
| *iced* | *freddo* |

# INDEX